## There Will Be the Devil to Pay

The European financial crisis of 1931 was a pivotal moment in the economic and financial history of the twentieth century. Based on extensive archival research and a cultural conceptual framework, *There Will Be the Devil to Pay* offers a new and much needed understanding of the European financial crisis. It tells the dramatic story of the five months that led to the breakdown of the gold standard, writing the history of the crisis from the perspective of central bankers, private bankers and government officials. It provides a new narrative of how those involved struggled to understand and respond to the crisis as it unfolded. Contributing to the emerging literature on radical uncertainty and narrative economics, this book provides a detailed analysis of how decision-makers confront uncertainty and shape narratives that create actionable knowledge and enable decision-making.

Per H. Hansen is a professor in the Department of Business Humanities and Law at Copenhagen Business School. He is a past president of the Business History Conference and the recipient of the Newcomen Article Prize (2008), the Henrietta Larson Article Award (2012) and the Hagley Prize for the best book in Business History (2019).

STUDIES IN MACROECONOMIC HISTORY

*Series Editor: Michael D. Bordo, Rutgers University*

*Editors:*



The titles in this series investigate themes of interest to economists and economic historians in the rapidly developing field of macroeconomic history. The four areas covered include the application of monetary and finance theory, international economics, and quantitative methods to historical problems; the historical application of growth and development theory and theories of business fluctuations; the history of domestic and international monetary, financial, and other macroeconomic institutions; and the history of international monetary and financial systems. The series amalgamates the former Cambridge University Press series Studies in Monetary and Financial History and Studies in Quantitative Economic History.

*Other Books in the Series:*

Simon Amrein, *Capital in Banking: The Role of Capital in Banking in the 19th and 20th Century: The United Kingdom, the United States and Switzerland* (2024)

Stephen Quinn and William Roberds, *How a Ledger Became a Central Bank: A Monetary History of the Bank of Amsterdam* (2023)

Simon Hinrichsen, *When Nations Can't Default: A History of War Reparations and Sovereign Debt* (2023)

Barry Eichengreen and Andreas Kakridis, *The Emergence of the Modern Central Bank and Global Cooperation: 1919-1939* (2023)

Alain Naef, *An Exchange Rate History of the United Kingdom: 1945–1992* (2021)

Barrie A. Wigmore, *The Financial Crisis of 2008: A History of US Financial Markets 2000–2012* (2021)

Max Harris, *Monetary War and Peace: London, Washington, Paris, and the Tripartite Agreement of 1936* (2021)

Kenneth D. Garbade, *After the Accord: A History of Federal Reserve Open Market Operations, the US Government Securities Market, and Treasury Debt Management from 1951 to 1979* (2020)

Harold James, *Making a Modern Central Bank: The Bank of England 1979–2003* (2020)

Claudio Borio, Stijn Claessens, Piet Clement, Robert N. McCauley, and Hyun Song Shin, Editors, *Promoting Global Monetary and Financial Stability: The Bank for International Settlements after Bretton Woods, 1973–2020* (2020)

Patrick Honohan, *Currency, Credit and Crisis: Central Banking in Ireland and Europe* (2019)

William A. Allen, *The Bank of England and the Government Debt: Operations in the Gilt-Edged Market, 1928–1972* (2019)

Eric Monnet, *Controlling Credit: Central Banking and the Planned Economy in Postwar France, 1948–1973* (2018)

Laurence M. Ball, *The Fed and Lehman Brothers: Setting the Record Straight on a Financial Disaster* (2018)

Rodney Edvinsson, Tor Jacobson, and Daniel Waldenström, Editors, *Sveriges Riksbank and the History of Central Banking* (2018)

Peter L. Rousseau and Paul Wachtel, Editors, *Financial Systems and Economic Growth: Credit, Crises, and the Regulation from the 19th Century to the Present* (2017)

Ernst Baltensperger and Peter Kugler, *Swiss Monetary History since the Early 19th Century* (2017)

Øyvind Eitrheim, Jan Tore Klovland, and Lars Fredrik Øksendal, *A Monetary History of Norway, 1816–2016* (2016)

Jan Fredrik Qvigstad, *On Central Banking* (2016)

Michael D. Bordo, Øyvind Eitrheim, Marc Flandreau, and Jan F. Qvigstad, Editors, *Central Banks at a Crossroads: What Can We Learn from History?* (2016)

Michael D. Bordo and Mark A. Wynne, Editors, *The Federal Reserve's Role in the Global Economy: A Historical Perspective* (2016)

Owen F. Humpage, Editor, *Current Federal Reserve Policy Under the Lens of Economic History: Essays to Commemorate the Federal Reserve System's Centennial* (2015)

Michael D. Bordo and William Roberds, Editors, *The Origins, History, and Future of the Federal Reserve: A Return to Jekyll Island* (2013)

Michael D. Bordo and Ronald MacDonald, Editors, *Credibility and the International Monetary Regime: A Historical Perspective* (2012)

Robert L. Hetzel, *The Great Recession: Market Failure or Policy Failure?* (2012)

Tobias Straumann, *Fixed Ideas of Money: Small States and Exchange Rate Regimes in Twentieth-Century Europe* (2010)

Forrest Capie, *The Bank of England: 1950s to 1979* (2010)

Aldo Musacchio, *Experiments in Financial Democracy: Corporate Governance and Financial Development in Brazil, 1882–1950* (2009)

Claudio Borio, Gianni Toniolo, and Piet Clement, Editors, *The Past and Future of Central Bank Cooperation* (2008)

Robert L. Hetzel, *The Monetary Policy of the Federal Reserve: A History* (2008)

Caroline Fohlin, *Finance Capitalism and Germany's Rise to Industrial Power* (2007)

John H. Wood, *A History of Central Banking in Great Britain and the United States* (2005)

Gianni Toniolo (with the assistance of Piet Clement), *Central Bank Cooperation at the Bank for International Settlements, 1930–1973* (2005)

Richard Burdekin and Pierre Siklos, Editors, *Deflation: Current and Historical Perspectives* (2004)

Pierre Siklos, *The Changing Face of Central Banking: Evolutionary Trends since World War II* (2002)

Michael D. Bordo and Roberto Cortés-Conde, Editors, *Transferring Wealth and Power from the Old to the New World: Monetary and Fiscal Institutions in the 17th through the 19th Centuries* (2001)

Howard Bodenhorn, *A History of Banking in Antebellum America: Financial Markets and Economic Development in an Era of Nation-Building* (2000)

Mark Harrison, Editor, *The Economics of World War II: Six Great Powers in International Comparison* (2000)

Angela Redish, *Bimetallism: An Economic and Historical Analysis* (2000)

Elmus Wicker, *Banking Panics of the Gilded Age* (2000)

Michael D. Bordo, *The Gold Standard and Related Regimes: Collected Essays* (1999)

Michele Fratianni and Franco Spinelli, *A Monetary History of Italy* (1997)

Mark Toma, *Competition and Monopoly in the Federal Reserve System, 1914–1951* (1997)

Barry Eichengreen, Editor, *Europe's Postwar Recovery* (1996)

Lawrence H. Officer, *Between the Dollar-Sterling Gold Points: Exchange Rates, Parity and Market Behavior* (1996)

Elmus Wicker, *The Banking Panics of the Great Depression* (1996)

Norio Tamaki, *Japanese Banking: A History, 1859–1959* (1995)

Barry Eichengreen, *Elusive Stability: Essays in the History of International Finance, 1919–1939* (1993)

Michael D. Bordo and Forrest Capie, Editors, *Monetary Regimes in Transition* (1993)

Larry Neal, *The Rise of Financial Capitalism: International Capital Markets in the Age of Reason* (1993)

S. N. Broadberry and N. F. R. Crafts, Editors, *Britain in the International Economy, 1870–1939* (1992)

Aurel Schubert, *The Credit-Anstalt Crisis of 1931* (1992)

Trevor J. O. Dick and John E. Floyd, *Canada and the Gold Standard: Balance of Payments Adjustment under Fixed Exchange Rates, 1871–1913* (1992)

Kenneth Mouré, *Managing the Franc Poincaré: Economic Understanding and Political Constraint in French Monetary Policy, 1928–1936* (1991)

David C. Wheelock, *The Strategy and Consistency of Federal Reserve Monetary Policy, 1924–1933* (1991)

# There Will Be the Devil to Pay

*Central Bankers, Uncertainty and Sensemaking in the European Financial Crisis of 1931*

**PER H. HANSEN**
Copenhagen Business School

CAMBRIDGE
UNIVERSITY PRESS

CAMBRIDGE
UNIVERSITY PRESS

Shaftesbury Road, Cambridge CB2 8EA, United Kingdom

One Liberty Plaza, 20th Floor, New York, NY 10006, USA

477 Williamstown Road, Port Melbourne, VIC 3207, Australia

314–321, 3rd Floor, Plot 3, Splendor Forum, Jasola District Centre, New Delhi – 110025, India

103 Penang Road, #05-06/07, Visioncrest Commercial, Singapore 238467

Cambridge University Press is part of Cambridge University Press & Assessment, a department of the University of Cambridge.

We share the University's mission to contribute to society through the pursuit of education, learning and research at the highest international levels of excellence.

www.cambridge.org
Information on this title: www.cambridge.org/9781009505314

DOI: 10.1017/9781009505307



When citing this work, please include a reference to the DOI 10.1017/9781009505307

First published 2025

*A catalogue record for this publication is available from the British Library.*

*Library of Congress Cataloging-in-Publication Data*
NAMES: Hansen, Per H., author.
TITLE: There will be the devil to pay : central bankers, uncertainty and sensemaking in the European financial crisis of 1931 / Professor Per H. Hansen.
DESCRIPTION: New York, NY : Cambridge University Press, [2024] | Series: Smeh studies in macroeconomic history | Includes bibliographical references and index.
IDENTIFIERS: LCCN 2024024524 (print) | LCCN 2024024525 (ebook) | ISBN 9781009505314 (hardback) | ISBN 9781009505284 (paperback) | ISBN 9781009505307 (epub)
SUBJECTS: LCSH: Financial crises–Europe–History. | Macroeconomics–History.
CLASSIFICATION: LCC HB3782 .H36 2024 (print) | LCC HB3782 (ebook) | DDC 332.1094/09043–dc23/eng/20240628
LC record available at https://lccn.loc.gov/2024024524
LC ebook record available at https://lccn.loc.gov/2024024525

ISBN 978-1-009-50531-4 Hardback

# Contents


1 Introduction 1
The House of Cards 3
Central Bankers, the Gold Standard and Dealing with Crises 6
The Focus of This Book 12
Sensemaking and Uncertainty 15
Analytical Strategy and My Sources 17
Structure of This Book 20

2 Central Bankers and Their World 22
Francis Rodd and Harry Siepmann 22
Montagu Norman, George Harrison and the BIS 25
Central Bankers, Nationals and Individuals 30
The World They Lived In: The Present World Depression 34
The Common Vision of the Future Has Been Destroyed 37
Beyond Understanding 40
The Fiction 42
Uncertainty 44

3 Preparing for Crisis (May 11–May 19) 47
Tomorrow Will Be Critical Day 50
The Plan 55
Organizing the BIS Loan 57
Board Meeting in Basle 61

4 Foreign Creditors (May 16–May 25) 66
The Government Loan 67
Credit Anstalt on the Move 69
Ask the Governor 74
A Wild Exaggeration 80

| | | |
|---|---|---|
| 5 | Moratorium or Guarantee? (May 25–May 27) | 84 |
| | We Must Rely Heavily on the Governor | 85 |
| | No One over Here Knows What the Situation Is | 88 |
| | At All Costs | 92 |
| 6 | Guarantee at Last? (May 26–June 1) | 96 |
| | Cause and Effect | 98 |
| | Unhappy about Vienna | 102 |
| | A Case for Common Action | 104 |
| | A Butcher, a Dictator and a Credit | 108 |
| 7 | Releasing the BIS Credit (May 29–June 5) | 113 |
| | We Cannot Afford to Fail in Vienna | 115 |
| | I Have No Information on Which to Act | 120 |
| | Absolutely Inseparable | 126 |
| 8 | Surrounded with Trouble (June 5–June 10) | 132 |
| | A German Visit to Chequers | 135 |
| | The Second BIS Board Meeting | 139 |
| | We Shall All Lose Our Money | 144 |
| 9 | Where and How to Place? (June 8–June 13) | 148 |
| | Nothing to Report | 150 |
| | Not an Hour to Lose | 153 |
| | Van Hengel Goes to Basle | 155 |
| | The Guarantee, Again | 159 |
| 10 | A World Political Problem (June 11–June 16) | 163 |
| | We Absolutely Cannot Afford to Wait | 166 |
| | James Gannon's Plan | 168 |
| | Bankers in Vienna | 170 |
| | What Is the Answer? | 175 |
| | Her Majesty's Government | 179 |
| | To Save the Ship before She Sinks | 181 |
| 11 | Francis Rodd Makes Sense – and a Plot (June 9–June 20) | 185 |
| | Rodd's Memorandum | 186 |
| | Narrating the Crisis | 196 |
| | Pierre Quesnay's Story | 199 |
| 12 | To Act Now If We Are to Act at All (June 16–June 27) | 204 |
| | Putting Money Down a Sink Hole | 205 |
| | The Hoover Moratorium | 212 |

$100,000,000 to the Reichsbank 220
George L. Harrison Takes Charge 224

13 Germany Will Collapse (June 19–July 10) 231
Strong Political Antagonism 232
The French Cabinet Is Now in Session 238
A Billion Dollars to Germany? 241
A Very Bad Frame of Mind 251

14 Anxiety within Germany at Climax (July 11–July 23) 256
In a State of Uncertainty 263
If Germany Goes into the Abyss 265
You Have Done a Fine Job 269
A Programme for Averting Disaster? 271
The London Conference 276

15 Going Off the Gold Standard? (July 14–August 21) 281
A Sudden Drop in Sterling 282
A Credit to the Bank of England 288
Working in Harmony 296
To Face the Music 300
Blind and Irrational Forces of Nature 303

16 We Must Not Fool Ourselves Now (August 21–September 17) 307
No Use in Doing the Thing Halfway 308
They Can Do All They Like 313
Convincingly Ample 317
No Place for a Tired Man 320

17 As for the Future of England (September 16–October 23) 325
The Avalanche 327
I Will Not Dwell upon the Feelings 329
Capital Is an Elusive Thing 333
We Lost Our Money and Achieved Nothing 335

The End (2024) 342
Understanding the 1931 Financial Crisis 344
Decision-Making under Radical Uncertainty 350
The Great Financial Crisis 353

*Timeline* 357

*Actors in the 1931 Financial Crisis* 363

*Acknowledgements* 371
*Archives* 375
*Notes* 377
*Bibliography* 459
*Index* 477

Épreuve d'artiste

Fancy skating on

MELCHIOR
MORET
Mc GARRAH
FRANQUI
SNOWDEN
BRÜNING
FLANDIN
LUTHER
LAVAL
MACDONALD
Derso et Kelen
frozen credits

# 1

# Introduction

The year 1931 was distinguished from previous years ... by one outstanding feature. In 1931, men and women all over the world were seriously contemplating and frankly discussing the possibility that the Western system of Society might break down and cease to work.[1]

Arnold J. Toynbee

This book is first and foremost about how central bankers struggled to overcome uncertainty and make sense of the worst financial crisis the world had ever seen. Over five dramatic months, they worked day and night to avert contagion and stop the European financial crisis of May to September 1931. It all began in Vienna.

By any standard, 1931 was already a bad year, when on Friday, May 8, it went from bad to worse. On that day, amid the Great Depression, the largest Austrian bank Österreichische Credit Anstalt für Handel und Gewerbe (Credit Anstalt) informed the Austrian National Bank and the government that it had suffered losses of almost 140 million schillings, leaving it close to insolvency with only about 25 million schillings or 15 per cent of its capital left.

The Credit Anstalt was not just any bank, *The Economist* explained to its readers. It had been a financial powerhouse since its creation in 1855. Promoted by the Austrian Rothschild banking house and the Austrian government, the Credit Anstalt grew steadily, and in 1931 its balance sheet amounted to 70 per cent of all Austrian bank assets. A so-called universal bank, the Credit Anstalt had become 'a central holding and finance company for Austria'.[2]

Typical of continental banking, this business model was the Achilles heel of all universal banks including the Credit Anstalt. It financed companies with long-term credits and capital, but it borrowed short-term, and could only 'keep going so long as the supply of short-term funds did not show any falling off'. That is exactly what happened from 1928 as financial markets in New York and London tightened, Wall Street crashed in October 1929 and was followed by American banking difficulties in 1930. As a result, not only Austria but the whole of Central Europe, including Germany, was increasingly deprived of an important source of money.[3]

The size and importance of the Credit Anstalt and its dependence on foreign short-term credits emphasized the seriousness and potential international significance of the bank's distress. The Austrian authorities realized that a solution must be found before Monday, and the weekend was spent in tense negotiations in Vienna between the Austrian government, the National Bank and the Austrian Rothschild banking house, the largest shareholder of the Credit Anstalt.

On Monday, May 11, the parties announced a reconstruction plan. The losses were to be covered by the shareholders, the Austrian state and the Austrian National Bank. In addition, the state, the Rothschilds and the National Bank would pay in new money, bringing Credit Anstalt's new share capital to 177.5 million schillings. More than 50 per cent of its capital was owned by foreign stockholders, leading to criticism that the rescue operation was a 'gift to foreign capitalists'.[4]

The National Bank and the Rothschilds each contributed 30 million in new capital, while the state covered the lion's share of 100 million schillings.[5] The only problem was that the government budget was in deficit and the money would have to be borrowed.[6] The Bank of England quickly realized this constraint and prepared a note on the 'Austrian Government Borrowing Powers'.[7]

The *New York Times* reported that the government loan would need to be a foreign loan, which required permission from the League of Nation's Control Committee. Adding a political dimension to the situation, Germany and Austria officially announced a plan for a customs union on March 21, unleashing 'the first true landslide of the Great Depression'.[8] The customs union would be a background theme throughout the crisis leading to frequent rumours about 'the withdrawal for political purposes of French short-term loans'.[9]

Nevertheless, at a press conference on Monday evening, the Austrian Finance Ministry announced that deposits were safe and that the Credit Anstalt would carry on business as usual.[10] The *Neues Wiener Tagblatt*, too, told its readers that the bank had ample liquidity and survival was not in question.[11] Unimpressed depositors withdrew their money anyway, and within the first four days after the announcement, a quarter of the deposits were gone. Two weeks later only half was left.[12]

Reassurances were made outside of Austria as well. The Credit Anstalt owed large sums abroad, primarily to American and British banks that had to be convinced to maintain deposits, loans and credit lines, lest a currency crisis develop. The Austrian National Bank cabled the Federal Reserve Bank of New York that 'Loans granted and other claims are in no way endangered and can safely be maintained'.[13]

At the Bank of England, Deputy Governor Ernest M. Harvey responded to a similar message, 'We were glad to receive such prompt and authentic information. I did not fail to let it be known in this market and I think it helped to form opinion here. My impression is that the market is taking a quiet and reasonable view.'[14]

It was not going to be that easy.

## THE HOUSE OF CARDS

Even if the initial sentiment in 'the market' seemed calm, both the Austrian authorities and international central bankers realized that uncertainty about the future had just increased dramatically. On Monday morning, May 11, Harry Siepmann at the Bank of England's Central Banking Department received telegrams from Richard Reisch, the president of the Austrian National Bank, and Otto Juch, the Austrian minister of finance, urging him to 'come to Vienna as soon as possible in order to advise us in a matter of extraordinary importance suffering no delay'.[15]

Siepmann, already aware of the Credit Anstalt situation, preferred to 'wait until the central banking aspects appear more clearly in a few days' time and then deal with them not by direct association between London and Vienna but rather by association of Vienna with central banks gathered by that time in Basle'.[16]

'Basle' referred to the Bank for International Settlements (BIS) where central bank governors were to meet the upcoming weekend for the monthly board meeting. Siepmann's response stressed two important principles, strongly promoted by Montagu Norman, the governor of the Bank of England and first among central bankers. First, central banks should only concern themselves with the risk of currency flight that might threaten the gold standard, and, second, 'individual action by central banks ... has been superseded by corporate action through Basle'.[17]

In fact, Reisch had also asked the BIS to send Pierre Quesnay to Vienna. Quesnay, a French economist and general manager of the BIS, was unable to leave Basle, and instead Francis Rodd, the British manager of the BIS's Central Banking Department, left Basle for Vienna on Monday, May 11.

According to Leon Fraser, the American vice president of the BIS, Francis Rodd's first task in Vienna would be to 'canvass situation and . . . discuss desirability of having available a central bank credit to counter-act effect of news and as second line of defense to reinforce existing satisfactory position of National Bank'.[18]

Fraser also wrote to George Harrison, the governor of the Federal Reserve Bank of New York, that it was too early to tell if an international credit would be needed, but 'we are prepared in principle to head and participate in any necessary credit, but first desire to secure data'.[19]

'I shall appreciate your keeping me informed', Harrison replied. Echoing Harvey's assessment for England, he reported that despite some uneasiness there was 'no real feeling of alarm' in New York.[20]

From his office at 33 Liberty Street in New York City's Financial District, Harrison was at a disadvantage as he was not familiar with the situation in far-away Vienna. He immediately had a staff member prepare a note on the history and current situation of the ailing Austrian bank. The note confirmed the international interconnectedness of Wall Street and the Credit Anstalt.

The bank did business with several large American banks and had been listed on the New York Stock Exchange since 1927. 'Issued at $80 per share, they were quoted on Monday at $48 5/8 and to-night (Tuesday) $12 bid, $37 ask with no sales transacted.'[21] The bid–ask spread left no doubt that uncertainty about Credit Anstalt's future had just increased dramatically.

The German Reichsbank, too, took notice of the news and cabled the New York Fed that Credit Anstalt's trouble had 'greatly surprised our market and heavily influenced rates of securities'. However, the Credit Anstalt did not have much business with Germany and vice versa. 'Therefore money market calm.'[22]

In a matter of a couple of days, then, the large central banks and financial markets in New York, London, Basle and Berlin were hard at work assessing the Austrian situation and potential effects in their own markets. Below the seemingly calm surface, there was an unmistakable sense among economic and political decision-makers that the situation was fragile, perhaps nearing a tipping point. Despite the 'quiet and reasonable view' in the financial capitals, central bankers feared contagion as they communicated across national and organizational borders.

Indeed, Harry Siepmann, the Bank of England official, imagined a wider economic and financial breakdown. On May 11, he called

Frederick Leith-Ross, a high-ranking expert on international finance at the British Treasury. 'This, I think, is it', Siepmann said, 'it may well bring down the whole house of cards in which we have been living.'[23] Two days later, Siepmann wrote another Treasury official airing his fear that everything 'seems to be boiling up now and I am mainly concerned in wondering where and when it will all boil over'.[24]

Siepmann, one of the protagonists and most well-informed actors in this story, worried that contagion would destroy the already fragile house of cards.[25] The world had never seen a year quite like 1931, and the financial crisis represented something new and unknown, an international financial panic with runs on both banks and currencies. Fraught with economic, financial and political problems and polarization stemming from the Great War and the Versailles Peace Agreement, many decision-makers already felt that Western capitalism was in dire straits. Would the Credit Anstalt crisis be the final straw?

Lacking any relevant historical analogies and experience, Siepmann imagined a future breakdown through fictional rather than rational expectations.[26] It did not look good. Like Francis Rodd, he was about to have a busy summer.

Siepmann's house of cards story imagined a future yet to be shaped and called for action in order to stop this future vision from becoming present. With what later happened, the house of cards story quickly came to identify, legitimize and empower central banks as 'fixers' in a 'particular causal framework'.[27]

What followed were five months of intense work trying to contain the Austrian crisis and preventing it from spreading to neighbouring countries, and Germany in particular. While apparently successful in mid-June, an even more serious emergency soon developed in Germany and in mid-July it crossed the Channel and led Great Britain to leave gold on September 21.

In their efforts to make sense of the situation and prevent an international financial crisis, the central bankers and other actors in this book aimed to shape an unformed future as they hoped for the best but feared the worst. The thoroughly interconnected transatlantic financial community was in for a bumpy ride over the summer of 1931.[28]

Their worst-case scenario was contagion from Austria to other countries, not least Germany. If that happened, they feared not only for the international financial and monetary system, but for capitalism itself.[29]

## CENTRAL BANKERS, THE GOLD STANDARD AND DEALING WITH CRISES

'Now we know how to deal with' periods when 'internal panic and external demand for bullion ... occur together', Walter Bagehot wrote in *Lombard Street* from 1873. Bagehot, a well-known writer on economic and social issues, was the editor of one of the most influential business magazines of the time, *The Economist*, between 1861 and 1878.

In *Lombard Street*, which became required reading for generations of central bankers, he noted that an external drain of gold could be stopped by raising the interest rate 'as high as may be necessary ... And at the rate of interest so raised, the holders ... of the final Bank reserve must lend freely. Very large loans at very high rates are the best remedy for the worst malady of the money market where a foreign drain is added to a domestic drain'. Bagehot added, 'At this rate ... advances should be made on all good banking securities.'[30]

In the interwar period, Bagehot's prescription was the operating model for a central bank's role as a lender of last resort, and in many ways it still is.[31] Bagehot was concerned with the Bank of England, but the idea could be applied elsewhere. The Austrian National Bank could create money to lend to the Credit Anstalt and other Austrian banks in financial distress. But, like other central banks, it could not create gold or foreign exchange such as dollars and sterling, so the only remedy to contain such a drain would be to borrow abroad and to raise the discount rate. If a high interest rate failed to stop the drain, sooner or later the central bank would run out of free gold and foreign exchange, 'one of the most difficult situations for a central bank to be in'.[32]

In that situation, the central bank would need assistance from an international lender of last resort, a concept that only arose out of the 1931 crisis.[33] It would have to borrow dollars and sterling, but how and where from? This was uncharted territory for central banks in 1931. Beyond the Bagehot model, they had no blueprint to act upon and few, if any, relevant experiences and historical analogies for their decision-making and actions. The crisis of 1931 was the first truly international financial crisis.[34]

What they did have was the BIS created the year before, in 1930, as part of the Young Plan to administer German reparation payments and facilitate central bank cooperation. Siepmann had referred the Austrians to the BIS, but it lacked experience, resources and, most significantly, the ability to create credit and issue notes like national central banks.[35]

Gates McGarrah, the American president of the BIS, envisioned the BIS to be 'the Central Bank of Central Banks' but as long as it could not create money, there were limits to this vision.[36] Still, the BIS provided a new venue for central bankers to meet and discuss common issues, and to develop a social network, trust and shared knowledge.

In February 1931, McGarrah argued that 'in addition to the meetings of the board, contact was maintained by repeated visits of central bank officials to Basle and return visits of the officers of the bank and by a "practically continuous series of gatherings of experts to study problems of common concern"'.[37]

These meetings included the exchange of views on 'how the world works and on objectives of central bank policy'.[38] During the financial crisis of 1931, as it became increasingly unclear how the world actually worked, the *New York Times* reported that the BIS became a clearing house and a nerve centre of financial information. Telegraph and telephone bills quadrupled from April to July, and the 'World Bank began to acquire an airplane bill and lose all notion of banking hours'.[39]

While central bankers in the 1920s and 1930s were familiar with and subscribed to the Bagehot model, they acted in a troubled world very different from what Bagehot and they themselves had known before the Great War. Indeed, the 'generation, to which the heads of the major central banks owed their basic outlooks, had known a world economy that was unified to a unique degree. . . . To this orderly, integrated, and expanding system, the world of the 1920's bore only a superficial resemblance'.[40]

Still, central bankers shared enough basic assumptions and practices to constitute a nascent transnational epistemic community with 'shared causal beliefs' and 'a set of common practices associated with a set of problems towards which their professional competence is directed'. The central bankers' primary policy goal was to maintain the gold standard, and that required financial stability. Epistemic communities such as the central bankers I follow in this book, take on increased importance during crises, such as the one that broke out in 1931, where uncertainty peaks.[41]

Personal characteristics, national identity and belonging as well as blueprints occasionally interfered with the assumptions and practices of this developing epistemic community of central bankers. Cohesion was certainly challenged at times as the community split over national and central banking logics. Still, despite these occasional signs of diverging visions, central bankers still shared worldviews, knowledge and specific core assumptions and causal ideas construed through mutual socialization at the BIS and during the crisis. Core assumptions like the Bagehot model and the commitment to gold acted as a blueprint that helped actors plot 'their course in uncertain conditions'.[42]

The concept of epistemic community is open to criticism. Any cultural community experiences occasional deviations and disagreements, and in the context of the interwar period's political and economic polarization it should not be surprising that this was the case in 1931 as well. Central bankers like everyone else belonged to and identified with both professional and national communities, but like identities national interests were not objective or given. In fact, they were construed and shaped on an ongoing basis while the identity and profession of being a central banker was a hallmark of Montagu Norman's vision of central banking in the 1920s.

The changes to the central banking community culture after the Great War illustrate how epistemic communities and their shared assumptions and knowledge were context dependent. The anthropologist Grant McCracken argues that members of a community act in 'conformity with the blueprint of culture . . . so that the world they create is made consistent with the world they imagine. In a sense, the members of a culture are constantly engaged in the construction – the constitution – of the world they live in'.[43]

That applies to central bankers as well. In 1924 Harry Siepmann wrote to Norman about the world he imagined, where the 'traditional and political means of associating nations' were substituted by other means including 'the association of central banks . . . supplemented by some kind of spiritual association'.[44]

Siepmann viewed central bankers like himself as a community apart, united by 'the idea of a professional and corporate responsibility, and of service to general interests which transcended those of national particularities', and other government officials.[45]

A mainstay of the identity and community of central bankers was shared causal beliefs and practices related to their strong commitment to the gold standard.[46] Linking currencies and exchange rates together, the classical gold standard from 1870 to 1914 was seen as more or less automatic in regulating the economy according to perceived 'rules of the game'. However, the outbreak of the Great War caused most countries with the exception of the United States to suspend the gold standard. The result was widespread inflation, and hyperinflation in Germany and Austria.[47]

After the war central bankers and policymakers had one goal; to beat inflation, get back on gold and re-establish the global economy they had known before the war. It was a nostalgic but widely shared dream.

It was also a costly dream. In Austria the League of Nations organized a stabilization loan at the price of a deflationary policy that cost almost 100,000 government workers their jobs. In Germany, the Dawes Plan in 1924 involved foreign intervention on a large scale with the American Seymour Parker Gilbert Jr. appointed Agent General for German reparation payments. These interventions left no doubt that some powers, first and foremost the United States and the UK, were more powerful than others.[48]

In Britain, the dream meant returning to gold at pre-war parity of $4.86 to the pound in 1925. In 'The Economic Consequences of Mr Churchill', John Maynard Keynes scorned the Chancellor for going back at a 10 per cent overvalued rate. France, in contrast, went back to gold in 1928 at 20 per cent of the pre-war level. The result was an overvalued pound and an undervalued franc giving France an advantage in trade and a steady inflow of gold.[49]

The re-established gold exchange standard had a built-in asymmetry forcing deficit countries to deflate their economy as surplus countries like France and the United States failed to inflate their economies according to what Keynes called the 'rules of the gold standard game'.[50] The problem was that there were no agreed-upon rules or enforcement of the game. Instead, these 'fixed ideas on money' were part of a worldview that Kenneth Mouré called the 'gold standard illusion'.[51]

While central bankers viewed the gold standard as natural as sunrise and sunset, monetary policy was in fact determined by 'political influences, economic ideas, and by institutions and individuals deciding policy within intellectual constraints they adopted willingly'.[52] Put differently, the gold standard was a cultural construct. Its 'rhetoric was deflation, and its mentality was one of inaction. Central banks stood ready to withstand financial panics . . . but not to preserve output and employment'.[53]

That, however, was certainly not the view of most contemporaries who saw the gold standard as the guarantor of prosperity and stability and not subject to discussion. Shortly after Britain had left gold in September 1931, Russell C. Leffingwell, a J.P. Morgan & Co. partner, stated that 'the gold standard is not something that economists, politicians and bankers have thought up and devised as a convenient expedient for the welfare of mankind. The gold standard is something deeply rooted in the appetites of men. The love of gold is instinctive in men like their love of land and women'.[54]

In the case of Britain, policy- and decision-makers had made their experiences under the pre-war gold standard that 'appeared to operate successfully for Britain and the international economy'. Montagu Norman himself, Bank of England's governor since 1920, came from a long line of bankers who had lived through 'three generations of gold-standard-dominated City life'.[55] This was the world they knew.

Francis Rodd, Montagu Norman, George Harrison, Harry Siepmann and their central bank colleagues in other countries shared a set of assumptions of how the economy and the monetary and financial system worked, and was supposed to work. Within specific areas, they subscribed to the same worldview, routinely enacting and re-shaping this system through their shared assumptions and daily practices and routines.[56]

There was a 'strong commonality of aims and objectives among central bankers, particularly when it came to the contribution of the gold standard to economic well-being'.[57] Part of that orthodox financial and economic worldview insisted on the sanctity of a balanced budget, which 'represented the surest guarantee for a better future'.[58]

Based on this blueprint, the community of central bankers, along with some private bankers and economic experts, could be termed 'money doctors', forming a 'remarkably cohesive social group'. During the 1920s, they advised and often worked as brokers between foreign investors and authorities in countries in need of money. Money in exchange for reforms was part of the process, and it was no coincidence that money doctors came primarily from the United States, Great Britain and France. After all, that was where the money was.[59]

Walter Stewart, an American economist and money doctor, believed that America's rise to prominence in international finance after the War had shifted disinterestedness from Britain to America whose 'representatives are usually the ones who are truly independent and neutral'.[60] This idea of the neutral expert economist gained momentum in the early twentieth century. The money doctors' job was to keep politics out of the economy. In fact, none of them were neutral or without interests; 'at the very heart of money doctoring is an inseparable combination of economics and politics'.[61]

As central bankers struggled to keep up with the Austrian, German and British crises, their orthodox worldview and Bagehot's operating model served as a default blueprint for how they made sense of, and made decisions and acted in the radical uncertainty about, the future that so strongly characterized 1931.

In 1927, Ralph Hawtrey, a British Treasury official and expert on the gold standard, noted the allegiance to Bagehot arguing that 'long and varied experience of financial crises has shown that it is very undesirable that the Central Bank should absolutely refuse to lend. That way lies panic'.

To avoid a panic, the central bank should 'continue to lend. It may insist on good security and may charge a very high rate for its loans'.[62]

Bagehot's model was still state of the art, based on both experiences of past financial crises and expectations for the future. It presented a blueprint for action in times of crisis and uncertainty, but knowing what to do and what to expect was not a simple thing for central bankers. There was nothing familiar about what they were witnessing in 1931.[63] Like so many others during the Great Depression, they were often struggling to make sense of the economy, and dominant economic theory including the Bagehot model often seemed of limited use if not useless.

The central bankers confronting the plethora of problems in the summer of 1931 would soon experience the contrast between their operating model and the situation on the ground in Vienna and Central Europe, where the 'crucial decisions had to be taken by the authorities under conditions of extreme uncertainty'.[64]

Siepmann, Rodd, Norman, Harrison and their colleagues had to deal with all the messy real-world characteristics of uncertainty, ambiguity, lack of information and coordination problems, as well as the various actors' conflicting motives, perceived interests, worldviews and perceptions. Still, as a nascent epistemic community, they shared some basic assumptions and knowledge, including the Bagehot model that enabled their struggle to contain the Credit Anstalt crisis.

If anything, economic and financial crises are characterized by and contribute to radical uncertainty and emotional stress. They change our outlook, our imagined futures, our hopes and anxieties, oftentimes with dramatic economic, cultural, social and political consequences following in their wake. Not to mention personal implications. 'Crises are the domain of multiple realities and conflicting cognitions.'[65]

Dealing with the financial crisis in the summer of 1931 was not for abstract rational agents. It was for humans of flesh and blood with a shared vision. It called for sensemaking and narrative emplotment by an epistemic community of concrete actors in a radically uncertain world.

The international financial crisis of 1931 was grounded in an international context of structural, economic and political problems that had grown bigger by the day since the end of the Great War in 1918 and the Versailles Peace Treaty of 1919. In early 1931, the world was already in a political and economic crisis that went far beyond financial issues.[66]

Historians and contemporary actors alike have agreed that the financial crisis of 1931 was a turning point in the Great Depression.[67] That year unemployment reached 25 per cent in the United States, 21 per cent in Great Britain and 34 per cent in Germany. Still, as one historian puts it, in 'the midst of the deepest deflationary crisis in modern history, the German people continued to worry about inflation!' Industrial production, prices and trade seemed on a never-ending downward slide, while banking systems in most countries grew ever more fragile. Protectionism was on the rise as well, exemplified by the American Smoot-Hawley tariff of 1930.[68]

As a strong undercurrent beneath everything that happened in 1931 lay political, economic and financial issues. Ever since the Versailles Treaty, security issues, war debts and reparations had poisoned international relations and given rise to nationalism and polarization within and between nations. France and Germany in particular were at odds over security, reparations and geo-politics.[69]

France was a strong defender of the Versailles Treaty and reparations, while Germany wanted to get rid of it altogether, and Britain supported a revision of the terms. The break-up of the Austro-Hungarian empire left a political and economic vacuum in Central and Eastern Europe that both Germany and France sought to fill and dominate. Relations between Europe and the United States in turn were strained by war debts, not least because the United States disputed any links between reparations and war debts.[70]

It was in this context, fraught with structural problems and national and personal tensions, that central bankers stepped up in the summer of 1931 and struggled to save capitalism from itself. Before I enter the world of Montagu Norman, George Harrison, Francis Rodd and Harry Siepmann in 1931, I want to elaborate on my conceptual framework and analytical strategy.

If you just want to read the dramatic story about how a group of central bankers struggled to rein in the financial crisis of 1931, you can skip this section and go directly to Chapter 2, without too much harm done.

## THE FOCUS OF THIS BOOK

A perceived failure of central bank cooperation has been the dominant frame among historians for explaining the international financial crisis of 1931.[71] In this book, I deliberately shift focus away from a backward-looking analysis of a perceived failure of central bank cooperation to how a community of central bankers dealt with the 1931 crisis on a forward-going basis. This shift in framing is necessary in order to consider anew and understand what happened in 1931.

I study the roads not taken and the roadblocks encountered by contemporary actors as they went along in their effort to halt the crisis. I provide a detailed historical narrative of a group of central – and some private – bankers of flesh and blood with different tempers, prejudices, allegiances and vantage points as their world turned upside down in the fateful year of 1931.

I show how they followed well-known blueprints for dealing with financial crises, and how they struggled to make sense of the situation under radical uncertainty when the blueprint failed to guide them, and it became clear that not all involved shared their views of what to do.

This book provides a new narrative of central and private bankers' response to the European financial crisis, and to our empirical and theoretical understanding of how decision-makers go about and deal with radical uncertainty, constraints and opportunities in crises.[72]

While the Bagehot model and the ideas of how the gold standard worked may have appeared readily applicable, neither actors nor events fit easily into this generalized blueprint. The future often unfolded differently than the actors imagined and expected, and they were often in the dark as to the future outcome of their actions. In addition, (in)actions and (in)decisions by other central actors occasionally seemed incomprehensible and irresponsible to them – and vice versa.

Moreover, perceptions and the relative power of various groups had changed, since Bagehot wrote his book in 1873. It was realized that an increase in bank rate would increase unemployment, and with unemployment at record height in 1931, that was politically sensitive.[73]

In writing the history of the 1931 crisis forwards, chance, contingency, ambiguity, coincidence, good luck and bad luck, doubts and fears about what would happen next, in short radical uncertainty, must be front and centre. I pay attention to how actors' worldviews, stories and practices as well as their emotions, hopes, fears and anxieties all influenced their sensemaking, their decision-making and their actions. At the same time, these very actors also shaped the crisis and events through their emplotment of events and actors into a narrative with chronology, cause and effect, heroes, villains and a moral.

I strive to leave hindsight aside and aim instead to understand and show in as great detail as possible how Harry Siepmann and Francis Rodd and their colleagues in London, Basle and New York struggled to impose order and direction on their perception of the crisis, of cause and effect, and of right and wrong.[74] I show how they worked 24/7, across borders and time zones, as events unfolded in real time, to deal with and halt the Austrian crisis from spreading to neighbouring countries in general, and to Germany in particular.

The European financial crisis of 1931 played out over five hectic months from May 11 to September 21. I tell the story of this period from the Credit Anstalt failure in May to Great Britain abandoning gold in September, in effect leaving the gold standard dead and gone.

While I zoom in on a group of central bankers from the Bank of England, the Federal Reserve Bank of New York and the BIS, many other actors are part of the story. They include central bankers from France and Germany, private bankers in New York and London as well as the occasional politician, civil servant and many others.

It matters what kind of persons these actors were, how they saw the world they lived and worked in, and how they perceived, categorized and assigned meaning to events and their counterparts. What kind of future did they imagine in the months and weeks up to, during and after the crisis? How did their past experiences and future expectations influence their thinking and practices as they had to deal with the next financial hotspot?[75]

In order to capture these elements, I take a thick description approach where 'phenomena previously considered to be sufficiently described and understood assume completely new meanings by altering the scale of observation'.[76] I am not only altering the scale of observation, but I am also changing the point of observation, following the actors, the human beings, as closely as my empirical material allows for.[77]

Yet, despite my claim to be writing history forwards, there's no denying that it is my conceptual framework and my selecting, ordering, reading and emplotting the empirical material that guides the story from beginning to end. While the empirical material – my sources – certainly sets limits to possible interpretations, it did not emplot itself into a – hopefully – coherent narrative. I did that.

In a way, I am an actor, too, in this history of the financial crisis of 1931 you are about to read. I see nothing wrong with that. If the role of humanistic historical research is to understand how humans in the past made sense of themselves and their world, is the historian – with their emotions, empathy, curiosity, blind spots, prejudices, abilities and limitations – not part of this process?[78]

At the end of the day, like everyone else, I cannot escape Clifford Geertz' description of the process where 'what we call our data are really our own constructions of other people's constructions of what they and their compatriots are up to'.[79]

My focus, or lens, is shaped by the concepts I have chosen and mentioned above. To repeat, they are radical uncertainty, sensemaking, imagined futures, narratives and epistemic communities. I use these concepts as an analytical and heuristic framework to understand the central bankers and their actions, as they struggled to save the gold standard and capitalism in 1931.

## SENSEMAKING AND UNCERTAINTY

Before returning to the financial crisis of 1931, I want to briefly discuss the main concepts and my analytical strategy for understanding what Ralph Hawtrey in his 1932 book called *The Art of Central Banking* as it played out in practice in 1931.[80] The central bankers who struggled to stem the financial crisis faced a deeply uncertain future that challenged their operating model and practices, based primarily on Walter Bagehot's work and their own past experiences.

As an emerging epistemic community, the central bankers involved in halting the financial crisis from spreading shared the operating model based on Walter Bagehot. I build, among others, on sociologist Mitchell Abolafia's work. He argues that 'operating models are intersubjectively shared within cultural communities. In policy-making groups, they often take the form of causal propositions. For example, if we do A, then B will happen'.[81]

Under radical uncertainty, the outcome of decisions is unknown as perceived causal relationships break down, leaving actors with a meaning loss that challenges their operating model. In 1931, this uncertainty called for sensemaking through narrative emplotment that outlined an imagined future outcome. In the words of Rosenhek, a 'fundamental facet in these processes is the ways in which influential actors make sense of the situation, formulating diagnoses of current conditions and causal accounts for explaining them. This is particularly important in highly uncertain and volatile times of crisis, when the taken-for-granted status of dominant institutional blueprints, as well as of their ideational foundations, is potentially jeopardized.'[82]

The central bankers in this story feared that the crisis would lead to a future radically different (worse, that is) from what they knew and hoped for. Ultimately, they feared the fall of the gold standard and capitalism. In fact, that was the essence of their idea of crisis.[83] Like Harry Siepmann, they imagined a future where the house of cards would come tumbling down, and they worked to shape a narrative that could make sense of and help navigate these unknown, unformed and scary futures. It was all about dealing with uncertainty and enabling action.

Sociologist Jens Beckert and economist Richard Bronk argue that actors navigate radical uncertainty through narrative emplotment of fictional expectations that imagine an as yet non-existing future. Narratives point to possible futures through the emplotment of selected elements into an ordered and meaningful explanation that enables decision-making and serves as a blueprint for action. No matter how much data they have, without narratives, actors have no basis for decision-making and action, let alone legitimizing their decisions and actions.[84]

Narratives and uncertainty are also central concepts in sensemaking, a social process in which people 'when confronted by discrepant events seek ... to negotiate and sustain meanings which permit coordinated, (putatively) rational action'.[85] In this process, members of an organization construct 'accounts that allows them to comprehend the world and act collectively.'[86]

Sensemaking involves 'the active authoring of events and frameworks for understanding, as people play a role in constructing the very situations they attempt to comprehend'.[87] Narrative constructions are acts of sensemaking, but they do not start from scratch. When actors assign meaning that shapes a specific understanding of a situation and what needs to be done, they use history as well as personal and institutional memory, and build on an existing framework for perceiving the world – an operating model such as the Bagehot model and the gold standard narrative.[88]

Within an epistemic community, the narrative that results from the sensemaking process will reflect, shape and frame the worldview and practices of this community. This means that narratives both reflect actors' perception of an already existing social reality and re-shape this social reality on an ongoing basis. Narratives are, in short, performative as they assign causality and blame, legitimize, silence or de-legitimize interpretations, actions and actors, heroes and villains. They shape worldviews and serve as a blueprint for actions, practices and decisions. And they represent and exercise power.[89]

In short, 'narrative provides a typical means of constructing the world without which we would be left "lost in a murk of chaotic experience".'[90] As such, the gold standard narrative was performative in that it shaped and legitimized the perceptions and practices of central bankers and policymakers.[91]

I use these concepts and ideas as a heuristic framework for understanding the various actors' points of view, practices and actions. It is this focus and the micro and forward-looking perspective that contribute to making the present study different from the abundant earlier research on the 1931 crisis.[92] Central bankers and other actors did not have direct and privileged access to an already established understanding of what was going on in Austria, Germany and Great Britain in the summer of 1931, and in contrast to historians they had no way of knowing how it would all 'end'.

Instead, central bankers and other actors in 1931 made sense by 'considering as much available information as they can, giving it meaning and relevance, applying a causal model of how they imagine things will evolve and then acting'. In fact, this is how 'actionable knowledge' is established in a context of radical uncertainty.[93]

Someone had to go to Vienna to figure the situation out for themselves and to construct a narrative that enabled them to produce 'actionable knowledge' needed to navigate massive uncertainty, imagine future consequences, and offer a blueprint for actions and remedies. This process does not happen in a vacuum. The central bankers I tail in this book were both helped and constrained by their broader social and cultural context and their experiences and worldviews as central bankers.

The way they made sense of events and cues framed the crisis in a specific way that may also have created blind spots. Colin Hay argues that decision-makers are acting in a context that favours some strategies over others. Actors must, therefore, 'rely upon perceptions of that context, which are at best incomplete, and which may very often prove to have been inaccurate after the event'.[94]

## ANALYTICAL STRATEGY AND MY SOURCES

How can I capture and understand how a group of central bankers from several countries worked to avert what they feared might well be the end of the world as they knew it? My approach is to follow these actors and the people they met, interacted and communicated with as closely as the empirical material allows. Through 'thick description' and using my conceptual framework as a heuristic lens, I seek to capture in the narrative that follows the meanings Rodd and Siepmann and their fellow central bankers assigned to events, their actions and their context.

My analytical strategy, then, focuses on the central bankers and their communications with and relations to each other and to groups outside of their community. I follow them as they worked to make sense of the crisis as it spread from Austria to Germany and then to Britain. I deliberately downplay the traditional frame in the historiography of central bank cooperation and focus instead on how these central bankers saw their world and how they made sense and acted as they worked on the ground in Vienna, Basle, London and New York.

I am telling the story of how Francis Rodd, Harry Siepmann, Montagu Norman and George Harrison and their fellow central bankers strived to piece the puzzle together and construct a narrative that could guide their decisions and actions in order to stop the crisis from spreading. To understand central bankers' perceptions, decisions and actions in the summer of 1931 requires not only that I follow them closely from day to day, sometimes from one hour to the next. It also entails that I inquire about the processes of signification involved in their endeavour. How did they explain their experiences and actions to themselves and to others?

The protagonists in this book lived in cities in Europe and America. Most of them worked in the offices of the Federal Reserve Bank of New York, the Bank of England in London and the BIS in Basle. They used whatever form of communication available depending on the expediency and urgency of the matter at hand. They communicated by letter, telegram, telephone and in person, and they wrote a large number of memos and notes for internal use. They were travelling between Basle and Vienna, London and Basle, or even between New York and Europe by train, aeroplane or ship as they attended meetings, or needed to assess the situation for themselves on the spot. And they relied on each other as well as on newspapers and magazines to keep updated about the situation as it developed.

As early as May 12, Francis Rodd arrived in Vienna by train from Basle. His first task was to figure out what was going on and to what extent there was a central banking issue at all. Though he was not alone and would not be making the final decisions, occasionally Francis Rodd was sensemaker-in-chief. He was the one who had to separate the wheat from the chaff.

There are many limits, however, to what I can know and show. I would have loved to know the many actors' thoughts and emotions, and to have been a fly on the wall during their many conversations, meetings and talks over a beer or dinner and a glass of wine. But all I have are the written traces they and the archives left behind, and my imagination properly constrained, I hope, by the historian's craft.

Thus, the book is based on the traces of the past, my empirical material, left in the archives of the BIS, the Federal Reserve Bank of New York and the Bank of England among others. It is on the basis of this material I have constructed a new narrative of how a relatively small group of central bankers sought to understand and narrate the crisis as they were trying to save the monetary and financial system and capitalism from itself.

These three organizations and their highly trained officials were front and centre in the first truly international lender-of-last-resort operation in history. My focus is on these organizations and individuals, and their interactions, with each other, and with other groups, firms, governments and individuals involved in the crisis. I also use contemporary newspapers and magazines, and other archives such as the Morgan Library, the Rothschild Archive, and Francis Rodd's archive.

What I do not use are archives from the Austrian National Bank, the Banque de France and the German Reichsbank or from, say, finance ministries. I also do not use archives of the Credit Anstalt or the Danatbank. The reason is, as stated already, that my interest, my research question if you will, lies with the perceptions and actions of the most important central bankers who worked to contain the crisis.

I cannot rule out that there may be relevant material in the archives not frequented. But I think it is fair to argue that, given the focus of this book, using these archives would not have changed the narrative that follows in any decisive way.

The BIS, the Federal Reserve Bank of New York and the Bank of England were without doubt the most important organizational actors. Therefore, I focus on them and their interactions with actors from other central banks such as the Banque de France and the Reichsbank. To the extent other authorities and actors played a role, and they did, I rely on the work of a great many colleagues.

To be clear, I am far from the first historian who has used one or parts of these archives to understand some aspect of the Austrian, German and British crises.[95] However, to my knowledge, I am the first who has combined such extensive use of the three central bank archives to study in a systematic way how central bankers made sense of and narrated the crisis on a forward-going basis. This book is also the first to include important private bankers from J.P. Morgan and the Rothschilds in London.

My claim to novelty, then, is not only based on the detailed narrative of the European financial crisis of 1931, though I do consider that an important new contribution. It is also based on the purpose, forward-looking and cultural approach of this book – to understand sensemaking and decision-making during crises and radical uncertainty in depth.

I do not pretend to tell the final truth about the financial crisis of 1931. In fact, I do not believe there is one. I also do not analyse or test in detail various cause and effect claims such as why the Credit Anstalt or Danatbank failed, or why the gold standard broke down. Many historians have dealt with these questions, and will continue to do so, but that is not what I am interested in. I am interested in human beings and how people act when they think their world is falling apart. I am interested in the 'natives' point of view' even though this time around, the natives were central bankers.

I am also not testing theories or hypotheses, and I am not operationalizing the conceptual framework in order to prove it right or wrong. I am using it as part of my analytical strategy, as a lens to select, order and read my empirical material, and narrating the story of the European financial crisis of 1931. The conceptual framework is embodied in the narrative that follows, not necessarily explicitly announced in every instance. This book is a humanistic and cultural analysis of central bankers in the hectic summer of 1931.

I have found it important, even necessary, to allow the actors to speak for themselves. Throughout the book, I therefore rely on many and extensive quotes to let their voices be heard. This does not mean that I take their statements at face value or to be true or to necessarily reveal what they were thinking. That is not my concern. My concern is to show the actors' sensemaking process from fictional expectations to imagining futures, to narrative emplotment, to actionable knowledge and decision-making as it unfolded during five hectic months from May to September 1931. The many quotes show sensemaking, meaning construction and narrative emplotment under radical uncertainty in action. They do not necessarily tell us what the actors believed or what was 'true'.

The result, which you are about to read, is a narrative. It is my story about what Francis Rodd, Harry Siepmann and their many colleagues and counterparts were up to in the summer of 1931. The resulting historical narrative is not an anecdote or the basis for further analysis and conclusions.

The narrative *is* the analysis.

## STRUCTURE OF THIS BOOK

In Chapter 2, I introduce some of the important actors and their perception of the world they lived in up to and as the financial crisis played out in 1931. In Chapters 3–10, I tell the detailed story of how central bankers prepared for a crisis somewhere in Europe and how they worked hard to deal with the outbreak in Austria in May and June 1931. This part is largely organized chronologically, which enables me to follow the actors closely in their daily interactions and deliberations.

In Chapter 11, I briefly change the perspective together with the actors, as they shifted from prospective to retrospective sensemaking. I show how Francis Rodd, Pierre Quesnay and others sought to emplot and narrate the Austrian crisis from their vantage points. In Chapters 12–14 I trace how central bankers' worst-case imagined future came to life as Germany was hit by a serious financial and exchange crisis in June and July. Finally, Chapters 15–17 trace the battle for sterling and Britain's departure from gold in September 1931.

Throughout this book, I try to show how Francis Rodd's, Harry Siepmann's, Montagu Norman's and George Harrison's and their colleagues' hopes and anxieties, prejudices, prior assumptions and blind spots as well as the available information shaped their decisions – decisions that may well have felt the most important ones they would ever have to make. I show how they worked together and sometimes against each other, and how different perspectives and conflicts influenced their tempers, actions and decisions.

I end the book by discussing the implications of writing history forwards from a micro-level perspective. I have deliberately left out of this introduction a discussion of the extant historical literature on the crisis of 1931. You can find much of it in the endnotes, and in the final chapter where I discuss the book's empirical and theoretical contribution to the historical scholarship into the European financial crisis of 1931. Finally, I briefly consider parallels with the Great Financial Crisis and discuss if there are any lessons to be made with regard to decision-making under radical uncertainty in other past and future crises.

But first, let's get to know some of the main actors and the world in which they lived.

# 2

# Central Bankers and Their World

Montagu Norman and George Harrison were in charge during the financial crisis of 1931, and as it spread across Europe they increasingly took centre stage. Their interactions with each other, with the Bank for International Settlements (BIS) and with other central banks and private bankers are an important part of the history of the crisis of 1931.

Still, below the level of top central bankers, there was a layer of highly competent and hard-working people who were instrumental in figuring out how to understand and stop the crisis from spreading. Francis Rodd and Harry Siepmann were important figures in this community of central bankers. In contrast to Norman and Harrison, we know next to nothing about them.

In the Austrian phase of the crisis, until mid-June, Rodd and Siepmann emerged as prominent sensemakers and human hubs of information. Nevertheless, with only a few exceptions, both contemporary observers and later historians have tended to overlook people like them and their role in the 1931 crisis.

As Governor Montagu Norman's right hand, Harry Siepmann spent most of the time at the Bank in Threadneedle Street in the City of London, while Francis Rodd spent weeks in Vienna to collect and screen information in May and June.

Without following people like Rodd and Siepmann, we cannot have a proper understanding of how central banks worked – or work – during crises. They, and many others, are important protagonists in this story, but who were they?[1]

## FRANCIS RODD AND HARRY SIEPMANN

Francis Rennell Rodd was born in London on October 25, 1895. He was educated at Eton and Balliol College, Oxford, and was a member of the

British aristocracy. His father, a diplomat, had been ambassador to Italy, and Rodd spoke fluent Italian along with French and German. Like so many others of his generation, he served in the Great War and then followed in his father's footsteps into the Foreign Service.[2]

In 1924 at twenty-nine, Rodd left the Foreign Service and took up a position at a stockbroking firm, becoming a member of the London Stock Exchange two years later. In 1929 he came to the Bank of England, and the following year he was seconded to the newly established BIS.

Travelling to new places to make sense of what he saw was by no means new to Rodd, who had been a fellow of the Royal Geographical Society since 1921. In 1922 and 1927 he went to Sahara to live among the Tuareg people.[3] His 1926 book *People of the Veil* on the Tuareg was well received by the *Daily Telegraph* noting that Rodd had a 'captivating literary style'.[4]

Rodd was perceived as shy and reserved but also confident, perhaps even brusque in public matters though with a 'great capacity for affection'.[5] He was also seen as 'toughminded and unsentimental' with 'leadership qualities'. Despite his distinctly British 'imperial' worldview, Rodd felt that he had the ability to see 'the other chap's point of view' and that his role as a traveller had been to 'try and understand people who live in other places'.[6] He would certainly have had to make use of these qualities as he arrived in Vienna on May 12, 1931, thirty-five years old.

Rodd was a central figure in the first phase of the crisis precisely because he spent a lot of time in Vienna, the eye of the storm in May and early June. Rodd himself noted that 'time and again in our history the man on the spot with the knowledge has found it necessary to act and his action has eventually been approved at home though their views and politics were different'.[7] He clearly saw himself as a decision-maker and man of action.

Francis Rodd spent several weeks in Vienna with his BIS colleague Hans Simon, an Austrian economist, and he was indispensable for collecting, making sense of and producing actionable knowledge for the BIS and for the Bank of England.

Harry Siepmann did not share Rodd's privileged background. He was born on October 1, 1889, and his father was a German-born educator in modern languages at Clifton College in Bristol. Six years older than Rodd, he too was educated at Oxford, at New College, where he received a brilliant first in Greats or Classics.[8]

Siepmann joined the Treasury in 1912 at age twenty-three. Two years later as the War broke out, his German background became a liability, and he volunteered for war service. He fought in Egypt, in

Italy and on the Western Front as a captain, where he suffered a poison gas attack in September 1918. The effects of war haunted him for the rest of his life.[9]

Back at the Treasury, in 1919 Siepmann was John Maynard Keynes's personal assistant at the Versailles Peace Conference. He remained an acquaintance of Keynes and shared his views of the Versailles conference and the economic consequences of the peace.[10] Siepmann also knew the economist Ralph Hawtrey, a treasury official and expert on central banking, who published *The Art of Central Banking* in 1932. The book was Hawtrey's response to the 1931 crisis and the need for an international lender of last resort.[11]

Before joining the Bank of England as an adviser in 1926, Siepmann served as an assistant to the finance member of the Viceroy's Council in India, and as an adviser to the National Bank of Hungary. As early as 1923, Siepmann had come to know Montagu Norman and they corresponded on a fairly regular basis, writing long letters on various matters. It was almost too much. At one point Norman had seven unanswered letters from Siepmann lying on his desk.[12]

Siepmann was a writing man, and an 'unusually expressive writer whose elegance sometimes conveyed a clarity of view beyond what was currently held by his masters'.[13] Intelligent, eloquent, modest and hard-working, he once finished a letter to Norman on the Austrian National Bank on a Sunday at 3 in the morning, earning a marginal note from Norman saying 'Shame!'[14] When the BIS was established in 1930, Siepmann declined to go to Basle, and instead Francis Rodd became the manager of BIS's Central Banking Department.[15]

Rodd and Siepmann were colleagues and in frequent contact, but as persons they were quite different. Rodd, with the self-consciousness of the British upper class, was different from Siepmann, who was haunted by self-doubt and found social contact difficult. In a letter to Rodd, the latter confessed, 'If it is a sin to dislike talkativeness, I had better admit this sin is in me native and original.'[16]

Siepmann was dedicated and focused on the tasks at hand, and not given to small talk. In late June 1931, a bank manager spent an hour of Siepmann's valuable time complaining about the French. 'Altogether, a superficial, gossipy, unimportant conversation', Siepmann noted afterwards.[17]

What bound Rodd and Siepmann together in 1931 was a dislike of wasting their time, and the need to save the world as they knew it – and Montagu Norman, the governor of the Bank of England.

## MONTAGU NORMAN, GEORGE HARRISON AND THE BIS

Born into a banking family in 1871, Norman went to Eton and Kings College, Cambridge, but he did not thrive and left Cambridge after a year and soon went into banking in both London and New York. Like his American counterpart, the sixteen years younger George Harrison, he was a bachelor in 1931 when the financial crisis struck.

Norman became a member of the Court of Directors of the Bank of England in 1907, and in 1915 he left private banking for the Bank of England. In 1917 he was elected deputy governor, and in 1920 he became governor of the Bank of England, a position he kept until 1944. He was the first 'professional' governor of the Bank.

The Bank of England was a private bank, and Norman was less constrained by the checks and balances most other central bank governors had to live with. At the same time, he professionalized the Bank, bringing people like Harry Siepmann and Francis Rodd on board. He held frequent meetings with the Committee of Treasury, Bank of England's 'board', and he encouraged discussion. Still, most often, within the Bank Norman's word was law, which enabled him to act faster and with more determination than most other central banks.[18]

A handsome man with a melancholic expression and a Van Dyke beard, Norman was a larger-than-life central banker with an image to die for. Without doubt he was the best-known, most experienced and best-connected central banker in the world. Besides his eccentric qualities, he was quintessentially British with a corresponding imperial worldview, which earned him some distrust from quite a few continental central bankers.[19]

Norman was 'temperamentally shy and retiring' and often travelled incognito, not least when he was visiting the United States. He was no fan of publicity but was nevertheless followed closely by the media as the central banker celebrity he undeniably was. One suspects that he may have enjoyed the attention, after all.

The contemporary prolific economic writer and journalist Paul Einzig described Norman as a friendly and kind man, but 'there is something in his personality which makes opposition to his will extremely difficult'.[20]

He not only had a strong will. He also had a temper, especially with people who did not live up to his expectations, whether reasonable or not. He was a conservative, a strong believer in the gold standard, the Bank of England's international status and sterling's exorbitant privilege.[21]

The Bank's and other central banks' primary purpose was to protect the exchange rate and the gold standard come what may in terms of unemployment and recession. In this view, Norman was joined by the City of London and bankers around the world, who favoured stable money above all else and worshipped the gold standard with almost religious fervour.

His role in reconstructing the post-war financial system and the gold standard was based on his idea of traditional central banking principles and his strong belief in central bank cooperation and independence. Norman was a 'political operator' who envisioned 'a global network of central banks, independent of governments, [that] would radically reduce the capacity of states to interfere with markets'.[22] This vision included Norman's hope that the BIS would come to improve and develop central bank cooperation. The management of BIS spent much time figuring out what to make of Norman's views. 'Of course the basis of all of Norman's criticism of our activities . . . is that we are in fact a central bank, save for the power to issue notes, and consequently should conduct ourselves as such.'[23]

On a larger scale, according to Pierre Quesnay, a French economist and central banker, and from 1930 General Manager at the BIS, the 'economic and financial organization of the world appears to him the great objective of the twentieth century'. In his work towards this objective, Norman opposed not only political intervention in financial markets but also French insistence on the Treaty of Versailles, including reparations, and he supported Germany's wish for a revision of the Treaty.[24]

To Norman, Britain and the Bank of England had a historical claim to be at the centre of a global economy. That required a return to the gold standard, which Britain achieved in 1925. But it also led to competition with the United States and France for economic dominance.[25]

There is no reason to assume that Norman had an easy life. Tormented by occasional nervous breakdowns and depressions and a pessimistic worldview, his perception of world events rarely touched an overly optimistic note. In early 1931 he wrote to Clément Moret, the governor of Banque de France, that unless 'drastic measures are taken to save it, the capitalist system throughout the civilized world will be wrecked within a year. I should like this prediction to be filed for future reference'.[26]

In fact, in early 1931, Edward Grenfell, senior partner in the merchant bank Morgan Grenfell, wrote to Jack Morgan that Norman 'felt very blue'. Grenfell and 'Monty' saw 'nothing to be cheerful about [in] our industrial or fiscal situation'. Jack Morgan was senior partner in J.P. Morgan & Co. and son of Mr American Finance, John Pierpont Morgan, who had passed away in 1913. Since then, Jack Morgan had been heading the House of Morgan.

He was a little more optimistic. Norman's view of the situation 'is very similar to my own', he wrote to Grenfell, but 'whatever its length like all tunnels it has light at the other end'.[27] To Norman, civilization would be 'wrecked'; to Morgan it was something they would get through. It was two very different imagined future narratives in a time of radical uncertainty.

The correspondence also revealed Norman's far-reaching network that went well beyond the world of central banking. One of his biographers likened him to a 'human spider' who spun a 'finely meshed web of private contacts radiating from his office into every nook and cranny of the City'.[28] He did, indeed, have close relations with prominent merchant bankers in the City and beyond, including Edward Grenfell and Jack Morgan in New York.

Edward Grenfell was an influential person, too. A senior partner of Morgan Grenfell, he was also Director at the Bank of England and a Conservative MP. Morgan Grenfell in London, Morgan & Cie in Paris and J.P. Morgan & Co. in New York together made up the House of Morgan. J.P. Morgan & Co. was the go-to investment bank not only in America but also for transatlantic transactions and loans. After the Great War, Jack Morgan led the firm into government financing and the firm had particularly close relations with France and Great Britain. This position gave the Morgan banks an important role in the final phase of the European crisis.[29]

To Norman, being governor of the Bank of England with a history going all the way back to 1694 meant that he worked in an organization with a heavy tradition and 'burden of history'.[30] It was a time- and life-consuming endeavour based on his strong belief in the gold standard, which went all the way back to 1717. As crisis struck in 1931, this involved even longer than normal hours of hard work. That, too, was the case for Norman's American colleague, George Harrison.

George Leslie Harrison was born in 1887 and was a graduate of Yale and Harvard Law School. He clerked for Supreme Court Justice Oliver Wendel Holmes before joining the Federal Reserve Board in 1914. In stark contrast to Norman and the Bank of England, Harrison did not join an organization with a long history and tradition. In fact, the Federal Reserve System and the Federal Reserve Banks opened for business in November 1914, the same year Harrison joined the System.

In 1920, the revered Governor Benjamin Strong of the Federal Reserve Bank of New York recruited Harrison from the Board in DC as his deputy governor. When Strong died in October 1928, Harrison was his logical successor.[31]

Lame in his left leg since childhood, Harrison used a walking stick. In 1931 he was forty-four years old and like Norman still a bachelor. He lived at the Yale Club close to the Grand Central Station from where he could take the subway to the New York Fed at 33 Liberty Street 'without getting his feet wet', as he liked to say. An American with British ancestors Harrison was fond of poker and chess as well as sailing his sloop. He was portrayed as a 'scholarly looking fellow who smokes a brier pipe and speaks in soft, cultivated tones. He has ... friendly blue eyes and a shy, warm smile'.[32]

He was a stoical man who rarely lost his temper, and in some ways Norman's opposite. He did not share Norman's pessimism and temper, and he stood up for the New York Fed's autonomy relative to the Federal Reserve Board. When Harrison became governor in 1928, Roy A. Young, the governor of the Federal Reserve Board, tried unsuccessfully to reclaim authority from the New York Fed to the Board in Washington DC. But 'Harrison was the clear victor. He stood firm' despite 'violent language'.[33]

Morgan partner R.C. Leffingwell described the difference between Benjamin Strong's and Harrison's leadership at the New York Fed as a 'transition from Ben's benevolent despotism to George's more gentle but perhaps ultimately more enduring democratic constitutionalism'. Leffingwell had 'complete confidence in George, in soundness of his views and his ability ultimately to put them into effect'.[34] Private bankers and central bankers were part of the same network and often shared worldviews.

As Wall Street crashed in October 1929, Harrison 'lowered interest rates and pumped billions of dollars in credit to buoy banks with heavy loans to brokers' and in his 'whatever it takes' moment announced, 'Gentlemen, I am ready to provide all the reserve funds that may be needed.'[35]

Like Norman and Benjamin Strong, Harrison 'believed fervently in the principle of the separation of the state and the central bank'.[36] Charles F. Whigham, a partner at Morgan Grenfell, argued that this 'is one of the fetishes of all Central Banks they will deal with central banks and not governments'.[37]

One should not underestimate the role of personality and personal relations, especially in times of crisis. In a way, Strong's death bound

Norman and Harrison closer together as they corresponded and reminisced about Strong whom they both admired.[38] Since then, they worked to strengthen their relationship, which came to go beyond the strictly professional though not without obstacles along the way.

Norman was aware of the criticism Strong had experienced in the United States, where he was suspected of managing a monetary policy that served the Bank of England's interests. In contemplating a visit to New York to see Harrison, Norman was concerned about such speculation, but Harrison assured Norman that 'there is no reason for embarrassment and great advantages in your coming'.[39]

In January 1931, as Norman returned from two weeks of holiday in southern France, Harrison wrote to him, 'I am glad that you were able to get a rest and I am still hopeful that some day we may both have one together. In the meantime however I hope to get away for a week or ten days fairly soon if possible.'[40] Two months later, a concerned Harrison, confirming their shared identity as central bankers, told Norman, 'You must take care of yourself. . . . This business of being a central banker requires much more than the average endurance and therefore much more than the average care.'[41]

Harrison and Norman did not agree about everything, but in 1931 they envisioned themselves as part of a community working together to save the international financial system from breaking down. Harrison was at a disadvantage, though, in terms of access to reliable information about the situation in Europe. Norman could rely on his close personal network of people with intimate knowledge of the situation in Austria and other European countries, and Harrison often asked him for updates. To some extent, two other Americans in Europe compensated for this problem.

Gates McGarrah was president of the BIS and a former chairman of the Federal Reserve Bank of New York, meaning that he already knew Harrison well. Leon Fraser, vice president of the BIS, was a former partner in a New York law firm and general counsel to the Dawes Plan representative S. Parker Gilbert from 1924 to 1927. In 1931 Gilbert went on to become partner at J.P. Morgan.

Fraser's European network and his knowledge and understanding of Europe were superior to most other Americans involved in the financial crisis. He and McGarrah played a central role in the Austrian phase. Though less so as the crisis moved on to Germany in late June, they were still well positioned to keep Harrison up to date.

## CENTRAL BANKERS, NATIONALS AND INDIVIDUALS

The socialization into what exactly it meant to be a central banker and to become a member of the community of central bankers was not a theoretical but a practical, cultural and social one. If there was one person at the top of this network, it was Norman who knew everything worth knowing about central banking and the City.

Like most of their fellow central bankers, Norman, Rodd and Siepmann had no formal economic training. What they knew about central banking they had learned through practice, studying on the side and being part of the inner circle at the Bank of England.

Norman, in particular, distrusted theory and academic knowledge, relying instead on instinct, experience and intuition. To be sure, there were economists at both the Bank of England and the New York Fed, but they were few and mostly held advisory and not policy-making roles. Norman, Rodd and Siepmann shared ideas of what it meant to be a central banker, and they were part of the emerging epistemic community of central bankers.

Sentiment was the same at the Banque de France. Officials there told Francis Rodd how they disliked 'theoretical consideration' and believed that 'central Banking could not be run by theorists or on statistics. It was a profession requiring experience and contact with realities not with figures'.[42]

At the same time, however, central bankers also had national outlooks, and in the Bank of England they certainly shared a distinctly British and imperial view.[43] They never lost sight of what they perceived as British interests, even when they were not aware of it, which was most of the time. In fact, the only thing Norman distrusted more than academic theorizing was the French, against whom he and many other British decision-makers were strongly prejudiced.[44]

Norman had a seriously problematic relationship with the Banque de France's governor from 1926 to 1930, Emile Moreau, who did not share Norman's view that politics and central banking had nothing in common and would not stand for his patronizing.[45]

While sceptical of the French, Norman was not only sympathetic to Germany's resistance to reparations, but he was also a friend of the controversial president of the Reichsbank until 1930, Hjalmar Schacht. A man with few friends, Schacht was highly intelligent and arrogant as well as a stern critic of the Versailles Treaty and reparation payments.

In contrast, Norman was reported to consider Hans Luther, Schacht's successor as Reichsbank president, a 'whinger'.[46]

What united them all as central bankers was their almost by definition conservative worldview and belief in sanctity of the gold standard and 'free markets'. When Norman testified before the Macmillan Committee on Finance and Industry on March 26, 1930, he told the Committee that 'the whole of the international machinery is bound together'. He continued that 'what is called the gold standard is the cement by which it is bound together'.[47]

In the 1920s, Benjamin Strong and Montagu Norman had developed both a friendship and a 'New York-London axis' of central bank cooperation, and they worked to expand the community of central bankers independent of politics.[48] Though Norman found little place for Banque de France in this network, Benjamin Strong developed a good relationship with Émile Moreau and he considered Norman's attitude towards Banque de France 'stupid beyond understanding'.[49]

A few months before he died in October 1928, Strong had grown tired of European ways. He thought that with currencies back on gold 'the old evils of cut-throat competition are again showing themselves. It even enters into the policies of the banks of issue. My belief is that the time has come to keep out of any complications of the sort which the banks of issue are likely to encounter. We have discharged our moral obligation to Europe'.[50]

Of course, Strong could not know what would happen three years later, and after he passed away, Harrison continued the good relationship with Moreau's successor Clément Moret, while also keeping in close contact with Norman. Norman's relation with the Banque de France also improved when Clément Moret replaced Moreau, but their relations in 1931 were still less than perfect.[51]

Bank of England's position at the centre of the dominant central banks was challenged by America's ascendance as a creditor nation, and by France's increased economic importance as it returned to gold in 1928.[52] The rivalry between the Banque de France and Bank of England partly stemmed from their competition over financial leadership in Europe, a position the Bank of England had traditionally held, but which the French central bank challenged, not least in Central and Eastern Europe.[53]

Occasionally, central bankers were torn between perceived national interests and their allegiance to the gold standard and the community of central banks. While their ultimate loyalty and worldviews often aligned with their national belonging, national interests were never given but culturally constructed and therefore needed to be interpreted and mediated before they could be translated into decisions and actions. Central bankers were aware of the importance of their actions to the world economy and to financial stability and did not always concur with their respective governments' ideas of national interests.[54]

In 1928 Benjamin Strong noted that human nature and 'differences of language, customs, beliefs and financial and political needs' would necessarily influence central bankers' views and policies.[55] Harrison and Norman would undoubtedly agree. Norman too argued that central bankers had to consider national interests but maintained at the same time that personal relations and community mattered as well.

The BIS, Norman argued, by bringing people together in Basle, contributed to shaping a sense of community and facilitated sharing of important ideas and values about what it meant to be a central banker. This double loyalty based on national, cultural and personal affinity meant, for instance, that central bankers agreed, at least in principle if not always in practice, on the role of monetary policy, the sacredness of the gold standard, the separation of politics from the economy and finance, and of central banking from the affairs of the state.

Exchange of information was facilitated with the establishment of the BIS, but old lines of communication were still used. Over the summer as financial conditions worsened, Norman was an important source of information and fellow sensemaker to Harrison and they both knew that. Less than two weeks before the Credit Anstalt failure, Norman sent information about the upcoming BIS board meeting to Harrison 'for your information because you complained that communications from Basle and indeed Europe was too few and far between'.[56]

Francis Rodd frequently communicated back home to Siepmann and Norman at the Bank of England; Pierre Quesnay kept the Banque de France informed and McGarrah and Leon Fraser informed Harrison – sometimes by way of Morgan & Cie in Paris, in order to keep the exchange confidential.

These communications along national lines occasionally created conflicts internally at the BIS or between BIS and one or more central banks.[57] But the most significant fault line was between Germany and France. The BIS was not popular in Germany where it was considered a 'vestige of the post-Versailles Reparations Commission and of the Dawes Plan Control Committee'.[58]

In March and April 1930, a conflict between the Reichsbank and the Banque de France came to a head, and Harrison took it upon himself to ease the troubled waters. At a BIS meeting in March, Hjalmar Schacht refused to endorse Pierre Quesnay of the Banque de France as General Manager of the BIS. As Schacht was forced to resign as Reichsbank president, Harrison tried to convince his successor Hans Luther to vote for Quesnay, but to no avail. 'The deep scruples against a French General Manager continue in Germany undiminished', Luther told McGarrah.[59]

Nevertheless, on April 22, Pierre Quesnay was elected by the BIS board of directors, but Luther voted against 'because the German nation and the Reichsbank considered that the manager of the bank should be chosen from a neutral nation and not from a former enemy of the Reich'.[60]

Compared to Hjalmar Schacht, Luther was a moderate, however. Schacht insisted that what Germany needed was open export markets and that reparations should be cancelled. In early 1930, S. Parker Gilbert, J.P. Morgan partner and former Agent General for Reparations under the Dawes plan, characterized Schacht as one who 'liked to pose as the only German who has the courage to say no to the foreigners ... his course of action is almost entirely unpredictable'.[61]

Harrison had met with Luther in Naples in March as he tried in vain to convince him to vote for Quesnay's position at the BIS. He nevertheless liked Luther, a former Chancellor of Germany. 'I do want to tell you about my visit with Luther', Harrison wrote to McGarrah. 'He came to lunch with me at my hotel in Rome Sunday. In general, he made an excellent impression – very earnest, sincere and evidently frank.'[62]

A financial crisis was the last thing central bankers needed in the spring of 1931. Distrust, conflicts and personal animosities, together with varying levels of access to information, came on top of the general uncertainty about the future of capitalism in Europe and the United States. It was not a given that the various groups involved in a future rescue operation would be able to cooperate smoothly towards a common purpose, or that they would even have identical views of means and purpose.

In fact, it would be surprising if they agreed about everything. Nevertheless, they were united in their shared belief in the gold standard and the need to avoid a breakdown of the international monetary and financial system. And whether they had read it or not, they knew Bagehot and the operating model well enough to realize what was expected of them if a financial crisis broke out.

That did not necessarily mean that they agreed on what exactly the underlying problems of the gold standard were. The reestablished gold standard was a gold exchange standard. This meant that some foreign exchange such as dollars and sterling were included in the cover ratios determining how much gold and foreign exchange central banks had to hold relative to their note issue.

The Bank of England and Banque de France had different monetary policy goals, meaning that the perceived 'rules of the game' of the gold standard was an illusion. Britain was economizing on the use of gold while France was seen as working to acquire gold 'as an instrument of power and to reestablish it as the sole monetary base'.[63]

The resulting so-called sterilization, by which France and the United States neglected to expand credit despite an inflow of gold, was a thorn in the side of Montagu Norman and other deficit countries.[64] France on the other hand considered the inflow of gold as a sign that markets and the gold standard worked and argued that it was Britain's responsibility to deflate the economy.[65]

Everywhere in Europe and America, the situation was dire as 1930 turned to 1931. In Basle and elsewhere they were in for a steep learning curve and some extraordinarily stressful months. If there ever was a time when finance and politics were separated, the interwar period was not that time.[66]

## THE WORLD THEY LIVED IN: THE PRESENT WORLD DEPRESSION

Even before May 1931, there was already much anxiety in Europe and the United States about the economic depression and the economic and political future. The outlook had taken a definite turn for the worse in mid-1930. On April 1 that year, the Morgan partners felt that 'there generally exists a feeling of optimism as to the future', and one month later in a case of seriously bad timing, President Hoover told the US Chamber of Commerce, 'I am convinced that we have passed the worst and with continued effort we shall rapidly recover.'[67]

The optimism was short-lived. On June 17, despite warnings from more than a thousand economists and bankers, the US Congress passed the Smoot-Hawley Tariff bill, and as 1930 turned into 1931, concern about the international economy only increased. At the BIS and the Bank of England, too, officers were concerned that 1931 might hold unpleasant surprises. Central bankers were keen observers of economic and financial indicators, and they were in regular contact with international colleagues, exchanging information, anxieties and hopes about the future.

In late November 1930, George Harrison and Allan Sproul, his assistant deputy, visited Europe to assess the situation in person. In Paris, they met with the governor of the Banque de France Clément Moret and Prime Minister André Tardieu. After the meeting, Harrison reported back home about an 'atmosphere of uncertainty in Paris . . . many fear economic and fiscal problems in Germany . . . and possible breakdown in capitalist system'. The European scene with 'political disturbances and bank failures have contributed to what they all call the crisis and general nervousness seem prevalent'.[68]

Harrison and Sproul also met with the prominent French economists Charles Rist and Pierre Quesnay, both of whom had previously held positions at the Banque de France. The gentlemen were gloomy as they discussed the role of gold and foreign lending in the 'present economic depression'. Investors had an 'extreme preference for safety as compared with yield', and the 'seriousness of the situation lies in the fact that capitalism itself is on trial in many countries'.[69]

The international press corps was well aware of the precarious and uncertain economic situation. As reporters approached Harrison outside of his hotel in Paris, all he said was 'I am simply talking over monetary affairs. . . . Of course, gold is always one of our problems.' This was noted by *Time* magazine in an article that discussed gold sterilization by France and the United States.[70]

Two weeks later, *Time* reported that Montagu Norman met with Harrison aboard the S.S. Bremen as 'France and the U. S. continuing their joint dominance of three-fifths of the world's monetary gold'.[71] The magazine summed up Britain's position that the gold sterilized by France and the United States had to be put into fruitful circulation before 'prosperity can return'.[72]

Ignoring such stories, the two surplus countries resisted inflating their economies despite the continuing inflow of gold. This policy put more pressure to deflate on deficit countries such as Austria, Germany and Great Britain. Norman hardly felt that the United States and France, who were accumulating gold at an unprecedented pace, were trying hard enough to expand credit and make gold re-enter circulation.

Ralph Hawtrey remarked in February 1931 that we 'complain of the drain of gold because it tends to cause a monetary contraction here and in the rest of the world'. France's reply, he said, was 'that we can prevent the drain of gold if we choose to effect a monetary contraction'.[73]

In January, Norman was highly disturbed by rumours that 'there is a distinct possibility of a revision of the value of the pound during 1931'.[74] A couple of weeks later, he expressed his concern about central banks' options, since 'the future here depends more on politics than on finance'.[75]

O.M.W. Sprague, an influential American economist and expert on financial crises, and adviser to the Bank of England, also spoke to Harrison and Sproul during their European tour. Sprague was a strong supporter of the gold standard and an equally strong believer in market forces and the economy's ability to correct itself.

Sprague told Harrison and Sproul that there were no patent medicines or central bank cure-alls for economic depression. England had to 'take her difficulties sitting down, instead of standing against them'. Sitting down, in Sprague's view, meant deflation, also called 'economy' at the time. It meant reducing 'costs of production – including salaries and wages – where they have been held up despite drastic declines in commodity prices'.[76]

This leave-it-to-the-market narrative was the dominant idea at the time with only a few dissenting voices. At the New York Fed, Harrison's deputy governor W. Randolph Burgess, who was trained as a statistician, believed central banks should do more to assist the markets. On February 21, 1931, he wrote to George J. Seay, the governor of the Federal Reserve Bank of Richmond, that 'it is the duty of the central bank in any country to throw its influence towards firm money in times of business expansion . . . and to throw its influence towards easy money at times of depression'.

The New York Fed, Burgess said, had 'recently reviewed the depressions of the 90s and 1908' but was unable to identify any useful historical analogies. Burgess noted that 'the world is going through a desperate economic depression, one of the most severe in its history, and the strain is made greater by the fact that we and France have not been operating the gold standard according to the old rules'.[77]

Two months later, Burgess again stressed 'the seriousness of the present world situation' and the uncertainty of how to deal with the 'obstacles which lie in the way'. Burgess noted that there was no willingness to increase foreign lending and no demand for bank loans in America. The credit system had come to a standstill.[78]

These were all signs that despite their common ground, central bankers and economists could not make sense of or agree about the situation in the spring of 1931. Their use of history in search of relevant historical analogies was not helpful, and the sense of meaning loss and uncertainty was widespread, feeding on the already overwhelming feeling of pessimism.

In one of his regular and 'strictly confidential' reports to the US Department of State, Merle Cochran, the American Consul in Basle, reported in February 1931 of a profound sense that the gold standard didn't work and that the 'functioning in the past few years had been subject to non-monetary conditions'. There was a need for 'external assistance' in order to make the system function according to the 'rules'.[79]

Cochran, who got most of his information from Gates McGarrah and Leon Fraser at the BIS, noted that the British saw French and American sterilization of gold inflows as the 'chief cause of the present world depression', and it required 'exterior measures being taken that will remedy England's gold situation'.[80]

Despite the gloomy sentiment, many were looking for small signs of economic recovery. Harrison's deputy Jay Crane noted in early March how 'the feeling here about prospects abroad has improved considerably in the last week or so', and Harrison wrote to Norman that sentiment was better, partly due to 'the new naval agreement and the apparently better feeling between France and Germany'.[81] Finance and politics seemed more connected than ever before.

### *The Common Vision of the Future Has Been Destroyed*

Always on the outlook for cues that could help them make sense of the economic situation, central bankers engaged in relatively intense communications during 1930 and early 1931. The Americans seemed a little more optimistic than their European colleagues, who did not see much light at the end of the tunnel.

One of the most important issues was the prevalence of short-term credits and the need to convert them into long-term investments in Europe. The problem was a real one. The BIS estimated that in 1930 global short-term debt amounted to $13.5 billion of which Germany owed $3.9, the United States $2.7 and the UK $1.9 billion. Only one-third of the total were estimated to be part of commercial transactions while the remaining $9.2 billion were 'hot money'.[82]

In February 1931, Gates McGarrah, the president of the BIS, gave a talk at the American Club in Paris, stressing that 'the active expansion of long-term credits and foreign lending' required national and international political stability, and 'it is upon Paris and upon New York that … the obligation fall to help themselves by helping others, through making long-term investments'.[83]

However, there were few visions for how to provide some measure of order and stability in dealing with the massive short-term indebtedness of Central Europe. Whatever plans there were failed to appeal to all parties. One such plan was the so-called 'Kindersley Plan'.[84]

Montagu Norman sent the plan for 'a corporation to start the wheels going round again' to McGarrah on February 2 and asked that it be discussed at the next board meeting. The four-page plan stressed that 'at a period like the present, when the capitalist system is largely under the microscope and is being attacked from many sides, it is of the greatest importance that capitalists as a whole should thus make an effort to find a remedy for at least one important difficulty which faces money markets of the world to-day'.[85]

After the BIS board meeting on March 8 and 9, 1931, Merle Cochran, the American Consul, reported to the US Department of State that the board had discussed a plan by Sir Robert Kindersley. Kindersley, a British representative at the Dawes Plan negotiations in 1924, was Chairman of the merchant bank Lazard Brothers & Co. and a director of the Bank of England.

The Kindersley plan concerned the establishment of an international bank with a capital of £25–50 million and the ability to borrow up to three times that amount by issuing bonds. These funds were to be lent against good collateral to governments and private organizations unable to borrow in the market. Promoted by Norman at the BIS board meeting in February, the plan expected the United States and France to provide most of the funding, without allowing them to dominate the board.

According to Cochran, 'The French . . . continued their . . . opposition to the project on the ground that it was a plan to draw upon France for capital to be managed by outsiders', meaning Great Britain. The president of the German Reichsbank, Hans Luther, on the other hand, felt that the BIS 'is merely dealing in theories and acting as a guide without itself entering into measures capable of bettering German economic conditions'.[86]

McGarrah informed Harrison and the Morgan partners in New York that Clément Moret would leave it to 'each market . . . to work out its own problems'. Norman and Luther, on the other hand, 'considered this approach inadequate since private initiatives had not yet produced any results'. They stressed the need for 'something striking, which would reestablish public confidence and give assurance that international bankers were collaborating and themselves had confidence in foreign investments and in the future'.[87]

Cochran reported that Norman would sail to New York on March 21 to discuss the Kindersley plan with Harrison and to convince him to maintain a low discount rate to avoid pulling American short-term credits from Great Britain.[88]

Oliver M.W. Sprague, the American economist and adviser to the Bank of England, would be accompanying Norman, but Harrison was first and foremost looking forward to seeing 'My dear Monty' and wrote 'I have so much to talk with you about that it is futile to attempt it by letter.'

Sentiment in the United States was improving, Harrison felt, 'and that, of course, is not a small part of the battle'. He did not foresee any improvement in securities markets, but 'all this we can talk over when you get here. In the meantime, I shall miss you'.[89]

On February 12, Harrison had cabled Norman and asked whether a *New York Herald-Tribune* article on the creation of an 'International Credit Bank' was true. Norman replied that the story was 'essentially correct and refers to a plan which originally reached me through Lazards from Paris ... To do any good it would be necessary for B.I.S. to become responsible sponsor for the plan which I might favour but which the board will never approve'.[90]

On March 3, a frustrated Norman complained to Harrison that the BIS 'is already slipping to the bottom of a ditch and in that position seems likely to do no more than helpfully perform a number of routine and Central Banking transactions. A change of direction and of spirit is needed in order that it may also fulfil the hope for its wider usefulness'.

Norman thought that the Kindersley plan would contribute to opening up capital markets, but he was getting nowhere. He complained that 'perhaps the principal obstacle is the unwillingness, which we have seen in certain quarters, to support a scheme of which the control and the funds are truly international'.[91]

The Kindersley plan not only evoked a discussion about the role of the BIS but also laid bare the fault line between creditor and debtor nations. Harrison, who was in Paris when he received the letter, did not share Norman's pessimistic view about 'certain quarters', meaning the French. In Harrison's opinion, the French central bank had real hopes for the BIS to promote cooperation and its focus on reparations 'will gradually shift as time goes on to other matters and to the field of action which you yourself had more in mind'.[92]

But for Norman, time was a scarce resource and so was any kind of support from private bankers for the Kindersley plan. Jack Morgan and his partners Thomas Lamont and S. Parker Gilbert all distanced themselves from the plan and its 'artificial means'. Never fans of interfering with markets, the Morgan partners had made sure that George Harrison, Owen D. Young and Jackson E. Reynolds, an American banker, agreed.

Like the French, they felt that 'putting American investment funds at the disposition of an international institution' was a bad idea.

Private bankers had little patience for government or central bank intervention into 'the market', which they considered their domain. They argued that 'Germany and other foreign borrowers will on the whole get as good credit as they deserve . . . without the intervention of artificial agencies and that we shall in the long run get the best and soundest results for the development of the foreign bond market in this country if new issues have to meet the test of the market'.

The Morgan partners shared Harrison's sentiment of the 'market's greater confidence in the German situation' and did not fear that Germany would stop its 'payments on her obligations to private investors'.[93]

Private bankers' dislike of interfering with the market was part of their shared worldview. Indeed, they saw themselves not as an integrated part of but as mere interpreters of the market's will.[94] This ideology was expressed by Jack Morgan to his partners in New York. On July 24, he wrote about his satisfaction that the London Conference was 'over without doing any harm to the situation and that politicians have turned matter over to bankers to handle which is what must happen. Hope that European bankers will take same line as ours and not allow politicians to govern their actions'.[95]

In Germany, where the situation was different, and where history, politics and the economy were viewed differently, the banker Carl Melchior took a different lesson from the London Conference. He commented to Hans Schäffer, an influential German civil servant, that what 'I have just experienced means the end of a way of life, certainly for Germany and perhaps other countries as well. We have repealed the rules of the game that have regulated commerce between the nations of the world. The common vision of the future has been destroyed.'[96]

## *Beyond Understanding*

As the debate about the Kindersley plan gained momentum and the fault lines surfaced, Norman was getting ready for his Atlantic trip. As the world's pre-eminent central banker, he wanted to minimize speculation as to the purpose of going to New York, a sign of how psychology was driving the markets but also of Norman's eccentric personality. Norman suggested to Harrison that he made an announcement in London that 'this is merely visit of courtesy to yourself without any special significance', an idea Harrison found 'very wise'.[97]

On March 21, Norman and Sprague left London aboard *RMS Berengaria*, the pride of Cunard Lines. On arrival in New York, Harrison picked Norman up at the dock and took him to his hotel. Despite invitations from Jack Morgan and other Morgan partners to stay with them while in New York, Norman declined in order not to 'appear too much attached to the Morgans', a decision Harrison also found wise.[98]

As Norman arrived in New York on March 27, Merle Cochran reported to the State Department about 'the most upsetting factor in several months'. The announcement of a plan for a customs union between Germany and Austria was political anathema to France in particular, and 'speculation is rife as to how far Germany may be inclined to go in creating economic ties to the east and south'. Moreover, rumours had it that Germany might declare a moratorium on its debt, probably the worst nightmare of every politician, banker and central banker.[99]

Despite the serious situation in Europe, Norman and Harrison enjoyed each other's company. 'Really it was a delightful visit – and interesting too', Norman wrote on his return trip to Europe on April 20. Delightful 'because of your welcome . . . to me especially'. The trip had even provided a longed-for opportunity for socializing 'on the last evening: Walter Stewart was charming and somewhat convincing – especially after several cocktails had quieted Sprague!!'

Norman also met with President Hoover and Secretary of State Henry Stimson, an unmistakable sign of his international standing. Nevertheless, he was not optimistic about the future, and without actionable knowledge he had trouble figuring out what to do. He told Harrison that 'conditions are perplexing, abnormal and beyond understanding'.[100]

A second banking crisis was menacing the United States in March 1931, and Harrison could hardly disagree about the uncertainty of the times. It was beyond difficult to come up with a coherent narrative that could make sense of the world economy and financial and monetary currents, not to mention point to a better and less uncertain future. At an April 9 meeting with his board of directors, Harrison briefly informed the board about Norman's visit to Washington and his own conversations with the Federal Reserve Board.

Harrison had 'again pointed out the three possible alternatives of Federal Reserve credit policy', which were '1) to make money firmer, 2) to make money easier, 3) to maintain existing money condition'.[101] He leaned towards the second option, but fear of inflation in a time of deflation, and the fact that the three conflicting alternatives could even be raised at the same time points to the loss of meaning among decision-makers.

Norman's letter and Harrison's statement can be seen as a 'cosmology episode' where people 'suddenly and deeply feel that the universe is no longer a rational, orderly system'.[102] It was a sign of how difficult it was even for experienced central bankers like Norman and Harrison to handle the situation and get the world economy going again.

As Norman returned to the UK on April 21, Harrison informed US Secretary of State Henry L. Stimson about Norman's visit. Norman, he wrote, did not expect Germany to cancel reparations, but he felt that the capitalist system 'is being put to a strong test in these days of depression'.[103] The same day, Cochran noted that the Kindersley plan, or the Norman Plan as he called it, 'is definitely killed'.[104]

Only two days later, the board of directors of the New York Fed met to discuss the Fed's monetary policy and the steady inflow of gold. During the discussion, Governor Eugene Meyer of the Federal Reserve Board searched for historical analogies to make sense of the situation but found none. He concluded that 'we are now in an era without precedent'.[105]

Less than a week later Randolph W. Burgess reported to Harrison about the severe economic depression and 'political and economic unsettlement'. The Federal Reserve System, Burgess argued, should 'put forth every possible effort within its power towards maintaining a measure of credit stability throughout the world and towards eventual business recovery'.[106]

## *The Fiction*

One of the more sanguine observers was R.H. Brand, a partner of Lazard Brothers. Some months earlier, he had spoken to Sproul about the 'world unsettlement and ... complete lack of confidence' since the Wall Street crash in October 1929. He was also sceptical of the re-constructed gold standard 'Why maintain the fiction?' he asked.[107]

The 'fiction', however, was a mainstay of the dominant narrative and ideology sustaining the economic and monetary system. It was an important part of central bankers' worldview and blueprint that laid the basis for their practices in good times and bad times. As Norman reminded Harrison in early 1931, 'our actions must be governed by gold movements'.[108] It was a 'frame borne of historical routine' and based on central banks' learning and practices during historical financial crises.[109]

It was also a system they had worked painstakingly to reconstruct in the 1920s with significant economic and social costs. Giving up the idea of gold as an anchor of value was unimaginable to most central bankers and economists.

In February 1931, Pierre Quesnay told a meeting in Paris, 'Gold is truly the basis of our civilization, and life as we live it would be impossible without a stable standard of value.'[110] It was hardly only economic value, Quesnay referred to. Even in June 1932, ten months after Britain had abandoned gold, when a friend asked Francis Rodd to recommend a few books about 'your complicated and unknown world', Rodd recommended Bagehot's *Lombard Street* and Hawtrey's *The Gold Standard in Theory and Practice* as important books 'on which I would recommend you to start'.[111]

These books were required reading for any aspiring central banker. After all, that was where they learned about the Bagehot rule as their operating model. But becoming a central banker also required practical on-the-job training, as Harry Siepmann emphasized in a letter to Francis Rodd in March 1931. Rodd was working to recruit a person from the Bank of England for a routine job at the BIS. Siepmann was concerned that 'to take one of my group of people, who has specialized in Central Banking and who is in the process of going through a systematic course of training, and plant him in Basle to do the work this job offers seems to me to be altogether wasteful, especially as my resources are as depleted as they are'.[112]

The gold standard may have been an illusion, but it was one that central bankers lived by and acted out. So, they maintained the fiction despite realizing it was under pressure and might even be part of the problem. On May 7, 1931, as Harrison arrived in his office, he could read in the *Wall Street Journal* about 'Mr. Norman's dark secret', the Kindersley plan.

Thomas F. Woodlock, editor of the journal, deemed it impossible, since in 'the present state of "sentiment" in this country, long-term credits to European countries generally are simply out of the question, and in France loans are made only to those countries which constitute her political group. Thus, the two nations who possess the resources which other nations desire and need, are, seemingly, unwilling to supply them'.[113]

The same day, Harrison reported to his board about comments he had made to the System Open Market Committee the week before. He had asked rhetorically, if the members of the committee wanted the gold imports to continue until other countries had 'been driven from the gold standard? There never was a time where it was so necessary that we do what we can to make gold useful and to support the gold standard'.[114]

The next day, the *New York Times* carried an article with the headline 'Germans skeptical of Norman's plan'. According to the newspaper, there was a perception in 'German circles' that France dominated 'the world's banking policies'. Quoting the *German Cologne Gazette*, the *New York Times* also reported the suspicion 'that the English move does not primarily aim so much at remedying existing gaps in credit facilities as at reinforcing Britain's influence on world capital.'[115] No matter where one looked, a shared understanding and diagnosis of the problem was out of sight.

The sense of urgency was not felt strongly enough, until the Credit Anstalt crisis tipped the scale and made action a matter of days and hours, not months.

## Uncertainty

Economic and political uncertainty was pervasive in the spring of 1931. Norman's 'perplexing, abnormal and beyond understanding' comment demonstrated decision-makers' struggle with plotting events into a coherent narrative with cause and effect properly accounted for. To them the world seemed chaotic. Unable to make sense of events, they had no real actionable knowledge to serve as a blueprint for action, and despite the seriousness there was no real sense of intense urgency.

The Bank of England and the Federal Reserve Bank of New York both held pessimistic expectations of the future and had no clear idea how to escape that imagined future, except perhaps to wait for the market. What they agreed on at the most general level was that the economic and political trouble mostly emanated from the repercussions of the Great War, the Versailles Treaty, reparations, war debts and the asymmetry of the gold standard.[116]

At the Bank of England, on May 1, Harry Siepmann confessed in a letter to Edmund Hall-Patch a British civil servant in Hong Kong about his gloomy view of the economic situation.

> In the last few weeks the general tone and temper both in this country and elsewhere seem to have suffered a relapse and I expect you would find us a good deal gloomier than there can be any occasion to be in Bangkok. A year ago, I suppose most of us expected that we should be looking hopefully towards America by now. But the market there still seems to be going from bad to worse and the prospect of restarting international lending on a grand scale still looks remote. The French have been quite responsive to criticism and are trying, in their way, to be helpful, though the difficulties of their legislation and of the public frame of mind are very great. However, there have been a few loans in Paris, to Roumania, Poland, Czechoslovakia and perhaps shortly to Yugoslavia, and I suppose we must not grumble if they all have a political as well as a financial aspect. . . .

All these little countries give rise to disproportionately great anxiety. But in the end, I suppose, everything turns upon Germany and upon Russia. The Germans at the present are being patted on the back by everybody, but a pat on the back may not be helpful to someone who is just learning to skate and their ice, I feel sure, is very thin. . . .

All the dove-cotes have been fluttered by the proposed Austro-German Custom Union, which is as disconcerting as any proposal to convert good theory into practice. The French are busy thinking out alternatives . . . less likely to be carried into action. The general feeling seems to be that the Germans will have to find some means of dropping their idea without loss of face and that the alternatives will all come to nothing. . . .

Excuse this gossipy letter. I have simply been thinking aloud, rather irresponsibly, about some of the subjects which we have daily in mind. To you they may seem rather remote and I sometimes wish that I could look at them from a distance and see them, as you can, with greater detachment and in better perspective. Write to me again soon about Bangkok. It is a refreshing change of subject.[117]

The ice did, indeed, seem very thin. The Belgian banker and BIS board member, Emile Francqui, stressed that the 'uncertainty of the future in the present crisis' called for the BIS to be able to act 'on a very large scale in times of crisis', but Norman did not agree with such a vision for the BIS.[118] In the end, as Leon Fraser wrote to Harrison, 'there is nothing sensational about it, and if this is the end of the agitation which was started in the first instance by Norman, then indeed the mountains have labored and begotten a ridiculous mouse'.[119]

The BIS was at a stalemate. There was no plan for dealing with the mountain of short-term debt in Europe, let alone an outbreak of a financial crisis. In the absence of a plan uncertainty prevailed. At least, there was always the traditional tool, the bank rate.

On May 5, Norman wrote to Harrison, 'the general economic outlook appears in every way so discouraging that for my part I should like now to try the effect of reductions of ½ per cent in your and our discount rates'. Harrison agreed and after waiting a couple of days so as not to give the impression that they had synchronized the action, the New York Fed reduced its discount rate to 1½ per cent. Harrison wrote to Norman that 'only time will tell how much good it and the rest of our policy will do'.[120]

Sprague wrote to Burgess at the New York Fed that your 'last reduction in the discount rate is an historic event – the lowest rate that has ever been established by a Central Bank in any country. It signifies, I suppose, that we are experiencing the worst depression that has ever been recorded. Hoping, without much confidence, that it may prove a potent influence in extricating the world from the present morass'.[121]

In early May, central bankers were running out of ideas. They were aware of the seriousness of the world economic outlook and the related political problems, but there was no real sense that Central Europe was about to implode. Even fewer expected it to happen in Austria. Nevertheless, both the BIS and the Bank of England feared that the ice was too thin. What would happen in the case of a major financial failure?

# 3

# Preparing for Crisis (May 11–May 19)

On May 17, 1930, Bank for International Settlements (BIS) President Gates W. McGarrah, informed central banks that the BIS was now open for business. Three weeks earlier, the Bank had held a board meeting in a 'most friendly and helpful spirit of co-operation'. McGarrah and Fraser wrote to Harrison and J.P. Morgan, 'We are greatly encouraged and optimistic about the future.'[1]

One of the first central banks to express an interest in central bank cooperation was the Austrian National Bank, whose president, Richard Reisch, replied that his bank was keen to establish relations with the BIS 'in the true spirit of international cooperation'. To show that he meant business, Reisch announced that his bank would make a deposit with the BIS.[2]

Soon after, the BIS began preparing for a less joyful future. From the beginning, it imagined itself as a 'Super-Central Bank' that could assist central banks in need but within the limits of central bank orthodoxy. In August 1930 Pierre Quesnay met with Governor Ivar Rooth of the Swedish Riksbanken and announced that the BIS expected to be able to perform small lending operations on its own to central banks. In cases where significant amounts were needed, the Bank would have to cooperate with national central banks. Quesnay asked whether Rooth would contribute to such a programme to be used in case of urgency.[3]

The BIS was focused on envisioning how to respond in case of financial trouble somewhere in Europe. In January 1931, Hans Simon prepared a note discussing what the BIS and central banks could do in case of a combined run-on banks and the currency of a European debtor country.

The note is a central piece of prospective sensemaking and fictional expectations. Implicitly based on past experience and central banks' operating model, it was a clear-cut case of imagining the future in the context of radical uncertainty.

Though it is rather unpleasant to deal with future dangers which, as one hopes, may never materialise it may still be worthwhile to consider what would be the attitude of the B.I.S. if it were approached by central banks in cases of serious trouble with private credit institutions within their area.

It seems as if dangers of that kind were limited to capital importing countries; in creditor countries where there is no danger of big foreign balances being withdrawn in case of spreading distrust, failures of private banks may have serious repercussions, but they are not likely to lead to a crisis which might endanger the economic life of the country itself. The situation might be quite different in countries which are, on a large scale, borrowers of foreign short term funds: difficulties of a single more important credit institution might easily induce the bulk of foreign lenders to withdraw their short term credits if distrust was spreading from one bank to the other, so that under these conditions a central bank might well be forced to intervene in order to avoid serious dangers. This is the more the case as in such circumstances as mentioned above the normal methods of filling a gap in the short term indebtedness of a country would, in all likelihood, fail. In cases of more serious banking troubles new short term borrowing in order to replace withdrawn credits would be just as impossible as the sale of securities, public or private, to foreign investors, as these, at such a moment, would not be inclined to consider fresh investments in an area of danger.

In these circumstances it does appear that a Central Bank might be driven to interfere in order to prevent the spreading of ~~general~~ distrust which might lead to a general withdrawal of funds. Whether it could do so without asking for assistance from abroad would depend mainly on the amount of foreign exchange at its disposal as compared with the private banking system's total short term indebtedness abroad which the Central Bank might be called on to repay.

The information about the short term indebtedness is rather difficult to obtain and not very reliable. In the case of Austria, for instance, according to a private estimate I have heard, the total short term indebtedness of banks and bankers amount to about 600 million schillings, whereas the central bank holds gold and foreign exchange serving as legal cover up to 395 million schillings, and other foreign exchange assets up to 513 million schillings; in this case, therefore, even the largest withdrawal of foreign funds could, apparently, be easily dealt with by the central bank. As, however, the situation might not be equally favourable in other countries it might be worthwhile considering what might happen in these cases.

If the Central Bank of such a country was asked to pay out considerable sums in foreign exchange towards repayment of foreign short term balances, it would probably not be able to proceed with a concurrent contraction of its own currency in order to keep its reserve ratio stable, so there is likely to be a run of home depositors at the same time, so that the Central Bank might be forced to discount even more freely than usual in order to satisfy these creditors. In the case of this character, the assisting Central Bank might, therefore, require help in the shape of foreign exchange reserves to be put at its disposal. This foreign exchange would have to serve a two-fold purpose: part of it might have to be used in order to repay foreign credit balances due to banks abroad, and would have to be really withdrawn; another part might be required only in order to comply with legal reserve regulations.

> The question arises therefore as to whether and how it might be possible to put foreign exchange reserves at the disposal of such Central Banks. Would any of the old examples of such measures of help be appropriate in our case, or would one not have to consider other methods? It does seem as if the old system of depositing gold and borrowing against that gold in foreign currencies would only be helpful where the gold was considerably in excess of legal requirements, which is not very likely to occur in cases such as which we have been discussing.
>
> As not only Central Banks, but also private banks are in the habit of keeping their foreign exchange assets, in so far they are not used for immediate payments – in other words, their foreign reserves – mostly in the shape of $ or £, it is particularly amounts in $ or £ which would be required in case of such a crisis. It seems as if, except in cases of very minor importance, the B.I.S. by itself could not, in view of the limitation of the resources at its disposal do very much in putting such foreign balances at the disposal of these Central Banks, even supposing that the principle was agreed to. As an alternative would it be possible to ask Central Banks of creditor countries, the private bankers of which wish to withdraw funds from the country where a banking crisis occurs, to advance to the Central Banks of debtor countries these funds in their own currency towards repayment of the withdrawn balances, taking as collateral, for instance, bills of exchange or bankers' acceptances endorsed by the borrowing Central Bank?
>
> Provided some assistance was to be given, would it be given solely with a view to the position of the Central Banks which were asking for help or would one have to go into the merits of the case, i.e. to examine the position of the private banks which were in trouble? Would one ask for additional guarantees, for instance, from the side of the Government?
>
> I realize that there are only questions here and no answers. All we mean to do is to draw attention to something, which might become a problem, and which it might be worthwhile to discuss with one or other of the Central Banks.[4]

The general context of the note was the economic problems that central bankers struggled to deal with and contain. It shows that Simon, and he was hardly alone among central bankers, expected the thin ice to break and a financial crisis to break out somewhere in Europe. He was clearly familiar with Bagehot's *Lombard Street* and the operating model, and he referred to past experience in order to deal with what could reasonably be called 'fictional expectations' about the future.

The note was an example of how decision-makers bridge past and future when navigating the present, but as Simon ended his memo, there were more questions than answers. The many 'might' and 'would' and references to danger, crisis and problems made it clear that Simon imagined worse times to come. Just not in Austria, though a sceptical reader, probably Harry Siepmann, had heavily underlined 'apparently' in the note.

The very fact that the memo was written, the many hypotheticals, the references to past experience, an unshaped future and the limited capabilities of the BIS show just how uncertain the world had become, and how difficult it was for the world's central banks and the BIS to know in advance how to deal with what was yet a hypothetical crisis.

In early December 1930, Gates McGarrah told a group of bankers that one of the BIS's 'principal functions is to assist exchanges in distress'.[5] A week after Simon wrote his note, Pierre Quesnay was in London to visit the Bank of England. He too was concerned that the BIS may have 'come too late to be of much effect in this present crisis' and risked being seen as a 'debating society'.

In that case, the BIS would be of no use, and the management of the new institution was adamant that this must not happen. The BIS was a 'mutual insurance society' where member banks could rely upon 'cooperative help . . . in the observance of' the gold standard.[6]

The ultimate purpose of Simon's January 22 note was to address uncertainty and discuss how exactly to do that, given the many known and unknown unknowns. It aimed at navigating the radical uncertainty of the times by establishing a plan, a blueprint for stabilizing an already troubled world economy if it was to be hit by financial disaster. It was – in Austria of all places.

## TOMORROW WILL BE CRITICAL DAY

On Monday, May 11, the same day as the Austrian finance minister Otto Juch urged Harry Siepmann to come to Austria, Francis Rodd boarded the 2.45 p.m. train to Vienna at Basle's railway station at Centralbahnplatz in the city centre. The station was only a short walk from the BIS headquarters at the former Grand Hotel et Savoy Hotel Univers, Centralbahnstrasse 7. Rodd was headed to Vienna and for all we know, he was accompanied by his colleague Hans Simon, an Austrian with a doctorate in economics.

Simon, his full name was Hans von Simon, had worked at the Austrian treasury with Viktor Brauneis in 1919, and in the 1920s he worked at the League of Nations, while Brauneis went on to become General Director of the Austrian National Bank in 1922. From 1930 to 1931, Simon, now in his mid-forties, worked at the BIS Central Banking Department as an assistant to the General Manager Pierre Quesnay.[7] It was a long train ride to Vienna, and Rodd and Simon had plenty of time to catch up on the Austrian economic situation and to make plans for their stay.

In London, Siepmann had enough on his plate already. In a letter to the French central banker Roger Auboin, he admitted that it was 'troubled times and I hardly know what to expect to happen next. Technical questions seem to have become quite secondary'. Still, he did find time to deal with technical questions, a significant part of his job. For instance, he sent a letter to the governor of the Bank of Finland with questions about its balance sheet.

Siepmann also wrote to Pierre Quesnay whom he was to meet in Paris on Friday that week. The American economist Walter Stewart, who had been adviser to the Bank of England before O.M.W. Sprague, would also be there and, 'like you, I am delighted that he is coming', Siepmann wrote to Quesnay. 'I should like best to go with you and him to the top of a mountain and stay there, but I am afraid my place is in the irrelevant rough and tumble of everyday life, from which I see little prospect of escaping, even for a period, until you give me back Rodd.'[8]

But there was no escape for central bankers in the summer of 1931, though it hardly resembled everyday life. On May 12, as Siepmann wrote these lines, Francis Rodd arrived in Vienna. He checked in at Hotel Sacher in Philharmoniker Strasse 4 and went to the Austrian National Bank at Otto Wagner Platz, where he settled into an office.

There, he set out to canvass the situation based on the few available facts. He quickly identified three main issues related to the Credit Anstalt crisis. First, he needed to understand Credit Anstalt's condition; next, he had to figure out the foreign exchange position of the Credit Anstalt, the other commercial banks and the National Bank; and, finally, he would have to come up with a plan for what to do.[9] It was quite a mouthful.

During his first day in Vienna, Rodd sent two letters and two telegrams and made a telephone call to Fraser in Basle. He wired Leon Fraser about a 'Critical position in treasury' and noted that '100.000.000 [schilling] needed for Credit-Anstalt must be found within three weeks ... Government is asking parliament tomorrow for authority to issue 150.000.000 ... real problem is 1) League permission to issue 2) Where and how to place ... Please think this over and cable me at National Bank where have office'.[10]

It was clear from day one that separating Credit Anstalt's situation from the foreign exchange position of the National Bank would not be easy. The Austrian government's commitment to pay 100 million schillings of new capital into the Credit Anstalt depended on both permission from the League of Nations and on the ability of the government to borrow the money either in Austria or abroad. And, while at it, the government planned to borrow an additional 50 million schillings. The budget could certainly use it.

But the key question, 'where and how to place', was uncertain. Would it be possible to raise the money at all? The distinction between private banking problems, central bank issues and fiscal questions could easily become blurred, as Simon had warned in his note. Rodd was also concerned that Credit Anstalt's actual losses were higher than 140 million schillings and that might endanger the reconstruction.[11]

Though the reconstruction plan agreed upon on the weekend of May 9 to 10 had, in principle, taken care of Credit Anstalt's solvency, there were plenty of things that could go wrong. Where and how to place the government loan was one, and a serious one, too. Another equally important problem was the size of the Austrian banks' foreign short-term debt. And finally, there was the question of Credit Anstalt's liquidity and collateral if it needed to borrow from the National Bank.

Rodd estimated the total foreign exchange liabilities of the Austrian banks at about $50 million of which 35 million were Credit Anstalt's, while the National Bank's foreign assets were estimated to be around $105 million excluding its gold reserves.[12]

This corresponded with Simon's January note, meaning there should be ample foreign exchange to cover withdrawals by foreign creditors. Even if the Austrians lost confidence in the schilling, Rodd believed that the National Bank's exchange reserves were 'at present more than enough to take care of any emergency even if there were a considerable demand on the part of the public for foreign notes'.[13]

Rodd was more concerned about the risk of a domestic run on the Austrian banks. Despite the reconstruction, there had already been a run on two Credit Anstalt branches and the National Bank's loans to the Credit Anstalt had increased from 69 million schillings on May 7 to 200 million on May 12. It was a warning sign that Credit Anstalt's liquidity was under pressure, and Rodd feared that the bank would need further support. In that case, the National Bank might have to ask BIS for assistance, as suggested by Simon in January. 'Tomorrow will be critical day', Rodd noted.[14]

Having sent the two telegrams and made a phone call to Basle, Rodd sat down to collect more information and to write two long letters to Leon Fraser with more detailed information. The foreign exchange position was reassuring, but rediscounting at the National Bank was higher than Rodd had reported earlier in the day.

In just two days the Credit Anstalt had rediscounted 116 million schillings, and Rodd had learned that the bank had only '40 million decent papers left'. This meant that the majority of Credit Anstalt's assets did not qualify as collateral for borrowing from the Austrian National Bank. Discounting beyond that level would be in conflict with the Bagehot rule and the National Bank's statutes.

The National Bank issued public statements every Tuesday, and if by then 'things are not calm or the runs continue they may ask us to help'. Nonetheless, Rodd was more concerned about the government loan. 'The crux of the matter is the treasury position.'[15]

He needed more data from Minister of Finance Otto Juch, though 'I will not vouch for his statements, but will reproduce what he has said.' The government needed the loan, and 'the circumstances are such that they would take money in any form'.

For the government to be able to issue the loan, permission was needed from the League of Nations' Control Committee, but even if that was taken care of, 'the problem of how to place the 100 millions of the contemplated issue must be considered at once. This is a subject which the Governors must discuss on Sunday', at BIS's monthly board meeting. The Austrian government and banks would have to assist, or 'it will be, to my mind, almost superhuman to place the issue abroad'.

While Rodd expected the League of Nations to allow the loan, this was a political issue. The BIS would have no influence over the outcome, but it was an emergency, and Rodd felt that most members of the Control Committee realized this. If political considerations were 'dragged in or the decision is postponed I do not think anyone will be answerable for the consequences'.[16]

Rodd's concern was that France might use the crisis as an opportunity to derail the planned Austro-German customs union. The Vienna-based reporter M.W. Fodor even claimed that the Credit Anstalt crisis was set in motion by France as part of a masterplan to force Austria to drop the customs union and to take over Austrian finance through ownership and control of the Credit Anstalt and '80 per cent of Austria's industries'.[17]

Governor George W. Norris of the Federal Reserve Bank of Philadelphia found the story 'interesting, if true', and sent the press clipping to Harrison, who questioned its 'accuracy'.[18] In times of uncertainty, rumours of all kinds contribute to destabilizing the situation further, and Rodd was aware of that as he wrote to Fraser.

> I wish you to understand that the longer it is postponed the greater risk there is not only of a continuance of runs on the Credit Anstalt but of the infection spreading to other banks and of the movement developing into a flight from Austria. Should that occur I think it is doubtful whether any of us have the sufficient resources to stop the movement.[19]

This was a worst-case scenario, and in the context of uncertainty and central bankers' general anxieties about the European and US economy, Rodd's fear of contagion resonated strongly with Siepmann's 'house of cards' scenario. The government loan was one of the pillars of the reconstruction plan, and if that failed, then what? The house of cards scenario involved contagion to Germany and a threat to the gold standard. On his first day in Vienna, Rodd was already plotting the various facts into a worst-case narrative.

This imagined future involved a situation where politics interfered with economic and financial matters and led to contagion from Austria to Germany and the possible breakdown of the gold standard; the perceived marker of monetary and financial stability, civilization even.[20]

During his first day at the National Bank, Rodd talked to several of his Austrian colleagues and scrutinized piles of paper and accounts. His identification of the successful placement of an Austrian loan of 150 million schillings, about $21 million, and the foreign exchange position as the most important priorities laid out the future path of his task in Vienna.

To be sure, the Austrian government did not have 100 million schillings to pay into the Credit Anstalt, and the adequacy of the National Bank's foreign exchange reserves depended on how foreign investors and the Austrian public responded to the situation. Siepmann's assessment in January that the National Bank's reserves were ample could easily change overnight if foreign banks pulled their short-term capital out of the country.

Rodd was also concerned that the rescue of Credit Anstalt might be construed as a 'deliberate invitation to other banks to play the fool. It may be so, but that eventually must be taken care of when we have a little more breathing space'. Indeed, the whole problem was the result of the fact that 'like all really bad positions everything has been left till the last moment'.[21]

Rodd made sure that Fraser and the central bank governors who were to meet at the BIS board meeting the upcoming weekend were aware that the reconstruction plan stitched together over the weekend had already locked in the options.[22]

> I do not know whether a better solution for the Credit Anstalt mess might not have been found, but I do know that it is now too late to reopen negotiations with all the political parties and foreign banks concerned upon any other basis. It is therefore no use any one suggesting that the plan is a bad one. I want this to be quite clear.[23]

Still on May 12, the day of Rodd's arrival in Vienna, Leon Fraser reported the gist of Rodd's work to Harrison in New York. Four American banks held dollar deposits above $200,000 with the Credit Anstalt, which had

$35 million of total foreign deposits, a third of which came from Great Britain. Fraser also noted that the National Bank believed that it would not need help 'unless abroad makes panic in withdrawals'. Richard Reisch hoped that central banks in the United Kingdom and UK 'will encourage calm'.[24]

Harrison in turn informed the relevant American banks about the situation and that the Credit Anstalt had received new capital contributions 'in excess of losses to be written off'.[25]

Rodd also found time to inform his hinterland at the Bank of England. He phoned Siepmann on Wednesday morning, May 13, to emphasize the urgency of getting the League of Nation's acceptance of the bond issue. Siepmann passed the information on to Orme Sargent, the Head of the Foreign Office's Central Department, and added, 'Rodd thinks that if this permission is given at once the situation will be remedied promptly, but if it is not given promptly, very grave difficulties will arise.'[26]

Rodd soon realized that it was impossible to separate the Credit Anstalt's and the National Bank's positions and that Austria's fiscal position was part of the equation as well. This awareness developed over the next couple of days, as he got a better overview of the situation.

Central bank issues also moved closer. Rodd learned that Credit Anstalt's foreign liabilities were $10 million larger than assumed the day before. They were now estimated at $45 million, but no withdrawals had taken place, and the schilling withdrawals had eased as well. That was the good news.

The bad news was that the National Bank's portfolio of discounted paper had reached 350 million schillings, with 'good paper exhausted and finance bills with security collateral now being used'. Summing up his first telegram of May 13 to Fraser in Basle, Rodd noted that the situation 'today much better than expected, yesterday worse than anticipated'.[27]

## THE PLAN

Francis Rodd and Hans Simon had been in Vienna for a day. So had the German private banker Max Warburg who like the London-based merchant bank N.M. Rothschild & Sons was interested in Credit Anstalt's fate. In fact, Warburg was on Credit Anstalt's board and on May 13 his son Eric made a phone call to Rothschilds in London to tell them about the reconstruction and that 'Rodd and Simon of the B.I.S. were already in Vienna and seemed very reasonable and quite sympathetic'.[28]

Before long, the two groups, private bankers and central bankers, would be communicating more frequently, but for now Rodd's job was to develop a more detailed plan that took future liquidity and currency risks into account and at the same time tried to manage expectations in Austria.

Rodd reported to Fraser that the National Bank believed it could manage the crisis without requiring any assistance from the BIS. However, he also laid out what a credit might look like should it come to that.

> At meeting this evening National Bank decided unless situation materially changed that it would not for present require any credit facilities and would prefer to publish on Tuesday statement as of Friday showing full extent of discounting if we can have arrangements with C.B. by Sunday or Monday, whereby not less than 100,000,000 could be made available at any time . . . in case of need. If you can assure this as a reasonable probability a communication would have to be published Sunday that N.B. in spite of having offers of help from BIS has not had to have recourse to assistance which, however remains available in case of need. This involves all necessary arrangements being made beforehand which I suggest should take form of . . . facilities from us for 40 millions and 2) joint C.B. credit for 60 millions. . . . Only circumstance which might modify this decision is if Friday's developments involved loss of a lot of foreign currency by N.B. when an immediate credit by us before publication of statement might be necessary. As things look this eventuality is not likely.[29]

This plan laid out by Rodd late at night on his second day in Vienna was partly about managing expectations. And, just in case that failed, he also detailed a plan for BIS and central bank assistance to the Austrian National Bank. With Rodd's plan for addressing the future, the BIS would be ready to invite its largest central bank members to take part in a credit to the Austrian central bank.

The National Bank wanted to avoid a BIS credit in order to reassure depositors and creditors, but if that proved impossible, precaution and the 'house of cards' scenario required a plan B. The unknown would be the public's response to the publication of the National Bank's balance sheet on Tuesday, May 19.[30]

The BIS credit would not be drawn upon unless the situation changed for the worse, but it needed to be ready. The *Financial Times* reported on the Austrian National Bank's statement of May 15 and 'the moral and material support' given by the BIS by granting a credit of 100 million schillings. However, the National Bank was quoted for saying that in view of the 'strong position of the Austrian National Bank, there was no need to take advantage of this offer of assistance'.[31]

The single most important indicator over the coming weeks, already identified by Francis Rodd, was the volume of the National Bank's rediscounts and foreign reserves on Fridays, which were published the following Tuesdays. If the figures were bad – whatever that meant – both the National Bank and Rodd feared that the public and foreign creditors would run for their money.

On Thursday, Rodd's cautious optimism seemed to endure, and he reassured Basle that 'immediate position is not so bad'. But there was another problem. The League's Control Committee would not decide whether to authorize an Austrian loan until the next day. The quality of whatever collateral Credit Anstalt had left was 'of course rotten', as Rodd put it, but he was optimistic that the Control Committee would permit the loan issue. In the meantime, he hoped that Credit Anstalt's liquidity shortage could be bridged with help from the government.

> But these are all tactical considerations only and we must all consider final solution which seems to present itself to me in the form of an international syndicate 1) to take over shares and stand between C.A. and Government and N.B. with money provided by latter 2) to run C.A. and clean up the mess since I expect when position is investigated losses will be greater.[32]

This was looking ahead. Strictly speaking, it was none of their business, but central bankers had no taste for state ownership of private banks – in particular a universal bank that controlled a big share of Austria's industry. The Austrian government's stock in the reconstructed Credit Anstalt was not to be taken lightly, and even before the government loan and the potential currency crises had been dealt with, Rodd was thinking about the future setup of the Credit Anstalt.

He had been in Vienna for three days and had worked hard to collect information and data and communicate it back to Basle. At the same time, he had to navigate a sea of uncertainty where local and global political issues were never far away. In these critical first days, decision-makers relied on the quality of Francis Rodd's work and the soundness of his assessments. After all, it was he who shaped the actionable knowledge on which the BIS, the Bank of England and the Federal Reserve Bank of New York would base their decisions and actions.

## ORGANIZING THE BIS LOAN

While Rodd collected information and thought of solutions from his temporary office at the Austrian National Bank, BIS's management in Basle began to coordinate the different tasks, such as the League of Nation's acceptance of an Austrian loan and the BIS-led credit proposed by Rodd. The latter was a challenge in itself, since the BIS had limited resources, hence Rodd's suggestion that 60 per cent of the credit should come from central banks.

Frederick Leith-Ross from the British Treasury would attend the Control Committee's meeting on Friday, May 15, and he was familiar with Rodd's reports from Vienna. An Austrian bond issue was necessary and if the Control Committee would not allow the issue, 'anything might happen'. Siepmann, was optimistic that the bonds could be placed, 'even Paris seems likely to come in. London will be expected to find some money'.[33]

On Thursday, May 14, Gates McGarrah, the BIS president, sent a telegram to Governor Harrison in New York informing him about Rodd's proposal for the arrangement of a BIS-coordinated credit to the Austrian National Bank. McGarrah stressed that it would be 'very helpful for public confidence to be able to announce simultaneously that though no foreign assistance has been utilized it is available'.

The 100-million-schilling credit was for 'emergency use only'; the BIS would supply 40 million and central banks the remaining 60 million 'in the form of rediscount credit'. McGarrah told Harrison that the German, Belgian and British central banks had already agreed in principle to participate, and he now asked Harrison to cable 'frankly whether you would desire me to raise officially question whether Federal cares to participate'.[34]

In contrast to the European and Japanese central banks, the Federal Reserve System was not a member or shareholder of the BIS. Congress had not wanted the United States to take part in the international monetary cooperation instituted by the BIS, and instead a few American commercial banks with J.P. Morgan & Co. in front had become shareholders in the Bank. Even participating in the BIS general meeting not to mention a credit was potentially problematic for the New York Fed.

In March Harrison had met with Secretary of State Henry L. Stimson to discuss the New York Fed's relation to the BIS, and Harrison knew that Secretary Stimson and the President would not be opposed to his participation in the credit.[35] Harrison's board of directors also agreed, and he wrote to McGarrah that the New York Fed would like to be invited.[36]

The next day, Eugene Meyer, the governor of the Federal Reserve Board in Washington, DC, confirmed this and on May 18, Harrison cabled to the BIS the Federal Reserve Bank's final acceptance to participate in the credit to the amount of 10 million schillings.[37] It is telling that Harrison could not make the decision himself. In contrast, Norman was often able to make that kind of decisions on his own.

While the BIS was recruiting the largest central banks to take part in the loan, Rodd was still working to figure out the situation back in Vienna. Leon Fraser cabled him that 'we all greatly appreciate your complete letters and telegrams', but that could not relieve Rodd of his increasing concerns about the Credit Anstalt's balance sheet.[38]

I am very much afraid that the foreign exch. liabilities will be much worse. I have no information – cannot get any – other than you have had but I don't think this or any other bank with a 2,000 million schillings balance sheet can only have some 350 million foreign deposits.

I am impressed by 1) the necessity of the money which is going to be put in being forthcoming as soon as possible and 2) the foreign creditors being quiet.

. . . some scheme must be put up to restore confidence here. The withdrawals have not been inordinately heavy but no bank can continue to lose £1,000,000 a day without things ending in a catastrophe. I repeat that the tactical position is as good as can be expected, but the further view is grim and if this goes on then we are really in for serious trouble in Austria and Germany.[39]

This letter was written on Thursday, May 14, in the evening, and something had made Rodd more concerned during the day. First of all, it was impossible to get the information he needed, and he was frustrated by the lack of cooperation from his Austrian counterparts. Second, the foreign exchange position and the risk of a run on the Austrian schilling made Rodd fear what the future might hold.

He had no confidence in Credit Anstalt's balance sheet and feared that foreign creditors would begin to move their money out of the Credit Anstalt and out of Austria. Third, and closely related to the first two points, the long-term consequences of an Austrian breakdown were frightening. Even worse, a panic might spread to Germany, and then what?

It was the first time Rodd mentioned Germany directly. It was the worst-case scenario of any imagined future. The fear of contagion made him insist that 'I would like to have a chance of talking to the Governors on Sunday. In case something happens to me collect Reisch at all costs and don't let him be too benignly optimistic.'[40]

Tiring of the Austrians, Rodd's last sentence suggested that he had been threatened but maybe he was just a careful man conscious of the heavy burden on his and his colleagues' shoulders. Either way, it was an ominous comment, and a sign of the extraordinary significance of the situation and the risk of contagion to Germany.

By now, several central bankers had identified restoring confidence as key to fight the risk of the crisis spreading to Germany, but no one had laid out in detail what such contagion would entail. They couldn't know, of course, so instead they imagined what might happen, without even daring or being able to spell it out. It was almost as if emplotting their worst fears and anxieties into a narrative would make it more likely to happen.

Germany's short-term foreign debt was many times larger than Austria's and its foreign exchange position was worse too. Rodd and Siepmann were well versed in the operating model, but they had no blueprint or historical analogy for this kind of crisis or their overwhelming sense of international financial fragility. Hence, they stopped short of tempting fate by trying to map out what exactly the worst-case narrative entailed. Even invoking the thought of the crisis spreading to Germany seemed quite enough. They just knew it would be bad.

The next challenge in Vienna was the upcoming weekly statement of the Austrian National Bank. It would be published on Tuesday, May 19, and report on the balance sheet as of Friday, May 15. The critical issue was how the Bank's loan portfolio and foreign exchange reserves had changed since the week before.

The statement would present a snapshot of the health of the Credit Anstalt and the whole banking system, and at the same time show if the resources of the central bank were about to be exhausted. A significant part of that story was symbolic and had to do with the psychology of the Austrian public and the foreign creditors. The foreign creditors had not panicked yet, but it might happen any moment now, and the National Bank statement could be the trigger.

When the balance sheet was drawn up, the National Bank's total portfolio of rediscounted paper was 375 million schillings against 69.5 million the week before. Since Monday when the reconstruction was made public, the Austrian National Bank had discounted more than 300 million schillings worth of assets for the Credit Anstalt and other banks. That was a dramatic increase, but Rodd had feared 'the total figure of being considerably over 400 millions'.

> I had thought that a figure up to 400 millions could reasonably have been published, but Stierhof [?] coming back from the Stock Exchange informed us that the public as well as the press had a quite unduly optimistic conception of what the effect of the C.A. developments had meant to the Nationalbank. He reported that the public is apparently under the impression that not more than 100 millions had been discounted at the Nationalbank.[41]

The National Bank's foreign exchange losses came to about 50 million schillings, or 7 million dollars. Rodd called the amount 'excessive' and Viktor Brauneis, the General Director of the National Bank, wanted to 'make certain adjustments in the various entries in the Statement'.[42]

This window-dressing exercise reduced the foreign exchange losses from 50 to 20 million schillings, and the portfolio of discounted bills from 375 million schillings to 300 million; not exactly 100 million, but less than 400 and in any case the best they could do.[43] A Bank of England official called the exercise a 'masterpiece in the art of presentation of Balance Sheets'.[44]

The effect of these arrangements would have to wait to be seen until the statement was published on Tuesday, May 19. In the meantime, there was enough to do, as the BIS governors' meeting would take place on Sunday, May 17, the board meeting on Monday, and the general assembly on Tuesday. As Rodd travelled to Basle in order to present his view to the governors, Hans Simon took over in Vienna. From the BIS, McGarrah cabled Harrison in New York that 'from late reports received today situation in Vienna improving'.[45]

## BOARD MEETING IN BASLE

The May 16 issue of *The Economist* was optimistic as it reported for the first time on the Credit Anstalt crisis. 'Fortunately it is already clear that the difficulties of the Credit-Anstalt are already being taken successfully in hand', the magazine proclaimed as it congratulated all concerned 'upon the frank, prompt and energetic manner in which the episode has been dealt with'.[46]

On Saturday Rodd boarded the train to Basle. It's easy to imagine him in deep thoughts and somewhat less optimistic than *The Economist.* He was probably thinking about what story to tell the governors and the board. In the meantime, Simon was busy in Vienna. With Rodd on his way to Basle, Simon sent a telegram to the BIS with an update on the most recent development.

The National Bank had decided not to mention the BIS credit after all, since they believed it would 'rather frighten public than reverse'.[47] Nevertheless, the foreign exchange reserves had declined further, and a US bank had withdrawn $50,000, by itself a small amount, but the kind of withdrawal that must not happen. Simon appealed, 'Please intervene as further withdrawals of foreign credits would create very serious position.'[48]

The next day, Simon reported that 'as matters stand the withdrawals for Schillings seem to have eased, and . . . the position here seems well in hand, provided that no new difficulties arise from the side of the foreign creditors'. Simon agreed with the National Bank, that 'distrust and trouble are bound to spread to other countries . . . unless the matter is organized by the

B.I.S. and by the central banks'. He added that it was 'almost impossible to extricate facts from the C.A. without which it is, of course, impossible to put down concrete proposals'.[49]

The National Bank's management seemed to have turned on a dime twice within the week, and the Credit Anstalt stuck to a policy of secrecy that seemed misplaced given its situation. What was Rodd to tell the board meeting in the BIS building at Centralbahnstrasse 7 in Basle?

Among the members of the board were central bank governors Louis Franck (Belgium), Clément Moret (France), Hans Luther (Germany), Vincenzo Azzolini (Italy) and Montagu Norman (Great Britain).[50] Besides the board meeting, there was a General Meeting of shareholders and a gathering for the first time ever of central bankers from twenty-four countries to discuss monetary and credit problems.[51]

At the governors' meeting, Rodd told the governors that the situation in Austria appeared to be under control. The alarm he had expressed earlier did not leave a mark on his presentation.

After Rodd's presentation, the governors discussed the situation. Their first concern was whether all of Credit Anstalt's losses had been written off. Rodd explained that according to Ludwig Neurath, the chairman of the Credit Anstalt, 'losses have all been written off to the full extent which prudent banking practice would require, if the Credit Anstalt is valued as a going concern'.

That did not reassure the meeting. Rodd had already aired his concern about Credit Anstalt's real position, and Norman, too, was sceptical. His Belgian colleague Louis Franck asked whether the National Bank had examined the Credit Anstalt, and Rodd replied that 'nobody has yet made a thoroughgoing investigation'.

If the Credit Anstalt was still fragile after the reconstruction, all plans would be in jeopardy. Both the solvency and liquidity of the bank were in question. Three-quarters of the bank's assets were placed outside of Austria, mostly in Poland, Romania and Hungary, and besides the difficulty of valuing them they were not eligible for discounting in the Austrian National Bank.[52]

Credit Anstalt had no more liquid assets. As Simon explained, the Bank 'have borrowed for short terms or at sight, whereas the borrowed funds are locked up either in frozen industrial loans or in securities which are unsaleable at the time being'.[53] It was the curse of a universal bank.

These questions could not be separated. If the Credit Anstalt failed, there was no way that the foreign exchange position of the National Bank could be maintained. The reconstruction must stand, as Rodd had strongly emphasized on the very day he arrived in Vienna. The Control Committee's authorization and the successful placement of the bond loan were also necessary for Rodd's plan to succeed.

Richard Reisch, the National Bank's president was in Basle, too, but did not participate in the meeting. He felt that the 'collapse of the Credit Anstalt would mean the collapse of Austria', but the board was unanimous that 'the only concern of the BIS was the National Bank'. The BIS's task was to secure 'the foreign exchange position of the National Bank and not . . . rescuing Austria or the Credit Anstalt'.[54] It was all about the gold standard and the risk of contagion.

Harry Siepmann and Norman had taken the same position when Austria had asked for assistance a week earlier. It was a matter of principle, but also an attempt to ringfence the BIS from wider financial and moral responsibility. How the governors envisioned that separation to work out in real life, no one apparently dared to ask.

The decision meant that the BIS's task and responsibility were more clearly delineated, even if it might prove difficult to exercise this distinction in practice. The purpose of the BIS action in Austria was to assist the National Bank in maintaining its foreign exchange reserves, to keep Austria on the gold standard, and ultimately prevent the crisis from spreading to Germany or other countries.

This opened a potential conflict between the ultimate goals of the Austrian government and of the international central bankers. If this conflict widened, it might harm the cohesion within the community and endanger a shared solution. In Austria the goal was first and foremost to protect the Austrian economy and the financial system. Outside of Austria, it was all about stopping the Austrian crisis from spreading to other countries and threatening the gold standard. And avoiding losses to their own banks in Great Britain and the United States.

All that did not matter much at the moment, however, since 'unless the treasury bills are first issued, the present plan of reconstruction falls entirely to the ground'. It was imperative to find banks ready to issue and investors willing to buy 150 million schillings of Austrian government three-year bonds. Leaving it to the market was not an option, because of the 'present world depression'. The placement had to be arranged in advance and that required a deal with international banks capable of and ready to take on the risk.

At the governors' meeting, it was debated how to approach international bankers who had issued Austrian stabilization loans in 1922 and 1930 and with whom it was agreed that no new government loans would be issued until 1933. Fraser and Rodd said that bankers were 'believed to be favourable to the issue of treasury bills', but nothing concrete was known.[55]

The *New York Times* claimed that Clément Moret, the governor of the Banque de France, had 'made it clear that France would be willing to assume a very large portion . . . provided Austria definitely renounced all future attempts to form a customs union with Germany'.

The newspaper also noted that although 'all the meetings of the members of the BIS are surrounded with deep secrecy, it was difficult to conceal the fact that such delicate issues as indicated provoked long and at times animated debate yesterday'. Still, the loan 'seems assured regardless of the French attitude'.[56]

No one knew anything for sure, however. It was all hearsay, and no bankers had actually committed themselves to take part in, let alone underwrite the loan. They might lose more money if they participated in the new loan than if they did not and Credit Anstalt failed. Sitting tight did not look like the worst strategy.

Rodd was very much aware that the uncertainty was bad for confidence and increased the risk of both an internal and external run. He repeatedly stressed that besides the government loan, the Austrian National Bank would need an international credit to maintain the rediscounting for the Credit Anstalt. This was where the BIS loan came in.

The board meeting took place on Monday, the day after the governor's meeting. The situation in Vienna appeared calm, but the crisis was nevertheless an important topic, which presented a rare opportunity for central bankers to get acquainted, and to discuss the failure of the Credit Anstalt and the BIS credit.[57]

Merle Cochran reported that the BIS had found the Austrian position 'considerably worse than it first anticipated'. It is unclear, Cochran noted, 'whether the accounts of the bank are in so arrear that the actual situation is not known, or whether the situation is so bad that the Austrians do not desire to disclose the exact conditions'. However, the BIS believed that the National Bank's position was sound, and a credit would be forthcoming.

As the BIS credit to Austria was 'definitely arranged', it was made clear that the BIS 'was not sponsoring an issue of Austrian Treasury Bonds'. Neither were J.P. Morgan or Lee, Higginson & Co., a Boston-based investment bank, and attempts to attract the interest of financiers in London or Paris had been unsuccessful so far.

On Tuesday, May 19, the General Meeting took place. Here, the conflicting views on the role of the BIS and its governance surfaced again. The Germans, French and British held very different visions for the BIS.

Germany wanted credits, Norman tried to revive the Kindersley plan, and France held 'to the idea that the desired help can be extended through existing private institutions'.[58]

But the loan agreement fell in place. The recognition that time was of the essence enabled a shared position. At the meeting, McGarrah formally invited the governors of the central banks to participate in the BIS credit suggested by Francis Rodd. With the exception of the three Scandinavian central banks, most central banks agreed to take part.[59] The final contributions to the Austrian credit were 40 million schillings from the BIS, and 7.7 million schillings each from the Federal Reserve Bank of New York, the Bank of England, the Bank of France, the Bank of Italy and the German Reichsbank.

The central banks of Belgium, the Netherlands, Czechoslovakia, Poland, and Greece each contributed 3.85 million schillings and the Swiss National Bank 2.25 million.[60] It all added up to 100 million schillings or $14 million. At this time, the Austrian National Bank had not yet asked for it, but the first truly international central bank credit ever was in place, organized by the BIS.

The *New York Times* was enthusiastic and called the BIS loan, 'one of the most significant decisions of its brief history'. The National Bank had not applied for the loan yet, but the newspaper felt that 'the psychological influence of the ... initiative may render such an appeal unnecessary, but the fact remains that Austria can now have this amount of money for three months by merely asking the World Bank'.

In a general reference to the economic situation, the paper noted in a less optimistic mood the 'widespread 'crisis of confidence' in all the investment markets. Bankers can scarcely recall a time when money for lending purposes was so difficult to find'.[61] That did not sound promising for the placement of the Austrian bond loan.

Still, McGarrah informed Harrison 'spirit of general meeting excellent'.[62] That evening, he had dinner with Norman. The next day May 21, Norman lunched with Pierre Quesnay and dined with Francis Rodd and his wife Mary before leaving Basle at 11.30 p.m. He arrived at Victoria Station at 3.30 p.m. the next day.[63]

# 4

# Foreign Creditors (May 16–May 25)

Even if the Basle meetings ended on an optimistic note, the general situation was one of confusion and rumours threatening to further destabilize confidence in Austria and elsewhere. On May 18 Harrison cabled Norman that 'persistent rumours have today run the gamut here regarding Barclays Bank in particular and also Schroeders and lastly Rothschilds. While these rumours are not taken seriously in important quarters nevertheless I think you should know of them'.[1]

With Norman still in Basle, Deputy Governor Ernest Harvey replied that the rumours were considered entirely groundless.[2] Still, rumours both reflected and contributed to the uncertainty and nervousness of the situation.

In Vienna, now in the second week of the crisis, central banks saw Credit Anstalt's management as dragging its feet and being difficult to deal with. For all the central bankers knew that the bank had not even been in touch with its foreign creditors to try and renew credit lines or attract new credits, or even to keep them informed about the situation. As the Bank for International Settlements (BIS) board meeting ended and central bankers returned home, the situation in Austria was still fragile.

The good news was that negotiations in the League of Nation's Austrian Control Committee had been successful. Frederick Leith-Ross, the British Treasury official on the Committee, observed that the French, Belgian and Czechoslovak governments had 'absolutely declined to agree to the Austrian proposal'. But the League and the Committee was dominated by the British, and Leith-Ross noted that after some convincing they reached a compromise, which was also accepted by the Austrian government.[3]

It was a green light to proceed with the Austrian bond loan. The first hurdle was overcome.

## THE GOVERNMENT LOAN

With the Control Committee's acceptance, most actors assumed that private banks and markets would now take care of Rodd's 'where and how to place' question. In fact, even 'the market' believed that France would be the answer to Rodd's question.

On May 16, Max Warburg wrote to Rothschild in London that 'the issue of treasury bills is being hastened to a greater extent than was expected with the participation of the Banque de Paris et des Pays-Bas and other houses'.[4]

The assumption that Banque de Paris et des Pays-Bas an investment bank, would take part of the loan was widespread. Max Warburg may well have heard it from one of the Morgan firms. The day before, Morgan & Cie in Paris had called and told Morgan Grenfell in London that the French government had asked Banque de Paris et des Pays-Bas to 'form a group to arrange to handle a block of three year 6% notes of Austrian Government'. The Banque de Paris et des Pays-Bas wanted J.P. Morgan & Co. to 'lead the whole business'.

The French bank assumed that the French market could take between 8 and 10 million dollars out of the total of $21 million. Morgan Grenfell wanted to know if J.P. Morgan & Co. would be interested in taking the 'lead in this business or handle any part of it in the event of your being asked to do so'.[5]

Morgans were delighted to hear that the French government and the French market appeared ready 'to play a part in Austrian financing'. But they did 'not see how we could under present conditions place any of these notes in our market. We have not been asked to participate in the proposed operation and we hope we shall not be asked to do so'.

Morgan also wanted to know why the Austrian government needed to raise 150 million schillings, when the reconstruction plan only mentioned 100 million. Had this plan broken down already, had a new emergency emerged or was the government using 'the occasion to borrow for budget purposes'?[6]

Good question. While the latter was the case, it demonstrated how private bankers like everyone else struggled to get the information needed to fit the cues into a larger story. On Monday, May 18, Morgan Grenfell met with partners from Baring Brothers & Co., N.M. Rothschild & Sons, and J. Henry Schroder & Co., a group of the City of London's most prominent merchant banking houses, to discuss the situation. After the meeting, they cabled J.P. Morgan & Co. that 'the situation is not by any means clear'. Uncertainty continued, as Rodd stressed there was no guarantee that the international loan would 'clear up the Credit Anstalt position'.

But it had to be tried. The idea was that 50 million schillings might be subscribed in Austria while the rest should be found abroad, primarily in France, since 'neither New York nor London could do anything with such a loan at the present times'. If Austria could borrow the money from continental bankers, it should certainly do so.[7]

The BIS was not about to go out on a limb by giving any statements about Credit Anstalt's situation. In a follow-up telegram, Morgan Grenfell noted that the 'Vienna situation is not as clear as we thought . . . However, as efforts are being made in highest quarters at Basle we feel that as any precipitate action might cause a critical situation we think it would be unwise for us to withdraw our lines of credit.'[8]

At this time, the telegram that J.P. Morgan hoped not to receive arrived at Morgan Grenfell's office at 23 Winchester Street in the City. It was addressed directly to Charles Whigham from the Austrian finance minister Otto Juch pleading that 'your firm would take the lead in organizing syndicate for such issue of bonds as will be placed abroad'. Juch believed that Banque de Paris et des Pays-Bas, Mendelssohn and Credit Suisse would participate, and he asked Morgan Grenfell to discuss the loan terms with them. Quick action was 'absolutely essential. Relying on your advice and support.'

Declining an appeal from a European finance minister to organize a loan was not business as usual for the House of Morgan. After all, this was what they did, and who knew what consequences it might have for future business opportunities. That is why they hoped the invitation would never come. But here it was. Whigham wrote to J.P. Morgan, 'while Juch mentions only Morgan Grenfell & Co. he doubtless means the Morgan Houses'.[9] What to respond?

Morgan & Co. replied that, despite sympathetic interest, they did not see how any part of the loan could be placed in the United States.[10] Whigham then informed Juch about the decision but in order not to exclude future business opportunities, he noted that it 'is with the greatest regret that we thus find ourselves unable to be of service to your Government at this time'.[11]

At least there was some hope that the loan could be arranged on the continent. The Banque de Paris et des Pays-Bas called Morgan & Cie on May 19 urging J.P. Morgan to 'reconsider your decision and accept to take the lead in the business'. It would be a 'great advantage ... having

American Bankers who are disinterested politically leading in this operation which is really a rescue party'. And, after all, New York and London banks had more money at stake with Credit Anstalt than French banks.[12]

If the latter was an attempt to put some moral pressure on J.P. Morgan, it did not work. In a lengthy response to Morgan & Cie, J.P. Morgan wrote that 'market conditions here with respect to foreign securities in general and the newspaper publicity which has heralded the current discussion of Austrian affairs in this market make the operation here impracticable'.[13]

Morgan & Cie replied with a short 'Many thanks. Have advised Banque de Paris et des Pays-Bas'.[14] With this decision communications between the Morgan offices on the topic went silent. The market and its representatives could not take care of the situation, and neither the involved central banks nor the private banks paid much attention to the loan for the next few weeks. Maybe they expected the French to take care of it.

## CREDIT ANSTALT ON THE MOVE

Around the same time as the Morgans dodged the bond loan, and Francis Rodd and Richard Reisch were in Basle for the BIS meetings, most unwelcome ideas about a moratorium surfaced in Vienna. They had not seen that coming, but on Sunday, May 17, as the BIS governors' meeting was well underway, Simon wrote a 'note on foreign exchange position of C.A'.[15]

Despite pressure from the government and the National Bank, Credit Anstalt's management remained passive and had done nothing to get in touch with foreign creditors to renew loans or obtain new credits. Simon's note was a gamechanger.

Armand Dreyfus, the managing director of the Schweizerischer Bankverein, had proposed to set up a syndicate of banks in countries with claims on the Credit Anstalt. These syndicates should convince Credit Anstalt's creditor banks in their respective countries to renew their credits and try to raise new money where renewals failed. Central banks in the creditor countries should support this effort by impressing on banks that withdrawals would cause a complete breakdown of the Credit Anstalt and lead to very considerable losses to the banks. Simon continued,

> Withdrawals of these funds would amount to a complete catastrophy. The Minister of Finance is, after consulting with the National Bank, preparing a moratorium for such an emergency case though, of course, everybody is aware of the fact that this would be a deadly blow for the credit of the country.[16]

Simon felt the position was 'well in hand' unless foreign creditors began withdrawing their money. Vice President Thaa and General Director Brauneis of the National Bank, and Otto Juch, the minister of finance, had pointed out to Simon that 'distrust and trouble are bound to spread to other countries'. The Credit Anstalt had failed to get in touch with its creditors, and Thaa and Brauneis 'are convinced that success is almost impossible unless the matter is organised by the B.I.S. and by the Central Banks'.[17]

With this note and the threat of a moratorium, focus was now on the foreign creditor banks and central banks. The Austrian authorities were putting pressure on the BIS and central banks by insisting they got involved with the foreign banks in their respective countries. By raising the idea of a moratorium as the means to avoid contagion and 'complete catastrophy', they were certain to be heard. It played right into the house of cards worst-case narrative.

No one outside of Austria believed that a moratorium would be less catastrophic. In fact, Norman told his Committee of Treasury that the position was dangerous and that a moratorium would be 'fatal to the whole credit of Austria'[18] It would also make foreign money in Austria illiquid and thus harm the creditor banks in the United States and Great Britain. And it would certainly not do any good for confidence in the deeply interconnected international financial system.

Armand Dreyfus's idea of involving central banks in convincing creditor banks to leave their money in Austria was exactly what they had tried to avoid by focusing exclusively on the National Bank's position. Rodd and Simon were realizing that it was not an easy task.

On Monday, Rodd learned that both the Credit Anstalt and the National Bank had acted upon Armand Dreyfus's proposal. Simon phoned a message to Rodd from Thaa and Brauneis. The Credit Anstalt was about to get in touch with prominent bankers abroad and ask them to contact other banks in their respective countries not to withdraw funds from the bank. Foreign withdrawals of credit would endanger Austria's monetary position and result in heavy losses for foreign banks. The National Bank was 'convinced that such losses will not occur if creditors proceed with the necessary care'.[19]

The Austrian initiative looked like an attempt to force the international creditors to accept a standstill agreement.[20] There were also echoes of Simon's January note, where he asked if creditor countries' central banks could step in to assist a debtor country's central bank under pressure. But this was different. It would implicate central banks in a way they did not want by involving them directly in the business of private banks and the Credit Anstalt.

The next day, Tuesday, May 19, Simon reported that the National Bank now considered the fear of foreign withdrawals somewhat reduced. 'Vice president and general manager wish to express their gratitude for support.'[21] There are no clues to tell what if anything Rodd or the BIS responded to Simon's note and telephone call, but the Austrian National Bank at least seemed to believe that the BIS and private banks would support the initiative. That was a mistake, as J.P. Morgan & Co.'s response would show.

The Credit Anstalt asked Morgan to convince other banks in the United States to maintain their loans to and deposits with the Credit Anstalt. This was Armand Dreyfus's idea. The Credit Anstalt wrote that in

> agreement with Government and Austrian National Bank we consider it necessary in order not to impede reconstruction programme that our foreign creditors grant extension for six months of credit facilities allowed for total utilized so far and that national syndicate be formed to assure co-operation in this respect, thereby serving best own interests. Are convinced that crisis will be overcome thereby definitely. We appeal to your friendship and good will asking you to kindly approach in the above sense our other creditors there, full list of which would be supplied to you immediately upon receiving your affirmative reply which we confidently anticipate and for which accept our hearty thanks in advance. Kindly also communicate with Federal Reserve Bank who will be advised by Austrian National Bank by way of B.I.S. and who we trust will support your efforts. Are convinced that you will, like ourselves, consider it essential that this matter is dealt with strictly private and confidential. Please reply by cable.[22]

The rather bold message must have led to a collective raising of eyebrows at 23 Wall Street, Morgan's New York headquarters. Partner S. Parker Gilbert had spent six years in Germany as Agent General for Reparations to Germany. His stay had made him fiercely anti-German while also being critical of Britain's motives and intentions. He considered France the true friend of the United States.[23]

European ways were not unknown to Gilbert, whether he liked them or not, but Credit Anstalt's request was highly unusual. He and the other partners at Wall Street's best-known investment bank did not like the idea at all. After clearing Morgan's reply with George Harrison, Parker Gilbert sent a telegram to the Credit Anstalt by way of Morgan Grenfell in London.

> We have given the most sympathetic consideration to all that you have told us about your program but we feel very clear that we could not be helpful in

organizing any approach to your creditors here for a six months' extension, and further that an appeal in the form that you suggest would be more likely to aggravate your difficulties than to cure them ... we should think that you would be much more likely to obtain results and that it would be better for your whole situation if you would communicate directly by cable with each one of your creditors here, advising them in detail of your situation and of the steps which are being taken to deal with it. . . . We have already informed Morgan Grenfell & Co. and we are glad to confirm to you that so far as our own line of credit is concerned we are prepared to act in this sense and to leave the present line undisturbed for the time being, assuming of course that you succeed in your plans for replenishing your capital and in obtaining the necessary co-operation from other foreign creditors and depositors. We should think it would also be helpful if the Austrian National Bank, directly or through the Bank for International Settlements, would take pains to keep the Federal Reserve Bank of New York advised of your situation and of your program of reconstruction, so that the Federal Reserve Bank may be in possession of full information and be in a position to answer inquiries that may be directed to it here.[24]

The next day, Thursday, May 21, the Austrian National Bank cabled the Federal Reserve Bank of New York what Harrison already knew, that the Credit Anstalt had contacted J.P. Morgan among others. The National Bank repeated what it seems to have considered its strongest argument that 'all endeavors made so far would be useless if creditors . . . could not be convinced that they will safeguard best also their own interest by waiting quietly'.[25]

The approach seemed amateurish and counterproductive to Parker Gilbert and Harrison. Waiting quietly was certainly not an option. Morgan Grenfell made the same decision as J.P. Morgan.[26] Charles F. Whigham of Morgan Grenfell wrote to Otto Juch that his and other London banks as well as J.P. Morgan in New York agreed that Credit Anstalt's and the National Bank's proposal 'is so unusual that it might even precipitate the withdrawal of credit facilities by foreign bankers'.[27]

Though J.P. Morgan and Morgan Grenfell maintained their current and relatively insignificant credit lines to the Credit Anstalt for the time being, a few banks were less forthcoming. Credit Anstalt's telegram may even have encouraged withdrawals, since a number of banks either cancelled acceptances or declined to renew credits.[28]

It was not even close to a full-scale run on the Credit Anstalt by international creditor banks, but these withdrawals were enough to show how the situation could quickly develop and become very serious indeed. As most of the banks involved were French or had French connections, they also raised suspicions that politics were at play.

In short, Credit Anstalt's proposal found no support anywhere. J.P. Morgan's response had made it perfectly clear that without a detailed plan and full information, the bank would not even consider further involvement. A plan, like a narrative, could be seen as a fictional expectation. It was a way to deal with uncertainty by imagining a specific future and enabling decision-making according to a blueprint. Morgan and other creditors were not about to expose themselves further without a convincing plan.

Nor were the central banks. The New York Fed, BIS and Bank of England all abstained from acting on the request from the Austrian National Bank. In London, Peter Bark asked Norman to support Credit Anstalt's request, but Norman and the Committee of Treasury had no wish 'to be formally associated with such meeting'.[29]

With J.P. Morgan and Harrison located in New York far from the epicentre of the crisis, Morgan Grenfell in London had better access to European sources of information. Morgan Grenfell had talked with Peter Bark, who was apparently behind Credit Anstalt's telegram, and explained the problem to him, and 'we believe he was impressed with the wisdom of those views'.[30]

Peter Bark, a former Russian finance minister who migrated to the UK after the October Revolution in 1917, was director of the Anglo-International Bank, which was closely intermingled with the Bank of England. He had close ties with Norman, and was on the board of the Credit Anstalt.[31] Nevertheless, Morgan Grenfell did not learn much new from the conversation with Bark, 'though the following points may be of interest: The bank's liability for foreign credit facilities . . . is very considerable; there being about £6,500,000 in London, the equivalent of about £5,500,000 in New York, and, say, about £2,000,000 on the Continent, but we would not wish these figures taken as definite, without further check. The number of foreign banks extending these facilities is quite large, including most of the more important banks and firms in your country and ours.'[32]

Nine days into the crisis, this was the first indication of the size and distribution of Credit Anstalt's foreign liabilities. And it was given to private bankers rather than the central banks, which were to be the last resort if the drain of foreign exchange continued. It was yet another sign of the difficulties of getting and processing information and how parallel lines of communication were not coordinated.

Maybe that, and the obvious failure of the attempt to put pressure on the creditor banks and central banks, was what led the Austrian National Bank to communicate directly with the New York Fed. On May 22 the Austrian National Bank wrote to Harrison that the reconstruction of Credit Anstalt was moving forward as planned and that the bank's balance sheet and liquidity were stable. An independent audit would be carried out soon, and the National Bank assured Harrison that things were under control.

After heavy withdrawals during the first days, the situation was now 'almost normal and cash payments yesterday exceeded entries by 3¼ million schillings only'. Still, even small foreign 'withdrawals are very undesirable and might imply serious complications'.[33]

## ASK THE GOVERNOR

Credit Anstalt's and the National Bank's first attempt at reaching out to foreign creditors achieved nothing. In fact, it backfired by moving the threat of a moratorium closer, though that may have been the idea, and by leaving private and central bankers in serious doubt as to how and when this situation would end. In fact, they were nowhere near the end. Saturday, May 23, would be another gamechanger as the BIS, Bank of England and N.M. Rothschild & Son were in for another surprise.

On Saturday, May 23, at 12.05 p.m., Rodd, still in Basle, made the first of three phone calls from the BIS to the Bank of England. Only five days earlier at the BIS board meeting, Governor Norman had again made it clear to Richard Reisch of the Austrian National Bank that Bank of England could not and would not take independent action in the crisis.[34]

Now, however, the National bank had requested the BIS to implore Norman 'to do what he can about the London market'. The upcoming Tuesday, May 26, 'certain deposits of Japhet and Rothschild with the CA fall due and it is understood that they will probably be withdrawn unless some action is taken'. The Austrian public was also withdrawing money, and the Credit Anstalt was running out of funds. If the two City merchant banks joined the flight, a moratorium would be next.

According to Rodd the 'only method of preventing a moratorium would be for the Austrian government to guarantee foreign deposits'. Moratorium or guarantee. These were two fundamentally different strategies, and time was a critical factor. Rodd said that 'the BIS would be greatly relieved if the governor could see his way to advising the President of the NB as to what lines should be adopted, by telephone or cable if possible'.[35]

Rodd's call on Norman for assistance reflected an increased sense of urgency and uncertainty about foreign withdrawals and when they would reach a critical point. It also demonstrated the limits of BIS's influence. While Norman kept insisting that BIS should head the operation, the BIS had neither the information nor the network to make things happen.

Whether Norman liked it or not, and he probably liked it, the Bank of England was now an indispensable part of stemming the crisis. Indeed, as the apparent threat of large foreign withdrawals came from two British merchant banks, it was imperative that Norman could be persuaded to act. After all, the City of London was his home territory.

Less than half an hour after his first call, Rodd was back on the phone. This time he stressed that 'if the governor's message yesterday through Rothschild to the Austrian NB was that he would do everything he could upon receiving a request from the BIS to do so, then the BIS do hereby request him to do everything he can. The B.I.S. could not themselves organize a committee of creditors or such like.' B.G. Catterns, the Bank's chief cashier, took the phone call and noted,

> Rodd afterwards amplified the message as follows: That the BIS have got neither the contacts nor the machinery for organizing anything from Basle but if the governor can do anything in the London market or with friends abroad, it would be a great help if he would do it. The president himself would be very grateful.[36]

As a recently established organization with two Americans at the helm, the BIS was unable to pull the threads the way Norman could. The BIS emergency loan to the National Bank agreed upon by the board on May 18 had not yet been finalized, though it was unclear why. And when it came to relations with the international creditors of the Credit Anstalt, the BIS had little influence compared to the extensive network Norman commanded from his position at 'the Old Lady of Threadneedle Street'.

Rodd and McGarrah may have been frustrated about the situation and the inability of the BIS to assume the role of an international central bank, but if anyone could do anything about the foreign creditors, it would have to be Norman.

The BIS could and did organize cooperation, and it contributed more directly to making sense of the Austrian situation through Simon's and Rodd's work in Vienna, and by bringing central bankers together. But Norman's network and his autonomy at the top of the Bank of England now seemed indispensable. In that perspective, Norman's insistence that the Bank of England must not be directly involved in the rescue operation was not helpful.

At this point, the situation was deteriorating from hour to hour, and Rodd's misgivings about Credit Anstalt's real position now proved warranted. At 1 p.m. he called Catterns for the third time that day. Rodd had learned that 'the position as a whole was very much worse than had been previously anticipated and the CA now say that unless they can obtain a credit in London for £10.000.000 sterling by Tuesday they will feel obliged to declare a moratorium'.

It looked like a game of chicken. The Austrians wanted a moratorium to save Credit Anstalt and the domestic economy. Contagion outside of Austria was not their greatest concern. The foreign creditors and central banks were less interested in the Credit Anstalt but worried about contagion, the gold standard and their own money. A government guarantee would take care of that. Who would give in?

And where did the 10-million-pound figure come from? It was a lot of money, about $48.6 million or almost 350 million schillings. On top of that, Rodd now believed that the Credit Anstalt held foreign deposits of 720 million schillings, or about $100 million, 'of which 120 mill. had already been drawn'. These figures were more than double Rodd's earlier estimates, and Japhet's and Rothschild's deposits of 2 and 1 million dollars, respectively, 'were only part of much larger claims'.

Even worse, perhaps, Rodd told Catterns that the National Bank had decided not to recommend a government guarantee for Credit Anstalt's liabilities as they 'did not believe that the government had sufficient resources to carry the position'. A moratorium would now most likely have to be for the whole country, but it was doubtful if it could be arranged fast enough to contain the crisis.

Painted into a corner, Francis Rodd and the BIS now felt that if the run on the Credit Anstalt continued it was the '£10,000,000 credit or nothing'. The already agreed upon but not yet finalized BIS credit of $14 million, about £2.9 million, paled in comparison. Before ending the call, Rodd emphasized that the BIS would not accept any direct or moral responsibility for such a credit, and he expected the Bank of England to share that view. 'Nevertheless, they would naturally be greatly relieved to hear that London financial interests were willing to provide the necessary credit.'[37]

It seemed like a long shot. If Japhets and the Rothschilds were about to withdraw 3 million dollars in deposits, it was not very likely that 'London financial interests' would be eager, or able for that matter, to grant a 10-million-pound credit.

Norman certainly had no wish of involving the Bank of England in the urgent request for 10 million pounds and referred the problem to Peter Bark. In the meantime, Ernest Harvey, the Bank's deputy governor, learned some disturbing details about Japhet's and Rothschild's claims on Credit Anstalt. Credit Anstalt and the Austrian National Bank had not told Francis Rodd and the BIS the full story.

Harvey, a long timer at the Bank of England where he was hired as a clerk in 1885 at age eighteen was one of the first of a new generation of professional central bankers. After holding positions as chief cashier and comptroller, he joined the Court of Directors in 1928, and a year later, he was appointed deputy governor. Harvey knew the Bank's organization and practices inside out, but what he now learned was a surprise.

During an already busy day, he met with Samuel Stephany, the general manager of N.M. Rothschild & Sons, who was there when Harvey learned about the deposits. Stephany noted that the 'Credit Anstalt had informed the B.I.S. that their difficulties were due to the withdrawal of deposits by two London Banks due for payment on the 26th May. I pressed Sir Ernest for the names of the banks. He told me Rothschilds and Japhets. I said that as far as we were concerned this was quite untrue. He spoke to Japhets on the telephone and Lindenberg was going over to see him.'

Paul Lindenberg, the managing director of S. Japhet & Co, explained to Harvey that the money Japhets were withdrawing was 'not an ordinary deposit', and if the Bank of England wanted, he could leave the money with the Credit Anstalt.[38]

It turned out that the money in fact belonged to the Austrian National Bank and that Japhet and Rothschild were only strawmen for the National Bank that was not 'able to make a deposit direct' into the Credit Anstalt. If the National Bank wanted to renew the deposit with Japhet the 'matter could be arranged. Japhets undertook to cable the NB of A to this effect'.[39]

The shady arrangement dated back to 1929 when the Credit Anstalt took over its ailing competitor the Bodencreditanstalt. To support the merger at the time, the Austrian National Bank had deposited part of its foreign exchange reserves with foreign banks, including Japhet and Rothschild, on the condition that the money was re-deposited with the Credit Anstalt. This dubious practice now meant that the National Bank was unable to mobilize part of its foreign exchange reserves since the money would end up being withdrawn from the Credit Anstalt.[40]

Very few people knew about this arrangement, which meant that the statement of the National Bank's reserves was unreliable. Norman was not amused. He insisted that the 'tainted money' should be 'taken completely out of the National Bank's Return'. Rodd agreed but pointed out that there 'is a good deal of nervousness in Vienna about showing any decrease of the National Bank's foreign exchange reserves'.[41]

It would seem that at least 3 million of the sudden request for a 10-million-pound credit were now accounted for. It was hard not to view the use of this tainted money by the Credit Anstalt and the National Bank as coming close to blackmail, hence Norman's anger. Even Peter Bark, a board member of the Credit Anstalt, could not explain why the bank suddenly needed 'such a large figure as £10 million Sterling', and in any case he saw little that could be done in London before Tuesday or even with more time at hand. The National Bank would have to save the position, as 'a moratorium would be a tragedy and . . . the repercussions would seriously affect not only the whole Austria but Central Europe generally'.[42]

Figuring out what to do was being urgently considered in Austria, Basle and London, as New York was about to be informed about the new situation in Vienna.

On Saturday, May 23, just one day after the 'almost normal' telegram from the Austrian National Bank, George Harrison at the New York Fed received an urgent and confidential cable from Gates McGarrah at the BIS. He was no less distressed than Francis Rodd.

Credit Anstalt's situation was 'very serious due to large foreign withdrawals' and the fact that foreign liabilities were larger than believed. A moratorium of a few weeks was considered by the government in order to 'give time for fundamental reorganization of . . . Credit Anstalt . . . if possible.' If there were any good news, it was that Monday was Whit Monday and there would be no business in Europe.[43]

Whit Monday, at least, gave the authorities and the private banks, which were about to get seriously involved too, a long weekend to figure out what to do.

The bad news had not only reached Norman, McGarrah and Harrison. A small group of private bankers in the City of London and on Wall Street was increasingly drawn into the fragile situation. After all, it was their money at risk in Austria. Against all odds, they had managed to keep their cool until now, but as they heard the disturbing news from Norman, they too got nervous.

Samuel Stephany wrote a letter and a memorandum to Lionel de Rothschild the merchant bank's managing partner informing him that Norman had returned from Basle the night before and had met with Peter Bark. Norman had told Bark that

> unless the Credit-Anstalt situation was taken in hand at once the whole affair would drift and a serious problem would arise. At the moment he considers the moment very serious mainly because it was desired to establish a moratorium in Vienna which in his opinion would be disastrous. He suggested to Mr. Bark that an informal committee representing creditors and shareholders should be set up at once in London.[44]

Armand Dreyfuss had also proposed the formation of a syndicate of banks, of course, but that was the only similarity with Norman's initiative. Norman already had a list drawn up of potential members of the committee: Lionel de Rothschild as chairman, a Morgan Grenfell partner representing London and New York, a Lazard partner to represent London and Paris, Peter Bark and 'a fifth person'.

Impressed by the events and strongly against a moratorium, Norman now followed Rodd's plea and abandoned his earlier position that it was up to the BIS to act. He also proposed to intervene directly in the affairs of the Credit Anstalt though without direct Bank of England involvement. The committee's role would be to arrange 'renewals and terms of existing and new credits, voting control, representation on Board, policy, administration, and Board of Directors, audit and/or investigation'.

Norman was aware that this was a controversial plan, but he had the process all worked out. Bank of England would not help the Austrian National Bank directly, but 'thought the formula should be: The Credit Anstalt to apply to the Austrian National Bank for assistance. The latter in turn would apply to the Bank for International Settlements, and the Bank for International Settlements would ask the Bank of England and other State Banks to participate in helping the Austrian National Bank.'[45]

Stephany's letter to Lionel de Rothschild continued with the sombre message that Credit Anstalt might 'close its doors next week or . . . a moratorium proclaimed in Vienna'. Stephany advised Lionel de Rothschild to join as chairman of the committee, 'which the Governor wishes to be formed'.

Norman's move towards organizing Credit Anstalt's creditors was brought about by the rising concern about the bank's position and the threat of a moratorium. May 23 stood out as the day when the uncertainty about Austria increased further, and the various actors came to realize that neither the BIS nor the market could take care of the problem. Bagehot and their past experience had not prepared them for this.

Stephany ended his letter that, 'this new situation now exposed is almost incredible and we must look forward to a long period of uncertainty whilst the bank's assets are realized or, alternatively, a scheme for its reconstruction is arranged'.[46]

An unholy alliance emerged out of the increasingly panicky atmosphere. The central bankers had no real interest in the Credit Anstalt, and the private bankers were not that interested in the Austrian National Bank. What united them was the simple fact that the two could not be untangled, that everyone outside of Austria wanted to avoid a moratorium at any price, and that the international monetary and financial system was at risk.

Rodd's comment on May 12 that it was 'no use suggesting the plan is a bad one' now seemed outdated as Credit Anstalt's survival was in question. The fear of foreign withdrawals, the discovery of the 'tainted money', Credit Anstalt's request for 10 million pounds, and not least the threat of a moratorium all added up to a dramatic increase in uncertainty and risk of contagion, as Stephany's letter and memorandum made clear.

A few days earlier, matters had seemed under control, but the outlook had once again changed overnight. It was unsettling, especially in the context of an already fragile economic and political situation in Europe. It was on that background that Norman had accepted BIS's request 'to do everything he can'. That meant pulling the private banks into the circle.

## A WILD EXAGGERATION

N.M. Rothschild & Sons had a strong interest in Credit Anstalt. The Vienna-based S.M. v. Rothschild headed by their cousin Louis Rothschild was closely related to the Credit Anstalt and Louis was chairman of its board. His firm was a major shareholder and had taken part in the reconstruction. From the perspective of the Rothschilds, the situation now escalated from hour to hour. In his lengthy memo, Stephany accounted for the same gradual realization about the seriousness of the situation that Rodd reported to the Bank of England on the same day.

Stephany's day consisted of an endless number of telephone calls and meetings held throughout the day in order to make sense of and emplot the developing situation. It began in the morning as he called Louis Rothschild in Vienna, who told him that a moratorium was 'possible but not probable'. He also said that Credit Anstalt needed 5 million pounds in new credits, which would be guaranteed by the government. This was completely new and was at best wishful thinking, and when Louis Rothschild asked 'how much we could do in London … I could not reply'.

Stephany's memorandum covered the whole day from morning to evening. Like Rodd and the people in the Bank of England, he received new information throughout the day and tried to fit it into a coherent understanding of what was going on. The parallel lines of communication complicated making sense of events and separating facts from rumours and outright wrong information.

As Rodd was on the phone with Catterns at the Bank of England for the second time that day, Stephany received a phone call from Vienna.

Dr. Brauneis, Vice-president of the Austrian National Bank, rang up and said he understood that the Bank of England and ourselves were against a moratorium. Dr. Brauneis agreed that it was undesirable, but in face of the situation of the Credit-Anstalt he considered it inevitable. The Directors of the Credit-Anstalt had asked for a credit of £10,000,000 an amount which the Austrian National Bank was unable to acknowledge. He said that unless this credit was available by Tuesday morning the Credit Anstalt would have to close its doors and come to an arrangement with its creditors. This would precipitate a very grave situation politically and financially because the currency problem would become involved. He was getting into touch with the B.I.S. at Basle with a view to obtaining their help and the help of the banks of issue. He asked me to inform the Governor of the Bank of England and enlist his help.[47]

After the conversation with Brauneis, Stephany took the short walk from New Court, the Rothschild's office at St. Swithin's Lane in the City, probably turning left along Lombard Street and right on Threadneedle Street where he entered the imposing Bank of England to see Ernest Harvey, the deputy governor. Harvey agreed about the seriousness of the situation but 'did not see what could be done between now and Tuesday'.

Harvey also told Stephany that he had been in touch with the BIS again and heard that 'unless London could provide a £10,000,000 credit by Tuesday morning the Credit-Anstalt would have to close its doors. The B.I.S. would be very pleased if London could do this, but they, the B.I.S., could take no responsibility. Sir Ernest thought that nothing could be done'.

At 5 p.m., Viktor Brauneis called again, this time asking if Rothschild or the Bank of England was able to arrange and make public a 3-million-pound credit for Credit Anstalt on Tuesday morning and an additional 7 million pounds 'would be made available as required after the whole position had been examined, the Credit Anstalt would probably be saved'. A government guarantee could not be arranged before Friday.

But it was impossible to consider a credit before Tuesday because of the holidays. Stephany asked if it could wait until Wednesday, and at 7.30 p.m. Brauneis called Stephany again, and

read out to me a prepared statement word by word to the effect that no delay was possible and any arrangement for a new Credit must be made by Tuesday. The Credit-Anstalt expected another run on Tuesday and it was impossible to estimate the amount. There were already rumours in circulation that extraordinary measures were to be taken.

The Austrian National Bank would not furnish the Credit Anstalt with currencies to meet these withdrawals as it would lead to inflation with the result that a large amount of Austrian currency would be offered in exchange for foreign currencies which could not be supplied; thereby the whole currency situation would be threatened. All the banks in Vienna would be involved and a great catastrophe was surely impending if the Credit or Guarantees for it was not forthcoming by Tuesday.[48]

Stephany remarked, 'I have informed the Bank of England of all the foregoing and also Mr. Bark, who the Bank of England informed me had the matter in hand on their behalf.'[49]

Like the story told by Rodd and McGarrah, Stephany's memo was a narrative of imminent economic and financial breakdown in Austria and beyond. This narrative came from Credit Anstalt and the Austrian National Bank, and it left no other option than a very substantial credit to the Credit Anstalt, or else a moratorium. Since the BIS and the Bank of England had already made it clear that they would not lend directly to the Credit Anstalt, the money would have to come from private banks. Brauneis's emphasis on the risk of inflation to legitimize the National Bank's position played right into the powerful memory of the hyperinflation of the early 1920s and served to legitimize the call on foreign banks and central banks to step in.

Despite all that, and the apparent consensus that a financial catastrophe was imminent in Vienna, very little happened over the weekend, and on Whit Monday, two days later, nothing much had been achieved.

In the morning Harry Siepmann and Simon, none of whom took the day off, spoke on the phone. There was 'relative calm' in Vienna, Simon said, but the Credit Anstalt's situation was constantly revised, and 'there is no reason to believe that the worst has yet been heard about the losses or their immobilization'.

Moreover, Brauneis believed that a flight from the Austrian schilling was now underway, and he was inclined not to discount more paper from the Credit Anstalt, even if the bank had any eligible paper left. Credit Anstalt's request for a 10-million-pound credit was 'believed to be merely a wild exaggeration by the CA, who do not wish to be caught underestimating any longer'.

Simon also told Siepmann that Norman's plan of organizing the international creditors was known in Austria. Reisch was optimistic that, if the upcoming maturities could be handled, 'there will be time to organize the foreign creditors before any further trouble arise'. Simon had also heard that Johannes Schober, the Austrian foreign minister and vice-chancellor, had returned from a League of Nations meeting in Geneva and reported that the German Reichsbank would be willing to put a 'substantial amount, say £1 million, at the disposal of the CA. It was also said that in that event further help would be forthcoming from France'.

From Simon, Siepmann heard about the phone calls between Brauneis and Stephany two days earlier, but with a somewhat different outcome than Stephany's memo mentioned. In Brauneis's version, 'Mr. Stephany is reported to have replied that £3 million might possibly be forthcoming during the holidays.'[50]

Maybe the Reichsbank would help. Maybe France would come to assistance. Maybe the Austrian S.M. v. Rothschild bank or the government would issue a guarantee. Or a moratorium. Or maybe N.M. Rothschild & Sons in London would help. Nobody knew anything for sure except that the pressure in and from Vienna was building. Simon's report made it clear just how difficult it was to establish and make sense of facts about what was going on in Austria. Who and what information to trust, what to do or not to do, what was possible, and what would happen?

They had no coherent narrative and therefore no actionable knowledge to come up with a blueprint for further action. All this uncertainty urged Montagu Norman to send a brief telegram to Harrison on Monday, May 25. 'Urgent cable following' it said.[51]

5

# Moratorium or Guarantee? (May 25–May 27)

Norman's urgent cable told Harrison that the 'situation in Austria may be even more serious than it appeared or perhaps dangerous'. Credit Anstalt's solvency and the 'internal banking position' could be dealt with. The real problem was how to handle the foreign creditors and ensure a proper administration of the Credit Anstalt in the near future.

Norman did not want the Credit Anstalt to be controlled by the Austrian government. 'We must not forget that Credit Anstalt virtually controls Austrian industries and that therefore Austrian Government should not be allowed to control Credit Anstalt.'

Norman's worldview did not leave room for state-owned enterprises, it would be a symbolic retreat of capitalism, and since the Austrian reconstruction he had been critical of the Austrian National Bank and its president, Richard Reisch. But his more immediate concern was the risk of a run on the Austrian schilling by Credit Anstalt's foreign creditors and contagion beyond Austria. He told Harrison that nor

> must we forget that a monetary breakdown in Austria might quickly produce a similar result in several other countries. Although a bank holiday I send this cable because matter is urgent and Oesterreichische Nationalbank seems helpless if not incapable.[1]

With the threat of a moratorium hanging, Norman was losing his patience. He told Harrison that 'on Wednesday morning formation of an informal and temporary committee will be announced under chairmanship of Lionel de Rothschild to concern itself particularly with the policy to be adopted in the near future'.[2]

Harrison had also kept up to date through the Austrian National Bank and the Bank for International Settlements (BIS), who 'have emphasized in particular the seriousness of a continuation of foreign withdrawals'.

He agreed 'that breakdown in Austria may have serious repercussions elsewhere' and if a committee of foreign creditor banks would improve the situation, 'it will be most important and useful'.

He suggested that Norman made it appear that the committee 'is organized with cooperation of or even at invitation of Credit Anstalt' to avoid the 'risk that it will be construed as a super-imposed creditors' committee with all that that implies?' Harrison once again asked Norman to keep him informed about the situation.[3]

In a parallel communication across the Atlantic, Morgan Grenfell informed J.P. Morgan & Co. about Norman's initiative to form a committee of creditor banks. The risk of contagion was again stressed as the main motive behind the idea. The proposal was not taken out of 'consideration for the Anstalt itself but by the belief that the whole Austrian financial fabric is dependent upon the maintenance of the Anstalt position and that any breakdown of the Austrian financial fabric would have disastrous results reaching far beyond Austria'.[4]

At this point, everyone agreed that the situation in Austria was increasingly fragile and that contagion beyond Austria was a real risk. But priorities differed. In Austria the concern was with the Credit Anstalt and the domestic economy including inflation. Outside of Austria, contagion and Siepmann's house of cards scenario dominated the narrative. Significantly, two weeks into the crisis, the centre of action had moved to London, as Norman, unhappy with the BIS and the Austrian National Bank, assumed responsibility for getting things done. His way.

## WE MUST RELY HEAVILY ON THE GOVERNOR

Two parallel transatlantic reporting lines emerged as the private bankers entered the stage. One between Norman, and occasionally the BIS, and Harrison, and another between the Morgan firms, J.P. Morgan & Co. in New York, Morgan Grenfell in London, and Morgan & Cie in Paris headed by the American banker Nelson Dean Jay since 1920.

Harrison's concern about being at an information disadvantage also extended to J.P. Morgan & Co., who relied on Morgan Grenfell and Morgan & Cie for updates from Europe. They acknowledged that 'the Governor and you are much closer to this situation than we are and we are ready to accept your judgment as to what is best in circumstance'.

In addition to these transatlantic channels of information, the House of Morgan, in particular, played an active role in establishing a communication line between the private banks on the one hand and the Bank of

England and the New York Fed on the other. Nelson Dean Jay also provided timely information from France and occasionally from the BIS.

J.P. Morgan forwarded the information from Morgan Grenfell about Norman's committee plans to Dean Jay. He believed that the idea and the choice of Lionel de Rothschild would be seen as reassuring in France and that more direct communication with France might also be beneficial for placing the Austrian loan. Since everyone relied on the French market to float the loan, he suggested that it would be 'good business for Bank of England to take the Banque de France into its confidence'.

In contrast to Norman, the Morgan firms had a direct line to France through their Paris office. Working closely with the French was not Norman's cup of tea, but it increasingly looked like the Austrian loan could not be placed without French banks taking the lead.

Norman's fear of contagion and a moratorium convinced him to step in and involve the private banks. Reaching out to the French was a different story. His dislike of the French made it unlikely that he would follow Morgan's advice. Still, Norman was now at the centre of any solution to the situation in Austria, and J.P. Morgan recognized that.

> We are so far away that we feel we must rely heavily on the Governor of the Bank of England and lend him our moral support at this juncture since the state of our market and the sudden adverse publicity about Austrian affairs make it impossible for us to do more. We are profoundly disturbed by the report that a moratorium is even being considered for the Credit Anstalt.[5]

Aware of the wider political context, Morgan also feared that 'the closing of Austria's principal private bank might have the gravest consequences with respect to the whole business of reconstruction not only in Austria but elsewhere'. In 1922 France and Great Britain, among others, had agreed to a reconstruction of Austria's economy, had set up the League of Nation's Control Committee and guaranteed a League loan. That the countries who made this possible, 'should let Austria go is unthinkable' and Morgan & Co. asked if Norman had considered this, and 'what do you yourselves think about it?'[6]

Morgan Grenfell was reluctant to involve the League of Nations because of the 'political atmosphere at Geneva', but in the last resort 'the league might have to be called into the picture'.[7]

It was not just the House of Morgan that struggled to make sense of all the new information and deal with the sudden increase in uncertainty that took place over the weekend. Norman, Harrison, Rodd, Siepmann, McGarrah, the Morgan partners and N.M. Rothschild were all involved.

So was Leon Fraser, the vice president of BIS, who met with Dean Jay while 'passing through Paris' on Tuesday, May 26. He also admitted to the uncertainty of the future and what to do. He confessed to Dean Jay that while 'our Basle data conflicting and change hourly, our best present view is salvage operation for OCAHG necessary to avoid bankruptcy'.[8]

Credit Anstalt's foreign liabilities were now estimated at $80 million after $20 million had already been paid out. This could not go on. Fraser feared that either the Credit Anstalt would have to close, or the government would declare a moratorium for private bank claims. The Austrian government was putting pressure on the National Bank to take over the liabilities of Credit Anstalt's foreign creditors, but the BIS and the National Bank were 'against this measure because it may bring down National Bank and currency'.

Fraser then made clear that BIS's unofficial view was that the 'Austrian state will have to choose between guaranteeing creditors or at least foreign credit of Credit Anstalt, if they agree to leave their funds, or permitting Credit Anstalt, which controls 70% of Austrian industry, to close, with the unemployment and other social consequences involved'.

Since this was the unofficial view, Fraser also emphasized that the BIS was careful to stay out of the Credit Anstalt's business and focused on assisting the National Bank. But it was impossible to completely neglect the Credit Anstalt, 'which is without competence or leadership'.

Separating Credit Anstalt's crisis from the National Bank's developing foreign exchange crisis was increasingly difficult. The BIS thought that an international creditor's committee must be formed with influence on the management of the Credit Anstalt. Even though the largest creditor countries were 'American and London Markets in for about $25,000,000 each', with Chase National Bank and National City Bank the largest creditors, Fraser stressed the need for 'some French and possibly one German on committee'.

Finally, Fraser told Dean Jay that the Austrian Parliament would meet two days later on Thursday, May 28, and that the question of a government guarantee might come up, 'unless aid from abroad found or withdrawal foreign funds ceases'. In any case a creditor's committee was needed.[9]

Of course, Norman had already set the establishment of a creditors' committee in motion. While Fraser met with Dean Jay, the formation of the committee was ready after 'two very long meetings at the Bank of England'. Lionel de Rothschild informed his Austrian cousins that a small and informal committee would be set up to calm the concern in London and to convince the creditor banks not to withdraw their credits. The house of cards scenario was never far away. 'It is obviously quite clear that if all credit facilities were withdrawn at the present time, the result would be disastrous.'

Lionel de Rothschild proposed that the Credit Anstalt should send somebody to Paris and London 'to explain the whole position to the various creditors' and to the Banque de Paris et des Pays-Bas. It would also be helpful if the Austrian Rothschilds would 'help keep us advised of the situation in Paris vis-à-vis the Credit Anstalt'.[10]

With preparations in place, shortly before 8 p.m. on May 26, Morgan Grenfell informed J.P. Morgan that a message would appear in the newspapers the next morning announcing that

> In agreement with the Governor of the Bank of England and at the suggestion of the OCAHGV the following committee has been informally and temporarily established
>
> Lionel de Rothschild (Chairman)
> Charles F. Whigham
> Sir R.M. Kindersley
> Peter Bark
>
> The committee will concern itself particularly with the policy to be adopted in the near future.[11]

The next day, Wednesday, May 27, the *Financial Times* carried the announcement.[12] The London Committee was now a fact, and Norman had followed Harrison's advice and arranged that 'announcement tomorrow will state that committee is formed at the suggestion of the Credit Anstalt'.[13]

The same morning, as the *Financial Times* announced the London Committee, the *New York Times* reported that the Credit Anstalt was not 'beyond all danger and that 'unofficial rumors ... are circulating to the effect that some kind of moratorium for the Credit Anstalt is under discussion'.[14] They were not out of the woods yet.

On Thursday, the *New York Times* told its readers that the 'gravity of the Austrian financial crisis is increasing so rapidly from hour to hour that it is difficult to see the end'.[15] As George Harrison read the morning paper, he must again have felt that he was sidelined and depended on Norman, McGarrah and Fraser, or Morgan for reliable news. To the extent that anyone had reliable news.

## NO ONE OVER HERE KNOWS WHAT THE SITUATION IS

Morgan Grenfell cabled Morgan in New York, 'We have already informed N.D. Jay by telephone asking him to advise the Banque de Paris et des

Pays-Bas this evening as knowing the cooperative attitude of the latter we were anxious to avoid in any way crossing wires with them.'[16]

The next day, Dean Jay informed the Banque de Paris et des Pays-Bas about the formation of the London Committee. In turn, the French bank told Dean Jay that the French government had asked it to send a representative to Vienna to negotiate the Austrian loan, but

> they declined, for they consider that there are political questions to be dealt with before Foreign Bankers can deal with the financial situation. They think the Austrian Government should assume the liabilities of the Credit Anstalt and, when this step has been taken, Foreign Bankers can study a plan for providing funds for the Government. They added that representatives of the Bank of France and of the French Treasury left for Vienna last night.[17]

This was perhaps the first real and troubling sign that the French banks might not take the Austrian loan after all. They, too, wanted a government guarantee first, and the suggestion that political questions should first be dealt with, played into the rumours that the French government might use the crisis to demand political concessions.

One of the representatives who had gone to Austria was Charles Rist, the prominent French economist and former Banque de France official, and now a money doctor. Before he left for Vienna, he called Dean Jay and said that he expected the Austrian government to arrange 'some form of external financing immediately' but he questioned if the bond issue would be possible 'without the guarantee of the principal European Governments'.[18]

The Morgan partners in New York were unimpressed. The lack of progress and the uncertainty about the future including the threat of a moratorium triggered J.P. Morgan's response to its French branch a few hours later. 'Hope you will find it possible to consult with us before issuing additional letters of credit under our Joint Line to Credit Anstalt. Please also cable us total amount of outstanding bills under franc line and also amount of credits open but unused. At present our total acceptances and unused balance of credits $185,155.08.'[19] Morgan's exposure to the Credit Anstalt was relatively small. Unable to assess the future outcome of the Austrian situation, they had no intention of increasing it.

The creditors' committee was seen as an important step, but its formation did not by itself solve any of the outstanding problems. Moratorium or government guarantee, the Austrian bond loan, who the foreign creditors were and how much they were owed, and the role of France and French bankers were all unresolved issues. And then there was the 'political atmosphere'.

At the moment, however, the need to identify the foreign creditors and establish their exact claims on the Credit Anstalt was the first step to be taken. In his report to Dean Jay, Fraser had mentioned that US and UK creditors each had claims of $25 million on the Credit Anstalt. Two weeks into the crisis, it was the first time specific amounts were mentioned, and both the BIS and Norman realized $50 million was more than enough to destabilize Austria and force it off the gold standard if withdrawn at the same time. But they needed more information.

The prominent American banker Paul Warburg, brother of Max Warburg, and Chairman of the International Acceptance Bank, tried to move things along. He had seen J.P. Morgan & Co and the New York Fed, he wrote to Rothschild in London, and they wanted to help. However, they could not come up with a plan until 'we know exactly who are creditors here and individual amounts involved'.[20]

J.P. Morgan reported on the same meeting to Morgan Grenfell, mentioning that the bankers they had talked to were inclined to maintain their credits if everyone else did the same. The BIS had suggested to the National Bank the 'necessity of an Austrian government guarantee for at least the foreign liabilities of the Credit Anstalt … In this connection we presume you already have in mind the case of the Danish Landmandsbank in 1922 1923 which may present some interesting parallels.'[21]

Morgan Grenfell responded the same day that Norman would send a list of outstanding credits to Harrison. However, the Bank of England did not have the individual amounts either. N.M. Rothschild had some information about withdrawals by American banks but not about when they had taken place. The banks and amounts were

National City Bank reduced from $2,000,000 to $1,000,000
Shawmut Corporation of Boston $600,000 withdrawn
Guaranty Trust Co. of New York $2,000,000 withdrawn
Chatham Phoenix National Bank & Trust Co. $1,000,000 withdrawn[22]

Like Charles Rist, Morgan Grenfell had learned that the Austrian Parliament would vote on a bill authorizing the government to guarantee Credit Anstalt's liabilities, but they had no specific information. They also mentioned that they had held the first meeting in the so-called London Committee formed on Norman's initiative.[23]

Harrison's meetings with Warburg and J.P. Morgan were not coincidental. In fact, Norman had suggested that he 'consult with J.P. Morgan & Co. as to getting into touch privately with Paul M. Warburg and other interested parties to help toward avoidance of foreign withdrawals and continuation of credits'.[24]

Since the BIS meetings the week before, focus had shifted to what Bagehot called a 'foreign drain'. Without knowing exactly who the creditors were and how much they had at stake, it was difficult to know how to proceed and how to coordinate the creditor banks' response. The problem with the London Committee was that it only organized banks in London. Since American and presumably other banks had large claims on Credit Anstalt, the effort to organize the creditors had only just begun.

With the discussions about moratorium or guarantee intensifying, the tipping point for foreign withdrawals from the Credit Anstalt was moving closer. But no one knew exactly where that point was. Only ten days earlier, Max Warburg, the German banker, was unable to imagine such a situation. In a letter to Lionel de Rothschild, he wrote that 'the fate of the Credit-Anstalt . . . is so bound up with the country that I think it quite out of the question that the government or the Nationalbank would decline to intervene . . . I therefore consider it justified to cooperate with the Credit-Anstalt now and consider that confidence will be maintained even by foreign friends'.[25]

If Warburg was right, the foreign creditors could rely on the Austrian government as the last resort, that is as guarantor of their claims. The problem was that the threats of a moratorium and uncertainty about a guarantee had changed the outlook dramatically in just a little over a week. What if Warburg was wrong?

Until now, the Credit Anstalt's foreign creditors had been patient, surprisingly so as a matter of fact. But things might change fast. If just a few of them began wondering if the Credit Anstalt would be allowed to fail, then what?

Apparently, no one outside of the Credit Anstalt knew for sure who the foreign creditors were, and even though the flight of capital from the Credit Anstalt and Austria had not yet taken on destabilizing proportions it might happen any day now. The spread of distrust and doubts about the intentions and abilities of the Austrians as expressed by Norman and Fraser were a bad sign.

The problem was that the Austrians preferred a moratorium or a foreign credit to restore confidence and avoid a bank failure. The BIS, Bank of England, the New York Fed and the foreign creditor banks on the other hand were concerned about a moratorium and contagion across the Austrian border and therefore demanded a guarantee.

The central bankers did not explicitly recognize these diverging narratives. But they increasingly felt the consequences as their frustrated statements about the Credit Anstalt, the government and the Austrian National Bank showed. In a wire to Morgan Grenfell on May 28, J.P. Morgan & Co. expressed this frustration.

We understand that National City Bank and Guaranty Trust Co. both reduced their lines immediately upon newspaper reports some time ago ... We think it is high time the Credit Anstalt gave its banks full information and let them know what it desires of them direct. No one over here knows what the situation is nor so far as we know is G.L. Harrison in a position to give any assurances.[26]

A little later, the firm repeated that Credit Anstalt should present its case directly to individual banks so that they got a 'clear understanding of the plans for dealing with the situation and be able to form their own judgment as to what they are asked to do'.

On the record up to date it is not surprising that individual banks should be taking steps to protect their own interests as best they can but we should still be inclined to hope for a good response to a direct appeal for full cooperation if they can be made to feel that the situation is definitely in hand and that the plans under way have reasonable prospects of success and of general acceptance.[27]

From the perspective of the foreign creditor banks, Credit Anstalt's response until now seemed like an object lesson of how not to handle a financial crisis. It was also not something Walter Bagehot had foreseen. In fact, he had not deal with an international crisis of the kind the world was struggling with during the summer of 1931, and he did not foresee the entanglement of all the different interests, actors, motives and perceptions.

Central bankers' operating model based on Bagehot came up short and offered only limited guidance. The uncertainty, lack of actionable knowledge and increasing sense of being kept in the dark by the Credit Anstalt and the National Bank was disconcerting. Without a plan, foreign bankers had no idea how to proceed. Morgan's telegrams suggested that a coherent narrative with a plan for providing actionable knowledge to act upon might change the situation.

## AT ALL COSTS

With the pressure on the Austrian currency mounting, and the linkage between the banking and the currency problems, the Austrian authorities were unable to solve the situation on their own. As they had done before, they appealed to Montagu Norman and the Bank of England.

On May 26 at 11.15 a.m. Harry Siepmann called Victor Brauneis at the Austrian National Bank. It was a critical moment in the crisis. The National Bank was inclined to stop discounting bills for the Credit Anstalt because the credit risk was too large and the solvency of the National Bank itself might be in danger. The Austrian government put pressure on the National Bank to continue discounting, and the Bank of England also encouraged this.[28] But Brauneis had reservations, so Harry Siepmann called him.

I rang up Dr. Brauneis at his request. He said that I had yesterday given some advice over the telephone which was confirmed later by the Governor to Dr. Reisch and to the Finance Minister. For his part, Dr. Brauneis said that he could not reconcile it with his conscience to carry out this advice. He was bound by oath at home and he had made promises in England which made it impossible for him to act proprio motu on the lines which we recommend.[29]

Brauneis wanted to know if Bank of England would advise the National Bank officially to keep rediscounting for the Credit Anstalt. He considered this advice to 'manufacture notes' and inquired whether the National Bank would be secured against losses of accepting bad collateral from the Credit Anstalt. The losses might be many times the National Bank's capital, and this would require either a government guarantee, 'which that Government would not give except perhaps on the strength of categorical advise' from the Bank of England, or 'some kind of international guarantee from outside'. Finally, Brauneis asked if

a telegram could be sent from here or from Basle – saying that the Central Banks of Europe would at all costs defend the Austrian currency from depreciation as a result of the Kredit Anstalt position.[30]

The conversation illustrated the dilemma from the point of view of a central banker. Brauneis was not intent on printing more money, and if he had to do it anyway, he would not accept responsibility for the consequences. The Bank of England or the BIS on the other hand had no intention of assuming the risk of losses emanating from the Credit Anstalt. It was two weeks into the crisis, and no one had even carried out an in-depth examination of the bank yet.

At 12.30 p.m., Siepmann called Rodd to discuss Viktor Brauneis's three questions. Norman did not want to involve the Bank of England in any of this, and 'the B.I.S. has to be the only mouthpiece of Central Banks'. Siepmann emphasized that the advice he had given to the National bank the day before was

given personally and individually as between friends and not as between institutions and . . . the alternatives before us yesterday were whether the National Bank should continue paying out or the Austrian Government should declare a moratorium.

We advised the National Bank to go on paying but we did not enter into the separate question of how they might properly require to be secured by the Government against the losses which might be incurred. On this subsequent question, which only arises if a moratorium is not declared, the B.I.S. view is that the Austrian Government has no business to require the National Bank to carry the whole credit risk of the Kredit Anstalt, and that unless the National Bank is secured against this credit risk it has no business to rely on other Central Banks to support the Austrian currency. The first duty of the National Bank is to look after the currency, which may be endangered even if the National Bank is covered by the Austrian Government against the credit risk. If through the immobilisations involved in taking Kredit Anstalt paper under Government guarantee the National Bank were to find its reserve unduly weakened, it might then count upon support from Central Banks.[31]

Siepmann re-stated the operating model and the purpose of it all, when arguing that 'the first duty of the National Bank is to look after the currency', and a moratorium was not part of that duty. The National Bank's president, Richard Reisch, and general manager, Brauneis, both placed phone calls to the BIS to try to get a statement that the BIS would defend the schilling and by implication the gold standard at all costs. Central banks on the other hand kept insisting on a government guarantee, as the BIS replied with a somewhat different 'at all costs' message.

we consider at all costs steps should be taken to avoid a moratorium. It is also essential that the ANB should not be impaired by such action as it has to take in order to provide the CA with liquid resources. We therefore desire again to emphasise the advice which you already have had that in present circumstances an adequate guarantee should be secured from the Austrian Government.... Provided that a division of responsibility is secured between the Government assuming full liability for the credit risks involved by the CA and the NB being responsible for the exchange position you may rely on the BIS and its associated central banks to assist you in maintaining the stability of the Austrian schilling. But neither the BIS nor such central banks as have been approached would be prepared to support the NBs exchange responsibilities if it has to take upon its shoulders the credit liabilities of the CA.[32]

The BIS telegram provided some leverage in the National Bank's negotiations with the government, but it also made clear what kind of support could be expected from the BIS and the central bank community and under what circumstances. An at-all-cost defence of the Austrian currency was not part of that, as the wording 'may rely on' and 'assist' revealed.

Still, the telegram served its purpose at the very last minute. Siepmann noted in a memo the following day, Wednesday, May 27.

This cable took some time to decode in Vienna and was not available at the Cabinet meeting held last night and attended by Dr. Reisch. At 11.30 p.m. the

Cabinet had reached the decision to proclaim a general moratorium this morning. Dr. Reisch then went to get a copy of the BIS cable, which he laid before the Cabinet, and the decision to proclaim a moratorium was immediately reversed. . . . Dr. Reisch has telephoned this morning that there is every prospect of a guarantee being proposed to Parliament tomorrow. The necessary law is being drafted and no particular objections are expected from the Opposition Parties. In the meantime the National Bank will continue paying out.[33]

A government guarantee suddenly seemed possible after all. The pressure piled upon the National Bank and the government by the BIS and central and private banks had worked eventually. It paved the way for a shift in frame from a moratorium to a government guarantee, despite the wishes of the Austrian government and to some extent the National Bank. This was exactly what both central bankers and private bankers had wanted.

McGarrah told Harrison that the BIS telegram was well received in Vienna by both the government and the National Bank, and 'we are assured that necessary law guaranteeing all of the indebtedness of the Oesterreichische Credit-Anstalt fur Handel und Gewerbe will be unanimously passed by parliament tomorrow. This must be taken with some reservation but we think chances good.'[34]

At last, there was, perhaps, a small light at the end of the tunnel. Norman wrote to Harrison that the prospect of a guarantee 'should satisfy foreign creditors and should encourage the National Bank to give and obtain necessary assistance'.[35]

# 6

# Guarantee at Last? (May 26–June 1)

As the dust settled after some hectic days, a guarantee suddenly appeared closer. Maybe the storm had been weathered this time around. There were repercussions, however, not least regarding the way the Austrian authorities and the Credit Anstalt had handled the situation.

An upset Fritz Dreyse, a vice president at the Reichsbank, complained to Siepmann that 'he did not understand how a demand for fresh money could be discussed at the same time as a moratorium is being threatened'. Dreyse had heard 'from Vienna', that a syndicate of British creditors would prolong the credits to the Credit Anstalt and provide new money of up to 6 million pounds. French creditors were said to have pledged 2 million pounds of new money. Siepmann said that 'there could be no question of new money being found direct for the KA in this market'.

The feeling that the Austrian authorities were playing the international financial community seemed widespread. They certainly saw the crisis through different lenses. The contact between Siepmann and Dreyse had been set up by Richard Reisch of the Austrian National Bank, and Dreyse 'very much resented the Austrian method of asking for help simultaneously in various quarters for the KA on the strength of promises said to have been already received'.

Despite German claims on the Credit Anstalt being quite small, 'if there were to be an international rescue party, the Germans would obviously be anxious to take their part', Siepmann noted. As the conversation ended, they agreed to keep each other informed of important developments, yet another sign that information and coordination were of the utmost importance; but hard to come by.[1]

Later that Tuesday, May 26, Hans Luther, the Reichsbank's president, called Siepmann inquiring 'whether there was not some intention of providing new money by international action either for Austrian

Government direct, or for the Kredit Anstalt with the guarantee of the Austrian Government. I said that I knew of no such intention'.[2]

They were now two weeks into the crisis, and the relative clarity Rodd had provided in the first few days, was increasingly replaced by uncertainty as the situation became ever more ambiguous. Fault lines, conflicts and divergent perceptions were surfacing, and Norman had not succeeded in leaving all responsibility for the rescue action with the Bank for International Settlements (BIS). His fear of a moratorium and contagion beyond Austria, and Rodd's call on behalf of McGarrah to 'do everything he can', had made him step in and organize the London creditors.

The committee of creditors could be an important step in reining in the crisis and reducing fears of contagion. In the week before the crisis took a turn for the worse, Fraser had expressed his feeling to Morgan & Cie that 'if all creditors remain calm the situation may be worked out but he is by no means certain of it'.[3]

The question of the international creditors and foreign liabilities of the Credit Anstalt and the National Bank now required all attention, as fears of a run on the schilling mounted. The central banking aspects certainly appeared more clearly, as Siepmann had put it in the first days of the crisis. The ball was back in Norman's court.

Harrison was happy to help, and his sense was that all important quarters wanted to 'play ball and as far as possible to avoid any unnecessary risk of a breakdown in Austria the seriousness of which everyone seems to appreciate'. There was one problem, though.

Harrison knew that total US claims on the Credit Anstalt was in the area of $25 million, but except for the larger New York banks he did not know who the creditors were. He needed full information about 'names and amounts of individual American lines' to figure out what could be done.[4] As so often since May 11, the link between the present and the imagined future was next to impossible to establish without actionable knowledge and a coherent narrative.

The next day, Wednesday, May 27, Norman sent Harrison the information he had asked for. The data were collected from 'various sources and may not be accurate', but with that reservation the Credit Anstalt owed $20.8 million to 33 US-based banks. The biggest creditors were Chase National Bank ($3.5 million), New York Trust Company ($2.2), International Acceptance Bank ($2.1), National City Bank ($1.5), First National Bank of Boston ($1.2) and Chemical Bank and Trust Co. ($1.1). Among the least exposed were J.P. Morgan ($0.19) and Lazard Freres ($0.24).[5]

Despite the lack of knowledge about Credit Anstalt's foreign creditors, the prospect of the Austrian government introducing a guarantee bill in Parliament, and the formation of the creditors' committee in London allowed for some optimism. Also, the Credit Anstalt reported on Tuesday, May 26, that the situation was a 'trifle calmer than at the close Saturday'. On Wednesday, McGarrah felt that perhaps 'the situation is more encouraging than seemed possible yesterday'.[6]

## CAUSE AND EFFECT

True to Harrison's wish to be kept informed, Norman wired him about the prospect of a guarantee. If the law was passed and enacted, it would both accommodate the foreign creditors and make it possible for the National bank to support the Credit Anstalt and get assistance from abroad. In a rare acknowledgement of the BIS, Norman added that this 'action follows on B.I.S. advise'.[7]

The bad news came on May 27 in a telegram from Harrison to Norman.

> In addition to all the talk about Vienna there has been much gossip and rumor both in and out of the press during the past two days about likelihood that German government will shortly ask for postponement under the Young Plan.
>
> . . . Most of these rumors purports to come from Berlin and while they may not be as much responsible for current weakness of reichsmark as conditions in Vienna nevertheless I should appreciate any comments you may feel free to send me.[8]

Concern about Germany and reparations was nothing new, but the surfacing of these rumours at this critical moment of the Austrian crisis was disturbing. After all, it was the worst-case imagined future that everyone feared. Norman was about to have a busy day due to developments in Vienna, but he nevertheless replied to Harrison admitting his own difficulties making sense of and emplotting the situation into a coherent story.

> In my opinion general situation is so confused and slippery that cause and effect cannot clearly be distinguished. But while I attribute current weakness of Reichsmarks mainly to condition in Vienna I think that belief is growing that German government will during 1931 seek some temporary easing under Young plan. This might be sought in many ways and personally I believe will be sought – especially if prices and markets continue as at present.[9]

In contrast, McGarrah, who also weighed in on the discussion about Germany, had a somewhat different view. He sent some 'in our opinion best available information' to Harrison.

The chronic condition of Germany, as evinced by the economic depression and the budget difficulties has long been known. No acute change has occurred. On the contrary, the Government is making every effort to balance the budget, and is likely to succeed in its endeavor.

The effect of these reconstructionary measures on private enterprise and on the money market can only be beneficial. There are no indications of any intentions on the part of the German Government to have recourse in the near future to the postponements for which the provision is made in the Young Plan. Moreover, it is common knowledge that postponements of the kind do not afford relief from an acute crisis.[10]

While Norman found it difficult or impossible to make sense of what was going on and what was cause and effect, he still expected a very different outcome in Germany than McGarrah. McGarrah stuck with orthodoxy and thought that Chancellor Heinrich Brüning's deflationary measures would balance the budget and be good for business and the money market. Going somewhat beyond 'available information', he had no eye for the political polarization in Germany where Nazis and Communists were fighting each other in the streets. Referring to 'common knowledge', he revealed a blind spot assuming that others saw the situation through the same cultural lens he did.

Despite McGarrah's confidence, the fear of a meltdown in the German economy had been the underlying nightmare scenario for quite a while as Siepmann's 'thin ice' and 'house of cards' metaphors demonstrated. Now, in late May, references to Germany became more frequent, as the central banks and the BIS struggled to contain the Austrian crisis. As the German worst-case scenario kept popping up, the uncertainty regarding the situation in Austria added weight to Norman's troubling inability to make sense of events and assess cause and effect.

Thursday, May 28, began quietly. At the BIS, Pierre Quesnay received a telegram from the National Bank, thanking him for the 'at all costs' statement of May 26, which 'had decisive significance for establishing distinct view here'. The statement had increased the chance that a guarantee for all creditors of the Credit Anstalt would be passed making it easier to attract foreign credit. 'Thus the defense of the schilling currency and the support you have promised will be considerably facilitated.'[11]

Quesnay's message had, indeed, shifted the balance towards a guarantee and away from a moratorium. If the telegram struck an optimistic tone that changed when Vice President Gustav Thaa called Simon with an SOS to the BIS management from Brauneis and himself. Things were getting out of hand in Austria, despite the fact that the country had followed all the advice given by the BIS. The National Bank was losing 30–40 million schillings of foreign exchange every day. A run on the Austrian schilling was underway.

Thaa feared that publication next Tuesday, June 2, of the National Bank's weekly balance sheet would accelerate the flight from the schilling, and then 'no foreign credits will be able to stop it, and he foresees in that case the entire collapse of Austrian currency unless support is given very quickly'. Simon's account of the phone call continued

The psychological and economic results of such a breakdown of Austrian currency would undoubtedly be from the point of view of the country itself as well as that of the whole world, even worse than those which have so far been luckily avoided.

In Thaa's opinion, there exists therefore only one salvation: either the government must receive very quickly foreign funds with which to meet the withdrawals of credit from the CA and to quieten the public, or the BIS and the bigger central banks must take effective measures to safeguard the stability of the schilling. Thaa thinks that the sums required for this purpose would be very small, and that no risk would be involved; if the BIS would publish the fact that it and a certain number of cooperating central banks would unite their efforts to maintain the stability of the schilling, all anxiety and all flight of capital would be removed in one moment. If this is not done, Thaa and Brauneis are afraid that, owing to the increase of circulation which they had to admit in order to avoid the bankruptcy of the CA, their funds . . . will be depleted very shortly and a collapse will become unavoidable. Thaa ended by saying that he and Brauneis implored me to submit this SOS to the management of the BIS. The management should not believe that their statements are exaggerated. They are indeed convinced that nothing short of one of the two above mentioned measures can avoid the worst.[12]

To this account of the conversation with Thaa, Simon added that he was convinced that the National Bank would 'agree to any sort of control or condition which the BIS might consider necessary'.[13] To make sure that the gravity of the situation was clear at the BIS, an urgent telegram arrived from the National Bank at 4.45 p.m.

We have been warned of a moratorium on account of destructive consequences on credit and reaction abroad.

Cannot believe that breakdown of currency would have less serious consequences here and abroad.

If we continue as at present rapid decrease of foreign exchange holding and of percentages of cover eventually must lead to suspension of Bank statutes.

As population is anxious on account of experience during time of inflation we must fear that bad bank's return will cause currency panic.

We think that restoration of confidence is the only means of rescue.

As a bill is to be passed by parliament today authorizing government to grant guarantee for new credit to Oesterreichische Credit Anstalt für Handel und

Gewerbe whereby conditions for support of currency by BIS and central banks are fulfilled we urgently request you to publish as soon as possible declaration of maintenance of stability of Austrian schilling.

As a consequence of such declaration we expect re-establishment of confidence and stoppage of large foreign exchange withdrawals.

Please do your best for procuring that expected new foreign credit OCAHG under governmental guarantee are granted as soon as possible.

Such credit would diminish demand for new credit at Oesterreichische Nationalbank and increase our stock of foreign exchange.

Any delay might endanger result of action for currency.

If our request be fulfilled we are ready to submit to any technical demands concerning our activity after having examined them.

Please inform big central banks accordingly.[14]

A key word in this message was 'new foreign credit OCAHG' indicating that existing credits to the Credit Anstalt would not necessarily be covered by a guarantee. And that the National Bank expected the BIS and central banks to either extend credit to the Credit Anstalt or to induce private banks to do so.

In the view of the English banker Harry Goschen, the 'risk of precipitating Austrian and possibly also German or still wider crisis far exceeds danger of loss by continuing with . . . Credit Anstalt'.[15] Nevertheless, it was hard to imagine existing creditor banks extending new loans, if their current credits were still at risk.

Harrison received a copy of the National Bank's urgent telegram to the BIS, and the Bank also cabled him directly to 'urgently ask you to approach New York City Banks' to maintain their business with the Credit Anstalt, 'which certainly serves best interest of creditors'.[16] Later that day, the National Bank cabled Harrison again to inform him that the New York Trust Company was reluctant to renew a $2 million credit due May 29, 'we call your special attention to this fact'.[17]

Harrison assured that he wanted to be helpful, but he was not going to spend his and the New York Federal Reserve Bank's reputation on convincing private banks to renew credits, 'especially as it is not yet known here what action will be taken in Vienna tonight with respect to the proposed law to guarantee creditors'.[18]

The trifle of calm had been short-lived, and the National Bank's foreign exchange reserves were dwindling. The weekly statement had to be drawn up the next day, Friday, May 29, and released on Tuesday, June 2. That could be the tipping point.

The BIS's patience had certainly tipped. The many requests from the Credit Anstalt and the National Bank without any of them having any plan in place began to take a toll and change how the BIS approached the Austrian authorities. This was clear in a May 28 message from the BIS to the National Bank.

> We consider that the authorities should as soon as measure has been voted in parliament announce to public that government has assumed full liability for the CA this guarantee covering both existing depositors as well as depositors of new money. Communique should make clear that this decision has been taken after careful consideration of various alternatives which have all been discarded in favour of guarantee. No other exceptional measures are therefore under consideration. When this communique has been issued we should be prepared to make a statement regarding support of BIS to ANB.[19]

The phrase about alternatives being discarded and no exceptional measure being considered pushed the Austrians to give up the idea of a moratorium. The telegram made clear that not only was a moratorium unacceptable, the guarantee would also have to cover both new and old deposits. If, and only if, these demands were fulfilled would the BIS make a statement of support for the National Bank. When the National Bank had accepted this by telephone, a second telegram would follow.

Around midnight after the National Bank had accepted these conditions by telephone the second telegram added a request, already implied by Simon. The National Bank 'will insist on Controller to be appointed by foreign interests being put in charge of CA and NB inviting an advisor.... Please telephone us as soon as possible tomorrow morning and before reaching final decisions.'[20]

The message did not leave much room for objections or interpretation. The next morning at 9.15 a.m., Brauneis called to say that the National Bank, the Credit Anstalt and the Austrian government accepted the 'proposal' of a controller to be appointed to the Credit Anstalt and an adviser to the National Bank.[21]

## UNHAPPY ABOUT VIENNA

While the National Bank seemed to consider the controller and adviser to be mostly communication exercises designed to improve confidence, the Bank of England and the BIS saw these measures as a way to make sure that the Austrian authorities conducted a proper policy. That is, the policy wanted outside of Austria.

The BIS informed the Bank of England about the request that 'a foreign controller shall be put in charge of the Kredit Anstalt and a foreign adviser shall be put into the National Bank' before 'further help is promised or announced by the BIS'.[22] At the Austrian National Bank, a few managers may have questioned the BIS and Bank of England's confidence in their abilities and intentions.

With the Austrian Parliament still in session late on May 28, there was not much central bankers and international creditors could do but wait. They hoped the guarantee would be passed and that it would ease the outflow of foreign exchange from Austria. Two and a half weeks had gone by since the Austrian finance minister Otto Juch had urged Harry Siepmann to travel to Vienna immediately, and since then nothing much had been achieved to effectively stem the financial problems.

The BIS credit to the National Bank had been organized but not yet released, the Austrian loan had been authorized by the Control Committee but not yet placed, and the discussion about a moratorium or a guarantee was still ongoing though the scale was tipping towards a guarantee as a result of massive pressure from the central bank money doctors and the BIS's 'at all costs' telegram.

It now seemed clear that the BIS and central bank credit would not be released until the moratorium was off the table and parliament had passed the guarantee. The delay was not a matter of clumsiness in arranging the credit, it was part of forcing the Austrian government's hand.

In the meantime, foreign exchange was flowing out of the country as both foreign creditors and the Austrian public were about to lose confidence in the Credit Anstalt and the schilling.

Montagu Norman's push for an international creditors' committee was not yet a reality, and the rationales for action were to some extent diverging. To the international central bankers, the fear of a moratorium and contagion was the dominant problem, while Austrian decision-makers were more concerned about their own banking system and inflation.

In his message to Harrison where Norman gave up on making sense of cause and effect, he also confessed that

> I am unhappy about Vienna where from the beginning situation seems to have been poorly handled: indeed some prompt action and boldness was needed both in national bank and in Bank for International Settlements.[23]

Despite all Norman's efforts to convince the BIS to manage the first real international financial crisis response, the case was back on his desk. And he knew who to blame. In Norman's narrative, the BIS and the Austrian authorities had either neglected or been unable to do what was necessary to halt the Credit Anstalt crisis from developing into a currency crisis.

On May 28, the Austrian National Bank finally informed the Federal Reserve Bank of New York about US banks' engagements with the Credit Anstalt. There were four lists of US-based banks. Lists A and B listed banks in New York City and Brooklyn 'having withdrawn or reduced credit' or 'still granting facilities' respectively, while lists C and D listed the same for banks outside of New York. The lists showed that, in total, out of $20.3 million, deposits of $4.7 million had been withdrawn.

The New York Trust Company had maintained its $250,000 credit and had, allegedly, promised to open a short-term position of 2 million dollars on May 29; Chase National Bank maintained a credit of $3.75 million to the Credit Anstalt, but National City Bank had reduced its exposure from 2 to 1 million dollars.[24]

This meant that almost a fifth of deposits by US-based banks had been withdrawn since May 11. These figures covered a diverse picture, but Harrison cannot have been too optimistic about his own backyard. The same day, his board of directors met in a sombre mood. Harrison argued that 'with conditions the world over as serious as they now are . . . the adoption of a program of mild inflation must be considered'.

Charles Mitchell, CEO of National City Bank and a member of the New York Fed's board, agreed with the diagnosis but not the cure. The risk of failure was big because 'at the moment, fear was the dominant element in business thinking' and this 'psychology of fear' stood in the way of success.[25]

## A CASE FOR COMMON ACTION

Norman, too, had strong reservations about the National Bank's appeal to Harrison to approach US banks, which resembled what the Credit Anstalt had already tried once. Instead, he suggested to Harrison that it was 'essential for New York and London to consolidate and make their position toward Credit Anstalt effective and helpful. I am pushing as best I can though unconnected with Rothschild committee and as you have list of American creditors please do your utmost immediately to bring about this active consolidation.'[26]

The Rothschild committee was the informal British committee of creditors with Lionel de Rothschild as chairman. Also called the London Committee, it had been formed on Norman's initiative and held its first meeting on Wednesday, May 27, at 3 p.m. in New Court, N.M. Rothschild's office since 1809 just around the corner from the Bank of England.

Present were the two Rothschild brothers and managing partners Lionel and Anthony as well as Samuel Stephany from N.M. Rothschild & Sons.[27] Charles F. Whigham from Morgan Grenfell, Robert Kindersley from Lazard Brothers, and a few others also attended. Lionel de Rothschild chaired the meeting and 'explained that the Governor of the Bank of England had considered the formation of the committee necessary to ensure that credit facilities were not withdrawn'.

A government guarantee was key in preventing withdrawals, and Charles Whigham of Morgan Grenfell 'referred to the case of the Danske Landmandsbanken in 1922, when the Danish government guaranteed the foreign credits granted to the bank'. Whigham suggested that 'the Austrian government might similarly guarantee the CA's foreign credits'.

That was any foreign creditor bank's dream scenario, but it was not yet clear what kind of guarantee the Austrian Parliament might pass, not to speak of how and when the government would actually implement it. The same uncertainty prevailed regarding the placement of the Austrian government loan, which had gone nowhere since J.P. Morgan turned down the request to take the lead.[28]

The committee agreed that it was urgent to involve American banks, in particular, but also other countries' banks. The day after the first committee meeting, Siepmann, who was in close contact with the Rothschilds, made a note to Governor Norman that the committee would meet at 3.30 p.m. with London representatives of American banks to update them and encourage them to maintain their credits.

Lionel de Rothschild 'is anxious that everything possible should be done to get New York in step with London'. He asked whether Norman would enlist Harrison's support 'in order to obtain concerted action by creditors in New York. Unless New York maintain their positions with the Credit Anstalt it will not be possible to ask London to continue doing so much longer'.

The Committee would also find it helpful if the BIS 'could make a public declaration that through them the stability of the Austrian currency will be supported, so far as possible, by central banks'. In a copy to Lionel de Rothschild, Siepmann added that the governor is 'doing all he can by cable and telephone' to enlist Harrison's support, and that he would deal with the BIS later.[29]

As the Committee met with all London-based creditors including American bankers at 3.30 p.m., Lionel de Rothschild welcomed the assembled bankers and informed them that the BIS and central banks had organized a 100-million-schilling credit to the National Bank and that the

Austrian government 'has decided to introduce a bill today guaranteeing all new liabilities of the Credit Anstalt'. He continued that 'unless we are willing to continue our credits and deposits the drain of currency will be too great. . . . I think you will all agree this is a case for common action.'[30]

After the Chairman's introduction, there was a brief discussion between the assembled bankers representing fifty-one banks. The influential banker and strong believer in the gold standard, Harry Goschen, supported Lionel de Rothschild's plea.[31] He argued that

> the meeting should seriously consider what might be the result of a refusal on the part of the international bankers to maintain their present positions – that such action might have repercussions in Germany and other countries and involve the breakdown of the European credit structure.[32]

As the meeting adjourned and the bankers left New Court and filed into Lombard Street, the Committee informed Credit Anstalt that they had agreed to maintain liabilities on a day-to-day basis on three conditions. First, no foreign creditors must be paid in preference. Second, effective measures were taken to 'allay local feeling and no more serious withdrawals are permitted in Vienna in detriment to foreign creditors'. Finally, the government guarantee must cover both existing and new deposits, and the committee asked for a reply 'to reach us first thing tomorrow morning'.[33]

In New York, George Harrison received a copy of these conditions and discussed the terms with the major American creditors of the Credit Anstalt. He wrote to Norman that the New York creditors realized the seriousness of the situation and its 'possible ramifications'. If the committee's three conditions were fulfilled, he thought the banks would be 'willing to continue facilities to extent now utilized at least from day to day'.[34]

In the meantime, the sense of urgency spread and increased the need for action. Hambros Bank in London had been asked to send dollar and sterling notes to Vienna by airmail, and Swiss banks had already sent 5½ million Swiss francs since May 13. Siepmann told the Reichsbank's Fritz Dreyse that the London market was not participating in the Austrian government issue because 'the best and most considerable contribution that they could make at present would be to refrain from withdrawing existing credits'.[35]

Only a guarantee could change the impasse. It was passed in Parliament late on May 28. The Austrian National Bank immediately cabled the good news to the Federal Reserve Bank of New York, which received it in the morning of May 29. The act authorized the government to fully guarantee loans to the Credit Anstalt until June 30, 1933.[36]

According to the National Bank, the law gave the government the right to guarantee both new credits and renewed existing credits. 'We firmly believe that this bill will essentially contribute to establish atmosphere of calmness indispensable for the realization of the reconstruction program of . . . Credit Anstalt . . . this bill will certainly give you material assistance in meeting our request as per our cable of May 27.'[37]

At a committee meeting on May 29 at noon, Chairman Lionel de Rothschild reported the good news together with encouraging reports from banks in the United States and France who agreed with the committee's purpose. 'The chairman said that in view of these developments the committee thought the time had now come for the informal London committee to give place to an international committee to be composed of 3 British representatives, 3 American representatives and 1 representative each from Switzerland, France and Holland.'[38]

That was the London committee's last meeting. Lionel de Rothschild, Charles Whigham and Robert Kindersley stayed on to represent British interests on the International Committee, which met for the first time on June 1 as the 'Credit Anstalt International Committee' with new representatives from the United States, Italy and France and the hope of more to come.[39]

What really mattered, was the addition of three American representatives. The American banks had been reluctant to join, but J.P. Morgan reported that 'the Banks are generally falling into line'. They elected three American bankers residing in London to represent them.[40] They were James H. Gannon, vice president of the Chase National Bank in London, the largest creditor with a claim of $3.75 million; D.B. Grant of the Guaranty Trust Co. with a claim of $750,000; and L.S. Chanler Jr. of the International Acceptance Bank with a claim of $2 million.

Harrison sent the names to Norman, who suggested to Lionel de Rothschild to co-opt the three Americans. 'If you will adopt this method and be content without formal procedure, I think you will find the result will satisfy everyone concerned; but I have left it to you to approach the three persons named above.' There was no doubt about the close relations between the central bankers and the private banks.[41]

On June 2, the *Financial Times* informed its readers that the International Bankers' Committee had been formed with the participation of Gannon, Grant and Chanler as well as representatives from France and Italy, and with Swiss, German and Dutch bankers to join them 'in due course'.[42]

For once, things seemed to be heading in the right direction. J.P. Morgan & Co. credited George Harrison, 'who has met the situation with great good sense and courage and has largely been instrumental in securing the cooperation of the interested parties on this side'.[43]

In France, too, things seemed to go smoothly. Governor Moret cabled Norman that 'Committee of the French creditors of the Credit Anstalt has been formed this morning. Credit Lyonnais will be the representative of the French creditors to the International Committee.' Norman responded the same day, 'I am glad that Paris and London should thus be marching in step and I shall be careful to keep in touch with you on the whole question in its Central Banking aspects.'[44]

Despite this progress, both the internal and external drain seemed to continue in Austria, and there were still significant unresolved questions as to how the guarantee would be implemented. *The Economist* remarked on May 30 that 'overcoming the difficulties . . . are proving more formidable than at one time seemed likely'. Still, the magazine was optimistic that organizing the creditors and the fact that the Austrian government had given 'some form of state guarantee' would soon provide 'breathing space'.[45]

The American *Commercial and Financial Chronicle* saw the Austrian crisis in a larger context and noted how the market feared that 'the reparations question may be reopened'. The paper pointed out that 'the German situation is doubtless influenced by the critical conditions in Austria' and was cautiously optimistic that alarm over reparations was groundless. The German government was 'firmly entrenched and Chancellor Bruening has repeatedly demonstrated his ability to hold control'.

Nevertheless, ominously but clear-eyed, the *Chronicle* also noted that the world was 'grievously harassed by unemployment, falling prices of commodities and securities, an appalling burden of public indebtedness, and unprecedented conditions in gold, silver and credit. Any attempt to draw a hard and fast line between what is political and economic . . . would obviously be futile.'[46]

## A BUTCHER, A DICTATOR AND A CREDIT

According to Norman, it was he who had insisted on the appointment by the international creditors of a controller in the Credit Anstalt, and an adviser to the National Bank. The butcher and dictator, he called them. He had informed Walter Stewart and Francis Rodd about this on May 28, and the BIS went along.[47] In a handwritten note on a telegram from Harrison, Norman wrote on May 29,

Friday 2.30 pm – answered above, HAS present. Also reported my talk with WWS & FR last night (10.30 pm) refusing further credit to A.N.Bk except with a Butcher with powers in Cr ans. Dictator in ANB and a definite forceful & new attitude somehow to be estab'd in Basle.[48]

This was Norman 'dealing' with the BIS. FR and WWS were Francis Rodd, and Walter Stewart, an American economist 'of wonderful insight and understanding', according to Harry Siepmann.[49] Stewart, another money doctor, had been invited by the BIS, to 'spend some time as economic adviser, and particularly to assist in strengthening its relations with Central Banks' and 'formulate recommendations for policies and practices of the B.I.S'.[50]

Though they used different words than butcher and dictator, the Credit Anstalt, the National Bank and the Austrian government accepted the 'proposal' of a controller to be appointed to the Credit Anstalt and an adviser to the National Bank. Viktor Brauneis at the National Bank wanted the adviser to share responsibility for all decisions. He proposed that the press should be notified about the appointments, 'such notification being in his opinion calculated to strengthen confidence in conditions in Austria'.[51]

The purpose was to make it look as if the Austrians themselves had asked for assistance. Siepmann noted from a telephone conversation with Rodd that 'the appointment of a dictator in the Kredit Anstalt is to be both suggested and made by the Austrian Government'. In fact, both the appointment of a controller at the Credit Anstalt and an adviser for the National Bank were orchestrated by the BIS and Bank of England and coordinated with the International Committee's secretary H.E. Davies from Rothschild & Sons.[52]

On May 30, the Austrian National Bank cabled the BIS that 'Government and National Bank request urgently adviser should be sent for … Credit Anstalt … National Bank invites Bank for International Settlements to send an adviser.'[53]

With the guarantee passed by the Austrian Parliament and the demands for a controller and an adviser in place, the BIS finally prepared a press communiqué announcing the joint 100-million-schilling foreign exchange credit arranged almost two weeks earlier. It was hardly a coincidence that the release of the credit was announced on the same day that the Credit Anstalt, National Bank and Austrian government finally accepted all the demands of the international financial community.

In fact, Francis Rodd called Siepmann on Thursday, May 28, to tell him that 'the B.I.S. have informed the Austrian National Bank that unless the Government gives a full and unconditional guarantee for all liabilities of the Kredit Anstalt they would get no support whatever from the B.I.S. or from any of its associated banks. This message has been taken by Dr. Brauneis to the Cabinet which is still in session.'[54] This was a reference to BIS's 'at all costs' message that shifted the balance away from a moratorium towards the guarantee.

Merle Cochran, the American Consul in Basle, told the State Department that the BIS credit and statement of confidence was announced 'only as the reciprocal part of an agreement which required that the Austrian Government guarantees the obligations of the Credit Anstalt'.[55]

It added up to a lot of pressure from the central banking community on the Austrian government and the National bank. And it worked. The plan for a moratorium had been dropped, at least for now, and instead the Austrian Parliament has passed the guarantee requested by the BIS, the central banks, and the International Committee. According to Pierre Quesnay 'Vienna is now much calmer'. Quesnay also believed that 'the Government communiqué showing that existing depositors are covered by the guarantee has made a good impression locally'.[56] That was somewhat premature as no such cover had yet been implemented.

But the foreign controller to the Credit Anstalt and foreign adviser to the National Bank had been accepted, as had the demands from the informal creditors' committee. The BIS communiqué on the international credit emphasized that

> The Bank for International Settlements is confident that with these resources, in addition to those already at the disposal of the Austrian National Bank and the support of the other Central Banks, the Austrian National Bank will continue its normal functions of ensuring the convertibility and stability of the Austrian currency. Close contact is maintained between the Bank for International Settlements and the Austrian National Bank and in order to provide direct personal contact a representative of the Bank for International Settlements is on his way to Vienna.[57]

The representative was Francis Rodd, who had flown back in from Basle and resumed his work in Vienna on the afternoon of May 29. From the BIS he heard that the press communiqué was 'favourably received and exchange markets are quieter'.[58]

It had been almost two weeks since Rodd had left Vienna and returned to Basle to brief the board and central bank governors. Since then, the situation had certainly gone from bad to worse, and now he was back with the same assignment: to collect information and make sense of the situation on the ground in Vienna.

His first report stated that Austria had lost 40 million schillings worth of foreign exchange on May 29 alone. That corresponded to BIS's share of the central bank credit gone in one day, and it was a sure sign of an accelerated flight from the schilling. The total losses of foreign exchange since May 12 now amounted to 250 million schillings or $35 million. The National Bank's foreign exchange position was still comfortable with 512 million schillings of foreign exchange, but most of it was illiquid and only 92 million were immediately available.[59]

Even if the BIS credit of 100 million schillings had come late, it was timely. And small. The National Bank statement for the week ending Friday May 29, would have to be made the following day, and 'they will probably require to make use of the Central Bank credit . . . they expect to have to take 20 more, that is to say 10 millions out of the 60 to be put up by the central banks'.[60]

Despite the fact that all the necessary signatures had not been collected at the time of the press communiqué 'in view of the urgency of the matter', on May 30 the BIS decided to allow the National Bank to draw up to 60 million schillings. 'We are placing at your disposal, value as per today, to your sight account with us £866,958 . . . and $4,218,222 being together the equivalent of 60 million Austrian Schillings'.[61]

Austria had lost 40 million schillings on May 29 alone, and 60 million schillings might not reassure increasingly nervous creditors or the Austrian public. Maybe the National Bank had a point that communication was important, but the actual implementation of the guarantee by the Austrian government was still not in place. Rodd felt that both the government and the National Bank were 'rather too optimistic' about the situation.[62]

On the day that the Austrian National Bank was given access to the credit, the foreign exchange losses of the Credit Anstalt were down to 12 million schillings from 40 million the day before. That was a good sign. Perhaps the news of the credit and the intended government guarantee was working after all? According to Rodd, the situation was 'quite quiet'.[63]

The guarantee and the BIS credit also gave the Austrian savings banks a reason to deposit money with the Credit Anstalt. Rodd reported that about 50 million schillings would be deposited by the savings banks. That should ease Credit Anstalt's need for rediscounting at the National Bank.[64] However, Rodd struggled to convince the minister of finance, Otto Juch, that the uncertainty about the guarantee was now the key issue.

The trouble about the position is that the Government guarantee is in such form that before any such deposits are made the assurance that they will be covered by the guarantee is required. No amount of plain speaking last night to the minister of the finances had any effect, his only retort being that he had already got more by the way of freedom to give the guarantee than a number of his colleagues in the cabinet were willing to give him. More he could not obtain.[65]

'I confess to consider the position unsatisfactory', Rodd wrote to McGarrah about the fact that there was no guarantee until depositors applied for it in each case. Juch had assured Rodd that the guarantee would be granted when applied for, and Rodd hoped that this would have an effect on the public, but he was not optimistic. On top of that, as hinted by Juch, political problems were brewing in Austria. The minister of justice threatened to resign and with him a group of politicians who supported the government. A cabinet crisis was imminent, and Rodd was 'afraid that the state of mind of the ministers at present is not conducive to extending the guarantee or to popularizing its application'.[66]

A national political crisis on top of the economic crisis was not really what was needed in Austria. The central bankers and the international financial community, or at least the Anglo-American part of it, had finally come up with and managed to push through their plan for stopping the Austrian crisis from spreading, and hopefully saving the gold standard as well as their own money. The BIS loan to the Austrian National Bank had been released, a moratorium had been averted at the very last moment, a guarantee was passed though the specifics were unclear at best, and the international creditors were organizing themselves while maintaining their credits on a day-by-day basis.

At long last there was some small if fragile hope for optimism, if only politics did not interfere. On June 1, Merle Cochran reported to the US State Department that

Since the acute situation arose at Vienna a large part of the time of the men at the head of the B.I.S. had been given thereto. Even while the Monthly and Annual Meetings were going on, from May 18 to 20, telephone calls were being had, night and day, with Vienna, and the B.I.S. has really guided the policy throughout. The BIS has necessarily been in close touch with Central Banks, financial experts, and international bankers in several centers. Protective committees have now been formed in New York, London and Paris, and representatives of creditors in other European banking centers have visited Vienna.[67]

7

# Releasing the BIS Credit (May 29–June 5)

By the end of May, the outlook had improved, and the future seemed a little brighter. The Austrian Parliament had passed a law authorizing the government to implement a guarantee for Credit Anstalt's foreign credits, and the threat of a moratorium had subsided for now. Bank for International Settlements (BIS) and the Bank of England had shown their strength by pushing these initiatives through, and by installing an adviser in the National Bank, and a controller in the Credit Anstalt.

With Norman's and Harrison's assistance, the foreign creditors had been organized in the International Committee of Foreign Creditors of the Austrian Credit Anstalt. This was an important move enabling them to speak with one tongue to their counterparts, the Credit Anstalt and the Austrian government. The Committee had managed to get Credit Anstalt to accept the conditions for maintaining their deposits and credits on a day-to-day basis.

Francis Rodd was back in Vienna monitoring the situation and the selection of the adviser to the National Bank and a controller to the Credit Anstalt.

The BIS and the Bank of England wanted the right man for the position as controller, or butcher, in the Credit Anstalt and considered the Swedish banker Oscar Rydbeck. The BIS noted that 'he must be placed in position of authority and not merely advisory'.[1]

Therefore, it caused some consternation when the Austrian National Bank asked for an adviser rather than a controller to be appointed to the Credit Anstalt.[2] The Credit Anstalt, too, accepted the appointment of an adviser, and noted that the government guarantee would have an effect on internal withdrawals, but a 'complete cessation of payment(s) in Austria would necessitate legal measures which you just(ly) like ourselves desire to avoid'.[3]

Harry Siepmann was already exhausted, 'I have had to be at the beck and call of the telephone and from morning till night my time has not been my own.'[4] And now this. Credit Anstalt's message was 'thoroughly unsatisfactory ... as I read it. Conditions refused or held in suspense. Withdrawals continue over the backs of the foreign creditors.'[5] The BIS shared Siepmann's view; they had asked for 'a foreign controller to be put in to the Kredit Anstalt and are not satisfied with the Austrian proposal of an adviser. This point is being cleared up.'[6]

It proved difficult to find a controller for the Credit Anstalt, but the International Committee agreed to appoint Adrianus van Hengel to represent their interests in Vienna. Van Hengel, a talented and frank Dutch banker with no problem speaking his mind, was 'invested with all necessary powers' and was already on his way to Vienna. His first task would be to figure out 'what steps were being or had been taken to limit withdrawals ... as if they continued on any scale it would constitute a grave danger to the success of any arrangement'.[7]

Morgan Grenfell reported to J.P. Morgan in New York, that with 'van Hengel now in Vienna we hope in the next day or two to get a much clearer picture of the whole situation and of the various questions which have to be solved'.[8] The International Committee was intent on using the appointment of van Hengel to its own best. On June 2 Morgan Grenfell wrote to J.P. Morgan & Co. about the situation.

> Now that practically all foreign creditors have agreed in principle to continue their credits to the extent in use at 28th May and van Hengel is on the spot to represent International Committee ... Committee has instructed van Hengel to communicate the following to Credit Anstalt: ... If Credit Anstalt has not sufficient funds it must get additional facilities necessary from the Austrian National Bank.[9]

So much for the market. That the National Bank should fund a private bank that increasingly looked like it might be insolvent in order to cover potential losses of private foreign banks did not seem farfetched to the Committee. If van Hengel was supposed to be both controller on behalf of the BIS and to represent the International Committee, he was wearing two hats. Apparently, the Committee had captured van Hengel's services.

Still, a few banks chose to challenge the newfound peace. Chatham Phoenix National Bank & Trust Co. were rumoured to have cancelled an $800,000 credit line, 'they will not fall into line with the general principles agreed by the other creditors', Morgan Grenfell reported to New York.[10]

A few days earlier, Francis Rodd had told the BIS that Bank of America's London affiliate had refused to join the International Committee and had rejected Credit Anstalt's attempt to draw £50,000 arguing that Credit Anstalt 'is in no funds'. That was true, of course, but an unwelcome position nonetheless, and Rodd alerted Pierre Quesnay and Walter Stewart to the problem.

'If it is known in the market here, there will be the devil to pay', he said. Something had to be done and Rodd was 'trying to find out and put the matter right at this end. Will you please get through to London, to the Bank of America, and find out the position?' In London, Robert Kindersley of Lazard called Bank of America's representative 'who was very tiresome over phone & finally hung up'.[11]

They were getting nowhere with Bank of America, but a few days later Siepmann reassured Stephany that such failure to follow the International Committee's policy was worst for Bank of America's prestige 'as it would be assumed that they did not fall into line not because they would not but because they could not'.[12]

Despite these road bumps, the situation was calmer than it had been since the 'tainted money' issue, Credit Anstalt's urgent request for £10 million, and the threat of a moratorium. That was one week ago.

Now, with the butcher in place, attention turned to the 'dictator' at the Austrian National Bank. The BIS suggested the Dutchman Gijsbert Bruins, a former business school professor who had been international commissioner to the Reichsbank and Royal commissioner to the Netherlands Bank. In addition, the French money doctor Charles Rist was recommended as adviser to the Austrian government.[13]

And then, of course, there was the question of where and how to place the Austrian loan. It could not be left alone forever.

## WE CANNOT AFFORD TO FAIL IN VIENNA

Back in Vienna, Rodd was thrown into the midst of yet another conflict. The Austrian loan, the appointment of Rist as adviser to the government and Bruins to the National Bank all had political ramifications. But nowhere near what happened when the controversial Hjalmar Schacht's name suddenly landed on the table. On Saturday, May 30, Rodd wrote a long letter to Norman. The letter demonstrated how closely entangled national, political, personal and financial matters were.

Dear mr. Governor,

At the time of writing Rist's departure has been delayed. As I understand from Basle, the delay is due to the proposal of certain names which was made, including that of Schacht.

When I had the pleasure of speaking to you on Thursday night, it was my understanding that the name of Schacht was made in connection with the Credit Anstalt, to act as a butcher. This suggestion appeared prima facie reasonable to me and I think to Walter Stewart, who was present at this conversation. Since then, however, I understand that the name of Schacht has been mentioned not in connection with the Credit Anstalt, but in connection with the National Bank. The effect of that name being mentioned has created such disturbances in the minds of the French in general and of Rist in particular as to involve the postponement of the latter's departure.

I must confess that the proposal of Schacht's name in connection with the National Bank does not appear to be one that can be considered for a moment. The political implications are such that I feel any French reaction against the proposal is entirely reasonable. The proposal moreover essentially brings the whole question into a purely political field, whether or not the theoretical division between budgetary duties and central bank duties can be sustained, which I confess to thinking both doubtful and in this place at the time irrelevant.

I think it is an awful pity that the suggestion of Schacht for the National Bank should ever have been made, for apart from the unavoidable political consequences, which in any circumstance must have occasioned delay, that we certainly cannot afford here, the situation created in the National Bank by his coming here as adviser would be perfectly impossible. Neither Reisch nor Thaa could have faced such a public rebuff.

I do not think Basle is in any way responsible for having put a political complection on the matter up to date; I am satisfied that they have been at particular pains to avoid the appearance of partiality. It seems to me that Rist's personality and history are alone sufficient safeguard against undue political influence being attributed to his arrival. On the other hand, nothing less than a report from Rist, however summary it may be, will satisfy the requirements of the French market, where a large part of the treasury bills presumably must be placed.

While the Austrian government might be able to place the whole issue here in the country, from the National Bank's point of view I think it is essential that as large a part as possible should be placed abroad. Every penny placed abroad means so much more foreign exchange for the National Bank, and so much smaller calls upon central banks for assistance in maintaining the position of the schilling. Placing the treasury bills abroad is indeed our best chance of getting repayment from the National Bank of the credit arranged for it by the BIS and the associated central banks.

I would like to say again what I have said before that the political implications which might arise from placing a large part of the treasury bills in Paris can best be avoided by a London participation however small in the operation, a proceeding with which I understand the French would be in entire agreement, indeed they would welcome it. Without a London participation, however small, the arrangements for placing these bonds abroad – in America, France and Germany – may fail and we cannot afford to fail in Vienna today.[14]

It may well have been a difficult letter for Rodd to write. Schacht antagonized most people, but not Norman, who against all odds had connected with Schacht at a personal level and was the godfather of his son. Norman knew very well how controversial Schacht was and had met with him secretly in London on May 12.

It was, in fact, Norman who had put Schacht's name on the table because he found the Austrian National Bank 'apathetic' and the BIS lacking in 'firmness and promptitude'. Bringing Schacht's name up seriously upset Clément Moret, the governor of the Banque de France, and earned Norman an official complaint from the French Embassy in London to the Foreign Office.[15]

Rodd had just returned to Vienna after a 'frightfully busy' day with 'one long series of telephone calls and cables'.[16] He made it abundantly clear that even suggesting Schacht could jeopardize the placement of the Austrian loan in France, as well as the relationship with the Austrian National Bank and Banque de France. Ironically, Rodd wrote his letter to Norman on the very same day that Norman was writing to Moret that he was happy about Paris and London working together and that he would stay in touch 'on the whole question in its Central Banking aspects'.[17]

George Harrison was also concerned. He had heard that the Austrian government might not accept Rist as adviser, and as always when feeling outside of the information loop, he turned to Norman. Had there been any changes in the plans about Rist advising the Austrian government?[18]

In fact, it was still about Norman's recommendation to the National Bank 'to take as their Adviser one of two men against both of whom the French have the strongest objections, namely Schacht and Bruins'.[19] Bruins was nowhere near as controversial, if at all, as Schacht, and Norman did not mention him again as he explained his view of the state of affairs to Harrison.

> As I told you on Saturday I insisted that more financial brutality was needed in Austria, that to this end Schacht was the right type, that there were probably irregularities in the Oesterreichische Nationalbank and that the same person e.g. Charles A. Rist could not advise the Oesterreichische Nationalbank and the Government, which positions would doubtless be conflicting. This has led to protests against my behavior from Paris to which I pay no attention. Such incidents would not occur if Basle contained more discretion and less gossip.[20]

In contrast to Rodd, Norman blamed the BIS for his blunder, if that is what it was. Despite the highly charged situation and tension created by bringing up Schacht's name, the matter was settled. Norman told Harrison that 'van Hengel is installed in the Credit Anstalt and G.W.J Bruins in the Oesterreichische Nationalbank, both I understand with adequate powers, while Charles A. Rist is temporarily helping the Austrian Government'.[21]

While Bruins may have been controversial to the French, he was nowhere near evoking as strong emotions as Schacht's name. Schacht was critical of his own government and against Germany's short-term borrowing, but he was most known for arguing that Germany should simply stop paying reparations. In September 1930, the Nazis won an astonishing 18.3 per cent of the votes against 2.6 per cent in 1928. As they took their 107 seats in the Reichstag, Schacht embarked on a lecture tour, which took him to the United States for almost two months. In March 1931, the English translation of his book *The end of Reparations* hit the book stores in America.[22]

To say that Schacht was not popular in France would be an understatement. But Norman was not bothered by self-doubt and rarely worried about what others thought. Maybe that is why he and Schacht were friends.

Norman ended his message to Harrison stressing again how uncertain the situation was; 'it is too early to know how safe or unsafe the monetary position will turn out to be in Austria and elsewhere or to foresee the amount of further credit that you and I may have to provide'.[23] Norman and Harrison were allies, and their central banks were at the centre of the efforts to halt the crisis. Norman's 'you and I' statement made it clear that it was their job, their responsibility, to save the gold standard.

The next phase of the Austrian crisis was about to begin. Rodd told Norman, 'Tonight, Rist, Bruins, van Hengel and I am all dining together to work out plans.' It was Monday, June 1, and they planned to publish a statement in the evening, 'so all is well though not before the press has made some statement about Anglo French rivalry and disagreement, which is a pity'.[24]

The ever-so-well-informed Merle Cochran reported to the US State Department that it was the BIS that had decided on van Hengel, Rist and Bruins. There had been 'some adverse comment from German and Austrian sources against the bringing of a Frenchman into the situation at present, lest France might endeavor to gain some political control over Austria', but Cochran believed that Bruins and van Hengel as neutral bankers and the cooperation of the BIS meant that politics would not interfere with solution to the crisis. 'It now remains to be seen what the next steps will be.'[25]

The next steps were on Harrison's mind as well. In a meeting with his executive committee, he discussed the situation in Austria and the possible repercussions 'in other countries, particularly in Germany'. He also told the committee about the efforts to induce international creditors 'not to withdraw funds', and Charles Mitchell pointed out that the 'current uncertainties' were to blame. Unless 'there was a radical change for the better in those countries, more funds would be withdrawn'.

The real issue was Germany, however. Harrison said that 'until the present world depression' Germany had been adjusting the economy through a 'reduction in the standard of living'. But he questioned, 'how much more can the German people and the German political structure stand.' Asked directly by Clarence Woolley, another executive committee member, it was clear that Harrison and Norman agreed about the role of central banks in currency crises and about last-resort credits. If, Harrison said,

> Germany should ask for a postponement of reparations transfers, and if that action should invite the withdrawal of short-term funds from Germany, driving down the German exchange and restricting the German credit supply, the Reichsbank would probably ask the help of the other central banks of the world. The central banks would then have to decide whether to let the situation go or to support it with a credit, and the latter alternative, at the moment, would appear to be the only acceptable choice.[26]

Harrison's emplotment of the future at the board meeting resonated with Norman's 'you and I' statement. Meantime, Siepmann met with Rothschild's Samuel Stephany and told him about the political difficulties regarding the appointments of van Hengel, Bruins and Rist. Stephany was particularly interested in van Hengel, who had already demonstrated his independence of mind. Despite representing the international creditors, he had apparently argued that 'the creditors generally had only themselves to blame for being in their present position and too much consideration should not be given to them'.

That was not Stephany's cup of tea, of course. Siepmann thought that 'at New Court van Hengel's attitude was calculated to put everybody's back up but that when he talked to the Governor he changed from a lion to a lamb and was very calm, reasonable and well balanced'. This would not be the last time they heard from van Hengel.

The discussion then shifted to the guarantee. It was very difficult to 'get anything definite' done about the guarantee. Siepmann called Vienna to get an update from Rodd, who explained that the law made almost any form of guarantee possible, but so far only deposits of a special category were guaranteed.

With Rodd still on the phone, they also discussed the issue of treasury bonds, which had been neglected for too long. Austria needed the foreign exchange and Credit Anstalt needed the capital, but no progress had been made. Rodd repeated that London would have to 'give a lead even if they only took a few hundred thousand before France and other countries would make a move'.

As they were wrapping up the phone call, 'Rodd said that conditions in Vienna were calm but people were depressed and the morals seemed to have gone entirely'. The dinner with Rist, van Hengel and Bruins the previous night had been held in a very friendly atmosphere, though Rodd seemed to think van Hengel was 'rather a tiger and that nobody else was allowed to speak'.

Before he left Stephany at New Court, Siepmann said that 'the whole thing was going to be a long business and that one ought to be prepared for it spreading to other countries, such as Roumania and Hungary'.[27]

The discussion between Stephany, Siepmann and Rodd was another sign that the guarantee was not going to be the all-round solution hoped for when Parliament passed it. The Austrian loan was not closer to being placed, and van Hengel was a loose cannon that no one really knew what to expect from. That was a bit of a problem for the International Committee since van Hengel had been 'given full powers to act for this committee' in his capacity as controller at the Credit Anstalt.[28]

The only progress seemed to be that Bruins was now settled at the National Bank, van Hengel at the Credit Anstalt, and Rist as special adviser to the Austrian government. It had not been an easy process, and it left a mark in the press, too. The *New York Times* reported that the appointment of Rist as adviser to the Austrian government had ramified 'through the field of international finance into that of international political intrigue'. The article continued that the shadow of the customs union plan loomed behind 'almost every phase of the Creditanstalt' crisis.[29]

The reporter, himself English, noted that 'only Britain and neutrals are left as possible rescuers of Austrian finance'. The Rothschilds were exerting 'every ounce of their enormous influence', with the approval of the 'British Government, which seems disquieted by the growth of French hegemony in Central Europe'.[30]

At this time, Norman and Harrison both had their belief in central banks' ability to halt the crisis intact. But politics was rearing its head. It was getting ever more difficult to pretend that politics were marginal to the financial situation.

## I HAVE NO INFORMATION ON WHICH TO ACT

On Tuesday, June 2, D.B. Grant of the Guaranty Trust Co. told the International Committee that 'his Bank's representative in Vienna reported a general flight of capital from the Country and a feeling of uncertainty regarding the attitude of the foreign creditors'.[31]

It was the same day that Harry Siepmann spoke to Rothschild's Stephany, but despite their concern, Hans Simon, Rodd's BIS colleague, was optimistic enough to sit down and write a lengthy memo about the lessons to be learned from the Austrian crisis.[32]

*The Economist* also struck a positive note. There was 'good ground for hoping that the corner has been turned', it noted, because 'ten of the leading central banks' and the Federal Reserve had agreed to support the Austrian National Bank. Moreover, the international creditor banks had formed a committee, 'and one great danger, namely, the withdrawal of foreign credits and balances at the end of May, has already been staved off'.

Now, what was needed was time and patience. *The Economist* saw the actions 'as proof of the reality of international co-operation in the spirit of Basle and Geneva'.[33] But Austria's economy was in depression and the budget was deteriorating, as the magazine reported about a 140-million-schilling fiscal deficit in the first four months of the year.[34]

Despite *The Economist's* cautious optimism, the political fault lines surfaced, and as May turned to June concerns about Germany spread. In early June it became clear that matters were not quite settled. The fact that the New York Fed was imagining a much worse future scenario in Germany and that Rodd was pessimistic about Vienna and the placing of the bond loan together with the tension between the Bank of England and Banque de France were all signs of this.

Rodd was not naïve about the political aspects. But he represented the BIS and was working on the spot in Vienna where he focused on stemming the crisis while trying hard to avert the intricacies that popped up all the time. International political tensions, though a fact of life, were not conducive to that goal, but Norman was not going to allow French interests to dominate. To Francis Rodd the Anglo-French rivalry was 'a pity', to Norman it was the order of the day. But Rodd felt that the French government and the Banque de France were not necessarily in agreement. He wrote to Norman that 'Rist is outspoken about all this being kept international ... I am sure that this position can be maintained from now on.'[35]

Meanwhile, troubles were spreading, as 'the BIS have provided $5 million for Hungary and they are doing the same for Italy'.[36] A few days later on June 4, problems intensified in Hungary, and the central bank would probably need more money from the BIS. Rodd noted that 'the foreign exchange management of the Hungarian National Bank seems to be very good but its reserves very scarce'.[37]

In Austria, the opposite was the case. On Monday, June 1 around noon, Vienna had been 'pretty calm'.[38] Only five hours later, at 5.30 p.m., Rodd reported that the morning's favourable position had deteriorated. Foreign exchange withdrawals had accelerated. By the day's closing the National Bank had lost 25 million schillings.[39]

Moreover, the issue of cross deposits, the 'irregularities in New York and London' mentioned by Norman, complicated the matter. Rodd reported to Pierre Quesnay in Basle that the tainted money ran to about 7 million dollars, including the deposits from Rothschild and Japhet.[40]

Another account put the total at 9 million dollars.[41] The implications were serious no matter what. Norman insisted that the money should not be counted as part of the National Bank's foreign exchange reserves, but if the next balance sheet was to show a decline of 7–9 million dollars in foreign exchange, anything might happen.

Except something good. If the National Bank withdrew the deposits from British and American banks, they in turn would claim the money from the Credit Anstalt, which would then have to resort to the National Bank for support. As long as the guarantee was not in place, it increased the risk of a flight from Austria and contagion to other countries.

Where and how to place the government loan and how to keep foreign creditors from withdrawing their money and closing credit lines? They were still the two most important questions. The real position of the Credit Anstalt was in doubt as well, despite the efforts of the BIS to avoid opening that can of worms. Three weeks into the crisis, Francis Rodd's agenda from the very first days was still unsolved. Progress had certainly been made, but the international loan was still in limbo, there was no agreement with Credit Anstalt's international creditors, and the guarantee had not been implemented by the Austrian government. At least not to the international creditors' liking.

As Simon was writing his 'Lessons of the Austrian Crisis' memo on June 2, there was still uncertainty about the real content of the government guarantee for Credit Anstalt's creditors. Rumours and stories were abundant. In London, Siepmann had a busy day on June 3 struggling to make sense of it all and shape a narrative that ordered chaos into something to act upon. He was already concerned that rumours 'had much too much to say right now; and that is another reason why we of the Fire Brigade, or of the Salvage Corps, should remain in close touch with one another, answering but not distributing alarms'.[42]

Still early on June 3, at 10.30 a.m., Siepmann received a phone call from Wilhelm Vocke, a director at the German Reichsbank. He had heard from

Karl Blessing, another German seconded from the Reichsbank to the BIS, that French banks were offering to lend 200 million schillings against the Austrian Tobacco Monopoly as collateral. In a later call at 1.15 p.m., Vocke told Siepmann that there had been a meeting the same morning between Rist, van Hengel and Bruins, and the finance minister, 'where it appeared that Sch. 100 millions are required by the Austrian Government today, if they are not to get into further trouble'.

According to Vocke, the National Bank would send Viktor Kienböck, a former minister of finance and member of the Austrian Parliament, to negotiate with the French about the loan. Siepmann noted that it was important that the loan was international, and 'Dr. Vocke urged the importance of direct British participation in order to make the transaction really international and exclude political conditions.'[43]

Later that day, Siepmann learned another version of the meeting with the Austrian minister of finance from Rodd, who had also been present. It appeared that Vocke had misinformed Siepmann. There 'is no question of any certain need for Sch. 100 millions, nor of any Exchequer difficulties in Austria at the moment', Siepmann noted.[44]

Rodd also phoned the BIS about the meeting where, in Rodd's version, 'the minister spoke in favour of an internal issue, the Bank for International Settlements in his opinion being responsible for procuring the necessary foreign exchange. Rodd said that the Bank for International Settlements will not give any new support if the Government does not apply for an external issue of 100 million schilling. The minister then decided to send abroad mr. Kienböck.' The minister's position had led to a 'big discussion' between Rodd, Bruins and van Hengel, and the minister of finance Otto Juch.[45]

During the 'big discussion', though argument might be a better word, van Hengel, Bruins and Rodd had 'all joined in threatening to leave Vienna unless the finance minister gave them immediate satisfaction on several points'. Siepmann wrote a note based on Rodd's story.

First, the troika demanded that negotiations to place the bond loan abroad 'must be immediately begun'. Otto Juch expected to place the loan in Austria and said that 'the BIS had promised to look after the currency position … Bruins replied that the BIS's promise was conditional upon bonds being placed abroad and that no assistance would be forthcoming unless this condition was fulfilled'.

Second, the Austrian Government must guarantee Credit Anstalt's schilling deposits, or the 'National Bank would refuse to go on rediscounting for the Credit Anstalt.' Juch told the troika that the Credit Anstalt had lost 500 million or one-third of its deposits. Of the remaining billion 'about half are foreign and half are in schillings'. In any case, the cabinet would not go any further with the guarantee.

Third, van Hengel had to be assured that all foreign credits were guaranteed. He did not need a public announcement, but he must 'have the guarantee in his pocket, because it was the only means of obtaining renewals'.[46]

After the meeting, Rodd called both Basle and Siepmann in London to tell them about the outcome. It was a forceful demonstration of power, with a lot of pressure being put on the Austrian authorities from all sides, including Charles Rist, who agreed with the demands.

The International Creditors Committee and the banks were also 'getting restless'. An 'immediate guarantee was essential', and the Committee cabled van Hengel that the banks would consider maintaining their credits for at least a year if the government guaranteed their claims. If not, 'retaining co-operation' among the bankers would be difficult, and the Committee hoped 'you will be able to give us necessary assurance tomorrow morning'.[47]

The same day, Wednesday, June 3, Norman informed his Committee of Treasury that he had been asked by the BIS whether the Bank of England would be prepared to participate in another credit to the Austrian National Bank. Norman recommended participation and pointed out that 'if the situation worsens in Eastern Europe, Germany must become involved and in that event the trouble would inevitably spread to this Country'.[48]

This was the first time that the ultimate house of cards scenario was imagined and spelled out in a narrative fictional expectation that stretched from Austria to Germany to Great Britain. Contagion to Britain, the perceived epicentre of the gold standard would take the situation to another level. The crisis had to be stopped before it got so far.

Rodd called both Basle and London again on Thursday, June 4, and said that the 'pressure made yesterday evening on the Austrian Government had had satisfactory result'.[49] Negotiations in Paris were about to begin and 'Professor Rist left on the 2 o'clock train for Paris' and expected to meet with ParisBas after the weekend. The whole Austrian loan was to be placed abroad, as 'Cabinet permission for this was given last night'.[50]

However, Rodd also reported that he, Bruins and van Hengel 'still have some fears regarding internal withdrawals. Further measures might have to be taken, and Rodd wanted the BIS 'to cable us here stating that BIS assistance is dependent upon Austrian Government giving further guarantees in form required by Bruins as and when situation requires.'[51]

To give Rodd more leverage, Pierre Quesnay sent a telegram identical to the one he had sent two days earlier, confirming that BIS's assistance 'is dependent upon Austrian Government giving in the form required by Dr. Bruins further guarantee as and when in his opinion situation requires'.[52]

In parallel communications, van Hengel cabled Lionel de Rothschild that the 'foreign representatives got all they wanted'. He also told Rothschild that the uncertainty about the Creditor's Committee's position on renewal of credits and deposits caused anxiety in Vienna. 'Mr. Rodd hopes that the Creditor's Committee will come to a definite conclusion as soon as possible.'[53]

Charles Rist was also worried. In telegrams to Harrison and Norman, by way of Governor Moret of the Banque de France he noted that the crucial point in Vienna was the risk of foreign withdrawals, 'which might give way to a general demand of foreign monies which would be impossible to check'. Rist asked Moret to prevail upon the Paris market to maintain and renew credits, and he urged Norman and Harrison to do the same in their markets.[54]

Norman replied that he shared Rist's view and, indeed, tried hard to influence his market, that is the bankers in the City of London. He added that the Austrian position must be held in the interest of Europe, and he was reassured knowing that Rist was in Vienna. 'Please rely on me for any support which I can give and accept my warmest personal greetings.'[55]

Despite his kind and obliging messages to Moret, Norman told Harrison he found the situation 'obscure' and 'I have no information on which to act'.[56] Harrison agreed and wrote to Rist that 'there are still a number of matters which are uncertain or obscure to the creditors and which will no doubt have to be settled before the position of the creditors vis-à-vis the Credit Anstalt will be satisfactorily settled'.[57]

The uncertain and obscure situation was the very same that had been discussed since the early days of the crisis. It was the government guarantee and the position of the foreign creditors, two problems that were very much interrelated and in urgent need of a solution.

The uncertainty and lack of actionable knowledge faced by the central bankers made it difficult to navigate the crisis, not to mention making any final decisions. There was concern that Austrians were withdrawing their deposits from the Credit Anstalt and converting them into pounds and dollars. That would leave the foreign creditors in a difficult position if they agreed to maintain their credits for a year or two, and it would put more pressure on the schilling. In addition, the situation in Germany was still fragile.

## ABSOLUTELY INSEPARABLE

German ministers were about to visit Great Britain's Prime Minister Ramsay MacDonald at Checkers, the PM's official country residence, where Norman would also be present. Harrison told Norman that the upcoming German visit caused much discussion and media coverage of 'previous widespread rumors' about a postponement of reparation payments. 'All of this talk coupled with Austrian problem has been and continues to be a depressing influence upon many of the foreign securities particularly the German ones.'[58]

The prospect that Germany's Chancellor Brüning might declare a postponement of reparation payments was a constant underlying threat against the fragile situation and the efforts to avert it. The fear of contagion from the Austrian crisis stressed the urgency of solving the two interconnected problems of a guarantee and the Austrian bond loan. Rumours that 'foreign deposits were being paid out by the Credit Anstalt' angered the International Committee, who feared for their claims if Credit Anstalt paid out to other creditors.[59]

There were enough signs that the situation reached another tipping point in early June. Simon's June 2 memo on the lessons of the crisis signalled that he believed the situation to be more or less under control, but the government guarantee still divided opinions. The ongoing discussions about the extent of the guarantee suggest that Simon was too optimistic when on June 3 he wrote that

> Now that the first storm has been weathered and that there no longer seems to be any immediate danger for the stability of the Austrian currency, it would appear necessary to consider the whole of Austria's position, as it has developed owing to the crisis of the Credit Anstalt and the unlimited guarantee which the Government had to undertake for the debts of this institution.[60]

In fact, there was no unlimited guarantee as the Austrian government kept dragging its feet implementing it. And both the National Bank and the Austrian budget were at a crossroads. The Credit Anstalt 'now owes approximately 400 million schillings to the National Bank', Simon noted, and sooner or later that would threaten the stability of the schilling if it was not reduced.

The bond loan would not solve all problems either, since 'the amount would hardly be sufficient to reduce the rediscount debt of the Credit Anstalt ... to a somewhat manageable size, whereas nothing would be left for the foreign and domestic creditors of the Credit Anstalt or for the requirements of its customers'.

The Austrian budget problem and the Credit Anstalt problem were now 'absolutely inseparable', and no solution was in sight. Perhaps another Austrian loan, but would the League of Nation's Control Committee allow that? And the first one wasn't even placed yet.[61]

Simon, an Austrian himself, tried to take a longer-term perspective and to imagine, what the future might look like for Austria. Despite his immediate optimism about halting the run on the schilling, the longer term looked bleak with risk of inflation and a breakdown of the schilling on top of a budget crisis. Simon did not have a quick or easy solution. In fact, there was no easy solution.

If the long term looked bad, the short term was desperate and needed to be dealt with. On June 4, less than a week after the BIS credit had finally been made available, the BIS learned that the Austrian National Bank were about to draw the remaining 40 million schillings of the credit. A quick solution was needed to calm investors and savers in Austria and abroad.

With the BIS credit exhausted, unless confidence in the market could be improved, more money would be needed very soon. Nevertheless, the BIS was taken aback when Viktor Brauneis asked for the credit to be increased.[62] To even consider it, the National Bank would need Bruins's endorsement, and a formal request had to be submitted before June 7 when the BIS board would meet again.

Only a few days after Simon's memo on Austria, Francis Rodd wrote some notes about 'coping with the situation'.[63] Based on these notes, he wrote a memo on the 'present position as at the 5th of June'. The memo was Rodd's attempt to make sense of the situation and it would provide an important basis for the board's negotiations and decision-making on June 7 and 8.

The government guarantee was still less than perfect, and the foreign creditors had not yet agreed to a two-year prolongation of their deposits, but Rodd expected them to do so, and 'further rediscounting from the C.A. on a large scale is unlikely'. However, 'it is impossible to stop withdrawals and so rediscounts entirely without closing the bank, which in turn would lead to the consequences everyone has sought to avoid'.

The total discount position of the National Bank had increased from 116 million schillings on May 17 to 628 million on June 5. There was more or less a one-to-one relationship between withdrawals from the Credit Anstalt and an increase in the National Bank's discounts. In May, the National Bank had lost 350 million schillings, or about $50 million, of foreign exchange, while its note circulation and sight deposits had increased by 250 million to 1,282 million schillings, 'which is the extent of the inflation that has taken place'.

Over the last two weeks, the National Bank had lost about 190 million schilling of foreign exchange as demand 'by the small people has assumed the proportions of a flight from the Austrian schilling'.[64] The problem of inflation and a flight from the Austrian currency were now seen as the single most important issue and the Austrian people's experience with hyperinflation only nine years earlier was used as a central historical analogy to make sense of events.[65]

The Austrian National Bank was one of the symbols of the reconstructed monetary regime following hyperinflation, and Rodd and Bruins feared that the symbolic value of the National Bank as a bulwark against a new period of monetary instability was at risk. This inflation frame had not been invoked much until now, and it got the attention of Bruins as adviser to the National Bank. It introduced yet another constraint on possible actions.

A reduction of the National Bank's note issue would require a contraction of its credits to the Credit Anstalt and that would mean 'the closing of the C.A. and serious difficulties possibly ending in the closing of the Wiener Bankverein as well'. Therefore, 'a limited amount of rediscounting must continue'. This was the National Bank's dilemma; how to continue assisting the Credit Anstalt and at the same time reduce the outstanding note issue? Rodd estimated that a reduction of between 300 and 400 million schillings was required to stop the demand for foreign currency, but as long as the Credit Anstalt needed further discounting facilities that was not going to happen.

On May 30 the National Bank increased the discount rate from 5–6 per cent, and management was authorized to raise it further to 7 per cent. It was an integral part of the Bagehot model, but it would not solve the problem, so another plan was to issue 'Kassenscheine' in order to 'sponge' up some of the additional credit held by banks and savings banks. A government loan in schilling might also contribute, but that would not take care of the National Bank's need for foreign exchange.

Time was of the essence as well. The 'present position is clear; the National Bank requires foreign devisen . . . to avoid a complete currency panic which is in the process of developing'. The cover ratio, which Siepmann had found so reassuring in January, had fallen from around 78 per cent to 57 per cent, and though this was way above the legal requirement of 30 per cent, a 'fall to about 40% would probably create a panic'.

Having presented this view of the situation in Austria, Rodd set forth his and Bruins's plan to avoid an Austrian breakdown.

> It is therefore considered that funds should be made available and that the public should learn that funds are available to support the position of the National Bank. But neither the public nor anyone else in Austria should know the exact amount of funds available. It is our opinion that if it can be made known, by whatever channels may be deemed most appropriate, that funds are available to the National Bank to meet the position, much can be done to allay present fears. This impression cannot be given unless further assistance is available. The amount of further assistance that has been estimated should be made available in the form of foreign exchange consists of the proceeds of the issue of 150 million schillings in Treasury Bills and an additional credit from the B.I.S. and Associated Banks of as much again as has already been provided namely an additional 100 million schillings.[66]

The 'morale of the Government and the National Bank are bad', Rodd noted as he emphasized the need for additional resources to the National Bank. However, the 'first essential is an adequate communication as a result of this meeting'.[67]

This was Rodd's combination of actionable knowledge and future-planning. He provided data on the actual situation of the National Bank and combined this with an imaginary for what would happen either if nothing was done or if more money was placed at the disposal of the National Bank. On this background, Rodd, and Bruins with whom the plan was made, estimated that the total amount needed to reassure the Austrian public and thereby to halt the imminent run on the schilling would be 250 million schillings in foreign exchange, about $35 million.

The success of this plan required, as the plan noted, that the announcement would re-establish confidence in the National Bank's position, and here Rodd relied on the Bagehot dictum, that the impression should be created that 'though money may be dear, still money is to be had'.[68]

This money should come from the Austrian bond loan of 150 million and a second BIS and central bank credit of another 100 million, which would only be released after the proceeds of the bond loan were gone. At that time, it would also be possible for the BIS to monitor the use of these proceeds and 'if the plan is unsuccessful or the Austrians do not carry into effect the conditions which have been imposed upon them, the additional credit to be provided by the B.I.S. will not be used, and in the interval the Austrian Government will only have expended its own funds'.

The idea of a second BIS loan was a response to Viktor Brauneis's question on June 4 of whether the first credit could be increased. In his note prepared for the governors' meeting, Rodd also requested that the credit could be used to bridge the time until the proceeds from the Austrian loan were received 'on the understanding that any advance so made shall be reimbursed out of the proceeds of the issue of treasury bills'.[69]

At this point, Rodd would not rule out that the efforts to stop the crisis might fail. The uncertainty, not only of the situation in Vienna but also of the general future if the crisis continued, was still very real. At this juncture, it was the flight of capital and the fact that Austrian citizens were contributing to the capital flight that was the real problem. In order to avoid a 'complete currency panic which is in process of developing' the single most important target was to keep the reserve ratio from falling further.

As Rodd prepared his note for the board meeting, he considered how best to convince the governors to follow the recommendation of a plan for a second BIS credit. It was an important meeting, and almost four weeks into the crisis it was still Francis Rodd who knew best what was going on in Vienna. Rather than bringing clarity, the three weeks since Rodd had first arrived in Vienna seemed to have brought more uncertainty. Though Rodd's and Bruins's plan seemed to provide a blueprint for further action, there was still no way to know what would happen next. Moreover, as Rodd had hinted early on, the reconstruction plan of May 11 constrained the options.

The technicalities of Rodd's note aside, it was still a story about the need to keep the Austrian public and foreign creditors from losing confidence in the financial and monetary system of the country. At the end of the day, all efforts made until then had served the single purpose of restoring confidence and avoiding contagion and a perceived financial and monetary breakdown in Europe. On the one hand, they had been relatively successful as Simon's note about having weathered the first storm signalled. On the other hand, Rodd's note was written on the premise that another storm would soon develop if confidence was not restored; 'there are certainly symptoms of nervousness among the population', he wrote.

Rodd felt that those who had been in Vienna in the last week 'have certainly had the impression that the demand for foreign currency by the public has become rather more acute and rather more dangerous'. Still, he believed that 'if the amount of new credit placed in circulation could be reduced, the foreign exchange situation could be readily kept in hand'.

The word 'panic' said it all and was why both Simon and Rodd spent some time drawing up the balance sheet in both real and metaphorical terms. The BIS board meeting was on Sunday, June 7, and Monday, June 8, and there were important and controversial decisions to be made. Only the board could decide whether to grant another credit to the Austrian

National Bank. Rodd's meticulous report provided the background, together with the National Bank's balance sheet. Rodd concluded his memo that

> Though Prof. Bruins considers the position serious, he does not consider it hopeless, an opinion which I entirely endorse, provided that the situation is not unduly aggravated by unpleasant developments in neighbouring countries, and here I regard a calm and broad-minded attitude by banks having credits in Austria not only in the C.A. but elsewhere, and also by banks having credits in neighbouring countries taking every possible step to prevent hasty withdrawals or panic decisions.[70]

Rodd's reservation regarding unpleasant developments was just one of the factors that could not be controlled. On Friday, June 5, the next weekly statement would be drawn up, to be published right after the BIS board meeting. The National Bank would have exhausted the first BIS credit, and 'they have no more foreign exchange immediately available'. Rodd asked for Harry Siepmann to come to Basle 'to say what the Bank of England is ready to do, i.e. within what limits and on what conditions, if any'.[71]

At 6.45 p.m. the same day, Rodd again called Bank of England and told Siepmann about 'some rather disquieting symptoms'. The 'trouble is now not so much the Credit Anstalt as a currency situation. Such technical measures as can be taken will be taken. Bank rate will go up tomorrow, either by 1% . . . or 2% immediately. It is proposed to issue National Bank Kassenscheine and the rise in Bank Rate should enable this to be done at a rate of interest sufficiently attractive to bring in Schillings.' Siepmann noted that

> Mr. Rodd complains of the extreme difficulty of getting anything done in good time. So far he says everything has been done a week too late and only in the face of the greatest opposition.[72]

# 8

# Surrounded with Trouble (June 5–June 10)

As Francis Rodd was getting ready for the upcoming board meeting in Basle, Gijsbert Bruins was writing a more general note. It represented his attempt at making sense of the situation after only five days in Vienna. His narrative ordered his impressions until now.

Though only made public in early May, Credit Anstalt's losses were not incurred overnight. 'The machinery is consequently disturbed. Much of what was thought a good basis for foreign credits now appears valueless.' Bruins argued that while the losses were already there, the budget was 'in order', and 'the position of the National Bank was very strong up to the crash'.

> From a currency standpoint, the difficulties therefore are in the first and foremost place, psychological ones. That the Austrian people, who have already passed through an inflation, and among whom many are rather pessimistic about the future of their country, have reacted on this event with a feeling of uneasiness about their currency – apart from the heavy but under such circumstances normal withdrawals from abroad – is not to be wondered at. The serious element in the situation is that, after the first excitement, their feelings have not gradually disappeared, but are still there like smouldering fire which some day might break out in a dangerous way.[1]

During his short time in Vienna, Bruins had seen nervousness over the schilling grow, and rather than a matter of economics, he explained the currency problems with the psychology, confidence, trust and emotions of the Austrian people. In the context of their recent historical experience of hyperinflation, this added to a view of the most recent development as homemade by Austrians who changed their schillings for foreign exchange.

Like Rodd, Bruins was critical of the Austrian government and the National Bank's reconstruction of the Credit Anstalt over the weekend of May 9–10. It had been inadequate and half-hearted, but the moment had passed for bringing an immediate end to the crisis. Important time had been allowed to lapse and now it was 'much more difficult to cope with the crisis'.

All eyes are instinctively turned abroad. Today again Mr Rodd and I had to tell the Finance Minister, who certainly is not a bad man, that foreign credits can never be more than a 'Rückendeckung' and that when the Government and the Central Bank do not do all in their power to put their house in order and to inspire the population with the feeling that the matter is in strong and efficient hands, there is a serious danger that fresh money from abroad will . . . go through the mill and disappear like the S.400 millions which the National Bank has already lost from its portfolio of Devisen.[2]

Even if the foreign creditors accepted a two-year standstill agreement very soon and if the placement of the 150-million-schilling treasury loan was agreed upon soon, domestic Austrian measures would still be needed. Credit Anstalt's schilling deposits 'must be guaranteed by the Government in a clear and unmistakable way as soon as possible'.

Bruins was very clear that the guarantee was absolutely necessary to stop the withdrawal of both schilling and foreign exchange – Devisen – from the Credit Anstalt. He pointed out that for political reasons, the government 'is very anxious to extend this guarantee as little as possible. It took us three conversations with the Finance Minister to put pressure on this matter, and still the promises given today are not fully satisfactory. Further pressure will most probably be necessary.'

However, credit restrictions, which Bruins strongly endorsed, 'might turn themselves against you' until an agreement was reached with the foreign creditors and the Austrian loan was placed. All other measures were 'mere palliatives'.

After this sombre analysis, Bruins ended the note by addressing the Board of the Bank for International Settlements (BIS) directly, recommending his and Rodd's plan for a second BIS credit to the National Bank. He admitted that the money will 'probably be used for further capital flight as was the case with the first Schillings 100 million credit. I must confess however that for the present moment I see no other possibility. . . . I fear that on the real danger spot, the rediscounting with the National Bank, no efficient measures can be taken before the feeling of confidence has been strengthened by an agreement between the foreign creditors and an agreement on the issue of the Schillings 150 millions Treasury Bonds.'[3]

At this point, the Bagehot operating model had lost most of its value as a blueprint for averting the Austrian crisis. The discount rate had been raised, and the National bank lent freely to the Credit Anstalt, but confidence did not return, and neither did the foreign exchange. To stop the Austrian crisis required a guarantee of Credit Anstalt's schilling and foreign exchange deposits, an agreement with the International Committee to maintain their credits, and the placement of the Austrian loan. If these issues were taken care of, the confidence of the Austrian public might return. In Bruins's analysis, domestic Austrian politics stood in the way, not international issues.

Bruin's analysis did not come as a surprise. His view was shared by the international central banks and the International Committee, but his forceful note and his stress on the role of confidence and psychology contributed to the sense of urgency. Minister of Finance Otto Juch and the National Bank, on the other hand, felt that the international community, through the BIS, should provide more credit to enable Austria to withstand the crisis. The Austrians still focused on the domestic economy and politics, while the central banks were concerned about contagion and the gold standard – the house of cards. The foreign creditor banks worried mostly about their own money and perhaps international financial stability. As long as their view of the situation converged, they were on the same side as the central banks.

The next morning, Gates McGarrah called Walter Stewart at the Bank of England and told him that Bruins was pushing for the bond loan to be placed. Stewart pointed out that London had not received any official request from the Austrian government and that 'London cannot be expected to take any decision in the matter until such a communication arrives.'[4]

He added that the drain of foreign exchange was now driven primarily by domestic depositors. McGarrah agreed with Stewart that since the internal depositors 'are getting out while the foreign creditors are virtually under a moratorium', they too should be put under 'a moratorium whether by legal means or by using such measures of compulsion as may be available'.[5]

A few hours later, at noon, a Bank of England official placed a phone call to Basle on behalf of Norman who was getting impatient. The flight from the Austrian schilling was serious, and 'the Governor wishes to have an opinion from the president and from the people who have been in control on the spot, namely messrs. Rodd, Bruins and Hengel, as to what can be done to stop this leakage'. Norman also wanted to know what would be done to 'consolidate the future'.[6]

Consolidating the future was all about reducing the uncertainty confronting the actors and thereby improving confidence. Norman was frustrated, and he needed actionable knowledge and a plan for how to stop the leakage of foreign exchange. The tensions were building as Bruins sent a message to McGarrah around midnight again stressing the importance of a second BIS credit. Bruins understood the reluctance to grant another 100-million-schilling credit, but together with the bond loan it was absolutely necessary. He ended the call remarking that 'in order to carry out the task I have undertaken in Vienna at the invitation of the BIS I think I am entitled to feel that I have their full support and to say so'.[7]

It was the upcoming board meeting that led to the frenzy of activity as frustrations over the lack of progress were growing in Vienna, London and Basle, while Harrison at the New York Fed was somewhat marginalized. The guarantee and the foreign loan which had been debated almost since the outbreak of the crisis were still in limbo, and the foreign creditors feared that Austrians hoarded foreign exchange at their expense. Something had to be done, and everyone was now looking to the board of governors to do it.

Austria was not the only problem, however. Politics interfered as the British-German meeting at Chequers was coming up at the same time as the BIS board meeting.

## A GERMAN VISIT TO CHEQUERS

While everyone held their breath hoping for a solution to the Austrian crisis, investors and speculators were highly uncertain about where to put their money. In Portugal, for instance, the need for an international loan had been postponed because Norman had 'asked the bankers not to commit themselves unless Austrian position improves'.

It was not at all good for international financial markets, and Norman was pessimistic after four weeks of problems in Austria. He confided in Harrison that

> I have only inadequate information from Vienna but enough to be disturbing. Internal and external confidence seems to be lacking. Devisen continues to trickle out so that further foreign credit may be required, under guarantee of Austrian Government and I know of no effective or final policy to maintain industrial and monetary position in Austria and/or adjoining countries.[8]

Austria was not Norman's only concern, and he seemed to be about to give up on the whole thing. Admitting that he knew of 'no effective or final policy', he was unable to plot a way forward, and below it all lay Germany. During the weekend of June 6 and 7, as the BIS board meeting convened,

Norman sent Siepmann to Basle, while he was getting ready to leave for Chequers. German Chancellor Heinrich Brüning and Foreign Minister Julius Curtius visited Britain's prime minister Ramsay MacDonald at his official country house about 40 miles north-west of London.

The visit had been planned since before the Austrian crisis, but there were more than enough issues to deal with anyway. Still, the Austrian crisis contributed to the sense of urgency in an already uncertain context, as *The Economist* noted on the first day of the visit, Saturday, June 6.

Since Easter . . . not only has the path of disarmament been once more obstructed by the hitch in the naval negotiations and the renewed strain in relations between Italy and France, but there has arisen a burning controversy over the Austro-German Customs union, and the ideas of an Anschluss, while the continuance of economic depression and falling commodity prices and the disclosure of the banking difficulties of Austria have brought into the picture once again the possibility of Germany applying for a postponement of transfer of the conditional annuities under the Young Plan, or even for a revision of the plan itself.[9]

It was a mess. If Norman read the new issue of *The Economist*, he must have speculated about the possible outcomes of the Chequers meeting. It was not at all clear what would happen, but according to the magazine, consensus in England was 'that reparations have demonstrably been, and are likely to be, a contributory factor in the international economic malaise'. However, this was not something Britain could solve. 'If Germany needs relief she must address herself in the last resort to France and America.'[10]

France and America were seen as breaking the rules of the gold standard. They were also the only two countries with the wherewithal to provide large-scale support to Germany, but that was unlikely to happen. The *New York Times* reported that French financial observers expected Germany to make 'an immediate request for a moratorium on the conditional payments'. That was not to France's liking, and since France linked German reparations to its own war debts to the United States, it would have much wider implications.

The reporter linked the German situation to the Credit Anstalt crisis arguing that a solution to the Austrian crisis would do much to ease the situation in Germany and contribute to the continuation of between 2 and 3 billion dollars 'in American short-term credits, upon which German industry and finance are now largely dependent'.[11] The stakes were high at Chequers.[12]

On the agenda were disarmament, the plans for an Austro-German customs union, and the all-important reparations, the most significant issue of all the interwar economic problems, as foreseen by John Maynard Keynes in 1919.[13] The economic depression with reduced trade, falling prices, unemployment, international imbalances, budget deficits, short-term capital flows of hot money, international political conflicts and fears for the future formed a sombre context for the meeting. The Austrian crisis did nothing to raise hopes.[14]

Germany's situation was precarious, to say the least. The country had gone through a number of politically induced deflationary initiatives. There were conflicts in the Reichstag and in the streets where clashes between Communists and Nazis had become an everyday occurrence. In May, if not before, it was clear that Chancellor Brüning and his government were planning yet another round of deflationary measures expected by many to further contribute to economic and social distress and to the fragile situation in the country.

On May 11, the very same day that the reconstruction of the Credit Anstalt was made public, Brüning's cabinet decided that it would announce the budget measures when the Chequers meeting took place. At the same time, Brüning would make public a statement on the reparations schedule under the Young Plan. It would not come as a complete surprise. Harrison and Norman had discussed the possibility of such a move on May 27 and 28, but the timing was spectacular.[15]

Fraser who had travelled to New York in late May reported on June 5 that there were 'wild rumors here concerning Germany including a revolution a moratorium . . . and even an early war'. He asked McGarrah for any concrete news about the Chequers meeting to deal with the 'wild guesses prevalent here'.[16]

Brüning's statement and timing may have aimed mostly at stabilizing the domestic political situation. Already on March 6, as he was warned about the deteriorating fiscal situation, he said that the 'German people cannot tolerate a further compression in the financial domain without being offered crucial steps on reparations'.[17]

As Brüning's declaration of June 6 became known during the meeting on Sunday, June 7, it shocked the English delegation and immediately changed the agenda of the Chequers meeting.[18] The British ministers and Norman were taken aback that Germany had not only introduced new deflation measures but also declared that

> The limits of the privations we have imposed on our people have been reached. The presuppositions upon which the Young plan came into being have been shown by the course of world development to have been wrong. The alleviations the new plan was to bring to the German people, as was the intent of the

participants and which at first it gave promise of bringing, have failed to be realized. The government is conscious of the fact that the directly-menaced business and financial position of the Reich calls imperatively for alleviation of the unbearable reparation obligations. The economic recovery of the world also depends upon it.[19]

Norman joined the meeting on Sunday morning, June 7, before the German announcement was known to the participants. While Brüning tried to turn the focus to the plight of Germany, Norman was preoccupied with the Austrian crisis and declared, 'Southeast Europe is in flames!' He went on, 'I do not wish to belittle the difficulties of the German Government, but it is a less urgent problem. Germany has already gone through two or three financial crises which would have been fatal to any other country; she has shown a wonderful power of recuperation, and she may well get through again.'[20]

At that time, telegrams from the British ambassador to the United States finally arrived with the news about the German declaration. Things went downhill from there. After a long discussion, the meeting issued a communique noting that special 'stress was laid by the German Ministers on the difficulties of the existing position in Germany and the need for alleviation'. With that the meeting ended. Brüning later recalled, 'The farewell was gracious, but depressed.'[21]

On Monday, June 8, Norman cabled Harrison about the meeting. It was planned many weeks ago and could not be cancelled 'although conditions have since so greatly changed as to alter the whole basis'. The German statement 'was entirely unexpected and so worded as to be a shock to the English and to make the ice thin in places'.[22] Shortly after receiving the telegram, Harrison called Norman, who

seemed concerned and worried . . . and indicated that in his judgment the situation is fraught with danger, the extent of which will be dependent primarily upon two factors: the effect of Chequers in Berlin and developments in Vienna during the next few days. . . . If withdrawals from Berlin continue he did not see how the Reichsbank could avoid seeking help from some of the other central banks in substantial quantities.

With respect to Vienna he was not at all happy. He said it was absolutely necessary for the Austrian government to raise externally 150,000,000 schilling to begin with and probably 100,000,000 schilling a little later on, that he did not see how it was going to be easy to place any bonds for the government but that without them it would not be possible for the Austrian government to subscribe the capital which it has promised to the Credit Anstalt. In this connection he mentioned that he had just heard that the Austrian National Bank has approached the Bank for International Settlements to raise another 100,000,000 schilling central bank credit for its accommodation.

> He said . . . that on the whole, as he expressed it, 'we seem to be surrounded with trouble'.[23]

It was easy to see where Norman's blues came from. Despite his ill-fated attempt to argue that the real problem was in Austria and that Germany had proven its ability to withstand financial trouble, the meeting at Chequers made it abundantly clear that both Germany and politics were now part of the problem.

Central bankers knew that they acted in a political world, of course, but they preferred not to. They also knew that the German problems and the reparations issue could not be ignored. They just hoped that by dodging the Austrian crisis, they would be able to establish a more stable environment in which to deal with the German problem.

The American weekly *Commercial and Financial Chronicle* covered the meeting at Chequers in a couple of long articles and stressed Germany's underlying problems with 'a turn toward Bolshevism or Fascism, unless a measure of relief is granted the sorely tried German people'.[24]

The BIS board meeting was the next step in trying to avert disaster. Merle Cochran reported about the Basle meeting that most of the 'meetings on Sunday and Monday was taken up by discussion of the Austrian situation. Mr. Rodd, an English expert of the B.I.S., who has been the principal contact officer with Vienna during the present crisis, returned to Basel by airplane to set forth the situation to the Directors.'[25]

## THE SECOND BIS BOARD MEETING

As Harrison was on the phone with Norman, the board meeting at the BIS was dragging to an end, and the board agreed to follow the recommendation by Rodd and Bruins to extend a new 100-million-schilling loan to the Austrian National Bank – with conditions. The Austrian bond loan must be successfully placed first, and the National Bank's holding of 3 million pounds of gold at the Bank of England should be deposited in the name of the BIS. The board also approved of Bruins's other proposals.[26]

Now there was a plan, but the question remained of where and how to place the bond loan and how to rebuild the Austrian public's confidence in the Credit Anstalt and the schilling. It was hard to imagine a solution to the Austrian crisis if these issues were not taken care of together with the foreign creditors.

The Rothschild house and the International Committee felt the same way. As the board meeting was underway, Lionel de Rothschild sent a telegram to his cousins in Austria. He was upset and asked 'what arrangements are contemplated by directors' about restoring confidence in the Credit Anstalt.[27] He complained that Austrian deposits

> are being rapidly withdrawn although foreign depositors are expected to renew their commitments. This is most unsatisfactory and we feel prompt and effective measures must be taken to force Austrian depositors to stop drawing otherwise we fear negotiations to bring foreign depositors into agreement may break down.[28]

Things were coming to a head, and there seemed to be an emerging consensus that a lot depended on understanding and reestablishing the psychology and confidence of the Austrian people. Both Bruins and Rodd had stressed that, and so did Pierre Quesnay as he addressed the governors on the first day of the board meeting.

Quesnay had spent five years in Austria working on the reform of the Austrian monetary system in the early 1920s. He therefore felt that he had a 'certain knowledge of the Austrian frame of mind'. According to Quesnay, confidence would only be restored when the treasury loan was successfully placed and the guarantee made effective.

Trust in their government was not a dominant characteristic of the Austrian people, Quesnay told the board. He added that in contrast to the foreign creditors, who are 'big banking firms' that were easier to organize, it was impossible to do the same with the individual Austrian depositors.

The Austrian public would have to 'feel that behind their National Bank there are other powerful forces, viz. ten Central Banks of Europe associated under the auspices of the B.I.S.' 'For, it had better not be lost sight of that a nation like the Austrians, which has gone through the terrible experience of monetary inflation, has not, and cannot reasonably be expected to have, absolute confidence even in their public authorities, be it the National Bank, be it the Government.'[29] The Austrian hyperinflation emerged as an important frame, as Quesnay stressed the importance of recent Austrian history for the public's behaviour and sceptical attitude. 'If, however, they came to see that their National Bank is henceforth going to be backed by so powerful an institution as the B.I.S. then things would look different to their eyes.'

Like Rist and he himself had shown before, Quesnay demonstrated that it was not all French that opposed helping Austria. As a central banker and an economist, he knew what was at stake, and as part of the epistemic community, he favoured central bank independence, and he supported Bruins's idea of another joint BIS and central bank credit. The Austrian National Bank had deposited double the amount with the BIS, so the risk to the BIS would be minor, even if Bruins should suggest that 'we were going to go to even greater lengths in favour of Austria'.[30]

Rodd agreed, arguing that since the National Bank had deposited a high proportion of its foreign exchange with the BIS from the outset, this 'alone would have given Austria a moral title for expecting adequate support from the B.I.S. even had her present plight not made such support imperative'.

Like Bruins and Quesnay before him, Rodd argued that numbers alone would not make it possible to understand what was going on in Austria and why the public behaved as it did. Psychological and historical factors mattered as well.

> These figures, however, are not sufficient to give a complete picture of the situation. It must be borne in mind that Austria, after the armistice, was the first country to suffer the whole shock of inflation, and that the memory of this event is still vivid in the minds of most people there. It is therefore not quite unnatural that with a nervous people, very soon after the first news had reached the public, a flight from the schilling set in, which might have taken dangerous proportions had it not been possible to stem the tide in due time. Under these conditions, the importance of the assistance given by the B.I.S. is obvious.[31]

This was sensemaking through narrative emplotment. Rodd continued that the loan and other support provided by the BIS to the Austrian National Bank could not by itself 'relieve the anxiety which was felt in Austria'. The flight of deposits from the Credit Anstalt had to be stopped, and a full guarantee for Credit Anstalt's liabilities implemented.[32]

Moral title or not, the meeting could not solve the real and ever more pressing problem, the issue of the Austrian bond loan. According to the *Financial Times*, the governors all heard 'Mr. Rodd's detailed report. It is rumoured that this report puts a very grave complexion on the banking position in Vienna.'[33]

On his return to London from Basle, Harry Siepmann wrote a note on the meeting. Rodd had reported on the Austrian position and the need for monetary contraction that both he and Bruins had recommended.

However, Siepmann noted, Rodd admitted that 'everything turns upon the successful placing' of the treasury bonds abroad. If the loan failed 'no currency programme would be of any use. But . . . it would be necessary to proceed on the assumption that this issue would be made'. In addition, a second BIS credit of 100 million schillings was needed as well, and 'if Dr. Bruins were to proceed immediately with the execution of his programme' that credit needed to be 'made temporarily available, pending the placing of the Treasury Bonds'.

The board was not impressed by the idea of another credit to Austria. 'The proposal that central banks should provide more money was first resisted in every quarter.' Louis Franck, the governor of the Belgian central bank, argued that 'if the Austrians had a prospect of obtaining more money, they would make every kind of difficulty about accepting the conditions which would necessarily be imposed upon them in connection with the issue of the bonds'.

The Italian banker Alberto Beneduce and Vincenzo Azzolini, the governor of the Italian central bank, were also reluctant to provide more assistance to Austria; a fact which raised some concern at the Bank of England that Italy too might be in financial distress.

Clément Moret, the French central bank governor, did not see any need for a temporary BIS loan, since he expected the bond loan to be placed within the next couple of days. Moret asked Siepmann, who represented the Bank of England in the absence of Norman, for the position of the 'London market'. Siepmann replied that the private bankers had not been approached about the loan but, if they wanted to participate, the Bank of England would encourage this.

At the end of a very long day, McGarrah proposed a resolution along the lines of Rodd's and Bruins's plan, but it was voted down by the board, and the meeting adjourned late in the evening without any conclusion. Francis Rodd was asked to prepare a new memorandum with a precise presentation of Bruins's proposal before the meeting resumed the next morning. As the governors met again Monday morning, it was 'with mr. Rodd's report before them'.[34]

Three pages long and held in a matter-of-fact style, it recounted the content of his own and Bruin's reports. Rediscounts by the National Bank was 420 million schillings, the Credit Anstalt had lost 500 million schillings, or one-third of its deposits, and about half of the remaining deposits were foreign. The National Bank's balance sheet had expanded by about 500 million schillings, while it had lost around 350 million schillings in foreign exchange. About 100 million 'are due to internal demands arising from lack of confidence in the stability of the currency'.

As a result, the note circulation and sight liabilities of the National Bank had increased by 200 million. 'In order to get command of the monetary situation it will be necessary to reabsorb these Sch. 200 millions, or preferably rather more.' This should happen through six measures including raising the bank rate, getting 50 million in new money into the Credit Anstalt from savings banks, issuing so-called Kassenscheine in both foreign and domestic currency, and reducing the rediscounting for the Credit Anstalt 'without, of course, refusing to go on paying out. Such a refusal would directly cause a moratorium'. Finally, Rodd informed the board that

in the opinion of Dr. Bruins, these measures taken all together should effectively stop the leak, by depriving people of the currency which they would otherwise convert into foreign exchange. If this program commands the assent of the B.I.S., Dr. Bruins would wish a B.I.S. communique to be issued in as generous terms as possible, so that the programme may be launched in a favourable atmosphere.[35]

Rodd did not get many hours of sleep that night. He probably also talked to Siepmann, who at the morning meeting 'took occasion to modify the commitment which I had given to M. Moret about London participation in the Treasury Bond issue'. Siepmann told Moret and the rest of the board that if the 'Central Banks declined to provide Dr. Bruins with the resources which, in his opinion, are required in order to safeguard the currency position, it would be morally impossible for the Bank of England to encourage private bankers to subscribe'.

This move supported Rodd's and Bruin's proposal, which was eventually agreed upon, but not before the board decided that the Austrian National Bank 'should be required to draw on its own reserves, and it was agreed that this should be done down to the psychological minimum, of which those on the spot would be the best judges'. In addition, the second BIS loan could not be used as a bridge loan, 'the proceeds of this credit will remain at the B.I.S.' until the bond loan was placed.

At this point, Moret 'admitted that, according to his latest information the placing of the Treasury bonds might take longer than he had expected'. The immediate problem of a bridge loan had not been solved, after all. Apparently, Siepmann had anticipated this situation, and he now presented an idea to the board.

In the course of the discussion on the previous day I had maintained that although several Central Banks represented in Basle were in a position, had they chosen to do so, to take charge of the Austrian situation by themselves, they are precluded by the existence of the B.I.S. from taking any such individual action. Monsieur Franck disputed this opinion, and I then asked the president whether, if one or more Central Bank judged the position to be so serious that they could not accept the responsibility of inaction, he would be willing that they should contribute the necessary resources to the B.I.S. on the understanding that they would be passed on and used by the B.I.S. in its own name without the origin of such contributions being disclosed. This would, of course, amount to lending the name of non-participants to the action taken by the B.I.S. on behalf of the participants. The President thought that this would be a perfectly proper proceeding, and Monsieur Franck and Monsieur Moret agreed.[36]

Whether Siepmann wanted to leave a door open for the Banque de France to do, what he found right, or if, in contrast, he wanted to reserve the right for the Bank of England to act on its own, or both, is not known. The idea had already surfaced in Simon's January note, and he surely imagined more trouble with the placing of the bond loan, or with political issues. Now, with the consent from the BIS and the Banque de France, the Bank of England at least had some degrees of freedom if the house of cards tumbled.

McGarrah was happy with the outcome of the meeting and praised Siepmann, who 'was splendid and very helpful' while the Belgian central bank governor Louis Franck 'was most difficult on the Austrian question. He lacks courage and ... when anyone takes the lead on a conservative tendency, Moret joins in'.[37]

## WE SHALL ALL LOSE OUR MONEY

Meanwhile, as central bankers were attending meetings in Basle, the members of the International Committee had their own problems to deal with. Negotiations with the Austrian government had been going on for a while and among other things the period that the creditors would be bound to maintain their deposits in return for a guarantee was contested. The Austrian government wanted a four-year period, but the compromise was two years, based on van Hengel's and others' advice that it would be 'the shortest reasonable time to enable the bank to properly liquidate its frozen credits'.

The committee ... very strongly brought out the fact that if the creditors raised technical points at this moment it may bring about bankruptcy next week.... We suggest that broad general view be taken because if anything happens to Credit Anstalt it will have a serious repercussion throughout Central Europe where most banks give large credits to other banks.[38]

Morgan Grenfell informed J.P. Morgan & Co. that 'the consensus of opinion is that time is the essence of the whole matter'.[39] J.P. Morgan & Co. was not 'much impressed by the argument that it would be impossible to get the Austrian Government guarantee unless the two-year period is accepted', but they were inclined to accept what the Committee was able to agree on.[40]

The two-year period was a point of contention between the creditor banks. Several members of the International Committee feared what would happen if Austria were to get a socialist government, not the most unlikely scenario. As Lazard partner Robert Kindersley put it at a meeting in New Court, N.M. Rothschild & Sons's office since 1809,

> There is nothing to assure us that there will not be socialist Government within the two years ... You may easily get a socialist Government which may, with this voting control in its hands, vote such salaries and such conditions to its employees or even vote such obligations that the Bank have got to undertake as to make it practically impossible for us to get our money and I personally feel very strongly that this voting control as long as we go on should be in the hands of the Committee of control.[41]

The chairman, Lionel de Rothschild, took a more balanced view and argued that if 'you say the Credit Anstalt is not good enough and we must have the guarantee of the Government, then we must take the guarantee of the Government, we cannot have it both ways. What we have agreed to do is to go on provided the Austrian Government gives us its guarantee, then the Government must control the Credit Anstalt. If you say we must control the Credit Anstalt and the Government give its guarantee, the Austrian Government would have the right to say no.'

Charles Whigham of Morgan Grenfell also felt uneasy about the two-year period. In the first place, he said, 'We are still in the air as to what the guarantee really means. We believe it means a day to day guarantee but we have not had that confirmed.' While Lionel de Rothschild was 'anxious to get something through so as to get the bank working again', Whigham wanted to use the time period of the guarantee as a lever to get a better result.

> I believe what we ought to do is to get down to a formula all round of what we want, one of the terms of which will be the time and if we get all the other things we want we may make it two years or some other period, but I do not like giving away our position until we get straight. The Austrian Government guarantee unsecured is all right but is not a first class guarantee and I think we want only to give away our position on the time we will allow when we get the formula made as to what we want.[42]

The chairman did not have an easy time with his fellow bankers who knew what they wanted. But so did he. More interested in gardening than in banking, he may silently have wished himself to be in his garden at Exbury.[43]

Lionel de Rothschild reminded his colleagues why they were there and said,

> Unless we can arrive at some agreement we shall all lose our money and I want to save the money of everybody who is in this boat and the only way I can see is to get the Bank going as soon as possible, and that is why I feel very strongly we have got to get something done at once about continuing the credit facilities. . . . Let us put down on paper, following Mr. Whigham's suggestion, what exactly the terms are that we can recommend for acceptance to all the people whom we represent.[44]

Some of the international creditors argued that theirs were special cases and that their claims on the credit Anstalt were privileged. That made it difficult to send a unified signal to van Hengel and the Austrian government. As the voice of reason, Lionel de Rothschild tried as best he could to manage a meeting on June 5, which increasingly started to look like a university faculty meeting. At one point he felt compelled to emphasize the need for an agreement, saying that he was

> only pointing out what the danger is. But what I am trying to get out from you people is whether you think I have to tell Van Hengel now that there are all these reservations asked for which means I cannot get a decision for Heaven knows how long, or whether you will tell me you will get on the telephone and say 'it is so urgent that we want you now to come in on this agreement, in principle, and let us publish it, and we will take up everything else afterwards'.[45]

It was not only internal disagreements and misunderstandings, however, that came to the surface. At a meeting five days later on June 10, the group tried to figure out a common position on a guarantee on internal deposits. Some of the bankers felt that would be a misunderstanding, and one argued that when schilling deposits were withdrawn, they were converted into foreign exchange, thus adding to the problems. Lionel de Rothschild agreed. 'Your point helps us considerably, because if we do not allow them to guarantee, money will be withdrawn, exchange will be pulled, and our position will be jeopardized.'

A discussion then erupted about van Hengel. Robert Kindersley understood that van Hengel might disagree about an internal guarantee, and 'if you agree to a thing like this over his head, even though he is away, you are apt to merely disgruntle him'. That was the final drop for Lionel de Rothschild.

CHAIRMAN: Well, let us do so. I am getting tired of Van Hengel. He never talks to me. Let us find someone else who will really get into touch with us. Someone said van Hengel rather pooh-poohs the suggestion, but he has apparently expressed no opinion that it will be contrary to the interests of the foreign creditors.

SIR ROBERT: Then all we need say is, he does not disapprove.

CHAIRMAN: After all, van Hengel does represent us. But we are the Committee sitting here and I think we take the opinion that it is in the interests of the Bank that the schillings should be protected by the Austrian Government, and van Hengel has no right to be cross about it. If he is, let us get someone else. Van Hengel goes all over the place playing his own game. I don't know what it is.[46]

At the end of a long meeting, the representative of the French banks raised doubts about the Austrian loan. 'If the French Government do not do it I am afraid that will be the end of it, because nobody else cares to do it.' The Chairman asked, 'You don't think you will be able to raise money in France?'. The reply was not encouraging, 'when I was in Paris nothing had been done'. As the meeting adjourned the Chairman concluded. 'Doesn't it come back to the same, old story – unless you keep the Credit Anstalt going, Austria goes. If Austria goes, it is going to collapse. It is in the interest of every country in Europe to keep Austria going and therefore it will be kept going somehow or other and we are doing our part. What will be done in the other part, I don't know.'[47]

# 9

# Where and How to Place? (June 8–June 13)

Among the central bankers, Rodd and Siepmann, and of course Norman, were at the centre of the epistemic community during the Austrian crisis because of Rodd's position at the Bank for International Settlements (BIS) and his presence in Vienna, and the Bank of England's position among central banks. Rodd also reported to the BIS where Fraser, McGarrah and Pierre Quesnay were well informed about the latest development, as was Bruins in the National Bank.

In contrast to Rodd and his compatriots, who not only had access to but often produced the most updated information and actionable knowledge, Harrison did not feel well informed. On June 9, the day after the BIS board meeting, he complained to the BIS that his most recent figures from the Austrian National Bank were from May 15. He would appreciate more recent information.[1]

Harrison benefited greatly from McGarrah and Fraser's updates as well as from his connection to the House of Morgan, but Norman remained his most important source of information and emplotment. As Norman and Harrison finished their phone call on Monday, June 8, Norman asked him to call again the following day. So, late next morning, Harrison was on the phone again to get the latest news on the European situation.

Norman painted a bleak picture, according to Harrison. The International Committee had not finished its work, and there were 'still many difficulties', while 'the currency situation in Austria is not at all satisfactory'. Norman told Harrison about the new BIS credit, 'but the real question is how are we to raise 150,000,000 for the Austrian Government'.[2]

Norman said that Paris would take half the bond loan, and 'it is essential that some should be placed in London and New York'. He doubted that the public would buy the bonds, so it was all about 'getting the bankers to take the issue', which would be very difficult in London, while Harrison thought he could place some on Wall Street.[3]

As usual, there were many rumours, but very little had actually happened since the House of Morgan had declined to take part in, not to mention lead, the Austrian loan. In early June, Charles Rist, the French adviser to the Austrian government, tried to get negotiations on track.

On June 4 and 5 there were meetings in Paris about the bond issue, and Rist arrived in Paris on Friday, June 5, for further negotiations with the French Foreign Ministry at Quai d'Orsay, and the Banque de Paris et des Pays-Bas.

But nothing much seemed to happen. On June 9, BIS's information about the negotiations was still scarce. Karl Blessing, a German BIS representative now in Vienna, could add little in a phone call to Basle, 'No further details are known of the Paris negotiations for the marketing of the bonds. The French group is said to have declared its readiness to take over up to 80% of the 150 millions of treasury bonds.'[4]

The same day, McGarrah cabled Fraser who was in New York that Harrison was considered by 'London', not to be 'fully informed' about the nature of the bond loan. McGarrah questioned that French banks would take as much as 80 per cent of the bond loan. Another estimate was that 'Paris is contemplating subscribing for 75,000,000 of these bonds, the second part being offered at London, Berlin, elsewhere in Europe and it is hoped New York will be willing to participate'.[5]

The well-connected Morgan & Cie knew about Charles Rist's visit to Paris and told J.P. Morgan & Co. that Banque de Paris et des Pays-Bas was considering 'a two year credit of 150.000.000 Schilling for use through drawings by the Austrian National Bank and endorsed by Austrian Government'.

Through Morgan & Cie the French Bank asked J.P. Morgan if American banks would take part 'in this operation which in our minds certainly is constructive and probably necessary to prevent a very bad situation developing throughout Central Europe with serious effects on other American credits there'.[6]

The idea was apparently drawn up as an alternative to a bridge loan from the BIS until the bond loan could be placed, but J.P. Morgan & Co. did not like it. The idea mixed up central banking and government issues.

> Would it not be wiser to follow the course which we had assumed would be followed namely, arrange for the Austrian National Bank to look to the B.I.S. and other central banks for co-operation as to the exchange and currency problems of the Austrian National Bank and arrange for the Government to take whatever steps are necessary to protect the Credit Anstalt situation?[7]

That did not leave much to the market, but Morgan was not alone in criticizing the plan, which was soon dropped because it 'encountered opposition'.[8] Instead, Nelson Dean Jay, the head of Morgan & Cie, wrote to McGarrah that he wished Austria would send a competent man to Paris to negotiate with the Banque de Paris et des Pays-Bas 'for meeting the present emergency'.

Dean Jay thought that Banque de Paris et des Pays-Bas was forthcoming and broadminded 'but they cannot be expected to formulate a programme without the full cooperation and support of the Austrian Government'.[9]

## NOTHING TO REPORT

Despite much hearsay, there was no progress with respect to the bond loan, and the situation was only marginally better with regard to the international creditors. On June 9, Norman informed Bruins that Robert Kindersley would go to Vienna to negotiate on behalf of the International Committee. Kindersley, a tall and imposing man at forty-nine with bushy black eyebrows and a deep voice, was 'fully acquainted with the general position in Austria and with the present state of affairs in London'. Norman suggested postponing any important steps 'until after Sir Robert Kindersley's arrival'.[10]

Early in the evening that Tuesday, Bruins called Siepmann and complained that the guarantee for internal deposits was only granted when depositors applied for it. Many preferred to withdraw their money instead, which forced the National Bank to go on rediscounting the Credit Anstalt's paper. This made it impossible to reduce the note circulation, Bruins's first priority.

Siepmann discussed the issue with the International Committee, which had no objection to Bruins's work to get a better guarantee of internal deposits. He also told Bruins that the BIS should resist 'putting up any new money until . . . the internal leak is stopped'. Otherwise, Bruins's currency contraction could not be implemented, and the new BIS credit would not serve its purpose. Bruins told Siepmann that he had 'already received by telegram the support of the B.I.S. for this contention'.[11]

The discussion demonstrates the complexity of both the issues themselves and of the communication and command lines at a time when speed and clarity were essential. Bruins spoke with the Austrian finance minister Otto Juch and van Hengel at the Credit Anstalt and passed his concerns on to Harry Siepmann at the Bank of England, who was in touch with the International Committee. It was a constant negotiation on several levels to make sense of the various positions and events and of what it all meant. No single person or central bank was in a leadership position to make a quick and final decision. As Norman had told Harrison a few days before he did not feel in position to make any final decisions either.

In principle, perhaps, authority lay with the BIS, but the BIS did not have the network, or the resources and historical legitimacy that the Bank of England did. It needed the support of its member banks. Therefore, even though Bruins informed the BIS and received Basle's consent to his plan, he still had to communicate with the Bank of England as well. The Bank of England then turned around and discussed with the International Creditors. Only then could Bruins go back to the Austrian authorities.

The Bank of England again emerged as the centre of the epistemic community of central banks. And the most powerful. When tensions increased, the initiative and the ability to act, even if on a limited scale, were drifting back to and reassumed by the Bank of England, mostly for historical reasons and because of Norman's standing and international network.

Norman accepted the role for the same reasons and because of his lack of confidence in the resoluteness of his counterparts as well as his fear that things were getting out of hand.

'Everything now turns upon the placing of the Sch. 150 millions Treasury Bills abroad', Siepmann wrote on Wednesday, June 10, as he summed up his impressions from the board meeting in Basle for Norman. It was like the world had stood still for a few weeks. The National Bank needed foreign exchange, and the Austrian loan would therefore have to be issued abroad.

The French still appeared ready to take half, but they wanted New York and London in on the loan. 'What they want more than our money', Siepmann noted, 'is the use of our name for the prospectus'. This was perceived to help restore confidence in Austria.

Siepmann also commented on the situation in Italy and Hungary, where things looked bad. The Italians seemed anxious but would not even 'unburden themselves to the president in private'. In Hungary on the other hand, the situation was even worse, but in contrast to the Italians they had no problem unburdening themselves. They complained that the central banks' support to Vienna made things more difficult for the neighbouring countries.

Siepmann told Norman, that Hungary 'have had to suffer at the hands of the First National Bank of Boston and the Irving Bank, and they fear either, that the patient in Vienna will die under ministrations of so many medicine men, or if the devil is exorcised, he will only go over the border'. The

Hungarian central bank would soon need more money, and 'Rodd will probably go to Budapest next week-end', Siepmann explained.[12]

The exception to the rule of the importance of the Bank of England was the Austrian bond loan. It did not want to have anything to do with a government loan. Instead, France took the lead, not least because it was one of the few countries where such a loan could be placed. Therefore, communication lines were also different.

Robert Lacour-Gayet, director of economic studies at the Banque de France, called Siepmann the same Wednesday.[13] Lacour-Gayet, a former financial representative for France in the United States and a staunch advocate of the gold standard and the free market, told Siepmann that 'there is nothing to report about the Austrian Treasury Bond negotiations in Paris'. The Banque de Paris et des Pays-Bas had set up conditions for the bond loan participation and was now waiting for a reply from the Austrian Government.[14]

Siepmann spent a lot of time on the telephone that Wednesday. The widespread use of the telephone for international calls was in itself a marker of the increasing intensity and urgency of the situation. The need to communicate faster and to get back to add new questions or ask for more information was best served by the telephone. At the same time, the compression of time and space allowed and shaped through international phone calls and air travel also increased the risk of contagion.

Rodd called Siepmann twice on the phone. The first message in the morning was not encouraging.

> The morale in Vienna is now bad. They are down on their luck and even Brauneis is saying that they now seem likely to suffer the disadvantages of all the three alternatives which originally presented themselves; namely, moratorium, inflation and guarantee. They were advised to avoid moratorium, but they seem likely to come round to it again by way of the other two.
>
> Juch does not seem to appreciate the difficulties and dangers of the position. He has lost grip and he is so tired that he now listens without hearing.
>
> The treasury bond negotiations are not going too well in Paris. The Austrians presented their case very badly to Paris Bas, as if they were offering a favour.[15]

At 5.15 in the afternoon Rodd called again reporting little 'progress in Paris, chiefly owing to the attitude of the Austrians'. He also told Siepmann that there was no 'progress on the question of the internal guarantee. Juch told Bruins this morning that he could place Sch. 150 millions internally if necessary and repeated his absurd proposal that it might be done in terms of dollars.'[16] No one was happy with the Austrian authorities.

## NOT AN HOUR TO LOSE

The sense that the Austrian crisis was running out of control increased the feeling of alarm. On June 11, one month after the Austrian finance minister and the National Bank first reached out to Siepmann, Norman told Harrison that 'the Austrian situation is not improved and not doing well'. He repeated that he had asked Kindersley to 'go out there as the best person he knows of to find out what is the situation and what it is all about. Kindersley would leave the next day.'

The sense of urgency was vivid. In Hungary, the situation was 'rather more difficult', and in Germany it was 'certainly more uneasy today than yesterday'. The Bank of England also felt the heat, Norman told Harrison, having 'released £7,000,000 gold and also bought back £2,000,000 in bills. He said that there was great uneasiness in Berlin both political and financial because of the withdrawals.' And yet, information was scarce with no news from Basle except that they were still considering the second credit to Austria and one to the Hungarian central bank as well. Norman had no news about the Austrian bond loan.

The situation in India was critical as well and Norman had been busy with that problem for most of the day. But Europe was also in limbo:

> Governor Norman said that he considered the next few days would be most critical in the development of the situation in Austria, Hungary, Germany, and Central Europe generally; that we must maintain a contact hour by hour, and in reference to my statement that I might possibly go abroad, he said that he hoped I would not consider doing so unless some one would be left here prepared to act immediately in case of emergency. He said, of course, he would love to have me over there to talk over the situation which he regards as serious but that if I left this week the situation might break while I am on the water. I told him that under no circumstances would I leave unless I was satisfied the bank was prepared to function without me, as I was sure it would be.[17]

For once, Norman may have understated the problems in Austria. At 5.15 p.m. Siepmann received a call from Quesnay in Basle, who told him that 'they are "very nervous" in Vienna and there is "not an hour to lose"'. The discussions in Paris about the treasury bonds 'went very badly yesterday but will be renewed tonight, and there is reason to hope that they may go better'.[18]

Only an hour and a half later, at 6.50 p.m., Rodd called Siepmann and reported that in Austria 'things seem to be going about as badly as they could go ... the leak has not been stopped but, on the contrary, reserves are dwindling at an alarming rate'. The National Bank had lost another 50 million schillings in the last three days, and Rodd stressed that this was 'for our information inside the Bank of England exclusively'.

Rodd's allegiance to the Old Lady in Threadneedle Street was not in doubt, but he was also beginning to question BIS's ability to deal with the crisis. And he certainly had no confidence in the Austrian government. He told Siepmann that the

Austrian attitude, especially that of the Government is difficult to understand. It may be deliberate, or it may be due simply to incompetence. The fact is that they appear to be willing to do nothing and that the foreign advisers can make no progress. Dr. Juch has made promises to Dr. Bruins which, it afterwards appeared, he never had any intention of keeping. . . .

The Paris negotiations are held up by the apparent unwillingness of the Austrians to make any proposals. Such Austrian proposals as there are have gone off to Paris today, but the day has been wasted in inconclusive discussions. . . . Unless something happens by Saturday midday it seems very possible that a moratorium may be declared on Sunday.[19]

It was Thursday, June 11, one month after Francis Rodd had left for Vienna. He had worked around the clock to untangle the situation and communicate his findings to Basle and London. He had held numerous meetings, written several memos on the situation and spent hours on the phone. He had had to reassess the situation over and over again as he encountered new information, unexpected developments and what he perceived as deeply uncooperative Austrian authorities.

Rodd may well have felt that the Tuareg people in Sahara had been easier to understand than the Austrians. If anything, he could use a break, but he was nowhere near being done. In fact, he was still trying to find a solution to the same issues he had identified during his first day in Vienna. And now the threat of a moratorium was rearing its ugly head again. Rodd was exhausted and perplexed, but he could not go back home just yet. After returning to Vienna from Basle he sent a personal telegram to his boss, Gates McGarrah, resorting to metaphors to make sense of the situation.

I regret not having been able to keep you personally so closely in touch as I should have liked but with situation changing so rapidly my information arriving when already out of date would have been misleading rather than otherwise. We are doing our best to bring ship which is constantly springing new leaks into harbour and I am optimistic . . . Until Harbour lights in sight and pilots are on board and in charge I cannot properly leave owing to personal situation of which you are aware and which are more difficult than you know. I hope therefore you will excuse my absence and remain at least as confident as I am. None of us are affected by prevailing atmosphere here but are having hard times to prevent all others becoming downhearted.[20]

In Basle, McGarrah immediately thanked Rodd for the note. McGarrah, too, was cautiously optimistic and wrote, 'We miss you but your return is left entirely to your judgement.'[21] In that case it could be a while before Rodd would be able to return to Basle. More and more cues pointed to a general European crisis, and the BIS officers on the spot(s) were essential for dealing with the contagion.

It was around June 10 and 11 that the Austrian crisis entered its final and most critical phase and signs of contagion were abundant. One of the persons who was able at this difficult moment to take a few steps back and take a more general perspective on the situation, and what needed to be done, was Adrianus van Hengel. Earlier he had sent a long letter to Norman. Now he asked to see Gates McGarrah in Basle.

A week earlier, Harry Siepmann called McGarrah and told him that it 'would be helpful to us all as well as enlightening and pleasant for van Hengel himself if you would invite him to go from Vienna by air to Basel on Sunday to pay you personally a visit early that day. He would only need an hour or so in Basel.'[22] But McGarrah declined to see van Hengel. Bruins and Rodd advised against it.[23]

## VAN HENGEL GOES TO BASLE

Nevertheless, on June 10, van Hengel showed up uninvited at the BIS headquarters in Basle and insisted on seeing McGarrah. Back in Vienna the next day, van Hengel sat down and wrote a long letter to McGarrah outlining his argument; just to be sure.

'In my opinion it is necessary that I confirm by writing what I said yesterday, to which I will add what is the gist of the letter, I wrote to Mr. Montagu Norman, and which you declined to read unless Mr. Montagu Norman requests you personally to do so.'

Van Hengel apologized 'for the frankness, perhaps even rudeness, in which I expose my views. As an excuse I reiterate that you forced me thereto by your unwillingness to discuss matters with me. If you either share my views or are prepared to show me that I am not right, I am sure there is every possibility of a fruitful co-operation.'

Part of what followed was a transcript of van Hengel's letter to Norman, where 'I expect that you will arrange an interview of you, Mr. MacGarrah, perhaps Mr. Quesnay, and me as soon as possible, unless one of the two procedures which I am going to describe below as necessary, is decided for at once'.

Van Hengel quoted the French diplomat and politician Baron Louis, 'Faites moi de bonne politique et je ferai de bonnes finances', and continued that none 'of us are politicians, but circumstances may force us to meddle with politics ... Finances now are Western world over absolutely unsound because of the stupid financing by short time investments of long-term capitalisation. This has to lead and has led to a "crise de confiance"'.

The letter dealt with two issues related to the Bagehot operating model: an internal drain and an external drain. In both cases, according to van Hengel, there were two options from which to choose: paying everyone who wants to get paid or stopping payments. In the case of the internal drain, the central bank could pay out in its own currency, backed by a state guarantee if necessary. This would restore confidence after which a 'contraction of currency comes automatically and that confidence will be restored is a basic axioma we have to work on'.

However, 'if losses are certain', meaning if the bank was insolvent, 'not paying is fundamentally the only solution. Here in Vienna the wrong solution has been chosen out of fear for revolution.' Van Hengel shared Rodd's concern that the Credit Anstalt might not have been solvent at the time of the reconstruction. Political concerns had taken priority, but that was water under the bridge and too late to do anything about, as Rodd had pointed out.

Van Hengel continued that in the case of an external drain of foreign exchange, the 'anxiety of the foreign creditor has to be dealt with in such a way that currency parities will not be disturbed'. No central banks would have enough gold and reserves to

> meet 100% of the short-term indebtedness to foreign creditors, so that B.I.S. and that will in practice have to be U.S.A. and France have to provide the balance. If the arrangements made foresee 100% withdrawal, the actual withdrawals will stop probably long before those 100% are reached. ... If arrangements are half-hearted – of which I am pretty sure – withdrawals will continue up to nearly the 100% and naturally we will be forced into ... [s]topping payments with all its consequences wished by none of us.

After this Bagehot 101, van Hengel set out the way forward with respect to Germany. 'We' van Hengel wrote, including himself in the action, 'have to bring about a willing stopping of payments ... for all credits by international banks to Germany'. Van Hengel had no confidence in German bank's capital levels, and support from central banks and the BIS would require a state guarantee. However,

> losses fundamentally ought to be borne by the creditors, even by foreign creditors. They may get state guarantees if they pay the price of acknowledging – in the shape of extension for long duration – that they invested for long term and not for short period. This way round the consolidation process will be comparatively easy to be carried out.[24]

This situation was very much the same as in Austria. Van Hengel was aware of the risk of contagion, and he shared the view that Germany would be the last straw. In contrast to the central banks and the BIS, he had little sympathy for the international banks that had lent short-term funds with little consideration of the risk. He therefore proposed to force the international creditors into a kind of standstill agreement turning their short-term claims into long-term credits.

'Measures ought to be taken', van Hengel wrote not short of confidence and addressing Norman directly, 'by you, by the B.I.S., the Federal Reserve Board, perhaps the Banque de France, on one side, and the Reichsbank and German State on the other. This decisive action I hope to discuss with you and the other gentlemen before it is too late.'

While at it, van Hengel also addressed McGarrah directly noting that

> the world expects something from the Bank for International Settlements. If it is really not that which its name would imply, an Institution to warrant confidence in International Finance, its foundation is a calamity, and I think it your duty to avoid that calamity by having the Bank for International Settlements intervene to the necessary extent.[25]

Finally, he turned to the Credit Anstalt. It was not a normal bank but a holding company embedded in both domestic and foreign politics. It was also the result of

> stupid banking practices generally spread. Those practices were initiated and boomed by American Banks with infantile knowledge of International banking and other conditions, and, unhappily, copied by a number of European Banks, which thought that in the U.S.A. wealth brought wisdom along with it.[26]

Van Hengel's criticism of American banks' 'infantile knowledge' and bad risk management practices was partly shared by Charles Mitchell of City Bank, though he put it differently. At a New York Fed meeting on June 1, Mitchell argued that the withdrawals of funds from Austria 'was a natural consequence of many lenders entering a field of banking with which they were not familiar and in which they were easily frightened'.[27]

Van Hengel felt that perhaps the creditors including the international banks should be forced to take the losses. That was not part of the thinking among the central banks and even less so among the private bankers who certainly cared about the financial system but also about their own money and survival. McGarrah, Harrison and Norman cannot have failed to imagine a bleak future where the already fragile American banking system and the British merchant banks were hit by losses in Austria and Germany.

Letting the creditors take the losses, no matter how appealing, was a controversial idea in the context of a financial crisis where every effort was focused on avoiding panic and contagion. No one or only very few even considered a haircut or questioned the rights of the international banks to be paid in full, except perhaps Adrianus van Hengel, but he was seen as an eccentric and not accepted as part of the community.

He certainly did not mince his words, telling both McGarrah and Norman what to do, and making some important and unpleasant points along the way. Handwritten notes on the letter suggest that besides McGarrah, Leon Fraser and Pierre Quesnay also read it, but there are no signs that anything came of it. Though the analysis was both insightful and frank, to say the least, it also displayed a know-it-all attitude that hardly made McGarrah and Norman want to meet with van Hengel. His reputation had surely preceded him.

The letter was also rather critical of the BIS and the general approach to the Central European debt crisis. If van Hengel had a forceful and independent mind and did not take no for an answer, one could always ignore him.

In November, after the house of cards had tumbled, Francis Rodd wrote about van Hengel that 'my father-in-law observed to me this weekend, after meeting him last week in London, that though he had been quite polite, it must be a fact that he has extraordinary ability to earn any salary at all since it cannot clearly come from personal charm'.[28]

While van Hengel was in Basle seeing McGarrah, Harry Siepmann noted how his own attention to the Austrian crisis and its possible repercussions meant that he 'see so much of the trees that I cannot give you a fair description of the wood'.[29]

That was not van Hengel's problem. His analysis was both insightful and incisive. And focused on the wood. In early June, then, van Hengel envisioned a future where the gold standard would break down. In a way, he had both a narrative and an actionable knowledge but not the means and the power required to do something about it.

Incidentally, at the same time, the German Reichsbank reported to both Harrison and Norman, that the exchange situation was 'very serious' with heavy withdrawals on June 10. 'The withdrawals are very evenly distributed between German banks and there is no sign of any coordinated attack . . . though of course the Americans are on the whole more ruthless than others.'[30]

Two days later, the situation was 'extremely serious' due primarily to withdrawals of foreign credits, Vocke reported to Siepmann. There were no signs yet of any 'important flight of capital from Germany'. The withdrawals happened because of political unrest and the Central European situation, 'in which America does not perhaps make a distinction between the countries that may be involved'.

There were rumours about the Darmstädter und Nationalbank, also known as the Danatbank, but the Reichsbank believed that 'the Darmstädter Bank and the Kommerz Bank are, of all German banks, in the soundest position'.[31]

The day after, on June 13, the Reichsbank raised the discount rate from 5 to 7 per cent. The Austrian crisis' influence was perceived to be clear if indirect, but Brüning's June 6 declaration certainly made things worse in an already fragile environment. On June 19, Ernest Rowe-Dutton, financial adviser to the British Embassy in Berlin, wrote that Brüning's announcement 'very much increased' distress in foreign centres and led to increased withdrawals. The increase in the discount rate had eased the pressure in the short term, but 'it remains to be seen whether a renewed flood of withdrawals will take place at the end of the month or whether confidence will by that date have been sufficiently restored'.[32]

Standing at the crossroads, views differed as to what action to take and who to blame. Everyone agreed about the growing risk of contagion to Germany – Hungary had already been hit – but despite van Hengel's explicit warning and plan for what to do, no one seemed to listen. They were too busy neglecting their own blind spots and focused on the trees in Austria rather than the wood in Germany. And who knew if van Hengel was right anyway?

## THE GUARANTEE, AGAIN

Around the time van Hengel wrote the letter to McGarrah, the situation was growing worse in Austria as well as in Hungary and Germany. In Austria, Viktor Brauneis threatened to resign unless the bond loan was soon placed in Paris and a two-year standstill agreement was reached with the foreign creditors. He also insisted that the internal guarantee for the Credit Anstalt had to be 'satisfactorily cleared up with the Austrian Government'.

Brauneis's demands corresponded well with those of the central bank community, and it was an unfortunate moment for the general director of the Austrian National Bank to step down, but Bruins failed to convince Brauneis to remain in his post. At 11.30 a.m. on Friday, June 12, Bruins called Siepmann at the Bank of England for assistance. There was to be a board meeting at the National Bank at 4 p.m., which left only about four hours to change Brauneis's mind.

Bruins asked Siepmann if the International Committee could announce their willingness to 'stay put for two years of which nobody in Vienna is yet aware'. Siepmann said that though all creditors had in principle agreed, the details were far from worked out, so there was little hope of a binding statement. 'But I would bring the point to the attention of the Committee.'

While on the phone with Siepmann, Bruins told him that Austria's position was snowballing, and all the figures had become 'worse from day to day'. The demand for foreign exchange was increasing, and there was a very strong demand for foreign bank notes, meaning that the public was increasingly fleeing the schilling.[33]

The situation was getting worse in Germany too. Hans Luther cabled Harrison in New York and told him that the Reichsbank was losing large amounts of foreign exchange. It was accelerated by a 'certain political nervousness abroad with concomitant uncertainty concerning reparations problems', and the Austrian crisis, which hit Germany indirectly.

Luther assured Harrison that the German government worked hard to balance the budget and maintain reparation payments. He also pointed out that German banks had little business with Austria and one 'cannot compare Austrian banking situation with that of Germany. Periodical publication of German Banks' statements provide safe means for judging their situation which is sound notwithstanding large foreign withdrawals.'[34]

Norman alerted Harrison to the difficult situation in Germany. He was concerned about politics and increasing uncertainty due to President Hindenburg's emergency decree that allowed Brüning to govern without a majority in the Reichstag. If this affected the German finances, Norman thought that Luther's assessment would have to be at least partly modified, and it 'may force the Reichsbank to adopt measures of stringency without delay. Indeed it seems to me the moment has come'.[35]

Luther, in contrast, claimed that 'the steadiness and stability of the Reich seems to me absolutely firm'.[36] But Norman's call for contractionary policies demonstrated the dilemma of the central banker's worldview, one he shared with Bruins and others. Despite the fact that Europe was in the midst of a banking and currency crisis, not to speak of a social crisis, Norman called for the Reichsbank to tighten monetary policy, just as Bruins and Rodd had called for a reduction of the Austrian note circulation.

This dilemma resulted from the unambiguous acceptance by the epistemic community of central bankers that the gold standard was the pillar of stability that had to be maintained at all costs. Those costs increased as the crisis spread to more countries and as political unrest escalated. Still, in Austria they got some respite, as the board of the Austrian National Bank convinced Brauneis not to resign after all.

Governor Norman had even contacted Brauneis, probably in order to convince him to stay, and Siepmann had let Brauneis know that everyone would be sorry if he resigned, and even though his 'friendship for him would remain the same . . . [he] wonders whether Dr. Brauneis would not expose himself to misunderstandings in doing so and whether he would act in the real interest of his own country'.[37]

The pressure worked. At 5.15 p.m. on June 12, Brauneis called Siepmann for the third time that day and informed him that all the board members of the National Bank had backed him 'in his demand for energetic measures'. As Brauneis had agreed not to resign after all, the Austrian cabinet would meet at 6 p.m. to discuss, once again, the question of an internal guarantee. Brauneis also told Siepmann that the 'attitude of the Government is still not helpful but pressure has been brought to bear upon them from Berlin', and 'Dr. Bruins hopes for a favourable decision'.

At least there was hope. Siepmann noted that 'the news from Paris today is pretty good', and the note circulation was down to 950 million schillings. Indeed, good news was sorely needed. There had been a run on an Austrian savings bank, and the Viennese savings banks in general were preparing themselves for trouble.[38]

Bruins's hopes were soon disappointed. The cabinet meeting would not support an internal guarantee for the schilling deposits of the Credit Anstalt. Finance Minister Juch had explained to Bruins that a guarantee would create a bad psychological impression. A frustrated Bruins complained to Juch. He disagreed about the psychological effects and stressed that any further help from the BIS would be endangered by the Austrian government's failure to enforce a guarantee.

Bruins explained that the guarantee was an absolute precondition for any further assistance to the National Bank's support for the Austrian currency. I have discussed this with you four or five times with and without Mr Rodd present, he noted. Bruins also stressed that 'it is not just a currency question, but also concerns the survival of the Credit Anstalt'.

He emphasized that if the guarantee had been granted in time, the problems would not have reached the current proportions. The resistance against an internal guarantee and the delay in the placement of the Austrian bond loan meant that the Austrian government could no longer count on foreign assistance and support.[39]

The finance minister did not share this view. He had to take a broader view as finance minister, he argued, whereas Bruins as a monetary expert and adviser to the National Bank was not obliged to do so. Juch emphasized the absolute necessity of protecting the currency. He hoped that the treasury loan, which was just about to be placed, and the expected agreement with the foreign creditors would have the necessary psychological impact on the Austrian public.[40]

Having presented his view of the situation, Juch thanked Bruins and the Bank for International Settlements for their support and advice. In short, nothing came of Bruins's letter. Pressure and the sense of urgency were building both inside and outside of Austria together with a feeling among central bankers that maybe they were in over their heads.

## 10

# A World Political Problem (June 11–June 16)

Harrison called Norman twice on June 13. The first time, at 9 a.m., he asked Norman 'how serious he considered the situation in Central Europe and whether, first, there was anything that he thought the Federal Reserve System could do, or, second, anything that the Government might do which would be really and constructively helpful'.[1]

These questions were the direct outcome of the worsening situation in Europe and of discussions at the presidential level in the United States. On June 11 Ogden Mills, the undersecretary of the treasury, had called Harrison 'to advise me of the conversations which he had with the President ... in reference to some sort of postponement of debt payments ... he had told the President that ... sooner or later this question would come up and that we would be drawn into it, ... that our position would be better if we initiated consideration of the matter rather than if we delayed to a point where we were pressed by difficulties or emergencies into an adjustment of our position'.[2]

Given the 'very disturbed conditions' in Central and Eastern Europe, President Hoover wanted to know how the French and the British would respond to an American initiative, and 'how acute conditions in Germany really are'. Mills suggested that Harrison should go abroad to see Norman and Moret. 'Tell him go ahead', Hoover said, but Harrison could not leave and instead called Norman to get a sense of the European situation.

Norman was seriously worried about the situation. On Saturday morning, before Harrison's call, he told Charles Whigham of Morgan Grenfell that the 'Berlin situation is growing dangerous partly on account of internal politics and still more as a result of the Austrian troubles'. He hoped that Kindersley's trip to Vienna might take care of the Credit Anstalt problem, but the treasury loan 'dragged dreadfully and presents great difficulties'. He would be talking to Harrison later that day, he told Whigham.[3] When Harrison called, Norman told him that

> it was difficult to measure the relative seriousness of the position in Vienna, Berlin or Hungary, but that you cannot overestimate the seriousness of the situation of Europe as a whole. He mentioned that the Bank of England, the Federal Reserve Banks and other central banks are trying to deal financially with a situation that involves a world political problem; that our efforts, which he believes we must continue to make, are palliatives only pending some correction of the fundamental difficulties.[4]

Norman's statement was a key turning point in the process of sensemaking and emplotment of the Austrian crisis and the broader European situation. He may have been inspired by an *Economist* editorial published the very same day, arguing that

> To organize effective steps for unravelling the knots of the whole intricate international problem of falling prices, growing debt burdens, fiscal obstacles to trade and obdurate unemployment is the task which statesmen, even more than financial authorities must face during the coming months. The opportunity is great; the penalties of failure may be greater.[5]

Norman pinpointed two important emerging facts. First, it was no longer a question of the possibility of contagion from Austria to other countries. Regardless of cause and effect, Hungary had already crossed the line, and since the Chequers meeting, he and other decision-makers could no longer pretend that Germany's economic situation and the reparations issue could be isolated or controlled.

Second, but closely related, for the first time in relation to the financial crisis, Norman changed the narrative stressing that central banks could not solve a problem that was political and structural at its core. Of course, he had always been aware of the underlying political issues, but with this comment, Norman also, if only indirectly, answered Harrison's two questions. Both the New York Fed and the United States government had a role to play. If only they played it right.

There was nothing new, of course, in the political problems haunting the world, and Norman had made that clear on several occasions. But it was in mid-June, as Germany was hit too, that Norman realized the structural constraints on his and his central bank colleagues' room for manoeuvre and possibilities to act and change the course of the crisis. His 'you and I' statement to Harrison on June 2 was not a relevant blueprint anymore.

That did not mean that the palliatives did not matter, and Norman encouraged Harrison to join the Bank of England and other central banks in the second Bank for International Settlements (BIS) credit. He also presented Harrison with a plan for placing the urgent and politically sensitive treasury loan. Norman wanted it to be split equally between Germany and France, who should each take 75,000,000 schillings. Since Germany did not have that kind of money, New York and London would each underwrite 37.5 million 'as an aid to Germany. This, he says, is very urgent and under this setup Germany would be the beneficiary, or, as he expressed it, we would be "holding the baby" for Germany'.

The Reichsbank was rapidly losing foreign exchange and had increased the discount rate to 7 per cent. Harrison noted that in Norman's 'judgment, the situation was the blackest today of any time yet and that as he saw it it is getting worse. He then mentioned that it was so critical he hoped I would not sail tonight; that there wasn't time to come in view of the fact that anything might break while I was on the water.' Norman then returned to the structural and political issues.

Finally, he explained that unless somebody grasps the problem of reparations and debts we cannot emerge from this mess. I asked him what he meant and he said he thought that the emergency is so great that all reparations and debts should be remitted for five years. He repeated that our financial efforts were merely temporary efforts to deal with a problem that was fundamentally a political one of two categories:

(a) There is a world crisis pending because of the situation in Germany arising out of the problem of debts and reparations;
(b) There is a larger and perhaps more fundamental problem relating to a number of countries, including Germany as well, arising out of the Versailles Treaty which left Austria in an unsound and almost impossible position economically. He believes that the question of debts alone would not settle all of the fundamental problems but that the situation at the moment is so critical that something should be done promptly if possible regarding reparations and debts.[6]

Harrison's question of what 'really and constructively helpful' the United States could do may have contributed to Norman's emphasizing the political and structural elements of the situation. It was a change of narrative with wide-ranging implications in terms of how to make sense of and imagine the future. It was one thing to halt a financial crisis on the basis of Bagehot's operating model and a great deal of improvising. That had proved difficult enough, but dealing with the legacy of the Versailles Treaty was not a task for central bankers.

Norman was overworked but it was not just that. It was a feeling of impotence and inability to change the course of events that jumps out of every sentence in Harrison's notes on this and earlier telephone conversations. Central banks should do their best to try to keep credit flowing and avoid liquidity shocks to the system, but they could not deal with the underlying issues that went all the way back to the Great War and 1919. That was a job for governments.

But one had to try. Norman's suggestion that Germany and France share the Austrian loan was an attempt to reconcile the two countries most locked into conflicting narratives and perceptions of how to deal with them.

Norman confirmed the idea in a telegram telling Harrison that Hans Luther had agreed to the plan for New York and London to underwrite the German part of the Austrian loan. Norman asked Harrison to discuss the plan with J.P. Morgan & Co. and let him know on Monday, June 15, if they were in. 'In that case I shall be responsible for the other half.'[7]

## WE ABSOLUTELY CANNOT AFFORD TO WAIT

As financial contagion in Europe spread and was integrated into a more general narrative emplotment about structural and political obstacles to a solution, the need for exchange of information and new ideas increased. The key central banks intensified communication, and Harrison and Norman in particular resorted to phone calls more frequently than in the early phases of the Austrian crisis. Other central bankers also stepped up their activity.

Governor Clément Moret of the Banque de France informed Harrison on June 13 that 'since the inception of the crisis' the Reichsbank had sold large amounts of gold to Banque de France. Gold leaving Germany put more pressure on the Reichsbank and added to the problems of the imbalances of the gold exchange standard, but it was not something France felt. Moret noted that in 'spite of seriousness of situation our market has so far kept very calm'.[8]

Two days later, on June 15, as the drama of the Austrian crisis was peaking, Moret cabled Harrison that the Reichsbank had sold another 75-million-franc fine gold, bringing the total to just over 1 billion francs. 'There is no change to mention in the attitude of our market. We advise our banks not to withdraw any deposits from Germany nor to cancel any acceptance credits.'[9]

Harrison appreciated the updates about the situation in Paris 'especially as affected by developments in Berlin. We are endeavoring to watch the situation closely and are trying to be helpful here.' He told Moret, that the

New York Fed, too, had acquired gold from Germany – some $64 million since June 1.[10]

At the same time, Harrison corresponded with Luther about developments in Berlin. The New York Fed was anxious to 'do anything that we can to be of help in the present circumstances'. Harrison asked to be kept informed from day to day about changes in the Reichsbank's position, or 'any other developments in the situation in Berlin which might relate to it'.[11]

The correspondence was testament to the increasing tensions and asymmetry of the gold exchange standard. If there had ever been any rules of the game, the illusion was reaching its end. Gold flowed from Germany to France and the United States, both of which held an increasing share of the world's gold reserves. Meanwhile, it put pressure on the deficit countries – Austria, Germany, and Britain to deflate their economies. Together with reparations and war debts, this was part of the structural or fundamental and political problems Norman had pointed out.

On Sunday, June 14, Norman and Harrison were back on the phone. Harrison asked Norman 'whether there was anything new in the situation'. One thing that had not changed over the night was Norman's mood, 'he is still extremely worried about conditions . . . they are as bad as ever they can be'.

Harrison told Norman about a meeting between US Secretary of State Henry L. Stimson and Ramsay MacDonald, the British prime minister in the minority Labour government. Their impression was that Norman wanted to see the effect of the German increase in the discount rate before doing anything.

> Norman said that did not represent his views at all, that 'we absolutely cannot afford to wait,' that the sooner something is done the better. . . . Norman . . . repeated that we cannot afford to wait until the end of next week, that he thinks complete suspension of all intergovernmental debts 'all around the lot' for a period would do more than anything else to turn the situation, but that the first and most important problem at the moment is to raise 150,000,000 schillings for the Austrian government which they in turn have undertaken to pay into the Credit Anstalt. He said that he was speaking to Bruins in Vienna this morning and that Bruins had advised him that unless the money or the promise of it is available tomorrow they probably cannot last until Tuesday and thought that there would then necessarily be a moratorium and likely complete collapse. . . .
>
> In my discussion with Norman about possible debt suspensions I made it clear that I did not know what, if anything, our government could or would do but that I was merely anxious to learn from him, first, whether he thought a suspension of debt payments for even a short period, say even a year or two, would be effective in accomplishing some good, and second, whether, if so, action should be taken at once or whether it might well wait a week. On the first

point he was clear in his opinion that it would do good, and on the second he felt that it was most essential that we should not wait for the end of the week.[12]

Harrison and Norman had been anxious about the economic situation for quite a while. As the fear of transmission to other countries, and Germany in particular, became ever more dominant, they – and Norman in particular – began to construct a narrative of a 'complete collapse'.

It was an act of prospective sensemaking that imagined future economic and political chaos. This narrative enabled navigating uncertainty and ambiguity in the sense that it provided actionable knowledge in relation to their imagined future breakdown. It pointed out who the important decision-makers were and what they had to deal with. It ascribed the root cause to war debts and reparations, thereby intensifying the call for political action. It was not something a central banker could deal with on his own, and there was not much they could do when it came to the underlying political and structural problems.

That was a job for statesmen, as *The Economist* noted. But as central bankers, Harrison and Norman were men of the practical world, and they knew their operating model. Averting a currency crisis was part of their modus operandi. It had to be tried, and that meant a moratorium and contagion must be avoided.

## JAMES GANNON'S PLAN

Norman and Harrison felt the pressure to do whatever they could to stabilize financial markets, and Harrison was in close contact with his government while trying to measure a response to a possible American initiative. Nevertheless, in the very short term, a successful placement of the Austrian loan was essential to avert the renewed risk of a last-moment unilateral Austrian moratorium.

It would soon be too late. The National Bank had to issue its weekly statement on Tuesday, June 16, and that day came to be construed as the one where the house of cards might come down. That gave them two days, not to save the world – that was out of their hands – but to avoid an Austrian moratorium and financial contagion to Germany.

Waiting time was over for Norman, who felt the extreme gravity of the situation. The same sense of urgency was clear at the BIS. At its June 8 meeting, the board had only reluctantly agreed to provide a new credit to the Austrian National Bank, and the BIS officers wanted to speed up the process compared to the first loan. On June 13, McGarrah sent a telegram to Harrison to ask if the Federal Reserve Bank would participate in the credit. The board had consented to the credit on the condition that the bond loan 'appeared to be nearing completion', and 'this condition seems now to be fulfilled', McGarrah wrote optimistically.

The credit would be in gold schilling, an ominous sign that even the BIS and the central banks were no longer confident that Austria would be able to successfully defend the schilling. Even though the telegram was sent from the BIS on Saturday, an answer was requested on Monday, June 15, so the credit could be opened on the same day, just in time.[13]

That Monday, Harrison met with his executive committee and explained the seriousness of the situation. He asked the committee whether the New York Fed should participate in the second credit on the condition that the treasury loan was placed. It could save the situation, but the matter was urgent, and the BIS needed an answer the same day.

Charles Mitchell, whose National City Bank had a large claim on the Credit Anstalt, 'did not think we had any alternative; that we must participate in the credit'. The other members of the committee agreed to participate with up to 10 million schillings. The Committee also agreed to take part in a BIS credit to Hungary, and the Federal Reserve Board agreed as well.[14]

Harrison informed Gates McGarrah about the decision, and he thanked Harrison for this 'splendid cooperation' and noted that with the second BIS credit in place, all 'now depends upon placing Austrian Treasury bills which as you know is important condition attached to our second credit'.[15]

That was a problem. Despite McGarrah's optimism, there had been no progress with the treasury loan since the Morgan firms declined the request to take the lead. Yet, everything was now contingent upon that loan being placed. On June 13, James Gannon, one of the American representatives on the International Committee who had left for Vienna together with Kindersley, cabled Albert H. Wiggin, his boss at Chase National Bank, a plan for how to deal with the situation.

The first step would be to 'stop the immediate breach in the dike by exchanging with Austrian Government the Creditor's Agreements … for the Government guarantee'. That would provide a 'breathing spell' in which to 'compel France and Germany to come together' and share the treasury loan. New York and London should underwrite Germany's half.

If France insisted that the Austro-German customs union was abandoned as a condition for taking part in the loan, this should be made public to the 'world opinion'. Gannon also suggested that Germany's reparation payments should be looked into, and central bank governors in the creditor countries should call a conference of bankers to set up an agreement to continue existing credits in Central Europe unchanged for one year. Gannon believed that the plan would 'certainly go far if not all the way to restore confidence in Europe and America and provide a basis for recovery'.[16]

The idea of splitting the bond issue between France and Germany was identical to the one Norman shared with Harrison the same day, June 13. Gannon and Norman had clearly been in touch on this issue, and the attempt to work with, and put pressure on, France would certainly not have met with resistance from Norman.

Gannon and Norman planned to stress-test France, should she insist on making the Austro-German plan for a customs union part of the negotiations. The plan also accounted for the fundamental and political issues, including German reparation payments, that Norman had emphasized in his talks with Harrison.

Something had to be done about the reparations, and the international creditors to Europe would have to agree to prolong all credits for a year. Whether Gannon's plan could be carried out, let alone restore confidence, was perhaps doubtful as it left out the political side of the equation. But it demonstrated that private bankers, too, were concerned about the Austrian and German situation. And their money.

## BANKERS IN VIENNA

On Monday, June 15, Norman learned from Robert Kindersley that the Austrian National Bank had agreed to abandon the idea of a moratorium 'for the time being'. Kindersley, a director of the Bank of England and chairman of the merchant bank Lazard Brothers & Co., was not optimistic about the situation, but there was still hope.

Norman told Harrison that it was he who had asked Robert Kindersley to go to Vienna, and it was discussed in the International Committee on June 11. Lionel de Rothschild announced that Kindersley had agreed to go to Vienna to see how things were going and to get the agreement straight. According to Rothschild, it was Kindersley who had 'started the ball rolling himself', to which Kindersley replied without much enthusiasm, 'I did not start the idea of my going to Vienna, but I started the idea the thing did want handling.'[17]

At a meeting on Friday, June 12, before Kindersley and Gannon left, cracks were apparent in the façade of international banks' solidarity. The Committee still struggled to keep all Credit Anstalt's creditors in line.

The Ottoman Bank had received a payment from Credit Anstalt on May 29, 'and they flatly refuse to give up this money – 250,000 dollars'. Lionel de Rothschild wanted to put pressure on Ottoman Bank, not least because such free riding could spread. Rothschild asked the meeting if 'any particular bank tries to stick out from this, is not the consortium of the banks strong enough to force them to come in by threatening to do no business with them? Could we not make it so unpleasant for them, that they had to come in?'

No one responded to that question, perhaps feeling a bit uncomfortable about where that kind of thinking might lead. But assuming that some bankers would not get in line, how many signatures were enough for the agreement to be efficient? Was 95 per cent enough?

One representative noted, 'I do not think that this thing will work if we get it signed and say "Subject to ratification by a lot of people afterwards" . . . Sir Robert must be able at some stage to tell them that this list has been ratified and that he was authorized to sign'. That made Kindersley sit up.

> I think that ought to be left free. I am going to do my utmost to get this thing through quickly, but I am not going to sit down and wait while all these creditors are squabbling among themselves. I am not going to sit there for ten days while these people discuss minor details. That is perfectly clear. I am not going to do it for anybody living. I am going there and I am going to try and force this thing through. I know enough about the whole situation to know that if it drags on, it will never go through. I am going to fight them when I am there. We have not the time to wait. I hate going there. My partners very much object to it. . . . Either they have to come in on the broad outline, or I shall take the next train back.[18]

On Friday, June 12, Kindersley and James Gannon travelled to Vienna to try to wrap up the International Committee's agreement with the Austrian government. They stayed at Hotel Bristol at Kärtner Ring next to the opera house and a short five-minute walk from Hotel Sacher, where Rodd stayed. Their task was simple but not easy.

To reach an agreement with the Austrian government and the Credit Anstalt about a guarantee and the terms of a standstill agreement. Quid pro quo. Meanwhile, the two bankers could only hope that their own hinterland would stand behind them rather than free ride. Kindersley's forceful character and deep voice might prove useful.

In fact, the International Committee spent quite some time coordinating the response of the involved creditor banks and avoiding free riding. After the June 12 meeting, the American representatives sent a telegram to Robert F. Loree, a vice president at Guaranty Trust. They emphasized the urgency of the situation and the need to authorize Kindersley and Gannon to sign an agreement with the Austrian government on their behalf. It was

> Absolutely essential that ... Committee can give this authority Tuesday morning early London time. ... Unless unanimous unconditional agreement of all banks immediately obtained bankruptcy of Credit Anstalt must follow at once almost certainly as you have doubtless fully realized involving complete collapse Central European financial structure ... we believe we offer not only the best solution but the only one.[19]

Now, Monday, June 15, with Gannon and Kindersley in Vienna, the endgame was about to begin. They cabled Lionel de Rothschild that the situation in Vienna was 'extremely critical', though they had 'succeeded in postponing declaration of moratorium till Wednesday night'.[20]

Kindersley cabled Norman that the situation was definitely critical not least owing to lack of 'leadership and decision'. They had met with Reisch, Brauneis and Bruins the night before, and learned that the National Bank would declare a moratorium 'because the negotiations with France for foreign loan which appeared to be concluded on Friday have since broken down ... unless 150 million foreign loan arranged within next two days moratorium inevitable'.

Kindersley and Gannon had persuaded the National Bank not to declare a moratorium right away, but that would only work if the treasury loan came through within forty-eight hours. If the loan was placed, it should be possible to hold the position through 'restoration of authority and leadership. ... I cannot too strongly urge you to use every means in your power to press paragraph 2A of Gannon memorandum or any other method.'[21]

Paragraph 2A was the plan to have France and Germany share the treasury loan. Norman immediately informed Harrison of Kindersley's view and stressed that there were only two days to place the Austrian loan and arrange the second BIS loan. If that could not be done, a moratorium would be 'inevitable'.

Kindersley's conditional optimism was qualified by his point that authority and leadership would have to be restored in order to halt the crisis. Five weeks after the outbreak in May, the general opinion among the central bankers involved in the rescue operation seemed to be that a disturbing lack of authority and leadership was the main problem at all levels in Austria.

Norman had been in touch with a number of private and central bankers including S. Parker Gilbert of J.P. Morgan, Charles Whigham of Morgan

Grenfell, Clément Moret of the Banque de France, and some private French bankers, 'but all this takes time', he noted, and he was not particularly encouraged by the talks. Luther had agreed to Gannon's idea, but Norman was 'wondering whether in this urgent and critical position it would be wise to sound out Albert H. Wiggin. What about it', he asked Harrison.[22]

Wiggin was chairman of Chase National Bank, the world's largest bank, and a potentially important player in raising the money for the Austrian loan. Chase National was Credit Anstalt's largest creditor and was believed to hold $120 million German bonds. As Germany entered the picture, Wiggin and Chase's importance increased. Moreover, J.P. Morgan's close connections with France might raise concern in the increasingly intricate negotiations over the Austrian bond loan.[23]

On Monday, June 15, the day before the Austrian threat of a moratorium was believed to take effect, Gannon provided Wiggin with fresh information from Vienna. At 10.15 a.m. he telephoned the text to London from where it was cabled to Wiggin in New York and copied to Norman and Grant.

There were two issues. The first was a threatening cabinet crisis as the socialist party no longer supported the treasury loan and the guarantee plan. The government might fall by Wednesday. It was, therefore, 'of extreme importance we have all consents by Tuesday at latest as Dr. Juch is not unhopeful he can persuade his Cabinet associates to sign prior to upset and we must persuade him to this step'.

The second problem was an 'international moratorium' threatened by the National Bank 'owing to increasing depletion foreign currency reserves'. According to the National Bank, France had agreed to take 'perhaps 80 per cent' of the treasury bonds but withdrew that commitment on Saturday and added political conditions, 'so we are told and believe'. Kindersley and Gannon assured the National Bank that they would do their best to place the treasury loan according to Gannon's point 2A. If they failed, a 'moratorium here would force practical repudiation in all Central European countries at once'. Gannon wrote to Wiggin,

> Summed up, we seem to have just two days to do two jobs to save disaster throughout Europe, the first job to get all consents so as to get our guarantee before this Government falls, the second to get 150,000,000 Schillings before the Bank must declare the moratorium which I agree inevitable otherwise.[24]

After only a few days in Vienna, Kindersley and Gannon realized that politics might well stand in the way of a solution. A lot depended on Paris.

Norman wrote Harrison, 'I now hear Paris requires direct participation of New York and London as well as Berlin, which is entirely suitable as far as I am concerned. I would also conform provisionally to forms and maturities required by Paris because the matter is urgent and needs action now or never.'[25]

Now or never. Since May 11, the sense of urgency had often emerged as a prime motivator for action. This time it was for real. Monday, June 15, was a busy day with a sense of doomsday hanging over it. At 12.45 p.m. Siepmann was on the phone with Lacour-Gayet, the Banque de France official, who explained the 'conditions required by the Paris bankers for the placing of Austrian Treasury Bonds'. According to Lacour-Gayet, the French banks would now only take 40 per cent of the loan and as bills with a maturity of six months and renewable three times.

Also, the League of Nations should conduct an 'enquiry into Austrian Finances', and a few other conditions 'are to be considered by a cabinet meeting this afternoon . . . If the Government agree . . . the matter will be settled so far as the French bankers are concerned'.[26]

That was certainly not 'the market' taking care of things, as preferred by most private bankers. Since before the crisis, politics of all sorts on several levels, but with a shared point of origin in the repercussions of the Great War, had interfered with the central bankers' struggle to contain the Austrian crisis. Separating politics and finance was never easy. Separating politics and finance in 1931 was out of the question.

A few hours later, Siepmann had more news from Paris by way of Charles Whigham of Morgan Grenfell. Whigham sent a memorandum to Siepmann about a meeting in Paris between Nelson Dean Jay, the head of Morgan & Cie, and the general director of Banque de Paris et des Pays-Bas, Horace Finaly. Paribas was the bank around which the hopes for a French lead in the treasury loan centred.

N.D. Jay has seen Finaly and got a very cold douche. Something has undoubtedly happened since last week to change attitude of Paribas. Finaly said situation has now got too big and important for the French banks to get into it alone and at present the matter is really in the hands of the Government. The French banks had had a meeting this morning and written a letter to the Minister of Finance which should be in his hands about 2.30 p.m. outlining the extent to which the banks feel they can co-operate which is an amount much less than 75,000,000 schillings and with very definite security.

Finaly did not at all like the idea of German banks being in for such a large amount as 75,000,000 schillings as everyone knows they are not in a position to deal with such figures. In his opinion New York and London should take their responsibilities direct. He pointed out that New York and London were more interested in Austria and Germany than Paris and therefore they should take an important position and Paris would be willing to co-operate. He would not object to a German participation for a moderate amount.[27]

On a card attached to the memorandum, Whigham wrote, 'Is there anything I can do?' That afternoon at 2.55 p.m. Siepmann sat down and wrote a note summing up the content of Dean Jay's memorandum. 'The French bankers . . . regard the position as now being too big to be handled by banking methods, and they think it should really be referred to governments'.[28] Dean Jay also suggested that perhaps Leith-Ross from the treasury should get in touch with the French treasury.[29] Imagining France as the saviour was getting harder by the hour.

In the middle of the night on June 16, at 3.35 a.m. Francis Rodd sent a telegram to Siepmann, briefly saying that Pierre Quesnay 'is going to Paris to help settle affairs. He will lunch Moreau and can be found care of Farnier. Please secure avoidance complications.'[30]

## WHAT IS THE ANSWER?

In New York, George Harrison could not avoid complications. He had spent the weekend in Washington, where he met with the Secretary of State Henry Stimson, the Undersecretary of the Treasury Ogden Mills, the Governor of the Federal Reserve System Eugene Meyer, and President Herbert Hoover.

Stimson had heard that Germany would soon postpone reparations payments, the French would accept a temporary suspension and 'will in turn make prompt use of the suspension clause in the Mellon–Berenger agreement'.[31] The Mellon–Berenger agreement was negotiated in 1926. It eased the terms and payments of France's war debts to the United States but was still unpopular in France.

Stimson's information came from Lacour-Gayet and reached Stimson through Russell C. Leffingwell, the J.P. Morgan partner. Even though they had 'hired the money', as former President Calvin Coolidge is reported to have said, France would suspend payments on its war debt to the United States if Germany ceased to pay reparations.

Any hope of isolating the Austrian problem from Germany and the more fundamental issues was falling apart. It was one big melting pot, and cause and effect were indeed hard to emplot into a coherent story, as Norman had told Harrison two weeks earlier. In fact, everything was coming together in what seemed like the perfect storm. Radical uncertainty meant that the outcomes were completely unpredictable, but Norman and his colleagues certainly imagined the worst. From the perspective of the central bankers and the International Committee, everything depended on whether they could dodge an Austrian moratorium that would stop the wheels of the international financial machinery, break the gold standard and endanger capitalism.

Wiggin and some other American bankers were hardly aware of the rumours, and though they too struggled to make sense of the situation as it moved closer to Germany, they did not quite understand the gloomy messages. Wiggin believed that 50 million of the Austrian loan could be 'handled here', but he confessed to Gannon that 'New York banks do not share your opinions of far-reaching effect of non-success. Are your convictions as strong as in today's message', he asked and continued that 'banks here naturally ask why not let all creditors wait instead of raising funds to pay off part of them. What is the answer?'[32]

It is not clear who Wiggin referred to as being paid off. The bond loan was a government loan of which 100 million schillings was supposed to be paid into the Credit Anstalt as new capital. How Credit Anstalt intended to use the funds were, of course, anybody's guess, but the critical point was that the foreign exchange would end up at the National Bank.

From their vantage point, some American bankers were unconvinced that there was reason for so much concern about Europe. Whether this was due to a difference in perception or in access to information or both, it exposed diverging expectations about the future among the actors.

In Europe, they certainly feared far-reaching effects, and Gannon who was on the ground in Vienna, made it clear to Wiggin that we 'firmly maintain our opinion regarding far-reaching effect and add following explanation for you'. The explanation emphasized that the National Bank's cover ratio had fallen from 85 to 54 per cent. If the loan was not placed on June 16 at the latest, the National Bank's statement would show a loss of $15 million withdrawn by the public since the last weekly statement.

> This in our view with which Bruins and Rodd advising National Bank agree would create a panic to guard against which the National Bank will insist on internal moratorium. We are all satisfied that latter contingency would involve not only this country but neighboring countries in financial collapse.[33]

It is not clear if Gannon managed to convince Wiggin, but the difference in meanings assigned to the situation, and the increasing uncertainty was difficult to navigate and deal with. The catastrophe narrative had in any case been locked in and now framed the outlook. Now as before, time was the critical factor.

The challenge was twofold. First, there was the practical issue of getting information about the negotiations in Paris and the details of the bond loan and so on. There was also a meaning loss about the general situation in Europe. It would be bad, yes, but what exactly would a failure to place the treasury loan mean?

Meantime, in Austria there were concerns about the solvency of the National Bank. On June 15, the day before the next statement would have to be published, the National Bank's board, the 'Generalrat', warned against the risk to the National Bank's capital posed by the Credit Anstalt's rediscounting which had now reached 523 million schillings.[34]

The strong warning from the board contributed to the National Bank's wish to introduce a moratorium immediately. The statement and the plans for a moratorium may also have been intended to put pressure on the BIS and other central banks, but in any case, the situation now seemed so obviously critical that inaction was no longer an option.

Nevertheless, the Austrian government's reluctance to cooperate continued. Bruins had complained to Juch on June 12, but the finance minister's response and continuing resistance to guarantee Credit Anstalt's internal deposits only added to Bruins's and Rodd's frustration. On Tuesday, June 16, this frustration grew to new heights, and Bruins wrote an indignant letter to Juch.

The evening before there had been a meeting in the finance ministry where Kindersley and Gannon had also been present. As they discussed an internal guarantee, Juch claimed that a Mr Schüller had returned from a visit to the BIS in Basle and told Juch the BIS no longer required an internal deposit guarantee. Late Monday evening, Rodd therefore cabled McGarrah and asked him to send yet again the telegram that Otto Juch had already received twice that 'the guarantee . . . is an absolute and necessary condition for the support from the BIS'.[35]

McGarrah cabled Juch that the BIS still considered it necessary to introduce the guarantee for domestic deposits.[36] Bruins noted, 'I fully support this statement.' He ended his letter saying, 'I would very much appreciate to receive your definitive decision concerning this as soon as possible.'[37]

While it seemed more or less impossible to make the government guarantee Credit Anstalt's schilling deposits, an agreement with the International Committee was finally signed in the eleventh hour on Tuesday, June 16, by the International Committee, Credit Anstalt, and the Austrian government.

Kindersley had 'shown his teeth' and declared that if the agreement was not signed, 'the credit of the government and of the country would be done for permanently', and 'no foreign banker would ever lend anything to Austria again whatever happened'.[38] Two brief telegrams from members of the International Committee spread the news to the United States:

Please advise all banks Austrian guarantee covering foreign creditors signed today. Austrian Government expected to fall at any moment probably this afternoon.[39]

Please advise all banks Credit Anstalt has also signed agreement which is now on its way to London by airmail. Austrian Government fell a few minutes ago all of which proves urgent necessity of committees prompt action this morning.[40]

The agreement was signed at the very last moment. On June 22, Lionel de Rothschild announced that the agreement 'is now in operation, and it will consequently now be in order for you to resume all Banking operations with the Credit Anstalt'.[41]

The agreement between Credit Anstalt and the International Committee covered total foreign credits of $71 million of which $51 million were granted by American and British banks.[42] With that, the first big issue was taken care of. What was left was the now five-week-old issue of how the Austrian government would find the funds to inject new capital into the Credit Anstalt. Where and how to place?

Most actors agreed that a failure of the Credit Anstalt would lead to financial disaster in Central Europe and, through contagion, the rest of the world. From the perspective of the central bankers and many other actors, the future was at stake.

There was not much time left to save that future, however. On June 16, at 10.45 a.m. Siepmann received a phone call from Lacour-Gayet who confirmed that discussions about the loan were still ongoing in Paris. Asked if there was any news from London about participation, Siepman said, 'Nothing since last night.' Next up was a phone call from Quesnay, who was at Banque de France. Quesnay told Siepmann that

he is counting upon us to provide Sch. 50 millions in cash to-day . . ., provided that things go well in Paris and the B.I.S. puts up its 100 millions. I told Monsieur Quesnay that he must not count upon anything of the kind. It seemed to me that the right people to provide the cash, perhaps by way of 30 day advance, are the private bankers who take the Treasury Bonds. Monsieur Quesnay asked me to communicate with Dr. Bruins on the subject.[43]

## HER MAJESTY'S GOVERNMENT

A few days earlier in London, on Friday, June 12, the Austrian minister to Great Britain had paid a visit to the British Treasury, where he saw the Chancellor of the Exchequer, Philip Snowden. The minister, Baron Franckenstein, appealed for assistance in the negotiations about the Austrian bond sale. Afterwards, Snowden, a social radical free trader and fiscal orthodox believer in central bank independence, wrote to Montagu Norman,

> I feel it only right to let you know that H.M. Government are deeply concerned at the dangers of the present crisis in Austria, which may at any moment disturb the stability of Germany and other countries in Central and Eastern Europe, and I need hardly emphasise to you the great importance in the public interest of providing financial assistance to Austria without delay. I feel sure that you will take any steps that may be possible to secure the provision of such assistance.[44]

Snowden's letter cannot have been entirely unexpected. On the same day, Charles Whigham of Morgan Grenfell wrote to Baron Franckenstein about the efforts to place the Austrian loan. 'I have discussed the matter with the Governor of the Bank of England who suggests that owing to the particular nature and reason of your Government's requirements you should first of all ascertain the attitude of the Chancellor of the Exchequer.'[45]

Norman shared Snowden's concern about the grave dangers of contagion and the stability of Europe if the Austrian crisis was not halted. He was also deeply concerned about the risk of a moratorium, which in his view amounted to the same thing. And they were both Francophobic and probably wouldn't mind standing in the way of the French. The many signs that the crisis was already crossing the borders to Austria's neighbours contributed to the sense of urgency.

Germany was losing foreign exchange daily, and in Hungary the situation had been worsening for a while, as Rodd reported from Budapest in early June.[46] The BIS decided to extend a credit to Hungary, since it 'appears to us that it is a matter of first importance to assist in every way possible in maintaining the gold standard in those countries where it has been adopted'.[47]

Norman could hardly ignore Snowden's appeal to intervene in Austria by 'any steps that may be possible'. If he needed a legitimization for acting, Snowden's letter provided it on a silver platter, and maybe that is why he sent Franckenstein to Snowden. Siepmann may also have envisioned a situation like this at the BIS board meeting a week earlier, when he asked if an individual central bank could take action. They now had the actionable knowledge, the fictional expectation and imagined future narrative necessary. It was time to make a decision and act.

On Tuesday, June 16, at 1 p.m. Siepmann wrote in a note that 'the Bank of England proposes to transfer to-day to the credit of the Austrian National Bank with the B.I.S. the equivalent, in various currencies of Sch. 150 millions'.[48]

The note laid out five premises on which this proposal was based: (1) The treasury loan could not be successfully closed within the deadline; (2) The second BIS credit is contingent upon the treasury loan being placed; (3) The National Bank's next statement would show a loss of about 100 million schillings in foreign exchange. This would lead to a general moratorium in Austria; (4) The new foreign exchange was needed to allow the National Bank to initiate immediately 'detailed programme of currency contraction'; (5) Without new foreign exchange the Austrian National Bank would 'refuse to rediscount any further paper for the Credit Anstalt.'

Thus, around noon on June 16, the Bank of England decided to intervene in order to avoid a moratorium and breakdown of the Austrian financial system, leading to further contagion outside of Austria. The decision was communicated to Bruins at the National Bank Tuesday night, and a copy was sent to McGarrah, who received it on Wednesday, June 17, at 8.40 a.m. The telegram set out some of the same premises and conditions as Siepmann's memo and stated, 'The Bank of England have therefore decided to transfer to-day to the credit of the Austrian National Bank with the BIS the equivalent in various currencies of schillings 150,000,000'.[49]

The loan was provided on the conditions that the money would be advanced for one week at a time at the Austrian bank rate. It would be treated as an 'advance to the Austrian Government in anticipation of the placing of the treasury bonds'. The government would also have to appoint 'one individual who will be responsible for negotiating and placing the bonds', and of the proceeds 100 million schillings should be used to provide the government's injection of new capital into the Credit Anstalt.[50]

In the British Foreign Office, someone wrote in hand on a copy of Snowden's letter to Norman that the 'answer took the form of an immediate advance to the Credit Anstalt'.[51] That was not precise, and Norman would hardly have appreciated the framing. Nevertheless, though the loan was paid to the credit of the National Bank, it was actually made to the Austrian government and two-thirds of it would end up on the Credit Anstalt's balance sheet as share capital.

It was not what Norman – or anyone else – had imagined, but, given his narrative of the situation, he now saw no other way. The loan was meant as a short-term emergency bridge loan, a palliative, at a time when no one else could or would do anything. It was a decisive demonstration of authority and leadership at the very last minute by Montagu Norman and the Bank of England.[52] Perceived self-interest was certainly involved. The loan would ease some of the pressure on sterling and on British banks who were creditors to Austrian and not least German banks. And, again, Norman may have appreciated the opportunity to snub the French.

As the crisis moved closer to Germany, it also became a threat to financial stability in Great Britain, and Norman had no illusions about the worst-case scenario if the house of cards fell. As the whole situation seemed to have reached a complete impasse, it was not the financially stronger American or French governments or central banks that stepped in. It was, in fact, Norman and the Old Lady at Threadneedle Street that construed a narrative stressing the acute need for action and acted, despite, or because of, a much weaker financial position than America and France.

Thus, the bridge loan of 150 million schillings to the Austrian government by way of the BIS and the National Bank was more than pure self-interest. To Norman, the loan concerned nothing less than rescuing the gold standard, the European economy and by implication Western Civilization, with Great Britain at the centre.[53]

The British central bankers sensed the necessity of averting the impasse, and Siepmann had prepared the ground at the BIS board meeting. Snowden's letter was significant in legitimizing what from the perspective of Norman and the Bank of England had to be done.

The planning and negotiations for the placement of the Austrian government loan had dragged on since May 12 when Francis Rodd first arrived in Vienna. Things had intensified dramatically in the week following the BIS board meeting, and despite many rumours, hopes, emotional fallouts and disappointed expectations, no definite progress had been made; quite the contrary, as a matter of fact. On June 16, the very same day that Norman stepped in with a loan, the placement of the Austrian treasury loan failed decisively.[54]

## TO SAVE THE SHIP BEFORE SHE SINKS

As George Harrison woke up in New York on Tuesday, June 16, he was, as always, six hours behind continental Europe. If he read the *New York Times* with his breakfast, he could be excused for believing that things were on track to a solution. The paper reported that 'it is virtually certain that a consortium of Paris credit institutions, backed by the Bank of France, will assume the placing of 150,000,000 schillings in fairly long-term Austrian Treasury bonds'.[55] In a sign of a renewed focus on the situation in Germany, the *Times* stressed,

> There is an impression in financial circles here that the French move to save the Austrian financial situation will react with substantial force on the whole Central European situation and, above all, on the German crisis. The difficulties of the Creditanstalt, while carrying no direct reflection on German finance and economy, nevertheless played a big role in the precipitation of the present German crisis. If public confidence in Austria can be restored it is the opinion in Paris that a great service will likewise be done to Germany.[56]

Harrison only learned about the Bank of England's loan to the Austrian government when he called Norman to ask if there was 'anything new in the situation over there, especially as respects Austria'.

Norman initially seemed as much in the dark as Harrison. 'He told me that the position in Vienna is still very uncertain . . . and he know nothing of the results of the negotiations . . . in Paris'. The same morning, Norman had talked with Kindersley and Bruins, who were very concerned about the situation. If the bond loan was not raised the same day and the second BIS loan ready the day after, a moratorium would be declared on Thursday, June 18. And then he broke the news to Harrison.

> If this is done both Kindersley and Bruins think it will likely spread to adjoining countries, possibly including Germany as well. Governor Norman said that he considered the situation so serious and so critical that on the advice of Kindersley and Bruins (somewhat on the insistence of Kindersley) the Bank of England, at a special meeting this afternoon, decided that the situation would not wait for the placement of the Treasury bonds and that, therefore, the Bank of England had of its own account advanced 150,000,000 schillings to the Austrian government as of today, instructing the B.I.S. to pay over to the Austrian Government, through the Austrian National Bank a total of 150,000,000 of which £1,450,000 is in French francs, £1,450,000 in dollars, and £1,450,000 in Sterling. Governor Norman explained that this transaction was in the nature of an emergency short-time advance to the government in an effort to avoid a crisis in Central Europe, and that the Bank of England hopes that this will afford the Austrian government some time to turn around and to negotiate for the sale of its bonds, the proceeds of which should be paid over to the Bank of England to recoup the short-time advance.[57]

In the Bank of England's rendering of the conversation, Norman explicitly argued that in order to 'avoid a moratorium it was necessary to have the money in their hands which has been done. . . . We thus become short creditors of the Austrian Government for the total of £4,350,000 (the equivalent of 150 million Austrian Schillings). We have done this unwillingly but because we believe that otherwise there would be a moratorium in Austria which would be quickly followed by a similar action in the adjoining countries and probably in Germany as well.'

Norman said that he hoped that the Austrian bond loan would soon be placed and that Harrison was the first person to be informed about the Bank of England's action. Norman also asked Harrison to 'induce his Market to relieve the Bank of this commitment; the Governor had gone in to save the situation but he could not contemplate carrying the investment permanently'.[58]

Norman also told Harrison that according to Kindersley, the 'situation can be held' if the bond loan and the second BIS loan came through. Harrison was less certain:

> I said in this connection that the New York bankers in discussing the situation in New York this morning raised the question whether this money would do the trick. Governor Norman said as to that only time will tell. . . . Norman . . . said that . . . he hopes our market will be induced to take up some long-time bonds when arranged. I told him that one of the difficulties in interesting our market in the last few days had been the fact that there is no definite negotiator on behalf of the Austrian government and no knowledge of terms, conditions, or circumstances adequate to enable any one here to form a judgment. Governor Norman sympathized with this and said that the Austrian government was going to appoint a negotiator at once to arrange for the loan in the different markets and I imagine from what he said that he himself would nominate the negotiator.[59]

Before ending the conversation, they briefly touched upon the situation in Germany. On the same day, they had learned from Luther that 'the emergency decree to affect a balance of the budget will go into effect and it assures the stability of Cabinet Brüning. I hope that this decision will bring about considerable relief in Germany's credit situation.'[60]

This led Norman to tell Harrison that the political situation had eased a little; but in spite of Luther's hopes he was less optimistic about the financial position, which was serious. If the withdrawal of foreign exchange continued in Germany, it would become a real threat to the financial position. Norman then returned to Austria and said that 'what had been done was a final effort "to save the ship before she sinks"'.[61]

In Austria, the Cabinet stepped down as a result of the government guarantee of foreign creditors' claims. Interior minister Franz Winkler would not 'consent to let the State assume such heavy liabilities on behalf of foreign capital'. Two different narratives were at play, as the *New York Times* reported.

The situation as it appears to foreign creditors differs notably from that presented to the Austrian public. The statement has been repeatedly made in Austrian newspapers that American bankers, by withdrawing all their short-term credits, had aggravated the present difficulties of the Credit Anstalt. . . . Your correspondent understands however, that since May 27, when the Austrian Government asked foreign creditors to continue their loans in return for the promise of a guarantee of the bank's liabilities, not a single American dollar . . . was to be taken out of the Creditanstalt.

Where Austrian newspapers have been asserting that foreign creditors having obtained a Government guarantee, had failed to provide new credits for the Creditanstalt, the position of foreign creditors is this – that while they invest every dollar, pound, guilder and franc of their loans in the bank, its Austrian depositors have been drawing these out in schillings, so that the bank no longer has the means to repay its short-term creditors.

While the foreign creditors have been using the prospect of financial quarantine for years to come as their bargaining factor, the government has been urging the danger of further crashes in Europe if the Creditanstalt . . . were allowed to perish, as its main argument.[62]

Norman was not bothered by self-doubt about his actions. He had done what needed to be done, and now he wanted to make sure that the money would serve their purpose. Two days after the Bank of England loan was made, he cabled Bruins. 'Now that the means are at your disposal I think it essential that you should proceed immediately with your programme of currency contraction. Do you believe that the execution of this programme will enable the National Bank to be in complete command of the monetary situation within ten days?'[63]

## 11

# Francis Rodd Makes Sense – and a Plot (June 9–June 20)

Norman and Harrison continued working to save the world as the crisis spread to Germany, but Francis Rodd's role as lead actor in the Austrian crisis was coming to an end. As director of the BIS's Central Banking Department, he had spent most of his waking hours since May 12 in Vienna and Basle working hard to make sense of the Austrian crisis and trying to contain it. At times during the five weeks, he had been cautiously optimistic about halting the crisis from spreading to other banks and countries, but the week between the Bank for International Settlements (BIS) board meeting and June 16 had been frustrating beyond his imagination. The way Rodd and his fellow central bankers saw it, international financial stability had been at stake.

The placement of the Austrian loan had failed miserably, and it was only because of the agreement between the Austrian government and the Creditor's Committee, and Norman's last-minute intervention that an imminent disaster was avoided. How was it possible that even as the world economy seemed to hang in the balance, it had not been possible to avoid such a cliffhanger?

For Rodd, the breakdown of the negotiations about the government loan was the exasperating climax of more than a month's stubborn effort to implement the plan he had developed on his first day in Vienna on May 12. It didn't go that way, and he felt a deep urge to make sense of the events of the last five weeks by telling his story.

On Saturday, June 20, back in Basle, he pulled the final page of a seventeen-page memo from the typewriter.

The memo was Rodd's compelling version of what had happened since June 8. It was also a fascinating piece of retrospective sensemaking, where uncertainty about the future was finally turned into present certainty, at least from Rodd's perspective. All the events, actions and actors, and perceived causes and effects called for emplotment; the ordering of a myriad of events, actors, decisions and actions into a coherent narrative that provided a clear understanding of what had happened why, who was to blame and who to celebrate. It was an act of sensemaking that framed these events into a specific narrative and way of understanding that final dramatic week of the Austrian crisis.

## RODD'S MEMORANDUM

Rodd had twelve copies of the memorandum made and sent to, among others, Gates McGarrah, Robert Kindersley, James Gannon, Gijsbert Bruins, Harry Siepmann and Walter Stewart. Of the six remaining copies Rodd wanted to send one to Alexander Loveday, director of the financial section at the League of Nations, Eric Phipps, the British minister to Vienna, and Ernst Hülse at the German Reichsbank.

It was personal now. All the hard work Rodd had done and the optimism about the success of the rescue operation that it had fed were in shatters. Rodd had no doubt whatsoever who the villains were: the French with the Austrians in the role of supporting actor.

Rodd wanted to make sure that his version of the events would be known and available for posterity. When he sent his memorandum to Kindersley on June 22, he wrote, 'I enclose a copy of my note on the events which culminated with the Bank of England credit for 150 million schillings on Tuesday evening.'[1]

This is Francis Rodd's story.[2]

Basle, June 20, 1931

Memorandum

This memorandum covers the period since the date of the Board Meeting of the Bank for International Settlements held on June 8th.

The Austrian financial representative in Paris commenced negotiations on Tuesday the 9th with the Banque de Paris et de Pays Bas. The principal subject under discussion at the time with the French bankers was the nature of the security, if any, which would be provided by the Austrian Government for the Treasury Bill issue. The Austrians gave the French a note of their legal position showing the difficulties in the way of pledging any security without the consent of a number of other parties. The French Minister in Vienna on Thursday was not satisfied that the Austrian demarches were being seriously pressed. The dilatoriness of the Austrians, and the legal difficulties disclosed in the Austrian note had given him the impression that the Austrian Government was not taking up the question in Paris very seriously. He was inclined to send a telegram to Paris saying that the dilatoriness was deliberate.

Professor Bruins and myself had seen the Chancellor on Thursday evening at 8 o'clock, and had urged upon him the necessity of pushing the negotiations in Paris with the utmost fervor, and of providing the guarantee required by the B.I.S. on the internal schilling depositors of the Credit-Anstalt. Both these points had been taken up by Professor Bruins and myself with the Finance Minister both on Wednesday and on Thursday, without very much success. When we heard of the attitude of the French Minister we arranged to see him late on Thursday night with Mr. Rodenbach, in order to dissuade him sending the proposed telegram to Paris. After explaining the position to him and undertaking to get the Chancellor to send a message to the Austrian Minister in Paris that he was to use every effort to conclude the negotiations successfully, the French Minister promised to send an alternative telegram to the Quai d'Orsay urging that, whatever might be the apparent attitude of the Austrians, it was essential to find the money in order to avoid serious difficulties. And this he did. On the next day, Friday, the British Minister in Vienna not only telegraphed in similar tone to the Foreign Office, but also placed himself in direct touch with Lord Tyrrell in Paris, who on that day saw M. Berthelot and impressed upon him the urgency of a quick decision. The effect of the communications made by the French Minister in Paris was apparently to satisfy the French bankers and the French Government that the objections to the pledges raised in the Austrian Note were reasonable, that the Austrians really needed the funds, and that instead of a guarantee only a form of negative pledge could be obtained whereby the issue of 150 million schillings Treasury Bills could be coupled with an undertaking that the Austrian Government would only issue such a lesser amount of the second tranche of the 1930 Loan as, with the amount of Treasury Bills, would make up the total of the tranche envisaged. The effect of this was to leave part of the revenues pledged to the second tranche of the 1930 Loan free to cover the Treasury Bills issue. Although no direct pledge for the bills could be given, the availability of some of the revenues for the 1930 Loan might be held to provide some sort of assurance.

On Friday night the 12th of June, we were informed by Paris that the negotiations with the French bankers on the terms of the issue of the Treasury Bills had, for all intents and purposes, been completed and only the final approval of the French Government remained.

But in the meanwhile, the week's delay in placing the Treasury bills had created increasing nervousness in Vienna and withdrawals of foreign exchange from the Central Bank were going on at an alarmingly heavy rate. It moreover transpired in the Press that the B.I.S. credit promised by the Board Meeting on June 8th was tied up with the placing of the bills.

On Saturday morning, June 13th, we were informed both from Paris directly and also through the Austrian Ministry of Finance that the Paris bankers had received news from Austria of such an alarming nature that they were now unwilling to proceed with the issue of the bills except in connection with a loan to be guaranteed like the 1924 Loan by the larger Powers. This alarming news was said to have been given by the Länder Bank to their Paris friends. The terms which were proposed on Saturday morning may be summarized as follows:

> The bills to be six month bills at par renewable three times, for a total period, therefore, of two years, bearing interest at 6 per cent., the Austrian Government to pay all the expenses, bringing the net cost of the money to them up to about 7½ per cent. It was understood that the French bankers would take a figure which was variously given as 80 million schillings, or as 80 per cent. of the issue, but only on condition that the bills were converted into a long term loan to be guaranteed by the Powers which guaranteed the 1924 Loan. The bankers were willing to act if the French Government undertook to recommend a guarantee on its own behalf, without however waiting for similar guarantees to be given by other Powers, it being presumably understood that the French guarantee of a part of the long term loan would cover such part of the bills to be converted into a long term loan as would be placed in Paris. The Austrian Government was to get into touch with the League of Nations about the issue of such a loan.

It was further understood at this time that participations in the bill operation would have to be found in London and elsewhere as the Paris bankers were only willing to take a part and probably not more than half the issue of 150 million schillings. Whatever amount they took the Paris bankers were unwilling to proceed without foreign and apparently especially without a London participation.

In the course of conversation which took place on Sunday, it appeared that the participation of the French bankers even upon the conditions stated was gradually diminishing, but it was understood that the French Government was considering the question of a guarantee.

The withdrawals of foreign exchange from the Central Bank by the five principal banks in Vienna up to and including Monday, June 15th, are interesting reading. In total the five banks since the beginning of the crisis had withdrawn 343 million schillings of which, of course, the largest amount, namely, 142 million schillings, was withdrawn by the Credit-Anstalt between the beginning of the crisis and Saturday, June 6th, inclusive. This was accounted for by withdrawals of foreign deposits before the Creditors' Committee was formed and the cashing in of valuta Kassenscheine. From June 8th onwards the Credit-Anstalt withdrawals of foreign exchange were comparatively moderate considering the position of the Bank; they amounted in all to 28.7 million schillings. The Wiener Bankverein, which was known to have lost and be losing foreign deposits had, by June 15th, withdrawn 56 million schillings, of which 15.4 were between the 8th and the 15th inclusive. The N.O. Escompte Gesellschaft had up to June 6th inclusive withdrawn 24.5 million schillings, but since that date had actually received foreign devisen on balance, the net plus being 1.6 million schillings, between June 8th and 15th inclusive. The other two large banks concerned are both banks either directly under French influence or having French sympathies; they are the Länder Bank and the large and active branch in Vienna of Zivnostenska Banka of Prague. The direct foreign commitments of the Länder Bank at the beginning of the crisis were known to be small. Nevertheless, by June 15th this bank had withdrawn 50.5 million schillings of devisen, of which 17.5 were withdrawn between June 8th and 15th, being the largest amount withdrawn in this period by any Bank in Vienna with the exception of the Credit-Anstalt. It is of course well known that this Bank has behind it the Banque de Pays de l'Europe Centrale in Paris. Demands by the Länder Bank for foreign exchange from the Austrian National Bank may therefore be considered wholly improper in the present circumstances. The Zivnostenska Banka in the period under review withdrew 25 million schillings of which 9 million between June 8th and 15th. It is a matter of interest that half way through May the Zivnostenska Banka had asked a prominent American Bank for the terms upon which the American Bank could take a deposit of no less than 18 million dollars. It is therefore clear that the Vienna Branch of the Zivnostenska Banka had no business to call upon the Austrian National Bank for devisen.

To return to the position in Vienna, while the negotiations with the bankers in Paris were reaching an impasse owing to their demand for the guarantees of other Governments for a loan into which the Treasury Bills were to be converted, Sir Robert Kindersley and Mr. Gannon representing the International Creditors' Committee in London had left for Vienna, where they arrived at 5 o'clock on Sunday the 14th. The situation they found on arrival was that the delays in placing the bills abroad and the fact that the B.I.S. credit was coupled with the successful prospects of this operation, combined with the losses of foreign exchange by the Austrian Bank which between Monday, June 8th, and Saturday, June 13th, had amounted to 99 million schillings, produced a situation which could not continue. The Austrian National Bank had therefore decided that at the Generalrat of the Bank, which was due to be held at 10 o'clock of the morning of Monday the 15th, a request would have to be made to the Ministry of Finance for an internal Moratorium. Some credit restriction on rediscounting had already been practiced, but owing to the impossibility of securing immediate results from these and other steps which I had discussed at the Governors' meeting on June 7th, it was felt by the National Bank that it was imperative to stop rediscounting altogether in order to avoid further losses in foreign exchange, in other words, to prevent withdrawals by the public from banks by declaring an internal Moratorium. The National Bank felt that another week of 100 million schillings loss, without any progress in the direction of getting new foreign devisen, would place them in a position in which they would be unable to maintain the stability of the currency. A credit restriction policy, with the existence of the Credit-Anstalt leak, and of the Wiener Bankverein withdrawals, not to speak of the Länder Bank and Zinovstenska Banka policy, could clearly only operate slowly. The dilatoriness of the Austrian Government in giving the guarantee on the Credit-Anstalt internal deposits which the National Bank, in company with Professor Bruins and myself had been urging for a fortnight, had of course accentuated the difficulties.

When, therefore, Sir Robert Kindersley and Mr. Gannon arrived they were faced with the situation that a moratorium was likely to be recommended by the board of the National Bank on Monday morning to the Ministry of Finance. On the other hand, the agreement between the International Committee and the Austrian Government, whereby the latter undertook to guarantee the foreign deposits if they were left with the Credit-Anstalt for two years, had not yet been signed. The prospects of a signature became altogether remote if a moratorium were declared on Tuesday morning.

A meeting held in Dr. Brauneis' house, attended by President Reisch, Vice-President Thaa, Dr. Brauneis, Sir Robert Kindersley, Mr. Gannon, Professor Bruins, Mr. van Hengel and myself at 9.30 p.m. on Sunday night did not produce any results except a statement from Sir Robert Kindersley and Mr. Gannon that they would do their best to impress upon London, New York and Paris the urgent necessity of placing the 150 million Schillings' worth of bills, and a declaration by Sir Robert Kindersley that the proclamation of an internal moratorium would not only have a disastrous effect upon Austrian credit for some time, but would also bring about a collapse in neighbouring countries. He urged the postponement of a decision about the moratorium pending negotiations in Paris and London, but he added that if it were decided to proceed with a moratorium, the foreign creditors would undoubtedly take appropriate steps.

Sir Robert Kindersley and Mr. Gannon had their first meeting with the Minister of Finance on Monday morning at 10 o'clock, followed by a later meeting on Monday night. A draft agreement which they had brought out gave rise to certain difficulties in negotiations, but by Monday night it appeared that there were reasonable prospects of signature. It had, however, been necessary in order to produce the right atmosphere, for such an optimistic attitude to be taken up by Professor Bruins at the Board Meeting at the National Bank on Monday morning, that the directors decided to postpone the discussion of the moratorium until Tuesday afternoon at 6 o'clock. There were two factors which made this possible. The first was an indication by Sir Robert Kindersley that Governor Norman was doing his best to secure the placing of the bills in one form or another in Paris, London and New York; the other was a message from M. Farnier on Sunday that he hoped that a decision would be reached not later than Tuesday night.

Professor Bruins therefore declared to the board and a communiqué in that sense was published, that he had had information that good progress had been made towards placing the bonds and that he hoped to have an answer on Tuesday. A discussion of the moratorium proposal was therefore postponed and after a defeatist statement by Vice-President Thaa, the Board proceeded to discuss the credit restrictions measures proposed by Professor Bruins. The Board decided to raise the discount rate to 7½ per cent and to accept the proposals which Professor Bruins had put forward.

The Board Meeting broke up at 2 o'clock noon June 15th in a more optimistic frame of mind, and the National Bank conveyed this feeling of optimism to the Ministry of Finance. This undoubtedly had considerable bearing on the attitude of the latter towards the International Committee's guarantee agreement. On the night of Monday-Tuesday at 1 a.m., Sir Robert Kindersley and Mr. Gannon informed me that they hoped to have the agreement definitely signed at noon on Tuesday.

We remained without news of the Paris negotiations on Monday except that we were told that the bankers having decided upon their conditions were now awaiting a decision of the French Government regarding the guarantee of a long term loan. On this day, however, their participation had apparently been reduced to about 40–50 million schillings, or only about 30 per cent. It was also on this day that M. Lacour-Gayet enquired of Mr. Siepmann whether if Paris only took 30 per cent. of the issue it was permissible to assume that London would not take 60 per cent. [the implication being that it was difficult for the Paris bankers to make onerous conditions for so small an amount of the total if the balance were placed in London. The bearing of M. Lacour-Gayet's telephone message to Mr Siepmann, and that of M. Farnier to us in Vienna, urging upon us to postpone a decision upon the moratorium until late on Tuesday night, since a decision from Paris could probably not be received before midnight, become clear when the developments of Tuesday are considered.]

In the course of Monday the Minister of Finance informed us that he understood from the Austrian representative in Paris that the delay of the French Government in making up their minds about the issue of the bills in Paris was due to certain conditions of political nature which they wished to make. The conditions in question had, however, not been brought to his knowledge.

On Monday the losses of foreign exchange by the National Bank were again considerable and rediscount figures fairly large, owing to the date being mid-month when there is usually a fairly heavy demand.

The position on Monday night may be summarized as follows:- The prospects of an issue of a substantial portion of the 150 million schillings in Paris, which had been good on Friday night, had become pretty dark. The French participation, even if the bills were converted into a guarantee loan, had been whittled down. The prospects of a guarantee, even by the French Government, were not very rosy owing to internal political difficulties in Paris. The Austrian Minister had been given to understand that certain political conditions would be made before money was found in Paris. On the other hand Professor Bruins had succeeded in creating an optimistic atmosphere in Vienna with the result that the decision to proclaim an internal moratorium had been postponed from Monday morning for discussion at 6 p.m. on Tuesday night. The prospects of Sir Robert Kindersley and Mr. Gannon's agreement for the guarantee of the foreign creditors were good. On the other hand, the position of the Austrian Government was wobbly owing to the resignation of another Minister.

This Minister, Dr. Winkler, had resigned owing to the pressure, albeit unwilling pressure, which was brought to bear upon him by the Minister of Finance and the Chancellor, at Professor Bruins' invitation to agree to a full and unconditional guarantee of the schilling depositors of the Credit-Anstalt. This, Professor Bruins and myself had been urging for some time past; the object of course was to assist in stopping withdrawals from the Credit-Anstalt and therefore further discounting. On Monday morning the Government had agreed in principle to give the guarantee.

In their conversation late on Monday night with the Minister of Finance, Sir Robert Kindersley and Mr. Gannon had both again urged on him the immediate necessity of such a guarantee, only to be told that no decision had after all been taken, because in the course of the day, the Minister of Finance had been informed by Mr. Schüller who had been in Basle that the B.I.S. was no longer of the opinion that such a guarantee was necessary.

Not only had Professor Bruins and myself been urging the necessity of such a guarantee, but it has formed part of the B.I.S. conditions of assistance; a condition which, as a matter of fact had never been carried out, though it is true certain steps had been taken by the Minister of Finance in this direction. The news that Basle was no longer convinced of the necessity of the guarantee had led to a further postponement of the question by the Cabinet in spite of its acceptance in principle of the demand. When I heard of this on Monday night late, I cabled to Mr. McGarrah asking him to confirm that the B.I.S. was still of its old opinion and on Tuesday morning received his reply to that effect. [It transpired that Mr Schüller had made his statement on an alleged expression of opinion by M. Quesnay in the sense indicated after dinner in M. Simon's house in Basle on Sunday the 14th of June. If this attitude was true] If the alleged change of attitude in Basle had been true it had not been brought to the attention of Professor Bruins, who would never have subscribed to such a change of front, and in any case, whose information on the subject as far as the B.I.S. was concerned was still that contained in the B.I.S. telegram to myself on June 12th making a guarantee for the internal schilling deposits in the form required by Professor Bruins, an essential condition of B.I.S. help. [Whatever may be true of the conversation of Sunday night the 14th of June] The effect of M. Schüller's remark, which it was reported was made on the strength of an alleged statement to that effect by M. Quesnay, was the postponement of the question of the guarantee of the internal depositors until the Cabinet fell, when it was too late to secure what both Professor Bruins and myself considered to be an essential condition for credit restriction in Austria.

After the meeting which had taken place at Dr. Brauneis' house on Sunday, Sir Robert Kindersley and Mr. Gannon despatched cables to London and New York: Sir Robert Kindersley also telegraphed privately to M. Moreau. These cables urged the necessity of reaching a decision as soon as possible in order to avoid a collapse in Austria. Reference was made in Sir Robert Kindersley's and Mr. Gannon's telegram to a certain plan, which Mr. Gannon had proposed to Mr. Wiggin on June 13th, consequent upon a meeting with Governor Norman to discuss the European situation. The plan inter alia proposed that the 150 million schillings which were required should be found by underwriting the German half share in London and New York and, if the French bankers were unwilling to take up a substantial part without political conditions being imposed by the French Government, by underwriting the French share as well. News was received on Monday that the proposal to underwrite the issue in London and New York did not meet with French approval. Governor Norman therefore went back on Monday to the proposal to place the bills partly in Paris, partly in London, partly in New York and partly in Berlin. In the meanwhile, however, Mr. Gannon had received from Mr. Wiggin a cable which was the reply to his cable sent from Vienna. From this cable and from discussions in London that the proposal to place the bills partly in each of the four markets was in hand, we in Vienna believed that such progress was being made as justified Professor Bruins being optimistic.

We now come to Tuesday. On Tuesday morning London reported that no definite progress had been made in finding the money. Paris reiterated that a decision on the subject might be expected late that night and the Bank of France begged us to postpone the meeting of the Board of the National Bank, which was to decide to ask the Minister of Finance to proclaim an internal moratorium, until Wednesday morning. The difficulties of this course were manifest, since the Austrian National Bank's next statement was due to appear on Wednesday afternoon, or at the latest on Thursday morning, showing the figures as of Monday night. These figures included a loss of foreign exchange of 111 million schillings. The publication of the statement in this form was in the opinion of everybody concerned calculated to produce a panic. The publication of the statement, therefore, had to be made coincident with the declaration of an internal moratorium. It was moreover clear to all that an internal moratorium would lead to a general moratorium, and it was also clear that matters could not be allowed to drift beyond Tuesday night. Both London and Paris had had this situation explained to them on Monday. The request therefore to postpone the meeting of the Board from Tuesday evening until Wednesday was in itself difficult. Professor Bruins nevertheless continued to impart optimism at the Bank and succeeded on Tuesday midday in achieving a further postponement of the meeting until Wednesday.

Events then began to follow one another with considerable rapidity. The meeting between Sir Robert Kindersley, Mr. Gannon and the Minister of Finance for the signature of the Foreign Creditors' guarantee agreement was postponed from 12 noon to 1 p.m. in order to get the agreement into final form consistently with certain requirements which the International Committee in London had cabled. The agreement was signed soon after 1 o'clock, but upon the return of the Finance Minister to Parliament he discovered that the Cabinet, of which he was a member, had resigned at 3 o'clock. [owing to the unfavourable reception which the guarantee agreement had made, not only upon the Opposition but also upon certain elements amongst the Government's supporters.] The Agreement however had been signed and the lawyers stated that the Minister of Finance had power to sign under the Guarantee Law and the decisions of the Cabinet in connection therewith. Therefore the foreign creditors' position was apparently in order.

In the meanwhile, as I subsequently learned, a Cabinet meeting of the French Government took place at 11 a.m. in Paris at which the conditions to be complied with by the Austrian Government before any money could be found in Paris were decided. These conditions were handed to the Austrian representative in Paris, presumably at or soon after lunch. They were handed to him, as I understand, by the

Minister of Finance and not by the Quai d'Orsay. It is perhaps necessary to add that these conditions were not communicated to the French Minister in Vienna beforehand, nor did he know what they were until he was informed of them by the Austrian Government.

The Austrian Minister in Paris, Grünberger, telephoned the contents of the Note which he had received from the French Government to Vice-Chancellor Schober. These conditions were taken round to Parliament where Schober consulted his colleagues. The French Minister, and about the same time or a little later, the British and Italian Ministers were asked to go round to Parliament to see the Vice-Chancellor. The three gentlemen there learnt of the conditions which had been made. The text of Grünberger's telephone message was subsequently shown to me and read to Professor Bruins. I have made a summary of the Note, which Professor Bruins agree is a true and correct rendering of the document. This summary is as follows:-

> The French conditions were introduced by the remark that, in connection with the financial assistance which the Austrian Government was seeking in Paris, the French Government wished to make certain conditions which had to be accepted by the Austrian Government by 8 p.m. that evening. Nothing was said in the Note as to whether all or part of the proposed issue of 150 million schillings of Treasury Bills was to be placed in Paris nor upon what terms. Nothing was said about a French guarantee for a loan, or any other participations either in the placing of the bills or in the guaranteeing of a loan. The Minister of Finance said that he understood that if the conditions were accepted a substantial portion of the 150 million schillings would be found in Paris, but no reference to this was made in the Note.
>
> Two conditions were made.
>
> The first condition was that the Austrian Government should publish an official announcement in the Press, under its own name and in the form laid down by the French Government according to the text in French which was provided. The text ran approximately as follows:
>
> > The Austrian Government has decided to make an application to the League of Nations to send a commission to make 'une enquete approfondie' into the economic and financial position of the country. The Austrian Government undertakes as from now to accept the findings and put into force the recommendations and advice which might be given by the Commission (whatever the recommendations might be and before knowing them – F.R.).
>
> The second condition was that the Austrian Government should address a note to the French Government in the terms of the French text which was recited in full. The text read approximately:-
>
> > The Austrian Government has the honour to inform the French Government that it pledges itself to refrain from taking any steps which might modify the existing political and economic relations of Austria pending the enquiry of

the League of Nations' Commission referred to in the Austrian Government's announcement on the subject.

The Note provided that the text containing the second condition was not to be published, but should take the form of an exchange of Notes between the Austrian Government and the French Government.

Grünberger was instructed to add that while the French texts of the two communications had been prepared by the Quai d'Orsay, they had not yet been submitted to the other interested Ministries in Paris, and while no modifications were probable they were, nevertheless, not to be considered final.

(That is to say, the Austrian Government was to accept the conditions provided by the Quai d'Orsay in a form which could still be altered by the French Government but not by the Austrian Government. F.R.).

Upon his arrival at Parliament the French Minister was informed that the Austrian Government had resigned, Schober was not in a position to accept the conditions. The British and Italian Ministers were informed that neither that nor any other Austrian Government could accept such conditions.

It seems doubtful whether any Government, Austrian or other could have accepted conditions presented in such a manner.

It is clear that the Note telephoned by Grünberger containing conditions for acceptance by 8 p.m. that same day constituted an ultimatum, for a country placed in the position that Austria was. The shortness of the ultimatum must surely be without precedent. The reason for fixing 8 p.m. was, however, clear. It would have enabled steps to be taken in Paris, if the conditions had been accepted, between that hour and midnight regarding the issue of the 150 million schillings of bills. It might then have just been possible to have had the money paid over or advanced to the Austrian Government through the Austrian National Bank in time for the foreign exchange assets resultant upon the operation to have been included in the statement of the Austrian National bank before publication. It is, however, also clear that it was the last possible moment for such money to be received before a statement, which would have led to a panic and a moratorium, was published. The French Note is therefore not only a peculiar document, in so far as it gave the Austrian Government only about four hours in which to decide matters of momentous importance to that Government, but it was also sent at a moment when the pressure of financial circumstances had reached breaking points in Vienna. These circumstances were well known in Paris.

In comment upon this Note, it may be worth pointing out that an announcement was made in the Paris Press (reproduced in the Vienna Evening Press on Monday June 15th) that the French Government in the course of a conference with the Governor of the Banque de France and directors of the larger banks in Paris, had decided to send a commission to Central European countries to study the position, and in particular, not only to consider the reorganisation of the Credit-Anstalt and the losses of the foreign exchange to the Reichsbank, but also to make proposals on the spot for working out international co-operation in financial and economic affairs. A League of Nations' Committee to study the Austrian position, as required in the French Note, may therefore be considered in connection with the proposed despatch of French enquirers.

The other element which is possible is that the proposal of the Austro-German Customs Union was referred by the League of Nations to the International Court, and that the middle of July has apparently been fixed for the matter to be deliberated by the latter body. The pledge of the Austrian Government contained as the second condition of the French Note would, therefore, have involved a delay which it may be calculated would have been of several months, and which would have prevented any steps being taken by the Austrian Governments for some time even in the event of the decision of the International Court being favourable to the thesis of a Customs Union.

The Austrian Government had, as stated, informed the French Minister that being in statu demissionis it was unable to accept the conditions. The decision was reached independently of the knowledge that the Bank of England was prepared to advance 150 million schillings against the placing of the Austrian bills. This information was received by Professor Bruins at the National Bank in the course of a telephone message from Mr. Siepmann which began at 5.40 p.m. and terminated a little before 6 o'clock. As soon as this message was received Sir Robert Kindersley and Mr. Gannon were asked to go round to the Bank and remained there discussing the conditions which the Bank of England had made with Professor Bruins and myself until 8.15 p.m. Dr. Brauneis brought this development to the notice of the Finance Minister at about 8 o'clock. At a meeting at the Finance Ministry at 10.30 p.m. attended by the Chancellor, the Finance Minister, President Reisch, Vice-President Thaa, Dr. Brauneis, Professor Bruins and myself the message containing the financial conditions made by the Bank of England was handed to the Finance Minister. The Chancellor who was present at the meeting had then not heard any of the details of the message and both the Finance Minister and the Chancellor were unaware that the money had been advanced by the Bank of England.

## NARRATING THE CRISIS

Rodd's account of the dramatic week in June 1931 deserves attention as an act of sensemaking through narrative emplotment. For five weeks, he had struggled to make sense of the Austrian crisis, not just for himself but for the BIS and Bank of England officials, who had to decide what to do under the radical uncertainty that prevailed. Rodd had written numerous notes, letters and memoranda; sent telegrams and made and received phone calls to and from Vienna, Basle and London.

His memorandum of June 20 put the final week of the Austrian crisis into narrative shape with causes and effects, villains and heroes. The Austrians and the French are the villains who out of incompetence or national political interests sabotaged the efforts of good, unselfish (mostly British) people to rescue the world from financial and monetary disaster. The failure in placing the bond loan and the near failure of the guarantee for the foreign creditors both rested on the 'dilatoriness of the Austrians' while the final breakdown of the Austrian–French negotiations was due to the scheming of the French government with the assistance of French banks.

Notably, the Banque de France does not appear as a villain in Rodd's story that juxtaposes the French government's self-serving actions with the British focus on saving the world from economic disaster. Rodd did not see the Banque de France as an antagonist. Quesnay, Moret and Rist had fought the same struggle as the rest of the epistemic community.

The French government, in contrast, was the villain. This fits well with the many allusions to French political action that surfaced ever so often in the communications between the main actors. Norman's suspicion, even dislike, of the French was well known and resonates with the fact that a Bank of England official a few weeks earlier, on May 9, had highlighted only one section in a four-page note about France.

The note stereotyped the French as being 'quite unconcerned with the general welfare ... without any conception of big business, international vision or of co-operation either with each other or anyone else – individually, commercially and politically they ask to be left alone'.[3]

That British officials categorized the French as distinctly different was also clear from a meeting between Leith-Ross and French experts from the Ministry of Finance. At one point during a discussion of Germany's public spending for borrowed money, Leith-Ross remarked that the 'Germans, like other Anglo-Saxon races, spent more money on public undertakings than the Latin countries', declining to go along with the French experts' criticism.[4]

The memorandum was Rodd's final say on the crisis, and he saw to it that others were made aware of his story. 'Indeed, I see no reason for keeping the facts confidential from anybody who wishes to know them', he wrote to Kindersley.[5] It was an act of sensemaking in a situation with extreme uncertainty and perceived high stakes regarding the future of the gold standard and, indeed, Western capitalism.

It was also a narrative with a heavy emphasis on the British point of view, and as such it contributed to the framing of both the prospective sensemaking that had dominated until now, and the retrospective sensemaking that was to replace it as the crisis subsided. As a piece of 'fiction in the archive', it was a performative story that framed the understanding of the Austrian crisis in a very specific way.[6] In a letter to Gannon, Rodd self-consciously used terms related to emplotment and narratives.

I enclose a copy of the note which I promised you regarding the events which occurred in Vienna and culminated with the Bank of England credit on Tuesday night. I am afraid the style is not quite appropriate to the facts. It should have been written in the manner of the good 20th century political spy or detective stories. The facts are certainly sufficiently in keeping with such novels to justify their being re-edited in more appropriate language.[7]

Robert Kindersley and James Gannon had worked closely with Rodd during the final hectic week in Vienna. They certainly shared his frustration about the events described in the memorandum. They were still in Vienna when they received Rodd's memo.

Kindersley was working to finalize the practicalities related to the guarantee and the standstill agreement. He was about to run out of patience. When he received Rodd's letter and the enclosed memorandum, he was unable to keep a stiff upper lip and he let go of his feelings.

Many thanks for your letter of June 22nd enclosing note on the events which culminated in the Bank of England credit. . . .

I am leaving on Saturday by the 2 o'clock Orient Express and shall be glad to say goodbye to this city and its people.

As far as my experience goes here I find the Austrians to be not only lacking in backbone but very unreliable and one has to waste an enormous amount of time in compelling them to implement their promises. . . .

We have got the general guarantee announced at last. It was agreed to on Tuesday but nothing published till Friday – these are the sort of delays which are so maddening and as far as one can see unnecessary. . . . I hope when next we meet the world may be in a better shape.[8]

Kindersley also expressed his view of the Austrian approach to Eric Phipps, who reported back to Arthur Henderson, the foreign secretary, that 'the Austrian treatment of the whole matter had been weak and flabby'. They had 'failed lamentably to respond to those efforts to help them by taking prompt action to help themselves'. The American minister to Vienna went as far as to say that 'the Government made a fatal error as far as Austria is concerned when it decided to attempt to save the Credit Anstal'.[9]

Gannon also recognized the receipt of Rodd's letter. Still in Vienna, he replied on June 25.

I have just now found a moment to acknowledge and thank you for the memorandum covering your exciting days here. I shall keep it always as a most interesting historical document.

We miss you. For my part I am almost inclined to foment trouble elsewhere in order that we might thus secure your helpful and happy presence with us.
With kindest personal regards, and in the hope of seeing you soon again.[10]

## PIERRE QUESNAY'S STORY

If the French were the main villain in Rodd's narrative, Kindersley felt pretty much the same way about the Austrians who had also tested Rodd's and the BIS's patience more than once by allegedly dragging their feet every inch of the way towards the climax on June 16. At the end of the day, it was all about different worldviews, perceived interests and agendas but the British had not been great at seeing 'the other chap's point of view' or to 'understand people who live in other places', as Rodd had put it.[11]

Like everyone else, they had their blind spots, and Rodd's version was not the only one. Though it was much less detailed and elaborate, on June 16 Merle Cochran retold Pierre Quesnay's version in one of his reports to the US State Department.

I had a long talk last night with M. Pierre Quesnay, General Manager of the B.I.S., just before he boarded the train for Paris, where he is returning at the request of Premier Laval. M. Quesnay had gone to Paris earlier in the week to present to the French political and financial leaders the B.I.S. viewpoint on the Austrian situation. He did not arrive in Paris on the morning of June 16 until after the French cabinet had assembled. He did not have the opportunity, therefore, of submitting his observations to the ministers before a decision had been reached. In my last letter, dated June 9, 1931, I told you that the B.I.S. hoped for a decision within the week upon the question of a foreign loan to Austria. Dr. Rist, as I reported, returned to Paris from Vienna and undertook negotiations with the French bankers. I am informed that French bankers were willing to consider favorably the assumption of a large part of the contemplated issue of 150 million schillings of Austrian Treasury Notes upon the following conditions. The bankers asked the French Government to agree to act as guarantor for a loan, under the auspices of the League of Nations, which would be floated to take care of the Treasury Notes. It was asked that France assume this position as guarantor in the same manner as it served as one of the sponsors of the 1923 loan to Austria. The French bankers insisted that they were not the ones who really had a great stake in Austria, British and American interests being much heavier. They were willing to take the present risk only with the above described French Government guarantee. The French Ministers refused, at the session above mentioned, to undertake such a guarantee. It should be borne in mind that the Ministers were aware that on the same afternoon, June 16, there was to be a debate in the French Parliament at which M. Franklin-Bouillon was expected bitterly to attack the Government particularly upon its foreign policies. They realized that if they granted the guarantee in question they would have this to answer for when interpellated, and might therefore run a very serious risk of being voted down. M. Tardieu brought up again the possibility procuring a promise from the Austrian Government that it give up the idea of Customs Union with Germany provided the French would arrange for the necessary financing at this time.

The Austrian Minister in Paris was called to the Quai d'Orsay the same day and M. Tardieu's suggestion was made to him. He reported that the Cabinet then in power in Vienna could not repudiate the action which had been taken under the leadership of Foreign Minister Schober, and pointed out that later Austrian Governments could not be held to a promise that might now be made to abstain from an economic rapprochement with Germany. Since this negotiation thus failed, in the afternoon of June 16, the French Ministers, after emerging successfully from the Parliamentary session, were unable to reach any decision favorable to Austria. M. Quesnay had let them understand that the B.I.S. directors had at their last regular meeting, on June 8, agreed that a further credit of 100 million schillings could be extended by the B.I.S. to the National Bank of Austria whenever it might be definitely determined that the 150 million schilling Treasury note issue could be taken care of abroad. Since the French decision was negative, M. Quesnay explained that the B.I.S. could not extend this second credit.

Realizing, therefore, the desperate situation of Austria, M. Quesnay got in touch with Mr. Siepmann of the Bank of England and arranged for the latter institution to extend a seven day renewable credit of 150 million schillings to the National Bank of Austria at the official Austrian rate of 7½ percent. This sum was telegraphed to Austria late on the night of the 16th. It was possible, therefore, to show this amount as a receipt on the statement of the Austrian National Bank which came out June 17. It is understood that if this sum had not been received in time to appear on the balance sheet, the Austrian National Bank would have been positively obliged to declare the general banking moratorium in Austria, which had been threatened from day to day since the beginning of the present crisis. (It is interesting to note that one German writer asserts, that German diplomacy had become aware of the political pressure which France was bringing to bear upon Austria in connection with the loan, and consequently approached the British to take over the urgent transitory credit arrangements for relieving Austria).

The Austrian Cabinet meeting on June 16 gave final approval to the agreement, based on the legislation I have previously reported, and arrived at between Austria and the foreign creditors of the Credit Anstalt, acting through the International Committee organized at London. This agreement provides for the guarantee by the Austrian Government of $80,000,000 of old credits extended to the Credit Anstalt, with the counter provision that the foreign bankers permit such credits to remain for two years. This is the restrictions which I mentioned in my last letter. To achieve the ratification of this agreement cost the withdrawal of the Minister of the Interior of Austria, and the entire Cabinet resigned later in the day when the unsuccessful result of the negotiations at Paris was learned.

Austria is faced today, therefore, with the organization of a new cabinet. The British loan is purely a temporary measure, which the Bank of England thought absolutely necessary to prevent a moratorium and consequent heavy loss to British capital. Negotiations will continue with the view to placing the Austrian Treasury notes abroad, possibly to be followed by a loan under the auspices of League of Nations, or by a second tranche of the Construction Loan. M. Quesnay told me frankly that he thought the French Minister regretted the decision they had made, particularly after seeing England going to the rescue of the Austrian National Bank. He said that Premier Laval telephoned him yesterday noon, only a few hours after he, M. Quesnay had returned from Paris, asking that he come up again to discuss the question with him. M. Quesnay will, therefore, lunch with Premier Laval today, and the questions will be reopened.[12]

Merle Cochran was well aware that this was Pierre Quesnay's version and that it might not fit with the official BIS version, if one existed. At the time of writing, Rodd had not yet written his account of what happened, but a few days later, on June 19, Cochran added a note that the information in his letter 'was based almost entirely upon my conversation with M. Quesnay'. 'This morning I have seen an American director of the B.I.S. The following additional facts are submitted to bring my Letter entirely to date.'

Mr. Quesnay has not returned yet from Paris and has not reported the results of his yesterday's conference with Premier Laval. The B.I.S. does not look, however, to the French bankers resuming the lead in negotiations toward floating the external Treasury bonds of Austria. The French lost their chance through insisting upon the political stipulations which I have hereinabove described, and in giving Austria an ultimatum as to the time (8.00 p.m. on June 16) by which a compliance therewith should be agreed. The German Press is today lauding the astuteness of the Bank of England in stepping into the Austrian situation and foiling French political aims. I can imagine that the American section of the B.I.S. itself might be just a little satisfied at this check to the diplomacy of the franc, in view of the sharp criticisms which the absolute insistence of the B.I.S. upon the French putting aside political factors when dealing through the Bank have drawn from French officials and the French press. Negotiations are now going on through the Bank of England for a consortium to take the 150 million schillings of Austrian Treasury notes, to replace the temporary advance made by the Bank of England.... Since the transaction did not involve the taking by the Bank of England of Austrian Treasury bonds, the requirement prescribed by the B.I.S. before making its second credit of 100 million schillings available to the National Bank of Austria has not been fulfilled. The B.I.S. hopes that the British bankers will now proceed with plans for taking the Austrian Treasury bonds. It is possible that a third thereof would be subscribed in England, a third in the United States, and perhaps the French will come forward and take the remaining third, although no political stipulations will enter into any agreement. There is furthermore the possibility that German banks will participate, and also those of the Netherlands and Switzerland. When once this flotation is accomplished, the B.I.S. will then extend the second credit, if still necessary in the opinion of Dr. Bruins.[13]

In his next letter, dated June 26, Cochran took a further step away from his lengthy report about Quesnay. At this time Rodd's report was known at the very least to a small group of people in his network, among them Walter Stewart, and through him most likely Cochran himself.

In my last letter . . . dated June 16, 1931, I reported that M. Pierre Quesnay . . . had returned to Paris the preceding night at the request of Premier Laval for consultation on the French attitude with respect to the flotation abroad of 150 million schillings of Austrian Treasury notes. M. Quesnay has been in Paris most of the time since that date, but is now back in Basel. President Gates W. McGarrah is in Paris today. Mr. Fraser, the American alternate to the president, who sailed for the United States on May 27, will return to Europe on the Steamship Paris, departing from New York July 1. Dr. Walter W. Stewart, the American economist who has been assisting the B.I.S. since the middle of May has now established his family some distance from Basel, for a holiday sojourn, and he comes in to the Bank two or three days in the week. I had a talk with him this morning in which he cleared up a few points, particularly with respect to the Austrian financial situation above mentioned.

While in conversation with me M. Quesnay definitely stated that it was he who put the proposition up to Mr. Siepmann of the Bank of England for emergency action on the part of that institution when developments at Paris turned out as they did, and Austria faced a moratorium the next day, Dr. Stewart gives the English version. According to the latter, Mr. Rodd, British expert of the B.I.S., and Sir Robert Kindersley, the London banker, were with the minister of finance in Vienna when news of France's insistence upon the dropping of the Anschluss as a condition to French participation in the Treasury bond flotation was received. Word as to Austria's dire situation was consequently forwarded to London through British channels. The National Bank of Austria received word, on the same afternoon, June 16, that the 150 million schilling would be forthcoming, even before the Bank was aware of the source from which the funds would emanate. Austrian conditions have, of course, improved with the developments centering around President Hoover's plan. It appears today that the second credit of 100,000,000 schillings which the B.I.S. had decided upon for the National Bank of Austria, contingent upon the 150,000,000 schilling note issue, will not have to be touched.[14]

To what extent Quesnay was aware of Rodd's memorandum is difficult to say, but Quesnay's conversation with Cochran did not suggest that he wanted to distance himself from the Bank of England's emergency loan to Austria. In fact, he tried to take ownership of it. Together with Clément Moret, Charles Rist and Lacour-Gayet's roles so far, Quesnay's narrative, though perhaps too self-congratulatory, shows that French central bankers were not completely aligned with the French government. Like the Austrians, they were occasionally torn between two communities, two identities – as central bankers on the one hand and their national belonging and their governments on the other.

Quesnay may have felt squeezed in his position as a central banker on the one hand, and the French government's expectations of him on the other. If the *Commercial and Financial Chronicle* was right, 'No secret was made in Paris this week over French displeasure at what was described as the "intrusion" of the Bank of England in the situation.'[15]

While the run on the Austrian currency subsided with the agreement between Austria and the international creditors, and Bank of England's loan, there was still an expectation that the Austrian bond loan would have to be placed. That would not be easy.

# 12

# To Act Now If We Are to Act at All (June 16–June 27)

The breakdown on June 16 of the negotiations to place the Austrian government loan occurred simultaneously with Norman's decision to provide a bridge loan on a weekly basis to Austria. It is possible that Norman did not yet know about the breakdown of the negotiations when he made up his mind about the loan. But he was certainly aware that the situation was critical, and he was frustrated by the lack of progress and the perceived inability by the Bank for International Settlements (BIS) and the Austrians to act in a timely and rational way, his way.

Most observers were unanimous in praising Norman's action. The *Financial Times* reported that the City of London celebrated Bank of England as the 'saviour of Austria and a good deal more'. The paper argued that the action had no political content and was not directed at France. 'La Belle France, it is to be hoped, will not look at the contribution made by the Bank of England to the house of Austria as a slight upon herself.'[1]

If a message from Governor Moret of the Banque de France was any indication, the newspaper's hopes were confirmed. Moret told Siepmann that 'the action of the Bank of England in making an advance to Austria is highly appreciated in the Banque de France. We must realize that the Banque de France is unfortunately tied by strict regulations and could not have undertaken such an operation for its own account. But Monsieur Moret wishes us to know that the Banque de France whole-heartedly welcomes the action which our greater liberty enabled us to take.'[2]

It may have been an attempt at pouring oil on troubled waters, but Moret's phone call implies that Banque de France, too, was part of the emerging epistemic community of central banks and did not sympathize with the French government's mixing of politics and finance in times of crisis.

At the Bank of England, emotions were running high, though. Regardless of Clément Moret's appreciation, they were upset by the French government's action.

In an unsigned note of June 17, a Bank officer wrote, 'I think that we should at once inform the French Government that we have heard with amazement of the ultimatum they addressed yesterday to the Austrian Government. It is obviously futile to talk about European co-operation if the French Government hold themselves free to provoke a financial collapse in Central Europe.'[3]

Rodd was angry, too. In a phone call he told Norman that 'he considers the action of the French one of the most scandalous manoeuvres of which we have ever heard'. That was Rodd's final call from Vienna. On June 17, he left the city 'for Basle at 1 p.m. and arrives there at 5 a.m. to-morrow'.[4]

From Basle, McGarrah wrote Norman, 'I want very much, Mr. Governor, to express our appreciation of your splendid help in connection with the Austrian situation at the critical juncture.'[5] Gijsbert Bruins concurred that without the intervention by the Bank of England, 'a catastrophe would in all probability have taken place in the next few days'.[6]

At the home front, the British Foreign Office was less enthusiastic about Norman's lone rider action. On August 24, Orme Sargent of the Foreign Office wrote to the British legation in Vienna that the Foreign Office 'do not want particularly to be identified with the original action of the Bank in lending the money, especially as the transaction has not in the end had the effect (which it presumably was intended to have) of freeing Austria from French dictation'.

Sargent continued that 'the loan is entirely a private affair of the Bank's. The Bank took the initiative originally without consulting us, and since then have perhaps purposely not kept us informed. The Bank, as you probably know, are always jealous of their independence.'[7]

The Foreign Office's perspective obviously differed from Norman's and demonstrated how different logics were at work. Norman was certainly no stranger to the idea of keeping France out, but his primary interest was to avoid a moratorium and a further destabilization of an already fragile world economy and monetary system. That his action dodged the French ultimatum was but a welcome side effect.

## PUTTING MONEY DOWN A SINK HOLE

The Bank of England's loan did not solve Rodd's initial puzzle about where and how to place. The appetite for the Austrian bond loan in the United

States was scant, though Albert Wiggin at the Chase National Bank had a change of heart regarding the European situation.

In a cable to Gannon, he commended Governor Norman, who 'as evidenced by his grasp of the situation, has shown tremendous courage and commands our admiration. We now have breathing space and I am confident that we can persuade New York to do its share. Some progress has already been made.'[8]

But Wiggin's view was an exception. J.P. Morgan & Co., the quintessential American investment bank, was sceptical as it made clear in a cable to its sister bank in London. While praising Norman's action on June 16, the bank had talked to some of the 'leading banks and banking houses in an effort to prepare the ground, and we find them all, as anticipated, very reluctant to put any new money into this situation'.

They admired the 'courage with which Governor Norman has met the situation' and would like to help, but the banks wanted more information and a plan before they would even consider participating in credits to Europe. In fact, Norman's action had been counterproductive in the sense that while 'indicating the extent to which he is ready to back his own judgment . . . will be offset to some extent by the sense of relief from the immediate emergency'.

The shift of leadership back to Governor Norman and Bank of England was recognized and appreciated. But it had also – for a short while – reduced the urgency and uncertainty of the situation. Now, the bankers sat on the fence and waited for Norman to 'develop his plan'.[9] An unintended consequence, indeed.

Still, on the Austrian side, conditions were improving. On June 22, a new Austrian government passed a bill guaranteeing Credit Anstalt's schilling deposits. Bruins commented that 'the new Finance Minister is not a banker but a fine man'.[10]

In fact, Austria was no longer the problem; the 'Austrian position appears to be developing satisfactorily', McGarrah reported to Harrison on June 29.[11] Still, the treasury loan was getting nowhere, and having had their guarantee and avoided a moratorium, private banks saw no reason to go out on a limb to help Austria.

In fact, they were growing tired of Austria. Morgan Grenfell did not like 'the attitude of the Austrians . . . They still cannot forget that Austria was one of the great world powers and they stand on their dignity. We personally feel that the banks and the politicians have so mismanaged the affairs of the small modern Austria.'[12]

J.P. Morgan agreed and explained that the 'only reason why we once thought it possible that our banks might be willing to contribute, even on the modest scale suggested for Austria's relief, was to avoid the graver catastrophe in Germany'.[13]

Though it took some time for the various actors to realize, placing the Austrian loan no longer seemed a realistic prospect. There were simply no takers. In a note from August 6, Simon noted that it 'is one of the many misfortunes of Austria that so much time has elapsed before it was possible to convince the Government of the necessity of issuing Treasury Bonds abroad, so that the opportunity of doing this was definitely missed'.[14]

As a perceptive memorandum from late July made clear, now 'that the creditors have received the Government guarantee they feel themselves safe as far as their old money is concerned. They are giving no new money so that they are indifferent whether the Credit Anstalt is reconstructed or liquidated.'[15]

Harrison and the New York Fed were reconsidering as well. Two days after the Bank of England loan, he discussed the effect of the Central European crisis on monetary policy with his board of directors. Gold increasingly flowed into the United States, and 'during the last two weeks ... such drastic changes have taken place in the world credit situation ... as to point to the necessity for reconsidering our policy in the light of these events'.

During a long discussion of the American gold sterilization, Charles Mitchell, in an apparent about-face on Austria, argued that 'putting money into Austria was putting money down a sink hole; that Austria was broken by the treaty of Versailles and that it was still broke and that all the money which might be poured in wouldn't save it.... Mr. Mitchell said that his idea would be to let the economically unsound countries go and to concentrate upon keeping the conflagration from spreading to Germany, which he thought was economically sound.'[16]

With an enormous RM10 billion, or $2.4 billion, short-term foreign debt, the real burden of which increased with deflation, record unemployment and budget deficits; not to mention social and political unrest and polarization, Germany was the epicentre of distress and uncertainty about what the future would bring.[17] Brüning's reparations statement on June 6, just before his visit to Chequers, only made matters worse and action more urgent. During the first eighteen days of June, the Reichsbank's reserve ratio fell from 60 to 48 per cent, getting closer to the regulatory minimum of 40 per cent. On June 13, the Reichsbank raised the discount rate from 5 to 7 per cent, and the following week credit restrictions were introduced despite the already weak German economy.[18]

As attention turned to Germany, the Bank of England and the New York Fed took centre stage, while BIS was further marginalized. It was symbolic of this development when the BIS on June 18 sent an urgent telegram to the Bank of England, asking about the status of the treasury loan. 'We are in the dark regarding developments since Tuesday.'[19]

The BIS was out of the loop after Rodd had left Vienna and Norman's attention was elsewhere. Andrew Mellon, the US treasury secretary, was travelling to London, and Harrison thought that it would be 'important for Washington to receive a direct report of your views through him as soon as possible'.[20]

Norman met with Mellon on June 18 in the morning, and around noon, US East Coast time, he called Harrison to give him an update. There was nothing new about the treasury loan, but things were quieter in Austria. Hungary was worse, and in Germany the exchange position 'is bad tonight ... he looks for a worse day tomorrow'.

Norman then reported on his meeting with Mellon and on Mellon's meeting with Prime Minister Ramsay MacDonald, where Norman was present. Harrison noted Norman's 'surprise at how far the Washington mind had progressed on the matter of debts'. Mellon believed something needed to be done soon, and Norman advised him to 'go to Paris to sound out the French, but Mr. Mellon apparently stalled on this, at least pending word from Washington'.

Harrison asked Norman what he thought about the timing of any possible action, and Norman replied that 'it would be much more favorable from every standpoint in view of the seriousness of conditions abroad to act now if we are to act at all'.

Before ending the call, Norman once again stressed that they confronted not only a financial problem but an economic and political problem 'which requires much broader treatment than can be offered through the central banks alone'.[21]

There were limits to central banking, after all. Politicians had to recognize that fundamental issues centred around Germany, reparations and debt problems that were destabilizing the European and the world economy. The initiative would have to come from the United States and involve at the very least French acceptance. Central banks could only play the role of supporting actor.

Like in Harrison's and Norman's earlier conversations on the subject, Harrison was trying to get an idea of Norman's view as to the urgency of

American action. Norman clearly saw two potential problems. The first would arise if the Americans did not sound out French opinion. The second was the risk of waiting too long.

On June 19, Norman and Harrison were in touch again, this time about another credit to the National Bank of Hungary. Norman told Harrison, that he 'does not feel he can go any further in view of his Austrian commitment. Is there anything we can do? . . . I did not believe we should go in alone . . . I asked him whether he thought the Bank of France would do anything and he said he thought that was hopeless.'[22]

In Germany, as Brüning had returned from Chequers, he faced strong protests against his latest emergency decree, and calls for an extra session of the Reichstag. Brüning threatened to resign, and Luther made it clear 'that the outbursts of opposition had already weakened Germany politically and financially, and that the overthrow of the Bruening Government would spell financial disaster'.[23]

Brüning stood fast, and the opposition backed down. 'Brüning's victory is complete', Wilhelm Vocke of the Reichsbank told Norman who believed things were 'letting up' in Germany. He wrote to Luther that he hoped 'that before long our financial and economic troubles will no longer be aggravated by the instability of governments'.[24]

The optimism was short lived. Next day, in the afternoon, Siepmann received a call from Friedrich Dreyse from the Reichsbank. Things had improved after increasing the discount rate to 7 per cent, and the day had begun quietly but 'the whole position changed after midday', Dreyse said. The Reichsbank was concerned that they would have to go below the 40 per cent cover and feared it would 'be very disturbing to public opinion'.

They had a standing $50 million credit through the Gold Diskont Bank, a subsidiary of the Reichsbank established by the Dawes Plan of 1924, but the Reichsbank was concerned that it might affect American banks if they began drawing on the credit. There was also the option of asking the BIS for a credit of, say, 100 million reichsmarks, but Dreyse told Siepmann that the

> Austrian experience does not make one hopeful that such a transaction could easily be arranged or that it could be put through in such a way as to avoid, instead of creating, disturbance. We are therefore asking ourselves whether it is conceivable that, in spite of the existence of the B.I.S. which is perhaps not yet in a position to help us as much as we require, the cooperation by central banks might be enlisted direct, for example, by the rediscounting of good Reichsmarks bills in London and New York. This idea has not yet been broached to anyone. It has not even been discussed with Dr. Luther.[25]

This was an open attempt at bypassing the BIS and going directly to the Bank of England, and Siepmann and Norman did not object. Having read Siepmann's note, Norman sent Harrison an urgent telegram that 'position in Berlin has worsened seriously this afternoon since our conversation and may become critical at any moment'.[26]

It was Friday night in London, but nothing pointed to a peaceful weekend. In fact, there had been no peaceful weekends for a while by now. There had been cries of wolf a number of times, but what if this was the real thing? Harrison needed to know what was going on, and, despite being typical, the short, mysterious, and melodramatic style of Norman's telegram really did not say much.

> After receiving Governor Norman's urgent cable . . . with reference to the seriously worsened condition in Berlin, I telephoned him about 3:30 pm., New York time, and asked him what was the significance of his cable. He told me that about one-half hour after our telephone conversation this morning (at which time he said he had heard nothing from Berlin) the Reichsbank telephoned him to say they had had a very distressing afternoon and that after some let-up in withdrawals the last two days and even this morning, they had suffered a loss of 70,000,000 reichsmarks late in the afternoon; that they were near their legal limit and that they were considering what to do.[27]

A loss of 70 million reichsmarks corresponded to about \$16.7 million or £3.4 million. It was a serious amount of money to lose in one afternoon. There were three possible steps, the first was to go below the legal cover ratio, but Luther did not want to do that. The alternatives were to borrow 'a large amount' from the BIS or from the Bank of England and the Federal Reserve Bank. However, Norman was not prepared to grant a credit to the Reichsbank 'just for the purpose of enabling them to pay reparations'.

Before ending the call, Norman 'pointed out furthermore that he had been sent for this afternoon by the Prime Minister and had reviewed the seriousness of the whole position with him. He still thinks and hopes that something may be done immediately about debts.'[28]

Luther cabled Harrison about the same situation, being laconically brief saying that the loss of 'foreign exchange increased today again to 70,000,000 reichsmarks. Stock exchange considerably weaker. I took up telephone conversation with Norman.'[29]

The next day, Saturday, June 20, Norman called Harrison at 11 a.m. New York time. After a brief discussion about the situation in Austria and Hungary, they turned to the situation in Germany, and Norman said,

Berlin had had another bad day; that in his opinion they cannot continue like this, and that they must decide in the next day or two whether they would turn to the left or to the right. . . .

Governor Norman asked me whether I would be within reach over Sunday and I told him that I would, and he likewise said that he could be reached at any time through the Bank of England.

In response to an inquiry, I said that I thought that if our Government is to do anything at all about debts it is likely it would be early next week, probably Monday; that I did not think it was possible to reach any conclusions earlier than that. He said that he hoped an early announcement would be forthcoming inasmuch as he considered the situation in Berlin now a matter of hours rather than days.[30]

The Austrian and Hungarian problems were not solved, and there was trouble elsewhere, too, including Chile 'which was almost prepared to lie down and quit'.[31] But, by this time, Germany was squarely in the eye of the storm.

Harrison and Norman had a lot on their plate, and with the situation in Germany escalating, the need for money to be poured over Central Europe increased dramatically. For that very reason, the need for something to be done about reparations and war debts was urgent, and Harrison and, even more so, Norman expected the US President to do something soon; they just did not know what and when.

Also on June 20, Harrison received a long telegram from McGarrah, who asked 'whether you can envisage making an operation in Hungary analogous to that which the Bank of England has made at Austria, namely a direct deposit with the Magyan Nemzeti Bank of $15,000,000. . . . If a breakdown occurs there our work in Austria may prove vain.'[32]

It raised the question how much did Harrison really want to support Central European countries far away? Charles Mitchell had already suggested letting the small countries go and focus on Germany. In terms of upholding the world as they knew it, the work in Austria had proved in vain as soon as the German trouble began. Harrison's reply was muted. At the very least the BIS and the Banque de France needed to take part as well, and even then 'I am not sure how much further we would be authorized to go.'[33]

McGarrah's inquiry demonstrated what most central bankers knew already, that the BIS did not have much independent firepower to assist troubled central banks and currencies. The BIS's ability to do something about Germany would be next to irrelevant. It was significant that McGarrah wrote about a credit to Hungary, while Norman and Harrison discussed an external drain in Germany.

Still Saturday, June 20, Hans Luther cabled Harrison that the day had seen 'further withdrawals of 60,000,000 Reichsmarks foreign exchange ... credit restrictions coming into operation Monday. I am in constant contact with Norman.'[34]

Luther did not entertain any illusions about the BIS's ability to help Germany either, and he knew he had a friend in Norman, who had demonstrated that he was able to act fast and decisively when needed.

The situation in Germany, and the German authorities' persistent pressure on the reparations issue, led the Hoover administration to realize the need for action. On June 13, journalists had asked the US undersecretary of state, William R. Castle Jr, if the administration was reconsidering the war debt question 'in the light of the severe economic depression in Europe, and especially in view of the developments in Germany'. Castle told the journalists that the government's debt policy was clear, but in case of a 'serious crisis, the government would have to consider whether a temporary change in its policy was necessary'.

On the same day, Fraser reported to McGarrah about massive uneasiness in the United States about Germany's position. Washington officials wanted to know how France would respond 'in eventuality of postponement or reconsideration of the whole position'. Fraser asked for Quesnay's opinion, 'but better not reveal Washington inquiry. They are very nervous there.'[35]

Back in Basle, McGarrah talked to Quesnay and let Fraser know that 'despite great confusion of thought Quesnay sure they will strongly object to any reconsideration of the whole reparation position'. McGarrah also revealed his own inability to make sense of the 'intensely nervous feeling regarding Germany in New York and Washington', while at the same time believing that 'help may be needed any moment to enable the gold standard to be maintained'.

Fraser believed that Norman's 'general pessimism' and his many phone calls to Harrison contributed to the nervousness in the United States.[36] In fact, Harrison 'is very much under the influence of Norman', Fraser told McGarrah and while 'the temporary panic has subsided' he expected some 'kind of action in the next few months – or even weeks'.[37]

## THE HOOVER MORATORIUM

The action came the next day. On Saturday, June 20, at 6.15 p.m. in Washington DC, President Herbert Hoover announced a proposal for a one-year moratorium on reparations and war debts.[38] Harrison had vented the ideas to Norman in order to measure the response to what was now a reality, President Hoover's plan for a debt moratorium.[39]

Norman surely expected an American initiative any time now, but the announcement took many by surprise. The idea was first put to Hoover by Morgan partner Thomas Lamont, who once confessed that he was more interested in politics and diplomacy than banking and economics.[40]

That was not a bad combination at a time where close connections between politics and banks predominated and where the House of Morgan's influence was significant, though not necessarily with President Hoover who was not a big fan of J.P. Morgan & Co. and vice versa.[41] After having consulted with numerous people, the President announced,

> The American Government proposes the postponement during one year of all payments on intergovernmental debts, reparations and relief debts, both principal and interest, of course, not including obligations of governments held by private parties. Subject to confirmation by Congress, the American Government will postpone all payments upon the debts of foreign governments to the American Government payable during the fiscal year beginning July 1, next, conditional on a like postponement for one year of all payments on intergovernmental debts owing the important creditor powers.[42]

The plan's purpose was to assist the economic recovery of the world, and Hoover made sure to point out that it was in the self-interest of the United States to help Europe. To please his home audience, he emphasized that reparations were 'wholly a European problem with which we have no relation', and that he did not 'approve in any remote sense of the cancellations of the debts to us'.[43]

The debt proposal was an attempt to address some of the structural and political issues frequently mentioned by Norman as underlying the crisis in Europe.[44] That it might also ease the pressure on the American financial system was not lost on the President and his administration. The European reception of the initiative would be decisive for what happened next.

On Sunday Harrison called Norman to gauge the effect of Hoover's announcement. If Harrison was anxious to hear good news, he may have been disappointed. Most of Europe had hardly even heard of Hoover's speech yet.

Norman told him that 'it had been received with the greatest possible relief in London but that he gathered that it was not generally known on the Continent this morning and in none of the continental newspapers'. Norman had been on the phone with both Vienna and Berlin the same morning, and it was not known there. 'He reiterated, however, that the London reaction was most excellent.'[45]

If Harrison had called the Banque de France, he would have heard a different story. As *The Economist* made clear, the first impression in France of the Hoover proposal was one of 'incredulous astonishment'. The French government was under intense pressure from newspapers and the public that was hostile to the idea and claimed that Germany had astutely used 'American anxiety to protect the large amount of capital invested by the United States in Germany'.[46]

The French were furious about what they considered a one-sided American ultimatum and a threat to the Young Plan.[47] Compared to Britain, France was set to lose much more from Hoover's proposal. France received about $225 million annually from Germany in reparations payments. Of that, $50 million went to the United States and $75 million to Britain in war debt payments. The remaining $100 million were 'earmarked to meet services on loans for reconstruction of the devastated regions'. France was also highly disturbed that the plan did not distinguish between conditional and unconditional payments as laid out in the Young Plan.[48]

The *New York Times* reminded readers and France that it was the United States that stood to lose the most. The reporter felt that 'French reasoning and French passion for security' left little space for 'any appreciation of the generosity of the offer ... or any concern for its beneficial result on the situation in Germany'.[49]

It's difficult to say how widespread these perceptions of the French were, but the American undersecretary of state William Castle Jr did not hold back when he said on June 27 that the 'French are the most hopeless people in the world. First, they were furious because their pride was injured. Now they are quibbling on methods while the house burns and we have got to waste hours in trying to make them see some sense. An acceptance of the plan would mean instantly good relations with Germany; it would mean the acceptance by this country of the Young Plan; it would mean a cordial atmosphere all round; it would stabilize the gains already made in commodity prices on the French market. And France is willing to risk all of this because French logic sees things in a different way.'[50]

A different analysis came from Morgan & Cie, who knew France and the French. Nelson Dean Jay had talked to several of 'our friends' in Paris and had noticed French concern that Germany might use 'this breathing spell to strengthen her military establishment and make advances to Eastern European countries, including Russia'.[51]

In a five-page response, J.P. Morgan & Co. stressed the need for France to accept the plan. 'To many of us here the American proposal seems like the greatest piece of good fortune that has come to the world since America entered the war. For any Nation to run the risk of throwing away or nullifying the effect of this great constructive gesture would appear incredible.'[52]

Very few took France's economic and security concerns seriously. One of the few sympathetic voices came from the *Commercial and Financial Chronicle* arguing that 'no harsh feelings ought to be entertained towards France on that account. France lies contiguous to Germany, and during the war suffered worse from invasion than any other country, and also sustained larger losses in men and material things than any other country.'[53]

What mattered to Norman was that conditions were 'very bad in Berlin yesterday'. He told Harrison that he had been on the phone with Luther who would fly to London to discuss a central bank credit. 'Norman dissuaded him from doing this, however, on the ground that he ought to be in Berlin. Whereupon Luther indicated that he was going to send one of his principal officers to London tomorrow or the next day.'

The Reichsbank's cover ratio was barely above the minimum of 40 per cent, and Norman found it 'likely inevitable that they must ask for a central bank credit', unless Hoover's debt plan changed the situation.[54]

There was ground for hope, as Norman told Harrison on June 22 that confidence was much improved in Berlin, and in 'London your announcement has given more hopeful feeling regarding Europe than I can easily remember'.

Nevertheless, Luther might need $50 million to tide the Reichsbank over the end of the month. He would stay in Berlin but send a representative to London. Norman told Harrison that the money 'may be essential for Reichsbank but will not be readily granted by Bank of England, in view of recent commitments in Austria and Hungary'.

Norman noticed Harrison's 'hesitation to grant accommodation alone' to Hungary, 'and the same question may arise regarding Reichsbank'. The BIS could not be of assistance, and he found it unlikely that the Banque de France 'would co-operate at least on any reasonable basis'.[55]

The failed negotiations about the Austrian bond loan had done nothing to change Norman's mind about the French, and since the Hoover proposal had seriously upset France, who knew what Banque de France's position would be. It was clear that Norman had a point when he had advised both Mellon and Harrison that Hoover should talk to France before announcing his plan. What he did not seem to appreciate was that the French government and the Banque de France did not necessarily have identical views. After all, they were French, and dislike of the French was part of Norman's and more generally a British worldview.

With both Hungary and – much more seriously – Germany in need of assistance to keep them on gold, the situation was critical. Norman frequently mentioned that the Austrian credit had strained the Bank of England's resources, and he was not optimistic about either the BIS or the Banque de France stepping in. That shifted focus to the New York Fed. Was Harrison ready to assist Europe on a massive scale, and on what terms?

On Monday, June 22, Harrison met with his executive committee to discuss foreign credits. He had received a request from McGarrah for the New York Fed to make a $15 million deposit with the BIS in support of the Hungarian central bank.

The executive committee agreed that the real issue was Germany. In the case of Hungary, several members felt that 'except in a great emergency' European central banks ought to step in first.

Harrison hoped that Hoover's debt plan would relieve the pressure on both Hungary and Germany. He also noted that the Fed was 'involved in the problems of these weaker countries because American banks had rushed into positions there and had now gotten scared and were running to get out again. This made it necessary, he said, to consider these problems in the light of the repercussions which they might have upon our markets.'

Harrison was the American central banker with the most international outlook, which included seeing the United States as a part of an international or trans-Atlantic economy. He was aware of the interconnectedness of the financial system, and though he agreed that Germany was the main problem, he also knew that it was part of general economic and political imbalances.

The New York Fed, Harrison emphasized, 'had responsibilities, as a great creditor nation, toward these other countries which we could not avoid. If, on balance, the rest of the world owes us four or five hundred million dollars a year, he said, and if we, in effect, temporarily demand payment in gold, we must help them to live until they can again pay us with goods and services.'

Then Theodore Whitmarsh, a longtime member of the New York Fed's board, though not a banker, asked a key question. Was there a strategy hidden somewhere between the individual support actions?

Mr. Whitmarsh asked if any sort of comprehensive program of financial relief and rehabilitation had been evolved. He felt that the Governors of the central banks might be jumping from one thing to another without looking at the whole picture to see what had to be done. Governor Harrison said that, by their nature, these problems had to be treated as they developed although it was, of course, essential to try and visualize the ultimate course which events would take. In the back of his mind there was always the thought, he said, that anything the central banks might do was merely a palliative and that the world credit and financial situation could not be cleared up without treating fundamentals such as international war debts and tariffs. Meanwhile, the question is whether we should stop leaks in the dyke or let the water in.[56]

From Whitmarsh's vantage point, it looked like the programme was 'to take care of each situation as it developed', and he was not convinced that was the best approach. Instead, he suggested that 'we should select the keystone situation – in this case Germany, he thought – and concentrate our forces there'.[57]

In principle, they did have a programme or a blueprint. It was implicitly based on the Bagehot operating model, even though they hardly followed that either. But this was a crisis far away from New York City. The fact that it was also international and involved banks on both sides of the Atlantic through their interconnectedness increased uncertainty and hence the need for sensemaking and narrative emplotment.

That is why Whitmarsh's question was to the point, signalling that there was no general plan for how to respond to the international crisis in a chaotic and complex reality where other things were never equal.

Harrison paraphrased Norman about politics and palliatives, and admitted that 'it was, of course, essential to try and visualize the ultimate course which events would take' – in short to imagine future outcomes. But except for Rodd's plan based on the reconstruction and set out in the early phase of the Austrian crisis, they never really got down to it.

With a few exceptions such as van Hengel, most actors were having trouble seeing the wood for all the trees, as Siepmann had framed it. Given the pervasive uncertainty and ambiguity, maybe it wasn't possible to see the wood, so they took 'care of each situation as it developed' and hoped that would do the job. They were certainly aware of what they were trying to do. It was just very difficult to plan a strategy under radical uncertainty about the future when the urgency of the situation took priority and demanded their attention. The financial crisis in Europe was part of bigger structural constraints such as reparations, war debts, short-term debt and hot money, political and cultural conflicts and so on that needed to be addressed as well.

Even if there were different opinions about what countries to support, why and how, the members of the executive committee agreed that Germany was, in fact, the 'keystone situation'. It was the prospect of capital flight from Germany and what might follow that prompted Hoover to propose a moratorium on intergovernmental debts. It was also the German situation that made Harrison accept the risk related to central bank credits, and to tell Charles Mitchell that 'our interest in the maintenance of the gold standard justified accepting that responsibility'.[58]

Germany was the big dike, but would Hoover's proposal stop the leak? The first signs were encouraging. 'The times have been dusty', McGarrah wrote to Harrison on Monday. 'Saturday evening I was very apprehensive, not only that the work that had been done by all in Austria and Hungary would be ineffective but that a serious situation would develop today in Germany.'[59]

Now, with the news of the Hoover plan, he felt relief. An anonymous BIS source told the *New York Times* that Hoover's 'very, very important' announcement 'can be the end of very great difficulties in Central Europe and Germany'.[60]

McGarrah and Fraser hoped France would accept Hoover's idea, but Pierre Quesnay was caught between a rock and a hard place. He congratulated Fraser 'on great progress realized in your country' and continued,

> I hope you realize in what impossible position my friends are. They have given up all their claims on Germany for war debts reimbursements, cut down several times their reparation claims, abandoned every pledge except Saar and accepted a reduced balance provided it is completely and definitively treated as a commercial one.
>
> No French Government after 15 months of Young Plan can get public opinion to give up special character of unconditional annuities ... Am afraid of possible reactions of my people.[61]

Quesnay was emotional about the situation. He was on his way to Paris to try to negotiate the French response to Hoover's proposal, but he was not optimistic. Fraser, who had spent some years in Paris, 'personally deeply sympathize with your difficulties as do all friends of France here'. The American Administration had to think about public opinion as well, but Fraser was 'explaining terrific French decisions to all comers'.[62]

At the Reichsbank, Luther's concerns were different. On June 22, at 10.35 a.m. he told Siepmann that he was not 'inclined to make forecasts about the effects of President Hoover's statement'. It all depended on how it was received in other countries, and he was 'uncertain about Paris'.

Luther thought the political situation had changed, but the technical position was the same. The Reichsbank still had to be ready to 'put into force their programme of credit restrictions' while trying to mitigate the effects on the economy. Siepmann, however, was more upbeat.

> I told Dr. Luther that in my opinion the whole position had now changed and that everything which was said on Saturday applied only to conditions which no longer exist. The Governor had more than once emphasized that he was only talking about what was possible or impossible in the circumstance of that moment, and if any of the same questions should arise again now, they could be approached differently. Dr. Luther understood me to be referring to the possibilities of a rediscount credit. I gave him to understand that what I had said would apply equally to that question and to any other which might arise.[63]

Later that day, at 3 p.m. Luther talked with Norman. He was still anxious about France's response to Hoover's plan, but 'the general situation in Berlin has undoubtedly improved. There is less tension, and public opinion is more hopeful.'

The Reichsbank would modify the planned credit restrictions, but Luther was still concerned about the month's end when private banks would need to rediscount 250 million reichsmarks at the Reichsbank. That might push the cover ratio below the minimum of 40 per cent.[64] This relatively optimistic message led Norman to cable Harrison that

> The calm and relaxation caused by Mr. Hoover's statement at home and abroad has made it possible for the Reichsbank to ease this morning sharply the management of the credit restrictions. Also an authorization from the General Council for the Reichsbank Directorate to lower the 40% cover limit, has been abandoned. The stock exchange reacted to Hoover's statement with lively optimism developing partly speculative increases. Exchange supply and demand were in equilibrium and improvement in Reichsmark quotations continued after official hours. I should be very grateful for any encouragement of returned confidence.[65]

The Reichsbank had been on the verge of lowering the cover ratio, an unmistakable sign that the withdrawal of foreign exchange had reached a highly critical point. According to *The Economist*, Friday, June 19, 'panic broke out' and the gold cover fell below the legal minimum. On Monday 'the situation was saved', and 'Mr. Hoover's move is naturally regarded here as the salvation from an imminent catastrophe'.[66]

The touch of optimism was even stronger the next day. The 'better sentiment which appeared yesterday has grown firmer', Luther told Norman and continued that 'for the first time in weeks we have been able to acquire a small amount of foreign exchange on the Boerse'.[67]

The American President's plan for a moratorium had changed the outlook, as Siepmann had told Luther the day before. Some confidence had returned, and there appeared to be a small opening for a new way of imagining the future, a new and more optimistic narrative.

The Reichsbank's balancing act with regard to the note cover was no secret in well-informed circles such as *The Economist*. Norman Crump, an assistant editor, and Walter Layton, the editor of the magazine, both visited Germany during these critical days. Crump had met with the economist Gustav Stolper and reported back to both Siepmann and Ernest Harvey.

Stolper knew his Bagehot. He believed that the Reichsbank would need a rediscount credit from Bank of England and the Federal Reserve Bank. 'Let it be known that this credit was there, and that it was adequate to meet all emergencies during the gap pending the execution of the Hoover plan, and it would tide the Reichsbank over, and would probably not be drawn upon at all.'[68]

Crump framed the situation in terms of national tensions and how France might respond to a credit to Reichsbank. 'France could still take gold in buckets from London' and Stolper wanted London and New York to act together, 'then France cannot be a real menace'.[69]

In contrast, Walter Layton went on to Paris and met with Governor Moret, who told him that the Reichsbank could get a loan in France. Moret 'could not understand why the Reichsbank did not apply to it for rediscounts if they need any'. Layton thought that Luther 'for fear of a snub, would do anything rather than approach the Banque de France direct'.[70]

Like in the case of Bank of England's unilateral loan to Austria, Moret's position indicated that Banque de France was capable of taking a different view than the French government and public opinion.

Luther did not approach Banque de France and never found out if Moret was sincere. Instead, he asked Norman. The Reichsbank was 5 million dollars short of the legal cover for the upcoming weekly statement. The Reichsbank representative who had travelled to London asked Norman for help and got it. 'I am going to advance that money for the night and take it back to-morrow. Everything is arranged', Norman told Harrison.[71]

## $100,000,000 TO THE REICHSBANK

Norman's overnight 5-million-dollar credit to the Reichsbank was not standard procedure, but the risk was limited and the timeframe short. It was all about window dressing the Reichsbank's balance sheet for the upcoming statement. But that was not the end of it. Norman also told Harrison about a more significant request from Luther.

Reichsbank require a credit from tomorrow until the 15th July of say, $80–100 million. Therefore, as you do not wish to do it alone, I propose that you and I equally grant to the Reichsbank from to-morrow a credit of $100/£20 million . . . I will invite the Bank of France to participate and to the extent that they do so your and my participation will be reduced. I do not think they will agree but the credit has to be fixed up before you get the Bank of France in . . .

It is true that if the whole thing goes ballyhack we are in the wet. I told you yesterday that I was very reluctant to do this but since then we have been impressed by the importance of the situation and the danger which will arise if nothing is done. I discussed this with Mr. Mellon last evening and asked him to send a message to Washington, and he said he would do so if he had time. He thought that what I am proposing ought to be done. It is useless to ask the little banks to go in and all the B.I.S. would do would be to talk about it all over Europe.[72]

When the Austrian National Bank had asked the Bank of England for assistance less than two months earlier, Norman had been very clear that it was the BIS that should be approached. That policy had changed now, as Norman worked to arrange a $100 million to the Reichsbank directly between Harrison and himself.

This was a significant shift revealing some of the fault lines that had already existed before but had deepened during the Austrian crisis. Norman's trust in the French was at a low point, and his confidence in the BIS had also vanished. In Austria, Norman assumed leadership at a time when the situation reached the tipping point, and no other international leader stepped up. This time, the challenge was many times larger, and for the first time Harrison was openly critical of Norman's approach.

I told him that while I was most sympathetic and agreed with him as to the urgency and importance of something being done, nevertheless, I felt the Bank of France should participate; that otherwise I was fearful lest some pressure might be removed from the French to go along with President Hoover's proposal. Norman said he did not think that would have anything to do with the debt negotiations and, furthermore, he did not believe that if he asked the Bank of France to participate they would do so. I said I did not quite agree with him as to either of these points, that frankly I did not feel that we should participate unless the Bank of France participates also.[73]

Adding insult to injury, Harrison also wanted the BIS to participate, and Norman had to give in. Jeopardizing Hoover's proposal, which had already upset the French, was not a risk Harrison wanted to take, and he viewed the French central bank and the BIS in a more positive light than Norman.

In fact, Harrison had a direct line to the BIS through McGarrah and Fraser, and he knew from the recent board meeting that his directors wanted European central banks involved.

Norman confirmed their conversation in a telegram, and Harrison agreed 'in principle' to participate in the credit. The condition was that 'the Bank of France participate in a substantial amount which we think should be approximately the same as the Bank of England and ourselves'. He also requested that the BIS and 'possibly other Central Banks' were invited to participate, and he 'would not expect that our participation would be in excess of $35,000,000'.[74]

Harrison needed acceptance from his own board and the Federal Reserve Board in Washington DC. After his talk with Norman, he called Eugene Meyer, the governor of the Federal Reserve Board, to get a green light for the New York Fed's participation in the credit. He emphasized the positive effects of Hoover's announcement. It was not the time for the Fed to be 'throwing a cog in the wheel by refusing to cooperate temporarily over the month-end period'.

Meyer told Harrison that the President was concerned that the credit would reduce the likelihood for 'the French to come through with a satisfactory reply to Mr. Hoover's debt offer'. Harrison did not share this concern because he would only join the credit if Banque de France did as well. But, if the Fed's participation in the credit might jeopardize the negotiations with the French, 'it would give an entirely different aspect to it'.[75]

After ending the call with Meyer, Harrison called Robert Lacour-Gayet, the French central banker, who was in London. With six years of work experience in the United States from 1924 to 1930, Lacour-Gayet was fluent in English, and he had a better understanding of the American point of view than any other French central banker.

Harrison told Lacour-Gayet about his talks with Norman about the need for a credit to enable Germany to 'maintain its 40% limit to carry through from now until the 16th of July'. He then asked whether the Banque de France 'would participate if invited'.

Lacour-Gayet had 'heard nothing whatever' about the credit, but he was certain that Banque de France would participate if invited. He would 'immediately get in touch with the Bank of England and then call Governor Moret and talk to me at 2:30 p.m. New York Time'.

Harrison pointed out that he had only heard about the credit through Norman the same morning. He also encouraged Lacour-Gayet to tell

Moret thus: 'I believed it to be important and hoped that the Bank of France would go along in such a credit if we did.'[76]

Back on the phone with Harrison at 2.45 p.m., Lacour-Gayet told him that he had talked to Harry Siepmann and Clément Moret. Moret had not heard about the credit either, but he was ready to join. 'He said he would prefer to be invited by the Federal Reserve Bank, but that if invited by the Bank of England it would make no real difference in their final decision.'

Perhaps unavoidably they also talked about the Hoover proposal. Lacour-Gayet thought that France would be reluctant to give up the unconditional payments, which were exempt from negotiation according to the Young Plan. 'He indicated that there was considerable feeling in France that this whole thing had been done over their heads and without consulting them at all. I explained that I understood it, it was all done so hurriedly that it was impossible to do that over the weekend.'

> I then mentioned that, of course, the real benefit of this proposal would be in its effect upon the world depression rather than upon any particular country; that our Government had acted largely with that in mind, and that I thought it might be better for all of us to consider it from that angle rather than from the benefits to accrue to any one debtor. Lacour-Gayet said he realized that but that he thought Germany ought to be willing to make some contribution to that recovery as well as everybody else.[77]

Harrison was treading carefully as he tried to convince Lacour-Gayet to see the positive effects of the Hoover plan. Much like the *New York Times* two days before, but with more sympathy, he tried to re-frame the proposal, but with only limited success. Before ending the call, Lacour-Gayet told Harrison that he had a meeting with Siepmann or Norman the next day at 11 a.m. He would call Harrison later that day to tell him about the outcome.[78]

Though Norman was still very much at the centre of the community of central bankers, the disagreement with Harrison and the latter's direct communication with Lacour-Gayet indicated that a shift might be underway, where Harrison would take up a more central and decisive role and challenge Norman's position. The Hoover proposal played a role in this shift.

They were at the frontier of complicated and urgent negotiations of great significance to world financial stability, and Harrison felt that Norman's attitude towards the Banque de France was still 'stupid beyond understanding' as Benjamin Strong had put it in 1928. Harrison was less emotional about the French, but he had also become more deeply embedded in politics since the announcement of Hoover's debt proposal. Would his and Norman's partnership to save the world of finance grow strained?

## GEORGE L. HARRISON TAKES CHARGE

Harrison had a busy Tuesday. After the second phone call with Lacour-Gayet, he went on to his 2 p.m. meeting with his directors, who authorized him to participate in a German credit with up to $50 million. At 4 p.m. he called Norman for the second time that day to tell him that he had not yet heard back from Eugene Meyer.

Harrison emphasized again that the Fed would only participate in the Reichsbank credit if the Banque de France was in with the same amount as the Bank of England and the Federal Reserve Bank.

> Governor Norman said he questioned whether it was possible to get the French to participate and that he had not as yet (it then being 9 p.m. London time) taken the matter up with the Bank of France, although he had arranged to see Lacour-Gayet tomorrow morning at the Bank in London for the purpose of inviting the Bank of France.[79]

Harrison interrupted him and said that he had already talked with Lacour-Gayet who believed that the Banque de France would participate on an equal basis with the Bank of England and the Federal Reserve Bank. He went on to insist that the BIS be invited to participate as well, even 'if they could do so only for a relatively small amount'. Harrison also hoped that Norman would invite others to participate, and 'Norman said he would see what he could do along these lines too'.

During their talk, Norman mentioned that the credit ought to have been arranged by the BIS, a first hint that he realized how his approach might strain relations not only with Harrison but also with the Banque de France and the BIS. Harrison did not ask why the BIS was not the organizer but 'assumed that it was because the Germans had come direct to London and in the emergency and press for time had asked them to take the credit rather than taking it up with Basle'.[80]

Harrison still needed a go from Washington, and after his talk with Norman, he called Governor Meyer several times. Finally reaching him at 5 p.m., he updated Meyer on the talks with Lacour-Gayet and Norman, and his board's decision to go along with the credit.

Meyer was concerned about repayment of the credit, but to Harrison 'the risks of not participating were greater than the risks of doing so'. Meyer also asked, 'What was the hurry', which provoked Harrison.

He impatiently reminded Meyer that he had phoned him at home on Sunday 'to forewarn him of what was now transpiring, that, as I had told him on Sunday, it was inevitable, in my judgment, that the Reichsbank would very quickly have to ask for a credit, possibly even the next day; that I felt that he had as much advance notice as it was possible to give him, that indeed we had talked about this thing for a week or two in advance, in any event'.

He asked Meyer 'to please arrange for approval or disapproval tonight so that I might cable Norman'. Meyer replied that he had already talked with his board this morning, and they 'all realized that it was imminent. I said that in that event I hoped they would be prepared to act this afternoon.'[81]

Two hours later, Meyer called back with the board's approval, and soon after Harrison cabled Norman agreeing in principle to take part in the Reichsbank credit with up to $50 million. The conditions were that the Banque de France participated with the same amount as the Bank of England and the New York Fed, and that the BIS and 'possibly' other central banks were also invited to participate.[82]

Norman's ways prompted Harrison to take charge and insist on bringing the BIS and the Banque de France into the credit. Norman was not used to being told what to do, and his animosity against Banque de France and the BIS was getting the better of him. It did not go unnoticed in Basle.

Fraser cabled McGarrah from New York about Norman's plan. 'Some people indignant here that Norman leaving out B.I.S.' and Fraser foresaw a public scandal in Germany if the BIS was not part of the credit.[83] That was the first McGarrah had heard about it, and on Wednesday, June 24, around noon, he called the Bank of England and insisted on talking to Norman, who was not available. He ended up talking to Siepmann, who noted,

> Mr. McGarrah telephoned at 12.15 that he thinks Dr. Vocke may have made a great mistake in coming to London instead of going through Basle. This is exactly the kind of credit which it is for the B.I.S. to do, and they need it for their prestige whereas the Bank of England does not. Mr. McGarrah is very upset about it and he does not see why this credit is being handled on different lines from any other credit. I told him that we heard of it for the first time yesterday and explained that money had to be provided by the 23rd and 25th June. Mr. McGarrah replied that he did not understand why the Governor could not have telephoned him last night at the same time as he communicated with Governor Harrison. I asked Mr. McGarrah whether he wished me to understand that he could not give a definite reply about B.I.S. participation until this question of procedure had been answered or dealt with. He said that of course the B.I.S. would come along, but that in his opinion they should organize the credit. He asked me to obtain a reply for the Governor while he held the telephone line, and eventually said that he would be at

> his own house for the next half hour where we could ring him up. He has already expressed his feelings freely to Dr. Luther on the telephone.[84]

Luther did not hesitate to write an apology assuring McGarrah that he 'fully appreciate the helpful spirit you have always displayed'.[85] Norman never called back, but later that day, he sent a letter to McGarrah with a copy to Luther. He explained how Dr Vocke 'arrived yesterday in London' and asked for a credit and how the best way to deal with the problem was to arrange a credit running from June 24 to July 16 in order to maintain the Reichsbank's cover ratio above 40 per cent. It was not much of an apology, but Norman did at least write, 'I assume that Monsieur Moret and Governor Harrison would wish, as I do, that the contributions of all of us should be made available through the Bank for International Settlements.'[86]

Norman's stubbornness about the Banque de France took a hit as well. Shortly after McGarrah's phone call, Harry Siepmann met with Lacour-Gayet, who told him that Moret was 'personally very favourable to a participation' and that he would summon the Board of Regents that afternoon. Like Harrison, Moret insisted that the BIS should participate and 'perhaps arrange the details of the operation with the Reichsbank'.[87]

In fact, in a strictly private message, Banque de France called McGarrah and said that not only would they participate in the loan to Germany, 'they would make a deposit if necessary with the B.I.S. to enable it to participate in Reichsbank credit'.[88]

Harrison heard about Moret's wish to participate in the loan, as he talked to Lacour-Gayet three times that Wednesday. Lacour-Gayet also told Harrison that the French government had sent its reply to Hoover's proposal to Washington suggesting that the unconditional payments should still be paid by Germany but to the BIS and in reichsmark and to be used in Germany and other Central European countries. According to Harrison, Lacour-Gayet

> said that public opinion in France would make it almost impossible to consider releasing the Reichsbank from making payments even in marks on the unconditional annuities and especially so in view of the fact that the Bank of France was today participating in the credit to the Reichsbank. . . . He said that he was telling me his views personally, hoping that I might relay them to Mr. Mills for he said in his own judgment the French reply was an earnest effort to accept the spirit of Mr. Hoover's proposal.[89]

After the talk with Lacour-Gayet, Harrison called Norman, who told him that the four banks were in with $25 million each in the Reichsbank credit.

He also told Harrison that Britain's response to the Hoover proposal 'being published today is very definite and affirmatively good'. Norman was less happy about the French position, which made it 'difficult for the Reichsbank, the German exchange not being so good tonight', and might make 'the general position ... extremely critical'.[90] Norman then again brought up the issue of organizing the loan.

Incidentally he said he hoped that there would be no bad feeling against the Reichsbank as a result of the way this credit has been handled; that he had gotten some repercussions along that line already, and that he wished I would do what I could to pour oil on the waters. I told him I rather gathered that from my conversation with Lacour-Gayet; that he had said very pointedly that the Bank of France had heard nothing at the time at which I was talking to him yesterday; that there was some feeling on their part on account of lack of direct information, but I did not know there was anyone else. Norman then referred to the Bank for International Settlements and hoped that I would straighten Fraser out and explain that this thing did not come up even with him until yesterday noon in London, and that it was only pressure of time that made it necessary for the Reichsbank to act as they did, an officer of the Reichsbank being then in London. I told him I would do everything I could to straighten things out.[91]

Harrison, the poker player, had the best hand. He came out of organizing the Reichsbank credit strengthened relative to Norman, who had angered McGarrah and Fraser by circumventing the BIS, with some encouragement from Luther. At the Banque de France, they were also upset about not being informed; that was another kind of rules of the game and of cooperation that Norman praised but did not quite live up to. He had overstepped a line and was forced to retreat and let the BIS be in charge.[92]

Norman's view on central bank cooperation was seriously challenged by his animosity against the French and the BIS. Even if he did not see the blind spots and contradictions himself, his idiosyncratic approach seriously backfired. He was proved wrong both by Moret's and by Lacour-Gayet's eagerness to cooperate on the Reichsbank credit and by Harrison's insistence that the Banque de France and the BIS should also be part of the credit.

At the same time, the increasing awareness of the significance of structural and political issues also changed the situation. Hoover's debt proposal made it very clear to the central bankers how big a role politics and the legacy of Versailles played in the question of European financial stability. This was, of course, a point that Norman had stressed several times.

It was also important for Harrison to control the way information about the credit was passed on to the public. At 5 p.m. he placed a call to Norman saying it should be Luther who announced the credit, and that he would like to have advance notice about time and content of the announcement. There were already rumours about the credit, and it was bound to leak anyway. Harrison also asked where the credit would be signed, but after Norman replied at the BIS or the Banque de France,

I said that I did not care how it was done . . . but that I wanted to know what was done. Governor Norman indicated that during the day he had turned over the whole thing to the B.I.S. at their request or suggestion, but that he would guarantee me that he would look after our interest and our position in the matter.[93]

Harrison also took the occasion to write directly to Luther to say how much he appreciated 'your cables informing me from time to time of your position. They have been most helpful.'[94] Luther replied that Hoover's debt plan had led to a 'complete reversal of tendency on Stock Exchange. Stock prices increased to quite an unusual extent and the already firm tendency of bond prices was considerably strengthened.' Demand for foreign exchange had fallen since Monday and the Reichsbank had even purchased gold and was able, if barely at 40.4 per cent, to stay above the minimum cover ratio 'without having recourse to credits'.[95]

On Thursday, June 25, the Federal Reserve Bank officially confirmed to the BIS its participation in the Reichsbank credit.[96] The same day, the joint $100 million credit to the Reichsbank was announced in the public.[97] The New York Fed also published a statement to the press and communicated the content to McGarrah and Luther.[98] Luther's reply seemed to indicate the beginning of a closer relationship between the two central bankers.

Confirming your yesterday's cable I thank you sincerely for your efforts on behalf of the rediscount credit for the Reichsbank. In connection with the extraordinary action undertaken by President Hoover in so vigorous and resolute a manner I feel that the co-operation with you dear Mr. Harrison, is particularly important and valuable to us.[99]

Norman too received a thank you cable from Luther for 'your vigorous action which I realise in its full significance in connections with the general developments of recent days'.[100]

Luther appeared optimistic in these ritualized letters, but there was still a long way to go before anyone could expect to get a good night's sleep without worrying about the situation in Germany. On Thursday, June 25 at 10.45 a.m. New York time, Harrison called Norman and said that Germany was in a bad situation as the Reichsbank had lost between 6 and 7 million dollars before 1 p.m.

That was new. The information channel usually went from Norman to Harrison, but now Harrison was informing Norman about the Reichsbank's situation.

Norman again blamed the French. He told Harrison that the French reception of Hoover's proposal 'is reacting on Berlin. . . . There is such uncertainty with respect to the French position that the reaction in Berlin is disappointing and serious. According to Norman, the French must come into line or the situation will become dangerous again.'[101]

But the French did not come into line. One week into the announcement of the Hoover plan, the always well-informed Merle Cochran reported to the State Department on the Hoover moratorium and how it was perceived in Europe.

The Chequers meeting had reinforced the perception in Europe of the stalwart American position on war debts, and Hoover's proposal had come as a surprise in Europe. According to Cochran, the German statement about reparations made it even harder for the British to discuss this matter out of concern for 'offending the American viewpoint'.

Cochran's privileged access to information was evident as he noted that the first sign of a change in US policy on war debts 'appears to have been received through a telephone conversation with Governor George Harrison of the Federal Reserve Bank of New York, who, in discussing the Chequers-German situation, asked Governor Norman of the Bank of England if there was anything the United States could do to help'.

Cochran's source may have been Walter Stewart, who also told Cochran how Pierre Quesnay had tried to influence the French response to Hoover's plan. But Quesnay's efforts backfired and angered McGarrah and Leon Fraser, who did not like the perception that the French reply was 'based upon the idea of M. Quesnay'.

In fact, it was not. According to Cochran, Quesnay had advised the French Ministry of Finance that France should unconditionally accept Hoover's proposal. However, France did not follow Quesnay's idea but wanted the unconditional payments to be paid to the BIS rather than be suspended.

'M. Quesnay is a man of many ideas, with little reluctance at disclosing them', Cochran noted. 'Some of them are too international in viewpoint to please the French. M. Quesnay, in turn, is distressed at the attitude France has been taking, with respect both to Austria and Germany, and he realizes the position of isolation in which his country might be found if this policy was uncompromisingly continued.'[102]

Pierre Quesnay appeared again to share the ideas of the central banking community with Clément Moret, Lacour-Gayet and Charles Rist. Though not completely immune from French politics and institutions, their practices implied that their identity as central bankers mattered and that within some constraints, they tried to distance themselves from French politics. Maybe Norman did them injustice.

That was certainly how it looked from Basle. Already in late 1930, Fraser admitted to McGarrah that Quesnay is 'frequently overenthusiastic and a little bit too "quick on the trigger", and everybody who do not know this think that everything is the consequence of a carefully considered plan. Our London friends do not at all like our rapid development', and 'almost anything Quesnay does is construed in London as being anti-English'.[103]

Cochran's report to the State Department was confidential and not widely read. In public, *The Economist* reported on June 27 that the 'French fear, . . . is that, as the result of Mr. Hoover's offer being put into operation, German reparation payments will not merely be suspended for 12 months, but for all time, and that with this the Treaty of Versailles itself would also be torn up'.[104]

*The Economist* felt a 'sense of relief and gratitude' for Hoover's proposal, which provided the possibility of 'regained assurance and hope for the future' not least because 'the crisis in Germany was coming to a head with disastrous swiftness, and that the heavy continued foreign withdrawals of funds, accompanied by growing signs of panic on the part of German depositors, constituted an imminent threat to the stability of the German banking system'.[105]

## 13

# Germany Will Collapse (June 19–July 10)

The Austrian crisis began as a banking crisis when the bad news about Credit Anstalt became public on May 11. It then developed into a foreign exchange crisis too in late May and June. In Germany, it was different. As problems intensified in June, the German Reichsmark was the first to come under pressure. The $100 million credit to the Reichsbank on June 25 was arranged by the three largest central banks and the Bank for International Settlements (BIS). The big question now was how to stem the German foreign exchange crisis and keep it from developing into a banking crisis as well.

Germany was the 'keystone situation' as Theodore Whitmarsh remarked. This was what van Hengel had addressed in his letters to Norman and McGarrah on June 11. German banks had too little capital, and as 'not paying' was not considered an option, he emphasized the need for a 'willing stopping of payments as far as possible . . . for all credits by international banks to Germany', in effect a standstill agreement. He also asked for energetic steps to organize Germany's foreign creditors and urged Norman that these measures 'ought to be taken by you, by the B.I.S., the Federal Reserve Board, perhaps the Banque de France, on one side, and the Reichsbank and German State on the other. This decisive action I hope to discuss with you and the other gentlemen before it is too late.'[1]

But nobody apparently wanted to listen or talk to van Hengel, and no initiative was taken to avoid a further deterioration of conditions in Germany until President Hoover's debt proposal on June 20. In fact, it was not until early July that the idea of organizing the creditor banks surfaced again. 'Instead of waiting to organize the foreign creditors when a crash comes could not a big syndicate of private banks be got together to deal generally with private European debtors', Pierre Quesnay asked in phone calls to Siepmann and others, but nothing came of it.[2]

Already on June 20, readers of *The Economist* understood that everyone's eyes were now on Germany's financial fragility. Even if 'the strain of a week ago has during the last two or three days been momentarily relaxed', the main question now was 'the vulnerability of the German banking system to foreign withdrawals of funds'. The author was optimistic and believed 'the claims could be met', but if not, there was always 'the possibility of assistance from the B.I.S.'[3]

Another article in the same issue by *The Economist*'s correspondent in Germany begged to differ. The German situation was 'most gravely disquieting' as foreign exchange left the country. The author blamed contagion from the Austrian crisis, and the 'wave of distrust . . . has now spread . . . into a general flood which has penetrated into Germany as well'.[4]

As Germany's foreign exchange position was challenged daily, Austria lingered on. The standstill agreement with the International Committee and Bank of England's unilateral action had worked. Bruins found the situation 'much quieter' and replied on June 19 to Norman's question about when he would be in control, that 'if no new difficulties arise Austrian National Bank will be in complete command of the monetary position within a few days'.[5]

For once, Sir Robert Kindersley also struck an optimistic note in a telephone call with Siepmann at 6.30 p.m. on June 19. Kindersley was still in Vienna, and he said, 'The situation there is very definitely better. The National Bank are happy, for the first time. . . . Sir Robert Kindersley says that for the first time since he arrived in Vienna, he now feels that things are going right, and he would hope that this development will very quickly be reflected in Berlin'.[6]

Then, on June 20 Hoover announced his debt plan in an attempt to address some of the underlying constraints, and a few days later, on Thursday, June 25, the BIS, the Bank of England, the Banque de France and the New York Fed stepped in with the $100 million credit to the Reichsbank. There was reason to be cautiously optimistic. At this moment, the known unknown and main source of uncertainty was how France would respond to Hoover's plan.

## STRONG POLITICAL ANTAGONISM

On Saturday, one week after President Hoover presented his plan for a one-year moratorium on government debts, Norman received a brief message from Harrison, saying 'have just arrived in Washington. Will telephone you about three London time tomorrow.'[7]

Norman replied that he 'received your plain cable and await telephone call.... You will agree that unless unconditional annuities are dealt with broadly in terms of President's announcement the credit of Germany is likely to suffer immediately.'[8]

Since political elements had forcefully entered the crisis in Central Europe, Harrison and Norman spoke more frequently and their views and logics were no longer as well aligned. At 9 a.m. New York time, Harrison called Norman from Washington to hear the latest news 'as they appeared to him'.

They didn't appear good at all. Norman told Harrison that Germany had lost $14 million that day and the previous day. Norman said that the debate in Paris was 'most unfortunate indeed' and 'we should put all possible pressure upon them'. French modifications to the plan 'would put the Germans back in the position they would have been in before the President's announcement'. Harrison disagreed and argued that Germany would 'have a real benefit' despite possible French revisions.[9]

But Norman argued that the psychology would be different. What mattered were not 'Brüning, Luther or Curtius' but the 'attitude of mind of the German public'.

> Of course they are better off than if nothing had been done but they are worse off than they believed themselves to be under the President's announcement and, with the German public in its present frame of mind, it is bad to excite their hopes and then disappoint; you are dealing there with strong political antagonism; the position is difficult and dangerous.[10]

About the time Norman tried to convince Harrison that raising hopes and then crushing them could trigger a political response, Siepmann was busy talking to Vocke and Dreyse on the telephone. At 2 p.m. Vocke called Siepmann on behalf of Chancellor Brüning. The Chancellor was interested in Norman's position on the Hoover plan, and Siepmann made it clear that the 'Governor's position is in general that the Hoover scheme stands or falls as a whole and that any modifications or exceptions would immediately damage German credit'. Siepmann also stressed that Norman's opinion was based 'on the faith of what he has been told by the Reichsbank' about conditions in Germany.[11]

Two hours after Norman had talked with Harrison, Siepmann called Vice President Dreyse at the Reichsbank and asked if there could be any modifications to the Hoover proposal without destroying its effect. Dreyse said the Reichsbank would consider any modification a 'real misfortune', 'there had been a "miracle" and a "promise" made last Sunday and ... the Germans have set their heart on its fulfilment'.[12]

Norman had chosen a side. His sympathy lay with Germany, who had fixated all hopes on Hoover's plan. He was also aware of the political polarization in Germany, and how French demands for modifications could worsen the situation. To Norman, France was the obstacle. In contrast, from a US perspective, Harrison saw France as much as the key to a solution as Germany, and he certainly did not want to see his president's plan fall apart.

The discussion continued in a follow-up telegram from Norman, who tried to look at the wood rather than the trees and started outlining some more general problems in the European situation.

> We must look at Germany, Hungary, Austria etc. as merely different parts of one problem and each part is equally dangerous to the whole. This is too complicated to discuss in the first instance by telephone but please think it over and cable me for Monday and at present avoid discussion with Europe.[13]

'Europe' was most likely a reference to the BIS, which Norman still didn't trust to be able to keep a secret. Harrison, whether he agreed or not, knew that the BIS was not the decisive player in this situation. When he needed to discuss with Europe a couple of days later, he called Lacour-Gayet at the Banque de France. On Monday, June 29, at 1.50 p.m. they briefly discussed the credit to Hungary, and Harrison hoped 'that the Bank of France would finally decide to go into the credit'.

The telephone connection was bad, but Harrison also talked to Andrew Mellon, who was with the well-connected Lacour-Gayet in his apartment. Harrison told Mellon that the market in the United States was weak 'no doubt due to the uncertainty over the negotiations in Paris'. Mellon was 'discouraged about the status of the negotiations', and Harrison said that if they broke down, he would not recommend a renewal of the Reichsbank credit 'merely for the purpose of enabling them ... to pay reparations'.[14]

Next up, Harrison called Hans Luther at 3.25 p.m. There were more withdrawals, primarily from the United States and France. Luther was enthusiastic about the Hoover plan, but the 'protracted delay of the French in coming to an agreement ... has undone some of the good effects of Mr. Hoover's action'. He feared that 'further delay might precipitate real difficulty in the matter of withdrawals'. They agreed that Luther should update Harrison about the Reichsbank's position every evening.

At this point Norman was no longer Harrison's exclusive hub to information about events in Europe. He was establishing his own communications channels now and talked directly with the Reichsbank and the Banque de France.

Still June 29, Lacour-Gayet called Harrison at home at 9 p.m. They discussed the debt plan and Lacour-Gayet 'said it was not at all satisfactory; that really the French needed more time ... that after all the things had been put up to them in a great hurry and that it took time to analyze the situation and to develop it soundly'.

Harrison asked about the outcome of the cabinet meeting 'tonight (it then being 2 a.m. Paris time) and he said he understood that they had adjourned until Wednesday. Lacour-Gayet said he thought it important that we keep in close touch with each other, even by telephone, so I said I would call him tomorrow, which he said he would be glad to have me do.'

As agreed, Harrison called Lacour-Gayet the next day at the Banque de France at 4.20 p.m. and asked for any news about the debt negotiations in Paris. Like Norman and the German Reichsbank had referred to the German public as an important factor, Lacour-Gayet now referred to the French public opinion. He 'was very much afraid that his government will not go much further, largely on account of public opinion which, in his judgment, is quite impossible at the present time'.

It was a legitimizing narrative hard to argue with. After all, what politician would go up against public opinion? Harrison found that Lacour-Gayet, like Mellon, 'seemed pretty much discouraged about any hopeful outcome'. A lot of members of the French senate thought the government had 'already gone much too far'. In fact, that was the sentiment throughout the country.

Harrison tried really hard to find a way to change the narrative and convince Lacour-Gayet that Hoover's proposal was a good thing. Perhaps, Harrison said, Lacour-Gayet and the French government overestimated the public opinion. What mattered was how it was 'presented to the people', how it was framed. Harrison told Lacour-Gayet how the Hoover proposal had been favourably received by Congress and the public.

> I pointed out that one of the reasons for this was that our government made it so clear that our offer was for a worldwide holiday for a period of one year without any implications that we would waive or in any other way amend the obligations due to us after that year.... I wondered whether his own people would not respond equally favorably if they could see the picture equally clearly.[15]

In Harrison's telling, Lacour-Gayet appreciated his very clear and impressive 'picture' but did not believe the French government could be turned around. They felt that 'they have been rushed into a position without prior consultation and which in the light of public opinion is very difficult for them indeed'.

That was a familiar argument, and Norman of all people had already pointed out the risk of not involving the French government before announcing the plan. Now, Harrison grabbed the opportunity to address the issue and make it personal. He emphasized, 'We were forced to act so quickly in view of the crisis in Central Europe that we had little opportunity for prior consultation, such as we would otherwise have wanted.'

> I then said I wanted to tell him a story which should convince him of the background of our action here and our lack of intention to do anything 'over the heads' of the French government, as he had implied; that I had no express authority to tell him this but I thought he ought to know it in the press of the present circumstances: That the President of the United States a few weeks ago, when this question first arose in his mind, said that he wanted to take no action whatever until he had been able to find out in some authoritative fashion, first, how serious the situation in Central Europe really was and, second, whether any action on our part would be of any real help; that this would necessarily depend in part on what would be the attitude abroad, especially in France; that on Friday, June 12, he asked me to sail for France on the next day; that I had purchased my ticket and procured my passport at the State Department and was prepared to sail in order to discuss the matter in Paris, with a view to finding out what might be the attitude of the French in the event that our government later saw fit to take some action along the lines which it has now taken. Unfortunately, I explained to him, that very night and the next morning – the morning of the day of which I was to sail – information from Austria, Hungary and Berlin evidenced such a critical condition in those countries that it became obvious to us that if we were to act we must do so promptly and without the advantage, which the President so much wished, of prior first-hand information from some authoritative person directly on the spot. Furthermore, it was felt that because of the development of these conditions it was better for me to remain at my desk, rather than to be at the water, when central bank operations of large size might become imperative.[16]

Lacour-Gayet regretted that Harrison had been unable to come to Paris. A visit might well have influenced the French attitude. He appreciated Harrison telling this story, and 'asked whether I would have any objection to his telling his government. I told him that while I had no authority, I could see no objection.'

Lacour-Gayet said that he would go see 'his ministers' as soon as the call was over to tell them Harrison's story and encourage a settlement. Harrison had, in his telling, convinced Lacour-Gayet that the Hoover plan was 'vitally important to avoid a complete breakdown in Central Europe with all its damaging repercussions on us and on the French'.

Harrison then asked Lacour-Gayet to imagine a future where debt negotiations broke down. All Lacour-Gayet could say was that it would be serious. Would Germany be able to pay the next reparations payment, even the unconditional one, on July 15, Harrison asked, and Lacour-Gayet said it would be very difficult. It would be impossible, Harrison replied, and withdrawals from Germany would accelerate 'unless some favorable news becomes public very shortly'.

The French would lose as well, since they would not get anything from Germany. The Fed was not going to renew the Reichsbank credit just to enable Germany to pay reparations. And, Harrison suspected, neither would the Banque de France, which Lacour-Gayet admitted.

> So, I asked, if this is true is there not all the more reason for him to make one final effort to procure a generous and broad acceptance of the President's proposal in order, in the interest of France as well as the rest of the world, to avoid possibly very disastrous events. He repeated again that he would make one more effort and would immediately go to his government to see what he could do.[17]

As they ended the call, Harrison assured Lacour-Gayet that he was the most qualified to do it because of his experience from living in America.[18]

No one could blame Harrison for not trying. Hoover's prestige and Europe's future were at risk, and Harrison put all his effort into getting France on board without alienating Germany. It might not be a central bank issue any longer, but central banks still had a role to play, not least because of their personal connections and the community to which they belonged.

Rather than discussing central bank credits, Harrison and Lacour-Gayet tried to figure out if and how to change the French government's position to Hoover's proposal. Harrison's narrative was one of rational deliberations, but at the same time he invoked fictional expectations to win Lacour-Gayet over. The French story was emotional. Whether Lacour-Gayet could change his government's position by using Harrison's narrative remained to be seen.

Whether for strategic or personal reasons, or both, Harrison was more sympathetic to the French perception of the situation than the occasionally ill-tempered Norman, and he played his cards wisely. As central bankers, Harrison and Lacour-Gayet understood each other well, and they both realized that the world was on the brink of economic collapse. The focus was still on saving the gold standard, but it was a hopeless task without considering politics.[19]

What was certain was that in order to have any chance of succeeding in their endeavour, Hoover's debt plan needed some momentum, fast. Luther cabled Harrison that withdrawals of foreign exchange had increased since June 24, 'chiefly attributable we assume to continuous calls of foreign credits'. Further credit restriction would have to be introduced 'If French assent is not given by tomorrow', July 1.[20]

If J.P. Morgan & Co.'s information was valid, that would not happen. A day earlier, Monday, June 29, the French Ministry of Finance had asked Morgan & Cie. to come for a meeting and discuss the negotiations, but the banking firm had declined getting involved and informed its US parent in New York.

J.P. Morgan nursed no illusions about who was right and who was wrong. Hoover's plan meant that the United States would give up about $240 million in payments, while France would only give up about $92 million. That was 'a basic fact which no one can escape'. Morgans had been in 'fairly close touch with Washington' and the administration was upset about 'what they deem to be constant fresh conditions'.

Morgans believed that 'in case the discussion breaks down the Washington Administration will be likely to invite every other European Country concerned to take advantage of the American proposition and France will be left out on a limb and accused by the world of having tried to sabotage the whole plan'. The French people might not care, but Morgans believed that it would be manifestly against their own interests.[21]

Without a solution, Germany would have to begin another round of deflationary measures in order to stay above the cover ratio of 40 per cent. But deflation would only make matters worse. On Wednesday, July 1, Norman told his Committee of Treasury that he expected Germany to declare a moratorium if France and America did not come to an agreement soon.[22]

## THE FRENCH CABINET IS NOW IN SESSION

The same morning, Harrison received a telegram from Norman. News from Hungary was bad, and 'in Paris prospects look pretty black for Germany and others'.[23] At 12.35 p.m. Harrison called Norman who told him that the 'delay in Paris is becoming critical in Berlin. The French can afford to wait, but Berlin cannot, for it is being bled to death in the meantime.'

Harrison agreed that speed was essential but did not see what could be done. Ogden Mills had suggested to 'get the French to agree to

Mr. Hoover's proposal in principle' and refer a number of points to a committee of treasury experts. Norman was sceptical as 'these points seem only questions of detail to him and to me as central bankers', but 'they are very big questions to the treasuries concerned'.

Meanwhile, the British government was debating whether to 'officially advise the French Government that the conditions imposed by the French are wholly unacceptable to the British'.

Norman was in favour of 'forcing an issue' with regard to withdrawals, especially from Germany, 'the country which Mr. Hoover intended primarily to help'. Harrison said that 'the French Cabinet is now in session' and added that 'speed is all important'. They would probably know more in an hour or two.[24]

It was not clear what Norman referred to with forcing an issue, but as he met with the German Ambassador Konstantin von Neurath on July 2, he certainly went beyond ordinary central banking practices. Norman 'advised Germany (through him) to make sure she can't pay BIS Rep'ns this month & to announce the fact at once'.[25]

They were extraordinary times. Harrison called Norman at 5 p.m. after having talked with 'Washington'. France seemed prepared to abandon some demands about the unconditional payments, if the Bank of England, the Federal Reserve Bank and the Banque de France would 'agree to participate to the extent of $10,000,000 each in providing funds in some fashion for central European countries requiring it'.

'Norman's general reaction to all this was that he did not like it, partly because it was political in its inception, and partly because he was already so heavily committed in central Europe. I told him I was not asking him to express himself now, that I just wanted to let him know what I had heard was the development and counter-proposals of the French; that I hoped he would consider it overnight, and I said he would probably hear about it from his own government in the morning as I understood Washington was getting in touch with them.'[26]

The central banks had taken centre stage during the first phases of the Austrian crisis. Now they were gradually being relegated to second position as the larger structural and political issues came to the fore. At the same time, Norman and Harrison shifted roles, as Harrison became an increasingly central player and representative of his government as both politics and the United States entered the scene. Now, Harrison provided Norman with new information on the American and French positions. This was a reversal of the usual pattern where Norman had information about the European situation that Harrison needed.

Norman was still worried about the demarcation line between central bank problems and political problems. Norman had no wish for central banks to get involved in politics or vice versa. Except when it came to himself as his advice to von Neurath demonstrated. That was another blind spot.

Norman was in a dilemma. He had little respect for politics and preferred central banking to be kept as far apart from politics as possible. But he certainly knew how to play politics, and as his overall view of the situation in 1931 shifted towards an insistence on political and structural issues going back to the Versailles Treaty came to dominate, he began to do so in the service of what he viewed as a good cause.

On Friday, July 3, at 1.50 p.m. he wrote an urgent telegram to Harrison that the Bank of England had lent as much as 'is convenient in Austria, Hungary and Germany in order to avoid financial collapse. For that purpose, it may possibly be necessary to go further'. He then confirmed what Harrison suggested, that he had received an official request around midnight to participate in the credits mentioned by Harrison.

> I do not know which country or countries are intended nor the general plan under discussion in Paris of which these advances apparently form a part. But I have refused to agree to such advances which inter alia are purely political and not proper business for Central Banks. I assume you will do the same and I may add that the B.I.S. will in my opinion be well advised to avoid any responsibility in this connection.[27]

If the short and matter-of-fact-like cable is any indicator, Norman was upset about the request. Harrison was better informed, and in any case he disagreed with Norman as he made clear in his equally formal reply. First, he pointed out that the Fed had also granted credits to Austria, Hungary and Germany in order to avoid 'serious financial difficulties'. These credits were quite substantial relative to United States' stakes there, and he would prefer to grant further credits only to avoid 'a breakdown'.

Harrison was also more positive towards the French credit proposal, and he reminded Norman of the similarities with Simon's idea from a few weeks ago about depositing money with the BIS to be used in emergencies.

> Indeed it seems to me that this is just the kind of work that the B.I.S. should be prepared to undertake and regardless of the origin of the present proposal if we are to expect much demands in the future in any event as seems likely I can see no forceful objection to our making such a deposit if requested and can see many advantages in our anticipating possible contingency especially if at the same time it will aid in avoiding a general breakdown and much heavier demands upon us which would no doubt follow failure of present negotiations in Paris. I would like to hope you agree with this very general outline of the picture.[28]

Harrison was reminding Norman about the 'Goose club' scheme that originated in Simon's 'Lessons of the Austrian Crisis' note of June 2, and which Norman had also promoted to Harrison in a phone call on June 13. It may have been Norman's dislike of the French that made him so critical of the idea, but he also had fundamental objections as he wrote to Harrison in the second of two telegrams on Saturday, July 4.

Norman again distinguished between political, and monetary and financial needs, and he saw the French proposal as budget assistance to countries, not central banks. Therefore, it 'is political and is a question for our Governments and not for you or me'.

In contrast, the BIS deposits discussed earlier 'would have been to avoid financial or monetary or currency collapse. The need is entirely Central Banking'. Norman added that since they had not heard more about the whole scheme, 'you and I are discussing what we do not understand precisely'.[29]

What seemed to be close to an argument between Harrison and Norman, was perhaps at least as much about Norman's increasing impatience with the French who he now accused of deliberately obstructing the attempt to rescue Central Europe from a financial breakdown. That would have grave consequences for the rest of the world, including Great Britain.

In a brief and intense telegram to Harrison which was sent just before the one mentioned above, Norman seemed pessimistic and angry. Despite an earlier request from Norman to Harrison about Hungary, he had heard nothing. 'I have been waiting for an answer ... in the hope of joint action by private bankers in several countries. But failing that, Hungarians have necessarily been left to help themselves and the result is threatening.'

What really upset Norman, however, was that 'while folk have been talking and arguing in Paris, the Reichsbank has been bleeding to death. Of course this result must have been foreseen', and it was now doubtful whether the Reichsbank could avoid a collapse.

> Thus I fear we may next week see just those happenings which President Hoover's announcement was designed to prevent, not because that announcement came too late but because it has been smothered by opposition.[30]

## A BILLION DOLLARS TO GERMANY?

There was no easy way to get Norman to change his narrative about the French. It was deeply embedded in his worldview, and if anything, Rodd's story about the French conditions for taking the Austrian loan only confirmed this view. He was part of an emerging epistemic community of central bankers, but at the same time – like most others – he also belonged to a national community with an imperial outlook. In Britain that meant being weary of – if not outright hostile to – France.

When Norman looked through that cultural lens, he saw only obstruction of the prime task of central bankers, to preserve the financial and monetary system. Only, Banque de France could hardly be put in the same category as the French government and administration, but Norman could not and would not recognize that.

But Harrison had forced Norman's hand in no uncertain words. He held a more balanced view of the French in the first place, and Hoover's plan had widened his job description. His talks on the phone with Lacour-Gayet, whom he knew already, and who knew America and spoke the language, assured him that, as central bankers, they were not as far apart, as Norman would have it.

On July 3, Harrison consulted a number of banks about withdrawals from Germany. Among them were J.P. Morgan & Co., Chase National Bank, National City Bank and the International Acceptance Bank, and Harrison noted that 'the general sentiment of everyone is that they would at least maintain their present position and in some cases indicated that they would even reopen unused lines'.[31]

That was the good news. The bad news came in the shape of a steady flow of foreign exchange out of the German Reichsbank. The central bank credit was already exhausted and even worse, it was public knowledge. Vocke 'suspects Basle', Siepmann noted.[32]

In a case of bad timing, of which there were many due to the uncertainty, on July 4, as Vocke told Siepmann that the $100 million credit was exhausted and Americans celebrated Independence Day, *The Economist* struck an optimistic note. The Reichsbank credit was 'a good augury for the future'. It 'may become historic as the opening of an era of closer central banking co-operation'.[33]

At the Reichsbank they did not share the magazine's cautious optimism. On July 5, Luther cabled McGarrah that not only was the credit exhausted, the Reichsbank had lost further exchange and would tighten restrictions despite 'the great dangers for the German economy in its depleted condition'. It was the result of 'dire distress' and also meant that the Reichsbank would not be able to 'put devisen at the disposal of the Reich on July 15th for . . . reparation payments'.[34]

On July 6, the United States and France finally reached an agreement about the Hoover proposal. In Washington, the French Ambassador Paul Claudel was reported to have opened a bottle of champagne and proposed a toast with his American visitors, 'To the crisis we have just avoided and to the catastrophe which will follow.'[35]

Pierre Laval, the French prime minister, was not enthusiastic, and neither was French public opinion, but now the ball was in the German court. The internationalist Aristide Briand, the French foreign minister, invited Brüning and Curtius to come to Paris to discuss French–German relations. In the meantime, *The Economist* summarized French sentiment. When France had been in economic and financial trouble in the 1920s, the nation had restored financial stability through savings and taxation.

Germany, in contrast, had relied on foreign aid to fight hyperinflation and squandered reckless amounts on public works, artificial expansion of trade and re-armament. The purpose, in the French view, was to bring 'about a situation in face of which a demand for a moratorium might be regarded as justified'.[36]

There was no lack of stereotyping narratives and divergence of perceptions during the worst financial crisis in history. In Germany, the French–American agreement averted 'incalculable disaster' at the last minute. In London and New York there was a feeling that the 'effects of the credit crisis which began in Vienna' were no longer confined to Germany and Central Europe. They too 'might suffer if the collapse of Germany was not staved off'.[37]

Reichsbank's vice president Vocke told Siepmann that the Berlin Bourse was 'very strong' on July 7. 'He spoke cheerfully there being a better feeling'.[38] Harrison too was 'very happy' as he cabled to Luther, that an agreement had been reached. He hoped that it would ease the pressure on and losses in the Reichsbank's reserves.

Harrison also told Luther that he had done what he could to discourage withdrawals from American banks, and he believed that they had complied. Then came the real message.

> But looking to the future and because of the possibility that certain foreign withdrawals may continue I cannot over emphasize what seems to me to be the importance of Germany itself doing everything possible to restore confidence by taking every sound and constructive step necessary to ensure the goodness of its obligations especially now that the relief contemplated in President Hoover's proposal seems assured. With that in mind it seems to me to be essential that news coming from Germany should be certain to indicate that Germany now has confidence in itself and should not be subject to the misinterpretation that other external commitments of Germany are subject to any risk whatever.[39]

The United States had done its part, and now it was up to Germany to conduct a policy that would ensure its own future stability. Harrison's message was a sign that a new narrative might be emerging, shifting from Germany's fate being a shared concern to being Germany's self-made problem.

Luther responded the following day by informing both Norman and Harrison what he had already told Siepmann.[40] A group of about a thousand German companies were entering into a syndicate to issue a deficit guarantee of 500 million reichsmarks for the Gold Diskont Bank, a subsidiary of the Reichsbank. Luther put much emphasis on this strengthening of 'the unimpaired safety of Germany's credit'.[41]

In a phone call to Harry Siepmann, Vocke commented on the recent failure of the Nordwolle company a large industrial company. He told Siepmann, that the 'Reichsbank authorize us to deny in the most categorical manner that any of the great German Banks will be allowed to get into difficulty as a result of the Nordwolle position. The Reichsbank would in all circumstances provide the necessary support, whatever the effect upon its proportionate cover.'[42]

That was a statement solidly based on the Bagehot rule, but of the kind that any central banker might easily come to regret. The next day, Dreyse called Siepmann to check the effect in London of the news about the syndicate and Gold Diskont Bank. 'He was also anxious about what might be thought here of the Nordwolle and Danatbank.'

Dreyse called Siepmann again at noon 'to say that Dr. Luther wishes to leave Berlin for Amsterdam to-night and to cross by air to London tomorrow morning. He would then go to Basle by way of Paris. I told him the Governor's arrangements and said that if Dr. Luther was in London tomorrow the Governor would no doubt make it possible to receive him ... though he leaves on the 5 o'clock train' for a board meeting in Basle.[43]

The French–American agreement on the Hoover proposal had not eased the drain of foreign exchange from Germany, and everything balanced on a knife edge. After talking with Dreyse at noon, Siepmann got a phone call from Luther on Wednesday, July 8, at 4.30 p.m. The $100 million credit, the agreement on the Hoover plan and the syndicate of German companies backing the Gold Diskont Bank had not restored confidence. Withdrawals continued, and 'the Reichsbank must urgently consider what next it could do'.

Luther thought that a 'spectacular demonstration of faith' was needed to restore confidence and wanted to ask Norman 'what form such a demonstration could take'. He also answered his own question. A rediscount credit to the Reichsbank for a very large unspecified perhaps even unlimited amount and for at least six months might do it.

Luther would travel to London immediately and then to Basle for the upcoming board meeting by way of Paris to discuss the plan. As soon as he had heard Norman's opinion, he would call Basle, Banque de France and Harrison to inform them. Siepmann then spoke with Dreyse who said that unless foreign confidence was restored,

it seemed hardly worth while for the Reichsbank to proceed with vigorous measures in order to hold the internal position. If they were to fight internal distrust and put the whole of their resources and prestige behind, for example, the Danat Bank and the Nordwolle, they could not afford at the same time to be exposed to continuous assaults from abroad. 'What makes our situation intolerable is the complete lack of confidence we meet with'.[44]

This certainly looked like a situation where Bagehot's advice on how to deal with a combined internal and external drain would be needed. Except that raising the interest rate further did not seem to ease demand for foreign exchange in Germany, and it was certainly not good for the economy. Harrison's appeal to American bankers might help, but for how long? What was left, for Germany to stay on the gold standard, was another credit. This time several times bigger than the $100 million that had just evaporated in a matter of a week.

No one knows what exactly Siepmann and Norman said to each other when they discussed Luther's idea of a 'very large' credit. But the fact that Norman was ready to meet with Luther indicated that he might be sympathetic. They were both supposed to go to Basle for the weekend's BIS meeting, so they could talk on the train. Taught by recent bitter experience, Norman also advised that Luther must inform Paris, Basle and New York about his plans.

Given the issue, Norman 'could not undertake to give an immediate reply even in general terms' to the plan, but since it was the only idea, they had to work with, Luther should discuss it with Paris and New York. Siepmann called Luther at 6.15 p.m. to inform him about Norman's response.

Siepmann also spoke to Gates McGarrah and Clément Moret about the situation. Siepmann told Moret at 6.55 p.m. that 'we had heard suddenly an hour ago that Dr. Luther was coming to London and going on to Paris. The occasion for this journey appeared to be a new proposal for credits on a grand scale from Central Banks and perhaps private banks.'[45]

Shortly after, Harrison called Norman, who had just talked with Siepmann about the situation in Germany. Norman, Harrison noted,

told me that things generally are going very badly; that conditions in Berlin have reached a crucial point; that about two hours ago (that is, 5 o'clock London time)

Dr. Luther had telephoned and said the position in Berlin is now desperate; that they had lost another $10,000,000 in exchange today and that Luther is going to London tomorrow by aeroplane just for one hour; that they would travel to Dover together and that Luther would then go on to Paris to see Governor Moret, and he, Norman, to Basle.

Norman said that judging by his conversation with Luther this afternoon, Luther will . . . ask that the central bank credit shall be renewed, and will further ask for an additional credit in an 'unlimited amount' otherwise, he will say, Germany will collapse. Governor Norman mentioned that Mr. Siepmann has already telephoned to Paris and Basle to advise them of what he, Norman, is now advising me of the German situation and the likelihood of the demand for a new huge credit. Norman then mentioned that while Luther had referred to an unlimited credit it was, of course, out of the question and that he gathered from the conversation with Luther that they would need accommodation anywhere from $500,000,000 to $1,000,000,000 to avoid a complete breakdown. Governor Norman mentioned that he would be willing to join in such a credit, which Luther said must be for at least six months, provided we and the Bank of France participated . . . Norman then mentioned that any such credit should be predicated upon arrangements being made by the private banks in the principal markets not to withdraw further funds from Germany. I said that I did not think under any circumstances that would be adequate; that it would be impossible to get effective agreements from so many private creditors; that I, myself, felt that if any such large credit is in contemplation the private bankers should do more than agree not to withdraw from Germany – they should take participations in the central bank credit, thus making them partners with us and much more satisfactorily assuring the maintenance of their present position. Norman said he thought this an excellent idea and that he would endeavor, if the credit is to be arranged, to procure the partnerships of the London banks. . . . Norman then reiterated that he agreed with Luther that Germany is on the verge of collapse and that something probably would have to be done to avoid a complete breakdown. . . .

Finally, I told Governor Norman that I was very skeptical about the idea of a credit in any event; that I felt the chief difficulty was a flight from the Reichsmark by German nationals and that the Reichsbank should resort of much more drastic credit control than apparently was the case. Governor Norman said he thought Luther was now rationing credit very strictly, but he was not sure how effective or how broad it was. He thinks that they need Dr. Schacht there; that Luther does not seem to have the force necessary to do the trick. In any event, I insisted that these credit restrictions should be adopted, in my judgment, before we could fairly be asked for a sizeable new credit. Norman generally agreed with this position.

Governor Norman mentioned that the next published statement of the Reichsbank will be as of Tuesday July 14, and that if anything was to be done it should be done before that time.[46]

That was a whole new ballgame. One billion dollars! It could not surprise that Norman ended the call noting that the 'less said openly about the position the better'.[47]

Nevertheless, McGarrah had already heard about it from Siepmann, and at 3.20 p.m. Harrison received a phone call from Basle. McGarrah wanted to tell him about Luther's request for a 'huge credit'. McGarrah agreed that something should be done but he thought that the Reichsbank's position might be better the next day 'because the strain on the Reichsbank today was increased largely by virtue of the failure of a large industrial concern which reflected itself in the condition of one of the big banks in Berlin'.[48]

McGarrah was referring to Nordwolle and Darmstädter und Nationalbank, generally known as Danatbank. He was surprisingly calm about the failure of a large industrial company and its effects on Germany's second-largest bank. For any central banker, struggling to contain a serious foreign exchange crisis such an occurrence was a sign of danger.

But Harrison was still thinking about the call with Norman. The magnitude and potential implications of the German situation lurked in his mind, and late in the evening on July 8, he sent a telegram to Norman. Again, it was held in a formal tone and insisting on more economy, that is deflation, in Germany before Harrison would even begin to think about a 1-billion-dollar credit.

'I was surprised and concerned', Harrison wrote, to learn 'of the huge amount . . . you now feel may be necessary to hold the situation. While you know I am sympathetic with taking any reasonable steps that may really be necessary to avoid collapse in Germany and perhaps throughout Central Europe as well . . . it would be difficult if not impossible for us to consider taking any steps to look towards further credit accommodation here unless we have some most definite evidence that the Reichsbank itself has first done everything within its power effectively to protect its own position.'

Harrison was confident that New York banks had maintained or even increased their credits following Hoover's announcement. That suggested to him that Germany's recent loss of foreign exchange was due to a 'flight of German capital which it seems to me might well have been limited or restricted through a firmer credit policy of the Reichsbank'.

> Rationing of credit is of course a drastic and disagreeable procedure but it has been applied effectively in Germany in the past without proving to be fatal. On the contrary in each other instance it has been most helpful in repatriating German capital and in checking further outflows of funds and I cannot see why it might not be equally effective at this time if applied with equal force.[49]

Harrison did not recognize that the situation was different now with Germany in the midst of a financial crisis. He had certainly changed his mind compared to early June, where he told his board that they could not 'let the situation go' in Germany and that 'to support it with a credit ... would appear to be the only acceptable choice'.[50]

Now, five weeks later as Germany faced a looming run on the Reichsbank and with emerging concern about the Danatbank, Harrison would not endorse a new credit before he was convinced that the Reichsbank 'has done all that it has in its power to do to protect its own situation and this I think should be done immediately'. Harrison expected an increase in the bank rate and strict credit rationing, which

> may well turn the tide not only by checking a further flight from the reichsmark but by drawing back exported capital. At least it seems reasonable that they should make the effort hard as it may be before rightfully expecting the co-operation of the Central Banks or private banks in maintaining present credit or extending further credits which would only facilitate a continued flight of German capital.[51]

Harrison's cable ended, 'You are perfectly free to show this to Luther who I am sure will realize full well the friendly and helpful spirit in which it is sent.'[52] At the request of Lacour-Gayet, Harrison sent a copy of the cable to Moret for his 'private information'.[53] He also told Lacour-Gayet that the export of capital from Germany was primarily by Germans, and he tried to convince Dreyse of 'the need for a more strict credit policy of the Reichsbank'.[54]

Luther was in no position to say whether he found Harrison's spirit friendly and helpful. He just needed a lot of foreign exchange immediately, and having failed to reach Harrison on the phone, he sent a telegram on July 9, where he explained what he had already told Norman, McGarrah and Moret the day before. What was needed was a

> long-termed large rediscount credit to the Reichsbank to prevent Germany from heavy distress. This idea is based on the expectation that such credit will – because of its large amount and period of time – finally stop the distrust against Germany without it being really used to a larger extent. It would have been of great importance to me if I could have explained to you this situation as well as my opinion of it by telephone. I ask for your help and co-operation with regard to the necessary measures which must be urgently taken.[55]

But Harrison did not offer much help and cooperation except for the usual phrases about being 'most sympathetic', 'desirous of co-operating' and 'really helpful'. What Luther got was a copy of Harrison's July 8 telegram to Norman, which he had also sent to Moret. Germany needed to clean up its own house before any further assistance could be hoped for.[56]

With Harrison's new approach, the ideology and standard operating procedure of the gold standard became very clear. Economy, or deflation, was the preferred tool and result of that ideology. It was not quite what Bagehot recommended in the case of both an internal and external drain. McGarrah's and others' references to the uncertainty about Nordwolle and Danatbank should have alerted Harrison and Norman to an increased risk of the house of cards tumbling down.[57]

Two conflicting narratives with diverging morals were at play. Was Germany an 'innocent' victim of hot money and structural and political problems arising out of the War? Or were Germany's problems self-inflicted by not taking the necessary action? For a moment, it almost seemed like the Hoover plan had taken a backseat. It played no explicit role in Harrison's cable. This was a moral tale more than a matter of economics or politics. Two imaginaries for how to save the gold standard were at play.

Harrison's telegram was received at 5.15, Thursday morning, on July 9 at the Bank of England, and as soon as Harrison was back in the office at 8 a.m. New York time, he followed up with a phone call to Norman. Norman had changed his mind since their call the day before.[58] As Harrison told his executive committee, 'subsequently . . . the Bank of England had adopted a similar attitude', but the different worldviews of Harrison and Norman were still evident.[59]

Before Harrison's call, Norman had met with his directors who were reluctant to grant a new credit to the Reichsbank. It seemed that there was a flight from the reichsmark rather than withdrawal of credits, and it was unclear if the Reichsbank would introduce further credit restrictions that might 'control this export of capital by German nationals'.

Also, the credit was too big and 'political rather than financial', and Norman expected France to raise political conditions if they were to go along.[60] Norman told his Committee of Treasury that this credit 'is not a question of temporary support for the Reichsbank alone, but of supporting the whole German economy and as such is mainly a political matter – not a central banking matter'.

The Committee agreed that 'the present position of Germany appears to be in a large measure due to an internal flight from the Mark, that there is no evidence of the imposition of adequate measures of restriction to check the movement, that in its international aspects the situation has become political rather than financial in character and that in these circumstances the Bank are not prepared to provide further assistance'.[61]

This analysis compelled Norman to a change of heart, though he may also have read a memo written by Rodd two days earlier. Here, Rodd stated in its 'baldest form ... that the B.I.S. and Central Banks have been providing the National Banks of Austria, Hungary and Germany with funds which ultimately flow directly into private banks in America, England, Holland and Switzerland. Directly or indirectly, therefore, Central Bank money is being placed at the disposal of private banks.'[62]

Norman focused once again on the structural and political background. He told Harrison that 'the reparations question has got to be finally settled as the Bank of England does not wish to participate in a credit which would facilitate or make possible continued payment of reparations to the French. I told him that we, too, had that question in mind although we did not think it necessary to include it in our cable of yesterday.' Before ending the call, Norman told Harrison that Luther

> is arriving in London by aeroplane in about an hour, and that he is going to tell him frankly all the points discussed by his directors, of which he had just advised me, and the reasons that they feel they cannot now participate in a large new credit to the Reichsbank.... Norman feel, however, that Luther is not capable of imposing adequate restrictions; that he is politically minded and such drastic restrictions would, of course, be extremely unpopular. He bemoaned the fact that Dr. Schacht is not now in control of the Reichsbank, but so far as he sees it would be impossible to make a shift in the Reichsbank's management just now without by that very fact precipitating a breakdown. He seemed much discouraged at the outlook and does not see what the solution is.[63]

Norman finally said to Harrison that if he wanted to talk to Norman, he should do it directly and not through the BIS. When Harrison replied that he had informed McGarrah confidentially about his latest cable to Norman, he 'laughed and said I ought to know by now that I could not send anything privately to Basle'.[64]

Norman was leaving later in the afternoon and would arrive in Basle in the evening of July 10 for the BIS board meeting. He met with Luther at Victoria Station, where they boarded the train for Basle. During the trip they discussed the Reichsbank credit and after crossing the Channel together, Luther said goodbye to Norman and boarded the train to Paris. Once there, he met first with Clément Moret and later with Pierre-Étienne Flandin, the minister of finance. Meanwhile, Norman proceeded to Basle.[65]

Luther's and Norman's movements were surrounded by newspaper drama. As Luther arrived in Paris at 11.15 p.m. on July 9, he was 'besieged by dozens of correspondents, who crowded the platform at the Gare du Nord with the hope of obtaining some direct indication of the significance of his visit'.[66]

## A VERY BAD FRAME OF MIND

The remote possibility that the central banks might end up granting a 1-billion-dollar credit to the German Reichsbank made it imperative that the governors consulted with their hinterlands. Even Norman had met with his directors, who convinced him to change his view towards that of Harrison.

Harrison and Moret would also have to talk to their boards and other relevant bodies. For Moret, it would be the Banque de France's Board of Regents and perhaps the government, and for Harrison both his own board, the Federal Reserve Board, and his fellow governors in the Federal Reserve System would have to be consulted.

Before even meeting with his own board or Eugene Meyer in DC, Harrison wrote a letter to his colleagues at the other Federal Reserve banks, informing them about the situation in Central Europe. He recounted the help to Austria, Hungary and Germany and told his fellow governors about Luther's request for a new credit. He also pointed out that while Hoover's proposal had at first improved the situation, the protracted negotiations in Paris had led to new withdrawals from Germany.

Harrison then made the point which had also impressed Norman and his Committee of Treasury. Germany had to conduct a strict credit policy because the withdrawals of foreign exchange were homemade. Rather than blaming the French and his own country for accumulating gold, Harrison blamed the deficit countries hit by financial crises and required them to deflate their economies further.

He admitted that the delay in the acceptance of Hoover's plan and some uncertainty about negotiations had 'minimized to some extent the good effects of the original announcement'. But he stuck to the orthodoxy and the 'fiction' or illusion of the gold standard.

Harrison did not mention the French and their role in the delay but merely mentioned in the passive form that we 'are hopeful, however, that conditions may suddenly right themselves as soon as all the doubts and confusion incident to all the discussions and negotiations that have been going on shall have vanished'. He then returned to Austria, Hungary and Germany.

> In my own mind, it is now most important for each of these countries to exercise the most rigorous self-control, for it is becoming increasingly clear that their present difficulties are more largely a flight from their own currencies by their own nationals, than a withdrawal by foreign creditors.[67]

Harrison's view was that an internal flight from the currency should be blamed on the country in question, while a foreign exchange drain originating from outside the country might be blamed on foreign banks and investors. In the first case, no outside assistance was warranted, in the latter central banks could come to the rescue.

George J. Seay, the Governor of the Federal Reserve Bank of Richmond, was impressed by the argument. He noted that while 'everything possible should be done to avoid a financial collapse in Germany', I got a 'better understanding of the situation to learn that, at least as far as you are aware, the German situation is caused by its own nationals through the export of capital. I had supposed that it was chiefly due to foreign withdrawals.'[68]

Harrison's new narrative was about to change the framing of Central Europe's problems.[69] That new narrative also implied a new solution, that is the shift from a foreign credit to German credit restrictions, and Seay now agreed that 'the Reichsbank should first do all within its power to right the situation with respect to its own nationals'. The situation had been allowed to get out of hand, 'if it was subject to control' at all.[70]

That seemed to be the general American narrative by now. J.P. Morgan & Co.'s partners wrote on July 10 to Morgan Grenfell in London that 'by this time the rest of the world is thoroughly tired of the incapacity which the Germans have shown to deal with their own problems and ... the Germans themselves might as well understand here and now that they are not going to be babied any longer and that if they get future credits it will be only because they deserve them.'[71]

The Morgan firms did very little business with Germany, something that served them well in 1931 and made their views potentially less costly.[72] Still, apart from the extra twist of Morgan's anti-German outlook, this view represented most bankers' orthodoxy at the time; praising the gold standard and balanced budgets, and deflation as the proper response to imbalances. After all, one historian points out, bankers 'are rarely innovative thinkers, and the Morgan partners were no exception'.[73]

Neither was the former governor of the Banque de France, Emile Moreau. Now Chairman of the Banque de Paris et des Pays-Bas, he pointed out to Morgan & Cie that

> Germany with her favorable balance of trade and with great relief obtained through President Hoover's Plan is not in such a bad position. He emphasizes the fact that present situation is mostly psychological and that it is for the responsible authorities in Germany to take all steps they can to meet their own situation. He says that matter is in the hands of Government and feels that France could intervene only if it is possible for German Government to take steps to stay internal panic and give definite assurance of amicable relations in the future.[74]

Morgan & Cie reported this back to New York and added that 'nobody here seems very clear yet as to precise form these assurances should take'.[75]

A 'short narrative of the week' in Germany since July 3 was sent by E. Rowe-Dutton at the British Embassy in Berlin to Frederick Leith-Ross at the Treasury. He forwarded it to the Bank of England, where they paid special attention to a passage on page 2. It appeared, Rowe-Dutton noted, that 'Germany would have to reckon with the continuance of withdrawals by foreign banks, especially American. It was considered particularly alarming when e.g. The Guaranty Trust cabled to many, though not all, of its German friends reducing their acceptance "lines" by one-third (which often amounted to one-fourth of the credits actually taken advantage of under the "lines").'

Though Rowe-Dutton also noted that there seemed to be a beginning development of internal flight from the Reichsmark, this was a different story than the one presented by Harrison. On July 5 the 'tension was extreme' and the question of dropping below the cover ratio became acute. The banker Franz Mendelsohn invited Luther and some leading German bankers to a meeting at his house, where they spent the whole day discussing their options. 'After much argument those in favour of maintaining the 40% cover at all costs prevailed.'

Things were 'rendered desperate' when Nordwolle got into trouble as a result of 'a mixture of speculation, idiocy and common swindling'. The most important German banks were involved with Nordwolle, and Danatbank in particular. Rowe-Dutton believed that Danatbank could manage, but it was this situation that had led German companies to issue a deficit guarantee to the Gold Diskont Bank. Whether that would solve the problem remained to be seen, and Rowe-Dutton had 'still no information as to what success Dr. Luther is having on his whirlwind tour of Europe'.[76]

Not much. Luther reported that Norman assured him on their train trip together that the British government was prepared to step in if no one else would or could. However, Luther also got the impression from the conversation that 'Great Britain would like to take the direction of affairs tightly into her own hands'.

Leopold von Hoesch, the German ambassador to France, met with Luther in Paris, and he was inclined to believe that 'with Norman personally, his wish to bring France to reason and his anger over French resistance to the Hoover Plan certainly play a great role'. He believed that if Norman 'maintains that the crisis in Germany must get still worse, in order to bring everyone to reason on the subject of the German burden, then it seems to me that these methods for bringing France to terms are rather dangerous for us'.

Von Hoesch also had lunch with Lord Tyrrell, the British ambassador to France, who told him that 'in keeping with Norman's whole mental orientation, which leads him to seek ideal solutions in spite of all obstacles, he now wants, so to speak, to go "all out" ... Thereby, and especially in relation to France, the preconditions would be created for a real relief of Germany and the world.'[77]

In France, Luther's 'whirlwind tour' had not accomplished much either, but at least the atmosphere had been friendly. Lacour-Gayet explained to Harrison on a very bad phone connection that Luther met with the Banque de France, had lunch with Emile Moreau and other prominent bankers, and also met with some ministers.

The conclusion from the meetings was, as far as Harrison could understand, that before the French would consider another credit, 'there are certain things that must be done in Germany; among others, creation of a better political atmosphere'.

What creating a better political atmosphere meant exactly was not clear to Harrison, but he assumed it was about the customs union and the German so-called pocket battleships. Lacour-Gayet categorically denied this, and they agreed that political conditions were no concern for central bankers who should focus 'entirely upon economic and financial conditions, rather than political ones'.

Lacour-Gayet told Harrison that 'even the French' would not impose such conditions. What the French wanted was for members of the German government to come to Paris 'to discuss matters frankly as Dr. Luther had done today'.

The two men then discussed the unconditional payments and whether France would insist on the upcoming reparation payment from Germany on July 15. Lacour-Gayet confirmed this unless the BIS board meeting accommodated some French demands. Harrison said that this would cause a German default and be a 'threat to the whole future of the Young Plan'. Lacour-Gayet agreed and said that Norman was against BIS accepting the French demands.[78]

As Governor Norman and other central bankers assembled in Basle for the BIS board meeting on the weekend of July 11 and 12, the centre of information gathering shifted to Basle for a while. On Friday morning, the day Norman was to arrive in Basle, Harrison called McGarrah 'to ask whether he has heard anything yet with respect to the position in Berlin today. He said he had not heard anything final but that he understands the condition there is no worse and probably a little better than yesterday . . . He said, however, that he would send me an urgent cable giving me the final report as soon as he receives it from Berlin this afternoon.'[79]

The next day at 1.30 p.m., Harrison telephoned McGarrah who 'said that the situation in Berlin is worse again today; the Boerse is very weak; Luther is back in Berlin after his visit to London and Paris'. McGarrah also said that Norman was 'in a very bad frame of mind' and 'the situation is so much political and governmental that he questions how it can be handled'.

McGarrah told Harrison that 'the Reichsbank has applied credit restrictions in the past four or five days, although he does not yet know what their effect has been, if any. In any event Mr. McGarrah commented there is nothing the Federal can do unless the Bank of England and the Bank of France also act.'

Harrison noted that both Norman and McGarrah believed that they had to wait and see 'what is being done in Berlin'.[80]

# 14

## Anxiety within Germany at Climax (July 11–July 23)

'Hope Revived?' asked *The Economist*'s editorial on Saturday, July 11. The situation was critical but 'not yet unmanageable', and much depended on international banks maintaining their credits and balances in Germany. Otherwise, 'concerted action by the central banks can scarcely succeed in averting a disastrous collapse'. The editorial concluded that 'though for the moment the fate of Europe is in the hands of financiers, the hope of recovery in the long run depends upon statesmen'.[1]

It was not going to be an ordinary weekend. Tension was increasing in London, Basle, New York, Paris and most of all in Berlin. As the board meeting in Basle was about to begin, there were few, if any, encouraging signs anywhere.

Harrison's leave-it-to-Berlin approach, and Norman's apparent acceptance of this, whether out of agreement or necessity, pointed in the direction of not to act at all.

That must have been Luther's feeling as well, as he returned to Berlin from his trip with empty pockets and no prospects of a credit. In Berlin frustration and desperation were rapidly increasing.

At 10 a.m. New York time, Harrison received a phone call from Dreyse at the Reichsbank. It was a difficult conversation, mostly because a very bad trans-Atlantic connection made it hard for Harrison to understand what the thirty-minute call was all about. It did not help that Dreyse's English was less than perfect.

> It appeared to me, however, that they were trying to convey the idea that unless something is done very promptly to aid Germany it would be unavoidable that the Bruening government would fall, and that the political situation would then become most dangerous; that the only hope was in preserving the Bruening government; that political conditions, if imposed upon the Bruening government at this time, would be impossible to accept because they would insure a collapse of

the government with consequent dangerous social and political reactions in Germany. I asked what he meant by political conditions, but he gave no satisfactory answer that I could understand. I asked whether he meant that in his discussions in Paris yesterday, Dr. Luther had been told that a credit would be forthcoming only if certain political conditions were agreed to. My understanding of the reply was that the French had insisted on an abandonment of the tariff union with Austria, and some statement about the so-called 'pocket' battleships – the opposite story to the one I got from Lacour-Gayet last night.[2]

A bad phone connection was not the ideal condition for a complicated discussion of an ominous imaginary with far-reaching consequences. Harrison asked for a cable summarizing the conversation, as he had also done with Lacour-Gayet. He added that while he was not interested in political conditions, the Reichsbank had to reach an understanding with the Banque de France and the Bank of England, and to take 'effective steps . . . to check the outflow of German capital which, to our minds, seems to be a good deal of their trouble'.

At this point Harrison referred to the person he was speaking to as Dr Luther, who may have taken over the call. Luther replied that the Reichsbank was already 'rationing credit . . . very seriously, and that their currency had constantly contracted to a large degree'. Harrison asked whether that was a seasonal contraction but did not get a response.[3]

This phone call took place on Saturday, the very same weekend that the German authorities met with private banks to try to save the Danatbank from failure. Harrison's demand for credit restrictions did not reflect any knowledge of or concern about impending banking troubles, or the wider consequences it might have for Germany.

After the call, Harrison received a report from Berlin via Otto Kiep, the German Consul General in New York. This might well have been the summary he had asked for. Dated July 11, the report said that the failure to get more credits from London and Paris had produced a 'most critical situation in Germany'. Political conditions would cause the fall of the government, while the lack of credit assistance would unavoidably result in 'a complete collapse of the financial and economic structure of the country'.

The report argued that the German economy was sound, but if the Reichsbank did not receive a credit immediately, the

most critical conditions will develop on Monday . . . and the Government is . . . not any more in a position to restore confidence in the financial situation without assistance from the outside. . . . Still more menacing, however, is the run on German Banks and Savings Banks at home, which has set in with great force and is expected to assume dimensions Monday, with which the Banks and Savings Banks will not be able to cope. This will bring about a general crisis with the probable collapse of large Banks and reverberations in all Central Europe and the rest of the world ... which ... will of certainty destroy all success of the action towards a general postponement of political debts inaugurated by the President of the United States.[4]

The report rejected Harrison's call for more contractionary policies and painted a bleak picture of the future if Germany was left alone. Moreover, 'Dr. Luther points out that the Reichsbank has already applied increasing restrictions during the last two weeks in particular towards all industrial demands.'[5]

The report made it clear that Monday could be the fateful day of a breakdown of the German financial system, Hoover's debt plan, and the world economy. It was a final desperate call for help, reflecting two completely different narratives. One in which Germany was in desperate need of help from the outside and where that help was also help to self-help. And another story, a moral tale, where Germany needed to clean up its own house before it deserved help from abroad.

No one outside of Germany seemed to pay much attention to the political risk related to the rise of extremism in that country. Harrison and others called for more economic measures, while the German house of cards was tumbling down the exact way all central bankers had feared since Siepmann first used the metaphor two months earlier.

Harrison's shift to a deflationary position as the German financial system was falling apart provoked Fritz Dreyse to lecture him on central banking and the importance of context. Dreyse had learned that banking circles 'over there of opinion credit restrictions not sufficiently effectively applied'.

Wish to point out that Reichsbank has repeatedly used general credit restrictions since 1924 in times of crises as most effective protective measure and has thoroughly studied their possibilities and effectiveness.... If the stability of the currency is at stake the Bank of Issue must of necessity place the fate even of very important economic interests into second place. This we have done in 1924 1929 and last in 1930. Today credit restrictions affect in the first place a credit organization which is weakened by weeks of foreign credit withdrawals and, as time passes, becomes even more undermined through rumors of heavy losses of one of the large banks known to you and through the increasing apprehension of domestic depositors so that rigid application of the measure would have meant immediate suspension of payments for quite a few banks and particularly those which primarily do business with foreign countries.

As the French–American negotiations over the 'magnanimous' Hoover plan dragged out, the initial optimism had evaporated, and the central bank credit proved inadequate. Dreyse noted that the Reichsbank had tightened credit restrictions, which further weakened the banking system and the economy. 'For us it is now a question whether it is possible to relieve the situation before the imminent collapse of essential parts of the economic structure occurs. In my opinion this is possible only through quick and comprehensive extension of credit.'[6]

There were no kind phrases and well-wishing in Dreyse's note. If he was agitated, it was understandable. In the midst of hectic weekend negotiations about the fate of the Danatbank and under extreme uncertainty, Dreyse and his colleagues desperately reached out for help from abroad. Instead, what they saw was French political conditions and American and even British demands for more credit rationing. That was certainly not part of the Bagehot operating model during a combined internal and foreign drain. And it was not a recipe for success, however defined.

On Sunday, July 12, Dreyse repeated that France had insisted that Germany renounce the customs union with Austria and stop building battleships as a condition for assistance. He stressed again the urgency of the 'monetary and banking crisis'.[7]

It seemed like everyone was against Germany. Dreyse and Luther both rejected Harrison's claim that Germans were behind the capital flight. Upon his return from Paris, Luther cabled Harrison questioning his claim. Based on detailed figures for withdrawals from the largest banks Luther argued that 'there is no doubt that only a very small ... amount of the devisen withdrawals from the Reichsbank has been used for hoarding or capital flight purposes. The cause of the devisen losses is therefore principally the withdrawals of foreign credits.'[8]

It is not clear whether Harrison had received and read this telegram when he composed one to Luther, also on July 12. It was a defence of his position and outlined his thinking in more detail. Harrison made it clear that he had never received a formal request for a credit, but

> even if we had been asked to take the initiative in organizing such a credit, which I do not understand that we were, it would have been impossible for us to do so, because our lack of direct contact and information and the lack of opportunity for easy conversation over the telephone would have made it practically impossible for us, even if asked, successfully or quickly to arrange a joint credit which you were already discussing in person in London and Paris.
>
> The heads of the principal central banks in Europe are now at Basle and it seems to me that the only effective procedure left open to you is for you to ascertain from them, if you have not already done so, what they would be willing to do and what they and you would want us to consider. In other words, I believe that if the situation is as desperate as you indicate, you should pursue the matter with the

heads of those central banks who are now together, present them with a complete program, show how it would work and how credits if granted could be repaid, and then if you and they reach an agreement as to what steps should be taken you could give us an opportunity to consider our participation if you and they agree that a joint central bank credit is advisable and necessary as a part of a complete program. In view of the pronounced need for haste I see no other practicable procedure at this time, especially as the steps to be taken might well involve affirmative action by the Reichsbank and other quite apart from any credit by the central banks.

As you know and as I assured you . . . we are desirous of cooperating with you and doing everything that we may properly do to be of help in this emergency. This I hope we have shown in the past several weeks through our advances and rediscount credit. But I am sure you will agree that it would be impossible for us to give you any adequate credit all alone or on our own initiative to attempt to organize a joint credit. For that reason I have offered the suggestion that you endeavor first to reach a general agreement with the other central banks on a definite program which you should submit to them.

But I still feel as I expressed in my cable . . . to you that there is real doubt whether any central bank credit will be effective even now unless steps have been taken or are taken promptly to protect your own position and, if necessary, to check the leakage of German capital from Germany. As to whether or not you have now taken all such steps as may be practicable, I do not know. But this is a matter which you may properly discuss with the other central bank heads and if they are convinced that sufficiently restrictive steps have been taken that would likely be satisfactory as to that aspect of the situation. Then if you and the other central banks agree that some joint central bank credit is necessary and possible in the present circumstances and in the time available, we would be free promptly to consider our participation on its merits as a part of a general program.

Because of the difficulty of direct telephone communication with you and because of the need for haste, I have taken the liberty of outlining our position as above to Dr. Kiep last night and again this morning. He has just informed me that he has already told you of our conversations, that you fully understand our position, and that you are in general agreement with it and especially with the possible procedure which I have suggested, and that you have already dispatched a representative to Basle to discuss the matter with the Governors there present. I presume that we shall hear from them as soon as they reach a final decision one way or another.[9]

In Paris, Clément Moret was on Harrison's side. He had read the copy of Harrison's cable to Norman and 'understand perfectly your position'. The problem in Germany went beyond monetary policy, 'it is above all essential that from the psychological standpoint Germany should be the first to restore confidence in the stability of the Reichsmark'.

Moret and Harrison did not propose how to improve confidence through more deflation and political conditions, and it was at odds with the Bagehot model's prescription of a central bank's behaviour during a financial crisis. Except that this was an external drain, which should be addressed by increasing the bank rate. But what if a rate increase didn't do the job? What if no credit, however large, could take care of the problem? And what if the banking system was about to crash as well?

In Paris, Luther had told Moret that the Reichsbank needed a credit of several hundred million dollars and Moret replied that he wanted to 'come to the rescue of Germany . . . by means of concerted action between the central banks'. But Germany had to demonstrate 'its very definite will to clear up the political atmosphere of which the actual condition has such an influence on the international movement of capital'.

Luther, Dreyse, Harrison and Moret all relied on historical analogies to make their arguments. Moret told Harrison that 'as in the case of France in year 1926 the restoration of the confidence in the Reichsmark depends less on an external monetary help than on a comprehensive action of which the German Government must take the initiative'.

Moret repeated Lacour-Gayet's claim that France had not posed any political conditions for granting a credit. Still, to Harrison he referred to Germany clearing up the 'political atmosphere', and he admitted that the minister of finance had said that 'a complete smoothing of the relations between the German Government and the French Government' would have an immediate psychological effect.

Moret himself said that he would remain on 'a purely financial ground' but also noted that 'psychological forces' could influence 'monetary matters . . . which the central banks, using the only means at their disposal, are unable to control'.[10]

Hans Luther, Fritz Dreyse and Wilhelm Vocke had been asking for help for several days, but apart from Norman no one really seemed to seriously reconsider the future scenario they imagined, and how it might enable action. And after Norman changed his mind, he appeared resigned while Luther, in particular, was under heavy pressure. His trip to London and Paris, unsuccessful as it was, had not done anything good. By now, Otto Kiep told Harrison, Luther was 'confused' and 'under great pressure . . . he was the type of man who always tried to do everything himself'.[11]

The Banque de France and the Federal Reserve Bank of New York were the only central banks with the resources to really do anything to assist the German Reichsbank. But while most others were concerned with the eruption of a crisis in Germany, which might well lead to a breakdown of the gold standard and contagion to Britain, Harrison and

Moret stuck to the narrative of Germany having to put its own house in order and restrict credit even more.

France seemed to have gone even further by – however muddled – alluding to how German political concessions would be helpful. Harrison's defence that he was not aware that Luther had actually applied for a credit seemed like pedantry. After all, only three days earlier, on July 9, Dreyse had asked Harrison for his 'help and co-operation with regard to the necessary measures which must be urgently taken'.[12]

Still, utterly exhausted, Luther ended up almost apologizing for himself. In response to Harrison's cable, he asked Otto Kiep to assure Harrison 'of their appreciation of all we had done; that he did not see how we could do more than we already had done to be of help, and that he very much appreciated my suggestion as to procedure which he says he would follow'.[13]

International financial leadership would not be forthcoming from the Federal Reserve Bank of New York, Bank of England or Banque de France – if for different reasons. And maybe it didn't really matter? Maybe Norman and *The Economist* were right that despite Europe's fate being in the hands of financiers, the need was for statesmanship? Norman, for one, increasingly took the position that structural and political roadblocks stemming from the Versailles Treaty were an integrated part of the problem and must be addressed.

In Basle, it was 6 p.m. on Sunday, July 12, and the Bank for International Settlements (BIS) board was in an informal session. To kill time, Ernest Moore, McGarrah's secretary, allowed himself a little 'back recreation' and wrote a letter to a former colleague at the New York Fed while 'waiting for what is to emerge from that gathering'.

A month ago you felt we were so far from being out the woods yet, and despite of the Hoover proposal and the amazing collaboration of Central Banks up to date, we find ourselves deeper than ever in the woods. The fact is that the Hoover proposal had a double edge – one in the direction of lightening a few burdens, and one pointing out what the vast majority of people didn't know (assuming it was true), i.e., that Germany was in a desperate financial situation. As this latter idea has gradually been sinking in, apparently, panic has seized the banks or the populace or both, and now indeed the situation might almost be termed desperate. At this moment we do not know whether our board will meet here as usual tomorrow or will proceed en masse to Berlin overnight – which is what Luther wants us to do, saying he finds at the last moment he cannot possibly come to Basle. However, such feverish times cannot last forever and I believe we shall have calm weather again soon and can then estimate what damage the storm has done. Then the cleaning up can begin.[14]

## IN A STATE OF UNCERTAINTY

On Monday morning, all hopes were shattered as the large German bank, Danatbank, suspended payments. It was Germany's Credit Anstalt moment, except that the gold standard and the New York Fed's and Bank of England's insistence on more deflation made it next to impossible for the Reichsbank to support the Danatbank.[15]

The *Financial Times* reported that 'the situation has political as well as financial aspects, but the financial aspects are rather more urgent. The fate of the Reichsbank and the German currency may be a matter of hours. Also, it would be fatal for the B.I.S. to confess inability to help in the present crisis.'[16]

A brief Bank of England note said that 'Germany is in a state of uncertainty in anticipation of the Reich Decree which has not yet been published'.[17] The expected government decree of a bank holiday for Danatbank and a guarantee of the bank's liabilities soon followed. Later that day, another decree ordered a bank holiday for all banks in Germany for July 14 and 15. It also prohibited payments and transfers in Germany and abroad and closed the stock exchanges. Going off the gold standard would increase Germany's foreign debt and instead the cover ratio was reduced from 40 to 30 per cent and exchange controls were introduced, effectively if not legally taking Germany off the gold standard.[18]

According to *The Economist*, Germany was going through an 'experience which has never before been heard of in a capitalist country with a sound currency, except in the days immediately following the outbreak of war – an almost complete cessation of payments'.[19] German bankers told the *New York Times* that if 'no backing from Basle or America comes within forty-eight hours, we are done for'.[20]

In the United States, the *Commercial and Financial Chronicle's* weekly edition's first lines noted that the world confronted 'one of the greatest and gravest financial crises of which history furnishes any record . . . Germany has been verging on utter collapse and drastic measures have had to be resorted to . . . It has been a time of great anxiety and solicitude for the managers of the Bank of England, the Bank of France, and the Bank for International Settlements, as well as our own Federal Reserve banks'.[21]

Germany was now in the midst of a severe financial crisis with both an internal and external drain, as Walter Bagehot called it. The house of cards scenario everyone in the central banking community had feared and struggled to avoid since May 11 was no longer a fictional expectation. It was right there, in the present.

Harrison received a dramatic cable from Dreyse on Monday. The German government had guaranteed Danatbank's liabilities including those of foreign creditors, but 'anxiety within Germany at climax'. Dreyse pleaded with Harrison to 'exercise your great and far reaching influence in New York and Washington also at Basle … furthering our request in order that the great benefits of the Hoover Plan may be realized before it is too late'.

It was a situation similar to late May when Rodd and the BIS had asked Norman to use his network to do something about the Austrian crisis 'in the London market or with friends abroad'. Only, this time Harrison and the United States were at the centre.

Luther had tried to convince McGarrah to move the board meeting to Berlin, but as this idea was turned down, he decided to go to Basle the same morning to present the board with Reichsbank's proposals.[22] As an exhausted Luther was on his way, McGarrah talked to the BIS directors about

> the great crisis of confidence which had developed in and as regards Germany. This crisis appeared now to have gone so far that it seemed doubtful whether technical financial measures alone would suffice to restore the situation. Concerted action by the governments might provide a solution and clear the atmosphere so that financial forces might work normally, but it was evident that neither Bank for International Settlements nor the Central Banks could deal with or solve questions of a political order.[23]

In the United States, the *New York Times* and other newspapers reported that William Castle Jr, the acting secretary of state, had returned to DC after meeting with President Hoover at his private retreat by the Rapidan River in Virginia.

Castle made a statement to the newspapers that 'any plan for a banking solution of the situation must originate from these banks [represented at Basle] which are at the ground, and it is my understanding that our bankers are prepared to consider assistance in any effective plan of relief that they shall evolve'.[24]

After reading this, McGarrah called Harrison and asked what, 'if anything concrete, does Castle's statement this morning mean?' Harrison was taken aback by the statement but thought it 'merely means that there is nothing more the American Government can do; that the situation now is a banking one, and if anything is to be done in a banking sense it must be done over there'.

McGarrah told Harrison that the governors now in Basle had the exact opposite view. They saw it as a government matter and not a banking one. Norman and Moret agreed that 'it is gone well beyond a central bank proposition and that it is necessary for the governments to take it in hand in some form'. Castle's statement had confused the governors, Harrison noted, into thinking that American banks 'were going to take some action. I told him I did not know of any proposed action, and I thought it would be up to the bankers now at Basle.'

McGarrah then updated Harrison on the situation in Germany. The Reichsbank had asked for a renewal of the $100 million credit and had stopped granting new credits. The German government had guaranteed Danatbank's creditors and the German Gold Diskont Bank, a subsidiary of the Reichsbank, would guarantee all existing foreign credits. Norman and Moret believed a central bank credit was out of the question; what was needed was a bank moratorium and 'government help'.

Both Harrison and McGarrah had strongly encouraged Luther to present a 'complete and workable program' for how the Reichsbank would deal with the crisis. On July 12 Luther told McGarrah 'that he had none worked out . . . except to ask for a credit when he arrived in Basle. I said I hoped he had one by this time.'

Harrison told McGarrah that if Luther submitted a complete programme, and if the governors in Basle were ready to grant a credit 'we will be prepared to consider our participation on its merits. In other words, I said, it is up to those fellows over there. I assured him we cannot do it over here alone, and cannot attempt to organize a joint credit at this distance and with the short time available.'[25]

Then the phone connection broke and the call ended abruptly. So did Luther's hope of returning to Germany with promises of a new credit. Without a narrative, a 'complete and workable program' that could present a believable imagined future where the German crisis was averted, central bankers could not be turned around.

After a two-hour presentation, Luther called Berlin to tell his colleagues that the meeting had 'completely ruled out' any BIS assistance.[26] All the board was willing to do was to support the German government's efforts to achieve financial support from other governments, leaving no doubt that this was now a political matter.[27]

## IF GERMANY GOES INTO THE ABYSS

Harrison's day was packed. After his call with McGarrah was interrupted, he met with his executive committee and updated them on the recent developments in Germany and Basle and his discussions with Norman. If the New York Fed received a request for a credit, Harrison thought that the private banks which had a large stake in Germany should go along with the Fed in providing a loan, maybe to the German government.

Both Owen Young and Charles Mitchell were uncertain as to whether central banks ought to become involved in the situation. Young, the 'father' of the Young Plan, had extensive experience with Germany and argued that

> if the situation were so controlled that German nationals could not export funds from Germany under cover of foreign credits, and if the Germans would proclaim a real program and stick to it, a loan of as little as $200,000,000 (one-half, perhaps, by central banks and one-half by private banks) might save the situation, the assumption being that under these conditions very little of the credit would need to be used. He thought that there was a danger of being too timid in crises of this sort, however, and that the Germans, faced with panic and burdened with fear, were not in the best position to formulate a wise program. In these circumstances, he said, an outside agency might conceivably take the initiative and, in this case, that outside agency might well be the United States, the greatest creditor nation in the world. He did not see, in fact, how this nation could sit back and 'observe' in the face of the breakdown of another great industrial nation, which was probably economically sound at the core, and in which our investments are large in amount. If Germany goes into the abyss, he said, something may be started in central Europe which can't be stopped for generations.[28]

As the executive committee meeting ended, Young's ominous statement, which went against Harrison's position, must have resonated with the board members. As Harrison made his second call to Basle that day, the board meeting was still going on though it was 9 p.m. there. The governors had reached an impasse. They all agreed that Germany's foreign trade position and budget were in good shape, and McGarrah told Harrison that 'it would be a pity if anything is allowed to happen in Berlin; that it would spread to other countries and threaten a complete breakdown in central Europe'.

Harrison agreed 'very strongly' and asked what they were going to do about it. McGarrah 'felt that there was little he could hope for; that all feel there should be a moratorium on private bank payments in Berlin at once ... in view of the attitude which Governor Norman and Governor Moret have taken'.

Harrison was 'somewhat' surprised by Norman's and Moret's position and found their proposal of a government loan futile. He said that 'time is the essence' and avoiding a breakdown 'could best be accomplished through private bank and central bank action, rather than through governmental action'.[29]

Now it was Harrison's turn to be ambivalent after Young's bleak future vision had made it clear what was at stake. It was clear to all what was at stake if Germany went into the abyss, and it was not just Germany and not only for a few years but for generations. They had to try.

Later in the evening at 10.20 p.m. Harrison called Basle again and asked for Norman, who was called out of the directors' meeting, which was still in session. Harrison asked how he imagined governments to support Berlin and Norman said it could be through a credit. Luther had no plan at all, Norman said, except to ask for a credit.

> Norman then said that he was leaving in an hour to go back to London and that the board was going to adjourn. I said, if that is true, what is going to happen? He said nothing is going to happen – absolutely nothing. I said I thought it was a great pity that they should adjourn before something was done. He said: 'Well, what do you have to suggest?' Well, I said ... I thought it would be better if possible to work it out through the private banks and the central banks of the world, rather than to throw it back on the governments, even though the matter, as he indicates, might now be so big as to require governmental interest in the situation. He asked me specifically what I meant and I asked him, as I had already suggested to Mr. McGarrah, whether it would not be possible if, as he says, the economic situation is fundamentally sound and if some financial accommodation is necessary, to have the private banks in the various markets of the world make a credit or a loan to the Gold Discount Bank secured by the German Government, and then if necessary or simultaneously to have central banks give a credit to the Reichsbank. Norman merely reiterated he thought it too big for the central banks, and the governments must interest themselves in it, and he did not see anything the central banks could do at this time. He said he had to go back to the meeting as they were still in session, and that he was leaving in an hour for London. He seemed tired, disgruntled and discouraged.[30]

It was a critical juncture. Everyone was resigned and exhausted, and there was still no agreement as to whether Germany's crisis was a job for Germany, central banks, private banks or governments. Harrison had insisted on more contraction and credit rationing in Germany but having met with his executive board, he now tried to turn the mood around in Basle and suggested that central banks and private banks in the creditor countries should do something.

But Harrison's idea did not find any supporters. The BIS meeting adjourned without result, and back in London on Wednesday, July 15, Norman informed his Committee of Treasury that there would be no new central bank credits to the Reichsbank 'until the political situation has been made clear'. That was not likely to happen, and Norman added that 'if Germany falls the collapse of other countries in Eastern Europe will follow'.[31]

In fact, Norman seemed to have given up and taken a defeatist attitude. He was reported to have said at the BIS meeting that 'he did not wish for further credits for Germany, and that it was much better that there should be a complete bankruptcy on the part of Germany as this would raise the whole question of reparations and revision of the treaty of Versailles, including the Polish corridor'. That comment earned him another complaint to the Foreign Office from France through Aimé-Joseph de Fleuriau, the French ambassador to London.[32]

The central bankers were way beyond the point where the Bagehot model was useless. If Norman was tired, disgruntled and discouraged, he was not alone. Francis Rodd called the Bank of England to say that the 'Governor's party, including Dr. Stewart, all left last night by train. They are very tired, having sat almost continuously until about 11 o'clock last evening.'[33]

It had been like that for quite some time. It was the third month of the European crisis and Norman, Harrison, Siepmann, Rodd and numerous colleagues had been working hard to figure out how to avoid contagion from Austria, but to little avail. Now Germany was in the eye of the storm, and if it collapsed it would be more than difficult to stop the dominos from tipping Great Britain as well. In fact, some reputed City merchant banks were already in trouble due to the German crisis, exchange controls and the steps towards a standstill agreement. Kindersley's Lazard Brothers was among the most exposed banks and had to get help from the Bank of England.[34]

Moreover, the Danatbank failure and the bank holiday and exchange controls backfired to Austria and Hungary. On July 14, Budapest declared three bank holidays 'following upon parallel decision in Germany', and unless the situation improved, 'parallel steps will have to be taken in Vienna'.[35]

In fact, that was about to happen. On July 16, Francis Rodd told Siepmann that the BIS had complained 'in very strong terms' to Bruins that 'any withdrawals of foreign exchange are now paid out of borrowed money'. Nevertheless, an Austrian Cabinet meeting the same morning had 'unanimously decided to do nothing'.[36]

Bruins wrote to McGarrah that things had been normal until July 14, when 'suddenly under the impression of the bank holidays in Germany and Hungary the public began to withdraw shilling notes'. As a result, rediscounts and note issue at the National Bank had increased again. Bruins wanted to avoid another shock 'even at the cost of very strong measures'.[37]

Unfortunately, the situation in Germany did not improve. Tuesday morning, Harrison could read in the *New York Times*' editorial that

'Never before . . . was the peril so great of a financial infection spreading from one country to another. . . . To extend credits to Germany may be described as a strictly business operation, as necessary for the other central banks as it is for the Reichsbank itself.'[38] The newspaper also reported from the Basle meeting that the central banks were eager to help but 'the next move must now be made by the governments'.[39]

Later that morning, Harrison spoke to McGarrah and Fraser on the phone. Fraser told him that Luther had made a bad impression at the directors' meeting in Basle the day before. He had no programme whatever and 'they could not find anything constructive from him; that he had left Basle at noon and had been quite helpless during the whole meeting'. The meeting had focused on governments and the political conditions, which 'the Hoover plan has now brought back to light'.

Behind it all, according to Fraser, 'is Norman's effort to clean up by embarking upon a reconstruction period; that we have had an economic war and that now it is time for an economic peace; that the Versailles Treaty and the Young Plan should all be reconsidered now'. Harrison asked Fraser what would happen now.

> He said he is not sure but that the French are asking the Germans today to go to Paris at once – perhaps they will do so. The next step then, says Fraser, is to let the Germans sweat a day or two and then the British will call a real conference of the heads of the various governments for a general rehash of the whole problem. I asked Fraser whether there was any disposition at the meeting to pass the buck back to America. He said no, on the whole there was a very good spirit and nothing against us; . . . my explanation of Castle's statement had made them get down to work and, as he expressed it, 'talk turkey'.[40]

Before ending the call, Fraser told Harrison that Hjalmar Schacht stood to be appointed 'commissioner of the currency' later that afternoon. It might raise great difficulties in Paris, and 'if Schacht is appointed there will inevitably be a conflict between Luther and Schacht sooner or later; that Schacht will come out on top and will eventually become financial dictator'.[41]

At least, the 'streets are perfectly quiet and calm in Berlin', Siepmann reported after a call with Vocke around five in the afternoon.[42]

## YOU HAVE DONE A FINE JOB

At 11.45 a.m. on July 15 Harrison received a phone call from Fraser who told Harrison that the $100 million credit to the Reichsbank had been renewed. In Hungary the bank holiday would be prolonged, Austria could follow the next day, while Berlin might 'renew bank holiday unless they issue rentenmarks, or unless they get a credit, which are the only two other alternatives'.[43]

The Reichsbank went with the orthodox response and raised the bank rate from 7 to 10 per cent on July 16. Though the banks would open for payments, they were limited to wages, pensions, etc. Foreign exchange transfers would still be restricted. Vocke told Siepmann that the banking situation was still extremely difficult, and the 'Dresdner Bank's position is beginning to look very like that of the Danat Bank a little time ago'.[44]

The banking crisis in Germany posed problems for international banks, too. How to deal with the various credits to Germany. If foreign banks closed down credit lines and stopped accepting drafts by German banks to pay creditors in these countries, the ramifications could be alarming. Both Norman and Harrison held meetings with bankers and managed to convince them to maintain credits and acceptances for the time being.[45]

Norman praised Harrison, 'I think you have done a fine job.'[46] That was not an everyday occurrence. Harrison thanked him and noted that he would get in touch with his colleagues in the other Federal Reserve Banks 'to see what we can do about other American banks'.[47]

Harrison also told Luther that the New York bankers had agreed to maintain German acceptance credits in use, 'provided London and other markets will do likewise and assuming that you are taking the necessary steps there to prevent the further export of German capital'. However, while they would maintain credits, 'it is my personal opinion that it would be unwise for you to approach the New York bankers for any further credit just now'.[48]

Harrison met with the bankers again on July 16 and after some arm-twisting the eleven New York banks present agreed to maintain their business with German and Hungarian clients.[49] After a couple of meetings at the Bank of England, similar efforts in London resulted in a strictly private and confidential letter from The Bankers' Clearing House to its members strongly recommending that acceptance lines should be maintained 'at least at about the amount actually in use'.[50]

It may have been impossible to agree about a central bank credit to Germany, but Harrison and Norman at the centre of the financial networks on Wall Street and in the City were successful in impressing upon banks to maintain their lines to Germany. It was not easy, and it was much less coordinated than in the case of Austria, and a far cry from van Hengel's idea. But it worked, and McGarrah appreciated the effort, though 'of course outside our mutual field of operation'.[51]

The downside of these agreements was that American and British banks' claims in Austria and Germany were immobilized, which created potential liquidity problems for them. As the crisis moved towards the UK, this interconnectedness added to the problems.[52] On July 16, a formal 'standstill' agreement was agreed to in principle. It took effect in September, freezing about $1.25 billion of short-term credits for six months.[53]

In the same week, the Hoover plan took effect 'with Germany making only the unconditional payment provided for in the new plan and receiving the sum back promptly from the B. I. S. in the form of a loan to the German railways'.[54]

## A PROGRAMME FOR AVERTING DISASTER?

As Norman and Harrison talked with their local bankers, Siepmann made a note of a telephone conversation between the two heads of state, Heinrich Brüning and Johan Schober, about the situation in Germany and Austria.

> Dr. Brüning said that the situation in Germany is serious but not hopeless.
> Dr. Schober replied that the situation in Austria is hopeless but not serious.[55]

It was a rare show of humour in a situation as bad as they come. Whether the two statesmen actually meant to joke about the situation or if Siepmann just picked up on the comments and was able to see the humorous angle is hard to say, but he even made sure to note what the two statesmen had said in German.

In any case, on the same Thursday, the New York Fed's board discussed 'inter-governmental and inter-central bank negotiations with respect to the situation in Germany'. The evident lack of 'a definite program for the rehabilitation of German finances' had contributed to the sense that the problem was 'now one for governments rather than central banks'.

The problem was that they lacked actionable knowledge. 'Some promise of action might be gleaned' from an upcoming conference in Paris on the weekend of July 18 and 19 with government representatives from France, Germany, Great Britain and the United States. However, 'sufficient facts were not yet available to permit of our taking any definite action'. Eugene Meyer, who took part in the board meeting, agreed that 'we don't know enough to warrant taking action'.

When Clarence M. Woolley, chairman of the American Radiator Co., asked if 'it might not be possible and desirable to develop and suggest a programme for averting disaster in the form of a complete breakdown in Germany', he got the same answer from Harrison. The 'facts are not yet sufficiently well established to permit of intelligent suggestion as to the remedy, and it was thought that it would be worse than useless to rush in prematurely with promises which, later, we might not be able to fulfill'.

Harrison added that even if they had 'more readily ascertainable facts' it would be difficult to safely grant any credits without the other central banks 'because our protection in these transactions was in the knowledge of our partners and in their combined judgment of a situation, the proximity of which made possible investigation and study by them'.[56]

The Bank of England and the New York Federal Reserve Bank were navigating a field with significant uncertainty, and they were unable to establish a coherent narrative and blueprint to assist their decision-making. On the American side of the Atlantic, there was the added issue of being less well informed than their European counterparts. All of this made it difficult to produce actionable knowledge and plot the events into a story that could assist their decision-making and actions.

There was some irony in the fact that Harrison demanded a plan from the Reichsbank, but he himself now resisted presenting a plan. He was simply unable to emplot events into a coherent story that could point them in a specific direction. It just demonstrated how difficult it all was. In the meantime, they faced the prospect of the crisis spreading to Britain as the outflow of gold accelerated.

The overwhelming conflict in mid-July stood between Germany and France. It was this conflict, in particular, that had led Norman to believe that there would be no solution to the crisis of 1931 without discussing politics. The BIS meeting had also been unable to do much, apart from insisting that it was time for governments to step up.

In response, on July 14, President Hoover had asked the British government to call a London Conference of Ministers on short notice. The purpose would be to 'smooth out the differences between Germany and France', and 'draw up a permanent and far reaching plan on the relief of Germany for the consideration of the bankers'.[57]

That was a tall order. First, a plan is all about reducing uncertainty through imagining the future, and everyone already struggled with that. In addition, 'far-reaching' did not really mean far-reaching. Hoover did not entertain any ideas of going back to the Versailles Treaty and reparation problems at all. That was Norman's project, and the French and the Americans had no sympathy for his idea.

The conference was called for July 20 to 23, but it was uncertain whether the Americans and the French would attend. On July 16, Norman told Harrison that the conference might be cancelled due to a French proposal 'that no change in the fundamental position toward Germany should be considered'.

Norman had also learned that France had proposed a huge credit to Germany to be guaranteed by governments. That was a preposterous proposal, he told Harrison. Philip Snowden would never agree to such a guarantee. Harrison 'had understood from Washington that the proposal might even have originated with Norman', but he 'categorically denied both'.[58]

Instead, Norman insisted that it was 'useless to expect the Germans to restrict credit further; that their restrictions had already put one bank down'. This was an interesting moment, demonstrating different views of cause and effect, as Harrison noted that 'I did not quite follow this statement, nor did I agree with him'.

What Germany needed, according to Norman, was the 'possibilities of credit. This credit is not available at present, not because there isn't a responsible basis for credit in Germany, but rather because of political obstacles. What Germany needs is some rearrangement of reparations and political conditions. Indeed, Norman said, this is what the conference is to be for.'

Harrison took this to mean that Norman wanted to use the conference to pave the way for a 'final adjustment of reparations, political conditions and even war debts'.[59]

That was certainly not what Hoover had in mind when he asked Ramsay MacDonald, the British prime minister, to arrange the London Conference. Concerned about the implications, Harrison spoke with Ogden Mills, the undersecretary of the treasury, after the call with Norman and told him that the conference would deal with these larger questions and not merely 'relate itself to emergency action in the present crisis'.[60]

The next day, William Tyrrell, the British ambassador in Paris, told Henry Stimson, the undersecretary of state, that 'Norman apparently wants to hold back everything until he has reformed European finance'. Stimson reported this to President Hoover and noted that the British government 'were not prepared to go the full length of Norman's views'.[61]

Norman was not endearing himself to the Americans or the French by his insistence on going far beyond Hoover's intention with the London Conference. Harrison warned Mills and the president that if the administration did not want to discuss 'reparations, treaties, war debts and whatnots . . . I am sure they are being trapped if they let Mr. Stimson and Mr. Mellon go to this London conference.' He admitted that 'sooner or later we will have to talk these problems over with the Europeans', he just wanted to prevent the administration from being 'tricked against its will' into it.[62]

On July 18, *The Economist* stated that the 'present crisis has been precipitated by the failure of the Credit Anstalt', but behind it all lay 'a ten years' history, the lesson of which is the heavy penalty that has to be paid for procrastination'.[63]

The magazine's German correspondent was pessimistic about the prospects arguing that 'what is needed is a large loan to Germany which would make it possible for the Reichsbank to satisfy the most urgent credit requirements, and to put an end to the foreign exchange drain by inspiring confidence through uninterrupted payments'. It was Bagehot all over again, but 'the very last possible moment for such a step has already arrived'.[64]

Ernest Rowe-Dutton from the British Embassy in Berlin was also short on optimism. In a report on 'The financial crash in Germany', he concluded that the 'situation on Friday, 17th July, is . . . still one of very great uncertainty'. The government, he noted, was faced with a choice between inflation or a 'restriction on banking . . . which must very quickly lead to the strangling of Germany's economic life'. Both alternatives were impossible but if the dilemma was not solved quickly, the result 'can only be chaotic'.[65]

Sharing George Harrison's general view on Germany, Gates McGarrah seemed a little more optimistic. Germany's cover ratio as per July 15 was at 36 per cent and the Reichsbank had lost 300 million reichsmarks since July 7, but he told Harrison that they were seeing the monetary effects of the bank rate increase and credit restrictions. Also, Chancellor Brüning and the Reichsbank were considering 'trying to work out [Germany's] monetary salvation without recourse to foreign credit, which in present political atmosphere they consider not available quickly enough'.[66]

They were making a virtue of necessity, of course, but there might also be a little light at the end of a very long tunnel. It was reached through dispensing with free capital movements, one of the commandments of the gold standard. On Saturday, July 18, Luther cabled Harrison that the German government 'has approved today the decrees concerning capital evasion . . . Foreign exchange situation yesterday and today was balanced'.[67]

After the weekend, Harrison called McGarrah in Basle 'to ask him for his present judgment with respect to the German position, and especially with respect to their requirements, if any, for new money at this time'.

McGarrah was relatively optimistic. If Germany, can 'keep their present foreign balances he thinks they can rock along satisfactorily . . . But . . . if the French revive or insist upon new political conditions the situation inside Germany may become so excitable and unstable as to re-start trouble there and necessitate the need for further credits. But if politics can be kept out for the moment at least, then the relief of $400,000,000 under the Hoover plan plus their present foreign balances, in McGarrah's judgment, should be enough.'

McGarrah also mentioned that 'Norman evidenced very clearly at Basle that he thinks this is a good time for a revision of the various treaties and that was his main purpose in wanting a conference in London. . . . Mr. McGarrah wanted to be sure that Stimson was warned about Norman's attitude. I told him I had made it clear to Ogden Mills just exactly what Norman felt . . . I communicated to Mr. McGarrah that the President, following that advice, had sought and found reassurance from Mr. MacDonald that these subjects would not be discussed, and that no doubt that is the reason the French and Stimson are both participating in the conference.'[68]

The American story of Germany's crisis was in conflict with Norman's. On July 19, the Day before the London Conference was to begin, William Castle Jr., the undersecretary of state, cabled Mellon and Stimson in London on behalf of the president. The

> present emergency is strictly a short-term credit crisis. Fundamental pressure upon German economy during the period of depression has been relieved by the joint action of the creditor powers in suspending all payments upon governmental debts during the period of 1 year. But Germany has financed her economic activities to a very great extent through the medium of short-term foreign credits. There is no reason to doubt the soundness of the basis upon which these credits rest, but the general uncertainty which has prevailed for the last few weeks resulted in such a loss of confidence that the German banking and credit structure was subjected to a very severe strain. This strain took two very definite forms, both of which resulted in a drain of banking resources and the depletion of German gold and foreign exchange holdings.[69]

This narrative was all for status quo and also pointed to Germany as the villain. Castle left out that on the other side of short-term borrowing, there was short-term lending. Charles Mitchell was aware of this when on June 1, he had noted that American banks had been 'entering a field of banking with which they were not familiar'.

Still, in Castle's story it was clear who was to blame, and there would be no revisiting the Versailles Treaty. In a follow-up telegram from Castle to Stimson and Mellon, it was stressed that it 'should be understood in Germany that because of their crisis the entire world of finance has been placed in a very precarious position and that it is much more difficult now to provide further credit than would have been the case 3 months ago. It is necessary first of all to bring back confidence.'[70]

## THE LONDON CONFERENCE

Uncertainty increased dramatically in the first week after the failure of Danatbank on July 13, and it was difficult to collect and make sense of new information. At the same time, the fault lines continued to be reconfigured, as Norman and Harrison increasingly looked differently at the same situation. Harrison worked quietly behind the scenes to thwart Norman's ambitions.

Beyond central banks there was concern, too. A few days before the London Conference, the Morgan partners in New York wrote to Nelson Dean Jay in Paris.

> We are a bit disturbed by the revival of talks about loans and credits to Germany. ... We are fearful to arouse hope of loans and credits here which hope is in our opinion foredoomed to disappointment and may bring about another and worse crisis than that which Dr. Luther's futile flying to London and Paris, Brussels and Basle in search of $500,000,000 loan provoked.[71]

According to Morgan, the US government and the New York Fed could not lend to Germany. The investment markets were closed for Germany, and 'the commercial banks have more than all the frozen German loans they want'. The German crisis had to be solved without 'fresh money from America ... This may be a good thing and it may not. We think it is good.'[72]

The telegram got J.P. Morgan in trouble with Washington. At a party at the residence of the American ambassador to France, Walter Edge pulled Stimson aside and told him that Dean Jay wanted to talk with him. In a quiet corner, Jay showed Stimson the Morgan cable, sent by Thomas Lamont, the Morgan partner interested, but maybe not that skilled, in diplomacy, about the problems arranging a credit to Germany. 'Then I blew up', Stimson noted in a memorandum. That kind of talk was uncalled for at a moment when it was all about getting France to cooperate.

As Stimson blew up over Lamont, a waiter pulled him aside and told him that Washington was on the phone. It was the president. He was worried that 'everything depended upon the London Conference, that all the safety of the banks in New York who had advanced money to Germany was dependent on the conference going to London'.

Stimson agreed but told the president that if he wanted to do something, 'you will not do it by calling me up, but by calling up Tom Lamont'. He then told Hoover about the Morgan telegram, 'the one thing which would prevent the French from going to London'. Hoover agreed and Stimson told Dean Jay that he had to 'hit the London Conference right plumb in the eye and I want you to know it.... I pointed out to him in unregulated language the folly of the bankers getting into a situation depending on psychology when the representatives of their Government were trying to control the psychology of a situation like this and that they could not take refuge in narrow banking axioms because banking depended on general psychology.'[73]

It didn't stop there. On July 18, J.P. Morgan & Co. cabled Dean Jay that both the 'Secretary of State and Secretary of Treasury are most upset over alleged effect of our recent message to you'. Moret had forwarded the message to the French minister of finance, who was now considering cancelling his participation in the London Conference since US participation in 'fresh German financing' would be unavailable, according to Morgan.

Obstructing President Hoover's prestige project on a debt moratorium was not a great strategy even for some of the most powerful bankers in the world. The Morgan partners were 'especially concerned and even distressed to think that Secretaries Stimson and Mellon should have gained an incorrect impression of our attitude ... we are most anxious to show full co-operation with the President of the United States in his endeavor to render effective the generous and helpful ideas embodied in the Hoover Plan'.[74]

Stimson was concerned that Morgan's attitude towards Germany 'might cause the French to decline to participate in the London Conference', while Secretary Mellon, himself a banker, told Dean Jay that 'the views we had conveyed were what any well-informed banker already knew'. Mellon added, however, that Secretary Stimson was 'fearing that the views expressed to the Minister of Finance last night might cause the French to decline to go to London'.[75]

In fact, the French did attend the conference, as did Stimson and Mellon. It was a meeting at the highest political level with even US officials attending. Since the Americans were not usually keen on being mixed up in European affairs, this was good news, but none of them wanted to discuss what Norman saw as the single most important issue.

As the conference convened in London from July 20 to July 23, the chance of any important outcomes looked negligible. The French and the Americans wanted a narrow focus on the present German crisis, while the British and Germans wanted to discuss the big questions of war debts and reparations.

In the evening of the first day of the conference, Edward Grenfell cabled Jack Morgan that there had 'been no developments at all' and he and Norman had no 'pointers as regards the outcome' of negotiations.[76]

The next day, Harrison called Walter Stewart who was back in London attending the conference. Harrison asked 'what his impression of things generally in London was'. What struck Stewart most was that 'everyone is so frightened and so paralyzed by fear, that they are afraid to express their own frank opinions lest they will be charged with breaking up the meeting'.

The German position did not appear alarming to him, but like McGarrah, he felt that political questions or other disturbances might quickly change that. The Reichsbank seemed to have decided to live with the situation.[77] In fact, on the same day, July 21, the Reichsbank decided not to increase the discount rate 'for some time'.[78] This decision was likely made out of concern for the domestic economy, and a loss of confidence in the effect of an increase in the bank rate on Germany's huge short-term balances.

Harrison had figures that 'show that the total short-term indebtedness of Germany to American banks and bankers on June 30 was between 500 and 600 million dollars and that during the month of June there was a decline of this total of not more than $15,000,000'.[79] That was a lot of hot money, and Luther and Vocke decided against applying for further credit. Vocke told Norman that they had made the decision because they 'could not foresee the possibility of its repayment at due date'.[80]

He also told Stewart that 'they are not expecting any long money and . . . Vocke was very doubtful whether the Reichsbank should have . . . [a short] credit'. Harrison and Stewart agreed that this was not 'a time to be talking about central bank credit' to Germany.[81] J.P. Morgan & Co. was of the same opinion. Like Harrison, they had heard that Tuesday

> afternoon's session of Ministers has recommended $300,000,000 of new Central Bank credits to Germany. To this we understand that Washington is replying that there appears to be no need for new credits at this time, that the thing for the Germans to do is to maintain credit restrictions and take other necessary measures to save their own situation, that there can be no question of additional credits from the Federal Reserve Bank under existing conditions and that as to private banks it is necessary to depend on the voluntary action of the banks themselves for even the maintenance of existing credits. This indicates at least some progress in Washington.[82]

Jack Morgan was pleased with Washington's response and wrote, 'I particularly like the reply to suggestions of further Federal Reserve credits.'[83] While private bankers, or at least J.P. Morgan, were happy about Harrison's decision, Norman told Edward Grenfell that he 'saw no daylight after talking with Stimson and A.W. Mellon'.[84]

As the conference dragged to an end, on July 23, at 9 p.m., Edward Grenfell wrote to Jack Morgan that Norman had probably been the one closest to guessing the outcome. The conference agreed on three recommendations 'for relieving the immediate situation in Germany:

1) That the Central Bank credit of $100,000,000 to the Reichsbank be renewed for three months.
2) That concerted measures should be taken by the financial institutions to maintain the volume of credits already extended to Germany.
3) That the B.I.S. be invited to establish a Committee dominated by the Central Banks to enquire into Germany's further immediate credit needs and study the possibility of converting part of the short term credits into long term credits.'[85]

None of these recommendations were particularly groundbreaking. Numbers 1 and 2 had already been taken care of, and the third recommendation, while potentially useful, might not change anything, and certainly not in the very short term. That was the view of Morgan Grenfell, who wrote to Jack Morgan aboard his yacht, the *Corsair*, 'I cannot see that the Conference has achieved anything at all either in settling the immediate financial difficulties or the fundamental political difficulties between the countries.'

Jack Morgan replied that he 'did not expect it could do more than it has since dealing with the fundamental political differences between the countries must necessarily be a matter of time'.[86]

*The Economist* also tried to make sense of the London Conference. It had 'met in the hope of checking the widening circle of distrust and financial difficulty that commenced to spread through Europe with the failure of the Credit Anstalt'. To check the German crisis required restoring confidence and that both the external drain and the internal flight from the mark were stopped. 'Behind the immediate financial problem … lie economic and political questions of a very far-reaching character'.[87]

Still, the magazine noted, the American and British banks' willingness to maintain deposits and credits to Germany was an important step. It was 'a measure of self-protection for the great money markets of the world, since, if they were to precipitate further collapse and panic, they would themselves be involved in widespread disaster'.[88]

Indeed, disaster was seen to be inching closer every day. No one had a convincing vision of how to deal with the radical uncertainty and imagine the road to a better future. The German crisis had also laid bare significant differences in Harrison's and Norman's views. Harrison was sticking to the orthodox advice of deflation, while Norman saw the only solution in dealing once and for all with reparations and war debts.

On July 23, Morgan Grenfell had told Jack Morgan that the Bank of England lost £20 million gold over the last few days and had raised the bank rate from 2.5 to 3.5 per cent. 'Governor Norman hopes you will give him an opportunity to have a long talk with him early next week.'[89] Jack Morgan would be 'delighted to see Governor of Bank of England on Monday and have as long a talk as he wishes'.[90]

If S.D. Waley of the British Treasury was right, they might need a lot of time. In a letter to Francis Rodd sent as the London Conference was wrapping up, Waley commented that no 'doubt on both sides of the Atlantic we are living in a house built on sand, and the whole edifice will certainly begin to crumble the first time that Germany postpones her transfer'.[91]

# 15

# Going Off the Gold Standard? (July 14–August 21)

In late July and early August, things eased up in Germany. Despite fears of a domestic run on the banks as the 'last curbs on payments' were 'removed ... apprehensions proved groundless'. With the introduction of exchange controls, a forced merger between Danatbank and Dresdner Bank, and the creditors' standstill agreement, the 'commercial banks, meanwhile, settled into a routine of smooth functioning'.[1]

Still, markets had not cast off 'the many uncertainties in financial and political affairs and the unalleviated economic depression'.[2]

As the German crisis unfolded in July, central banks and private banks looked with increasing apprehension to the worst possible future outcome, they had hardly dared to imagine since the Austrian crisis broke out. While most communication since late June was about Germany and what to do about the nightmare scenario, the Austrian loan popped up every once in a while, but it didn't sound like anyone really meant or had the capacity or imagination to do anything about it.

In early August, McGarrah realized as much, when he wrote to Harrison that both Hungary and Austria would have to repay part of their loans from the Bank of England. The transactions 'reflects desire of London to strengthen its own present position'. The second Bank for International Settlements (BIS) credit had not been drawn upon and would probably be cancelled 'because there seems no likelihood placing Austrian treasury bills ... Austrian situation drifting in direction of League control under controller of large powers, as it has become a general economic, private banking and Government problem instead of a central bank problem'.[3]

Again, meaning loss and pessimism seemed to spread. On August 6, W. Randolph Burgess of the New York Fed wrote to his colleague Jay Crane, who was visiting the Bank of England. Burgess had spoken with Walter Stewart, who was very gloomy about the European situation and the world situation generally. He felt that the economic pressure would be so great this winter that important social and economic upheavals were to be expected in many countries. In particular he felt that there might be a revolt against the financial system and the gold standard plan.[4]

Norman had a point after all. The financial crisis of 1931 was not a central bank problem but a political and structural problem. That did not mean that there was no need for central banks. Now it was sterling's turn to feel the heat.

## A SUDDEN DROP IN STERLING

On Tuesday, July 14, the day after the Danatbank crisis and the publication of the British Macmillan Committee's report on Finance and Industry, the *Financial Times* reported with pride that 'London, the financial centre of the world, returned to business yesterday morning to face a serious situation and, as might have been expected, did so with calmness. . . . London is facing the situation quietly and calmly.'[5]

Not more calmly, though, than the Bank of England immediately after the BIS board meeting on July 13 informed the BIS that it intended to withdraw a $12 million deposit at maturity on August 15.[6] New York too was concerned about both the impact of the German crisis and the Macmillan report, which noted that British banks had claims on Germany for £267 million.[7]

Sterling was under pressure, as the *Commercial and Financial Chronicle* reported. 'Sterling exchange and the entire foreign exchange market have been utterly demoralized this week as a consequence of the German financial crisis. In Wednesday's trading on a wild market sterling collapsed, selling as low as 4.83¼ for cable transfers, the lowest price witnessed since April 1925, just prior to the amalgamation of British currency.'[8]

Harrison had noticed, of course. He cabled Norman on July 15, 'We are concerned and surprised at sudden drop in sterling exchange to-day. Can you throw any light on this?'[9] Norman was puzzled too.

I cannot explain the drop in sterling in relation to dollars and most European currencies. It was sudden and unexpected and resulted in engagement of over £7,000,000 gold for these days . . . We were perplexed this morning about a change in Bank Rate because exchanges are still so disorganized that 2½% is hardly justified. But to cope with such disorganization would require 7% or 8% rather than 3½% and as no more gold is being withdrawn we hope to ride at least another week.[10]

Harrison called Norman at 3.50 p.m. It was almost 9 p.m. in London, but Norman was still in his office at the Bank of England. He told Harrison that 'the situation now looks very bad and as though we were in for a bad weekend as the whole thing is boiling up'. There was pressure on the gold position, and he hoped that the London conference might improve conditions in Central Europe and 'clarify the situation'.[11]

A couple of days later, on Saturday, July 18, the two central bankers could read *The Economist*'s version. 'After comparative steadiness on Monday and Tuesday the Foreign Exchange market was thrown into a state of complete chaos with the reopening of the Paris Bourse on Wednesday, when an apparent loss of nerve in that centre led to the heavy withdrawal of funds from London with devastating results on sterling.'[12]

In practice, the French losing their nerves meant that gold would be leaving the Bank of England vault to be shipped to countries demanding gold. The *New York Times* reported that on July 16, the Bank of England lost £5.14 million gold, a record, as the 'outflow of precious metal represented about 40 tons, and tonight six big airplanes left Croydon for Paris and Amsterdam with gold'.[13]

The pressure on sterling was mounting. On Tuesday, July 21 at 7 p.m. Norman felt compelled to send a confidential and distressed message to Harrison. The Bank of England had lost £10 million in gold to France, Holland and Switzerland, and Norman thought the Bank would lose another £2 million daily.

> The normal remedy would be progressive increases in Bank Rate but with present conditions in Europe and with Conference perhaps approaching an impasse we hesitate to begin at once. I do not see any other protective measures open to us. Of course London has well nigh eliminated the granting of foreign credits. How do you view prospects and what is your advice.[14]

After receiving the cable, Harrison called Norman at 10 p.m. London time. In a brief handwritten note, Norman explained the latest developments, and they talked about a bank rate of 3½ per cent.[15] Since Norman's cry for help in figuring out what was going on with sterling, Harrison and Norman had been on the phone a couple of times about how to deal with the withdrawals. The Bank of England had lost over 100 million dollars of gold since July 13 as the 'drain began in real earnest' suggesting contagion from the German crisis to Britain amplified by the Macmillan report.

On Thursday, July 23, as the London Conference was drawing to a close, the Bank of England raised the bank rate from 2½ to 3½ per cent, as Norman had indicated to Harrison. It was the first increase since September 1929.[16]

At the New York Fed, Harrison was getting ready to support sterling. His board agreed that sterling's weakness was a 'disturbing factor in the world credit situation' and supporting it might have a positive psychological influence on markets.[17] Governor Meyer and the other governors of the Federal Reserve System consented to supporting sterling with up to $25 million – approximately 5 million pounds.[18] On July 23, Harrison told Norman that he was ready to support sterling, and the same day the Fed purchased £85,000.[19]

Despite this promise of American assistance, there was no way around getting in touch with the Banque de France, as a lot of Britain's lost gold went to France. Norman had to approach Clément Moret. But that didn't mean he had to do it himself.

Indeed, Harrison had already beat him to it. As he went away for the weekend, Harrison asked Jay Crane, his deputy, to inform Clément Moret about the arrangement to support sterling 'because of the pivotal position' it held. The pressure on sterling had a 'depressing psychological influence' in the New York market, and Harrison hoped that 'at least one cause of uncertainty may be removed at a time when the world so much needs a restoration of confidence'.[20]

The next day, Saturday, July 25, Jay Crane received a call from Robert Lacour-Gayet, who told him that 'the Bank of France had been approached by the Bank of England to give them a credit of about £20,000,000 or £25,000,000'. The Banque de France could not give an answer until Monday, but if there was to be a credit, they wanted the New York Fed to join them.

With Harrison out of town, Crane called Norman, who told him that Robert Kindersley was already in Paris 'talking tentatively with the people at the Bank of France regarding the possibility of arranging a credit'. Norman had written a cable to Harrison but would not send it until Monday, July 27, when he returned to New York. There would also be a meeting at the Bank of England to decide whether to proceed with a loan.[21]

On Monday, Norman sent the cable and informed Harrison that owing 'to continuing gold exports to France and to weakness of Exchange Kindersley went on Saturday to Paris in order to explore position and prospects. He saw Moret who suggested a rediscount credit of Sterling Bills up to £20,000,000 to 30,000,000 for a period of six or nine months.'[22]

In the evening, Norman wrote in his diary 'Danger of suspension of gold payments'.[23]

On Tuesday and with still no reply from Harrison, Norman wrote again that the arrangement discussed with Moret was 'in abeyance. The reason is that there are two schools of thought favouring either self-help with action at home or else Credits abroad. So I expect 4½ % Bank Rate on Thursday.'[24] Norman wanted to raise a credit but met with resistance from the Committee of Treasury. The members could not agree on whether to raise the bank rate or try to take care of the problem with a foreign credit.

Philip Snowden, the Chancellor of the Exchequer, was not happy about the idea of a credit. Norman had told him and the Committee that Moret had been very forthcoming when meeting with Kindersley about a credit.

Norman had asked Snowden if the British government would guarantee such a credit, but the chancellor replied that any 'arrangement for raising foreign credits should be purely a banking arrangement without any Government guarantee. . . . If credits cannot be arranged and gold continues to be withdrawn, British Banks must be entirely free to withdraw credits from Germany.'

That was a really bad idea, and difficult as well because of the standstill agreement. Consultations with the clearing banks, the five largest joint-stock banks, indicated that they too were critical of a credit, and in particular a French one, unless it was needed to avoid an immediate collapse. The bankers preferred that 'the Bank would not hesitate to have recourse to the weapon of Bank Rate to whatever extent might prove necessary'. Based on this information and after some discussion, the Committee of Treasury decided to tell Kindersley that 'he should try for the moment to leave the position open with the Bank of France'.[25]

BIS's Leon Fraser talked to Crane about the negotiations between the Banque de France and Kindersley. He told Crane that 'it had been suggested in Paris that there might be some way of bringing the B.I.S. into the matter in much the same way as the B.I.S. had been brought into the Reichsbank credit and . . . the B.I.S. would be glad to be drawn into the picture . . . because he felt that that would make the transaction appear more of an international one'.[26]

Still looking to strengthen the international position of the BIS, McGarrah wrote to Harrison that he had heard confidentially that 'British Government is objecting to acceptance by Bank of England of help from French market and that Sir Robert Kindersley is greatly annoyed . . . Suggest to you possibility that Bank for International Settlements might be helpful neutral instrument through which French or any other market might act.'[27]

Having heard that, Harrison called Norman on Wednesday, the day before he was to go to Basle, to talk about a possible credit. Norman told him about Moret's credit proposal, which was 'now tabled because . . . Parliament was adjourning Thursday or Friday of this week without any possibility of action along the lines required'.

Harrison was surprised that Norman thought a credit would be necessary, and Norman repeated what he had said in the telegram, that 'there were two schools of thought: one, that action at home should be taken to correct their position; the other that a credit would be desirable. He, himself, favored the credit but insisted that because of the early adjournment of Parliament without the necessary legislation the whole matter was now dead.'[28]

The *New York Times*'s Carlisle MacDonald reported that it was Norman who had made a 'last-minute decision ... to await developments before using the French credit offer'.[29] At the same time, it may not have been easy for Norman to accept the fact that the Bank of England relied on the Banque de France and Moret for help.[30]

When asked by Harrison if the Fed's support of sterling was not enough, Norman said that 'it would probably not be in sufficient amounts; that while sterling has temporarily improved and is at or about the gold point, nevertheless, he sees no reason "for permanent improvement" and on that account would prefer to have a credit'.[31]

Harrison sensed that something was not as it used to be. Norman seemed uncomfortable with the whole situation, Harrison noted. Norman

> then said rather cryptically that if this whole thing had not happened on a Saturday and Sunday they would not have gotten into this jam which they now appear to have been in; a position where Kindersley is reported to have been arranging a credit in Paris which is being defeated by the fact the British Government either disapproves or will not act. Governor Norman said the Bank had lost $6,000,000 today and that while this amount is less than yesterday, the great question in his mind is whether the position will hold. He said the domestic situation is not at all clear; the European situation all confused; Parliament is adjourned, and the report of the Economic Committee is to be published this week. He implied that this report would be bearish and its effect 'devilish'.[32]

They ended the call with some more cryptic talk as Norman asked 'whether I were coming abroad soon, that he wanted very much to see me, but hoped I would do absolutely nothing before talking with Walter Stewart, who is now on the water and who understands the whole situation inside and out as well as any one; that he has told him the whole story to relay to me. Governor Norman was obviously very cautious over the telephone in his use of words and names, and made it difficult for me to understand in some cases what he specifically had in mind.'[33]

After the talk with Harrison, Norman attended a Committee of Treasury meeting, which began at 12.30 p.m. It was decided to proceed with the arrangement of a credit. The Committee 'realized the impossibility in the time available of obtaining any guarantee that HM Government will take effective action to secure a balanced budget: they agreed, however, that the Chancellor be informed that while the Bank would recommend the acceptance of such credits in order to allow the Government time in which to formulate plans for balancing the budget, the proposed credits would, in their opinion be of no permanent avail unless followed by such action by the Government.'[34]

With this decision, the Bank of England effectively framed the sterling crisis as a result of the budget deficit, and therefore something that needed governmental action. It was the first, but not the last, Committee meeting where it was made very explicit that the Bank of England expected the Labour government to balance the budget.

It was also Norman's last Committee meeting in a while. He collapsed during the meeting and noted in his diary 'left C. Treas.y & went home about 3 oclock. Queer'. The next day, July 30, he wrote 'Plodge, Queer'. 'Plodge' referred to Norman's beloved home Thorpe Lodge in Kensington, to which he retreated after falling ill. It was the last entry in his diary until late September. Except from a brief return on August 5, he would not be back in the Bank until late September.[35]

With Norman out of the picture, Ernest Harvey, his deputy, was in the hot seat. Now it was on him to lead the Bank of England through the looming exchange crisis. His first task was to tell Harrison that the Bank had changed its mind and was seeking a credit after all. That had been Norman's position all the time.

Shortly after, Harrison phoned Lacour-Gayet and told him that Harvey had called and said that the Bank of England 'has revived the question of a credit and wants us to participate in such a credit with the Bank of France'.

Lacour-Gayet told Harrison that the Banque de France had been ready to sign a £20 million credit to the Bank of England on the night of Monday, July 27. The signing never took place, however, as Harvey wrote the Banque that the matter 'was being left open for a few days longer'. Having received an official request for a credit, Harrison would now discuss it with his directors.[36]

At J.P. Morgan & Co. the partners were concerned about sterling too, and they were getting ready in case their services were needed. In the morning of July 29, Thomas Lamont spoke on the phone twice with Charles Whigham and then followed up with a long telegram to Jack Morgan, who had just arrived in London on board his yacht, the *Corsair*. They were concerned about the heavy withdrawals, and a British operation of some sort was now being discussed. Morgans worried that rumours in 'the Street' would induce American banks to withdraw their money from London banks and make matters worse.

It would be a great pity if the British situation which per se is impregnable should be allowed to drift into uncertainty largely on account of some of the same loose talk which on a large scale in Germany precipitated the German crisis. In other words while we do not for a moment believe that the British have lost confidence in themselves, the sentiments attributed to the Governor of the Bank of England and British Ministers have certainly been most gloomy as to the British situation and have had their repercussions upon it.

An improvement in confidence would change the situation and make a credit feasible, if it was needed. The Morgan firm did not find a bond loan likely to succeed, but a credit 'analogous to the co-ordinated operation of the Federal Reserve Bank and ourselves in 1925 would be the best thing to consider'. Because of the German crisis and the pessimistic reports from London, even such a credit 'would by no means be an overnight job and would really be most difficult'.[37]

Jack Morgan had talked to Norman, who was 'much disturbed because the Government pays no attention to his repeated warnings and seems to be looking forward to an indefinite period of unbalanced budgets and obtaining necessary cash by short term borrowing'. Before government borrowing in the United States was likely, 'the Government would have to show at least some plan of restoration of financial stability and should at least have expressed the intention to reduce the expenditures to come within their means'.

Norman agreed, and Jack Morgan believed that apart from some 'operation' between the Bank of England and the New York Fed, a loan in America was unlikely. Jack Morgan ended his cable regretting 'to say I found Governor of the Bank of England showing the effects of the terrific strain which has been on him for so long'.[38]

*The Economist* also took part in these attempts at reining in future uncertainty. The magazine argued that 'the German crisis has drawn the leading central banks into still closer co-operation with each other, and it may be assumed that any passing emergency in any financial center will be dealt with by joint action, if and when the occasion arises. So far as London is concerned, it has not arisen.'[39] Ever the optimist.

## A CREDIT TO THE BANK OF ENGLAND

The *Financial Times*'s editorial discussed the Anglo-French negotiations and used history to legitimize a possible French Credit. It may be recalled, the paper wrote, that such a credit 'would be no new thing in history. It was done in 1907 and also in 1890, the year of the Baring crisis. A similar instance is recorded of 1839. Indeed, without delving back too far, it is not uninteresting to observe that in 1825 the Bank of France opened a credit ... for the Bank of England at a time of stress, and thus demonstrated ... "the solidarity of the world's markets"'.[40]

The New York Fed's board of directors also discussed a credit to the Bank of England. Would £20–25 million be enough, or was a larger amount called for? Owen Young again demonstrated that he understood Bagehot and the psychology of lender of last resort actions. The credit 'should be too large rather than too small. To quibble about $25,000,000 or $50,000,000 more or less was ridiculous, ... He would regard a credit of $200,000,000 as involving less risk than a credit of $100,000,000, he said, because there would be much less chance of the $200,000,000 credit being used.'

Harrison and other directors agreed in principle but doubted that the Federal Reserve Board in Washington would approve. A phone call to Governor Meyer confirmed this, and the directors voted to grant a credit of $125 million or about £25 million to the Bank of England.[41]

Harrison called Ernest Harvey and told him about the credit. He stressed that if it was too little, the British Treasury would have to borrow from private banks in New York. If 'a total of $250,000,000 credit to the Bank of England is inadequate, the problem is then one of such size that their own government should of necessity take part'.[42]

In the following weeks Harrison and Harvey would be in daily contact. They still had a role to play, but politics and statesmen and bankers were about to take over as lead actors. The 'central bankers were not now the real negotiating parties. Harvey in London and Harrison in New York became little more than channels of information, whose duty it was to ascertain the conditions in which dollars could be borrowed from a number of independent commercial bankers.'[43]

That Thursday, July 30, Harvey cabled Harrison that another increase of the discount rate from 3.5 to 4.5 per cent had been well received, but it was 'too early to judge full effect'. Sterling was still weak, and Harvey hoped that the credit could be 'concluded as soon as possible'.[44]

It was only one week ago that the rate had been raised from 2.5 to 3.5 per cent, and the new increase signalled that sterling was in trouble. Harrison wanted to speed things up. Back in his apartment on Thursday evening, he called Lacour-Gayet in Paris to update him on the progress and to talk him out of including French private bankers in the French credit to the Bank of

England. Lacour-Gayet told him that it had already been arranged and would be difficult to change. Harrison argued,

> We are the two banks with the greatest gold supplies in the world, and a credit granted by us, in which we each take equal shares without any other participants, would have an electrifying effect, in my judgment, and would do more than anything else to convince the world of our constructive cooperation in the interest of the gold standard.[45]

A combined credit from the Banque de France and Federal Reserve Bank of New York would provide the 'greatest psychological advantage', Harrison added, and Lacour-Gayet 'was very nice about it; said he would get in touch with Governor Moret as soon as possible tomorrow and let me know their views'.[46]

Back in Paris, an agreement inched closer. Harvey was satisfied with the result and in particular that Harrison had apparently been successful in 'excluding the French private bankers ... the Bank of England wanted to take a credit only from central banks and not from private bankers in either market'.[47]

On Saturday, August 1, *The Economist* discussed the Anglo-French negotiations and, like the *Financial Times*, used a historical analogy to the Banque de France's assistance to the Bank of England in a 'somewhat similar period of stringency in 1907'. It was a problem, however, that 'huge amounts of British and American short-term capital [is] locked up in Germany'. French bankers were also unhappy that their loans to the London market 'has been re-lent at much higher interest rates to Germany and other Central European borrowers'; money that could not be withdrawn because of the stillstand agreement.[48]

As the loans from the Banque de France and the Federal Reserve Bank of New York to the Bank of England were finalized, Harrison thanked Lacour-Gayet for his contribution to the negotiations. 'Your efforts to coordinate our points of view were always evident and were I am sure most influential in bringing about an ultimate conclusion of the agreement with the Bank of England. It will I hope prove a most constructive force in restoring confidence and certainly is striking evidence of the sympathetic cooperation between our two institutions. Please accept my best personal regards and thanks.'[49]

The loan was split half and half by the two lenders; $125 million from the New York Fed and 3.1 billion franc from the Banque de France. Harrison also sent warm regards to Ernest Harvey and Norman and expressed his hope that the loan would solve some of the Bank of

England's problems and 'in some measure restore confidence in a world situation which affects all of us alike'.[50]

Finally, Harrison wrote to Moret, who expressed his pleasure with the cooperation between the Banque de France and the New York Fed, which will be 'I hope most influential in every country and which proves at any rate the solidarity between our markets and London.'[51]

The loan was everything Norman had dreamt about in terms of central bank cooperation. But he had hardly imagined that it would be arranged by the Banque de France and the New York Fed to assist the Bank of England. They were the only two countries with the resources but for a long time they had been blamed for worsening the economic and financial situation rather than contributing to solving it. It was a great success for Harrison and showcased once again Clément Moret and Lacour-Gayet as part of the emerging epistemic community of central bankers. Ironically, it all happened while Norman was sidelined due to stress.

The sterling crisis brought the Banque de France and the New York Fed closer together.[52] Lacour-Gayet played a special role in the transaction and in bringing Banque de France and the New York Fed together. It was him, Harrison called, and his background as financial attaché in the United States in the 1920s played an important role in his self-perception.

You know, he wrote to Harrison, 'to what extent I remain faithful to the memories I keep of the United States. Nothing can be more pleasant to me than to see the Federal Reserve Bank of New York and Banque de France cooperate in close agreement.'[53]

*The Economist* was jubilant despite the serious situation. In an editorial on August 8, the magazine again used recent history and referred, like J.P. Morgan had done, to 1925 when Britain borrowed £200 million from the New York Fed with an option of 'a further credit secured from Messrs J. P. Morgan and Company by the Treasury'.

The magazine continued with what was certainly the best remembered take-away from Bagehot, and also referred to by Owen Young, that if 'such credits are to be opened at all, it is best for them to be so big as to make it clear beyond question that they are able to give the protection they promise. As our experience of 1925 showed, the bigger such credits are the less is the likelihood that they will have to be used.'

*The Economist* blamed the whole situation on the maldistribution of gold, the plethora of short money and lack of long-term capital. The German crisis and widespread destruction of confidence now 'gave rise to doubts as to the ability of Great Britain to maintain the value of sterling'.

The magazine then singled out the interconnectedness of the post-war financial system arguing that

> it is doubtful if there has ever been a situation, since the great commercial centres of the world have been linked to one another by financial ties, in which such a large amount of short-time obligations were outstanding between the different nations or the basis of international business in the near future so uncertain.

The magazine also acknowledged the support from the Banque de France and the Federal Reserve Bank of New York, and the Bank for International Settlements, which 'has undoubtedly done much to create the atmosphere in which alone such negotiations could be quickly brought to fruition'. Finally, both Moret and Harrison received honorary mention, as the 'financial world has given proof of its unity and of the close friendship between its various members'.[54]

The *Commercial and Financial Chronicle* was less jubilant. It insisted on context and rejected the analogical reference to the 1925 stabilization loan. There 'is no analogy between the situation at that time and the situation at the present time. . . . No menace then threatened. . . . To-day the situation is entirely different. The Bank of England is now in a state of great distress.' And besides, as always when the *Chronicle* commented, the Federal Reserve should not be in the business of lending money to Europe. There was a private market for that.[55]

Despite *The Economist*'s optimism, the *Chronicle* proved right. The ink had hardly dried on the loan agreement before it became clear that the Bank of England was nowhere out of the woods yet. Perhaps, as the French newspaper *Le Temps* put it, the credits could 'in no way dispense the British Government and Parliament from putting an end to the disorder in their public finances'.[56]

The publication of the May Report on July 31 certainly contributed to that narrative. In the face of 2.5 million unemployed and 7 per cent annual deflation, the May Committee set up to consider economic measures to reduce the fiscal deficit, predicted a deficit of £120 million and suggested a dramatic cut in fiscal expenses and a tax increase of £20 million. The report questioned the credibility of sterling and the country's determination and ability to remain on the gold standard.[57]

The May Report was bound to split the Labour government. According to John Maynard Keynes, it was 'the most foolish document I have ever had the misfortune to read'.[58] Still, the pound kept losing value, puzzling the officers at the Bank of England but not Keynes. He wrote to Prime Minister MacDonald on August 5 that 'it is now nearly certain that we shall go off the existing gold parity at no distant date. . . . We can put off the date for some time, if we are so foolish to borrow in terms of francs and dollars and so allow a proportion of what are sterling liabilities to be converted into franc and dollar liabilities . . . when doubts as to the prosperity of a currency, such as now exist about sterling, have come into existence, the game's up.'[59]

And conflict erupted too. As sterling dropped heavily on August 5 and gold flowed to Paris, it became clear that the Banque de France and the Bank of England did not agree on how the credit should be used and for what purpose. Harry Siepmann called Governor Moret at 7.10 in the evening.

I said we had been surprised by the day's events and would be grateful for Monsieur Moret's advice about the course to be taken tomorrow.

Monsieur Moret said that he also had been surprised that the recently arranged credit to the Bank of England had so little psychological effect. But he was even more puzzled to know why we had withdrawn exchange support.

I said that the credit was taken as a measure of precaution and not because we were at the end of our resources. We should not have been so desperate as to take it unless we were prepared to lose more gold than would be required for its repayment. This implied, I thought, that we would suffer further gold losses, if necessary, before drawing on the credit; or in other words that we should cease, for the time being, to support the rate by sales of franc exchange.

Monsieur Moret replied that such intentions could only have been carried out successfully if they had been explained beforehand. Continental opinion failed to understand why the rate should be allowed to slump if the credit is available. His own view was that the credit was intended to put a stop to gold shipments, and he would have expected us to go on intervening on the exchange market.

Despite the civilized tone, the tension was evident. Siepmann also commented on the 'tone and tenour of the conversation', which led him to conclude that the Banque de France expected the Bank of England to use the credit to prevent 'further gold shipments to Paris until the credit has been used or, perhaps, exhausted'. He also speculated that 'knowing we have no francs . . . the Bank of France are more than willing that we should become indebted to them, almost indefinitely, for gold – provided that we do not ship them any'.[60]

It was not only Moret who was upset about the event of August 5. Allan Sproul, Harrison's assistant deputy, cabled deputy Jay Crane who was aboard the steamship Bremen on his way to Europe. 'Sterling very weak in London this morning', he wrote. The Bank of England had asked him to support sterling 'outside' of the newly arranged credit. It annoyed Sproul, but he accepted to go along for a few days.[61]

Crane, too, was disappointed by the weak sterling and found that it 'shows something more than a credit needed to correct position. Credits should be regarded only as temporary stop-gap while fundamental correctives are set in motion. I think they must come to a long term foreign loan.'[62]

The Bank of England's actions did not make sense to the Banque de France and the New York Fed. Harrison and Lacour-Gayet spoke on the phone on August 6 around midnight in Paris and agreed that the credit was inadequate. Britain would have to seek an external loan as Crane had suggested. They had both discussed this with the Bank of England, and Lacour-Gayet agreed with Harrison who 'was very sorry that it had not been made simultaneously with or in conjunction with the central bank credit'.[63]

But another credit was not part of the Bank of England's thinking just yet. The Committee of Treasury met on August 6 to discuss Siepmann's conversation with Moret. It was not a good time for another conflict with the Banque de France, so it was 'essential to establish an effective understanding with the Bank of France'. The Committee decided to send Siepmann to Paris to straighten out things and to 'take measures to support the Exchange'.[64]

The Committee was also not keen on using the bank rate, the traditional weapon in an exchange crisis. They believed that raising the bank rate would further intensify the lack of confidence. In fact, since the return to gold in 1925, the Bank had been more reluctant to raise the rate because of the political and economic consequences.[65]

Instead, Harvey was authorized to tell the government that 'measures for the adjustment of the present budgetary position' should be immediately adopted, and at the same time, 'the bank desire to be allowed to lay their views before the leaders of the Opposition Parties'.[66]

The Bank of England was increasing its pressure on the Labour government to cut the budget. Norman would not have been a stranger to that view, of course, and 'the market' certainly agreed both at home and abroad. Nevertheless, Harvey's approach was unusual.

As the Committee of Treasury meeting came to an end, Harvey wrote a confidential letter to Philip Snowden, the Chancellor of the Exchequer.

> I am very sorry to have to inform you that the position this week has worsened rather than improved. We had greatly hoped that the credit arranged on Saturday last would have gone far to restore confidence: in fact the position has become even more anxious than can be gathered from the published accounts.... I wish to explain to you that in less than four weeks we have to date lost more than £60 millions in gold and foreign exchange and, apart from the credits, we have virtually

no foreign exchange left. If the flood does not abate we cannot maintain ourselves long. . . .

As I tried to explain to you last week, the reports which reach us all show that the sign which foreigners expect from this country is the readjustment of the budgetary position, and this attitude on their part has again been forcibly expressed to-day in messages from both Paris and New York. I am most anxious not to step beyond my province but I feel I should be failing in my duty if I did not say that with the prospects as they present themselves to-day the time available for the Government to reach decisions on this subject (as a means of safeguarding the value of sterling) may be much shorter than recently seemed likely.[67]

The narrative presented to Snowden was not false, but Harvey left something out. He did not mention that in order to push the government to cut the budget, Harvey had engaged the Bank of England in a rather unorthodox move by deliberately not using the newly obtained credits to protect sterling and stop the outflow of gold.

Later that day, Lacour-Gayet heard that Siepmann would be visiting Paris, and around midnight he called Harrison and told him that he would see Moret the next day to discuss the use of the central bank credit.

Lacour-Gayet also said that the Bank of England had just placed $10 million at the disposal of the Banque de France to support sterling. They had already purchased £2 million, spending the full amount, and the Bank of England would soon have to ship gold abroad again. Lacour-Gayet told Harrison,

This cannot go on forever, . . . they will have to use the credit and . . . the Bank of France, who are worried about the situation, believe that they should have been using the credit in the last few days rather than exporting gold. The failure of the Bank of England to adopt this course, in the judgment of the Bank of France, is already resulting in a loss of the moral effect of granting the credit. I told Mr. Lacour Gayet that we had also bought small amounts of Sterling for our own account . . . that I had told Harvey that we could not go on doing so, and that they must use the credit sooner or later.[68]

As Harry Siepmann arrived in Paris on Friday, August 7, he went directly to the Banque de France at the Place de la Bastille to see Moret, who was taken aback when Siepmann told him that

the Bank of England considered it necessary to lose gold and to raise the discount rate again, in order to make the British Government understand the seriousness of their position. Governor Moret advised Mr. Siepmann that he considered it very dangerous to let the situation drift that way merely with a view to convincing the British Government of facts which they ought to understand anyway, that the necessary consequence of this policy had been to create misunderstanding by the public in France and to undo much that had been accomplished by the announcement of the credit.[69]

The disagreement between the central bankers concerned something central to the epistemic community. This time, the Bank of England had stepped outside of the boundaries by involving itself directly in politics while leaving its primary purpose, the protection of the currency and the gold standard on the sidelines.

While substituting for Norman, Harvey actively used the Bank of England's authority to try and force the British Government's hand. In the process Harvey had at the very least made Harrison, Crane and Sproul raise their eyebrows; alienated Clément Moret, the governor of the Banque de France; mixed politics and central banking and misled the markets.[70]

## WORKING IN HARMONY

The criticism from both the New York Fed and the Banque de France regarding how and when to use the credit forced Harvey to change direction. In a phone call he told Harrison that the Bank of England would now draw the full French credit and start using the Fed credit as well.

Harrison said that sooner or later the British government would have to issue a loan abroad. It could have easily been placed three weeks ago, but now the situation had changed. 'He thinks however that the operation would again become possible provided steps are taken to restore some measure of confidence in New York.'

That could take some work. The feeling in New York about 'sterling was thoroughly bad; indeed worse than he had yet known it', Harrison pointed out. Any further loss of gold from the Bank of England could be disastrous. The newspapers were 'full of a variety of alarmist reports', and, according to the press, the Banque de France and the Bank of England had fallen out and would no longer cooperate.

The French government was reported to have asked for Norman's resignation, important English banking houses were in financial distress, and the government was doing nothing about the budget. Harvey assured Harrison that all these rumours were baseless.[71]

The rumours may have been exaggerated, but they were not without foundation. They not only made the American public nervous, but they also concerned central and private bankers in France and America. There was something deeply unsettling about the Bank of England, traditionally the pillar of central banking and the Atlantic economy, depending on help and advice from the Federal Reserve Bank of New York and the Banque de France.

The problem of making sense of and plotting events into a coherent narrative capable of dealing with the uncertainty of the moment was deepening. The question of what was going on in financial markets and exchange markets kept popping up. On August 6, *Financial Times* published an editorial amounting to a chaos theory of the financial and economic system:

> Events in the world of finance of late can have left no illusion as to the state of nervous tension prevalent on every hand. The difficulties in Austria of the Credit Anstalt, the Hoover war debt moratorium plan and the temporary suspension of banking operations in Germany, the nature of exchange movements and record gold withdrawals from the Bank of England, followed by the arrangement of supporting credits in France and the United States – all these things are symptoms of a condition in which the most vague influence may exercise an altogether unwarranted effect.[72]

The *Financial Times*' editorialist had more or less given up on the usual assumptions about cause and effect. The situation left observers almost clueless as to how to explain what was going on in the summer of 1931.

For central bankers, though, focus was on sterling. On August 7, Lacour-Gayet called Harrison at 7 p.m. New York time to tell him that the Bank of England had now decided to draw the French credit. Harrison was pleased that the Banque de France and the Bank of England were 'now working in harmony' to address what was seen around the world as a fundamental weakness of sterling. He also appreciated that Harvey would now use the credits to keep sterling above the gold point. It would all contribute to an easing of nervousness in New York.

Lacour-Gayet and Harrison agreed that the British government ought to seek a long-term loan in Paris and New York, and Moret had impressed the same on Siepmann during their talk. Harrison felt that a request for a loan should 'wait till the situation clears up', and they would also have to discuss the size of the loan. The call ended with Harrison without a hint of irony telling Lacour-Gayet that he was glad 'we were all three now in agreement as to the procedure to be followed by Bank of England'.[73]

Harrison also asked J.P. Morgan & Co. 'whether in our judgment a British Government operation would be feasible at this time'. The partners told Harrison that they were always ready to serve the British government 'to the full extent of our power'. Despite that, it was very unlikely that a loan could be placed in the American market at the moment, and 'even raising the question … might do more harm than good'. Morgan also pointed to the

> apparent confusion this week as between the Bank of England and the Banque de France in handling the sterling exchange and in administering the central banking credit. The banks and the public here do not understand how such difficulties could arise and they feel correspondingly confused and bewildered. A display of steady nerves in Great Britain and a better working understanding between the Bank of England and the Banque de France would go very far in our opinion to change the attitude of this and other markets towards sterling and the British situation generally.[74]

As interpreters of the market's emotions, the Morgan partners noted that Harrison seemed to agree. If the sentiment calmed down and the British came up with a plan, a credit might be relatively easily arranged.[75]

The relationship between the French and the British central bank was important enough that J.P. Morgan & Co. sent a follow-up telegram to Jack Morgan shortly after. Apart from Britain's budget problems, 'the thing which would help most to clear up the present situation would be the establishment of better working relations between the Bank of England and the Banque de France'.[76]

The market in New York did not understand how 'these two great central banks close together as they are and with so many mutual interests should fail to assure the orderly administration of the central banking credit arranged between them for the protection of sterling'. The Morgans even believed that friendly relations between the Banque de France and the Bank of England was a precondition for 'Germany's troubles … to be solved by agreement rather than a continued series of crises', and for a 'peaceful settlement in Europe'.[77]

Jack Morgan agreed. He did not know 'exactly where the difficulty lies but know the matter is actively under consideration by the Bank of England authorities and as I see it I am not in a position to butt in on the transaction'.[78]

Jay Crane arrived in London by ship around August 10 and learned from Siepmann that Hungary might soon be forced to leave gold. The position in Austria was also bad, but Germany's position was improving, and the continent worried about sterling.

Crane noted that Harvey believed that the pressure on sterling was caused by an 'unsound budgetary position and extravagant governmental policies'. The credit to the Bank of England would not solve the problem, but it could provide some breathing space and time to turn things around. The Bank of

England was therefore 'exerting utmost pressure on government to economize and is hopeful steps may be taken in that direction promptly'.

Crane could not ease Harrison's concern about the relationship between the French and the British central bank. 'Feeling against Banque de France is strong', he reported. The Bank of England felt 'maneuvered into a corner' to take the French credit and the Banque de France did not cooperate on 'Tuesday last when sterling was allowed to drop precipitately in Paris'. Finally, the way the French credit was arranged forced the Bank of England to draw the full credit at once imposing further costs on the Bank.[79]

The latter point led to rumours in the market that quickly reached J.P. Morgan. It was said that the French credit was almost used up, and bankers therefore assumed that 'the Federal Reserve Bank of New York's participation has also been substantially availed of'.[80] J.P. Morgan thought this was 'unfounded gossip' and asked Dean Jay if he knew anything. It was false. The Bank of England had only drawn one-sixth of the Banque de France credit.[81]

All these issues and rumours made Harvey's and Siepmann's jobs more difficult, but they did not change the Bank of England's strategy. Harvey and the Committee of Treasury had already made clear that they saw the exchange crisis as a budgetary rather than a bank rate problem. In a meeting on August 11, this was emphasized once again.

Harvey wanted to meet again with MacDonald and Snowden to emphasize how serious the situation was and what needed to be done. He was concerned that they 'were not yet prepared to face the position and … he feared that the Chancellor might even be considering … abandonment of the Gold Standard'.

The Bank had now used £6 million of the dollar credit and £2 million of the franc credit. If 'that rate is continued the position cannot be maintained for many days and it is essential for the Government to be convinced of the necessity for prompt action'. After further discussion, the Committee agreed that

> every effort should be made to persuade the Prime Minister and the Chancellor of the absolute necessity for maintaining the Gold Standard; … that the Government be urged to cause Parliament to be summoned immediately and to issue a public statement at the earliest possible moment to the effect that it is the intention of the Government to take some action based upon the recommendations of the Report of the Economy Committee and to introduce an Emergency Tariff.[82]

At the same meeting, it was reported that Norman was still not feeling well, but 'he was prepared to return to the Bank if the Committee considered his presence necessary. The Committee agreed that the Governor should be advised not to return to the Bank until sufficiently restored to health to assume his full duties.'[83]

That same day, Harvey and Edward R. Peacock, a director of the Bank of England and a close friend and adviser to Norman, met twice with MacDonald and Snowden and impressed upon them the need for 'early and effective action'. A next day Committee Meeting agreed not to raise the bank rate, but 'it is necessary to maintain pressure upon the Government to act speedily'. The Bank would also inform the five leading clearing Banks about the position, and as announced in his August 6 letter to MacDonald, Harvey held meetings with the leaders of the opposition parties, the Conservatives, and the Liberal Party. The Bank was tightening the thumbscrews on the government.[84]

## TO FACE THE MUSIC

On Wednesday, August 12, Crane reported from the Bank of England to Harrison that people 'at the bank here are working hard with Ramsay MacDonald and Philip Snowden to persuade them to take prompt action to balance budget and reduce expenditures'. They were also considering a long-term foreign loan. The pressure on sterling had eased slightly 'but the only safe way out is for the government to face the music and put its financial house in order'.[85]

To the extent it was any consolation, there remained at least one major shared interest between the Banque de France and the Bank of England. As Siepmann put it, 'The Bank of France recognise that the maintenance of sterling on the gold standard is a major interest of their own.'[86]

Indeed, for all the animosity between the French and the British, they tried to focus on the ball and reach a shared understanding. On the afternoon of August 11, Frederick Leith-Ross received three French treasury experts at the British Treasury. The French minister of finance had sent them to 'have a general discussion with me on the present economic situation', Leith-Ross reported.

Much of the discussion concerned Germany where there was little common ground about reparations. Even if the French agreed that something needed to be done, they maintained that it was politically impossible to do anything. Much like in the United States, Leith-Ross noted.

On the United Kingdom, Leith-Ross echoing his minister said that the banking system had been 'subjected to a very heavy strain and we could not undertake to maintain our credits in Germany unless the withdrawals from London were checked'. The French and American central bank credit was much appreciated, but the drain on sterling continued, and Leith-Ross asked the French experts what 'steps that we could take to restore confidence'. The group discussed economic theory for a while, and then turned to the budget;

there was no doubt that our budget arrangement had given rise to a good deal of criticism, and it was felt that we had failed to maintain our traditions in this matter. On this general foundation had come the German crisis in which the London market was known to be heavily involved. ... When the Central Bank credit had been arranged, a much better sentiment was created but, unfortunately this was spoilt through bad technical arrangements which allowed sterling to fall within a few days below the gold export point. There was no doubt that exports of gold for the time being would be inadvisable as they would be taken to be a sign of weakness.[87]

This view went against Harvey's policy of exporting gold to push the British government to introduce budget cuts, but the French group was not opposed to economy measures, quite the contrary. Governor Moret expressed a view similar to the French treasury officials in a conversation with Jay E. Crane.

During a period of economic depression Governor Moret feels that the Bank of France should keep its rate fairly high to prevent improper use of its credit and to hasten a healthy liquidation and return to prosperity. To maintain a very low rate does, in his opinion, merely put off the evil day of settlement, foster unsound positions and prolong the depression.[88]

Crane noted that these views 'are of course not the generally accepted doctrine of central banks, rather the reverse'. He went on to categorize Lacour-Gayet as an even 'worse deflationist than Governor Moret. He strongly favors a major surgical operation to relieve the economic body of diseased parts ... but I do not think he has great influence with Moret'.[89]

So, that was the state of things. Unable to export gold because of French and American resistance, the credit about to be exhausted and reluctant to use the bank rate, the Bank of England was painted into a corner.[90] The only option they could see, besides sitting still and hoping that this too would pass, was to convince the British government to face the music and embark on a deflationary policy. In the meantime, a government loan would be needed very soon.

What would Norman have done? No one had apparently asked where Norman was, but it was being noticed that Harvey had taken over since late July. Jack Morgan had already seen how Norman was 'showing the effects of the terrific strain which has been on him for so long'.[91]

In fact, Norman's normally full diary had almost no entries in August, and on August 7, Siepmann had a brief conversation with Vocke from the Reichsbank, who mentioned that a German press agency had announced that Norman was ill.[92] In a conversation with Harrison on August 8, Harvey told him that 'Norman had gone to the country last night, that he had a pretty good night and seemed better this morning'.[93]

But he wasn't better. He was 'worn out', Peacock wrote to Harrison on August 14. He told Harrison that it 'is a heartbreak to him to leave the country at the present time, but his doctor says he must and he is taking ship tomorrow, sailing on the S.S. Duchess of York. He would like to go to Bar Harbour ... but he has been warned that the Press would make such a mysterious fuss of his visit to America that it might under present conditions do great harm. I cannot tell you how we who know appreciate your help and sturdy confidence, as shown in the past few weeks.'[94]

On Saturday, August 15, the Bank of England issued a statement.

> The Governor of the Bank of England has been indisposed as the result of the exceptional strain to which he has been subjected during recent months. Acting on medical advice, he has had to abandon all work for the present, and has gone abroad for rest and change. He has been assured that a period of complete quiet and entire freedom from work should be sufficient to enable him to resume his full normal duties at the Bank.[95]

'I think the trip will do me good', Norman told the *Financial Times*. The newspaper commented that it 'is singularly unfortunate that his guidance should be absent at the present juncture'.[96] On Saturday, August 15 at 9 a. m., Norman boarded the train at Waterloo station to take him to the Duchess of York destined for Quebec, where he would be staying at the Chateau Frontenac.

It didn't take long for the news to spread, and on Saturday, August 15, the same day Norman left, Jack Morgan cabled Edward Grenfell:

> So sorry about Monty. If he would like it I will have the yacht meet him in any port in Europe or North Africa about September 10th and he can take any party he wishes and a doctor of his selection and go anywhere say India or the Further East if he wants to. There are rooms for six besides himself and for all the servants he could want. See what he thinks about this and I will come down and talk it over with him if there is any chance of him doing it.[97]

Grenfell forwarded the message to Norman aboard the Duchess of York and added, 'I think you may like to have this message from your affectionate friend. Yacht is in U.S.A. now. My best love, Teddy'.[98]

What are friends for? But one thing is friendship or strong professional networks; another is what happens when the head of an organization is suddenly forced to let go. The week before he left, Norman 'had completely given up active work', and it was important for the financial community to be assured that things were under control despite Norman's absence.

Grenfell was aware of that and wrote J.P. Morgan & Co. that Norman's deputy governor, Ernest Harvey, 'is carrying on in most efficient manner. We have utmost confidence in his powers and judgment.'[99]

With Norman out of the picture, Harvey was in charge. To what extent he made other decisions than Norman would have, is unknown, of course, but he certainly made some controversial ones. It was the Bank of England's turn to be exposed to hot money, the illusion of the gold standard and the temper of the market, and it was Harvey's turn to be in the driver's seat. It's not hard to imagine that he may have dreamt of this opportunity.

## BLIND AND IRRATIONAL FORCES OF NATURE

The central bank credit to the Bank of England was at best a temporary help. Everyone seemed to agree that the British budget deficit was the underlying problem and that a long-term government loan in the United States or France or both places was needed very soon. In mid-August, the Treasury asked the Bank of England to inquire with Harrison about the prospects of a new American credit.

Harrison thought that it was the British government that should raise such a loan and that France would have to be involved as well. The amount might be £50 million from each country and 'he was further of the opinion that the British Government would be able to borrow in America provided their programme of economy was adequate and obtained the approval of Parliament'.[100]

Norman had certainly been right about the political nature of the 1931 crisis. Whether he had referred to his own bank and country was less certain, but with Harvey at the wheel and sterling evaporating at an increasing speed, that was now a fact. Now it was Britain that was asked for a programme of economy. The Committee of Treasury met almost daily in these weeks, and the topic was the same. On August 18, Harvey told the Committee that less than half of the credits were left.

He had yesterday evening acquainted the Chancellor of the position and had pointed out that at the present rate of progress the credits would be exhausted in about 10 days. He had told the chancellor that in the opinion of the Bank nothing short of the approval by Parliament of an adequate programme of economy would have the desired effect on foreign opinion, and that it was therefore urgently necessary that the Government's proposals should be completed and parliament summoned at the earliest possible moment. He proposed to emphasize these points again in a letter to the Chancellor to-day. . . .

It was further agreed that Dr. Sprague be requested to consider the results which would be likely to follow an abandonment of the Gold Standard by this Country and to prepare a memorandum as to the measures which should be embraced in any advice which the Bank might tender to the Government in that event.[101]

This was serious. Almost overnight, leaving the gold standard in the near future had become a possibility. It used to be an unimaginable step to most observers, but now the Bank of England's Committee of Treasury was getting ready for it.

At the same time, they worked to convince the British government to do something about the budget while they tried to figure out what kind of loan would be best. In mid-August the Bank's Chief Cashier Basil G. Catterns wrote some notes emphasizing the 'fundamental unsoundness of the British Budgetary position', and a 'failure of confidence'.

'The only really effective measure to cover our overlent position is the flotation of a long-term loan', he wrote, and asked 'whether the loan should be floated in the United States or in France or both countries together. £100 million should be the minimum amount.' Catterns concluded the final note on August 20 arguing that too 'much attention must not be paid to prestige. The assets backing a currency at a given moment are of more importance than its history. . . . A long term loan would restore complete confidence in sterling . . . and leave the Bank of England with a "masse de manoeuvre" sufficient to meet any sudden demand for francs or other currency for several years to come.'[102]

But there was no loan yet, and no government measures to balance the budget, so on August 19, Siepmann wrote the memo he had never imagined he would have to write. Entitled 'Going Off the Gold Standard', the memo used history, theory and imagination as a guide. Since his January memo, the Austrian and German crises had provided useful if troubling experience, but at the end of the day, Siepmann was dealing with yet another case of radical uncertainty: planning for a future that did not yet exist but was beginning to take shape in their imaginations. A future with sterling off the gold standard suddenly seemed a realistic prospect. That raised a lot of new questions.

As Siepmann finished the note on August 19, he had discussions with O.M.V. Sprague, the economic adviser to the Bank of England, and with

John Maynard Keynes.[103] But no one could actually know what going off the gold standard would mean. The memo was an act of prospective sensemaking. What else could he do?

The memo contained a large number of uncertainty-indicators such as 'seems probable', 'would probably', 'to be expected', 'suppose', 'must be expected', 'might even happen', 'should be ... assumed', 'seems to be', 'I believe', 'I imagine' 'without pretending to foresee', and so on.

Siepmann believed that the market forces of 'supply and demand' would eventually persist. After all, even if the gold standard was a human construct, supply and demand were forces of nature, he wrote. If Britain left gold, the exchange rate would have to find its own level.

First off, Siepmann wrote, it 'is to be expected that there would be wholesale liquidation and flight of capital from the country', but sellers would probably realize that it was unlikely for sterling to 'go the way of the Mark'. If sellers thought the authorities aimed for an exchange rate of $4 as opposed to the current rate of $4.86, '$3.60 might be the rate to which sterling would fall rapidly, perhaps within a week or even less'.

While 'blind and irrational forces of nature' might govern exchange markets for 'perhaps a day or two', the panic would end soon, and markets would 'again be governed, as usual, by intelligent anticipation'. Still, the new equilibrium would be 'very unstable', and with 'continued uncertainty'.

In one area, Siepmann nursed no doubt whatsoever. He saw 'no practicable alternative to returning, sooner or later, to the gold standard, and it would be assumed, rightly, by everyone from the first that this must be the eventual objective'.

The only unknown was whether to return to 'the original parities of exchange, or to resume control with a view to stabilizing the gold standard at or about the new equilibrium'. He thought sterling should return to a new parity. 'Without pretending to foresee the complicated economic reactions', the process 'would cause far more material loss to us through dislocation than it would bring gain by readjustment'.

Before setting out his recommendations, Siepmann considered whether it was immoral for Britain to go off the gold standard. On the contrary, he believed 'that it would bring us a twofold moral advantage: we should be admired for having stuck to our principles so long, and admired again (not without some admixture of Schadenfreude) for having shown practical good sense in admitting the necessities of the situation'. And then he delivered a blow to the deflationists.

To say that the fall in prices should be endured as an act of God while devaluation should be abjured as an unwarrantable interference with contractual rights is equivalent to saying that we are morally bound to suffer the effects of natural forces without any attempt to control or counteract them.

Siepmann concluded, 'If we went off the gold standard, we should go off only to come on at a new level, not easily predictable, but fairly remote from present parities.' At the end of the day, market forces would determine the new exchange rate, and he did not expect any significant economic advantages from the devaluation.

To be sure, Siepmann finally stressed that 'we ought to stay on, at all costs, unless – for this, to my mind, would be the ideal – we could arrange for a general abandonment of the gold standard and the adoption of new parities which would leave France and America high and dry with their gold. In other words, an international redistribution seems to me to be what is really required.'[104]

Siepmann sent the memo to Francis Rodd, who responded quickly in a personal and confidential letter. He agreed with most of Siepmann's conclusions and noted that 'purely on an economic basis I think it would pay us to go off whether or not we could determine in advance the point at which we will come on again. But it would not pay us to go off if there were any shadow of doubt that we were being forced off owing to incompetence and bad management. Therefore I would like to make the effort to stay on and then go off at any time when circumstance again became too hard to bear.'[105]

# 16

# We Must Not Fool Ourselves Now (August 21–September 17)

Siepmann's report contributed to shaping the emergent view that the Bank of England might leave the gold standard, but the decision had not been made and there was no way of knowing what would happen over the next month. Only very few considered leaving gold anything but a very remote possibility. After all, a government loan and deflation might change the outlook.

J.P. Morgan & Co. told Morgan Grenfell that the conditions for placing a loan in the United States had not improved 'largely due to gossip regarding the rapidity with which the Central Bank Credit has been used'. Nevertheless, the firm was ready to assist with a long-term loan if the British government announced a plan for 'a balanced budget and other satisfactory reforms in their finances', and if 'a favourable sentiment' had time to develop.

Lacour-Gayet had sent Morgan partner R.C. Leffingwell a letter 'suggesting French and neutral participation in the event of a British foreign loan', impressing 'us considerably as indicating a desire on the part of the French to cultivate the better relationships … and the fact that such participations is most important for the successful marketing of the American tranche'.[1]

The British government still hesitated, Morgan Grenfell replied and continued that as 'regards Lacour-Gayet's letter I would tell you for your very private information that we have not here a very happy opinion of his ability or professed friendliness and would be on our guard as regards his information and advice'.[2]

British dislike of Lacour-Gayet might partly stem from a pamphlet he wrote in November 1930 arguing that France had no responsibility for the gold accumulation and that England itself was responsible for its troubles by granting too much credit. The pamphlet reached the *Times*, which published a summary and provoked both Frederick Leith-Ross and Ralph Hawtrey to publicly reject Lacour-Gayet's story.[3]

Ironically, the Bank of England and the British government were now in a position not that different from Austria's 'how to place' problem. The issue gained momentum in the final days of August, with no prospect still of any government action.

*The Economist* was worried. Its editorial on 'the British "Crisis"' noted the urgent need for MacDonald's government to come up with an economic plan to balance the budget. In addition, it must also allay 'all doubts . . . as to our ability to hold firmly the gold standard, notwithstanding the strain placed, directly and indirectly, on London by the Central European crisis'. The magazine called for driving down prices, wages and salaries in order to restore Britain's competitiveness.[4]

Edward Grenfell wrote to Jack Morgan, who stayed at his Gannochy Lodge in Scotland for the grouse shooting season. 'Ramsay and Snowden have met the leaders of both the other parties. They have not been unreasonable but up to now I do not think the P.M. has been able to control his party and make his colleagues and the Trade Unions follow him. Meanwhile, time passes and the position becomes more unpleasant each day. . . . I am glad to hear that you have had plenty of grouse.'[5]

The same day, Friday, August 21, Harvey told Harrison that he would approach the Banque de France about a loan. Eager to help, Harrison suggested that Harvey consider if 'there would be any psychological advantage in doing this through a personal visit of one of your lieutenants rather than over the telephone'.[6]

Though the government was seen to be dragging its feet, preparations for a loan operation were gaining momentum.

## NO USE IN DOING THE THING HALFWAY

Saturday morning all Morgan partners received a telegram from J.P. Morgan & Co. that called upon them to return to New York on Sunday if they were out of town. Morgan Grenfell was asked to send by cable its 'consensus . . . opinion as to what the situation is and their advice'.

The reason for the all-hands-on-the-deck haste was that Harvey and Harrison 'think that a large operation should be undertaken next week' on Wednesday, August 26. Morgan had heard that the Banque de France would also be involved, something they found highly important. There were rumours that a loan of $500 million would be called for, a 'stupendous sum to contemplate', and it was 'absolutely impossible to say at this time how much our market could provide'.[7]

The bankers did not 'see how a public transaction of such magnitude could be made without prior Parliamentary action'. Yet, here they were with no sound fiscal policies, no real amendments and an American public that 'still looks upon the whole European situation as in a bad mess'. Morgan referred to the recently published Wiggin Report, the third outcome of the London Conference a month earlier.

Chaired by Albert H. Wiggin, the chairman of the Chase National Bank, the Wiggin Committee pointed out the political complications of the European crisis and urged a stillstand agreement between international banks and Germany, which was finally reached on the night of August 18.[8] Morgan wrote that the Wiggin Report noted that 'nothing sound can be looked for in a general European situation until such time as the political European difficulties have been measurably cleared up as between France and Germany'.

The uncertainty about Europe was a warning that 'any too urgent operation should be avoided'.[9] Still, there were small signs of progress in the government's plan to deal with the budget issue. Harvey and Peacock considered the proposal 'quite inadequate', leading the Chancellor to say that 'he intended to press for a reduction in the dole and to inform the Cabinet that a decision must be taken to-day'.

The Committee of Treasury met again later that day. Harvey had seen MacDonald and Snowden again. They had submitted a new proposal 'including a reduction of the dole and had asked him to obtain Mr. Harrison's view as to their adequacy'. The Conservatives and the Liberals were also sounded out by the Bank of England, pursuing its self-imposed role as a catalyst for fiscal contraction.

Meantime, Harrison told Harvey that 'if the programme of proposed economies was approved by all three Parties it would be possible for the British Government to raise a loan in New York but that the matter was one for consideration by Messrs. J.P. Morgan & Co. who would, he understood, be meeting to-morrow'.

The Committee decided to send Siepmann to Paris to talk with Pierre-Eugène Fournier, a deputy governor at the Bank of France, about a credit. 'The way would thus be paved for a direct approach to the French Authorities by H.M. Treasury.'[10]

Late on August 22, at 10 p.m., Harvey outlined the British government's plan to Harrison. The budget deficit for the fiscal year 1932–33 was expected to reach £170 million, £50 million more than estimated by the

May Committee, and was to be covered by cuts in dole benefits and wages, as well as increased taxes among other things. In addition, the government would 'undertake that future Budgets shall be balanced out of income'.

The telegram ended optimistically with Harvey stressing the expected psychological effect 'of a cut in social services ... by a Socialist Government'. Finally, the government would seek loans in New York and Paris, '£50 million each or £100 million in all, none of which to be used to meet Budget charges'.[11]

Harrison called Norman at Chateau Frontenac to inform him about recent developments and advise him against going to Bar Harbor. The 'situation in England', he said, is 'too critical to run the risk of any unnecessary publicity or false rumors as to the possibility of his seeking an additional credit'.

Norman told Harrison that he would go to Novia Scotia and sail back to England from there. Then, something unusual happened. Norman asked Harrison how things were going. It was typically the other way around, but Harrison now told Norman about the British Government's plan for saving £50 million through a 'ten per cent cut in the dole, salaries and wages, and other expenditures' and another £60 million by increasing taxes. They did not discuss the program, 'as I was not sure how well Norman is and I did not want to bother him unnecessarily'.

But Norman could not let go, and despite Harrison's concern, they arranged for him to call Norman again the next day, Sunday, August 23. Harrison asked about Norman's travel plans, but Norman 'wanted to know what the situation is today'.

> I told him I had been out at Glen Cove with the Morgan partners most of the day; that they had sent us numerous cables and exchanges of cables with their partners in London about a possible credit; that the Cabinet was now in session in London to determine whether they would agree to the program drawn up by the Government. Incidentally, I mentioned ... that some of the messages to Morgan's today indicated that MacDonald would resign if either Morgan's or I thought the program was not adequate. I told Norman that both Morgan's and I thought that was not a fair question to put up to us; that while we were certain that a very definite budgetary program must be put through if they are to float a loan here, nevertheless it was impossible for us at this distance to determine whether the proposed program was adequate enough and that I thought that the question was not a fair one to ask us. Norman agreed with this one hundred percent. He said that was obviously a question to be determined in London; that we could not do so here. I told him that Morgan's had finally cabled them to ask whether the program was satisfactory to the Bank of England and the City, including their own partners; that I thought that was the best way they could leave it. To this Norman also agreed. I then mentioned I had asked Harvey several times whether he thought the program was adequate and while he generally implied he

> thought it was, I got no definite answer from him. Norman intimated that I probably would not get a definite answer from him but that he, Norman, felt that the program was inadequate; that we must not fool ourselves now; that any inadequate program would cause trouble in a year or so and that it is essential that we must force an economic adjustment now and not in a year or so from now; that the program, in his judgment, must be sufficiently drastic to place the cost of output and wages on a competitive basis with the rest of the world and unless that were done he was certain the program would not be adequate; that if the Government attacked the situation courageously and did enough by way of drastic readjustment then, in his judgment, they would not need a credit at all. I said the difficulty with that was that the time was so short and the central bank credit so nearly exhausted, it was a risky thing to take the chance on even a drastic budgetary reform checking the withdrawals. Norman allowed there was something in this point. The sum and substance of our conversation indicated pretty clearly, however, that Norman felt the proposed program was not sufficiently severe to avoid trouble later on and that there was no use in doing the thing halfway.[12]

By preferring an even more drastic plan from the government, Norman went all in on the classic deflationary path. On the other hand, Harvey's apparent free riding and the British government's question to J.P. Morgan & Co. and Harrison if the plan was adequate was highly sensitive. Any banker would try to avoid such a question. J.P. Morgan & Co. and the New York Fed were no exceptions.

Harrison's and Norman's relationship was much closer and more personal than with Harvey. Their talks were more intimate, and they frequently used each other to try out their arguments and possible outcomes of various decisions. Harvey did not have anything close to such a relationship with Harrison and in some important decisions, he did not appear to listen to his colleague in New York.

In a Committee of Treasury meeting the same Sunday, August 23, Harvey told the Committee that MacDonald 'wished to know, if possible before the meeting of the Cabinet at 7 o'clock, whether these proposals would be acceptable abroad'. Harvey had sent a letter to Morgan Grenfell and asked them to 'communicate at once with J.P. Morgan & Co.'[13]

J.P. Morgan & Co. asked Morgan Grenfell if they were 'right in assuming that the programme under consideration will have the sincere approval and support of the Bank of England and the City generally and thus go a long way towards restoring internal confidence in Great Britain'. Harvey handed this message to MacDonald, who read it to the Cabinet meeting Sunday evening.[14]

Then the Labour government resigned. Prime Minister Ramsay MacDonald could not get his party behind his plan for cuts in social benefits, and Morgan's question, meant for Harvey's eyes only, had not been helpful. On Monday, MacDonald submitted his resignation. Or so he thought, but at the request of the King, MacDonald then formed a 'National Government' the same day, consisting of members from the Conservative Party, the Liberals and National Labour.

At a Committee of Treasury meeting, Harvey read Morgan's message, which he had mistakenly handed to MacDonald the evening before. He also told the Committee that he had been asked about the Bank and the City's view of the formation of a National Government 'to carry through the proposals already prepared by Mr. MacDonald and Mr. Snowden'. The Committee thought this the 'best possible arrangement' and agreed that Harvey should also 'ascertain the view of the leading Clearing Bankers'.

Before the Committee meeting adjourned, Harvey informed them that the demand for foreign exchange had been very heavy and that 'it was essential for arrangements to be made at the earliest possible moment for some further Credit'. Harvey received acceptance from the Treasury to begin negotiations with Morgans for a short-term loan.[15]

The Bank's position was strained. On August 24, the Bank of England asked the New York Fed if they would purchase or sell on the market securities for about $28 million for the Bank of England 'in case we should require to dispose of these'. It might have to be done quickly and the Bank of England hoped that it would not 'embarrass you if we were to ask you to realise the whole amount at short notice'.[16]

Harrison replied to Harvey that they had taken delivery of the securities from J.P. Morgan and could arrange the sale the next day if needed.[17] It was yet another sign of the pressure on sterling.

Much now depended on the reception of the new government and the US market's response to a British loan. Jay Crane, who was still at the Bank of England, cabled Harrison.

> Tomorrow ought to give us a good line on the public reaction here and abroad but I think much depends upon whether the new government issues a satisfactory statement tonight of its financial program. While the change of government in itself should inspire some feeling of confidence, nevertheless the important thing is for them to tell the public what their program is. If they do that and state that the dole is to be cut 10% my own feeling is that we shall see a prompt demonstration of renewed confidence in sterling.[18]

Crane added that the Bank of England had used £11 million of the central bank credit and had only £9 million foreign exchange left, including the proceeds from the $28 million of American securities they had asked the New York Fed to sell.[19]

To emphasize the urgency of the situation, Harrison cabled Harvey Monday evening that 'owing to heavy withdrawals you now have only' £1 million left of the credit meaning that after the sale of securities the Bank of England held £9 million in foreign exchange. At least, the news about the National government had been 'most favourably received and commented upon here and if there is appropriate publicity to-morrow it should do much to offset bad publicity of to-day thus substantially checking if not stopping to-day's rate of withdrawals'.

Harrison hoped for a loan to be organized by private bankers on Wednesday, but there was a Tuesday in between and few resources left at the Bank of England to withstand further withdrawals. Harrison was prepared to help bridge the Bank over, if 'your present holdings are not sufficient for to-morrow and if credit to the Government seems assured by Wednesday we could ... tide you over to-morrow and ... unwound by Wednesday night your statement night'. Harrison ended his message, 'Many thanks for keeping me so fully informed during days which I know have been difficult and strenuous for you.'[20]

With the Bank of England's foreign exchange almost exhausted, the situation was tightening up. It was only a matter of a day or two before a new credit must be in place. No one knew if that would even be possible.

## THEY CAN DO ALL THEY LIKE

Two months earlier, it had proved impossible to arrange a long-term credit to the Austrian government over several weeks. Now the British government needed a much larger loan within thirty-six hours, and both France and the United States had to participate.

At a Committee of Treasury meeting, Harvey told the members that the New York Fed had agreed to arrange a bridge loan if needed. Edward Grenfell, who was invited to the meeting, had been in touch with J.P. Morgan and Co., who thought that it would be possible to arrange a credit of between $150 and $200 million to the British government if negotiations were opened for a similar loan in France.

The Committee agreed to inform the new government that, 'in the opinion of the Bank, a definite announcement as to the policy of the new Government should be issued without delay and that negotiations should be commenced by H.M. Treasury as soon as possible for a government loan both in the United States and in France'.[21]

As the Bank of England continued to push for deflation, the Labour Party went into opposition. On August 25 the widely read *Daily Herald* with a close relation to Labour carried a front-page story on how US banks had posed an ultimatum to the government. This was the so-called bankers' ramp story claiming 'a startling, and apparently successful, attempt by American bankers to dictate the internal policy of Great Britain'. According to the *Daily Herald*, there would be no American credit to Great Britain, 'unless and until measures which the United States bankers consider satisfactory are put into operation by the new Cabinet'.[22]

Even worse, the article was illustrated with a photo of George Harrison, pointing to him as the main villain behind the claimed plot. Harrison was furious. In a phone call with Harvey, he demanded that the Bank of England issue a denial. In a somewhat vague statement, the Bank issued a communication to the *Financial News* and 'several other important newspapers' saying that 'it was authoritatively stated in London last night that there was no foundation' for the claims that the New York Fed had insisted on fiscal economy and cuts in the dole. 'I hope you will consider this satisfactory', Harvey wrote to Harrison.[23]

The connection between Bank and government, politics and finance, got closer almost daily. McDonald sternly rejected the bankers' ramp story. 'The situation is a financial one. It belongs to the world of finance', he said, and continued that the 'only way to secure necessary money is to afford those who have money to lend a security that it will be paid back when required.... One thing, and one only, will put British credit in a position of security at this moment, and that is a scheme consisting in economies on the one side and further revenue on the other.'[24]

Bankers' ramp or not, if anyone got the impression from Harvey's and Peacock's money doctoring that central bank independence was less an issue than government independence of the Bank of England, they could be excused.

The relationship between politics and finance was in a new place. On August 27, Harvey informed the Committee of Treasury that the new government's conservative and liberal leaders had announced their visit to the Bank of England 'in order to discuss ... the effect on City opinion of certain measures including economies which the Government are considering'.[25]

On the same day that the *Daily Herald* published the bankers' ramp story, Harrison placed a morning call to Lacour-Gayet in Paris. Though the British were apparently not enthusiastic about him – or anyone French, really – if this loan was to be arranged, the good relationship between Harrison and Lacour-Gayet could be instrumental. Two weeks earlier, Lacour-Gayet had sent Harrison a memorandum about the possibility of a British long-term loan. Now, Harrison suggested that Lacour-Gayet might have a prophetic talent.

'He laughed and said he did not realize at the time he wrote how true it would be.' Harrison had heard from 'the Corner', a common nickname for J.P. Morgan & Co. located on the corner of Wall Street and Broad Street, that the formation of the National government had improved the sentiment, and they now believed that it would be possible to arrange a credit to the Treasury of between $200 and $250 million if the French market would do the same.

Lacour-Gayet told Harrison that Harry Siepmann had arrived in Paris the same morning to talk with Moret about a credit. Siepmann had mentioned an amount between 3 and 6 billion francs, but Moret thought a credit nearer to 3 billion, or about $118 million, would be more realistic. Lacour-Gayet and Harrison agreed that it would be impossible to arrange a long-term bond loan, but a one-year loan against three-month treasury bills might be possible.

> I then asked him how quickly it would be possible to place the credit in Paris. He said he thought three or four days. I told him that I thought it ought to be done immediately if it were timed. He, figuratively, threw up his hands and said it was not possible, that it was now 5 o'clock in Paris and that Moret has not even yet been authorized to speak to any of the private bankers. I was astounded at this, and Lacour Gayet said that neither he nor Moret got any impression from Siepmann that there was any imminence about this credit; that he had come to talk in the most general terms; that he was now flying back to London, and that until they were authorized to talk to the private bankers there was nothing more he could do about it. I asked whether, if they got immediate authority to approach the private banks, it would be possible to talk to some of the bankers tonight. He said possibly, but that many of them had already left for the day and gone out of town.[26]

Harrison and Lacour-Gayet could not make sense of Siepmann's 'apparent indifference to speed'. They were convinced about the urgency of getting the loan arranged, as the Bank of England's resources were about to be exhausted. Harrison 'felt in any event it was necessary to do something by tomorrow night or Thursday morning at the latest'.[27]

Later that Tuesday, Harrison received a telegram from Moret telling him that the British Treasury would send a representative to Paris the next day, to negotiate an issue of treasury notes. He also confirmed that there were 7 million pounds left of the Paris tranche of the central bank credit and that Lacour-Gayet would keep Harrison updated by telephone.[28]

On Wednesday afternoon, a British delegation consisting of Frederick Leith-Ross and S.D. Waley from the Treasury and Harry Siepmann arrived in Paris. They first met with Clément Moret at the Banque de France at

5 p.m., and he assured that if the private bankers 'undertook to place any given amount, it could be taken as perfectly certain that they would succeed in doing so. In fact "they can do all they like"'.[29]

Shortly after, Leith-Ross, Waley and Siepman met with Pierre-Étienne Flandin, the French minister of finance, and Moret. Having coordinated the terms and form of a credit with Harrison in New York, what remained to be sorted out was the amount. Leith-Ross said that the issue was for Britain to 'be in a position to meet any possible foreign drain. We had been advised from Paris and . . . New York that any exports of gold', here Moret interrupted and finished the sentence, 'would ruin your credit . . . and I am still absolutely of the same opinion'.

Asked by Moret about Britain's short-term foreign obligations, Leith-Ross estimated it to be 'in the neighbourhood of £300 millions and M. Moret said that, after all, a credit of $400 millions amount to more than a quarter of this total and should be adequate'. Leith-Ross emphasized that the success of the operation depended upon the full support of the Ministry of Finance, which Flandin assured that they had 'without any condition whatever'.

Then the conversation took a sensitive turn, as Flandin said that he wished 'that the intimate and cordial relations established between the British and the French Treasury in November and December last should be renewed'. Leith-Ross agreed but noted that while everyone could agree about the problems to be overcome, there was no consensus about how to get there. That led to a longer discussion about the Wiggin Report, Germany and Washington, and at one point, Leith-Ross asked 'whether M. Flandin was deliberately linking these questions with the immediate question under discussion'.

The French minister denied that he was in any way associating the two problems, and then the meeting adjourned after agreeing to meet again the next day when they 'might reasonably hope to reach agreement on all essentials in the course of the day'.[30]

That was not quite to happen but after some long technical negotiations on August 27 and 28, a deal about a French loan was reached.[31] Since the French and the American loans were contingent on each other, a loan was also arranged in the United States, where J.P. Morgan & Co. had organized the process. On Friday, August 28, the bank issued a statement.

> We have arranged, in association with a Group of American Banks and Banking Houses, to extend a one-year credit of $200,000,000 to the British Government. We are informed by the British Authorities that they are arranging in the French market for one-year credits and loans in the aggregate amount of approximately $200,000,000.[32]

It was a moment of relief, and a powerful demonstration of Morgan's position on Wall Street that it managed to arrange the loan with the participation of more than 100 US banks in such a short time. In fact, it should have been impossible. A J.P. Morgan partner claimed that 'there is not a single institution in our whole banking community which actually desires the British Treasury Notes on any terms'.[33]

J.P. Morgan & Co. earned a commission of $2.5 million for using its network and placing power in the service of the British government.[34] There was cause for celebration. The day after the loan was concluded, Edward Grenfell sat down and wrote a letter to Jack Morgan, who was still in Scotland.

> My dear Jack,
>
> . . . It is no good trying to express to you how grateful we are to you for your support and broadminded treatment of the whole situation. . . .
>
> Snowden and Hopkins have to consider the political sentiment at all times and especially now when the whole Socialist Party is joining with the Trades Unions to put the blame on the blood-sucking bankers, but they both fully appreciate the feeling you showed and the exhibition of strength which J.P.M. & Co. alone could make to carry out such an operation. . . .
>
> Charlie Whigham and I cracked a bottle very lightheartedly before having a profound but light-hearted sleep.[35]

At last, the Bank of England and, indeed, Britain might be out of the woods. Ernest Harvey took the opportunity to send a letter to Morgan Grenfell & Co. to 'tender to you our most sincere thanks for the part which you have taken to bring the negotiations to a satisfactory conclusion'.[36]

The Bank of England, on the other hand, agreed to 'impress upon the Government the need for immediate steps to be taken to secure an adequate presentation to the public in popular form of the case for the maintenance of sterling and of the measures necessary to that end'.[37]

## CONVINCINGLY AMPLE

In the Treasury Chambers in Whitehall, Philip Snowden signed a letter to Charles Whigham expressing his 'sincere thanks to you and the members of your firm for the valuable assistance you gave in the negotiation of the dollar credit. I have just written to Mr. Morgan to express my thanks to him and to his partners.'[38]

Maybe the credit would do the trick and ease the troubled waters? With all the congratulating going around, it did seem like the mood might be about to change for the better. But the situation was still critical. Indeed, *Financial Times*'s editorial on September 2, warned that there would follow once again upon any departure from the gold standard the vicious circle of wages in pursuit of prices . . . hardship to many classes in this country, the uncertainty due to chaotic exchanges, and the effects of loss of confidence upon our external business generally. There is, moreover, the far wider consideration that our defection would strike a heavy blow at the efforts which have been made to restore stability throughout the whole world, and which have been hampered, not by the gold standard itself, but by the disturbance of commercial and financial equilibrium attributable to the war.[39]

Merle Cochran reported from Basle that the Bank of England had burned through the $250 million central bank credit from the Banque de France and the Fed and was already drawing on the government loan. 'Aside from the Hungarian situation, that of British finances is considered by the B.I.S. to be the most serious at present.' Bank of England's balance at the Bank for International Settlements (BIS), usually around $15 million, was at $27,000 and the Banque de France had had to support sterling.

Both Dutch and Swiss banks were withdrawing money from London, and it 'is difficult to forecast future events on that financial market. At the Bank of England people were especially unhappy to receive this week the visit of Dr. Vissering, president of the Netherlands Bank, who wanted to know what security the Bank of England would give for Dutch funds on deposit.'[40]

Crane had just learned about this incident as well and reported to Harrison that it concerned £11 million. The people at the Bank of England were 'extremely angry with him and offered to repay money immediately. Dr. G. Vissering went home without security and decided to leave his money in the Bank of England. There is no doubt however that Dutch, Swiss and Belgians are concerned about position in England and have been withdrawing substantial sums.'[41]

With the situation looking worse, not better, Merle Cochran told the US State Department that Norman's 'position as Governor is now considered quite unstable. He will probably be charged with an unsuccessful program, since such heavy borrowing has necessarily been resorted to, and since his recommendations with respect to funds for Germany, Austria, Hungary, Brazil, Chile, et cetera, may now be considered to have been unfortunate. As you are aware, Mr. Norman, on vacation in Canada, did not attend to the negotiations with New York that ended in the second credit above.'[42]

Norman had, in fact, been away from the Bank throughout August, but Cochran's letter also reflected Gates McGarrah and Leon Fraser's dislike of Norman's actions, especially during the German crisis. Though not for lack of trying, the BIS was not involved in the credits to Britain. The New York

Fed and the Banque de France were completely in charge and the BIS had been sidelined.

And of course, Norman was not on vacation, but a discussion about his position as governor of the Bank of England, a position he, in a significant break with tradition, had held since 1920, was yet another sign of the uncertainty and the fragility of the global financial situation.

There was a massive need to restore confidence. At a meeting at the New York Fed on Thursday, September 3, everyone agreed with W.R. Burgess that the only way to bring back confidence was to fix the European situation along with the banking crisis in the United States. Burgess reported that Walter Stewart and the Morgans 'were very pessimistic about the future in Europe' and

> vigorously agreed that before confidence could be restored abroad something more was required than a more permanent readjustment of reparations. The difficulty lies deeper and is social and political, and an agreement can only be reached by a fundamental political adjustment accompanied by changes in national feeling.[43]

This was not a job for central banks but would 'require a conference of representatives of the governments' that would deal with both economic and security issues 'so that Germany again felt easy with respect to Poland, and necessary guarantees so that France felt her security to be properly safeguarded'. And America needed to officially engage with Europe rather than keep sending unofficial representatives.[44]

As these discussions of political and structural problems took place, sterling continued to leave Britain at a disconcerting speed. The former was seen, problematically, as a longer-term and separate issue, while the latter was urgent and required immediate sensemaking, decisions and actions. At a cabinet meeting on September 3, Harvey was unable to explain why the drain of sterling continued, except that the 'future course of events depended largely upon the attitude of the British public towards the Government's proposals'.

The fact that the government's proposals had been strongly encouraged, even demanded, by Harvey, and the $400 million credit apparently had not strengthened sterling, did not lead Harvey to accept any responsibility or to take charge. Now, with the bankers' ramp attacks, and the situation being critical, the prime minister suggested that when the crisis was over, the Bank of England should 'make some statement as to the principles which had guided them in dealing with the general financial situation'.[45]

With confidence evaporating, the Bank of England's legitimacy was under pressure, not only in terms of the foreign exchange crisis but also because of Harvey's crisis policy. Harvey also got into a discussion with Harrison about how to use the government credit, and to what extent and at what rate sterling should be supported. Harvey wanted to peg the pound above $4.86, which worried Harrison. Though they agreed in principle, their discussions by telephone and cable demonstrated, that it was not easy to figure out or agree on what the best strategy would be.

Harvey felt that it was all a matter of confidence, and he hoped that the new government's programme to be announced next week might provide a test of 'the underlying strength of the market'. Harvey told Harrison that 'our Paris friends' strongly advised against letting the exchange rate decline as it would 'immediately increase the existing nervousness on the continent'.[46] He also met with the foreign exchange managers of the clearing banks and discussed if they were ready to support the sterling forward market.[47]

*The Economist* celebrated the credit and welcomed 'that their total size £80 millions, is convincingly ample, judged by the needs of any immediate threat to the stability of sterling'. However, in the long run it was not the credits but the actions of the new government that would determine confidence in sterling. According to the magazine, France's and America's actions proved that they had confidence in the government.[48]

On September 9, Crane, who was still travelling in Europe and visiting central banks, reported from Berlin that while Luther 'seemed terribly tired and discouraged', the people at the Bank of England 'were much more cheerful and said things were going better'.[49] On the same day, Siepmann wrote a letter, in which he admitted that 'after a rather long period of stress, I am now by no means overworked'.[50]

If there was some cautious optimism, however, it did not last long. On September 10, Sproul wrote to Crane that sterling had weakened and that the 'new government financial proposals evidently being at best no more than was expected. Bank of England sold $3,600,000 . . . and we purchased £626,000'.[51]

## NO PLACE FOR A TIRED MAN

In mid-September there was a curious situation with very practical and urgent matters such as Britain's and the Bank of England's worsening situation, on the one hand, and high-brow economic discussions, on the other. The New York Fed was more sophisticated in using and debating economic theory in relation to the depression than the Bank of England and most other central banks.

From the vantage point of economic theory, the depression was a conundrum, and among central bankers the explanation was mostly about psychology and confidence. It was a matter of restoring confidence in the public and the world of finance and business. W.R. Burgess, Harrison's deputy, addressed this issue in a note to Harrison on September 12 in which he argued,

The economics of this situation has in considerable part changed from a question of specific economic problems to a broad question of public psychology. The public both in this country and abroad has become unwilling to make future commitments and this unwillingness at the moment appears to be increasing rather than decreasing ... In a civilization so highly depending upon credit this state of discredit, as Bagehot calls it, might easily lead to disaster and to an overturn of the existing social and economic order.

A prerequisite to some return of public confidence and willingness to make commitments is a willingness on the part of the recognized leaders to make future commitments. The people generally cannot be expected to make commitments until their leaders will do so. The important question then is whether there is any practical constructive program which might be adopted by the leaders in finance to start things moving and whether the time for starting such a program is in sight.[52]

This was sensemaking under radical uncertainty, where even capitalism might be under threat. In his search for meaning, Burgess focused on the connection between a lack of confidence, a state of discredit and a lack of financial leadership in the United States and Europe. His call for a programme was in effect a call for a new powerful narrative that could change people's outlook and hopes by envisioning a better future. Unfortunately, they were few and far between and part of an as-yet unshaped future. In the United States, they would have to wait for Franklin Delano Roosevelt to become president for it to happen. In Germany, the dream of a better future turned into a nightmare.

Burgess may have had his fears and hopes, but at the time of writing, he had no knowledge about the course of future events. He was focused on searching for a way out of the hole. He stressed the problems of bank failures and the economic troubles of railroads in the United States, and the 'foreign situation in particularly Germany and England'. In Europe, apart from the German and British situations, there were 'other foreign problems centering in part around reparations and in part around the general disequilibrium ... The solution of these problems depend on politics.'[53]

Burgess also aired some ideas for a programme for economic improvement in the United States, but his plan aimed at restoring confidence applied to Europe as well. In a discussion a few days later with Willford I. King, a 'monetarist' and professor of economics at New York University,

Burgess argued that the problem could not be solved by merely increasing the quantity of money. The single most important thing, Burgess argued, was to deal with the European political situation and straighten out the English financial situation.[54]

Burgess realized that political and structural issues were at the centre of both the problem and the solution. But the situation in Britain needed to be taken care of as well. Indeed, as Burgess wrote to Harrison, Britain was entering the decisive week. On Wednesday, September 16, at 1.20 p.m. New York time, Harvey called Harrison to ask what the effect of a general election in the UK might be in relation to the exchange situation. Harrison noted,

They are still having a troublesome time with their exchange situation . . . 52% of the New York credit has already been used or contracted for and 40% of the French. The most disturbing factor is that the last four days have developed unusually heavy pressure and it was on that account that he is particularly concerned. The rate closed today (Sept. 16) in London at $4.86 1/32. The principal withdrawals are on account of Holland although Switzerland is also troublesome. I reminded him of earlier conversations which he and I had as well as an exchange of views by cable, with respect to the best and most appropriate method of handling the exchange situation in all the circumstances; that I had understood that he agreed with me that it would be better not to peg sterling but to let it go its own way . . . He said that he remembered our conversation very well; that he agreed now as he did then, with the principle; that the delay in removing the peg was due to causes which he had already explained: (a) the fact that the French public issue had not been placed and (2) that the British government had not presented its program to Parliament. I added that those two reasons for delay were now disposed of and that it seems to me that if the principle was the direct one there was no longer any justification for delay in its application. He repeated that he agreed with me but that the exchange situation was being handled by a special committee of his directors who had been of the impression that it would be wise to peg exchange at 4,86 or over. I said I could not emphasize too strongly, in his own interest, the effect of the present policy upon sentiment in New York; that maintaining exchange at such a high rate was encouraging sales and discouraging purchases; and that furthermore no one seems to be satisfied with continued use of the credit to maintain sterling at such a high point. Sentiment generally was questioning and restless and I thought his directors were entitled to know that. . . . He then stated that he had to appear before his government tomorrow morning to give the benefit of his judgment as to the effects of the different procedures upon the present disturbing exchange situation; that he was inclined to express his opinion along the lines that he had mentioned to me. In conclusion he asked specifically what he said was in the minds of a great many over there, that is, whether there was any prospect of helping the British situation from Washington. I asked what he meant and got no very satisfactory answer. I rather gathered that he and they are wondering whether there is any likelihood, as the press has been indicating in the past several days, of Washington taking any affirmative position regarding inter-allied debts and reparations. I hinted that I did not think it was possible to expect Washington to take any further initiative in this matter. It was left that way.

During the course of my conversation with Harvey I told him that I had just seen Norman, that he was much disturbed about the way the exchange situation was handled and he agreed with us that it was most important not to peg it, that every peg in the past history had proved disastrous, that he saw no occasion for it at this tie and that the chief reason he was hurrying home before he was quite ready to do so was to see if he could not make some headway in handling the exchange situation more satisfactorily.[55]

That could hardly be seen as anything but a snub by Harrison and Norman of Harvey. Harrison and Harvey had discussed pegging the pound before, and Harvey kept neglecting it while the credit was, in Harrison's opinion, being wasted on keeping sterling artificially high against the dollar.

A week earlier, J.P. Morgan & Co. had expressed the same concern in a cable to Morgan Grenfell and asked 'why the Bank of England does not use the classic remedy of Bank Rate instead of apparently pegging the exchange'.[56] Morgan Grenfell replied that the Bank of England had not 'abandoned the classic remedies of the Bank Rate, gold shipments etc. when in its judgment such action is desirable'. Like Harvey, they did not really explain why such action was not desirable at the moment.[57]

Confidence in Harvey was waning, and the final verdict came from Norman by way of Harrison. Whether Harvey cared is another question. As Harrison tried to get in touch the following Thursday, September 17, Harvey had an assistant send a cable to Harrison that 'owing to his engagements in meetings he is unable to speak to you today but that at present he has nothing special to say'.[58] It was probably the first time Harvey did not have time for the governor of the Federal Reserve Bank of New York.

But it was not just Harrison, Norman and J.P. Morgan that had a bad feeling about the Bank of England's policy. The always well-informed Edward Grenfell wrote a letter to Jack Morgan on September 17. He noted that the 'National Government is not a really happy family'. Although many people in the City and New York and Paris 'hoped the present Government would be a strong one and carry on for some time', they would probably be disappointed.

Harvey's question to Harrison about his view of the impact of an election implied as much, and financial matters were in no better condition. The New York and Paris credits were heavily drawn upon, and Grenfell continued, 'I cannot see how we can carry on if it is used at the present average and, in fact, I am doubtful if they will last till the 15th October – they will certainly not last over the election.' The positive news, if there were any, was that the 'French Government and Bank of France sterling balances still are very high in London and they have not attempted to withdraw them'.

Harrison has been seeing Monty in Quebec and has talked with the Deputy on the telephone. Monty sailed yesterday for England and is reported to be much better physically though still ragged in his nerves. For the moment we certainly do not want him back as there is no place here for a tired man.[59]

In a postscript Grenfell added that since 'writing the above the position has become somewhat more acute and Charlie and I may regretfully have to suggest that we should be comforted by seeing you in London'.[60]

Only the week before, *The Economist* had noted that the new National government 'will balance the Budget; it will curtail the national expenditure within its means; and it will endeavour to distribute the burden and the sacrifice equitably among all sections and classes'. To emphasize the point about sharing the sacrifice, the magazine celebrated the solidarity shown by the King, who announced that he would forego £50,000 of his annual income. The Prime Minister would take a 20 per cent cut to his annual salary of £5,000. They did this to do what they can to 'help during the present emergency'.[61]

Despite *The Economist*'s confidence, it was difficult to find optimists with regard to the situation in Britain, the Royal Navy included. On September 15–16 a 'mutiny' took place at the British Atlantic Fleet as about 1,000 sailors refused to carry out their duties in protest against a 10 per cent cut in salaries and wages.

*Financial Times* was not amused and commented that proof 'of the instability of the foreign mind and the narrowness of the view of Continentals was provided yesterday when foreign exchange dealers received calls from a number of foreign centres as to the situation with regard to the Navy. . . . It may not be out of place to point out to continental peoples that the British Navy has great traditions. Whatever may happen in other parts of the world its personnel has a strong sense of discipline and voice their complaints in the right spirit through the proper channels.'[62]

Continental or not, the BIS was not happy either. According to Merle Cochran, the 'B.I.S. is unable to forecast future British credit needs but realizes that the situation is still very serious. The present B.I.S. rating of the seriousness of financial conditions in countries on this side of the Atlantic would be as follows: (1) Great Britain; (2) Hungary; (3) Austria; and (4) Germany, with the last named much more favorable situated than the rest and offering the highest promise of recuperation to a strong position.'[63] Who would have believed that?

# 17

# As for the Future of England (September 16–October 23)

On September 16, Jay Crane, Harrison's deputy governor, returned to New York after a couple of months in Europe. The same day, he finished a 'Note on visit in England'. Crane discussed the sterling crisis in August, which now seemed far away.

> However, one or two remarks may be made in retrospect. In looking back, one is impressed by the really serious nature of the crisis and how close England actually came to being forced off the gold standard. It was almost a matter of hours, and certainly a delay of a few more days in the formation of a new government would have seen the exhaustion of the Bank of England's resources abroad and the necessity to let gold go again in large amounts, which would probably have been the last straw.[1]

Crane continued that the budget needed to be balanced through increased taxes and a reduction of wages and cuts in the dole. He urged 'economy', another word for deflation, and cited Henry Clay, professor, and economic adviser to the Bank of England. Clay had 'just returned from a trip in Wales, and he confirmed from his own observations . . . that the standard of living of the unemployed in England must be reduced'. Crane felt that Keynes was doing a 'great disservice to his country'.

> On the Continent particularly the fear that England might deliberately abandon the gold standard, or at least go off temporarily to return later at a lower level, has been widespread and can be charged to the influence of Keynes and his followers, who are many in England. Even at the Bank of England one hears men like Siepmann and Rodd admit quite frankly that the only way out is for England and most of the other European countries to go off the gold standard temporarily, leave France and the United States high and dry, and then return to gold at a lower level. As for the future of England, I must say that I have great confidence in their being able to solve the difficulties now that they have been squarely faced, but I do not wish to minimize the hard task which they have before them and which will take time to accomplish.[2]

As Crane wrote these lines, Bank of England's foreign exchange reserves were dwindling, and Harvey was discussing the situation with Harrison. Norman was on his way back to London after having met with Harrison in Quebec. Harrison had told him how critical the situation was, and he decided to return to England. It was not a vote of confidence in Harvey.

Harrison cabled Norman, who was aboard the Duchess of Bedford, 'It was so good to see you again though I too am sorry it was so short. Take care of yourself and let me hear from you when you get home. Good luck and good bye. George.'[3]

In the Committee of Treasury meeting on Wednesday, September 16, Harvey still resisted raising the bank rate. He told the members that 'on general grounds he would welcome a higher Rate, but in existing conditions with an actual increase in the stock of gold and an appearance of steadiness in the exchanges, any rise in the Rate might, he thought, have a disturbing effect'.

He therefore recommended holding the bank rate steady, and the Committee concurred.[4] The following day, Harvey told the Committee that he and Peacock would see the prime minister to inform him of 'the views of the Bank as to the steps to be taken to meet the situation'. Harvey continued that

> at the present rate the Credits would probably last less than a fortnight and after discussion it was agreed that the Prime Minister be informed that in the opinion of the Bank ... It would be impossible with the existing resources to maintain the Gold Standard during the period necessary to conduct a general election.
>
> That if the Government were to announce without delay that in view of the National Emergency a General Election is not contemplated at the present time, but that the present Government will immediately introduce measures designed to correct the adverse balance of trade ... the announcement might induce some return of confidence at home and abroad and lead to some diminution in the withdrawal of foreign balances. ...
>
> The announcement should be followed by diplomatic action in France and the United States, with the object of prompting international co-operation to maintain the situation.[5]

Harvey's decision to abandon the traditional central bank instrument went against Bagehot and involved the Bank directly in politics. Meanwhile, withdrawals continued. On September 18, Harvey 'informed the Committee that yesterday's demand for exchange had been very heavy, and there were indications of even greater demands to-day'.

Harvey and Peacock had pointed out the 'urgency of the position' to the Cabinet Committee, and Ramsay MacDonald said that he saw three options. To propose an emergency tariff immediately; to hold an election the next month and hope that France and the United States would be willing to provide further support until then. Finally, Britain could 'abandon the Gold Standard'. MacDonald was in favour of the second option and, as a consequence, 'Mr. Siepmann has gone to Paris and will see M. Moret to-day.'

It was about to get real. The Committee decided to approach the clearing bankers about how to restrict 'the export of capital by British Nationals', and to ask the Chancellor to prepare 'a letter authorizing the Bank to suspend Gold payments and to make provisional arrangements to enable an Act of Parliament to be passed at the earliest possible moment after the issue of the letter'.[6]

## THE AVALANCHE

As British decision-makers in the government, Whitehall and the Bank of England read the September 19 issue of *The Economist*, they learned that there was only one way forward. The editorial 'Devaluation Delusions' went against John Maynard Keynes and argued that leaving the gold standard would be a 'disaster for the whole world'.[7] There was no easy fiscal or monetary way out, only 'tightened belts and hard work', that is lowering wages and prices, would do the job.[8]

Still, as those lines were written and read, 'the avalanche . . . came down on Friday and Saturday with its full force', in the words of *Financial Times*.[9] As the Committee of Treasury met on Saturday, the mood was sombre. Harvey told the members that

> yesterday's demands had been exceedingly heavy, that the credits were now almost exhausted and that there had, in addition, been a demand for gold from Holland. He had told the Prime Minister yesterday that without further assistance the position could no longer be maintained and that in his opinion the Governments of the United States and France should be informed of this at once.[10]

The United States had declined additional help, and even though France might be able to extend another loan, the game was up. There was no way around suspending Subsection 2 of Clause 1 of the Gold Standard Act of 1925, that is to end Britain's adherence to the gold standard. The Committee recommended that the bank rate should be increased to 6 per cent from Monday, September 21, the same day the suspension of the gold standard would take effect. The Committee also recommended that the London Stock Exchange should remain closed on Monday but that the banks should open as usual.[11]

At 6.30 Saturday morning at home in his apartment at 25 East End Avenue, Harrison received a phone call from Harvey, who told him 'that they have come to the definite conclusion, for which they saw no option, to suspend gold payments Monday morning'.

I asked him whether there was not anything left to do . . . He said he was afraid not that they had reached the end of their tether and that so far as he could see there was nothing left to do. But, I said, you have $75 million left in the Paris credit and with that as a backlog and possible change in conditions and some restrictions, might they not be able to control the situation. He said that the $75 million left in Paris was but a drop in the bucket considering the rate of withdrawals . . . Harvey was of the definite impression that there was nothing left for them to do; . . . and that he did not see any way of effectively stemming the tide. I said it seems a great pity to let it go and asked whether there was anything we could do within reason. Harvey replied that he thought we had already done a great deal and that he saw nothing else which we could do to help, that there was no alternative left.[12]

Two hours later, Harvey called back and told Harrison that the Bank had lost another £7.3 million, and he asked Harrison to support the exchange rate with up to 10 million dollars for the rest of the day. Harrison pointed out that if the Bank was suspending gold payments on Monday anyway, was that not a waste of 10 million, but Harvey thought that was a 'reasonable expenditure of dollars' if it could prevent 'a wide open break here today' that the press would write about.

Harrison said again, 'The whole situation was a great shock to me and a great pity and that I hoped we could keep our backs up and fight to the last minute hoping that something might happen'. But Harvey had given up, and 'despondently said' that nothing would happen to change their 'final judgment'.[13]

On Sunday, September 20, at 9 p.m., the Bank of England sent Harrison the text of the announcement that was about to be handed to the press.[14] Harry Siepmann called Francis Rodd to let him know that we 'suspend gold payment as from tomorrow & will not support the exchange. Stock Exchange will be closed tomorrow for 1 day. Banks will do business as usual without restrictions. We do not expect any banking difficulties.'[15]

The British government's statement noted that 'it has become necessary to suspend for the time being the operation . . . of the gold standard act of 1925, which requires the Bank to sell gold at a fixed price'. They saw no alternative, and Britain was not to blame. The decision was made 'not because of internal financial difficulties but because of excessive withdrawals of borrowed capital'.[16]

The departure was front-page news. What had started in Austria in May, spread to Germany in June and reached the UK in July, taking down the gold standard in September. Despite concerted efforts, it had proved impossible to withstand the centrifugal forces unleashed after the Great War.

The *Commercial and Financial Chronicle* made it clear that Britain's departure from gold 'is one of the catastrophic events of the century, sure to be attended by a long train of ill consequences, from which Great Britain and perhaps the world at large is bound to suffer'.[17]

## I WILL NOT DWELL UPON THE FEELINGS

Jack Morgan was surprisingly calm about the decision and framed it as an opportunity. Having returned to London from grouse hunting in Scotland, he met with a reporter at Morgan Grenfell's offices in London. In a rare interview, Jack Morgan told the journalist that this 'step seems to me to be the second necessary stage in the work of the National Government, the first being the balancing of the budget. . . . The completion of the Government's work will be the restoration of trade in this country. This being the case, it seems to me to be a hopeful and not a discouraging event, and one which brings the great work of the government much nearer to accomplishment.'[18]

Owen Young sent Jack Morgan his 'heartiest congratulations on your statement. Your reserves of silence accumulated through many years make your statement extraordinarily effective here and everywhere in the world. In form and spirit it is exactly right.'[19]

Not everyone agreed, least of all Jack Morgan's partners. Thomas Lamont, the senior partner and second only to Jack Morgan, was upset and had to get it out. On September 25, he wrote to his boss,

> The point that we must make to you – a point that we fear you little realize – is to have you know fully the uncomfortable position in which the New York firm has been placed before the whole American world and the public generally. What the banks here, without exception, fail to understand, is why this enormous credit operation should have been permitted to blow up in our face overnight so to speak.

The House of Morgan had promised the more than 100 participating banks that the credit would save the gold standard, and

> Now the outcome has manifestly and inevitably diminished our prestige, not only publicly but with the American banking community which has for years so largely supported us in our efforts for the preservation here of British credit. And this is a fact that every partner of the firm, which (under you and your Father before you) has built up its American reputation upon careful judgment and prudent dealing,

must keep in the forefront of its mind for a long time to come . . . with you so far away, it has been we have thought, quite important to acquaint you with the unpleasant facts which have come to us all.[20]

It was as close to a mutiny as one could come. But what was Lamont, a partner since 1910 and second only to Jack Morgan, to do when his boss preferred spending his time sailing around the world and hunting for grouse in Scotland rather than taking care of the business? Had the firm broken the principle, Jack Morgan had expressed to Edward Grenfell seven years earlier, that we must 'be very sure not to let our desire to help the politicians to straighten out the tangled affairs of Europe lead us away from the fundamentals'?[21]

Or had the interview with the reporter set a new narrative in motion that might potentially reverse the loss of confidence and contribute to a new vision for the future?

Either way, the house of cards had come tumbling down. Britain had been on the gold standard since 1717 interrupted only by two war-time suspensions. Leaving gold was a genuinely symbolic event; it was what the community of central bankers had struggled to avoid since May 11 when Credit Anstalt's problems were made public. Great Britain was no longer on gold. Sterling was fiat money.

It was a 'time for cool courage', *Financial Times* argued. Britain could not be blamed, however. After having played 'the gold standard game to the best tradition for six years, Great Britain has been forced to call a halt. . . . Stated bluntly, the main reason is that foreigners for no cause associated with our own internal condition have . . . prevented gold from fulfilling its proper function . . . It is proper to emphasize that no internal weaknesses account for the emergency decision'.[22]

This was a convenient narrative that resonated with Siepmann's memo seeing no moral issues in a British departure from gold. It was, after all, not their fault since they were 'forced' off by external events.[23] The framing also resonated with the government's statement that foreigners were to blame; they had played a different game.

It even looked like financial markets were at ease. As the Committee of Treasury met on Monday, September 21, there was not much to report. Harvey told the Committee that 'the situation so far appeared to be generally satisfactory. The Bank have reported that business everywhere is proceeding as usual', and the Stock Exchange reopened on Wednesday, September 23.[24]

The next day, the New York Fed's Board of Directors discussed the significance of Britain's departure. Mr Wooley saw an opportunity for New

York to 'become the financial center of the world', missing the point that this was already more or less the case. The other directors were more concerned about how to save the remains of the gold standard.

Charles Mitchell saw little chance of the United States providing further credits, and he stressed how financial crises were always dominated by uncertainty. It's always a question 'just how much credit will be required to save a particular situation; one can never tell in advance'. First, they thought that the central bank credit would suffice to take care of the situation, 'and then that the private bank credit to the British Government would be sufficient, but . . . it had subsequently been proven that these amounts were not enough'.[25]

Britain's departure from gold called for sensemaking and emplotment of the events in order to imagine new futures in what *The Economist* called 'a situation of almost unparalleled uncertainty'.[26] The most predictable effect was that sterling depreciated in value, as Siepmann noted. The pound had fallen from $4.86 on Monday to around $3.90 on Thursday, a 20 per cent depreciation. This should mean an improvement of Britain's balance of trade ending the consequences of the decision in 1925 to return to gold at the pre-war parity of $4.86 to the pound.

However, foreign central banks and others holding sterling exchange were not amused. The Banque de France, which had been most helpful during the crisis and had not withdrawn money from the Bank of England, had every reason to be upset. On September 20, Harvey had written to Moret to confirm Britain's suspension of gold payments and to thank him for the Banque de France's support. 'I will not dwell upon the feelings', Harvey wrote, 'for they are feelings which I know you share'.[27]

But for Moret it must have been mixed feelings. Merle Cochran reported to the US State Department that 'The B.I.S. estimates the Bank of France's sterling assets at £80,000,000. A 20 per cent loss, calculated on today's depreciation of the pound would, therefore, amount to £16,000,000. The stockholders of the Bank of France are very much worried.' Ten days later, Cochran noted that if 'the Bank of France be liquidated tomorrow, it could be considered bankrupt'.[28]

The *Financial Times* speculated that 'before long only the United States, France, Belgium and Switzerland would remain on a gold basis'.[29] Rodd and Siepmann discussed the uncertainty of the situation, and what might happen if several countries left gold, to some extent echoing Jack Morgan's statement.

In New York they do not seem yet quite to have come to grips with the new realities, but Paris argues that in default of a new grouping on a common basis, we are likely to find one country after another going off the Gold Standard and taking to a managed currency. Nobody quite knows whether this would be workable, especially with independent management in each country. Even if it were workable it would have the effect of leaving France and America high and dry, whereas if it failed, it would lead to chaos. . . . Opinion generally seems to be veering round from the view that what has happened in England is a disaster which the rest of the world is entitled to resent. Perhaps it is an opportunity to group ourselves together afresh and to cooperation.[30]

One week after the departure from gold, Harvey sent a letter to a number of central bank governors, including Hans Luther, Clément Moret and Richard Reisch regretting the 'inconvenience and trouble' the action would cause. 'As to the future I can tell you no more than you can judge for yourself about the probable course of events. . . . Even if for a time, our normal banking relationships may be interrupted or curtailed, I hope and believe that the day will come when we shall be able to continue our co-operation on the stable basis which the gold standard alone can provide.'[31]

That Monday, September 28, Harvey told Committee of Treasury members that the prime minister wanted to know if the Bank had yet 'decided on any general line of financial policy', and what 'in the Bank's view would be the effect on sentiment in financial quarters at home and abroad of the announcement that a General Election is to take place in the near future?'

The Committee agreed that it was too early to 'formulate any definite future policy or objective but speaking generally the Bank are taking whatever steps possible to discourage speculation and will strive to prevent inflation, whilst seeking to avoid any steps likely to check improvement in trade; they will also aim at the maintenance of London as an international market.'

The Bank was not ready to commit itself to anything and would not advise on policy but played the ball back in the government's court. Harvey expressed the hope that the Government would remove the uncertainty as soon as possible by deciding upon a 'course which will permit of the adoption of a steady and consistent financial policy over an extended period'.[32]

The departure from gold increased the urgency of making sense of the situation. On the one hand, the new situation called for prospective sensemaking that could provide a new vision for and contribute to shaping the future. At the moment, nostalgia was prevalent in the shape of an often-repeated assurance that it was a matter of time only before Britain would be back on gold.

On the other hand, and because of the need to make sense of the future, the actors also need to retrospectively make sense of what they had just gone through, of what on earth had happened. It was in this meeting between 'space of experience' and 'horizon of expectations', between past and future, that central bankers and other actors struggled to figure out where to go from here. What did it mean to be a central banker or banker in a world with Great Britain off the gold standard?

## CAPITAL IS AN ELUSIVE THING

Among bankers, Britain's departure from gold was well received according to *The Economist*.[33] Jack Morgan considered the decision a 'hopeful' event, but the partners at J.P. Morgan & Co. were not happy about the process, which caused the 'whole American community ... an almost unprecedented shock'.[34] The Bank of England had spent credits totalling $650 million on supporting sterling by insisting on pegging the pound at an exchange rate above the gold point – the exchange rate below which it would pay to export gold.[35]

It was a seriously costly decision and exactly what Keynes had warned Prime Minister MacDonald against on August 5, 'if we are so foolish to borrow in terms of francs and dollars'.[36] Some may have felt a nagging doubt whether the outcome had been Harvey's plan all along, in order to force the government's hand.[37]

Now, the peg was gone, and so was the money. In a long telegram to Jack Morgan and Morgan Grenfell, the Morgan partners challenged the victim narrative of the Bank of England and the British government.

> Whatever it may have seemed best politically to say about foreign difficulties being the cause of the sterling crisis it seems to us that heavy foreign withdrawals might not have occurred if foreign bankers had not believed that there was an English flight from the pound in progress resulting from the growing fear of Socialist politics....
>
> Now that the crisis of last week is past we feel that we ought with an eye upon the future to acquaint you with the feeling existent in the American banking community. These comments may sound harsh but we do not mean them to sound so as they are only interpretative of the situation here.
>
> Whatever the reasons may be political or otherwise the collapse of sterling after $650,000,000 ... had been borrowed in France and America in six weeks to support it ... seems to thoughtful people to reflect on the judgment of the British Treasury and the Bank not to mention their bankers here. Having obtained the credits why did they dissipate the whole fund in a futile effort at pegging instead of using it to get control of the situation themselves with the help of the

traditional central banking measures that were open to them? Pegging the exchange above the gold point with money borrowed short was known by experience to be full of dangers as giving an invitation to speculators and as facilitating rather than discouraging a flight from the pound. The use of a substantial part of the credit during the last few days to peg sterling after decision to abandon it had practically been reached is also gravely criticized.

Having diagnosed Britain's departure from gold as a result of a flawed Bank of England policy, the Morgan partners continued with an 'eye on the future', using the historical analogy of the franc Poincaré.

Everything depends on the degree of confidence that the British Authorities succeed in creating at home and abroad in their ability and determination to restore budgetary and economic equilibrium and to enable British industries to compete in world markets and British capital to find renewed hope of profit at home and freedom from the fear of special taxation or confiscation. . . .

But above all it is a question of the restoration of confidence at home and abroad. So it was you will recall in France. Poincare and Moreau restored public confidence in the Treasury and the Bank and reversed the flight from the franc almost overnight. French capital was voluntarily repatriated without any measures to force mobilization being adopted so that within six months the Franc had risen from 2-1/4 cents to 4 cents where it had to be pegged down – not up – by buying pounds and dollars and selling francs. In this process the Banque de France showed the greatest skill in handling its exchange operations and was able to accumulate large reserves of foreign currencies for its own account. Capital is an elusive thing. It is readily enticed by the hope of profit. Fear drives it away but rarely brings it home.

The British authorities are now face to face with the practical problem of determining what course to pursue during the coming weeks and months while sterling is seeking a new level. We are glad to learn . . . that there is to be no pegging. And we are profoundly relieved that once it became apparent that the break must come our British friends did do the wise thing on the whole and while letting the exchange go maintained open markets all around and did not follow the course adopted by the Germans with their disastrous moratorium programme and stoppage of payments. But the authorities will undoubtedly be considering that some general plan of action is necessary if violent fluctuations in the exchange are to be avoided. . . . This is primarily a problem of planning and good management and no doubt your friends at the Treasury and the Bank have already in mind some of the practical measures that must be taken.[38]

Jack Morgan responded the next day, Wednesday, September 30. He understood well the criticism of Harvey's and the Bank of England's insistence on pegging sterling to the very last day. But he was more forgiving than his partners in the United States. With a nod to the uncertainty of the moment he noted, 'I am not sure that the time has yet come to discuss the details of or the reasons for past decisions. They were taken with the best judgment available and have turned out in some glaring instances to have been mistaken which everyone regrets.'

Norman and Harrison had also been critical of Harvey's decision to peg the pound above the gold point. It meant that the credits had evaporated into thin air, without serving their purpose. But now was a time to look forward and deal with the future. Jack Morgan wrote to his partners at J.P. Morgan & Co. in New York on September 30.

> Every day brings its own puzzle and until we can get at least an idea of the situation as a whole it is impossible to make any definite plan. All that can be done now as I see it is to meet the various difficulties as they come up and try to meet them in the right way and avoid making more mistakes than you have to.[39]

Jack Morgan expressed in a nutshell the conditions that called for sensemaking and emplotment. Hopes about controlling events and cause and effect were doomed to fail. His statement pinpointed the problem with radical uncertainty, even though his colleagues in New York were less perceptive.

The world had changed, as *The Economist*'s amply titled editorial 'The End of an Epoch' made clear. 'It is safe to predict that Monday, September 21, 1931, will become a historic date; the suspension of the gold standard in Great Britain on that day, after the six years of painful effort which followed this country's return to gold in 1925, marks the definite end of an epoch in the world's financial and economic development.'[40]

Norman's statement to the Macmillan Committee in March 1930 on the gold standard as the cement that bound the whole international economy together was no longer valid.[41] The cement had crumbled away, and the building had come down. The big question was what to build instead.

*The Economist* noted that after the overnight suspension of the gold standard, 'no one knows when or how we shall return to it, or whether some new order will eventually take its place. . . . No one can say what may follow.'[42]

## WE LOST OUR MONEY AND ACHIEVED NOTHING

As the various actors and observers struggled to navigate and make sense of the departure and its future implications, Norman returned to Britain and the Bank of England. On September 23 at 7 a.m., he arrived in Liverpool from Quebec on board the *Duchess of Bedford*. According to the *New York Times*, he had been travelling with his sister and before the ship reached the dock, he boarded a dinghy and caught an early train to London, where upon arrival he was protected from prying eyes and reporters by a 'police inspector, two sergeants and ten constables'.

At the station Norman was picked up by Josiah Stamp, a Bank of England director, who met him with a 'Hello old boy, how are you?' and updated him on the situation. Even if it felt good to be back home, rumours that he might not complete his term at the Bank cannot have been welcome.[43]

In Liverpool, Norman was handed a letter from Harvey apologizing for not being able to greet him on arrival. It continued that we 'have been through terrible times and at present I am feeling rather stunned. Though the outlook is dark I hope for the best. But we have terribly missed your guidance in our troubles. Indeed we seem to have been inflicted with every possible kind of misfortune. I hope you are going to rest quietly for a bit.'[44]

Hope springs eternal, but Norman was not going to rest or stay away from the Bank. On September 20, he had received a message from Harvey while still aboard the *Duchess of Bedford*, saying, 'Sorry we have to go off tomorrow and cannot wait to see you before doing so. Hope you are well. All send greetings. Ernest.'

Norman was upset with Harvey and Peacock, who had run his Bank during his absence, and when he returned to the Bank and the new world of fiat money, the day after he arrived in London, he let them know.[45]

On October 2, Norman was on the phone with Harrison who had called both him and Harvey to discuss 'the general situation and learning what, if any, plans they have for the immediate future. They said that they have formulated no plans whatever as yet; that it is impossible for them to do so until the political plan straightens out.'

Norman also told Harrison that there were rumours about the state of the American banks in general and Chase Manhattan in particular. Harrison was not concerned about the New York banks, but he did not know what to do about the rumours. Harrison said that he had first heard the rumours from Paris to which Norman replied that 'he would not be surprised if that is where they originated'.[46] Some things never change.

Even though Norman had been absent during most of the sterling crisis and had not been involved in the decision to leave gold, he too had to face the music. In October, he attended a Bank for International Settlements (BIS) board meeting in Basle where he 'spent some unpleasant days'. Many of his fellow central bankers asked him how to file claims for 'compensation for the losses their Banks have sustained by this Country's temporary suspension of the Gold Standard'.

Worst of all was Norman's painful and emotional experience in Basle. The 'status and authority of the Bank of England Representatives on the Board of the Bank for International Settlements have in great measure been destroyed'.[47] The Bank of England and Norman could no longer lay claim to any symbolic or moral superiority.

A new chapter could begin; indeed, had to begin. In November 1931, Francis Rodd left the Bank for International Settlements and Basle to return to London and the Bank of England. Norman wrote to Rodd that 'the second half of November Siep (still protesting) has promised to go right away for two or three months. Before he goes you will have settled in here and all the time he is away you will I hope do his work.'[48]

Siepmann left for holiday in Las Palmas at the Canary Islands on November 21, and 'at the moment I can think of nothing else. I shall not be back in the Bank until the beginning of February. By then, I imagine, things will look quite different.'[49]

Upon Siepmann's return from his well-deserved extended holiday, Francis Rodd by some irony became liaison to the Banque de France. On February 4, 1932, he and his wife, the artist Mary Vivian Smith, had a daughter and a few weeks later he cabled the ever-so-popular Walter Stewart, 'Will you be Godfather to new daughter?'[50] On January 1, 1933, Rodd left the Bank of England to become a partner at Morgan Grenfell.

George Harrison moved on October 1, 1931, to a new address close to his old apartment on 25 East End Avenue. In fact, he only moved a little up the road to a newly constructed building with a great view over the East River.[51] But he did not have much time to enjoy the view as the European financial crisis now crossed the Atlantic and led to massive withdrawals of gold from the United States at the same time as a serious banking crisis hit parts of the country.[52] But that is another albeit no less important story.

In 1940, Harrison, a long-time bachelor like Norman, married Alice Gordon Grayson, a widow of a friend, and the same year he stepped down as governor of the Federal Reserve Bank of New York to take up the position as president of the New York Life Insurance Company.

At the Bank of England, on November 11, 1931, the Committee of Treasury recommended to the Court of Directors that Norman and Harvey be 'invited to allow their names to be submitted to the Proprietors in April next for Election to their respective offices for a further year'.[53] When Harrison heard the news about the re-appointment, he cabled Norman, 'I am very happy about it for so many reasons. My love and congratulations. George'.[54]

How the relationship between Harvey and Norman developed after Norman's return is unknown. There is an interesting counterfactual in considering what would have happened had Norman not fallen ill and left the Bank of England during the most critical of times.[55]

Not many contemporaries turned that stone, but J.P. Morgan did cable Morgan Grenfell on November 30, 1931, that Norman's 'illness seems to us to have been one of the major misfortunes of recent months'.[56]

In a response, Morgan Grenfell noted that much 'are now matters of history . . . If you ask what can be done to improve matters, we believe both the Governor and Sir Otto Niemeyer would say that they have no suggestion to offer beyond the hope that from the labours of all who are working incessantly on these problems will come eventually some relief.'[57]

It took another thirteen years before Norman stepped down in 1944 after twenty-four years as the governor of the Bank of England. Things had never been the same since September 1931. Even though he married Priscilla Reyntiens in 1933 at age 62, with time his pessimistic mood increasingly got the better of him. He complained to an American friend,

> As I look back, it now seems that, with all the thought and work and good intentions which we provided, we achieved absolutely nothing. . . . By and large nothing that I did, and very little that old Ben did, internationally produced any good effect – or indeed any effect at all except that we collected money from a lot of poor devils and gave it over to the four winds. . . . And yet we lost our money and achieved nothing for all our blood and sweat because of the *politicians*, and all that sort makes me hate and despise politicians more and more.[58]

Harry Siepmann was hardly done thinking about the past either. He and many other central bankers, private bankers and decision-makers in Britain and abroad had taken the gold standard for granted and 'truly the basis of our civilization' as Pierre Quesnay put it in February 1931.[59] Even though Siepmann had foreseen that September 21 might happen, he was disillusioned and haunted by the thought of what more they could have done or done differently. On October 20, he wrote to Rodd.

> My Dear Francis,
>
> The criticisms about which I spoke to you yesterday on the telephone, and which I should be glad if you would do your best to kill, run more or less on the following lines.
>
> The suspension of the Gold Standard in England was bound to cause a great loss of prestige and moral authority. But in fact, the events leading up to the suspension have caused an additional and quite unexpected loss, to the Bank of England in

particular. The Bank of England have always been regarded as the chief exponent of sound financial and monetary principles and their technical competence has been above all criticism. Consequently, the surprise is all the greater now that the very doctrines which the Bank of England have been preaching all over Europe for years past appear to have been completely ignored in the defense of sterling.

If any Continental Central Bank went on paying out its foreign exchange reserves without effecting an equivalent contraction of the monetary circulation of the basis of credit, it was rightly considered to be unequal to its job. The Bank of England borrowed £130 millions abroad and paid out 130 millions of foreign exchange in the course of two months. During this period, the most attentive study of the Bank of England's Returns reveals no internal contraction of credit whatever. In other words, the Bank of England itself was providing buyers of foreign exchange with the sterling delivered to the Bank of England against the foreign exchange which the Bank of England had borrowed.

At this point I generally interrupt. I say that the criticism betrays complete misunderstanding of the technical working of the London market. We are not in the position of a Bank of Issue in a country where the total note circulation is an accurate guide to the volume of available credit. The only meaning to be attached to the criticism as applied to London is that market rates should have been in a closer relation to Bank Rate. In other words, the whole argument has to do with a difference of 1/8% or 1/4% and the amount of contraction possible without driving the market into the Bank amounts not to 130 millions but to, shall we say £5 or £6 millions. The most charitable way of ascribing some meaning to the criticism is to suppose that it is to be directed against the level of our Bank Rate.

At this point the other fellow interrupts and also shifts his ground. He says: precisely. Whoever heard of anybody going off the Gold Standard with a Bank Rate of 4½%. Did not the Governor of the Bank of England tell the Governor of the Bank of Spain that in order to stabilize at all it would be necessary to make money scarce and dear and to maintain a high effective Bank Rate? But the Bank of England Rate was not only kept low throughout the period of crisis; it was actually kept at 4½% after the date at which England had borrowed £80 millions in Paris at 4¼%. This was a direct invitation to any foreign, or indeed domestic, holders of Treasury Bills to transfer their holding at once into the new issue as of course many of them did. The one fact that the Bank of England Rate was not raised to 6% on the morning after the Paris arrangements had been concluded is sufficient evidence that the Bank of England proved themselves technically incompetent to manage the position.

Here I generally interrupt again, but with less conviction, therefore by counterattack. I say that our mistake may have been to listen perhaps a little too attentively to the disinterested advice which was being given us from abroad. For the fact is that we were consistently told by all our friends abroad that there were two things which, given the state of the public mind, we could not afford, namely a rise in the Bank Rate and a loss of gold.

The next count on the indictment has to do with our forward exchange operations. A fantastic blunder, since once again we were ourselves providing the means with which the sterling rate could be destroyed. Specifically, Belgium was long of sterling at the beginning of the crisis and was definitely short of sterling when we went off gold. More specifically still the Société Générale de Belgique succeeded in covering the whole of their losses in copper out of the profits in sterling which we were kind enough to present to them.

At this point I generally blow up.[60]

Siepmann was, of course, a close ally of Norman, and his letter to Rodd was a devastating critique of Harvey's conduct of Bank of England's policy during the critical weeks from early August to when Britain left gold on September 21, 1931. It was also his own – unsuccessful – attempt to construct a coherent narrative that could make sense of what had happened in August and September of 1931, probably the most dramatic and exhausting period in his life, except from the Great War.

The problem was that he could not make sense of it, and Francis Rodd could not help him. He too was at a loss as he responded a few days later.

My dear Harry,

... The summary which you give accurately describes what I have also been subjected to. There are, however, one or two points which I would like a little more comment on before I take up the cudgels. I have myself often wondered why we did not tighten up the market a great deal more ... by actually raising the bank rate. I did not for one moment suppose we were guided entirely by 'disinterested advice' from abroad against raising the bank rate. I presume it was felt that such a course was useless. Of course, it may be necessary in that particular aspect of the problem to go back to the time when the German market broke in July when, as you know, I would have preferred to see a rise in the bank rate immediately to 5 or 6%. The Governor, as you will remember, always used to say that we would break within three weeks of the Germans going. Reusch reminded me that the Governor had said this to him in May and Reusch, in the light of after events, commented on the perspicacity of the Governor.[61]

Like Norman's 'it's politics' narrative, Siepmann's story, though more thoughtful and loaded with doubts, was a search for meaning. Both enacted retrospective sensemaking trying to order their experience into a narrative that gave meaning and direction to their experiences. To take their meaning loss and turn it into something deeply connected with what they were first and foremost: central bankers.

From May to September 1931, they and their compatriots had been focused on the future, more precisely their imagined future constantly searching for signs and clues about what might come, and at the same time trying to shape that future. Now, they were looking backwards in order to understand what had been. The strange thing was that it did not get much easier that way.

While Norman had more or less given up on emplotting 1931 and the years that preceded it in a way that could legitimize the hard work, he was left with blaming politics and politicians, the villains of his story. It resonated, of course, with the story he had developed during the summer of 1931, that central bankers could not solve the crisis, because at the end of the day the legacy of the War and Versailles stood in the way. The crisis of 1931 was a job for statesmen, and in Norman's view they had failed miserably.

Siepmann on the other hand stayed closer to home, disillusioned about the Bank of England's actions and decisions during the sterling crisis of August and September 1931, as Norman was away from the Bank because of illness. He was desperately searching for a way to emplot the events into a narrative that would enable him to conclude that the Bank of England, his Bank of England, had done the right thing but lost anyway because of uncontrollable outside forces.

It would not be Siepmann's last disappointment. In 1945 he was appointed executive director, but his dream of becoming governor of the Bank of England, never materialized, as Cameron Cobbold was appointed governor in 1949. Siepmann was left a 'bitterly disappointed man'.[62]

# The End (2024)

The universe is under no obligation to make sense to you.[1]

Neil deGrasse Tyson

In January 1932, Foreign Affairs published 'The Crisis of the Gold Standard' by Harvard Professor of Economics John H. Williams. The retrospective sensemaking had begun. 'We have', he wrote,

> passed through the most acute international money crisis that has ever occurred in time of peace. The panic which began with the failure of the Austrian Kreditanstalt in May, forced the Hoover debt holiday and the freezing agreement on German short-time debts in June and July, wrecked the British Labor government in August and drove England from the gold standard in September, and then drained $738,000,000 of gold from the United States by the end of October, has no parallel for speed and magnitude in the history of international finance.[2]

Williams's introductory paragraph is a condensed, backward-looking narrative of the same crisis that I, more than ninety years later, have unfolded over several hundred pages. Williams and I both tell the story of the financial crisis of 1931.

The difference between the two is that in the Williams quote the process, the uncertainty, the in-betweens, the roadblocks, the roads not taken, the conflicts and the struggle to contain the crisis are left out. And so are the human beings, their relations, emotions, interactions, their sensemaking and the meanings they assigned to each other and to events as they unfolded between May and September 1931.

I think the brief quote in isolation is an example of what anthropologist Clifford Geertz calls thin description.[3] The Credit Anstalt crisis and the following crises in Germany and Great Britain have to some extent become a sort of meme that is mentioned and used in scholarly books as well as newspapers and magazines for various purposes. It has in a way taken on a life of its own, with silences, errors and inaccuracies being repeated as it has traversed over ninety years from one article or book to another.[4]

My ambition has been different. I wanted to provide a thick description of the 1931 financial crisis through a detailed forward-looking history written from central bankers' and other actors' perspective(s). I wanted to alter the scale of observation to see, as Giovanni Levi has put it, 'phenomena previously considered to be sufficiently described and understood' in a completely new way.[5]

In the introduction, I claimed that this approach would contribute in two ways to our current knowledge and understanding of 1931.

First, this study provides deep new knowledge and a new understanding of central bankers' struggle to contain the European financial crisis as it spread from Austria to Germany and to Great Britain over the summer of 1931. Second, the book contributes with an empirically based knowledge and understanding of how actual decision-makers, as opposed to abstract, presumed rational agents, work in a context of radical uncertainty.

Now, it is time to draw up the balance sheet and consider if altering the scale of observation and applying a humanistic and cultural approach and conceptual framework have led to new and different insights into and understanding of the European financial crisis in 1931? Do we understand the events of 1931 better or differently?

I resist calling this final chapter a conclusion. *The narrative is the analysis*, I argued in the introduction. I cannot stress this enough. I agree with Bent Flyvbjerg who argues that 'the narrative itself is the answer', and readers 'will have to discover their own path and truth inside the case'.[6] Still, this being 'The End' calls for a discussion of my contribution to the ongoing scholarly debate on the financial crisis of 1931, and of the contribution of my approach.[7]

What does this new micro-level, thick description, forward-looking narrative of the European financial crisis of 1931 tell us that we did not already know?[8]

At the most general level, writing history forwards with a focus on uncertainty and sensemaking calls for caution with respect to passing judgement. The actors of the past must be seen as individuals and part of the world in which they lived and acted, with the possibilities and constraints it offered. As a bonus, trying hard to exclude hindsight also keeps us from falling into the trap of believing that we are so much smarter today.[9]

But hindsight is not the only issue. Equally important is the theoretical or conceptual framing of the analysis and the scholar's (i.e. my) own worldview. In this book, I have aimed, however imperfectly, to figure out what actors in 1931 looked for and how they made sense of what they saw. Still, like all narratives, my framing of the analysis surely silences or marginalizes some parts of what happened over the summer of 1931. I too have blind spots.

The most important contributions of this book are related to the two points mentioned above. First, by writing history forwards, the story provides new knowledge and a new understanding of the financial crisis of 1931 as it unfolded. Second, the analysis provides an empirically grounded case of how decision-makers work in and shape crisis situations. As such the book contributes to emergent research in decision-making under radical uncertainty.

Though my ambition has not been to theorize or generalize, this book shows that there is an enormous difference between textbook and real-world context-specific decision-making.

In the remainder of this final chapter, I first discuss these two contributions respectively. I wrap up the book by briefly addressing the financial crisis of 2008 and the question of what, if any, lessons we may learn from this new history of the European financial crisis of 1931.

## UNDERSTANDING THE 1931 FINANCIAL CRISIS

Throughout this book I refer to and discuss the historiography on the European financial crisis of 1931 or parts of it. It is all in the endnotes and tells us that most historians have focused on either the Austrian, German or British phase of the crisis, on specific particulars and aspects of the events of 1931, or have examined these events as part of a broader analysis of the Great Depression, the interwar period, or of central banking or financial crises. Most of this work has focused on causality, for example, what caused the Credit Anstalt crisis, the German crisis, Britain's departure from gold, the Great Depression or some other cause-and-effect relationship.

In contrast, when Leon Fraser arrived in New York on June 3, 1931, he was met by reporters who wanted to know what had caused the world depression. To their frustration, his reply was 'any cause you wish.... I don't know of any explanation'.[10] Like Fraser, I have focused less on explaining why and more on understanding the processes and the actors involved. My interest has been how they made sense of the crisis in the context of radical uncertainty, their imaginations, frustrations, actions and decisions. How do this approach and my story relate to and add to existing scholarship?

Arguably, the dominant narrative about the causes of the Great Depression, in which the 1931 crisis, and not the Wall Street crash of 1929, is front and centre, is shaped by Barry Eichengreen's seminal book *Golden Fetters*. Together with Peter Temin's *Lessons from the Great Depression*, it has become the standard interpretation of the causes of the Great Depression. Eichengreen and Temin coin this problem the gold standard mentality. The irony is that while central bankers of the interwar period struggled to re-establish, maintain and rescue the gold standard, given the asymmetries and illusion of the gold standard, letting it go would have been the better thing to do.[11] That, however, was light years away from the dominant view at the time.

Within this gold standard mentality narrative, lack of cooperation has emerged as a, if not the, key frame in the historiography of the financial crisis and the Great Depression.[12] The dominant narrative begins at least with Stephen Clarke, who concluded that after mid-1928 central bank cooperation 'must be judged a failure'.[13] In addition, Milton Friedman and Anna Schwartz famously blamed the Great Depression in the United States on the Federal Reserve's 'inept' monetary policy and the death of Benjamin Strong.[14]

Recently the economic historian Mary O'Sullivan has argued that *A Monetary History* is 'suffused with ideology'. Since Milton Friedman and Anna Schwartz and up to and including Eichengreen and Temin, O'Sullivan argues, historians have reduced the Great Depression from a crisis of capitalism to 'a recession that turned into a depression because of central bankers' and political leaders' mentalities about money'.[15]

This does not imply that the gold standard mentality explanation is without foundation, as the evidence in this book also shows. But the focus on money and central banks has framed scholarly discussion and to some extent marginalized other perspectives and approaches. In particular, O'Sullivan forcefully argues that heterodox views of capitalism as inherently unstable and the Great Depression as a crisis of capitalism have been silenced.[16]

Hindsight has played a significant role as well in the strong critique of central banks.[17] Perhaps the most direct and unforgiving verdict came in 1986 from a group of economic historians concluding that 'what happened in 1931 was that the world saw the consequences of central bankers not understanding central banking'.[18]

This view makes it very clear why writing history forwards with a focus on uncertainty, sensemaking and context matters. That is this book's most significant contribution to the historiography on the crisis of 1931, which reveals varying degrees of presentism and hindsight, ideology and a deep belief in the Bagehot operating model as the solution to financial crises.

History written backwards silences the radical uncertainty and the unshaped futures imagined by contemporary actors and replaces them with certainty and a stable historical past. It marginalizes the experience of contemporaries, let alone trying to understand them and their world.

Writing history forwards lays bare the implicit counterfactual in much of the historiography: if only the central banks had lived up to and cooperated on the basis of the Bagehot model, the financial crisis (or crises) of 1931, the breakdown of the gold exchange standard and the Great Depression might have been avoided. But what if, as Forrest Capie asks, the breakdown of the gold standard was 'part of the disintegration of the system, about which little or nothing could be done'?[19] Then the counterfactual breaks down, and so does the dominant retrospective too-little-too-late narrative. And it opens up for Mary O'Sullivan's suggestion that the Great Depression should be understood as a crisis of capitalism.

Despite historians' claim to the opposite, no one could blame the central bankers for not trying.[20] The criticism of central banks' actions in 1931 is at least partly based on Walter Bagehot's operating model and a problematic framing. It is against this lens that the actors of 1931 have been measured and found failing. To be clear, historians have not neglected context in 1931. Most have been very much aware of the underlying structural and political issues complicating the situation in 1931. Nevertheless, most analyses have assumed that the financial crisis of 1931 would have been halted if surplus countries had played according to the 'rules of the gold standard' and if central banks had cooperated and followed Walter Bagehot's model.

In 1931, however, it soon became clear to contemporary actors that the operating model did not provide a solution in a complex world full of surprises, different worldviews, perceived diverging interests, uncertainty and chaos. Hans Simon discussed the role of central banks in a crisis in his January note and again in his 'Lessons of the Austrian Crisis' note from June 2. He and Siepmann both demonstrated their awareness of the accepted practices of central banking, but they also recognized the limitations and inadequacy of theory, historical analogies and past experience. And, significantly, in the midst of the crisis Norman realized that central banks were dealing with a 'world political problem'.

This book shows how Bagehot's statement that before 'we had much specific experience, it was not easy to prescribe for this compound disease [of an internal panic and a foreign drain]; but now we know how to deal with it', was and is much too optimistic, too modern.[21]

Perceiving the world is a tricky thing. It cannot be done without at the same time emplotting and shaping that world through narrative. During radical uncertainty where 'conditions are perplexing, abnormal and beyond understanding', and where 'cause and effect cannot clearly be distinguished' as Norman remarked, sensemaking and narrative emplotment are called for.[22]

My study shows that in such a radically uncertain world, models and blueprints are at best insufficient guides to actions and decisions. Sensemaking and narrative emplotment not only describe the world, but they also contribute to shaping the world and help navigate uncertainty. That was also the case in the European financial crisis of 1931.[23]

Another insight from this study is how chance, ambiguity, good luck and bad luck, tempers and personalities, animosities and friendships, experiences and expectations and networks all play a role. Human beings and individuals matter also below the top level of organizations. In 1931, events and situations called for sensemaking and emplotment by people like Francis Rodd, Pierre Quesnay, Robert Lacour-Gayet, Harry Siepmann, and, of course, Montagu Norman, George L. Harrison, Hans Luther and Clément Moret and many others. They provided and dealt with actionable knowledge while at the same time shaping their perception of the many connected events.

In short, they constituted an emerging epistemic community of central bankers with at least partly shared worldviews and practices. Occasionally, other identities and communities challenged the logics of this epistemic community, but it proved its strength several times, not least in the case of the Banque de France and its generally cooperative attitude. This epistemic community enabled decision-making and action. Radical uncertainty and problems of sensemaking and narrative emplotment during crises need to be integrated into future theory and practices.

This is why writing history forwards is necessary if we want to understand historic actors, human beings, rather than judge their practices, decisions and actions during situations fraught with uncertainty and anxiety about the future. It is also why, by altering the scale and examining in great detail how actors went about their daily business, we get to see the way they made sense of events in a complex context with ever-moving targets.

That may well be the most important insight from this book.

The central bankers of 1931 were not clueless. From the outset they and other actors knew that their ideas of the world economy and capitalism were already being challenged by events. They realized what was at stake and tried to prepare for the thin ice. They discussed the causes of deflation, maldistribution of gold, the legacy of the Versailles Treaty, German reparations, and war debts to the United States.

They debated the loss of confidence in, and survival of, capitalism, and they used words and expressions such as catastrophe, disaster, abyss, house of cards, there will be the devil to pay and so on to make sense of and shape the situation in which they found themselves. They did not always perceive these and other issues in the same way, and the narratives they constructed sometimes assigned different causes and meanings to the same events and changed over time as the 1931 crisis spread in Europe.

Still, during the first part of the European crisis, Norman and Harrison as well as the Bank for International Settlements (BIS) occasionally seemed optimistic that central banks could stop the crisis from spreading. As mentioned above and shown in the narrative, personalities, emotions, networks and trust mattered here as well.[24]

With time, they – and Norman, in particular, an emotional and intuitive rather than rational man if there ever was one – became convinced that the financial crisis was entangled in the political and structural issues, and that central bank action was a 'palliative' only. It would not be far off to say that Norman was proved right, but it is also an example of how narratives are performative. Norman's narrative about politics ultimately led him and Harrison to give up on the idea that central banks could do much.

A similarly forgotten part of the 1931 crisis is the role played by central bankers below the top level. Focus has been on Montagu Norman, Benjamin Strong (but not so much Harrison), Hjalmar Schacht (but not Luther) and Emile Moreau (more than Clément Moret). Meanwhile, highly competent and hard-working central bankers like Francis Rodd, Harry Siepmann, Pierre Quesnay, Robert Lacour-Gayet and others have been more or less neglected. But without them and many more, the interventions in Austria, Germany and Great Britain could not have been carried out. This is not exactly history from below, but it does indicate that a focus on the top layers marginalizes or silences important actors and events and disturbs our understanding of events.

Central banks were in frequent contact and cooperated more than granted in most of the historical literature. Yes, there were obstacles, prejudices and animosity, not least against the French. But the Banque de France nevertheless participated in the BIS loan to Austria, the $100 million credit to the Reichsbank and the $200 million credit to the Bank of England. In the case of Austria and Germany, the French government at the same time intervened with 'political conditions'. This again points to an emergent epistemic community among central banks, which allowed them not to follow their governments at all times. Still, both the Reichsbank and the Austrian National Bank ended up following their own routes, as domestic concerns and politics conflicted with the logic of the epistemic community's demand for deflation and guarantee, respectively.

Information problems came on top of struggles to make sense of the situation. They arose from geographical distance, different networks and shifting communication lines. In addition, at least in the Austrian case an apparent lack of will to communicate because of perceived diverging interests mattered too. The problem of geographical distance was partly taken care of through the community of central bankers, partly eased by technology such as the telephone and the telegraph, and aeroplane flights were used as well, signalling how the compression of time contributed to contagion and the intensity of the crisis. Networks, personal relations and trust were important, too, as just mentioned with Harrison and Lacour-Gayet, and with Norman and Harrison.

Also, J.P. Morgan & Co. had very different and at least partly personal and emotional views of Germany and the UK, which clearly influenced their willingness to assist. Harry Siepmann had a wide reach beyond the UK and into Central Europe. From his correspondence, it is clear that he knew many of the central bankers of Europe and nurtured these relationships. It was professional, but personal too.

The divergence of construed interests, distribution of power and not least perceptions were apparent in all three phases of the crisis, including and particularly in Austria. The Austrian government and to some extent the National Bank were focused on the domestic situation, the banking system and the national currency. That is why Austria introduced the idea of a moratorium and was most reluctant to enforce a guarantee for the Credit Anstalt's liabilities. The central bankers and the BIS on the other hand worried about contagion from Austria to the neighbouring countries and about the gold standard and the future of capitalism. This led to the conflicting narratives concerning a moratorium and guarantee, a topic to which historians have paid little attention until now.[25]

The role of private banks has not been known in much detail before and their inclusion in this book is a significant contribution to the historiography.[26] Rothschild & Sons and the House of Morgan played important roles in organizing the Austrian creditors and negotiating and forcing through the standstill agreement and the guarantee. They served their own perceived interests, of course, which occasionally converged with the public good of financial stability. Notably, private bankers had surprisingly close relations with the central banks. At times Morgan Grenfell and Rothschild in London and J.P. Morgan & Co. in New York communicated on a daily basis with Norman and Harrison and their colleagues, and they took part in the planning and discussion of the next steps.

To sum up, if we compare my narrative with other analyses of 1931, there are significant differences. By writing this history forwards as thick description, new actors and their struggle with uncertainty have emerged, silences have been heard, information problems identified, conflicts and diverging perceived interests and power exposed, and new key events, actors and networks have been drawn into and made part of the historical narrative of the 1931 crisis.

By writing history forwards and using a humanistic and cultural approach focused on human beings as actors and based on concepts not normally used in economic and financial history, uncertainty, doubts, worldviews, prejudices and emotions have been shown to matter a lot in central banking and during financial crises.

The limits of an operating model as a blueprint when confronted with real events, real human actors and pervasive uncertainty have been highlighted as well. As I argued in the introduction, understanding the actors, the human beings of flesh and blood, as they struggled to halt the 1931 crisis called for a conceptual framework able to deal with the uncertainty of the situation central bankers faced from May to September 1931.

## DECISION-MAKING UNDER RADICAL UNCERTAINTY

'What is this a case of?' A frequently asked question, which is also fair to raise here. On the one hand, this book is a study of one of the most important and consequential financial crises in history, and as argued above it provides a new and detailed narrative of the 1931 crisis. Every financial crisis is unique, and as such *There will be the devil to pay* is not a case study but a narrative in its own right of how central bankers and other actors struggled to contain the European crisis from May to September 1931. It does not have to be a case of anything. It can stand on its own.

On the other hand, there are similarities, parallels and patterns across financial crises and other situations and events loaded with uncertainty.

Therefore, this book also addresses important issues that go beyond the specific events and context of 1931. Though I do not want to generalize from this history in any statistical sense of the word, my historical narrative of the financial crisis of 1931 can be seen as a case of decision-making under radical uncertainty.

The idea of uncertainty is not new in economics. Most well known and basic is Frank Knight's *Risk, Uncertainty and Profit* from 1921 in which he distinguishes between calculable risk and uncertainty. George Schackle, another economist who worked on decision-making and uncertainty, emphasizes that many decisions are unique and concern an unknown future. In fact, the future does not yet exist in the present. Decisions, Schackle writes, 'are not choices amongst actual but amongst imagined consequences'.[27]

As mainstream economics in the post-war period marginalized uncertainty and grew increasingly mathematical, it came to focus almost exclusively on risk where future outcomes could be calculated on the basis of probability, the normal distribution and historical data, and by implication on general models for decision-making and behaviour in a perfect world.[28]

But the world is not perfect. In recent years, scholars have therefore reintroduced radical uncertainty into economic thinking about decision-making.[29] This book provides an example of how that unfolds in the real world. Below, I very briefly consider some broader implications of my conceptual framework.

I have employed five concepts, embodied in the narrative, to understand the process that unfolded during the 1931 financial crisis in Europe. The litmus test here is whether this conceptual framework can be helpful in understanding how financial or other crises play(ed) out, and how decision-makers and epistemic communities, can deal with these situations as they unfold. Can the framework of uncertainty, sensemaking, imagined futures and narrative emplotment be used retrospectively to understand historical crisis responses in situations similar to the one in 1931? And can it be used prospectively together with Bagehot's model or other relevant models and calculative technologies, to improve blueprints for dealing with future crises? My answer is yes. Not as a directly applicable lesson or general solution mechanism, but as food for thought and to reflect upon and with.

Radical uncertainty such as in 1931 – or the Great Financial Crisis, the Euro crisis, Covid-19, the wars in Ukraine and the Middle East, or the sudden rise of inflation – always calls for sensemaking by various epistemic communities and related actors. Actors emplot narratives that assign cause and effect, imagine specific futures and provide actionable knowledge and direction, thereby enabling decisions and actions to shape that future. Though these narratives will always be contested, they are necessary. Actors enter any situation with a model or modus operandi as a blueprint for action but given the uncertainty, the specificity of time and place and competing logics, they often find that the model is inadequate for decision-making.

Bagehot's rule for a lender of last resort is such a model, and throughout this book, I have argued that the actors knew their Bagehot. His operating model appears im- or explicitly in their communications, ideas and practices. We see it in Simon's January note and in the many references to concrete decisions and actions when changing the bank rate, halting runs on banks and currencies, contagion and capital flight, or providing emergency credits.

As Bent Flyvbjerg argues and this book demonstrates, rule-based knowledge cannot stand alone. It must be combined with context-dependent knowledge and experience. Only then can, say, central bankers become experts in their field. Knowing Bagehot's recipe for averting what is known today as a twin crisis is a good beginning, but meaningful narratives are necessary as well. Flyvbjerg notes, 'Narratives not only give meaningful form to experiences we have already lived through but also provide us a forward glance, helping us to anticipate situations even before we encounter them, allowing us to envision alternative futures.'[30]

Narratives, then, are catalysts between sensemaking, decisions and actions as they shape our perception of the world. As Francis Rodd, Harry Siepmann, Montagu Norman, George Harrison and many others realized, the rules may have been useful abstractions. But they also shaped their fictional expectations about what would happen if the house of cards tumbled because a moratorium was introduced, Germany halted reparations, a run on banks or on sterling developed and so on. The central bankers in this book shaped narratives that called for and enabled action and replaced or complemented the Bagehot model as a blueprint. These stories were updated or changed over time as the situation developed and various constraints appeared or were removed.

Throughout the book, there are numerous references to the uncertainty of the situations in which the actors found themselves, sometimes even amounting to a so-called 'cosmology episode' related to a deep meaning-loss.[31] They expressed this uncertainty both directly and indirectly, and it forced them to try to make sense of the situation by imagining what might happen next and what it would take to change particular fictional expectations about the house of cards metaphor.

Planning was a central part of the sensemaking process that should enable central banks to deal with the radical uncertainty. That explains the many calls for a plan or a programme by various actors in this history; without a plan, they had no blueprint and did not know how to act. Any plan or programme imagined a future and implicitly or explicitly contained a narrative on how to shape that future. That was the case all through 1931 from Simon's January note to central bankers' many references to contagion and disaster to the shifting narratives about how to deal with the situation as it spread from Austria to Germany to Great Britain, and to the time after September 21 as one epoch of capitalism ended.

The uncertainty they faced forced central bankers in 1931 to draw partly on their theoretical knowledge from Bagehot and the economy more generally and partly on their historical and practical experience to form ideas about the future and how to realize or avoid it. Most of the actors in this book referred to the unshaped future again and again, directly or indirectly. Experience and expectations went hand in hand.

The German historian Reinhart Koselleck has developed the concepts 'space of experience' and 'horizon of expectation' to describe how actors are situated in the present, between the past and the future.[32] This was the case with central bankers in the hectic months from May to September 1931. It always is, and it means that decision-makers must pay attention to the past as well as the future.

As argued above, historians have passed judgement, sometimes harsh judgement, on central bankers' actions in 1931. Indeed, a certain flavour of hubris or over-confidence can sometimes be traced in the historiography. After all, the most recent decades of financial history including central banking do not suggest that we have become so much smarter with regard to central banks' ability to manage the economy whether it concerns financial crises, inflation or other unexpected events entailing radical uncertainty. The financial crisis of 2007 to 2009 is a case in point.

## THE GREAT FINANCIAL CRISIS

On Martin Luther King Jr. holiday, January 21, 2008, Ben Bernanke, the Chairman of the Federal Reserve Board, called an unplanned meeting of the Federal Open Market Committee (FOMC). This was no ordinary measure, and at the meeting Bernanke argued, 'We have to address this crisis. We have to try to get it under control. If we can't do that, then we are just going to lose control of the whole situation.'[33]

At a later FOMC conference call, on March 10, as it became increasingly clear that global financial markets were in trouble and that the Wall Street investment bank Bear Sterns, in particular, was fragile, Tim Geithner, the president of the New York Fed, admitted that there were limits to the 'capacity to understand in real time what is actually happening'.[34]

At the first FOMC meeting after Lehman Brothers' spectacular failure on September 15, Ben Bernanke confessed, 'Frankly, I am decidedly confused and very muddled about this.'[35] A few days later, on September 18, Bernanke and the secretary of the treasury Hank Paulson went to Capitol Hill and met with members of Congress to persuade them to pass the $700 billion Troubled Asset Relief Program bill. As the audience sat dumbfounded by the magnitude of the amount, Bernanke reportedly said, 'If we don't do this tomorrow, we won't have an economy on Monday.'[36]

These examples demonstrate the similarities between the 1931 financial crisis and the Great Financial Crisis. To be sure, they were two distinctly different events with more than seventy-five years in between in what may be termed the long twentieth century. They played out in very different contexts with different actors and with a wealth of details setting them apart. What united them was that the actors faced radical uncertainty.

The so-called 'first responders' and 'firefighters' of 2008 shared a number of features with their predecessors in 1931. Ben Bernanke, Tim Geithner and Hank Paulson recognize the role of uncertainty in their books on the 2008 financial crisis. 'History was moving at warp speed', they note, 'and consequential decisions had to be made every day in the fog of uncertainty'.[37]

As always, uncertainty led to sensemaking and a search for relevant historical analogies. As early as August 26, 2007, *Financial Times*' Gillian Tett realized that increasing uncertainty in financial markets meant that 'the indifference towards the past is being replaced by a violent thirst for historical knowledge'.[38]

She was certainly right, and Barry Eichengreen reflected this in his important 2012 article on the use of historical analogies in decision-making.[39] Actors and observers published books and articles, as well as films, fiction and non-fiction, on their experiences.[40] Indeed, Ben Bernanke, stressed how during the Lehman Brothers crisis, his 'mind went back to my own studies of the Great Depression of the 1930s. The most catastrophic financial failure of that period was the collapse of the Kreditanstalt . . . it toppled other banks and, perhaps, helped derail nascent economic recoveries in the United States and Europe.'[41]

Historians, too, soon began to revisit the history of the Great Depression and the financial crisis of 1931 to make sense of and learn lessons from history.[42] It was once again open season for sensemaking, historical analogies and uses of history.

*The Economist* very directly used history to make sense of the present and future in 2011 when it referred to the 1931 crisis, arguing that 'It is all dreadfully familiar'.[43]

The magazine invoked the 'lessons of the 1930s' to stress how the financial crisis and the European debt crisis could be understood with the Great Depression as a historical analogy.[44] The implication was that by studying and learning from history, policymakers could flesh out policy lessons that would help them avoid repeating the mistakes of the past.

While history is certainly useful for reflection and prospective sensemaking, it is also contested and there are few directly applicable lessons to be learned from it. After all, history provides context-dependent knowledge. *The Economist* article was not a lesson learned but an act of prospective sensemaking through narrative emplotment. The magazine invoked the past to try to avoid an imagined future disaster. That is what we do when our daily routines and practices are upset by dramatic events that do not fit within our usual frameworks of understanding. We rely even more than usual on analogies and stories of past experiences in order to make sense of the situation.

That is the final contribution of this book. The conceptual framework I have used is not only a matter of approach. The ultimate lesson from history, including *There will be the devil to pay*, is that uncertainty, sensemaking, narrative emplotment and imagined futures are not just a framework.

Uncertainty and unknown and unshaped futures are facts of life, in which actors of the world are, for lack of a better word, embedded, and which like the 'burden of history' we cannot escape. Sensemaking, narrative emplotment and imagined futures are how we go about living and navigating that world, not some tools we pull out when we are in trouble.

This also explains why learning from history is difficult, if not impossible. Looking back at events with hindsight erases the context as well as the uncertainty and urgency faced by contemporary human decision-makers and therefore cannot deliver generalizable lessons. But history provides a context and a mirror in which we can better understand historical actors and their situations, and reflect upon our present and future society and its challenges.

This way of thinking is useful when we are in trouble like in the financial crisis of 1931, the financial crisis of 2008 or the Covid crisis. And we will get in trouble again.

# Timeline

1873

Walter Bagehot publishes *Lombard Street: A Description of the Money Market.*

1919

June 28, Versailles Treaty is signed.

John Maynard Keynes's *The Economic Consequences of the Peace* is published.

1920

Montagu Norman becomes governor of the Bank of England.

1921

May 5, German reparations are fixed at 132 million reichsmarks by the Reparations Commission.

1922

August 1, Balfour Note announces that Great Britain is willing to surrender its share of reparations if inter-allied debts are written off.

1923

Hjalmar Schacht is appointed president of the Reichsbank.

1924

September 1, Dawes Plan for German reparations takes effect, and S. Parker Gilbert is appointed Agent General for Reparations.

1925

April 28, Winston Churchill announces that Great Britain will return to gold at the pre-war parity.

1926

April 29, Mellon–Berenger debt agreement is signed by the United States and France.

Émile Moreau is appointed governor of the Banque de France.

1927

Ralph G. Hawtrey publishes *The Gold Standard in Theory and Practice.*

1928

June 25, France returns de jure to the gold standard at 20 per cent of the pre-war parity.

October 16, Benjamin Strong dies, and George L. Harrison becomes governor of the Federal Reserve Bank of New York.

1929

October 24, Black Tuesday, Wall Street Crash begins.

1930

Émile Moreau resigns as governor of the Banque de Franc.

Clément Moret takes over after Moreau as governor of the Banque de France.

March 7, Hjalmar Schacht is forced to resign as president of the Reichsbank.

March 11, Hans Luther is appointed president of the Reichsbank.

May 17, Young Plan replaces the Dawes Plan, and the Bank for International Settlements is established.

May 17, Gates McGarrah declares the BIS open for business.

June 17, President Herbert Hoover signs the Smoot-Hawley Act, which raises US tariffs.

November, George Harrison and Alan Sproul visit Europe.

1931

January 22, Hans Simon writes note on how to deal with a financial crisis.

March 8–9, Kindersley plan is discussed at the BIS board meeting.

March 21, Germany and Austria announce plan for a customs union between the two countries.

March 27, Norman and Sprague arrive in New York to meet with Harrison.

April 20, Montagu Norman writes to Harrison that 'conditions are perplexing, abnormal and beyond understanding'.

May, Federal Reserve Bank of New York reduces discount rate to 1½ per cent, the lowest rate ever. The Bank of England reduces rate to 2½ per cent.

May 8, Credit Anstalt informs the government and the National Bank that it has lost 140 million schilling, about 85 per cent of its capital.

May 11, the reconstruction of the Credit Anstalt is made public. Francis Rodd and Hans Simon travel to Vienna.

May 15, League of Nation's Control Committee authorizes Austrian loan issue of 150 million schillings.
May 16, Francis Rodd leaves Vienna for Basle to participate in BIS board meeting.
May 17, Hans Simon informs Francis Rodd that the Austrian National Bank and the Austrian finance minister are preparing plans for a moratorium.
May 17–19, BIS board meeting in Basle agrees upon central bank credit of 100 million schillings, or $14 million, to the Austrian National Bank.
May 19, Credit Anstalt writes to J.P. Morgan & Co. asking them to organize creditors in the United States.
May 23, Credit Anstalt announces that it needs 10 million pound sterling.
May 23, Montagu Norman suggests the formation of a creditors' committee.
May 27, The Rothschild Committee (or London Committee) meets for the first time.
May 28, Austrian Parliament passes law authorizing the government to guarantee Credit Anstalt's foreign deposits.
May 29, the BIS releases 100-million-schilling credit to the Austrian National Bank.
May 30, the Austrian National Bank raises the bank rate from 5 to 6 per cent.
June 1, 'International Committee of Foreign Creditors of the Austrian Credit Anstalt' meets for the first time.
June 1, Adrianus van Hengel becomes controller to the Credit Anstalt and representative of the International Committee, Gijsbert Bruins adviser to the National Bank, and Charles Rist adviser to the Austrian government.
June 2, Hans Simon writes 'Lessons of the Austrian Crisis' note.
June 6, the Austrian National Bank raises the bank rate from 5 to 6 per cent.
June 6–7, German Chancellor Heinrich Brüning and Foreign Minister Julius Curtius meet with British Prime Minister Ramsay MacDonald and the Bank of England Governor Montagu Norman (among others) at Chequers.
June 6–8, BIS board meeting agrees to extend a second loan to the Austrian National Bank on the condition that the Austrian bond loan is placed first.

June 13, Reichsbank raises bank rate from 5 to 7 per cent.

June 14, Robert Kindersley and James Gannon arrive in Vienna to negotiate a guarantee and stillstand agreement on behalf of the International Committee.

June 15, the Austrian National Bank raises the bank rate from 6 to 7½ per cent.

June 16, The International Committee signs agreement with the Austrian government and the Credit Anstalt guaranteeing foreign deposits and a stillstand agreement with foreign creditors who agree to maintain their deposits etc. in Austria for two years.

June 16, The French government demands that Austria renounces the planned customs union with Germany in exchange for an unspecified French loan.

June 16, the Bank of England extends a 150-million-schilling loan to the Austrian government for one week. The loan is prolonged several times.

June 20, Francis Rodd writes a memo on events in Austria between June 9 and June 16.

June 20, US President Herbert Hoover announces his plan for a one-year debt moratorium on intergovernmental debts, reparations, and relief debts.

June 25, The BIS, the Banque de France, Federal Reserve Bank of New York, and the Bank of England organize a $100 million credit to the German Reichsbank.

July 9, Hans Luther, president of the German Reichsbank, flies to London to meet with Montagu Norman seeking a second credit to the Reichsbank.

July 10, Hans Luther is in Paris negotiating for a loan.

July 11, Hans Luther returns to Berlin without any loan commitment from France.

July 11–12, Board meeting at the Bank for International Settlements in Basle.

July 12, German Cabinet meetings with private banks to try to rescue Danatbank.

July 13, Danatbank suspends payments. The German government declares a bank holiday, guarantees Danatbank's liabilities, and begins to introduce various regulations, including exchange controls. Berlin stock exchange is closed.

July 13, The Macmillan report is published in the UK.

July 16, Reichsbank raises bank rate from 7 to 10 per cent. All foreign exchange transactions are made subject to control by the Reichsbank.
July 20-23, The London Conference (the Seven Power Conference) meets in London to discuss how to assist Germany.
July 22, the Austrian National Bank raises bank rate from 7½ to 10 per cent.
July 23, the Bank of England raises bank rate from 2½ to 3½ per cent.
July 25, Robert Kindersley meets with Clément Moret in Paris to negotiate a loan to the Bank of England.
July 29, Governor Norman collapses at Committee of Treasury meeting and Deputy Governor Ernest Harvey takes over.
July 30, the Bank of England raises bank rate from 3½ to 4½ per cent.
July 31, The May Report recommending budget cuts is published.
August 1, the Federal Reserve Bank of New York and the Banque de France extend a loan to the Bank of England of $125 million each.
August 18, The Wiggin Report resulting from the London Conference is published in Basle by the Bank for International Settlements.
August 19, Harry Siepmann writes the memo 'Going Off the Gold Standard'.
August 28, J.P. Morgan & Co. in the United States, and a group of French banks in France organize loans of about $200 million each to the British government.
September 3, Germany and Austria abandon plan for a customs union.
September 15, Increasing rumours that the National government in the UK will seek an early general election.
September 15–16, Royal Navy 'mutiny' at the Atlantic Fleet.
September 18, British Treasury consults with French and American governments about opportunities for further credits, but none are promised. PM Ramsay MacDonald confers with Treasury and Bank of England at 9 p.m. It is decided to suspend the Gold Standard Act on Saturday if capital flight continues.
September 19, the Bank of England informs the government that credits are exhausted and that it cannot meet the demand for gold.
September 21, Great Britain leaves the gold standard and raises bank rate to 6 per cent. London Stock Exchange is closed. Banks remain open.
September 23, Governor Norman returns to London. London Stock Exchange reopens.
November, Francis Rodd returns to the Bank of England.
November 21, Harry Siepmann goes on vacation.

1932

July 9, Lausanne Conference reaches agreement cancelling the Young Plan and ending Germany's reparations payments with a final settlement of three billion reichsmarks.

Ralph G. Hawtrey, publishes *The Art of Central Banking.*

# Actors in the 1931 Financial Crisis Archives

(This list of actors is meant as a help for readers to recall the identity of the various actors in the crisis of 1931. It does not provide full information about their positions before and after.)

Azzolini, Vincenzo (1881–1967). Director General, Bank of Italy, 1928–30, governor, 1931–44. BIS board member, 1930–44.

Bark, Peter (1869–1937). Russian minister of nance, 1914–1917. Managing Director of Anglo-International Bank, Great Britain. Board member, Credit Anstalt.

Beneduce, Alberto (1877–1944). Italian banker, and BIS board member, 1930–39. Representative of Italian creditors on The International Committee of Foreign Creditors of the Austrian Credit Anstalt.

Berthelot, Philippe (1866–1934). Secretary general, French Foreign Office.

Blessing, Karl (1900–71). German Reichsbank, 1920–31. Bank for International Settlements, 1931–34, posted by the Reichsbank.

Brand, Robert H. (1878–1963). Partner and Managing Director, Lazard Bros. & Co. Ltd. London. Member of the Macmillan Committee on Finance and Industry.

Brauneis, Viktor (1876–1938). General Manager of the Austrian National Bank, 1922–38.

Briand, Aristide (1862–1932). Foreign minister, France, 1925–32. Former prime minister.

Bruins, Gijsbert W.J. (1883–1948). Professor Nederlandsche Handels-Hoogeschool, 1913–25. International Commissioner of the German Reichsbank, 1925–30. Adviser to the Austrian National Bank, 1931.

Brüning, Heinrich (1885–1970). German Chancellor of the Reich, 1930–32.

Burgess, W. Randolph (1889–1978). Federal Reserve Bank of New York, 1920–38; deputy governor from 1930.

Castle Jr, William R. (1878–1963). US undersecretary of state, 1931–33.

Catterns, Basil G. (1886–1969). Chief Cashier, Bank of England.

Chanler Jr, Lewis. S. (1891–1963). American banker, International Acceptance Bank. International Committee of Foreign Creditors of the Austrian Credit Anstalt.

Claudel, Paul (1868–1955). France's Ambassador to the United States, 1928–33.

Clay, Henry (1883–1954). Professor of Economics and adviser to the Bank of England.

Crane, Jay E. (1892–1973). Deputy governor, New York Federal Reserve Bank, 1930–35.

Crump, Norman (1896–1964). Assistant Editor, *The Economist*, 1929–39.

Coolidge, Calvin (1872–1933). President of the United States, Republican, 1923–29.

Curtius, Julius (1877–1948). Foreign minister of Germany, October 1929 to October 1931.

Davies, H.E. (?). N.M. Rothschild & Co. Secretary of the International Committee of Foreign Creditors of the Austrian Credit Anstalt.

de Fleuriau, Aimé-Joseph (1870–1938). French Ambassador to London, 1924–33.

de Rothschild, Anthony (1887–1961). Managing Partner, N.M. Rothschild & Sons, London.

de Rothschild, Lionel (1882–1942). Managing Partner, N.M. Rothschild & Sons, London. Chairman, International Committee of Foreign Creditors of the Austrian Credit Anstalt.

Dreyfus, Armand (1875–1942). Vice-Chairman and Managing Director Schweizerischer Bankverein.

Dreyse, Friedrich (Fritz) W. (1874–1943). Vice president, German Reichsbank.

Edge, Walter, Evans (1873–1956). American Ambassador to France, 1929–33.

Einzig, Paul (1897–1973). British economic author and journalist.

Farnier, Charles (1894–1980). Assistant governor, Banque de France.

Finaly, Horace (1871–1945). General Director, Banque de Paris et des Pays-Bas, 1919–37.

Flandin, Pierre-Étienne (1889–1959). French minister of finance, 1931–32.

Fodor, Marcel W. (1890–1977). Journalist, foreign correspondent in Vienna to UK and US newspapers.

Fournier, Pierre-Eugène (1892–1972). Deputy governor, Banque de France.

Franck, Louis (1868–1937). Governor of the Belgian Central Bank, 1926–37. Board member of BIS, 1930–37.

Franckenstein, Georg von und zu (1878–1953). Baron, Austrian minister in London.

Franklin-Bouillon, Henry (1870–1937). French politician and Member of Parliament.

Fraser, Leon (1889–1945). Vice president, Bank for International Settlements.

Gannon, James H. (1876–1935). Vice president, Chase National Bank. International Committee of Foreign Creditors of the Austrian Credit Anstalt.

Gilbert Jr, Seymour Parker (1892–1938). Agent-General for Reparations Payments in Germany, 1924–30. Partner J.P. Morgan & Co., 1931–38.

Goschen, Henry (Harry) Neville (1865–1945). British Banker, Partner, Goschen & Cunliffe. Chairman, National Provincial Bank.

Grant, Daniel B. (1893–1948). Guaranty Trust Co. International Committee of Foreign Creditors of the Austrian Credit Anstalt.

Grenfell, Edward (Teddy) C. (1870–1941). Senior Partner, Morgan Grenfell & Co., London. Director Bank of England, 1905–40. MP, 1922–35.

Grünberger, Alfred (1875–1935). Austrian minister in Paris, 1925–32.

Gunston, Charles A. (?). Deputy Head, Overseas Department, Bank of England.

Hall-Patch, Edmund (1896–1975). British Foreign Office.

Harrison, George L. (1887–1958). Governor of the New York Federal Reserve Bank, 1928–40.

Harvey, Ernest M. (1867–1955). Deputy governor, Bank of England, 1929–36.

Henderson, Arthur (1863–1935). Foreign secretary in Ramsay MacDonald's minority government, 1929–31.

Hoover, Herbert (1874–1964). President of the United States, Republican, 1929–33.

Hülse, Ernst (1881–1949). German Reichsbank, 1906–30. Assistant General Manager, Head of Banking Department, Bank for International Settlements, 1930–35.

Jacobsson, Per (1894–1963). Financial adviser, Swedish Kreuger & Toll. Economic adviser, Bank for International Settlements, 1931–56.

Jay, Nelson Dean (1883–1972). Senior Partner, Morgan & Cie, Paris.

Juch, Otto (1876–1964). Austrian minister of finance.

Keynes, John Maynard (1883–1946). British economist.

Kienböck, Viktor (1873–1956). Member of Austrian Parliament, former minister of finance.

Kiep, Otto C. (1866–1944). German Consul General, New York.

Kindersley, Robert (1871–1954). Chairman, Lazard Brothers & Co. Director, Bank of England.

King, Willford I. (1880–1962). Professor of Economics, New York University.

Lacour-Gayet, Robert (1896–1989). Director of Economic Studies, Banque de France, 1930–36. France's financial representative in the United States, 1924–30.

Lamont, Thomas W. (1870–1948). Partner, J.P. Morgan & Co.

Laval, Pierre (1883–1945). Prime minister of France, 1931–32.

Layton, Walter (1884–1966). Editor, *The Economist*, 1922–38.

Leffingwell, Russell C. (1878–1960). Partner, J.P. Morgan & Co.

Leith-Ross, Frederick (1887–1968). Deputy Controller of Finance, British Treasury.

Lindenberg, Paul (1871–1941). Managing Director, S. Japhet & Co, London.

Loree, Robert F. (1889–1979). Vice president, Guarantee Trust Company of New York.

Loveday, Alexander (1888–1962). British Economist. Director of the Financial Section and Economic Intelligence Service, League of Nations.

Luther, Hans (1879–1962). President, Reichsbank, 1930–33. Reichskanzler, 1925–26. Board member, Bank for International Settlements.

MacDonald, J. Carlisle (1894–1974). American journalist, foreign correspondent in Paris, New York Times.

MacDonald, Ramsay (1866–1937). British prime minister, 1929–35.

McGarrah, Gates (1863–1940). President and Chairman, Bank for International Settlements. Chairman of the Board, Federal Reserve Bank of New York, 1927–31.

Melchior, Carl (1871–1933). Partner, M.M. Warburg & Co. Board member, Bank for International settlement. German representative on League of Nation's Finance Committee.

Mendelsohn, Franz (1865–1935). Senior Manager, Mendelssohn & Co.

Meyer, Eugene (1875–1959). Governor, 1930–33, Federal Reserve Board, Washington DC.

Mills, Ogden L. (1884–1937). Undersecretary of the treasury, 1927–32.

Mitchell, Charles E. (1877–1955). Chairman and president, National City Bank. Member of the board and executive committee, New York Federal Reserve Bank.

Moore, Ernest (?). Secretary to Gates McGarrah, Bank for International Settlements.

Moreau, Émile (1868–1950). Chairman, Banque de Paris et des Pays-Bas, 1931–40. Governor, Banque de France, 1926–30.

Moret, Clément (1886–1943). Governor, Banque de France, 1930–35. Board member, Bank for International Settlements.

Morgan, John Pierpont (1837–1913). Senior partner, J.P. Morgan & Co., 1890–1913.

Morgan Jr, John (Jack) Pierpont (1867–1943). Senior partner, J.P. Morgan & Co.

Neurath, Ludwig (1866–1941). Chairman of the Credit Anstalt.

Niemeyer, Otto (1883–1971). Director and adviser to the governor, Bank of England. Director, Bank for International Settlements. Board Member, Credit Anstalt.

Norman, Montagu (1871–1950). Governor, Bank of England. Board member, Bank for International Settlements.

Norris, George W. (1864–1942). Governor, Federal Reserve Bank of Philadelphia, 1920–36.

Peacock, Edward R. (1871–1962). Partner, Barings Brothers & Co. Director, Bank of England.

Phipps, Eric (1875–1945). British minister in Vienna.

Quesnay, Pierre (1895–1937). General Manager, Bank for International Settlements, 1930–37. Head, Department of Economic Analysis, Banque de France, 1926–29. Member of Young Plan Commission, 1929.

Reisch, Richard (1866–1938). President, Austrian National Bank, 1922–32.

Reusch, Paul (1868–1956). German industrialist. Board member, Bank for International Settlements, 1930–38.

Reynolds, Jackson E. (1873–1958). President, First National Bank of New York.

Riefler, Winfield (1897–1974). Economist, Federal Reserve Board.

Rist, Charles (1874–1955). Economic and financial adviser to governments and central banks. Deputy governor Bank of France, 1926–29.

Rodd, Francis (1895–1978). Director, Central Banking Department, Bank for International Settlements, 1930–31, posted by Bank of England. Partner, Morgan Grenfell & Co., 1933–40.

Rodenbach, Constantin (1892–?). Central Banking Department, Bank for International Settlements, 1930–46.

Rooth, Ivar (1888–1972). Governor, Swedish Central Bank, 1929–48. Board member, Bank for International Settlements, 1931–33, 1937–49.

Rowe-Dutton, Ernest (1891–1965). Financial adviser, British Embassy, Berlin.

Sargent, Orme G. (1884–1962). Head of the British Foreign Office's Central Department.

Schober, Johan (1874–1932). Austrian vice-chancellor and foreign minister, 1930–32. Chancellor, 1921–22, 1929–30.

Schäffer, Hans (1886–1967). State secretary, German Finance Ministry.

Schüller, Richard (1870–1972). Head of Trade and Economic Policy Section, Foreign Ministry, Austria.

Seay, George J. (1862–1952). Governor, Federal Reserve Bank of Richmond, VA, 1914–36.

Sprague, Oliver M.W. (1873–1953). Chief economist, Bank of England, 1930–33. Professor of Banking and Finance, Harvard Business School, 1913–41.

Sproul, Allan (1896–1978). Assistant deputy governor, Federal Reserve Bank of New York, 1930–41. President, Federal Reserve Bank of New York, 1941–56.

Stamp, Josiah (1880–1941). Director, Bank of England. Chairman, London, Midland and Scottish Railway.

Stephany, Samuel (1876–1951). General Manager, N.M. Rothschilds & Sons, London.

Stewart, Walter W. (1885–1958). American economist, associated with the BIS. Director of Research, Federal Reserve Board, Washington DC, 1922–28. Chief Economist, Bank of England, 1928–30.

Stimson, Henry L. (1867–1950). Secretary of state, United States, 1929–33.

Stolper, Gustav (1888–1947). German economist. Editor in Chief, Der Deutsche Volkswirt, 1926–33.

Strakosch, Henry (1871–1943). British banker and businessman. Board member, Credit Anstalt.

Streit, Clarence, K. (1896–1986). American journalist, foreign correspondent, New York Times.

Tardieu, André (1876–1945). French minister of agriculture in 1931. Prime minister, 1929–30 and 1932.

Thaa, Gustav (?). Vice president, Austrian National Bank.

Tyrrell, William (1866–1947). British Ambassador to France, 1928–34.

van Hengel, Adrianus Johannes (1886–1936). Representative of the International Committee of Foreign Creditors of the Austrian Credit Anstalt, 1931–32. Former Director of Amsterdamsche Bank. Director of Credit Anstalt, 1932–36.

Vissering, Gerard (1865–1937). Governor, Netherlands Central Bank, 1912–31. Board member, Bank for International Settlements, 1931.

Vocke, Wilhelm (1886–1973). Member, Board of Directors, German Reichsbank, 1919–39.

von Hoesch, Leopold (1881–1936). German ambassador to France.

von Neurath, Konstantin (1873–1956). German ambassador to Britain, 1930–32.

von Rothschild, Louis Nathaniel (1882–1955). Head of S.M. Rothschild banking house in Austria. Chairman of Credit Anstalt's board of directors.

Waley, Sigismund D. (1887–1962). Civil servant, overseas finance, British Treasury.

Warburg, Eric. (1900–90). German banker, partner in M.M. Warburg & Co. Son of Max Warburg.

Warburg, Max M. (1867–1946). Director, M.M. Warburg & Co., Hamburg. Board member, Credit Anstalt.

Warburg, Paul M. (1868–1932). American banker born in Germany. Chairman of the International Acceptance Bank.

Whigham, Charles F. (1873–1938). Partner, Morgan Grenfell & Co., London.

Whitmarsh, Theodore F. (1870–1936). Member of the board and executive committee, Federal Reserve Bank of New York. Chairman of Francis F. Leggett & Co.

Wiggin, Albert H. (1868–1951). Chairman, Chase National Bank.

Williams, John H. (1887–1980). Professor of Economics, Harvard University, 1921–57.

Winkler, Franz (1890–1945). Austrian interior minister, 1930–33.

Woodlock, Thomas F. (1866–1945). Editor of the *Wall Street Journal.*

Woolley, Clarence M. (1864–1956). Board member, Federal Reserve Bank of New York. Chairman, American Radiator Co.

Young, Owen D. (1874–1962). Deputy chairman, Federal Reserve Bank of New York. Chairman, General Electric.

Young, Roy A. (1882–1960). Governor, 1927–30, Federal Reserve Board, Washington DC.

# Acknowledgements

There. I have reached the limit of my abilities and cannot make this book any better. I hope you have enjoyed reading it. As mentioned in Chapter 11, Francis Rodd at one point apologized for the style of his June 20 memorandum on the final week of the Austrian crisis. It should have been written, he noted, in "the manner of the good twentieth century political spy or detective stories".

I feel the same way about this book. I believe it could have become a bestseller and made into a movie, if only I had the talent for writing detective stories. Alas, I do not, but I have done my best to write the story in as interesting a way as possible, while at the same time making it acceptable to the academic community of which I am part. I hope that you as a reader have at least occasionally sensed that ambition.

I first had the idea for this book in the fall of 1997 as a visiting scholar at the Center for Monetary and Financial History at Rutgers University, New Brunswick, NJ. Now, more than twenty-five years and countless cases of despair and frustration later, I am finally done. It feels good. And, believe me, it would not have been possible without the help, support, encouragement and assistance from the many institutions and persons who have nudged me along the way with actual and moral support and sometimes with more belief and trust in the project than I myself was able to muster.

Among the institutions that supported me are my employer until 2002, the Department of History at the University of Southern Denmark, and my academic base since 2002, the Department of Business Humanities and Law (formerly known as the Department of Management, Politics and Philosophy) at Copenhagen Business School. Both have supported me financially and enabled my travelling to archives in the UK, the US and Switzerland. In addition, I have received generous travel grants from the Danish central bank, Nationalbanken, and the Carlsberg Foundation (2008-01-249).

Among other things, this financial support enabled me to visit a number of archives, some of them more than once. Beginning in 1998, I was warmly welcomed to the newly opened historical archive at the Bank for International Settlements by Piet Clement and Edward Atkinson. Since then, I have visited several other archives and always been met with expertise, kindness and interest in my project.

At the archive of the Federal Reserve Bank of New York, Rosemary Lazenby, Joseph Komljenovich and Julie Sager were most helpful as was Sarah Millard at the Bank of England's historical archive, and Melanie Aspey and Natalie Broad at the Rothschild Archive. So were the archivists at the National Archives in Maryland, Columbia University's Rare Book & Manuscript Library, the Morgan Library & Museum in New York and the University of Oxford's Bodleian Library. Only historians and others who have actually used archives know how instrumental archivists are for identifying and retrieving the material you need. I thank you all.

Over the last quarter of a century, I have presented paper after paper at so many conferences and seminars that I have lost track. But I do want to thank the participants and commentators at the Business History Conference and European Business History Association conferences over the years as well as seminar participants at Newcastle Business School, the Department of Economic History at University of Geneva, the Department of Economics at Stern School of Business, the Business History Group at University of Rotterdam, the Danish Society for Economic and Social History, the Department of History at University of Southern Denmark, Centre for Business History and the Annual Writing Seminar at Department of Business Humanitics and Leadership, Copenhagen Business School, Norges Bank, the Business History Group at Harvard Business School, Uses of the Past in International Economic Relations (UPIER) at the University of Oxford, Historical Economics and Development Group (HEDG) at the University of Southern Denmark, and the Department of Finance at Copenhagen Business School (CBS). Last but not least, I thank my academic and social home at CBS, the Centre for Business History and all my great colleagues.

At these seminars as well as talks over coffee, beer, lunch or dinner or by email correspondence, I have received helpful comments and suggestions from a lot of really smart people including Kim Abildgren, Mitchel Abolafia, Olivier Accominotti, Sebastian Alvarez, Melanie Aspey, Hartmut Berghoff, Philip Boobbyer, Michael Bordo, Ludovic Cailluet,

Philip Cottrell, Jeffrey Fear, Olivier Feiertag, Gerry Feldman, Juan Flores, Neil Forbes, Eric Helleiner, Robin Holt, Martin Horn, Harold James, Joost Jonker, Hans Kernbauer, Chris Kobrak, Niels Kærgård, David Lando, Håkan Lindgren, Nathan Marcus, Paolo di Martino, Tom McGovern, Alan McKinlay, Stephen Mihm, Rory Miller, Frank Müller, Charlotte Natmeßnig, Jeppe Nevers, Lucy Newton, Kay Lundgren Nielsen, Torben Nielsen, Susie Pak, Catherine Schenk, Aurel Schubert, Paul Sharp, John Singleton, George Smith, Anna Spadavecchia, Dieter Stiefel, Roy Suddaby, Anders Ravn Sørensen, Alice Teichova, Gianni Toniolo, Gail Triner, Andrea Whittle and Lars Fredrik Øksendal. To those I have forgotten, please know that I have appreciated your help, too.

Most directly, I have benefitted greatly from the helpful support from a group of scholars and friends who have read various versions or parts of the manuscript as it developed and fell apart and reemerged over time. I know how time-consuming it is to read and comment on a manuscript when you really should be working on your own stuff. I am incredibly thankful to Per Boje, Michael Bordo, Youssef Cassis, Piet Clement, Barry Eichengreen, Walter Friedman, Richard S. Grossman, Christina Lubinski, Mary O'Sullivan, Andrew Popp, Alfred Reckendrees, Hugh Rockoff, Tobias Straumann, Dick Sylla and Dan Wadhwani. You have all, one way or the other, influenced the final product, though I, of course, am the only one to blame for not always following your advice; and for any errors, misunderstandings or questionable interpretations.

As usual, I am most indebted to my wife, Anne Magnussen, a historian too, who has read and commented on the manuscript more times over the years than I – and she – care to think about. It is safe to say that without Anne this book would never have been finished.

# Archives

Bank for International Settlements, Basle (BISA)
Bank of England Archive, London (BEA)
Federal Reserve Bank of New York Archive (FRBNY)
Harrison Papers, Columbia University, New York (CUL, HP)
J.P. Morgan Archive, Morgan Library, New York (JPM)
Lord Rennell of Rodd Archive, Bodleian Library, Oxford (LRRA)
Merle Cochran's International Bank Notes, RG39, Records of the Bureau of Accounts (Treasury), National Archives, at College Park, MD (NARA, RG39)
Rothschild Archive, London, RA

# Notes

When two or more paragraphs are based on the same material, the note is placed at the end of the final paragraph that draws on that specific piece of material.

## Chapter 1

1 Arnold J. Toynbee, *Survey of International Affairs 1931* (London: Oxford University Press, 1932), 1.

2 'The Austrian Credit Anstalt', *The Economist*, June 27, 1931.

3 'The Austrian Credit Anstalt', *The Economist*, June 27, 1931. See also Gianni Toniolo, with the assistance of Piet Clement, *Central Bank Cooperation at the Bank for International Settlements, 1930–1973* (Cambridge: Cambridge University Press, 2005), 88–89; Olivier Accominotti and Barry Eichengreen, 'The Mother of All Sudden Stops: Capital Flows and Reversals in Europe, 1919–32', *Economic History Review* 69, no. 2 (2016): 469–92.

4 Dieter Stiefel, *Finanzdiplomatie und Weltwirtschaftskrise. Die Krise der Credit-Anstalt für Handel und Gewerbe 1931* (Frankfurt am Main: Verlag Fritz Knapp, 1989), 19–20.

5 Aurel Schubert, *The Credit-Anstalt Crisis of 1931* (New York: Cambridge University Press, 1991), 7–9; 'Aktion der Regierung Für die Creditanstalt', *Neues Wiener Tagblatt*, May 12, 1931.

6 Stiefel, *Finanzdiplomatie und Weltwirtschaftskrise*, 13.

7 Memorandum, 'Austrian Government Borrowing Powers', May 11, 1931. BEA, OV28/3, Austria Country File, January 14–June 15, 1931.

8 Adam Tooze, *The Deluge: The Great War and the Remaking of Global Order* (London: Allen Lane, 2014), 494.

9 'World Bank's Aid Sought by Austria', *The New York Times*, May 13, 1931; 'The Financial Situation', *Commercial and Financial Chronicle*, May 23, 1931. On the customs union, see also Edward W. Bennett, *Germany and the Diplomacy of the Financial Crisis, 1931* (Cambridge, MA: Harvard University Press, 1962), 40–81.

10 'Aktion der Regierung Für Die Creditanstalt', *Neues Wiener Tagblatt*, May 12, 1931.
11 'Sanierung der Creditanstalt', *Neues Wiener Tagblatt*, May 12, 1931.
12 Stiefel, *Finanzdiplomatie und Weltwirtschaftskrise*, 28.
13 Telegram, May 11, 1931, from Austrian National Bank to Federal Reserve Bank of New York. FRBNY, C261.1, National Bank (Austrian Nat'l Bank) Credit, May 1931–December 1932, 1 of 2.
14 Telegram, May 13, 1931, from Harvey to the Austrian National Bank. BEA, OV 28/3: Austria Country File, January 1–June 15, 1931.
15 Telegram, May 10, 1931, from Juch to Siepmann. BEA, OV 28/3: Austria Country File, January 1–June 15, 1931. See also Meeting, May 11, 1931, of Bank of England's Committee of Treasury. BEA, G8/60, Minutes of the Committee of Treasury, March 1931 to June 1932.
16 Telegram, May 11, 1931, from Siepmann to Reisch. BEA, OV28/3, Austria Country Files, January 1–June 15, 1931.
17 Letter, May 13, 1931, from Siepmann to Reisch. BEA, OV 28/3, Austria Country File, January 1–June 15, 1931. See also Liaquat Ahamed, *Lords of Finance: The Bankers Who Broke the World* (New York: The Penguin Press, 2009), 404; Toniolo, with the assistance of Clement, *Central Bank Cooperation*, 91. For the view that the establishment of the BIS led to a new institutional framework for central bank co-operation, see Olivier Feiertag, 'Les Banques d'émission et La BRI Face à La Dislocation de l'étalon-or (1931–1933): L'entrée Dans l'âge de La Coopération Monétaire Internationale', *Histoire, Économie et Société* 18, no. 4 (1999): 719.
18 Telegram, May 11, 1931, from Fraser to Harrison. CUL, HP, Box 16, binder 36, Personal Cables, 1930–35.
19 Telegrams #4501 and 4502, May 11, 1931, from Fraser to Harrison. CUL, HP, Box 16, binder 36, Personal Cables, 1930–35.
20 Telegram, May 12, 1931, from Harrison to Fraser. CUL, HP, Box 16, binder 36, Personal Cables, 1930–35, and telegram, May 12, 1931, from Harrison to Austrian National Bank. FRBNY, C261.1, National Bank (Austrian Nat'l Bank) Credit, May 1931–December 1932, 1 of 2.
21 Press Clippings and Memo of May 12, 1931, by D. Starr on 'Oesterreichische Credit-Anstalt Für Handel und Gewerbe'. FRBNY, C261, Austria – Oesterreichische Creditanstalt, Wiener Bankverein, March 1929–.
22 Telegram #107, May 13, 1931, from Reichsbank to FRBNY. CUL, HP, Box 3, binder 7, Reichsbank (Germany), January 7–December 1931.
23 Frederick Leith-Ross, *Money Talks: Fifty Years of International Finance* (London: Hutchinson, 1968), 133; Ahamed, *Lords of Finance*, 404.
24 Letter, May 13, 1931, from Siepmann to E. Rowe-Dutton. BEA, ADM25-5, Papers of Harry Arthur Siepmann Correspondence, January 1–June 3, 1931.
25 For a recent discussion of contagion channels during the 1931 crisis, see Gary Richardson and Patrick Van Horn, 'In the Eye of a Storm: Manhattan's Money Center Banks during the International Financial Crisis of 1931', *Explorations in Economic History* 68 (2018): 72–74; Olivier Accominotti, 'London Merchant Banks, the Central European Panic, and the Sterling Crisis of 1931', *Journal of Economic History* 72, no. 1 (2012): 1–43.

26 For fictional expectations, see Jens Beckert and Richard Bronk, 'Uncertain Futures: Imaginaries, Narratives, and Calculative Technologies', MPIfG Discussion Paper 19/10, 2019.

27 Deborah A. Stone, 'Causal Stories and the Formation of Policy Agendas', *Political Science Quarterly* 104, no. 2 (1989): 290, 295–97.

28 See, for instance, Olivier Accominotti, 'International Banking and Transmission of the 1931 Financial Crisis', *Economic History Review* 72, no. 1 (2019): 260–85; Mark Billings and Forrest Capie, 'Financial Crisis, Contagion, and the British Banking System between the World Wars', *Business History* 53, no. 2 (2011): 193–215.

29 Nathan Marcus has argued that overall 'the various bankers involved in managing the crisis from Vienna, Basle and London did not mention the crisis spreading beyond Austria'. However, there are numerous references to contagion in the material. See Nathan Marcus, *Austrian Reconstruction and the Collapse of Global Finance: 1921–1931* (Cambridge, MA: Harvard University Press, 2018), 318. Marcus also argues that fear of exchange rate risk was rational and therefore would not signify fear of contagion.

30 Walter Bagehot, *Lombard Street: A Description of the Money Market* (Westport, CT: Hyperion Press, 1962 [1873]), 27–28, 97. See also Rockoff who in a perceptive analysis points out that 'Bagehot provides a clear guide only to the most obvious situations. Ambiguous cases will remain so even after they are examined in the light of Lombard Street', see Hugh Rockoff, 'Walter Bagehot and the Theory of Central Banking', in *Financial Crises and the World Banking System*, ed. Forrest Capie and Geoffrey E. Wood (London: Macmillan, 1986), 160–80. Grossman and Rockoff argue that 'perhaps there is no general rule to follow and central banking will remain, as R.G. Hawtrey suggested, an art rather than a science', Richard S. Grossman and Hugh Rockoff, 'Fighting the Last War: Economists on the Lender of Last Resort', in *Central Banks at a Crossroads: What Can We Learn from History?*, ed. Michael Bordo et al. (New York: Cambridge University Press, 2016), 246–50, and 273 for the quote. See Richard S. Grossman, *Unsettled Account: The Evolution of Banking in the Industrialized World since 1800* (Princeton: Princeton University Press, 2010), 98–101, for a discussion of the Bagehot rule. The Bagehot rule also corresponds well with Milton Friedman and Anna Schwartz' explanation of the causes of the Great Contraction in the United States. They blamed the Federal Reserve for not acting as a lender of last resort, and this narrative has been influential as an analogy and a frame in the response to the Great Financial Crisis of 2007–9, see Milton Friedman and Anna J. Schwartz, *A Monetary History of the United States, 1867–1960* (Princeton: Princeton University Press, 1963); Allan H. Meltzer, *A History of the Federal Reserve. Volume 1: 1912–1951* (Chicago: The University of Chicago Press, 2003), 404–13; John Singleton, *Central Banking in the Twentieth Century* (Cambridge: Cambridge University Press, 2011), 80–83; Barry Eichengreen, 'Economic History and Economic Policy', *The Journal of Economic History* 72, no. 2 (2012): 289–307; Barry Eichengreen, *Hall of Mirrors: The Great Depression, The Great Recession and the Uses – and Misuses – of History* (New York: Oxford University Press, 2015). For a powerful critique of Friedman and Schwartz, see Mary A. O'Sullivan, 'History as Heresy: Unlearning the Lessons of Economic Orthodoxy', *The Economic History Review* 75, no. 2 (2022): 297–335.

31 Grossman and Rockoff, 'Fighting the Last War'; Michael D. Bordo, 'An Historical Perspective on the Quest for Financial Stability and the Monetary Policy Regime', *Journal of Economic History* 78, no. 2 (2018): 324, 332.

32 Stiefel, *Finanzdiplomatie und Weltwirtschaftskrise*, 31.

33 On the International lender of last resort, see Schubert, *The Credit-Anstalt Crisis*, 157–67; R.G. Hawtrey, *The Art of Central Banking* (London: Longmans, Green and Co., 1932), 273–78; Charles P. Kindleberger and Robert Z. Aliber, *Manias, Panics and Crashes: A History of Financial Crises*, 6th ed. (New York: Palgrave Macmillan, 2011), 229–56. See also the special issue of *Jahrbuch für Wirtschaftsgeschichte*, vo l. 63, no. 2, for example Emmanuel Carré and Laurent Le Maux, 'Financial Instab ility and International-Lender-of-Last-Resort Theory from the Gold Standard to the Dollar System', *Jahrbuch für Wirtschaftsgeschichte* 63, no. 2 (2022): 311–44; Hans Michael Trautwein, 'International Lending of Last Resort in Historical and Theoretical Perspectives: Introduction', *Jahrbuch Für Wirtschaftsgeschichte*63, no. 2 (2022): 303–10.

34 See, for instance, Stephen V.O. Clarke, *Central Bank Cooperation: 1924–31* (New York: Federal Reserve Bank of New York, 1967), 185. More generally for historical analogical reasoning, Eichengreen argues that analogical reasoning is used when there is limited time for making a decision, when decision-makers have limited 'information processing capacity', and when they disagree about what 'theory' on which to base their decision-making. Eichengreen also stresses that analogical reasoning can lead to problematic decisions, see Eichengreen, 'Economic History and Economic Policy'; Eichengreen, *Hall of Mirrors*. Eichengreen also points to 'incompatible conceptual frameworks' as reasons for disagreements, see Barry Eichengreen, 'Central Bank Co-operation and Exchange Rate Commitments: The Classical and Interwar Gold Standards Compared', *Financial History Review* 2, no. 2 (1995): 99–118.

35 For a discussion of the BIS as lender of last resort in 1931, see Juan Flores Zendejas and Gianandrea Nodari, 'Central Bank Cooperation 1930–1932, A Reappraisal' (Geneva, 2023). On the role of the BIS in 1931, see also Eleanor Lansing Dulles, *The Bank for International Settlements at Work* (New York: The Macmillan Company, 1932), 50–53; Barry Eichengreen, *Golden Fetters: The Gold Standard and the Great Depression, 1919–1939* (Oxford: Oxford University Press, 1992), 261–64, 282; Beth A. Simmons, 'Why Innovate? Founding the Bank for International Settlements', *World Politics* 45 (April 1993): 361–405; Toniolo, with the assistance of Clement, *Central Bank Cooperation*, chapter 2; Kazuhiko Yago, *The Financial History of the Bank for International Settlements* (London: Routledge, 2013), chapters 1 and 2. For a recent discussion of the Dawes and Young Plans and the Versailles peace agreement, see the excellent Tobias Straumann, *1931. Debt, Crisis, and the Rise of Hitler* (Oxford: Oxford University Press, 2019), 18–38; Albrecht Ritschl, 'Reparations, Deficits and Debt Default: The Great Depression in Germany', in *The Great Depression of the 1930s: Lessons for Today*, ed. Nicholas Crafts and Peter Fearon (Oxford: Oxford University Press, 2013), 112–18. On the establishment of the BIS, see also Jamie Martin, *The Meddlers: Sovereignty, Empire, and the Birth of Global Economic Governance* (Cambridge, MA: Harvard University Press, 2022), chapter 3. See also Piet Clement, 'Institutionalizing Central Bank Cooperation: The Norman-Schacht Vision and Early Experience of the Bank for International

Settlements, 1929–1933', in *The Spread of the Modern Central Bank and Global Cooperation, 1919–1939*, ed. Barry Eichengreen and Andreas Kakridis (Cambridge: Cambridge University Press, 2023), 80–102.

36 Clarence K. Streit, 'The World Bank Feels Europe's Pulse', *The New York Times Magazine*, August 30, 1931.

37 'The B.I.S. at Work', *The Economist*, February 28, 1931, 434. The quote is *The Economist*'s part paraphrasing and part quoting McGarrah. See also 'The Bank for International Settlements', *The Economist*, May 9, 1931.

38 Richard N. Cooper, 'Almost a Century of Central Bank Cooperation', in *Past and Future of Central Bank Cooperation*, ed. Claudio Borio, Gianni Toniolo, and Piet Clement (Cambridge: Cambridge University Press, 2008), 79–80.

39 Streit, 'The World Bank Feels Europe's Pulse'.

40 Clarke, *Central Bank Cooperation*, 18, 185. Meltzer argues that Fed officials knew Bagehot's work but ignored his analysis of the lender of last resort and did not follow his advice, Meltzer, *A History of the Federal Reserve*, 281–82, 381, 407, 729. For a prime example of how experiences may shape the worldview of a generation, see Ulrike Malmendier and Stefan Nagel, 'Depression Babies: Do Macroeconomic Experiences Affect Risk Taking?', *Quarterly Journal of Economics* 126, no. 1 (2011): 373–416.

41 Peter M. Haas, 'Introduction: Epistemic Communities and International Policy Coordination', *International Organization* 46, no. 1 (1992): 3; Peter Haas, 'Epistemic Communities', in *The Oxford Handbook of International Environmental Law*, ed. Daniel Bodansky, Jutta Brunnée and Ellen Hey (Oxford: Oxford University Press, 2008), 792–805. For a more recent discussion of epistemic communities, to which I subscribe, see Mai'A K. Davis Cross, 'Rethinking Epistemic Communities Twenty Years Later', *Review of International Studies* 39, no. 1 (2013): 137–60. For a discussion of central bankers as an epistemic community, see Ethan Barnaby Kapstein, 'Between Power and Purpose: Central Bankers and the Politics of Regulatory Convergence', *International Organization* 46, no. 1 (1992): 265–87. See also Eric Helleiner, *States and the Reemergence of Global Finance: From Bretton Woods to the 1990s* (Ithaca: Cornell University Press, 1994), 198–201. For a different interpretation based on network theory and trust between the actors in the 1931 financial crisis, see Peter Aykens, '(Mis)Trusting Authorities: A Social Theory of Currency Crises', *Review of International Political Economy* 12, no. 2 (2005): 310–33. At a general level, central bankers' community was an imagined community held together by the allegiance to the gold standard and similar worldviews and practices, see Benedict Anderson, *Imagined Communities: Reflections of the Origin and Spread of Nationalism*, rev. ed. (New York: Verso, 1991).

42 Haas, 'Epistemic Communities', 795; Cross, 'Rethinking Epistemic Communities Twenty Years Later', 147ff. This line of argument aligns with the one put forward by Jamie Martin in relation to the BIS. It was possible, he argues, that central bankers 'shared more in common with their counterparts in other countries than with an elected government in their own'. See Martin, *The Meddlers*, 125–26.

43 Grant McCracken, 'Culture and Consumption: A Theoretical Account of the Structure and Movement of the Cultural Meaning of Consumer Goods', *Journal of Consumer Research* 13 (1986): 73. For a similar view in finance, see Karen Ho,

*Liquidated: An Ethnography of Wall Streeet* (Durham: Duke University Press, 2009); Karen Ho, 'Disciplining Investment Bankers, Disciplining the Economy: Wall Street's Institutional Culture of Crisis and the Downsizing of Corporate America', *American Anthropologist* 111, no. 2 (2009): 177–89; Barry Eichengreen and Andreas Kakridis, 'Interwar Central Banks', in Eichengreen and Kakridis, *The Spread of the Modern Central Bank and Global Cooperation, 1919–1939*, 23

44 Philip L. Cottrell, 'Norman, Strakosch and the Development of Central Banking: From Conception to Practice, 1919–1924', in *Rebuilding the Financial System in Central and Eastern Europe, 1918–1994*, ed. Philip L. Cottrell (Aldershot: Scolar Press, 1997), 55–56.

45 Quoted from Kenneth Mouré, *The Gold Standard Illusion: France, the Bank of France, and the International Gold Standard, 1914–1939* (Oxford: Oxford University Press, 2002), 151, see also p. 150 n. 29. Singleton, who also quotes Siepmann, mentions the similarities to an epistemic community 'but this was not fully realized in the 1920s and 1930s'. See Singleton, *Central Banking in the Twentieth Century*, 94. However, as I argue in this book, an epistemic community was certainly emerging. See also Eichengreen and Kakridis, 'Interwar Central Banks', 6, 10; Hans Kernbauer, 'Central Bank Policy under Foreign Control: The Austrian National Bank in the 1920s', in Eichengreen and Kakridis, *The Spread of the Modern Central Bank and Global Cooperation, 1919–1939*, 132–33.

46 For a brief and precise description of the gold standard, see Max Harris, *Monetary War and Peace: London, Washington, Paris, and the Tripartite Agreement of 1936* (Cambridge: Cambridge University Press, 2021), 19–27.

47 Harris, *Monetary War and Peace*, 32–40. For different views on the workings of the gold standard, see Eichengreen, *Golden Fetters*; Eichengreen, 'Central Bank Co-operation'; Marc Flandreau, 'Central Bank Cooperation in Historical Perspective: A Sceptical View', *The Economic History Review* 50, no. 4 (1997): 735–63.

48 Martin, *The Meddlers*.

49 John Maynard Keynes, 'The Economic Consequences of Mr. Churchill', in *Essays in Persuasion*, ed. John Maynard Keynes (London: W.W. Norton, 1925), 244–70. Though many historians agree that sterling was overvalued in 1925, Harold James argues that this was not the case. See Harold James, *The End of Globalization: Lessons from the Great Depression* (Cambridge, MA: Harvard University Press, 2001), 68–69.

50 Keynes, 'The Economic Consequences of Mr. Churchill', 259.

51 Mouré, *The Gold Standard Illusion*, 2, 10–13; Nikolaus Wolf, 'Europe's Great Depression: Coordination Failure after the Great Depression', in Crafts and Fearon, *The Great Depression of the 1930s*, 78–79. For 'fixed ideas on money', See Tobias Straumann, *Fixed Ideas on Money: Small States and Exchange Rate Regimes in Twentieth-Century Europe* (New York: Cambridge University Press, 2010). While Schuker does not necessarily disagree about this mechanism, he argues that Temin and Eichengreen focus too much on these technicalities and the gold-exchange standard, and too little on politics and German obstruction as the cause of the gold standard's breakdown. See Stephen A. Schuker, 'The Gold-Exchange Standard: A Reinterpretation', in *International Financial History in the 20th Century: System and Anarchy*, ed. Marc Flandreau, Carl-Ludwig Holtfrerich and

Harold James (Cambridge: Cambridge University Press, 2003), 77–93. For Temin's and Eichengreen's positions, see primarily, Peter Temin, *Lessons from the Great Depression* (Cambridge, MA: MIT Press, 1989); Eichengreen, *Golden Fetters.*

52 Mouré, *The Gold Standard Illusion*, 15.

53 Barry Eichengreen and Peter Temin, 'The Gold Standard and the Great Depression', *Contemporary European History* 9, no. 2 (2000): 199; Barry Eichengreen and Peter Temin, 'Fetters of Gold and Paper', *Oxford Review of Economic Policy* 26, no. 3 (2010): 370–84.

54 Robert Skidelsky, *John Maynard Keynes: The Economist as Saviour, 1920–1937* (London: Macmillan, 1992), 399. When Meltzer says, that we can only speculate why deficit countries deflated rather than leave gold, it is a question ridden with hindsight, that is, writing history backwards, see Meltzer, *A History of the Federal Reserve*, 403.

55 Donald E. Moggridge, *British Monetary Policy, 1924–1931: The Norman Conquest of $4.86* (Cambridge: Cambridge University Press, 1972), 3. See also Henry Clay, *Lord Norman* (London: Macmillan & Co, 1957), 3–10.

56 Again, for these ideas, see McCracken, 'Culture and Consumption'.

57 Patricia Clavin, *The Great Depression in Europe, 1929–1939* (London: Macmillan, 2000), 66.

58 Diane B. Kunz, *The Battle for Britain's Gold Standard in 1931* (London: Croom Helm, 1987), 99–100.

59 Marc Flandreau, 'Money and Doctors', in *Money Doctors: The Experience of International Financial Advising 1850–2000*, ed. Marc Flandreau (Taylor & Francis, 2003), 1–9; Stephen A. Schuker, 'Money Doctors between the Wars: The Competition between Central Banks, Private Financial Advisers, and Multilateral Agencies, 1919–39', in *Money Doctors: The Experience of International Financial Advising 1850–2000*, ed. Marc Flandreau (Routledge, 2003), 49–77. The quote is from Schuker, p. 52. See also Eichengreen and Kakridis, 'Interwar Central Banks', 10.

60 'International Bank Notes (Letter No. 14)', by Merle Cochran, June 1, 1931. NARA, RG39, Box 104, Entry 145, Folder: 'G783.5 Special Report Confidential Letters (1–24)'.

61 Flandreau, 'Money and Doctors', 5. See also Schuker, 'Money Doctors between the Wars', 69–70. For the role of League of Nations, central banks and the BIS in relation to money doctoring, see Martin, *The Meddlers.*

62 R.G. Hawtrey, *The Gold Standard in Theory and Practice* (London: Longmans, Green and Co., 1927), 53–54.

63 See, for instance, James Ashley Morrison, 'Shocking Intellectual Austerity: The Role of Ideas in the Demise of the Gold Standard in Britain', *International Organization* 70, no. 1 (December 14, 2016): 180–82. See also Haas, 'Epistemic Communities', 795, who argues that causal ideas may be path dependent 'once they are institutionalized'.

64 Schubert, *The Credit-Anstalt Crisis*, 151.

65 For a discussion of crises from a symbolic perspective, see Paul t' Hart, 'Symbols, Ritual and Power: The Lost Dimensions of Crisis Management', *Journal of Contingencies and Crisis Management* 1, no. 1 (1993): 38–40. The quote is from p. 46.

66 For an excellent and recent discussion, see Straumann, *1931*. For an institutional and structural approach to the Great Depression, see Wolf, 'Europe's Great Depression'.

67 See, for instance, Straumann, *1931*; Clavin, *The Great Depression in Europe*, 110.

68 The quote is from Clavin, *The Great Depression in Europe*, 126; Eichengreen, *Golden Fetters*, 258–60. For the interwar period and the Great Depression, see also Charles H. Feinstein, Peter Temin and Gianni Toniolo, *The European Economy between the Wars* (Oxford: Oxford University Press, 1997); Nicholas Crafts and Peter Fearon, eds., *The Great Depression of the 1930s: Lessons for Today* (Oxford: Oxford University Press, 2013).

69 See, for instance, Clarke, *Central Bank Cooperation*, 27, 34. See also Eichengreen, *Golden Fetters*, 263 et passim.

70 See, for instance, Stiefel, *Finanzdiplomatie und Weltwirtschaftskrise*, 142; Tooze, *The Deluge*, 365–66; Robert Boyce, *The Great Interwar Crisis and the Collapse of Globalization* (Basingstoke: Palgrave Macmillan, 2009), 140–41. For a perceptive analysis of the various national interests, see also Piet Clement, 'Between Banks and Governments: The Records of BIS', in *European Banking Overseas, 19th–20th Century*, ed. Ton de Graaf, Joost Jonker and Jaap-Jan Mobron (Amsterdam: ABN AMRO Bank N.V., 2002), 156–62.

71 Among the most damning books in terms of blaming central banks for the Great Depression is Ahamed, *Lords of Finance*. For a devastating review of *Lords of Finance*, see Stephen A. Schuker, 'Central Bankers in the Dock. H-Diplo Review Essay on Liaquat Ahamed. Lords of Finance: The Bankers Who Broke the World', *H-Diplo*, 2011. See also Friedman and Schwartz, *A Monetary History of the United States*. And then there are contributions from the Austrian school who want to do away with central banks altogether. See, for instance, Murray N. Rothbard, *Economic Depressions: Their Cause & Cure* (Auburn, AL: Mises Institute, 1969). For an overview, see Singleton, *Central Banking in the Twentieth Century*, 91–109; Claudio Borio, Gianni Toniolo and Piet Clement, *Past and Future of Central Bank Cooperation* (Cambridge: Cambridge University Press, 2008); Harold James, 'The Creation of a World Central Bank? The Early Years of the Bank for International Settlements', in *The Interwar Depression in an International Context*, ed. Harold James (München: R. Oldenbourg Verlag, 2002), 165; Eichengreen, *Golden Fetters*, 259. Eichengreen, 'Central Bank Co-operation', 100; Charles P. Kindleberger, *The World in Depression, 1929–1939*, 2nd ed. (London: Penguin, 1986), 144–47; Piet Clement, 'Introduction: Past and Future of Central Bank Cooperation', in Borio et al., *Past and Future of Central Bank Cooperation*, 1–15; Beth A. Simmons, 'The Future of Central Bank Cooperation', in Borio et al., *Past and Future of Central Bank Cooperation*, 174–210; Toniolo, with the assistance of Clement, *Central Bank Cooperation at the Bank*; Beth A. Simmons, *Who Adjusts? Domestic Sources of Foreign Economic Policy during the Interwar Years* (Princeton: Princeton University Press, 1994); Beth A. Simmons, 'Rulers of the Game: Central Bank Independence during the Interwar Years', *International Organization* 50, no. 3 (1996): 407–43. Clarke, *Central Bank Cooperation*; Mouré, *The Gold Standard Illusion*, 145–79; Kenneth Mouré, 'The Limits to Central Bank Co-operation, 1916–1936', *Contemporary European History* 1, no. 3 (1992): 259–79. Meltzer takes a different perspective and argues against Eichengreen that the New York Fed did

cooperate during the European crisis of 1931, Meltzer, *A History of the Federal Reserve*, 336, 344. For a discussion of different levels of central bank cooperation, see Cooper, 'Almost a Century of Central Bank Cooperation', 79–80.

72 The concept of uncertainty is important. The current use of the concept can be traced back to Frank Knight, who distinguished between uncertainty and calculable risk, see Frank H. Knight, *Risk, Uncertainty and Profit* (New York: Houghton Mifflin, 1921). In the post-war period, the concept of uncertainty was increasingly marginalized, as academic finance focused on the idea of calculable risk based on probabilities, see Kevin R. Brine and Mary Poovey, *Finance in America: An Unfinished Story* (Chicago: The University of Chicago Press, 2017). In recent years, the concept of uncertainty has gained attention again, and the idea of radical uncertainty has been introduced, see Jens Beckert and Richard Bronk, eds., *Uncertain Futures: Imaginaries, Narratives, and Calculation in the Economy* (Oxford: Oxford University Press, 2018); John Kay and Mervyn King, *Radical Uncertainty: Decision-Making beyond the Numbers* (New York: W.W. Norton, 2020); Jonathan Levy, 'Radical Uncertainty', *Critical Quarterly* 62, no. 1 (2020): 15–28; Mervyn King, 'Monetary Policy in a World of Radical Uncertainty', *Economic Affairs* 42, no. 1 (February 28, 2022): 2–12. For an excellent study of how the emerging forecasting profession sought to deal with uncertain futures in the interwar period, see Walter A. Friedman, *Fortune Tellers: The Story of America's First Economic Forecasters* (Princeton: Princeton University Press, 2014).

73 Barry Eichengreen and Olivier Jeanne, 'Currency Crisis and Unemployment: Sterling in 1931', in *Currency Crises*, ed. Paul Krugman (Chicago: University of Chicago Press, 2000), 15–20.

74 Until now, to my knowledge, Youssef Cassis is one of very few who have noticed the problem of ex post evaluations and called for analysis of 'the perception of the contemporaries', see Youssef Cassis, *Crises & Opportunities: The Shaping of Modern Finance* (Oxford: Oxford University Press, 2011), 92–93. In consequence, he also questions the 'too little, too late' verdict that most historians of the 1931 crisis have subscribed to. See also Feiertag, 'Les Banques d'émission et la BRI Face à la Dislocation de l'étalon-or (1931–1933)', 728–32. For support of the 'too little too late' argument, see, for instance, Kindleberger, *The World in Depression*, 147; James, *The End of Globalization*, 54–55.

75 I refer here to what Reinhart Koselleck calls 'space of experience' and 'horizon of expectation'; see Reinhart Koselleck, *Futures Past: On the Semantics of Historical Time* (New York: Columbia University Press, 2004), chapter 14.

76 Giovanni Levi, 'On Microhistory', in *New Perspectives on Historical Writing*, ed. Peter Burke (Cambridge, MA: Polity Press, 1991), 98. For thick description, see Clifford Geertz, 'Thick Description: Toward an Interpretive Theory of Culture', in *The Interpretation of Cultures*, ed. Clifford Geertz (London: Fontana Press, 1973), 3–30.

77 To be sure, other historians have written rather detailed histories of parts of the crisis, focusing on a single country or 'event'. But to my knowledge, there is no detailed micro-level history (not to be confused with microhistory) of central bankers' response to the 'full' crisis from May to September 1931.

78 I am indebted to my colleague at CBS, Dr Anders Ravn Sørensen for his insights and for several stimulating discussions about this topic.

79 Clifford Geertz, *The Interpretation of Cultures: Selected Essays* (New York: Fontana Press, 1973), 9.
80 Hawtrey, *The Art of Central Banking.*
81 For the central idea of an operating model and the role of narrative construction in sensemaking, see Mitchel Y. Abolafia, 'Narrative Construction as Sensemaking: How a Central Bank Thinks', *Organization Studies* 31, no. 3 (2010): the quote is from p. 353; Mitchel Y. Abolafia, *Stewards of the Market: How the Federal Reserve Made Sense of the Financial Crisis* (Cambridge, MA: Harvard University Press, 2020), 77 et passim.
82 Zeev Rosenhek, 'Diagnosing and Explaining the Global Financial Crisis: Central Banks, Epistemic Authority, and Sense Making', *International Journal of Politics, Culture, and Society* 26, no. 3 (2013): 256.
83 For an interesting discussion of the narrative of crisis, and what it does (i.e. performativity), see Rüdiger Graf, 'Either-or: The Narrative of "Crisis" in Weimar Germany and in Historiography', *Central European History* 43, no. 4 (2010): 592–615. See also Wesley W. Widmaier, 'Constructing Monetary Crises: New Keynesian Understandings and Monetary Cooperation in the 1990s', *Review of International Studies* 29, no. 1 (2003): 61–77.
84 The important point about the future is that it is not only unknown, it does not exist, and narratives contribute to shaping the future through performativity. Beckert and Bronk, 'Uncertain Futures'; Jens Beckert and Richard Bronk, 'An Introduction to Uncertain Futures', in Beckert and Bronk, *Uncertain Futures*, 1–333. See also Andrew Popp, 'Making Choices in Time', *Enterprise and Society* 14, no. 3 (2013): 467–74. For narratives, see also Mads Mordhorst and Stefan Schwarzkopf, 'Theorising Narrative in Business History', *Business History* 59, no. 8 (2017): 1155–75; Per H. Hansen, 'Business History: A Cultural and Narrative Approach', *Business History Review* 86, no. 4 (2012): 693–717.
85 Andrew D. Brown, Ian Colville and Annie Pye, 'Making Sense of Sensemaking in Organization Studies', *Organization Studies* 36, no. 2 (2015): 273. More generally, for Karl Weick's seminal work on sensemaking, see Karl Weick, *Sensemaking in Organizations* (Thousand Oaks, CA: Sage, 1995); Karl Weick, 'Sensemaking in Organizations: Small Structures with Large Consequences', in *Making Sense of the Organization*, ed. Karl Weick (Malden, MA: Blackwell Publishing, 2001), 3–31; Karl Weick, 'The Collapse of Sensemaking in Organizations: The Mann Gulch Disaster', *Administrative Science Quarterly* 38, no. 4 (1993): 628–52. See also Tor Hernes and Sally Maitlis, 'Process, Sensemaking, and Organizing: An Introduction', in *Process, Sensemaking, and Organizing*, ed. Tor Hernes and Sally Maitlis (Oxford: Oxford University Press, 2010), 27–37.
86 Sally Maitlis, 'The Social Processes of Organizational Sensemaking', *Academy of Management Journal* 48, no. 1 (2005): 21.
87 Sally Maitlis and Marlys Christianson, 'Sensemaking in Organizations: Taking Stock and Moving Forward', *The Academy of Management Annals* 8, no. 1 (2014): 58, 109.
88 Eichengreen, 'Economic History and Economic Policy', 293 and 299.
89 See Per H. Hansen, 'Making Sense of Financial Crisis and Scandal: A Danish Bank Failure in the First Era of Finance Capitalism', *Enterprise and Society* 13, no. 3 (2012); Hansen, 'Business History'; Stone, 'Causal Stories'. Graf argues that 'crises

are narrative structures that transform a complex world into a dramatic plot . . . In other words, historical analyses should not end by pointing at the crisis, but rather start from there'. Graf, 'Either-or', 614. See also Colin Hay, 'Narrating Crisis: The Discursive Construction of the "Winter of Discontent"', *Sociology* 30, no. 2 (1996): 253–77. For an economic perspective on narratives, which is less developed and differs from the use of narratives in this book, see Robert J. Shiller, 'Narrative Economics', *American Economic Review* 107, no. 4 (2017): 967–1004; Robert J. Shiller, *Narrative Economics: How Stories Go Viral & Drive Major Economic Events* (Princeton: Princeton University Press, 2019); Mary S. Morgan and Thomas P. Stapleford, 'Narrative in Economics: A New Turn on the Past', *History of Political Economy* 55, no. 3 (2023): 395–421. For an example of how specific frames create blind spots, see Neil Fligstein, Jonah Stuart Brundage and Michael Schultz, 'Seeing Like the Fed: Culture, Cognition, and Framing in the Failure to Anticipate the Financial Crisis of 2008', *American Sociological Review* 82, no. 5 (2017): 879–909.

90 David Tuckett, 'Conviction Narrative Theory and Understanding Decision-Making in Economics and Finance', in Beckert and Bronk, *Uncertain Futures*, 69. Tuckett is quoting the classic text by Jerome S. Bruner, *Acts of Meaning: Four Lectures on Mind and Culture* (Cambridge, MA: Harvard University Press, 1990).

91 Wolf, 'Europe's Great Depression', 100. Of course, the gold standard was also an economic theory, but that only means that economic theories, too, are performative. For this general argument, see Donald Mackenzie, *An Engine, Not a Camera: How Financial Models Shape Markets* (Cambridge, MA: MIT Press, 2008).

92 The most thorough analysis of the Credit Anstalt crisis from an economic perspective remains Schubert, *The Credit-Anstalt Crisis*. See also Flora Macher, 'The Austrian Banking Crisis of 1931: A Reassessment', *Financial History Review* 25, no. 3 (January 10, 2018): 297–321; Hans Kernbauer, *Währungspolitik in Der Zwischenkriegszeit. Geschichte Der Oesterreichischen Nationalbank von 1923 Bis 1938* (Wien: Der Oesterreichischen Nationalbank, 1991), 291–304. Like Marcus, mentioned later, Hans Kernbauer analyses the 'pre-history' of the Austrian crisis; see Hans Kernbauer, 'Central Bank Policy'. For other perspectives, see Clarke, *Central Bank Cooperation*; Stiefel, *Finanzdiplomatie und Weltwirtschaftskrise*; Philip L. Cottrell, 'The Bank of England in Its International Setting, 1918–1972', in *The Bank of England: Money, Power & Influence, 1694–1994*, ed. Richard Roberts and David Kynaston (Oxford: Clarendon Press, 1995), 83–139; Philip L. Cottrell, 'Austria between Diplomats and Bankers 1919–1931', in *Konstellationen Internationaler Politik 1924–1931*, ed. Gustav Schmidt (Bochum, 1983), 292–311; Philip L. Cottrell, 'The Bank of England and Credit-Anstalt's Collapse, Spring 1931', in *Auf Heller und Cent. Beiträge zur Finanz- und Währungsgeschichte*, ed. Karl Bachinger and Dieter Stiefel (Vienna: Uberreuter Wirtschaft, 2001), 407–33; Iago Gil Aguado, 'The Credit Anstalt Crisis of 1931 and the Failure of the Austro-German Customs Union Project', *The Historical Journal* 44, no. 1 (2001): 199–221; Toniolo, with the assistance of *Clement, Central Bank Cooperation*, 84–114. For the role of the Austrian crisis in the contagion to other countries, see also Michael J. Oliver, 'Financial Crises', in *Economic Disasters of the Twentieth Century*, ed. Michael J. Oliver and Derek H. Aldcroft (Cheltenham: Edward Elgar, 2007), 204–5; Eichengreen, *Hall of*

*Mirrors*, 142–43; Boyce, *The Great Interwar Crisis*, 300–4. In contrast to most other narratives, Boyce is more understanding of the role of the French and the demand that Austria should reject the plans for an Austro-German customs union. So is Schuker, who explains the breakdown of the gold-exchange standard with political disagreements and assigns prime importance to Germany's efforts 'to repudiate the efforts of Versailles', see Schuker, 'The Gold-Exchange Standard', 88. Peter Temin sees the Austrian crisis as a precursor, not the cause of the German crisis, Peter Temin, 'Currency Crises: From Andrew Jackson to Angela Merkel', in *The Oxford Handbook of Banking and Financial History*, ed. Youssef Cassis, Richard S. Grossman and Catherine R. Schenk (Oxford: Oxford University Press, 2016), 469; Marcus, *Austrian Reconstruction*, argues that the Austrian crisis was contained by mid-June and that it was the German crisis and the failure of the Danatbank that led to the Austrian currency crisis in July and August. See also Kernbauer, *Währungspolitik*, 321.

93 David Tuckett et al., 'Monetary Policy and the Management of Uncertainty: A Narrative Approach', *SSRN Electronic Journal*, Staff Working Paper, 2020, 3. See also Tuckett, 'Conviction Narrative Theory'; Abolafia, *Stewards of the Market*, 129, 161.

94 Colin Hay, 'Constructivist Institutionalism', in *The Oxford Handbook of Political Institutions*, ed. R.A.W. Rhodes and Sarah A. Binder (Oxford: Oxford University Press, 2006), 63.

95 Works that are based on one or more of the archives on which this book is based, are, among others, Mouré, *The Gold Standard Illusion*; Marcus, *Austrian Reconstruction*; Harold James, *The German Slump: Politics and Economics, 1924–1936* (Oxford: Oxford University Press, 1986); Toniolo, with the assistance of Clement, *Central Bank Cooperation*; Bennett, *Germany and the Diplomacy*; Clarke, *Central Bank Cooperation*; Cottrell, 'The Bank of England'; Aguado, 'The Credit Anstalt Crisis'; Kernbauer, 'The Policy of the Austrian National Bank before and during the 1931 Crisis', *The 1931 Crisis and Its Aftermath*, 1982; Kernbauer, *Währungspolitik*, 291–332; Kunz, *The Battle*; Boyce, *The Great Interwar Crisis*; Martin Horn, *J. P. Morgan & Co. and the Crisis of Capitalism* (Cambridge: Cambridge University Press, 2022); Morrison, 'Shocking Intellectual Austerity'; James Ashley Morrison, 'Shocking Intellectual Austerity: The Role of Ideas in the Demise of the Gold Standard in Britain. Extended Citations', International Organization, 2016.

## Chapter 2

1 Among the few exceptions that recognize Rodd's role without explicitly emphasizing how he was in some ways one of the main actors in the Austrian crisis are Aguado, 'The Credit Anstalt Crisis'; Cottrell, 'The Bank of England'; Marcus, *Austrian Reconstruction*. A recent biography of Rodd includes his role in the 1931 crisis; see Philip Boobbyer, *The Life and World of Francis Rodd, Lord Rennell (1895–1978): Geography, Money and War* (London: Anthem Press, 2021).

2 Philip Boobbyer, 'Francis Rodd, Lord Rennell (1895–1978)', in *Geographers: Bibliographic Studies*, ed. Hayden Lorimer and Charles W.J. Withers, vol. 35 (London: Bloomsbury, 2016), 10–31.

3 'Obituary: Lord Rennell of Rodd, KBE, CB, JP', *The Geographic Journal* 144, no. 2 (1978): 392–93.
4 Francis Rennel Rodd, *People of the Veil* (London: Macmillan & Co, 1926). For the Telegraph quote, see Boobbyer, 'Francis Rodd, Lord Rennell (1895–1978)', 14. See also R.S. Sayers, *The Bank of England, 1891–1944* (Cambridge: Cambridge University Press, 1976), 624.
5 'Obituary: Lord Rennell of Rodd, KBE, CB, JP'.
6 Boobbyer, 'Francis Rodd, Lord Rennell (1895–1978)', 15, 24–25; Boobbyer, *The Life and World*, 47–48.
7 Boobbyer, *The Life and World*, 42.
8 Mary Wesley and Eric Siepmann, *Darling Pol: The Letters of Mary Wesley and Eric Siepmann 1944–1967*, ed. Patrick Marnham (London: Harvill Secker, 2017), 53.
9 Harry Siepmann, *Echo of the Guns: Recollections of an Artillery Officer, 1914–18* (London: Robert Hale, 1987), 9–10.
10 John Maynard Keynes, *The Economic Consequences of the Peace* (London: Macmillan & Co, 1919); Siepmann, *Echo of the Guns*, 177–83.
11 Donald E. Moggridge, *Maynard Keynes: An Economist's Biography* (London: Routledge, 1992), 278, 357, 674; Donald Moggridge and Robert Skidelsky, 'Critique of Schuker "J.M. Keynes and the Personal Politics of Reparations"', *Diplomacy & Statecraft* 26, no. 4 (January 1, 2015): 740; Hawtrey, *The Art of Central Banking*; Jérôme de Boyer des Roches and Ricardo Solis Rosales, 'R.G. Hawtrey on the National and International Lender of Last Resort', *European Journal of the History of Economic Thought* 18, no. 2 (2011): 175–202. See also Hawtrey, *The Gold Standard.*
12 Cottrell, 'Norman, Strakosch', 55–56, 72 n. 173.
13 Sayers, *The Bank of England*, 344 n. 1.
14 Letter, October 30, 1926, from Siepmann to Norman. BEA, ADM25–14, Papers of Harry Arthur Siepmann, Correspondence, August 5, 1923–October 18, 1933.
15 Sayers, *The Bank of England*, 356.
16 Letter, September 5, 1931, from Siepmann to Rodd. LRRA, Folder 145/1/6, Private; Siepmann, *Echo of the Guns*, 48–49.
17 Note #73 to the Deputy Governor on conversation with E. Cecil Jones, July 29, 1931, by Siepmann. BEA, OV45–4, France Country File, January 6, 1931–October 31, 1931.
18 Harold Callender, 'The Diplomat of Threadneedle Street', *The New York Times*, November 6, 1932; Paul Einzig, *Montagu Norman: A Study in Financial Statemanship* (London: Kegan Paul, 1932), 25.
19 Mouré, *The Gold Standard Illusion*, 158–59. For the case of Austria, see Marcus, *Austrian Reconstruction*, 7–9, 339–41.
20 Einzig, *Montagu Norman*, 30.
21 On exorbitant privilege, see Barry Eichengreen, *Exorbitant Privilege: The Rise and Fall of the Dollar* (Oxford: Oxford University Press, 2011).
22 Boyce, *The Great Interwar Crisis*, 148. For insightful contributions on Norman and his ideas about central banking, see Cottrell, 'Norman, Strakosch'; Einzig, *Montagu Norman*, chapters 6, 7 and 8; Clement, 'Institutionalizing Central Bank Cooperation', 82–83, who uses the term 'political operator'. See also Diane B. Kunz, 'American Bankers and Americas Fall from Gold', in Flandreau and

Holtfrerich, *International Financial History in the 20th Century*, 36. For a wider perspective on the issue of central bank independence in the 1920s, including that of the BIS, see Martin, *The Meddlers*, chapter 3.

23 Letter of September 18, 1930, from Fraser to Quesnay. BISA, 7.18.2. MCG.5. Notes from and for General Manager Pierre Quesnay, 1930–31.

24 Quoted from Andrew Boyle, *Montagu Norman: A Biography* (London: Cassell, 1967), 204–5. See also Boyce, *The Great Interwar Crisis*, 148; Singleton, *Central Banking*, 74.

25 Frank C. Costigliola, 'Anglo-American Financial Rivalry in the 1920s', *The Journal of Economic History* 37, no. 4 (1977): 911–34; Schuker, 'Money Doctors', 56–57, 60–61; Schuker, 'The Gold-Exchange Standard', 84.

26 The quote is from 'Germany: Ein Feste Burg', *Time*, July 27, 1931. See also Boyle, *Montagu Norman*; Kunz, *The Battle*, 79, 185 et passim; Boyce, *The Great Interwar Crisis*, 146.

27 Letter, February 6, 1931, from E. Grenfell to J.P. Morgan. JPM, ARC1195, Box 5: Folder 5/18, 1931; telegram #31/2060, February 16, 1931, from Jack Morgan to E.C. Grenfell. JPM, ARC 1216, Box 38A, Folder 34. For the House of Morgan network, see Ron Chernow, *The House of Morgan: An American Banking Dynasty and the Rise of Modern Finance* (New York: Grove Press, 1990), 324ff.

28 Boyle, *Montagu Norman*, 128, 134–38.

29 Horn, *J. P. Morgan & Co.*, 28–29, 59–61; Kathleen Burk, *Morgan Grenfell, 1838–1988: The Biography of a Merchant Bank* (Oxford: Oxford University Press, 1989), 135–36. See also Chernow, *The House of Morgan*.

30 Hayden White, 'The Burden of History', *History and Theory* 5, no. 2 (1966): 111–34; Per H. Hansen, 'Organizational Culture and Organizational Change: The Transformation of Savings Banks in Denmark, 1965–1990', *Enterprise & Society* 8, no. 4 (2007): 920–53.

31 'George L. Harrison Dead at 71; Headed Federal Reserve Here', *The New York Times*, March 6, 1958; 'G.L. Harrison Heads Reserve Bank Here', *The New York Times*, November 24, 1928.

32 Matthew Josephson, 'Money Men Are Different Now', *The Saturday Evening Post*, February 26, 1949, 16.

33 Friedman and Schwartz, *A Monetary History*, 256 and n. 26.

34 Copy of telegram #29/2178, March 7, 1929, from Leffingwell to E.C. Grenfell. BEA, G14–23, Governor's File.

35 Chernow, *The House of Morgan*, 319.

36 Josephson, 'Money Men Are Different Now', 60.

37 'International Committee Meeting. Thursday, 11 June 1931. 2.30 p.m.' RA, 31/26, 1931 Correspondence (A.C.A.) Shorthand Minutes June 1931.

38 See, for instance, Personal letters, November 2, 1928, from Norman to Harrison, and November 9, 1928, from Harrison to Norman. BEA, G14–23, Governor's File.

39 Telegram, January 1, 1929, from J.P. Morgan to E.C. Grenfell, and 'Note of telephonic conversation with Mr. Harrison at 3.35 p.m. Tuesday, 15th January 1929'. BEA, G14–23, Governor's File.

40 Telegram no. 9/31, January 10, 1931, from Harrison to Norman. BEA, OV32/7, Federal Reserve Bank of New York, Confidential Cables, 1931. With respect to Harrison's visit, see telegram no. 16/31, January 17, 1931, from Harrison to

Norman and no. 31/31, and February 6, 1931, from Norman to Harrison. BEA, OV32/7, Federal Reserve Bank of New York, Confidential Cables, 1931.

41 Letter, March 26, 1931, from Harrison to Norman, BEA, G14–23, Governor's File.

42 'Memorandum', December 17, 1931, by Francis Rodd. BEA, OV45–82, Banque de France, January 1, 1931–February 25, 1932.

43 For an extensive analysis of the British Empire and its significance, see John Darwin, *The Empire Project: The Rise and Fall of the British World-System, 1830–1970, The Empire Project* (Cambridge: Cambridge University Press, 2009). See also Martin, *The Meddlers.*

44 Boyce argues that the British (and American) elite's attitude towards the French was imbued with racial stereotypes, the French being of the 'Latin race' while the British and the Germans were the 'Anglo-Saxon' or 'Teutonic race', see Boyce, *The Great Interwar Crisis,* 14–21, 58–59 et passim. While Martin, *The Meddlers* seem to support Boyce, Mouré and others question Boyce's idea of racism as an explanatory category and instead suggest that it was a matter of stereotypes and prejudice, see Talbot C. Imlay et al., 'H-Diplo Roundtable Review of Robert Boyce: The Great Interwar Crisis and the Collapse of Globalization', H-Diplo, 2011.

45 Boyle, *Montagu Norman*, 142–43, 231–38. See also Clay, *Lord Norman*, 13, 58–59. For Moreau's perspective, see Emile Moreau, *The Golden Franc. Memoirs of a Governor of the Bank of France: The Stabilization of the Franc (1926–1928*, English ed. (Boulder, CO: Westview Press, 1991), 433–53.

46 Toniolo, with the assistance of Clement, *Central Bank Cooperation*, 517 n. 108.

47 Einzig, *Montagu Norman*, 185.

48 Mouré, *The Gold Standard Illusion*, 149. See also Lester V. Chandler, *Benjamin Strong: Central Banker* (Washington, DC: Brookings Institution, 1958), 247–90.

49 Mouré, *The Gold Standard Illusion*, 171; Schuker, 'Money Doctors', 62–63.

50 Quoted from Clarke, *Central Bank Cooperation*, 144.

51 Clavin, *The Great Depression in Europe*, 29, 61, 65; Ahamed, *Lords of Finance*, 259–61, 300–4. On Clément Moret, see Leith-Ross, *Money Talks*, 139 n. 1.

52 Mouré, *The Gold Standard Illusion*, 166–67, 179.

53 See, for instance, Clarke, *Central Bank Cooperation*, 134–35; Kunz, *The Battle*, 24–25.

54 For a discussion of the role of personal and national relations at the BIS, see Toniolo, with the assistance of Clement, *Central Bank Cooperation*, 66–67; Eleanor Lansing Dulles, 'The Bank for International Settlements', *American Economic Review* (June 1938): 58–59; Paolo Baffi, *The Origins of Central Bank Cooperation: The Establishment of the Bank for International Settlements* (Rome: Editori Laterza, 2002). For the concept of national interests, I do not subscribe to a realist view; see S. Burchill, *The National Interest in International Relations Theory* (London: Palgrave Macmillan, 2005); Toniolo, with the assistance of Clement, *Central Bank Cooperation*, 3, 9–13. See also Cross, 'Rethinking', 149; Martin, *The Meddlers*, chapter 3.

55 Clarke, *Central Bank Cooperation*, 40. See also Schuker, 'The Gold-Exchange Standard', 78.

56 Copy of telegram 115/31, April 30, 1931, from Norman to Harrison. BEA, OV32/7, Federal Reserve Bank of New York, Confidential Cables, 1931.

57 Baffi, *The Origins*, 65–84. For the BIS's organization and personnel, see Dulles, *The Bank for International Settlements*, 55–67.
58 Bennett, *Germany*, 287.
59 Letter, April 1, 1930, from Luther to McGarrah. BISA, 7.18.2. MCG.1. Reichsbank, 1930–31.
60 'World Bank Plans Meeting April 22', *The New York Times*, April 11, 1930; 'World Bank Names M'Garrah as Head', *The New York Times*, April 23, 1930.
61 Strictly confidential telegram, January 12, 1930, from Parker Gilbert to Gates W. McGarrah, George Harrison, J.P. Morgan, Thomas W. Lamont, Pierre Jay and Leon Fraser. FRBNY, Box 128149, Folder 797.3 Bank of International Settlements, January–May 1930.
62 Private letter, March 26, 1931, from Harrison to McGarrah. FRBNY, Box 128149, Folder 797.3 Bank of International Settlements, January–May 1930.
63 Toniolo, with the assistance of Clement, *Central Bank Cooperation*, 30. See also Mouré, *The Gold Standard Illusion*. According to Johnson, the French Monetary Law of June 25, 1928, which returned the franc to gold at an undervalued level and prohibited foreign exchange holdings to be counted as part of the legal reserves contributed to France's 'hoarding' of gold, H. Clark Johnson, *Gold, France, and the Great Depression, 1919–1932* (New Haven, CT: Yale University Press, 1997), 3–4 and chapter 9; Olivier Accominotti, 'The Sterling Trap: Foreign Reserves Management at the Bank of France, 1928–1936', *European Review of Economic History* 13, no. 3 (2009): 351.
64 For sterilization see, for instance, Eichengreen, *Golden Fetters*, 205–6. For a discussion and different views of the role of and reasons for French sterilization, see Mouré, *The Gold Standard Illusion*; Kenneth Mouré, *Managing the Franc Poincare: Economic Understanding and Political Constraint in French Monetary Policy, 1928–1936* (New York: Cambridge University Press, 1991); Johnson, *Gold, France*; Accominotti, 'The Sterling Trap'.
65 Mouré, *The Gold Standard Illusion*, 181–91.
66 See also Kunz, *The Battle*, 5, 68 et passim. Kunz stresses how the relationship between politics and central banking changed during the 1931 crisis.
67 Quoted from Horn, *J. P. Morgan & Co.*, 109.
68 Telegram, November 24, 1930, from Harrison to Case. CUL, HP, Box 16, binder 34, European Trips, 1927–32.
69 Record of certain conversations in London and Paris, November 11–December 17, 1930. FRBNY, FR credits'31, . . . 1931–32, 1936, 1939.
70 'International: Gold, Gold, Gold', *Time*, December 1, 1930.
71 'International: Again Gold, Gold', *Time*, December 15, 1930.
72 'International: Again Gold, Gold'.
73 Mouré, *Managing the Franc Poincare*, 63.
74 Letter, January 27, 1931, from Norman to Donald Ferguson, BEA, G1–468, Governor's Papers – Miscellaneous, January-December 1931.
75 Telegram 40/31, February 12, 1931, from Norman to Harrison. CUL, HP, Bank of England. Box 9, binder 20, Bank of England, January–December 1931.
76 'Record of certain conversations in London and Paris, November 11–December 17, 1930', FRBNY, FR credits'31, . . . 1931–32, 1936, 1939. On O.M.W. Sprague, see Hugh Rockoff, 'O.M.W. Sprague (the Man Who "Wrote the Book" on Financial

Crises) and the Founding of the Federal Reserve', *Journal of Financial Stability* 17 (April 1, 2015): 35–45; Hugh Rockoff, 'O.M.W. Sprague (the Man Who "Wrote the Book" on Financial Crises) Meets the Great Depression', *Jahrbuch Für Wirtschafts geschichte* 63, no. 2 (2022): 527–57. For a contemporary description of Sprague's view of the depression where he blames 'overproduction', see 'Prof. O. M. W. Sprague, Financial Adviser to Bank of England, Said to Be at Odds with Sir Josiah Stamp', *Commercial and Financial Chronicle*, June 20, 1931.

77 Letter, February 21, 1931, from Burgess to Seay. FRBNY, FR credits'31, . . . 1931–32, 1936, 1939.

78 'Report of the Chairman of the Open Market Conference to the Governors' Conference April 27, 1931'. The report is enclosed with a letter of April 27, 1931, from Burgess to Harrison. FRBNY, FR credits'31, . . . 1931–32, 1936, 1939.

79 'International Bank Notes (Letter No. 3)', by Merle Cochran, February 6, 1931. NARA, RG39, Box 104, Entry 145, Folder: 'G783.5 Special Report Confidential Letters (1-24)'.

80 'International Bank Notes (Letter No. 4)', by Merle Cochran, February 11, 1931. On the source of Cochran's information about BIS matters, see letter, April 10 from the undersecretary of state W. Castle to Ogden Mills, the undersecretary of the treasury. NARA, RG39, Box 104, Entry 145, Folder: 'G783.5 Special Report Confidential Letters (1-24)'. According to Harris, Cochran participated in the BIS board meetings. I have found no evidence to support this. See Harris, *Monetary War and Peace*, 40.

81 Letter, March 6, 1931, from J.E. Crane to Leon Fraser, BIS. FRBNY, 797.3 Bank for International Settlements, January–March 1931, and telegram 72/31, March 3, 1931, from Harrison to Norman, BEA, OV32/7, Federal Reserve Bank of New York, Confidential Cables, 1931

82 Harold James, 'Financial Flows across Frontiers during the Interwar Depression', *The Economic History Review* 45, no. 3 (1992): 597.

83 'The B.I.S. at Work'. *The Economist*, February 28, 1931.

84 For a brief discussion, see Clement, 'Institutionalizing Central Bank Cooperation', 89–91.

85 Letter and memorandum, February 2, 1931, from Norman to McGarrah. BISA, 7.18.2. MCG.1. Bank of England, 1930–31.

86 'International Bank Notes (Letter No. 6)', by Merle Cochran, March 11, 1931. NARA, RG39, Box 104, Entry 145, Folder: 'G783.5 Special Report Confidential Letters (1-24)'. See also Clarke, *Central Bank Cooperation*, 179–81; Boyce, *The Great Interwar Crisis*, 294–95; James, *The End of Globalization*, 45–47; Martin, *The Meddlers*, 128–29.

87 Telegram, March 12, 1931, from McGarrah to J.P. Morgan, sent by Morgan & Cie, Paris. FRBNY, 797.3 Bank for International Settlements, January–March 1931.

88 'International Bank Notes (Letter No. 6)', by Merle Cochran, March 11, 1931. NARA, RG39, Box 104, Entry 145, Folder: 'G783.5 Special Report Confidential Letters (1-24)'.

89 Letter, February 11, 1931, from Harrison to Norman. BEA, G14–23, Governor's File.

90 Telegrams, February 27, 1931, from Harrison to Norman, March 2, 1931, from Norman to Harrison, and March 3, 1931, from Harrison to Norman. FRBNY, 797.3

Bank for International Settlements, January–March 1931. See also Clement, 'Institutionalizing Central Bank Cooperation', for a discussion of Norman's plans for the BIS.

91 Personal letter, March 3, 1931, from Norman to Harrison. CUL, HP, Box 51, Norman, Montagu Collet, Governor of the Bank of England, I (May 1926–December 1931).

92 Letter, March 15, 1931, from Harrison to Norman. BEA, GL14–23 Governor's File. Correspondence between Norman and Harrison.

93 Telegram, March 13, 1931, from J.P. Morgan to Gates W. McGarrah. FRBNY, 797.3 Bank for International Settlements, January–March 1931. For further correspondence about the Kindersley plan between J.P. Morgan and McGarrah, see BISA, 7.18.2. MCG.1. Correspondence with and regarding J.P. Morgan & Co, Morgan Grenfell & Co, 1930–31.

94 Schuker, 'Money Doctors between the Wars', 63. For a discussion of bankers and the market in the 1990s and 2000s, see Ho, *Liquidated*; Ho, 'Disciplining Investment Bankers'.

95 Telegram, July 24, 1931, from J.P. Morgan to J.P. Morgan & Co., New York. JPM, JPM, ARC 1216, Box 38A, Folder 33.

96 Quoted from Kunz, *The Battle*, 70.

97 Telegrams 77/31, March 17, and 85/31, March 21, 1931, from Norman and Harvey respectively to Harrison and 86/31, March 18, 1931, from Harrison to Norman. CUL, HP, Bank of England. Box 9, binder 20, Bank of England, January–December 1931.

98 Telegram, February 24, 1931, from R.C. Leffingwell to Montagu Norman via Morgan Grenfell. JPM, ARC 1216, Box 38A, Folder 34. Personal telegrams 65/31, March 4, 1931, from Norman to Harrison, and 78/31, March 4, 1931, from Harrison to Norman. CUL, HP, Box 9, binder 20, Bank of England, January–December 1931. For an analysis of the social networks of J.P. Morgan, see Susie J. Pak, *Gentlemen Bankers: The World of J. P. Morgan* (Cambridge, MA: Harvard University Press, 2013).

99 'International Bank Notes (Letter No. 7)', by Merle Cochran, March 27, 1931. NARA, RG39, Box 104, Entry 145, Folder: 'G783.5 Special Report Confidential Letters (1–24)'.

100 Letter, April 20, 1931, from Norman to Harrison. CUL, HP, Box 51, Norman, Montagu Collet, Governor of the Bank of England, I (May 1926–December 1931).

101 'Memorandum: Meeting of the Board of Directors April 9, 1931. Subject: Credit Policy and Discount Rates'. CUL, HP, Box 23, binder 50, Discussion Notes: Volumes I, II & III, April 17, 1930–September 21, 1933.

102 Weick, 'The Collapse of Sensemaking', 633.

103 Letter, April 21, 1931, from Harrison to Stimson. CUL, HP, Box 51, Norman, Montagu Collet, Governor of the Bank of England, I (May 1926–December 1931). See also Kunz, *The Battle*, 42–45.

104 'International Bank Notes (Letter No. 9)', by Merle Cochran, April 21, 1931. NARA, RG39, Box 104, Entry 145, Folder: 'G783.5 Special Report Confidential Letters (1-24)'.

105 'Memorandum: Meeting of Board of Directors April 23, 1931. Subject: Credit Policy'. CUL, HP, Box 23, binder 50, Discussion Notes: Volumes I, II & III, April 17, 1930–September 21, 1933.
106 'Report of the Chairman of the Open Market Conference to the Governors' Conference April 27, 1931'. The report is enclosed with a letter, April 27, 1931, from Burgess to Harrison. FRBNY, FR credits'31, . . . 1931–32, 1936, 1939.
107 'Record of certain conversations in London and Paris, November 11–December 17, 1930', FRBNY, FR credits'31, . . . 1931–32, 1936, 1939.
108 Telegram, January 13, 1931, from Norman to Harrison, BEA, OV32/7, Federal Reserve Bank of New York, Confidential Cables, 1931.
109 For 'frame borne of historical routine', see Ian Colville, Annie Pye and Mike Carter, 'Organizing to Counter Terrorism: Sensemaking amidst Dynamic Complexity', *Human Relations* 66, no. 9 (2013): 1217.
110 'Summary of an Address by Mr. Pierre Quesnay at the Ecole de la Paix, Paris', February 18, 1931. FRBNY, 797.3 Bank for International Settlements, January–March 1931. See also Feiertag, 'Les Banques d'émission', 719–20.
111 Letter, June 7, 1932, from Rodd to R.H. Hadow. LRRA, Folder 146/4, Mr. Rodd's Personal Correspondence.
112 Letter, March 11, 1931, from Siepmann to Rodd. LRRA, Folder 59, 'A Few Bank of England Papers'.
113 Thomas F. Woodlock, 'Post-War War', *Wall Street Journal*, May 7, 1931.
114 'Memorandum: Meeting of Board of Directors May 7, 1931. Subject: Credit Policy and Discount Rate'. CUL, HP, Box 23, binder 50, Discussion Notes: Volumes I, II & III, April 17, 1930–September 21, 1933.
115 Guido Enderis, 'Germans Skeptical of Norman's Plan', *The New York Times*, April 21, 1931.
116 For this general point, see, for instance, Eichengreen, *Golden Fetters*; Ahamed, *Lords of Finance*; Boyce, *The Great Interwar Crisis*.
117 Letter, May 1, 1931, from Siepmann to E.L. Hall-Patch. BEA, ADM25–5, Papers of Harry Siepmann, Correspondence, January 1–June 20, 1931.
118 Note, May 5, 1931, from Siepmann to Mr. Skinner. BEA: ADM25–14 Papers of Harry Arthur Siepmann, Correspondence, August 5, 1923–October 18, 1933. 'International Bank Notes (Letter No. 10)', April 30, 1931, from Merle Cochran to the undersecretary of state, William N. Castle, Junior. NARA, RG39, Box 104, Entry 145, Folder: 'G783.5 Special Report Confidential Letters (1-24)'.
119 Letter, May 8, 1931, from Fraser to Harrison, with attached 'Report of the Committee created to examine the question of middle term credits', dated Brussel, May 5, 1931. FRBNY, Box 128149, Folder 797.3 Bank of International Settlements, April–June 1931.
120 Telegram 121/31, May 5, 1931, from Norman to Harrison. CUL, HP, Bank of England. Box 9, binder 20, Bank of England, January–December 1931. Telegram no. 144/31, May 6, 1931, from Harrison to Norman, and telegram no. 123/31, May 7, 1931, from Norman to Harrison; BEA, OV32/7, Federal Reserve Bank of New York, Confidential Cables, 1931, and telegram no. 150/31, May 8, 1931, from Harrison to Norman. FRBNY, C261, England, Bank of England, 1931–32, General.
121 Letter, May 8, 1931, from Sprague to Burgess. FRBNY, C261, England, Bank of England, 1931–32, General.

## Chapter 3

1 Strictly confidential telegram no. 2486, April 25, 1931, from McGarrah and Fraser to George L. Harrison, J.P. Morgan, Owen D. Young and Jackson E. Reynolds. CUL, HP, Box 23, binder 50, Discussion Notes: Volumes I, II & III, April 17, 1930–September 21, 1933.

2 Letter, May 19, 1930, from Reisch to McGarrah. BISA, 2.23, Central Bank of the Republic of Austria, Vienna, May 1, 1930–December 31, 1958.

3 'Konfidentielt. Samtal med monsieur Pierre Quesnay vid hans besök i Stockholm den 4., 5. og 6. augusti 1930', sent from Rooth to Nationalbanken, August 14, 1930. NA, Supplement no. 2642. See also Per H. Hansen, 'Cooperate or Free Ride? The Scandinavian Central Banks, Bank for International Settlements and the Austrian Financial Crisis of 1931', *Scandinavian Journal of History* 37, no. 1 (2012): 87–107. For 'Super-Central Bank' and orthodoxy, see Dulles, *The Bank for International Settlements*, 181–97.

4 Note, January 22, 1931, prepared by 'CB' – probably the BIS's Central Banking Department. BEA, OV28/3, Austria Country File, January 14–June 15, 1931. The note is unsigned, but it is likely that Hans Simon was the author. See also Cottrell, 'The Bank of England', 96. The first part of the note ends abruptly. However, the remaining two pages of the note is located in the same file between supplements 123A and 124. For an explanation of the acceptance market, see Accominotti, 'London Merchant Banks', 6–9.

5 'International: Again Gold, Gold'.

6 'Siepmann's Note on Monsieur Quesnay's Conversations in London' on January 27/29, 1931. BISA, 7.18.2. MCG.5. Notes from and for General Manager Pierre Quesnay, 1930–31.

7 Simon resigned from the BIS in October 1931 to return to Austria as a financial adviser to a private banking house, see Charles T. Thompson, *The Peace Conference Day by Day* (New York: Brentano's Publishers, 1920), 221; Dulles, *The Bank for International Settlements*, 59. For the name von Simon, see Merle Cochran's 'International Bank Notes (Letter no. 19)', July 18, 1931, where he refers to 'Dr. Von Simon, an Austrian in the B.I.S.', who was in Vienna with Rodd 'during the Credit Anstalt crisis'; and Merle Cochran's 'International Bank Notes (Letter no. 12)', May 19, 1931, and letter no. 29, October 16, 1931. NARA, RG39, Box 104, Entry 145, Folder: 'G783.5 Special Report Confidential Letters (1-24)'.

8 Letter #315, May 12, 1931, from Siepmann to Roger Auboin; letter #313, May 12, 1931, from Siepmann to the Governor of Bank of Finland, Risto Ryti; and letter #317, May 12, 1931, from Siepmann to Quesnay. BEA, ADM25-5, Papers of Harry Arthur Siepmann. Correspondence, January 1, 1931–June 30, 1931.

9 Letter no. 1, May 12, 1931, from Rodd to Fraser. BISA, 6.30. II/1 Granting of Credit of 100,000,000 Schilling to Austrian National Bank, 1931.

10 Telegram no. 1, May 12, 1931, from Rodd to Fraser. BISA, 6.30. II/1 Granting of Credit of 100,000,000 Schilling to Austrian National Bank, 1931.

11 Letter no. 1, May 12, 1931, from Rodd to Fraser. BISA, 6.30. II/1 Granting of Credit of 100,000,000 Schilling to Austrian National Bank, 1931. In fact, Rodd was right. The Credit Anstalt losses were seven times larger than the 140 million schilling.

The Austrian government soon learned that the losses were larger, but kept this secret; see Kernbauer, *Währungspolitik*, 295–96.

12 Telegram no. 1, May 12, 1931, from Rodd to Fraser. BISA, 6.30. II/1 Granting of Credit of 100,000,000 Schilling to Austrian National Bank, 1931.

13 Letter no. 1, May 12, 1931, from Rodd to Fraser. BISA, 6.30. II/1 Granting of Credit of 100,000,000 Schilling to Austrian National Bank, 1931.

14 Telegram no. 2, May 12, 1931, from Rodd to Fraser. BISA, 6.30. II/1 Granting of Credit of 100,000,000 Schilling to Austrian National Bank, 1931.

15 Letter no. 1, May 12, 1931, from Rodd to Fraser. BISA, 6.30. II/1 Granting of Credit of 100,000,000 Schilling to Austrian National Bank, 1931.

16 Letter no. 2, May 12, 1931, from Rodd to Fraser. BISA, 6.30. II/1 Granting of Credit of 100,000,000 Schilling to Austrian National Bank, 1931. For the League of Nations and the Austrian stabilization loan, see Martin, *The Meddlers*, 76–88; Marcus, *Austrian Reconstruction*.

17 Newspaper clipping, M.W. Fodor, Austria, 'Paris seen guiding Viennese finance'. FRBNY, FR credits '31, . . . 1931–32, 1936, 1939. Stiefel argues that this idea was a myth, but it may, of course, have influenced decision-makers anyway, see Stiefel, *Finanzdiplomatie und Weltwirtschaftskrise*; Aguado, 'The Credit Anstalt Crisis', 210.

18 Letter, May 15, 1931, from Norris to Harrison. FRBNY, FR credits '31, . . . 1931–32, 1936, 1939. And letter, May 18, 1931, from Harrison to Norris. FRBNY, C261, Austria - Oesterreichische Creditanstalt, Wiener Bankverein, March 1929–.

19 Letter no. 2, May 12, 1931, from Rodd to Fraser. BISA, 6.30. II/1 Granting of Credit of 100,000,000 Schilling to Austrian National Bank, 1931.

20 Eichengreen and Temin, 'The Gold Standard'; Eichengreen and Temin, 'Fetters of Gold and Paper'.

21 Letter no. 2, May 12, 1931, from Rodd to Fraser. BISA, 6.30. II/1 Granting of Credit of 100,000,000 Schilling to Austrian National Bank, 1931.

22 For a discussion of this point, see also Stiefel, *Finanzdiplomatie und Weltwirtschaftskrise*, 70.

23 Letter no. 2, May 12, 1931, from Rodd to Fraser. BISA, 6.30. II/1 Granting of Credit of 100,000,000 Schilling to Austrian National Bank, 1931.

24 Telegram no. 5, May 12, 1931, from Fraser, BIS to Harrison, NY Fed. FRBNY, Box 128149, Folder 797.3, Bank of International Settlements, April–June 1931.

25 Memorandum by Harrison, May 12, 1931. CUL, HP, Box 27, binder 59, Office Memoranda: Volume II, 1928–31.

26 Letter, May 13, 1931, from Siepmann to Sargent, #23. BEA, OV28/3, Austria Country File, January 14–June 15, 1931.

27 Telegram no. 3, May 13, 1931, from Rodd to Fraser. BISA, 6.30. II/1 Granting of Credit of 100,000,000 Schilling to Austrian National Bank, 1931.

28 Note, May 13, 1931, of phone call from Eric Warburg. RA, Correspondence Department, 111/521.

29 Telegram no. 4, May 13, 1931, from Rodd to Fraser. BISA, 6.30. II/1 Granting of Credit of 100,000,000 Schilling to Austrian National Bank, 1931.

30 See also three notes, May 14, 1931, by Siepmann on telephone conversations with Pierre Quesnay, BIS, on the BIS credit. BEA, OV28–35, Austria Oesterreichische Nationalbank, January 5–December 31, 1931.

31 'Austrian Bank Bills', *Financial Times*, May 21, 1931; 'Settlements Bank: Support for the Credit Anstalt', *Financial Times*, May 21, 1931.
32 Telegram no. 5, May 14, 1931, from Rodd to Fraser. BISA, 6.30. II/1 Granting of Credit of 100,000,000 Schilling to Austrian National Bank, 1931.
33 Note on 'Austrian Credit Anstalt', May 13, 1931, probably by Siepmann. BEA, OV28/3, Austria Country Files, January 1–June 15, 1931.
34 Telegram no. 6, May 14, 1931, from McGarrah to Harrison. CUL, HP, Box 16, binder 36, Personal Cables, 1930–35.
35 Note, April 2, 1931, by Harrison on telephone conversation with Stimson on April 1, 1931. CUL, HP, Box 16, binder 36, Personal Cables, 1930–35.
36 The Federal Reserve regulations did not allow member banks to make advances secured by bills. Instead, the Federal Reserve Bank purchased individual bills when it participated in central bank credits. Telegram no. 4, May 14, 1931, from Harrison to McGarrah. FRBNY, C261.1, National Bank (Austrian Nat'l Bank) Credit, May 1931–December 1932, 1 of 2.
37 Telegram, May 14, 1931, from Harrison to Meyer; letter, May 15, 1931, from Meyer to Harrison; and telegram no. 308, May 18, 1931, from Harrison to the BIS. FRBNY, C261.1, National Bank (Austrian Nat'l Bank) Credit, May 1931–December 1932, 1 of 2.
38 Telegram, May 14, 1931, from Fraser to Rodd. BISA, 7.18.9, Confidential papers on Austria and Hungary by Mr Rodd, 1931.
39 Letter, May 14, 1931, from Rodd to Fraser. BISA, 7.18.9, Confidential papers on Austria and Hungary by Mr Rodd, 1931.
40 Letter, May 14, 1931, from Rodd to Fraser. BISA, 7.18.9, Confidential papers on Austria and Hungary by Mr Rodd, 1931.
41 'Note on the Austrian National Bank Statement of the 15th May'. BISA, 6.30. II/1 Granting of Credit of 100,000,000 Schilling to Austrian National Bank, 1931.
42 'Note on the Austrian National Bank Statement of the 15th May'. BISA, 6.30. II/1 Granting of Credit of 100,000,000 Schilling to Austrian National Bank, 1931.
43 'Note on the Austrian National Bank Statement of the 15th May' probably written by Rodd on May 16, and telegram no. 7, May 16, 1931, from Rodd to Fraser. BISA, 6.30. II/1 Granting of Credit of 100,000,000 Schilling to Austrian National Bank, 1931.
44 'Note on the Austrian National Bank Statement of the 15th May'. BEA, OV28–35, Austria Oesterreichische Nationalbank, January 5–December 31, 1931.
45 Telegram no. 7, May 15, 1931, from McGarrah to Harrison. FRBNY, C261.1, National Bank (Austrian Nat'l Bank) Credit, May 1931–December 1932, 1 of 2.
46 'The Credit-Anstalt', *The Economist*, May 16, 1931.
47 Telegrams, May 16, 1931, from Simon to Rodd. BISA, 6.30. II/1 Granting of Credit of 100,000,000 Schilling to Austrian National Bank, 1931.
48 Telegram no. 3, May 16, 1931, at 7 p.m. from Simon to Rodd. BISA, 7.18.9, Confidential papers on Austria and Hungary by Mr Rodd, 1931.
49 'Note on foreign exchange position of the CA', May 17, by Simon. BISA, 7.18.9, Confidential papers on Austria and Hungary by Mr Rodd, 1931.
50 For a full list of board members, see Toniolo, with the assistance of Clement, *Central Bank Cooperation*, 661–66.

51 Bank for International Settlements, 'Second Annual Report. April 1, 1931 – March 31, 1932' (Basle, Switzerland, 1932), 21.
52 'Note on the meeting of governors held in Basle on Sunday, the 17th May 1931'. BEA, OV28/3, Country Files Austria, January 1–June 15, 1931.
53 'Note on the foreign exchange position of the C.A.' May 17, 1931, by Simon. BISA, 7.18.9, Confidential papers on Austria and Hungary by Mr Rodd, 1931.
54 'Note on the meeting of governors held in Basle on Sunday, the 17th May 1931'. BEA, OV28/3, Country Files Austria, January 1–June 15, 1931.
55 'Note on the meeting of governors held in Basle on Sunday, the 17th May 1931'. BEA, OV28/3, Country Files Austria, January 1–June 15, 1931.
56 Carlisle MacDonald, 'French Seek to Win Vienna with a Loan', *The New York Times*, May 18, 1931.
57 Telegram no. 308, May 18, 1931, from Bank for International Settlements to the Federal Reserve Bank of New York. FRBNY, C261.1, National Bank (Austrian Nat'l Bank) Credit, May 1931–December 1932, 1 of 2.
58 'International Bank Notes (Letter No. 12)', by Merle Cochran, May 19, 1931. See also 'International Bank Notes (Letter No. 13)', by Merle Cochran, May 21, 1931. NARA, RG39, Box 104, Entry 145, Folder: 'G783.5 Special Report Confidential Letters (1-24)'.
59 Hansen, 'Cooperate or Free Ride?'
60 Toniolo, with the assistance of Clement, *Central Bank Cooperation*, 91–93. For the distribution of the credit, see p. 108. See also Cottrell, 'The Bank of England'. See also telegrams, May 26, 1931, from Bank of Greece to BIS and telegrams, May 27, 1931, from Bank Polski and Nederlandsche Bank to BISA, 7.18.2. MCG.1. Papers Gates W McGarrah and Leon Fraser. Credit Anstalt Crisis, 1931.
61 Carlisle MacDonald, 'World Bank Offers Austria $14,000,000', *The New York Times*, May 19, 1931.
62 Telegram no. 8, May 20, 1931, from McGarrah to Harrison. CUL, HP, Box 16, binder 36, Personal Cables, 1930–35.
63 See 'Diary of Montagu Collet Norman – May 1931', www.bankofengland.co.uk/-/media/boe/files/archive/montagu-norman-diary/1931/may-1931.pdf (accessed December 26, 2023).

## Chapter 4

1 Telegram no. 163/31, May 18, 1931, from Harrison to Norman. CUL, HP, Box 9, binder 20, Bank of England, January–December 1931.
2 Telegram no. 136/31, May 19, 1931, from Harvey to Harrison. CUL, HP, Box 9, binder 20, Bank of England, January–December 1931.
3 Letter, May 18, 1931, from S.D. Waley, Treasury Department to B.G. Catterns, Bank of England. BEA, OV28/3, Country Files Austria, January 1–June 15, 1931. See also Aguado, 'The Credit Anstalt Crisis', 211.
4 Letter, May 16, 1931, from Max Warburg to Lionel de Rothschild. RA, Correspondence Department, 111/521.
5 Telegram #31/4734, May 15, 1931, from Morgan Grenfell to J.P. Morgan. JPM, ARC 1221, Morgan Bank European Papers. Austrian Bonds (I0), February 18–May 15, 1931.

6 Telegram #31/2201, May 16, 1931, from J.P. Morgan to Morgan Grenfell. JPM, ARC 1221, Morgan Bank European Papers. Austrian Bonds (II), May 16–June 29, 1931.
7 Telegram #31/4740, May 18, 1931, from Morgan Grenfell to J.P. Morgan, 1931. JPM, ARC 1221, Morgan Bank European Papers. Austrian Bonds (II), May 16–June 29, 1931. See also Minutes of the Meeting between Morgan Grenfell, Rothschild & Sons, Schroders and Barings: 'Austria. Meeting at 23 Great Winchester Street, E.C. on 18th May 1931'. RA, 111/521, Correspondence Department.
8 Telegram #31/4741, May 18, 1931, from Morgan Grenfell to J.P. Morgan. JPM, ARC 1221 Morgan Bank European Papers. Austrian Bonds (II), May 16–June 29, 1931. See also Minutes of the Meeting between Morgan Grenfell, Rothschild & Sons, Schroders and Barings: 'Austria. Meeting at 23 Great Winchester Street, E.C. on 18th May 1931'. RA, 111/521, Correspondence Department.
9 Telegram #31/4743, May 18, 1931, 7.50 p.m., from Morgan Grenfell to J.P. Morgan. JPM, ARC 1221 Morgan Bank European Papers. Austrian Bonds (II), May 16–June 29, 1931. See also telegram, May 18, 1931, from Dr. Juch to Charles Grenfell. RA, 111/521, Correspondence Department.
10 Telegram #31/2205, May 19, 1931, from J.P. Morgan to Morgan Grenfell. JPM, ARC 1221 Morgan Bank European Papers. Austrian Bonds (II), May 16–June 29, 1931.
11 Copy of cable #31/4755, May 20, 1931, from Morgan Grenfell to Dr. Juch, Finance Minister, Vienna. RA, Correspondence Department, 111/521.
12 Telegram #87/427, May 19, 1931, from Morgan & Cie to J.P. Morgan. JPM, ARC 1221 Morgan Bank European Papers. Austrian Bonds (II), May 16–June 29, 1931.
13 Telegram #66.874, May 20, 1931, from J.P. Morgan to Morgan & Cie. JPM, ARC 1221 Morgan Bank European Papers. Austrian Bonds (II), May 16–June 29, 1931.
14 Telegram #87.432, May 20, 1931, from Morgan & Cie to J.P. Morgan. JPM, ARC 1221 Morgan Bank European Papers. Austrian Bonds (II), May 16–June 29, 1931.
15 'Note on the foreign exchange position of the C.A.' May 17, 1931, by Simon. BISA, 7.18.9, Confidential papers on Austria and Hungary by Mr Rodd, 1931.
16 'Note on the foreign exchange position of the C.A.' May 17,1931, by Simon. BISA, 7.18.9, Confidential papers on Austria and Hungary by Mr Rodd, 1931.
17 'Note on the foreign exchange position of the C.A.' May 17, 1931, by Simon. BISA, 7.18.9, Confidential papers on Austria and Hungary by Mr Rodd, 1931.
18 Meeting, May 27, 1931, Bank of England's Committee of Treasury. BEA, G8/60, Minutes of the Committee of Treasury – March 1931 to June 1932. For a discussion of the moratorium vs a guarantee, see Stiefel, *Finanzdiplomatie und Weltwirtschaftskrise*, 31–35.
19 Note on telephone message from Dr. Simon to Rodd, May 18, 1931, 4.10 p.m. BISA, 6.30. II/1 Granting of Credit of 100,000,000 Schilling to Austrian National Bank, 1931.
20 Toniolo, with the assistance of Clement, *Central Bank Cooperation*, 92.
21 Telegram, May 19, 1931, from Simon to Fraser. BISA, 7.18.2. MCG.1. Papers Gates W McGarrah and Leon Fraser. Credit Anstalt Crisis, 1931.
22 Letter, May 20, 1931, from Parker Gilbert to Harrison with attached telegram no. 31/2208, May 19, 1931. FRBNY, C261.1, National Bank (Austrian Nat'l Bank) Credit, May 1931–December 1932, 1 of 2.

23 Horn, *J. P. Morgan & Co.*, 125–27.

24 Letter, May 20, 1931, with attached telegram no. 31/2208 from Gilbert to Harrison. FRBNY, C261.1, National Bank (Austrian Nat'l Bank) Credit, May 1931–December 1932, 1 of 2.

25 Telegram, May 21, 1931, from Austrian National Bank to Federal Reserve Bank of New York. CUL, HP, Box 17, binder 37, Miscellaneous Cables, 1925–32.

26 Letter, May 19, 1931, from Morgan Grenfell to Morgan & Cie. JPM, ARC 1221, Morgan Bank European Papers. Austrian Bonds (II), May 16–June 29, 1931; Telegram, May 20, 1931, from Morgan Grenfell to J.P. Morgan. FRBNY, C261.1, Oesterreichische National Bank (Austrian Nat'l Bank) Credit, May 1931–December 1932, 2 of 2.

27 Telegram, May 20, 1931, from Morgan Grenfell to Dr. Juch. See also 'Austria, Meeting at 23 Great Winchester Street, E.C. on 18th May1931'. RA, 111/521, Correspondence Department.

28 Telegram, May 19, 1931, from Simon to Fraser. BISA, 7.18.2. MCG.1. Papers Gates W McGarrah and Leon Fraser. Credit Anstalt Crisis, 1931; telegram no. 4, May, 20, 1931, from Simon to Fraser. BISA, 7.18.9, Confidential papers on Austria and Hungary by Mr Rodd, 1931. For an explanation of the acceptance market, see Accominotti, 'London Merchant Banks', 6–9.

29 Letter, May 20, 1931, with attached telegram no. 31/2208, from Gilbert to Harrison and telegram #31/4756, May 20, 1931, from Morgan Grenfell to J.P. Morgan. FRBNY, C261.1, National Bank (Austrian Nat'l Bank) Credit, May 1931–December 1932, 1 of 2. Meeting, May 20, 1931, Bank of England's Committee of Treasury. BEA, G8/60, Minutes of the Committee of Treasury - Mar 1931 to June 1932.

30 Telegram #31/4756, May 20, 1931, from Morgan Grenfell to J.P. Morgan. FRBNY, C261.1, Oesterreichische National Bank (Austrian Nat'l Bank) Credit, May 1931–December 1932, 2 of 2.

31 Geoffrey Jones, 'Public Policy and British Multinational Banks, 1914–1982', *Business and Economic History* 21 (1992): 209–18; Bernard Pares, 'Sir Peter Bark', *The Slavonic and East European Review* 16, no. 46 (1937): 189–93. Peter Bark was not the only British on the board of Credit Anstalt. Other members were Otto Niemeyer, an adviser to Governor Norman, and Henry Strakosch, an Austrian born British financier. The German banker Max Warburg was also member of the Credit Anstalt's board. Clemens Jobst and Hans Kernbauer, *The Quest for Stable Money: Central Banking in Austria, 1816–2016* (Frankfurt: Campus Verlag, 2016), 176.

32 Telegram #31/4756, May 20, 1931, from Morgan Grenfell to J.P. Morgan. FRBNY, C261.1, Oesterreichische National Bank (Austrian Nat'l Bank) Credit, May 1931–December 1932, 2 of 2.

33 Telegram, May 22, 1931, from Oesterreichische Nationalbank to Federal Reserve Bank of New York. CUL, HP, Box 17, binder 37, Miscellaneous Cables, 1925–32.

34 'Note on the meeting of governors held in Basle on Sunday, the 17th May 1931'. BEA, OV28/3, Country Files Austria, January 1–June 15, 1931.

35 'Telephone message received from mr. Rodd at 12.5 p.m.' May 23, 1931. BEA, OV28/3, Country Files Austria, January 1–June 15, 1931.

36 'Telephone message received from mr. Rodd at 12.30 p.m.' May 23, 1931. BEA, OV28/3, Country Files Austria, January 1–June 15, 1931. See also Cottrell, 'The Bank of England', 417.
37 'Telephone message received from mr. Rodd at 1 p.m.' May 23, 1931. BEA, OV28/3, Country Files Austria, January 1–June 15, 1931.
38 Memorandum, May 23, 1931, by Stephany. RA, 111/521, Correspondence Department.
39 'Memorandum of 23 May, 1931, by B.C.G.' BEA, OV28/3, Country Files Austria, January 1–June 15, 1931.
40 This story is analysed in detail in Aguado, 'The Credit Anstalt Crisis'.
41 'Telephone message sent to Dr. Bruins at the Austrian National Bank at 1.30 p.m. to-day at the Governor's request', dated June 2, 1931. BEA, OV28/3, Austria Country File, January 14–June 15, 1931.
42 'Memorandum of 23 May 1931 by B.G.C.' BEA, OV28/3, Country Files Austria, January 1–June 15, 1931.
43 Telegram no. 11, May 23, 1931, from McGarrah to Harrison. FRBNY, C261.1, National Bank (Austrian Nat'l Bank) Credit, May 1931–December 1932, 1 of 2.
44 'Memorandum, 23rd May 1931'. RA, 111/521, Correspondence Department.
45 'Memorandum, 23rd May 1931', by Stephany. RA, 111/521, Correspondence Department.
46 Letter, May 23, 1931, to 'Dear Mr. Lionel'. The author of the letter is unknown, but it is probably Samuel Stephany, general manager of Rotschild & Sons. RA, 111/521, Correspondence Department.
47 'Memorandum, 23rd May 1931'. RA, 111/521, Correspondence Department.
48 'Memorandum, 23rd May 1931'. RA, 111/521, Correspondence Department.
49 'Memorandum, 23rd May 1931'. RA, 111/521, Correspondence Department.
50 'Note of a Conversation with Dr. Simon at 10.45 a.m. on the 25th May 1931' by Siepmann. BEA, OV28/3, Country Files Austria, January 1–June 15, 1931.
51 Telegram no. 142/31, May 25, 1931, from Norman to Harrison. CUL, HP, Box 9, binder 20, Bank of England, January–December 1931.

## Chapter 5

1 Telegram no. 143/31, May 25, 1931, from Norman to Harrison. CUL, HP, Box 9, binder 20, Bank of England, January–December 1931. For Norman's and the British view of the National Bank and the appointment of Reisch as president, see Marcus, *Austrian Reconstruction*, 147–50; Kernbauer, 'Central Bank Policy', 112–13.
2 Telegram no. 143/31, May 25, 1931, from Norman to Harrison. CUL, HP, Box 9, binder 20, Bank of England, January–December 1931.
3 Telegram no. 172/31, May 25, 1931, from Harrison to Norman. CUL, HP, Box 9, binder 20, Bank of England, January–December 1931.
4 Cable #31/4766, May 25, 1931, 12 noon, from Morgan Grenfell to J.P. Morgan. RA, 31/8, file 31/1, Secretariat Department, Correspondence (ACA). American Committee, Files 1+2, May 1931–December 1932.

5 Cable #31/2222, May 26, 1931, 10 a.m., from J.P. Morgan to Morgan Grenfell dated. RA, 31/8, file 31/1, Secretariat Department, Correspondence (ACA). American Committee, Files 1+2, May 1931–December 1932.
6 Cable #31/2222, May 26, 1931, 10 a.m., from J.P. Morgan to Morgan Grenfell. RA, 31/8, file 31/1, Secretariat Department, Correspondence (ACA). American Committee, Files 1+2, May 1931–December 1932.
7 Copy of telegram #31/4768, May 26, 1931, from Morgan Grenfell to J.P. Morgan. RA, 31/8, file 31/1, Secretariat Department, Correspondence (ACA). American Committee, Files 1+2, May 1931–December 1931.
8 Copy of telegram #87.444, May 26, 1931, from Morgan et Cie to J.P. Morgan. RA, 31/8, file 31/1, Secretariat Department, Correspondence (ACA). American Committee, Files 1+2, May 1931–December 1931. See also telegram in JPM, ARC 1221 Morgan Bank European Papers. Austrian Bonds (II), May 16–June 29, 1931.
9 Telegram, May 26, 1931, from Morgan et Cie to J.P. Morgan. RA, 31/8, file 31/1, Secretariat Department, Correspondence (ACA). American Committee, Files 1+2, May 1931–December 1931.
10 Letter, May 26, 1931, from Lionel de Rothschild to 'My dear Cousins'. RA, Correspondence Department, 111/521.
11 Copy of telegram #31/4768, May 26, 1931, from Morgan Grenfell to J.P. Morgan. RA, 31/8, file 31/1, Secretariat Department, Correspondence (ACA). American Committee, Files 1+2, May 1931–December 1931.
12 'Credit Anstalt Affairs. London Committee Appointed', *Financial Times*, May 27, 1931.
13 Telegram no. 145/31, May 26, 1931, from Norman to Harrison. FRBNY, C261.1, National Bank (Austrian Nat'l Bank) Credit, May 1931–December 1932, 1 of 2.
14 'Vienna Credit Bank Still in Need of Aid', *The New York Times*, May 27, 1931.
15 'Austria Fights off Financial Crash', *The New York Times*, May 28, 1931.
16 Copy of telegram #31/4768, May 26, 1931, from Morgan Grenfell to J.P. Morgan. RA, 31/8, file 31/1, Secretariat Department, Correspondence (ACA). American Committee, Files 1+2, May 1931–December 1931. See also letter, May 26, 1931, from Morgan Grenfell to Morgan & Cie. JPM, ARC 1221 Morgan Bank European Papers. Austrian Bonds (II), May 16–June 29, 1931.
17 'Austria'. Letter, May 27, 1931, from N.D. Jay, Morgan & Cie to Morgan Grenfell partners. JPM, ARC 1221 Morgan Bank European Papers. Austrian Bonds (II), May 16–June 29, 1931.
18 Telegram #87/452, May 29, 1931, from Morgan & Cie to J.P. Morgan. JPM, ARC 1221 Morgan Bank European Papers. Austrian Bonds (II), May 16–June 29, 1931.
19 Telegram #66.898, May 29, 1931, 6.40 p.m., from J.P. Morgan to Morgan & Cie. JPM, ARC 1221, Box 14, Morgan Bank European Papers. Folder, Cables received, May 16–June 30, 1931, 4-B, (111-248).
20 Telegram, May 26, 1931, from Paul Warburg to Rothschild. RA, 31/8, file 31/1, Secretariat Department, Correspondence (ACA). American Committee, Files 1+2, May 1931–December 1931.
21 Telegram #31/2223, May 27, 1931, from J.P. Morgan to Morgan Grenfell. RA, 31/8, file 31/1, Secretariat Department, Correspondence (ACA). American Committee,

Files 1+2, May 1931–December 1931. See also telegram in JPM, ARC 1221, Morgan Bank European Papers, Box 36, Folder, Austrian Bonds (II), May 16–June 29, 1931. In 1922 the Danish bank 'Landmandsbanken' found itself in trouble and was reconstructed with new capital. In 1923 the Danish Parliament passed a law guaranteeing the bank's liabilities. Finally, in 1928 the bank had to be reconstructed again, and this time the government took full ownership of the bank. See Per H. Hansen, 'Making Sense of Financial Crisis and Scandal: A Danish Bank Failure in the First Era of Finance Capitalism', *Enterprise & Society* 13, no. 3 (2012): 672–706; Per H. Hansen, 'From Growth to Crisis: The Danish Banking System from 1850 to the Interwar Years', *Scandinavian Economic History Review* 39, no. 3 (1991): 20–40.

22 Telegram #31/4771, May 27, 1931, from Morgan Grenfell to J.P. Morgan. RA, 31/8, file 31/1, Secretariat Department, Correspondence (ACA). American Committee, Files 1+2, May 1931–December 1931. See also telegram in JPM, ARC 1221, Morgan Bank European Papers. Box 36, Folder, Austrian Bonds (II), May 16–June 29, 1931.

23 Telegram #31/4771, May 27, 1931, from Morgan Grenfell to J.P. Morgan. RA, 31/8, file 31/1, Secretariat Department, Correspondence (ACA). American Committee, Files 1+2, May 1931–December 1931. See also telegram in JPM, ARC 1221 Morgan Bank European Papers. Austrian Bonds (II), May 16–June 29, 1931.

24 Telegram no. 145/31, May 26, 1931, from Norman to Harrison. FRBNY, C261.1, National Bank (Austrian Nat'l Bank) Credit, May 1931–December 1932, 1 of 2.

25 Letter, May 16, 1931, from Max Warburg to Lionel de Rothschild. RA, 111/521, Correspondence Department.

26 Telegram #31/2224, May 28, 1931, from J.P. Morgan to Morgan. ARC 1221 Morgan Bank European Papers. Austrian Bonds (II), May 16–June 29, 1931.

27 Telegram #31/2225, May 28, 1931, from J.P. Morgan to Morgan. ARC 1221 Morgan Bank European Papers. Austrian Bonds (II), May 16–June 29, 1931.

28 Kernbauer, 'The Policy', 16–17.

29 'Note of a telephone conversation with Dr. Brauneis held at 11.15 a.m. on the 26th May, 1931' by Siepmann, May 26, 1931. BEA, OV28/3, Austria Country File, January 14–June 15, 1931.

30 'Note of a telephone conversation with Dr. Brauneis held at 11.15 a.m. on the 26th May, 1931' by Siepmann, May 26, 1931. BEA, OV28/3, Austria Country File, January 14–June 15, 1931.

31 'Austria', note, May 26, 1931, by Siepmann. BEA, OV28/3, Austria Country File, January 14–June 15, 1931. The conversation between Siepmann and Rodd is also mentioned in 'Conversation between mr. Siepmann and mr. Rodd from London'. Note, May 26, 1931. BISA, 6.30. II/1 Granting of Credit of 100,000,000 Schilling to Austrian National Bank, 1931.

32 Telegram, May 26, 1931, from BIS to the ANB. BISA, 7.18.9, Confidential papers on Austria and Hungary by Mr Rodd, 1931.

33 Memo, May 27, 1931, by Harry Siepmann. BEA, OV28/3, Austria Country File, January 14–June 15, 1931. Copy of memo is also in RA, Box 31/7, file 31/7, Secretariat Department, Correspondence A.C.A. Credit Anstalt (General), File 5 of 5, June–December 1931.

34 Telegram no. 13, May 27, 1931, from McGarrah to Harrison. FRBNY, C261.1, National Bank (Austrian Nat'l Bank) Credit, May 1931–December 1932, 1 of 2.

35 Telegram no. 150/31, May 27, 1931, from Norman to Harrison. FRBNY, C261.1, National Bank (Austrian Nat'l Bank) Credit, May 1931–December 1932, 1 of 2.

## Chapter 6

1 Note on 'Austria', May 26, 1931, by Siepmann. BEA, OV28/3, Country Files Austria, January 1–June 15, 1931.
2 Note 'The Kredit Anstalt' on telephone conversation with Dr. Luther at 5.30 p.m., May 26, 1931, by Siepmann. BEA, OV28/3, Country Files Austria, January 1–June 15, 1931.
3 Telegram #87.429, May 19, 1931, from Morgan & Cie to J.P. Morgan. ARC 1221, Box 14, Morgan Bank European Papers. Folder, Cables received, May 16–June 30, 1931, 4-B, (114-254).
4 Telegram no. 177/31, May 26, 1931, from Harrison to Norman. FRBNY C261.1, National Bank (Austrian Nat'l Bank) Credit, May 1931–December 1932, 1 of 2.
5 Telegram no. 148/31, May 27, 1931, from Norman to Harrison. CUL, HP, Box 9, binder 20, Bank of England, January–December 1931. See also telegram no. 13, May 27, 1931, from McGarrah to Harrison. FRBNY, C261.1, National Bank (Austrian Nat'l Bank) Credit, May 1931–December 1932, 1 of 2. For a full list of New York credit lines, see 'Kredit Anstalt', #65A, note, May 28, 1931. BEA, OV28/3, Austria Country File, January 14–June 15, 1931. According to Cohan, Lazard Brothers' claim on Credit Anstalt was actually £200,000, a much higher amount, maybe explaining Kindersley's engagement in the International Committee, see William D. Cohan, *The Last Tycoons: The Secret History of Lazard Freres & Co.* (New York: Doubleday, 2007), 34.
6 Telegram no. 12, May 26, 1931, from McGarrah to Harrison. FRBNY, C261.1, National Bank (Austrian Nat'l Bank) Credit, May 1931–December 1932, 1 of 2, and letter, May 26, 1931, from McGarrah to Jay, Morgan & Cie, Paris. BISA, 7.18.2. MCG.1. Papers Gates W McGarrah and Leon Fraser. Credit Anstalt Crisis, 1931.
7 Telegram no. 150/31, May 27, 1931, from Norman to Harrison. BEA, OV32/7, Federal Reserve Bank of New York, Confidential Cables, 1931.
8 Telegram no. 181/31, May 27, 1931, from Harrison to Norman. FRBNY, C261.1, National Bank (Austrian Nat'l Bank) Credit, May 1931–December 1932, 1 of 2.
9 Telegram no. 152/31, May 28, 1931, from Norman to Harrison. FRBNY, C261.1, National Bank (Austrian Nat'l Bank) Credit, May 1931–December 1932, 1 of 2.
10 Telegram no. 14, May 28, 1931, from McGarrah to Harrison. FRBNY, C261.1, National Bank (Austrian Nat'l Bank) Credit, May 1931–December 1932, 1 of 2.
11 Telegram, May 27, 1931, received on May 28, at 8.05 a.m. from 'Devisenleitung' to Pierre Quesnay, BIS. BISA, 7.18.9, Confidential papers on Austria and Hungary by Mr Rodd, 1931.
12 Note, May 28, 1931, by Simon or Rodd. BISA, 7.18.9, Confidential papers on Austria and Hungary by Mr Rodd, 1931.
13 Note, May 28, 1931, by Simon or Rodd. BISA, 7.18.9, Confidential papers on Austria and Hungary by Mr Rodd, 1931.
14 Telegram, May 28, 1931, 4.45 p.m., from Austrian National Bank to BIS. BISA, 7.18.9, Confidential papers on Austria and Hungary by Mr Rodd, 1931.

15 Quoted in telegram, May 28, 1931, from Chanler Jr. FRBNY, C261, Austria – Oesterreichische Creditanstalt, Wiener Bankverein.

16 Urgent telegram, May 28, 1931, from the Austrian National Bank to Federal Reserve Bank of New York, and telegram no. 319, May 28, 1931, from the BIS to FRBNY. FRBNY, C261.1, National Bank (Austrian Nat'l Bank) Credit, May 1931–December 1932, 1 of 2.

17 Telegram (#4635), May 28, 1931, from Austrian National Bank to Federal Reserve Bank of New York. FRBNY, C261.1, National Bank (Austrian Nat'l Bank) Credit, May 1931–December 1932, 1 of 2.

18 Telegram no. 54, May 28, 1931, from Harrison to Austrian National Bank. FRBNY, C261.1, National Bank (Austrian Nat'l Bank) Credit, May 1931–December 1932, 1 of 2.

19 Telegram, May 28, 1931, from BIS to 'Devisenleitung'. BISA, 7.18.9, Confidential papers on Austria and Hungary by Mr Rodd, 1931.

20 Telegram, May 28, 1931, from BIS to ANB. BISA, 7.18.9, Confidential papers on Austria and Hungary by Mr Rodd, 1931.

21 Note, May 29, 1931. BISA, 7.18.9, Confidential papers on Austria and Hungary by Mr Rodd, 1931.

22 Note on 'Kredit Anstalt', May 29, 1931, by H.A.S. BEA, OV28/3, Country Files Austria, January 1–June 15, 1931.

23 Telegram no. 152/31, May 28, 1931, from Norman to Harrison. FRBNY, C261.1, National Bank (Austrian Nat'l Bank) Credit, May 1931–December 1932, 1 of 2. In the telegram, an 's' is added in handwriting to 'national bank', but it's fair to assume that Norman was referring to the Austrian National Bank.

24 Telegrams, May 28, 1931, from Austrian National Bank to Federal Reserve Bank of New York. FRBNY, C261.1, National Bank (Austrian Nat'l Bank) Credit, May 1931–December 1932, 1 of 2.

25 'Memorandum: Meeting of Board of Directors May 28, 1931'. CUL, HP. Box 23, binder 50, Discussion Notes: Volumes I, II & III, April 17, 1930–September 21, 1933.

26 Telegram no. 152/31, May 28, 1931, from Norman to Harrison. FRBNY, C261.1, National Bank (Austrian Nat'l Bank) Credit, May 1931–December 1932, 1 of 2.

27 For an interesting description of Rothschild & Sons and New Court in 1931, see Michael Bonavia, *London before I Forget* (Upton-upon-Severn: The Self Publishing Association Ltd, 1990), 105–25. I am grateful to Melanie Aspey, Director of the Rothschild Archive, for telling me about this text.

28 'Credit Anstalt London Committee. Minutes of Committee meeting held at New Court on Wednesday, 27th May 1931, at 3 p.m.' RA, 31/8, 31/24, Secretariat Department, Correspondence (A.C.A.) Original Minutes (being the basis for the draft minutes) May–June 1931.

29 'The Governor', note, May 28, 1931, from Siepmann to Norman. BEA, OV28/3, Country Files Austria, January 1–June 15, 1931. The note was forwarded to Lionel de Rothschild on the same day by Siepmann. RA, Box 31/7, file 31/7, Secretariat Department, Correspondence A.C.A. Credit Anstalt (General), File 5 of 5, June–December 1931.

30 'Statement made by the chairman at the meeting of Banks interested in Credit Anstalt held on 28/5/31'. RA, Box 31/7, file 31/7, Secretariat Department, Correspondence A.C.A. Credit Anstalt (General), File 5 of 5, June–December 1931.

31 'Sir Harry Goschen, British Banker, 79', *The New York Times*, July 10, 1945.
32 Note that 'credit' is added in hand. 'Minutes of a meeting held at New Court, . . . on Thursday, the 28th May, 1931, at 3.30 p.m.' RA, 31/8, 31/24, Secretariat Department, Correspondence (A.C.A.) Original Minutes (being the basis for the draft minutes) May–June 1931.
33 Telegram no. 31/4772, May 28, 1931, from Morgan Grenfell & Co. to J.P. Morgan. FRBNY, C261.1, National Bank (Austrian Nat'l Bank) Credit, May 1931–December 1932, 1 of 2.
34 Telegram no. 183/31, May 28, 1931, from Harrison to Norman. FRBNY, C261.1, National Bank (Austrian Nat'l Bank) Credit, May 1931–December 1932, 1 of 2.
35 'Kredit Anstalt', note for the Governor, May 28, 1931, by H.A.S. BEA, OV28/3, Country Files Austria, January 1–June 15, 1931.
36 For a discussion of the guarantee and the process in Austria that led to it, see Stiefel, *Finanzdiplomatie und Weltwirtschaftskrise*, 45–55.
37 Telegram, May 28, 1931, from Austrian National Bank to Federal Reserve Bank of New York. FRBNY, C261.1, National Bank (Austrian Nat'l Bank) Credit, May 1931–December 1932, 1 of 2.
38 'Minutes of a meeting held at New Court, . . . on Friday, the 29th May, 1931, at 12 noon'. RA, 31/8, 31/24, Secretariat Department, Correspondence (A.C.A.) Original Minutes (being the basis for the draft minutes) May–June 1931.
39 'Draft Minutes of Credit Anstalt International Committee meeting held at New Court . . . on Monday 1st June, 1931, at 2.30 p.m.' RA, 31/8, 31/24, Secretariat Department, Correspondence (A.C.A.) Original Minutes (being the basis for the draft minutes) May–June 1931.
40 Cable #31/2228, May 30, 1931, from J.P. Morgan & Co. to Morgan Grenfell. RA, 31/8, file 31/1, Secretariat Department, Correspondence (ACA). American Committee, Files 1+2, May 1931–December 1932.
41 Copy of telegram, May 29, 1931, at 11.00 p.m., from J.P. Morgan to Morgan Grenfell, and telegram no. 154, May 30, 1931, from Norman to Harrison. FRBNY, C261.1, National Bank (Austrian Nat'l Bank) Credit, May 1931–December 1932, 1 of 2. For the Norman quote, see letter, May 30, 1931, from Norman to Lionel de Rothschild. RA, 111/521, Correspondence Department.
42 'Credit Anstalt Affairs. International Bankers' Committee', *Financial Times*, June 2, 1931. See also Cable #31/4776, May 29, 1931, from Morgan Grenfell to J.P. Morgan & Co. RA, 31/8, file 31/1, Secretariat Department, Correspondence (ACA). American Committee, Files 1+2, May 1931–December 1932.
43 Cable #21/2232, received June 2, 1931, from J.P. Morgan & Co. to Morgan Grenfell. RA, 31/8, file 31/1, Secretariat Department, Correspondence (ACA). American Committee, Files 1+2, May 1931–December 1932.
44 Telegram (90), May 30, 1931, from Moret to Norman, and letter (90A), May 30, 1931, from Norman to Moret, May 30. BEA, OV28/3, Austria Country File, January 14–June 15, 1931.
45 'The Credit-Anstalt', *The Economist*, May 30, 1931.
46 'The Financial Situation', *Commercial and Financial Chronicle*, May 30, 1931.
47 Telegram, May 28, 1931, from BIS to ANB. BISA, 7.18.9, Confidential papers on Austria and Hungary by Mr Rodd, 1931.

48 Handwritten note on copy of telegram no. 183/31, May 28, 1931, from Harrison to Norman. BEA, OV32/7, Federal Reserve Bank of New York, Confidential Cables, 1931.
49 Letter (460), June 29, 1931, from Siepmann to Réné Charron. BEA, ADM25-5, Papers of Harry Siepmann Correspondence, January 1–June 20, 1931.
50 'International Bank Notes (Letter No. 13)', May 21, 1931, by Merle Cochran. NARA, RG39, Box 104, Entry 145, Folder: 'G783.5 Special Report Confidential Letters (1-24)'.
51 Note, May 29, 1931. BISA, 7.18.9, Confidential papers on Austria and Hungary by Mr Rodd, 1931.
52 'Kredit Anstalt' (91), note, May 30, 1931, by Siepmann. BEA, OV28/3, Austria Country File, January 14–June 15, 1931.
53 Telegram no. 16, May 30, 1931, from McGarrah to Harrison. FRBNY, C261.1, National Bank (Austrian Nat'l Bank) Credit, May 1931–December 1932, 1 of 2.
54 Note, May 28, 1931, 5.45 p.m. of phone call from Rodd, Basle to R.H.P., Bank of England. BISA, 7.18.9, Confidential papers on Austria and Hungary by Mr Rodd, 1931. See also Clarke, *Central Bank Cooperation*, 187.
55 'International Bank Notes (Letter no. 14)', June 1, 1931. NARA, RG39, Box 104, Entry 145, Folder: 'G783.5 Special Report Confidential Letters (1-24)'.
56 Note on 'Kredit Anstalt', May 29, 1931, by Siepmann. BEA, OV28/3, Country Files Austria, January 1–June 15, 1931.
57 'Press Communique', May 29, 1931, Bank for International Settlements. FRBNY, C261.1, National Bank (Austrian Nat'l Bank) Credit, May 1931–December 1932, 1 of 2.
58 Telegram, May 29, 1931, at 5 p.m., from BIS to Rodd. BIS, HA 6/30. II/1 Granting of Credit of 100,000,000. Schilling to Austrian National Bank. General Information.
59 Telegram, May 29, 1931, from Rodd to BIS. BISA, 6.30. II/1 Granting of Credit of 100,000,000 Schilling to Austrian National Bank, 1931.
60 Note on 'Kredit Anstalt', May 29, 1931, by Siepmann. BEA, OV28/3, Country Files Austria, January 1–June 15, 1931.
61 Letter, May 30, 1931, from McGarrah to Austrian National Bank. BISA, 6/30b II/I, Correspondence with Austrian National Bank, 1931.
62 Telegram, May 29, 1931, from Rodd to BIS. BISA, 6.30. II/1 Granting of Credit of 100,000,000 Schilling to Austrian National Bank, 1931.
63 Telegram, May 30, 1931, from Rodd to BIS. BISA, 6/30b II/I, Correspondence with Austrian National Bank, 1931.
64 Letter, May 30, 1931, from Rodd to McGarrah. BISA, 6/30b II/I, Correspondence with Austrian National Bank, 1931. Note, June 1, 1931, at 6 p.m., on telephone message to RHP/EL at BIS, and on 'Telephone message from mr. Rodd', June 4, 1931, at 4 p.m. BISA, 6.30. II/1 Granting of Credit of 100,000,000 Schilling to Austrian National Bank, 1931.
65 Letter, May 30, 1931, from Rodd to McGarrah. BISA, 6/30b II/I, Correspondence with Austrian National Bank, 1931.
66 Letter, May 30, 1931, from Rodd to McGarrah. BISA, 6/30b II/I, Correspondence with Austrian National Bank, 1931.
67 'International Bank Notes (Letter no. 14)', June 1, 1931. NARA, RG39, Box 104, Entry 145, Folder: 'G783.5 Special Report Confidential Letters (1-24)'.

## Chapter 7

1 Telegram, May 29, 1931, from BIS to Rodd. BISA, 6.30. II/1 Granting of Credit of 100,000,000 Schilling to Austrian National Bank, 1931. For the suggestion of Rydbeck, see note on 'Kredit Anstalt', May 29, 1931, by Siepmann. BEA, OV28/3, Country Files Austria, January 1–June 15, 1931.

2 Telegram no. 16, May 30, 1931, from McGarrah to Harrison. FRBNY, C261.1, National Bank (Austrian Nat'l Bank) Credit, May 1931–December 1932, 1 of 2. See also telegram, May 29, 1931, 2.45 a.m., from Dr. Reisch to BIS. BISA, 7.18.9, Confidential papers on Austria and Hungary by Mr Rodd, 1931.

3 'Copy of telegram received from Austrian Credit Anstalt, Vienna, dated 29th May, 1931'. BEA, OV28/3, Country Files Austria, January 1–June 15, 1931.

4 Letter (359), May 30, 1931, from Siepmann to Dr. J. Nathan. BEA, ADM25-5, Papers of Harry Arthur Siepmann. Correspondence, January 1–June 30, 1931.

5 Handwritten note, May 29, 1931, at 5.35 p.m., by Siepmann on 'Copy of telegram received from Austrian Credit Anstalt, Vienna, dated 29th May, 1931' BEA, 28/3, Country Files Austria, January 1–June 15, 1931.

6 Note on 'Kredit Anstalt', May 29, 1931. BEA, OV28/3, Country Files Austria, January 1–June 15, 1931.

7 'Draft Minutes of Credit Anstalt International Committee meeting held at New Court ... on Monday 1st June, 1931, at 2.30 p.m.' RA, 31/8, 31/24, Secretariat Department, Correspondence (A.C.A.) Original Minutes (being the basis for the draft minutes) May–June 1931.

8 Cable #31/4781, June 1, 1931, from Morgan Grenfell to J.P. Morgan & Co. RA, 31/8, 31/1, Secretariat Department, Correspondence (ACA). American Committee, Files 1+2, May 1931–December 1932.

9 Cable #31/4785, June 2, 1931, from Morgan Grenfell to J.P. Morgan & Co. See also cable 21/2232, June 2, 1931, from J.P. Morgan to Morgan Grenfell; and cable, June 2, 1931, from Gannon, Chanler and Grant to 'Head Office'. RA, 31/8, 31/1, Secretariat Department, Correspondence (ACA). American Committee, Files 1+2, May 1931–December 1932.

10 Cable #31/4785, June 2, 1931, from Morgan Grenfell to J.P. Morgan & Co. See also cable 21/2232, June 2, 1931, from J.P. Morgan to Morgan Grenfell; and cable, June 2, 1931, from Gannon, Chanler and Grant to 'Head Office'. RA, 31/8, 31/1, Secretariat Department, Correspondence (ACA). American Committee, Files 1+2, May 1931–December 1932.

11 Note, 'Urgent message from mr Rodd by telephone from Vienna', May 30, 1931, at 12.15. BISA, 7.18.9, Confidential papers on Austria and Hungary by Mr Rodd, 1931.

12 Note #54, '2nd June 1931'. RA, Box 31/7, file 31/7, Secretariat Department, Correspondence A.C.A. Credit Anstalt (General), File 5 of 5, June–December 1931.

13 Telegram no. 16, May 30, 1931, from McGarrah to Harrison. FRBNY, C261.1, National Bank (Austrian Nat'l Bank) Credit, May 1931–December 1932, 1 of 2.

14 Letter, May 30, 1931, from Rodd to Governor Norman. BISA, 7.18.9, Confidential papers on Austria and Hungary by Mr Rodd, 1931.

15 Meetings, May 13, and June 3, 1931, of Bank of England's Committee of Treasury. BEA, G8/60, Minutes of the Committee of Treasury – March 1931 to June 1932.

Boyce, *The Great Interwar Crisis*, 301. See also Cottrell, 'Austria between Diplomats', 299–300.

16 Cable #2 from BIS to Fraser. BISA. MCG.5. Correspondence regarding Leon Fraser's trip to New York in June 1931.

17 Telegram (90), May 30, 1931, from Moret to Norman and Norman's letter (90A) to Moret, May 30, 1931. BEA, OV28/3, Austria Country File, January 14–June 15, 1931.

18 Telegram no. 184/31, June 1, 1931, from Harrison to Norman. FRBNY, C261.1, National Bank (Austrian Nat'l Bank) Credit, May 1931–December 1932, 1 of 2.

19 Note (58), June 1, 1931, from Siepmann to 'The Governor', dated June 1, 1931. BEA, OV28-35, Austria Oesterreichische Nationalbank, January 5–December 31, 1931.

20 Telegram no. 155/31, June 2, 1931, from Norman to Harrison. FRBNY, C261.1, National Bank (Austrian Nat'l Bank) Credit, May 1931–December 1932, 1 of 2.

21 Telegram no. 155/31, June 2, 1931, from Norman to Harrison. FRBNY, C261.1, National Bank (Austrian Nat'l Bank) Credit, May 1931–December 1932, 1 of 2.

22 John Weitz, *Hitler's Banker: Hjalmar Horace Greeley Schacht*, 1st ed. (Boston: Little, Brown and Company, 1997), 108–15.

23 Telegram no. 155/31, June 2, 1931, from Norman to Harrison. FRBNY, C261.1, National Bank (Austrian Nat'l Bank) Credit, May 1931–December 1932, 1 of 2.

24 Letter, June 1, 1931, from Rodd to Governor Norman. BISA, 7.18.9, Confidential papers on Austria and Hungary by Mr Rodd, 1931.

25 'International Bank Notes (Letter no. 14)', June 1, 1931. NARA, RG39, Box 104, Entry 145, Folder: 'G783.5 Special Report Confidential Letters (1-24)'.

26 'Memorandum: Meeting of Executive Committee, June 1, 1931'. CUL, HP. Box 23, binder 50, Discussion Notes: Volumes I, II & III, April 17, 1930–September 21, 1933.

27 Note #54, '2nd June 1931'. RA, Box 31/7, file 31/7, Secretariat Department, Correspondence A.C.A. Credit Anstalt (General), File 5 of 5, June–December 1931.

28 Note, June 1, 1931, at 6 p.m., on telephone message to the RHP/EL at BIS. BISA, 6.30. II/1 Granting of Credit of 100,000,000 Schilling to Austrian National Bank, 1931.

29 G.E.R. Geyde, 'Vienna Bank Crisis Laid to Paris Plot', *The New York Times*, June 7, 1931.

30 Geyde, 'Vienna Bank Crisis'.

31 'Draft Minutes of CA International Committee meeting held at New Court . . . on Tuesday, 2nd June, 1931 at 2.30 p.m.' RA, 31/8, 31/24, Secretariat Department, Correspondence (A.C.A.) Original Minutes (being the basis for the draft minutes) May–June 1931.

32 'Lessons of the Austrian Crisis', June 2, 1931, by Simon, pp. 15–16. BEA, OV28/3, Country Files Austria, January 1–June 15, 1931.

33 'The Credit-Anstalt', *The Economist*, June 6, 1931, 1211.

34 'Austria', *The Economist*, June 6, 1931.

35 Letter, June 1, 1931, from Rodd to Governor Norman. BISA, 7.18.9, Confidential papers on Austria and Hungary by Mr Rodd, 1931.

36 Telegram no. 4, June 1, 1931, at 5.30 p.m. BISA, 6.30. II/1 Granting of Credit of 100,000,000 Schilling to Austrian National Bank, 1931.

37 Note on 'Telephone message from Mr. Rodd', June 4, 1931, at 4 p.m. BISA, 6.30. II/1 Granting of Credit of 100,000,000 Schilling to Austrian National Bank, 1931.
38 Note, 'One p.m. Basle report on the telephone', June 1, 1931, by Siepmann. BEA, OV28/3, Country Files Austria, January 1–June 15, 1931.
39 Telegram no. 4, June 1, 1931, at 5.30 p.m. BISA, 6.30. II/1 Granting of Credit of 100,000,000 Schilling to Austrian National Bank, 1931.
40 Note on 'Telephone message from mr. Rodd to P.Q. at the BIS, June 1, 1931, at 6.30 p.m.' BISA, 6.30. II/1 Granting of Credit of 100,000,000 Schilling to Austrian National Bank, 1931.
41 Note #54, '2nd June, 1931'. RA, Box 31/7, file 31/7, Secretariat Department, Correspondence A.C.A. Credit Anstalt (General), File 5 of 5, June–December 1931.
42 Personal and confidential letter (371), June 1, 1931, from Siepmann to Roger Auboin. BEA, ADM25-5, Papers of Harry Arthur Siepmann. Correspondence, January 1, 1931–June 30, 1931.
43 Note #109, 'Credit Anstalt', June 3, 1931, by Siepmann. BEA, OV28/3, Country File Austria, January 14–June 15, 1931. Also in RA, Box 31/7, file 31/7, Secretariat Department, Correspondence A.C.A. Credit Anstalt (General), File 5 of 5, June–December 1931.
44 Note #122, 'Credit Anstalt', June 3, 1931, by Siepmann. BEA, OV28/3, Country Files Austria, January 1–June 15, 1931. Also note 64 in RA, Box 31/7, file 31/7, Secretariat Department, Correspondence A.C.A. Credit Anstalt (General), File 5 of 5, June–December 1931.
45 Note on 'Telephone message from Rodd to BIS, June 3, 1931, at 5 p.m.' BISA, 6.30. II/1 Granting of Credit of 100,000,000 Schilling to Austrian National Bank, 1931.
46 Note #122, 'Credit Anstalt', June 3, 1931, by Siepmann. BEA, OV28/3, Country Files Austria, January 1–June 15, 1931. Also note 64 in RA, Box 31/7, file 31/7, Secretariat Department, Correspondence A.C.A. Credit Anstalt (General), File 5 of 5, June–December 1931.
47 Cable #31/4788, June 3, 1931, from Morgan Grenfell to J.P. Morgan & Co. RA, 31/8, file 31/1, Secretariat Department, Correspondence (ACA). American Committee, Files 1+2, May 1931–December 1932.
48 Meeting, June 3, 1931, of Bank of England's Committee of Treasury. BEA, G8/60, Minutes of the Committee of Treasury – March 1931 to June 1932.
49 Note on 'Telephone message from Mr. Rodd', June 4, 1931, at 4 p.m. BISA, 6.30. II/1 Granting of Credit of 100,000,000 Schilling to Austrian National Bank, 1931.
50 Note #68 'Credit Anstalt', June 4, 1931, by Siepmann. RA, Box 31/7, file 31/7, Secretariat Department, Correspondence A.C.A. Credit Anstalt (General), File 5 of 5, June–December 1931.
51 Telegram, June 4, 1931, at 5 p.m., from Rodd to BIS. BISA, 6.30. II/1 Granting of Credit of 100,000,000 Schilling to Austrian National Bank, 1931.
52 Telegrams, June 3 and June 5, 1931, from BIS to Rodd. BISA, 6.30. II/1 Granting of Credit of 100,000,000 Schilling to Austrian National Bank, 1931.
53 Note #68 'Credit Anstalt', June 4, 1931, by Siepmann. RA, Box 31/7, file 31/7, Secretariat Department, Correspondence A.C.A. Credit Anstalt (General), File 5 of 5, June–December 1931.
54 Telegram no. 57, June 3, 1931, from Moret to Harrison. CUL, HP, Box 14, binder 29, Bank of France, 1931.

55 Telegrams (126 and 127), June 4, 1931, from Norman to Moret and Rist. BEA, OV28/3, Austria Country File, January 14–June 15, 1931.
56 Telegram no. 159/31, June 3, 1931, from Norman to Harrison. CUL, HP, Box 9, binder 20, Bank of England, January–December 1931.
57 Telegram no. 77, June 3, 1931, from Harrison to Moret. CUL, HP, Box 14, binder 29, Bank of France, 1931.
58 Telegram no. 188/31, June 3, 1931, from Harrison to Norman. CUL, HP, Box 9, binder 20, Bank of England, January–December 1931.
59 Note, 'Vienna, June 3rd, 1931' by Rodd. BISA, 7.18.9, Confidential papers on Austria and Hungary by Mr Rodd, 1931.
60 'Notes on some aspects of the present Austrian situation', June 3, 1931, by Simon. BEA, OV28/3, Country Files Austria, January 1–June 15, 1931.
61 'Notes on some aspects of the present Austrian situation', June 3, 1931, by Simon. BEA, OV28/3, Country Files Austria, January 1–June 15, 1931.
62 Note of 'June 4, 1931. Herr Blessing has communicated the following' by Hülse. BISA, 7.18.9, Confidential papers on Austria and Hungary by Mr Rodd, 1931. See also telegram, June 5, 1931, from BIS to central banks. BISA, 7.18.2. MCG.1. Papers Gates W McGarrah and Leon Fraser. Credit Anstalt Crisis, 1931.
63 'Notes for report to Governors' meeting in Basel 7/8 June, 1931', June 5, 1931, probably by Rodd, p. 11. BISA, 7.18.9, Confidential papers on Austria and Hungary by Mr Rodd, 1931.
64 'Mr. Rodd's note prepared for the Governors' meeting at Basel, 7 & 8 of June', June 8, 1931, by Rodd. BISA, 7.18.9, Confidential papers on Austria and Hungary by Mr Rodd, 1931.
65 'Notes for report to Governors' meeting in Basel 7/8 June, 1931', June 5, 1931, p. 9. BISA, 7.18.9, Confidential papers on Austria and Hungary by Mr Rodd, 1931.
66 'Mr. Rodd's note prepared for the Governors' meeting at Basel, 7 & 8 of June', June 8, 1931, by Rodd. BISA, 7.18.9, Confidential papers on Austria and Hungary by Mr Rodd, 1931.
67 'Notes for report to Governors' meeting in Basel 7/8 June, 1931', June 5, 1931, probably by Rodd, pp. 10–11. BISA, 7.18.9, Confidential papers on Austria and Hungary by Mr Rodd, 1931.
68 Bagehot, *Lombard Street*, 32.
69 'Mr. Rodd's note prepared for the Governors' meeting at Basel, 7 & 8 of June', June 8, 1931, by Rodd. BISA, 7.18.9, Confidential papers on Austria and Hungary by Mr Rodd, 1931.
70 'Notes for report to Governors' meeting in Basel 7/8 June, 1931', June 5, 1931, probably by Rodd, pp. 11–12. BISA, 7.18.9, Confidential papers on Austria and Hungary by Mr Rodd, 1931.
71 Note on 'Telephone message from mr. Rodd at Vienna at 1.30 p.m. on the 5th of June, 1931' by C.A.G, June 5, 1931. BEA, OV28/3, Country Files Austria, January 1–June 15, 1931.
72 Note on 'Telephone message from mr. Rodd in Vienna received at 6.45 p.m. on the 5th June, 1931', June 5, 1931, by Siepmann. BEA, OV28/3, Country Files Austria, January 1–June 15, 1931.

## Chapter 8

1 Note by Bruins, Vienna, June 5, 1931. BISA, 7.18.9, Confidential papers on Austria and Hungary by Mr Rodd, 1931.
2 Note by Bruins, Vienna, June 5, 1931. BISA, 7.18.9, Confidential papers on Austria and Hungary by Mr Rodd, 1931.
3 Note by Bruins, Vienna, June 5, 1931. BISA, 7.18.9, Confidential papers on Austria and Hungary by Mr Rodd, 1931.
4 Note on 'Credit Anstalt', June 6, 1931, by C.A.G. BEA, OV28/3, Country Files Austria, January 1–June 15, 1931. On Walter W. Stewart, see Gardner Jackson, 'The American Signer of the Basle Report', *The New York Times*, January 3, 1932 and William P. Yohe, 'The Mysterious Career of Walter W. Stewart, Especially 1922–1930', *History of Political Economy* 14, no. 4 (1982): 583–607.
5 Note on 'Credit Anstalt', June 6, 1931, by C.A.G. BEA, OV28/3, Country Files Austria, January 1–June 15, 1931.
6 'Telephone message from the Bank of England', noon, Jun 6, 1931. BISA, 7.18.9, Confidential papers on Austria and Hungary by Mr Rodd, 1931.
7 'Message sent from Professor Bruins to the President last night', June 7, 1931. BISA, 7.18.9, Confidential papers on Austria and Hungary by Mr Rodd, 1931. See also 'Report on the position in Vienna given by Mr. Rodd to the Governors in Basle on Sunday, 7th June, 1931', June 11, 1931, by Siepmann. BEA, OV28/3, Country Files Austria, January 1–June 15, 1931.
8 Telegram no. 165/31, June 6, 1931, from Norman to Harrison. CUL, HP, Box 9, binder 20, Bank of England, January–December 1931.
9 'Conversations at Chequers', *The Economist*, June 6, 1931.
10 'Conversations at Chequers'.
11 '90-Day Debt Notice by Reich Forecast', *The New York Times*, June 2, 1931.
12 For an in-depth discussion of the Chequers meeting, Germany's positioning, and its impact on the US and the Hoover moratorium, see Bennett, *Germany and the Diplomacy*, 113–65.
13 Keynes, *The Economic Consequences of the Peace.*
14 'Conversations at Chequers', *The Economist*, June 6, 1931; 'And After Chequers . . . ?', *The Economist*, June 13, 1931.
15 Simon Banholzer and Tobias Straumann, 'Why the French Said "Non": A New Perspective on the Hoover Moratorium of June 1931', *Journal of Contemporary History* 56, no. 4 (October 1, 2021): 1046.
16 Cable #30, June 5, 1931, from Fraser to McGarrah. BISA, 7-18.2. MCG.5. Correspondence regarding Leon Fraser's trip to New York in 1931.
17 Banholzer and Straumann, 'Why the French Said "Non"', 1046. Banholzer and Strauman's text in general is an important contribution to the understanding of France's position on Germany.
18 See Bennett, *Germany and the Diplomacy*, 113–32 and Straumann, *1931*, 127–51.
19 'The Reich Government. Text of the German Manifesto', *The New York Times*, June 7, 1931.
20 For the 'flames' quote, see Bennett, *Germany and the Diplomacy*, 127. For the 'I do not wish' quote, see Straumann, *1931*, 147–48.
21 Straumann, *1931*, 149–50.

22 Telegram no. 166/31, June 8, 1931, from Norman to Harrison. CUL, HP: Box 9, binder 20, Bank of England, January–December 1931.

23 'Telephone conversation with Governor Norman at Bank of England', June 8, 1931, by Harrison. CUL, HP: Box 21, binder 45, Harrison, Conversations, Vol. 1, 1926–31.

24 'The Financial Situation', *Commercial and Financial Chronicle*, June 13, 1931. The quote is from page 4091. With hindsight, the *Chronicle* – and the many German observers including the Reichsbank – were right; see, for instance, Győző Gyöngyösi and Emil Verner, 'Financial Crisis, Creditor-Debtor Conflict, and Populism', *The Journal of Finance* 77, no. 4 (2022): 2471–523; Manuel Funke, Moritz Schularick and Christoph Trebesch, 'Going to Extremes: Politics after Financial Crises, 1870–2014', *European Economic Review* 88 (September 1, 2016): 227–60; Sebastian Doerr et al., 'Financial Crises and Political Radicalization: How Failing Banks Paved Hitler's Path to Power', *The Journal of Finance*, June 22, 2022.

25 'International Bank Notes (Letter no. 15)', June 9, 1931. NARA, RG39, Box 104, Entry 145, Folder: 'G783.5 Special Report Confidential Letters (1-24)'.

26 Minutes from the Board Meeting, June 8, 1931. BISA, 1.3a, Board of Directors, Agenda and Minutes. Meetings 10–19. Vol. II, 1931–32.

27 Telegram #17, June 8, 1931, from N.M. Rothschild to S.M. v Rothschild. RA, 111/521, Correspondence Department.

28 Telegram #17, June 8, 1931, from N.M. Rothschild to S.M. v Rothschild. RA, 111/521, Correspondence Department.

29 'Short resume of Statement made in French by the General Manager, M. Quesnay in the Meeting of Governors held at Basle in the B.I.S. on Sunday, June 7, 1931, from 4 till 7.45 p.m.', June 8, 1931. BISA, 7.18.2. MCG.1. Papers Gates W McGarrah and Leon Fraser. Credit Anstalt Crisis, 1931.

30 'Short resume of Statement made in French by the General Manager, M. Quesnay in the Meeting of Governors held at Basle in the B.I.S. on Sunday, June 7, 1931, from 4 till 7.45 p.m.', June 8, 1931. BISA, 7.18.2. MCG.1. Papers Gates W McGarrah and Leon Fraser. Credit Anstalt Crisis, 1931. See also Martin, *The Meddlers*, 113–15 et passim. Harold James's assessment of Pierre Quesnay's role differs. On the basis of French material, he argues, that Quesnay (and Moret) identified with the interests of the French government. James, *The End of Globalization*, 54–55.

31 'Report on arrangements in connection with the Austrian situation', June 8, 1931, the report was probably written by Rodd or Simon. BISA, 6.30. II/1 Granting of Credit of 100,000,000 Schilling to Austrian National Bank, 1931.

32 'Report on arrangements in connection with the Austrian situation', June 8, 1931. BISA, 6.30. II/1 Granting of Credit of 100,000,000 Schilling to Austrian National Bank, 1931.

33 'Settlements Bank. Board and Credit Anstalt Affairs', *Financial Times*, June 9, 1931.

34 'Note of the meeting of Governors held in Basle on Sunday, the 7th, and Monday, the 8th June, 1931', June 11, 1931, by Siepmann. BEA, OV28/3, Country Files Austria, January 1–June 15, 1931.

35 'Report on the position in Vienna given by Mr. Rodd to the Governors in Basle on Sunday, 7th June, 1931', June 11, 1931, by Siepmann. BEA, OV28/3, Country Files Austria, January 1–June 15, 1931.

36 'Note of the meeting of Governors held in Basle on Sunday, the 7th, and Monday, the 8th June, 1931', June 11, 1931, by Siepmann. BEA, OV28/3, Country Files Austria, January 1–June 15, 1931.
37 Cable #3, June 10, 1931, from McGarrah to Fraser. BISA, 17.8.2. MCG.5. Correspondence regarding Leon Fraser's trip to New York in June 1931.
38 Telegram no. I-5, June 5, 1931, from Gannon, Chanler and Grant to Loree. FRBNY, C261.1,2 Austria-Oesterreichische Credit Anstalt fur Handel, June 1931–April 1932.
39 Cable 31/4796, June 5, 1931, from Morgan Grenfell to J.P. Morgan & Co. RA, 31/8, 31/1, Secretariat Department, Correspondence (ACA). American Committee, Files 1+2, May 1931–December 1932.
40 Cable 31/2242, June 5, 1931, from J.P. Morgan & Co. to Morgan Grenfell. RA, 31/8, 31/1, Secretariat Department, Correspondence (ACA). American Committee, Files 1+2, May 1931–December 1932.
41 'Thursday, 4th June. 2.30'. RA, 31/26, 1931 Correspondence (A.C.A.) Shorthand Minutes June 1931.
42 'Thursday, 4th June. 2.30'. RA, 31/26, 1931 Correspondence (A.C.A.) Shorthand Minutes June 1931.
43 Bonavia, *London before I Forget*, 105–25.
44 'Thursday, 4th June. 2.30'. RA, 31/26, 1931 Correspondence (A.C.A.) Shorthand Minutes June 1931.
45 'International Committee meeting, 5th June, 1931, 12 noon'. RA, 31/26, 1931 Correspondence (A.C.A.) Shorthand Minutes June 1931.
46 'International Committee Meeting. 10th June, 1931. 3. p.m.' RA, 31/26, 1931 Correspondence (A.C.A.) Shorthand Minutes June 1931.
47 'International Committee Meeting. Wednesday, 10th June 1931. at 3 p.m. (continued)'. RA, 31/26, 1931 Correspondence (A.C.A.) Shorthand Minutes June 1931.

## Chapter 9

1 Telegram no. 212, June 9, 1931, from Harrison to BIS. FRBNY, C261.1, National Bank (Austrian Nat'l Bank) Credit, May 1931–December 1932, 1 of 2.
2 Note of telephone conversation with Norman, June 9, 1931. FRBNY, 3115.2 Harrison Papers. Harrison's conversations with M. Norman, 1931.
3 'Account of telephone conversation between – The Governor and Mr. Harrison', June 9, 1931, at 4.30 p.m. BEA, OV32/7, Federal Reserve Bank of New York, Confidential Cables, 1931.
4 'Telephone message from herr Blessing', June 9, 1931, by Hülse. BISA, 7.18.9, Confidential papers on Austria and Hungary by Mr Rodd, 1931.
5 'Copy of cable received by mr. Fraser from Mr. McGarrah', June 9, 1931. FRBNY, C261.1, National Bank (Austrian Nat'l Bank) Credit, May 1931–December 1932, 1 of 2.
6 Telegram #87.471, June 8, 1931, from Morgan & Cie to J.P. Morgan & Co. JPM, ARC 1221 Morgan Bank European Papers. Series 9. Austrian Bonds 1919–1958 Boxes 36, Austrian Bonds 1929–30, Austrian Bonds (II), May 16–June 29, 1931.

7 Telegram #66.919, June 9, 1931, from J.P. Morgan & Co to Morgan & Cie. JPM, ARC 1221 Morgan Bank European Papers. Series 9. Austrian Bonds 1919–1958 Boxes 36, Austrian Bonds 1929–30, Austrian Bonds (II), May 16–June 29, 1931.
8 Telegram #87.481, June 10, 1931, from Morgan & Cie to J.P. Morgan & Co. JPM, ARC 1221 Morgan Bank European Papers. Series 9. Austrian Bonds 1919–1958 Boxes 36, Austrian Bonds 1929–30, Austrian Bonds (II), May 16–June 29, 1931.
9 Letter, June 12, 1931, from Nelson Dean Jay to Gates McGarrah. JPM, ARC 1221 Morgan Bank European Papers. Series 9. Austrian Bonds 1919–1958 Boxes 36, Austrian Bonds 1929–30, Austrian Bonds (II), May 16–June 29, 1931.
10 'Message from Governor Norman to prof. Bruins dictated by mr. Siepmann to Blessing'. Not dated, but probably June 9, 1931. BISA, 7.18.9, Confidential papers on Austria and Hungary by Mr Rodd, 1931.
11 'Credit Anstalt' June 10, 1931, by Siepmann. BEA, OV28/3, Country Files Austria, January 1–June 15, 1931.
12 Confidential note, June 10, 1931, by Siepmann. BEA, OV28/3, Country Files Austria, January 1–June 15, 1931.
13 On Lacour-Gayet, see Olivier Feiertag and Pablo Martin Acena, 'The Delayed Modernization of the Central Banks of France and Spain in the Twentieth Century', in *The Emergence of Modern Central Banking from 1918 to the Present*, ed. Carl-L. Holtfrerich, Jaime Reis and Gianni Toniolo (Aldershot: Ashgate, 1999), 44–45.
14 Note #164, June 10, 1931, by Siepmann. BEA, OV28/3, Country Files Austria, January 1–June 15, 1931.
15 'Credit Anstalt', note (154A), June 10, 1931, 4 p.m., by Siepmann. BEA, OV28/3, Austria Country File, January 14–June 15, 1931.
16 'Credit Anstalt', note (160), June 10, 1931, 5.15 p.m., by Siepmann. BEA, OV28/3, Austria Country File, January 14–June 15, 1931.
17 Note, June 18, 1931, on telephone conversation June 11, 1931, between Harrison and Norman. CUL, HP, Box 21, binder 45, Harrison, Conversations, Vol. 1, 1926–31.
18 'Credit Anstalt' (#170), June 11, 1931, 7.45 p.m. by Siepmann. BEA, OV28/3, Country Files Austria, January 1–June 15, 1931.
19 'Austria'. Note, June 11, 1931, on telephone conversation between Rodd and Siepmann. BEA, OV28/3, Country Files Austria, January 1–June 15, 1931.
20 Telegram, undated (but probably June 10, 1931) from Rodd to McGarrah. BISA, 7.18.9, Confidential papers on Austria and Hungary by Mr Rodd, 1931.
21 Telegram, June 10, 1931, from McGarrah to Rodd. BISA, 7.18.9, Confidential papers on Austria and Hungary by Mr Rodd, 1931.
22 Handwritten note, June 4, 1931, by Siepmann. BEA, OV28/3, Austria Country File, January 14–June 15, 1931.
23 'Telephone message from Mr. Gunston, Bank of England', June 6, 1931, by OEM. BISA, 7.18.2. MCG.1. Papers Gates W McGarrah and Leon Fraser. Credit Anstalt Crisis, 1931; note on 'Telephone message from Mr. Rodd', June 4, 1931, 4 p.m. BISA, 6.30. II/1 Granting of Credit of 100,000,000 Schilling to Austrian National Bank, 1931. See also 'Memorandum' (135), June 4, 1931, by C.A.G. BEA, OV28/3, Austria Country File, January 14–June 15, 1931.

24 Letter, June 11, 1931, from van Hengel to McGarrah. BISA, 7.18.2. MCG.1. Papers Gates W McGarrah and Leon Fraser. Credit Anstalt Crisis, 1931.
25 Letter, June 11, 1931, from van Hengel to McGarrah. BISA, 7.18.2. MCG.1. Papers Gates W McGarrah and Leon Fraser. Credit Anstalt Crisis, 1931.
26 Letter, June 11, 1931, from van Hengel to McGarrah. BISA, 7.18.2. MCG.1. Papers Gates W McGarrah and Leon Fraser. Credit Anstalt Crisis, 1931. See also Toniolo, with the assistance of Piet Clement, *Central Bank Cooperation*, 112–14, for a discussion of van Hengel's letter to McGarrah.
27 'Memorandum: Meeting of Executive Committee June 1, 1931'. CUL, HP, Box 23, binder 50, Discussion Notes: Volumes I, II & III, April 17, 1930–September 21, 1933. A case could be made for a comparison between the interwar period and the time up to and beyond the financial crisis of 2008. The evidence is massive, of course, but for a cultural perspective, see Per H. Hansen, 'From Finance Capitalism to Financialization: A Cultural and Narrative Perspective on 150 Years of Financial History', *Enterprise & Society* 15, no. 4 (2014): 605–42; Ho, 'Disciplining Investment Bankers'; Ho, *Liquidated.*
28 Letter, November 23, 1931, from Rodd to Sir Otto Niemeyer. LRRA, Folder 59, 'A few Bank of England Papers'.
29 Letter, June 11, 1931, from Siepmann to Roger Auboin. BEA, ADM25–5, Papers of Harry Arthur Siepmann. Correspondence, January 1–June 30, 1931.
30 'The Governor. Dr. Vocke telephoned at 5.45 p.m. as follows' (#60) note, June 10, 1931, by Siepmann. BEA, OV34–80, Germany Reichsbank, January 2–July 14, 1931. See also telegram #125, June 10, 1931, from Reichsbank to Harrison. FRBNY, C261, Germany, Reichsbank, Policy and Procedures 1931–32.
31 'Telephone message received from Dr. Vocke at 4.30 p.m. on 12th June, 1931', by Siepmann. For 'entirely indirect', see telegram #64, June 12, 1931, from Luther to Norman (#63). BEA, OV34–80, Germany Reichsbank, January 2–July 14, 1931.
32 'Raising of Reichsbank discount rate, 13 June, 1931', note #72A, June 19, 1931, by E. Rowe Dutton. BEA, OV34–80, Germany Reichsbank, January 2–July 14, 1931.
33 'Austria', note, June 12, 1931, 11.30 p.m., by Siepmann. BEA, OV28/3, Country Files Austria, January 1–June 15, 1931.
34 Telegram no. 129, June 11, 1931, from Luther to Harrison. CUL, HP, Box 3, binder 7, Reichsbank (Germany), January 7–December 1931.
35 Telegram no. 173/31, June 12, 1931, from Norman to Harrison. CUL, HP, Box 9, binder 20, Bank of England, January–December 1931.
36 Telegram no. 135, June 12, 1931, from Luther to Harrison. CUL, HP, Box 3, binder 7, Reichsbank (Germany), January 7–December 1931.
37 'Message from Mr. Siepmann to dr. Brauneis through the intermediary of prof. Bruins'. No date. BISA, 7.18.9, Confidential papers on Austria and Hungary by Mr Rodd, 1931.
38 'Austria', note, June 12, 1931, 5.45 p.m., by Siepmann. BEA, OV28/3, Country Files Austria, January 1–June 15, 1931.
39 Letter, June 12, 1931, from Bruins to Juch. BISA, 7.18.9, Confidential papers on Austria and Hungary by Mr Rodd, 1931. Original is in German. Translation by the author.
40 Letter, June 13, 1931, from Juch to Bruins. BISA, 7.18.9, Confidential papers on Austria and Hungary by Mr Rodd, 1931.

## Chapter 10

1 Note, June 18, 1931, on telephone conversation between Harrison and Norman on June 13, 1931. FRBNY, no. 3115.2, Harrison Papers, Harrison's conversations with M. Norman, 1931.
2 'Conversations relative to debt settlements', June 11, 1931, Governor Harrison. HP, Box 21, binder 45, Harrison, Conversations, vol. 1, 1926–31.
3 Telegram #31/4809, June 13, 1931, from Morgan Grenfell to J.P. Morgan & Co. JPM, ARC 1221 Morgan Bank European Papers. Series 9. Austrian Bonds 1919–1958 Boxes 36, Austrian Bonds 1929–30, Folder, Austrian Bonds (II), May 16–June 29, 1931.
4 Note, June 18, 1931, on telephone conversation between Harrison and Norman on 13 June. FRBNY, no. 3115.2, Harrison Papers, Harrison's conversations with M. Norman, 1931. See also Mouré, *The Gold Standard Illusion*, 194, 200; Boyce, *The Great Interwar Crisis*, 304–5.
5 'And After Chequers . . .?'
6 Note, June 18, 1931, on telephone conversation between Harrison and Norman on June 13, 1931. FRBNY, no. 3115.2, Harrison Papers, Harrison's conversations with M. Norman, 1931.
7 Telegram no. 174/31, June 13, 1931, from Norman to Harrison. CUL, HP, Box 9, binder 20, Bank of England, January–December 1931.
8 Telegram no. 64, June 13, 1931, from Moret to Harrison. CUL, HP, Box 14, binder 29, Bank of France, 1931.
9 Telegram no. 67, June 15, 1931, from Moret to Harrison. CUL, HP, Box 14, binder 29, Bank of France, 1931.
10 Telegram no. 81, June 15, 1931, from Harrison to Moret. CUL, HP, Box 14, binder 29, Bank of France, 1931.
11 Telegram no. 80, June 15, 1931, from Harrison to Luther. CUL, HP, Box 3, binder 7, Reichsbank (Germany), January 7–December 1931.
12 Note, June 15, 1931, on telephone conversation between Harrison and Norman on June 14, 1931. FRBNY, no. 3115.2, Harrison Papers, Harrison's conversations with M. Norman, 1931.
13 Telegram no. 348, June 13, 1931, from McGarrah to Harrison. BISA, 7.18.2. MCG.1. Papers Gates W McGarrah and Leon Fraser. Credit Anstalt Crisis, 1931.
14 'Memorandum: Meeting of Executive Committee June 15, 1931'. CUL, HP, Box 23, binder 50, Discussion Notes: Volumes I, II & III, April 17, 1930–September 21, 1933. See also telegram, June 15, 1931, from Harrison to Federal Reserve Board, letter and telegram of June 16, 1931, from FRB to Harrison, and telegram no. 221, June 16, 1931, from FRBNY to BIS. FRBNY, C261.1, National Bank (Austrian Nat'l Bank) Credit, May 1931–December 1932, 1 of 2.
15 Telegrams no. 11, June 15, 1931, from Harrison to McGarrah and no. 18, June 16, 1931, from McGarrah to Harrison. CUL, HP, Box 16, binder 36, Personal Cables, 1930–35; and telegram no. 223, June 16, 1931, from FRBNY to BIS. CUL, HP, Box 1, binder 2, Bank for International Settlements, April 2, 1930–December 1931.
16 Telegram, June 13, 1931, from James H. Gannon to Wiggin. BISA, 7.18.2. MCG.1. Papers Gates W McGarrah and Leon Fraser. Credit Anstalt Crisis, 1931.

17 'International Committee Meeting. Thursday, 11 June 1931. 2.30 p.m.' RA, 31/26, 1931 Correspondence (A.C.A.) Shorthand Minutes June 1931.
18 'Austrian Credit Anstalt International Committee. Report of a meeting held at New Court, Friday morning, 12th June 1931, at 12 noon'. RA, 31/26, 1931 Correspondence (A.C.A.) Shorthand Minutes June 1931.
19 'Cable to Head Office' #2912, June 12, 1931, from Gannon, Chanler and Grant. RA, 31/8, file 31/1, Secretariat Department, Correspondence (ACA). American Committee, Files 1+2, May 1931–December 1932.
20 Letter #28, June 15, 1931, from Lionel de Rothschild to 'my dear Cousins' with enclosed telegram from Kindersley and Gannon to Lionel de Rothschild. RA, 111/521, Correspondence Department.
21 Telegram, June 15, 1931, from Kindersley to Norman. BIS, BISA, 7.18.2. MCG.1. Papers Gates W McGarrah and Leon Fraser. Credit Anstalt Crisis, 1931.
22 Telegram no. 176/31, June 15, 1931, from Norman to Harrison. CUL, HP, Box 9, binder 20, Bank of England, January–December 1931.
23 'International: Nothing Resounding', *Time*, August 24, 1931.
24 Telegram, June 15, 1931, most likely from Gannon to Wiggin. BISA, 7.18.2. MCG.1. Papers Gates W McGarrah and Leon Fraser. Credit Anstalt Crisis, 1931.
25 Telegram no. 177/31, June 15, 1931, from Norman to Harrison. CUL, HP, Box 9, binder 20, Bank of England, January–December 1931.
26 'Note of a telephone conversation with Monsieur Lacour-Gayet at 12.45 p.m. on the 15th June 1931', taken by Siepmann, June 15, 1931, at 1.15 p.m. BEA, OV28/3, Austria Country File, January 14–June 15, 1931.
27 'Memorandum' (187), June 15, 1931, by C.F. Whigham. BEA, OV28/3, Austria Country File, January 14–June 15, 1931. See also telegrams #31/4811 and 31/4815, June 15, 1931, from Morgan Grenfell to J.P. Morgan & Co. See also Memorandum on Austria, June 15, 1931, by Nelson Dean Jay. JPM, ARC 1221 Morgan Bank European Papers. Series 9. Austrian Bonds 1919–1958 Boxes 36, Austrian Bonds 1929–30, Folder Austrian Bonds (II), May 16–June 29, 1931.
28 Note (188), June 15, 1931, at 2.55 p.m., by Siepmann. BEA, OV28/3, Austria Country File, January 14–June 15, 1931.
29 'Memorandum' (187), June 15, 1931, by C.F. Whigham. BEA, OV28/3, Austria Country File, January 14–June 15, 1931.
30 Telegram (6), June 6, 1931, at 3.35 a.m., from Rodd to Siepmann, BEA, OV28-4, Austria Country File, June 16–July 30, 1931.
31 Memorandum, June 15, 1931, by Harrison. CUL, HP, Box 27, binder 59, Office Memoranda: Volume II, 1928–31.
32 Copy of telegram, June 15, 1931, from Wiggin to Gannon. BISA, 7.18.2. MCG.1. Papers Gates W McGarrah and Leon Fraser. Credit Anstalt Crisis, 1931.
33 Copy of telegram, June 16, 1931, from Gannon to Wiggin. BISA, 7.18.2. MCG.1. Papers Gates W McGarrah and Leon Fraser. Credit Anstalt Crisis, 1931.
34 'Resolution des Generalrates der Österreichischen Nationalbank vom 15. Juni 1931'. BISA, 6.30. II/1 Granting of Credit of 100,000,000 Schilling to Austrian National Bank, 1931.
35 Letter, June 16, 1931, from Bruins to Juch. BISA, 6.30. II/1 Granting of Credit of 100,000,000 Schilling to Austrian National Bank, 1931. Quotes are translated into

English from German by the author. For the discussion in the 'Generalrat' and the request for a moratorium, see also Kernbauer, *Währungspolitik*, 310–12.

36 Telegram, June 16, 1931, from McGarrah to Rodd. BISA, 7.18.9, Confidential papers on Austria and Hungary by Mr Rodd, 1931.

37 Copy of letter of June 16, 1931, from Bruins to Juch. BISA, 6.30. II/1 Granting of Credit of 100,000,000 Schilling to Austrian National Bank, 1931. Quotes are translated into English from German by the author.

38 Stiefel, *Finanzdiplomatie und Weltwirtschaftskrise*, 58. Schubert is critical of the guarantee and the terms of the standstill agreement and argues that Kindersley and Gannon's approach 'came very close to blackmail'. He also argues that the Austrian authorities were overly dependent on foreign interests, 'Too late, the Austrian authorities recognized that the only interest of the foreign creditors was self-interest. They wanted to get as much as possible out of the CA or out of Austria.' See Schubert, *The Credit-Anstalt Crisis*, 154, 157, 165. Stiefel has a somewhat different perspective on the international creditors in that he stresses their interest in maintaining the international financial system, see Stiefel, *Finanzdiplomatie und Weltwirtschaftskrise*, 38–40.

39 Telegram no. I-30, June 16, 1931, from Grant to Loree. FRBNY, C261.12 Austria – Oesterreichische Credit Anstalt fur Handel, June 1931–April 1932.

40 Telegram no. I-31, June 16, 1931, from Wallace, Chanler and Grant to Loree. FRBNY, C261.12 Austria–Oesterreichische Credit Anstalt fur Handel, June 1931–April 1932.

41 'Cable to Head Office' #3911, June 22, 1931, from Chanler and Wallace. RA, 31/8, 31/1, Secretariat Department, Correspondence (ACA). American Committee, Files 1+2, May 1931–December 1932.

42 Kernbauer, *Währungspolitik*, 300.

43 'Austria' (4), 'Telephone message received from Monsieur Lacour-Gayet at 10.45 a. m. on the 16th of June 1931'. BEA, OV28/4, Country File Austria, June 16–July 30, 1931.

44 Letter, June 15, 1931, from Snowden to Norman. BEA, OV28/3, Country Files Austria, January 1–June 15, 1931. The letter from Snowden demonstrates that Norman also acted in accordance with the wish of the British government. See also Cottrell, 'The Bank of England', 432–33; Cottrell, 'Austria between Diplomats'. Cottrell is – to my knowledge – the only scholar who refers to Snowden's letter and establishes the link to the Bank of England's loan to the Austrian National Bank. Aguado, 'The Credit Anstalt Crisis', argues that it was the fear of a moratorium alone that drove Norman to lend the money. For the characterization of Philip Snowden, see William H. Janeway, 'The 1931 Sterling Crisis and the Independence of the Bank of England', *Journal of Post Keynesian Economics* 18, no. 2 (1996): 259.

45 Letter, June 12, 1931, from Morgan Grenfell to Baron Franckenstein. RA, Correspondence Department, 111/521, #25.

46 'Memorandum', June 5, 1931, probably written by Rodd. BISA, 7.18.9, Confidential papers on Austria and Hungary by Mr Rodd, 1931.

47 Telegram no. 349, June 14, 1931, from BIS to FRBNY. CUL, HP, Box 1, binder 2, Bank for International Settlements, April 2, 1930–December 1931.

48 'Austria', note (7), June 16, 1931, at 1 p.m., by Siepmann. BEA, OV28/44, Austria advance by Bank of England to Austrian Government, May 12, 1931–March 31, 1932.
49 Telegram, June 16, 1931, from Siepmann to McGarrah. BISA, 6.30d, Credit of Sch. 150,000,000 to Austrian National Bank by Bank of England (16th June 1931), 1931–32.
50 Telegram, June 16, 1931, from Siepmann to McGarrah. BISA, 6.30d, Credit of Sch. 150,000,000 to Austrian National Bank by Bank of England (16th June 1931), 1931–32.
51 Cottrell, 'Austria between Diplomats', 309.
52 This is not the framing used by Charles Kindleberger and the many historians who have carried his interpretation onwards. Kindleberger incorrectly argues that Bank of England's credit was only 50 million schillings or $7 million, and marked the 'end of Britain as a lender of last resort', see Kindleberger, *The World in Depression*, 144–47. The quote is on p. 147.
53 Boyce argues without citing evidence that Bank of England's action was caused by the need to avoid bankruptcy among the City's leading merchant banks, see Boyce, *The Great Interwar Crisis*, 303. It seems likely that this case refers to mid-July when the German banking crisis intensified, see David Kynaston, *The City of London. Volume III. Illusions of Gold, 1914–1945* (London: Pimlico, 1999), 227–30.
54 For a discussion of the Bank of England's loan and the French ultimatum, see Stiefel, *Finanzdiplomatie und Weltwirtschaftskrise*, 150–67. The timing and process of the loan is described on page 159 and does not quite fit with the evidence presented in this book.
55 Carlisle MacDonald, 'Paris Fears Abate on German Crisis', *The New York Times*, June 16, 1931.
56 MacDonald, 'Paris Fears'.
57 Note, June 18, 1931, by Harrison on telephone conversation, June 16, 1931, with Norman. FRBNY, No. 3115.2, Harrison Papers. Harrison's conversations with M. Norman, 1931.
58 'Telephone message to – Governor Harrison' June 16, 1931, at 4.45 p.m. BEA, OV32/7, Federal Reserve Bank of New York, Confidential Cables, 1931.
59 Note, June 18, 1931, by Harrison on telephone conversation, June 16, 1931, with Norman. FRBNY, no. 3115.2, Harrison Papers. Harrison's conversations with M. Norman, 1931.
60 Telegram, June 16, 1931, from Luther to Harrison. CUL, HP, Box 3, binder 7, Reichsbank (Germany), January 7–December 1931.
61 Note, June 18, 1931, by Harrison on telephone conversation, June 16, 1931, with Norman. FRBNY, No. 3115.2, Harrison Papers. Harrison's conversations with M. Norman, 1931.
62 John MacCormac, 'Austrian Cabinet Quits on Bank Deal', *The New York Times*, June 17, 1931.
63 Telegram (29), June 18, 1931, from Norman to Bruins. BEA, OV28/4, Austria Country File, June 16–July 30, 1931.

## Chapter 11

1 Letter, June 22, 1931, from Rodd to Kindersley. BISA, 7.18.9, Confidential papers on Austria and Hungary by Mr Rodd, 1931.
2 Memorandum, Basle, June 20, 1931, by Francis Rodd. This rendering of the memorandum is based on two versions: a draft, deposited in BISA, 7.18.9, Confidential papers on Austria and Hungary by Mr Rodd, 1931, and a final version from BEA, OV28/69, Credit Anstalt Reconstruction, 20.6.31–31.12.31. Some important parts are left out in the final version. In my rendering of the memorandum, I have put left-out passages in square brackets: []. Changes in the final version due to these revisions are italicized.
3 Note 'France', May 9, 1931. BEA, OV45/4 France Country File, January 6–October 31, 1931. It's difficult to read who wrote the note, but it may say 'by Ingrams, ... Chemical Bank', which means that the note was not written by a Bank of England officer.
4 'Note of a Discussion with French Treasury Experts 11th August, 1931'. By Leith-Ross, August 13, 1931. BEA, OV45-4 France Country File, January 6–October 31, 1931. Notably, this is the only reference to race I have found in the empirical material. This may support Mouré's and others' claim that rather than race, British scepticism towards the French was based on national stereotypes and prejudice. See Mouré's argument and Boyce's reply in Imlay et al., 'H-Diplo Roundtable Review of Robert Boyce', 20, 42–43; Boyce, *The Great Interwar Crisis*, 14–21, 58–59 et passim.
5 Letter, June 22, 1931, from Rodd to Kindersley. BISA, 7.18.9, Confidential papers on Austria and Hungary by Mr Rodd, 1931.
6 Natalie Zemon Davis, *Fiction in the Archives: Pardon Tales and Their Tellers in Sixteenth-Century France* (Stanford: Stanford University Press, 1987). For performativity, see Hansen, 'Business History'; Ho, 'Disciplining Investment Bankers'. The classic work on finance and performativity is Mackenzie, *An Engine, Not a Camera*.
7 Letter, June 22, 1931, from Rodd to Gannon. BISA, 7.18.9, Confidential papers on Austria and Hungary by Mr Rodd, 1931.
8 Letter, June 26, 1931, from Kindersley to Rodd. BISA, 7.18.9, Confidential papers on Austria and Hungary by Mr Rodd, 1931.
9 Quoted from Stiefel, *Finanzdiplomatie und Weltwirtschaftskrise*, 65.
10 Letter, June 25, 1931, from Gannon to Rodd. BISA, 7.18.9, Confidential papers on Austria and Hungary by Mr Rodd, 1931.
11 Boobbyer, 'Francis Rodd', 15, 24–25; Boobbyer, *The Life and World*, 47–48.
12 'International Bank Notes (Letter no. 16)', June 16, 1931. NARA, RG39, Box 104, Entry 145, Folder: 'G783.5 Special Report Confidential Letters (1-24)'.
13 Note, June 19, 1931, added to 'International Bank Notes (Letter no. 16)', June 16, 1931. NARA, RG39, Box 104, Entry 145, Folder: 'G783.5 Special Report Confidential Letters (1-24)'.
14 'International Bank Notes (Letter no. 17)', June 26, 1931. NARA, RG39, Box 104, Entry 145, Folder: 'G783.5 Special Report Confidential Letters (1-24)'.
15 'The Financial Situation', *Commercial and Financial Chronicle*, June 20, 1931.

## Chapter 12

1 'Bank of England and Austria. Resolving a Crisis', *Financial Times*, June 19, 1931.

2 Note, June 18, 1931, by Siepmann on telephone conversation with Moret. BEA, OV28/4, Austria Country File, June 16–July 30, 1931. Some historians have argued that the Banque de France, seeking revenge, liquidated sterling holdings with the Bank of England; see Karl Erich Born, *Die Deutsche Bankkrise 1931. Finanzen Und Politik* (Münich: R. Piper & Co. Verlag, 1967), 66; Kernbauer, *Währungspolitik*, 317.

3 Unsigned note (40), June 17, 1931. BEA, OV28/4, Austria Country File, June 16–July 30, 1931.

4 'Telephone message from Mr. Rodd for the Governor', June 17, 1931, 10.10 a.m. by C.A.G. BEA, OV28/4, Austria Country File, June 16–July 30, 1931.

5 Letter, June 16, 1931, from McGarrah to Norman. BISA, 6.30d, Credit of Sch. 150,000,000 to Austrian National Bank by Bank of England (16th June 1931), 1931–32.

6 'Strictly confidential' note, July 9, 1931, by G.W.J. Bruins. BEA, OV5/3, Bank for International Settlements, Minutes August 6–December 10, 1931.

7 Quoted from Aguado, 'The Credit Anstalt Crisis', 216.

8 'Extract of telegram received by mr. Gannon from mr. Wiggin and telephoned by mr. Gannon from Vienna on the 18th'. BISA, 7.18.9, Confidential papers on Austria and Hungary by Mr Rodd, 1931.

9 Telegram no. 31/2264, June 16, 1931, from J.P. Morgan to Morgan Grenfell. FRBNY, C261.1, National Bank (Austrian Nat'l Bank) Credit, May 1931–December 1932, 1 of 2.

10 Note, June 22, 1931, by Siepmann of telephone conversations with Kindersley and Bruins respectively. BEA, OV28/4, Austria Country File, June 16–July 30, 1931.

11 Telegram no. 387, June 29, 1931, from BIS to FRBNY. FRBNY, C261.1, National Bank (Austrian Nat'l Bank) Credit, May 1931–December 1932, 1 of 2.

12 Cable no 31/4853, July 3, 1931, 1.44 p.m. from Morgan Grenfell & Co, London to Whigham, J.P. Morgan. FRBNY, C261.1, National Bank (Austrian Nat'l Bank) Credit, May 1931–December 1932, 1 of 2.

13 Cable no 31/2314, July 10, 1931, from 'RCL' J.P. Morgan to Morgan Grenfell & Co, London. FRBNY, C261.1, National Bank (Austrian Nat'l Bank) Credit, May 1931–December 1932, 1 of 2.

14 'Certain measures referring to currency and credit to be considered in the case of Austria', note, August 6, 1931, by Simon. BISA, 6.30. II/2 Granting of Credit of 100,000,000 Schilling to Austrian National Bank, 1931–32.

15 The memorandum is not signed but may well be written by a member of the Warburg banking house. See 'Memorandum' attached to letter, July 23, 1931, from Max Warburg & Co. to N.M. Rothschild. RA, 111/521, Correspondence Department.

16 'Memorandum: Meeting of the Board of Directors June 18 1931'. CUL, HP, Box 23, binder 50, Discussion Notes: Volumes I, II & III, April 17, 1930–September 21, 1933.

17 For the relationship between debt and deflation, see Irving Fisher, 'The Debt-Deflation Theory of Great Depressions', *Econometrica* no. 1 (1933): 337–57. See

also Ben Bernanke and Harold James, 'The Gold Standard, Deflation, and Financial Crisis in the Great Depression: An International Comparison', in *Essays on the Great Depression*, ed. Ben Bernanke (Princeton: Princeton University Press, 2000), 70–107.

18 Clement, 'Between Banks and Governments', 141–42.

19 Telegram, June 18, 1931, from BIS to Bank of England. BISA, 7.18.9, Confidential papers on Austria and Hungary by Mr Rodd, 1931.

20 Telegram no. 199/31, June 16, 1931, from Harrison to Norman. CUL, HP, Box 9, binder 20, Bank of England, January–December 1931.

21 Note, June 19, 1931, Harrison telephone conversation with Norman, June 18, 1931, at 12.30 p.m. FRBNY, no. 3115.2, Harrison Papers, Harrison's conversations with M. Norman, 1931. See also 'Telephone call to - Governor Harrison', June 18, 1931, at 5.28 p.m. BEA, OV32/7, Federal Reserve Bank of New York, Confidential Cables, 1931.

22 Note, June 20, 1931, Harrison telephone conversation with Norman, June 19, 1931, at 10.45 a.m. FRBNY, no. 3115.2, Harrison Papers, Harrison's conversations with M. Norman, 1931. See also 'Telephone call to - Governor Harrison', June 19, 1931, at 3.45 p.m. BEA, OV32/7, Federal Reserve Bank of New York, Confidential Cables, 1931.

23 'Political Stress in England and Germany - The Reparations Issue', *Commercial and Financial Chronicle*, June 20, 1931.

24 'Telephone message from Dr. Vocke of the Reichsbank' (#71), June 17, 1931, by C.A.G. BEA, OV34-80, Germany Reichsbank, January 2–July 14, 1931, and letter, June 18, 1931, from Norman to Luther. BEA, OV34/2, Country Files, Germany, February 14, 1930–July 31, 1931. For an analysis of the political situation in Germany, see Straumann, *1931*, 155–59.

25 Confidential 'Note of a telephone conversation with Dr. Dreyse at 4.45 p.m. on the 19th of June, 1931'. Note #73, June 19, 1931, 6.25 p.m. by Siepmann. BEA, OV34-80, Germany Reichsbank, January 2–July 14, 1931. See also Clement, 'Between Banks and Governments', 142–43. Toniolo, with the assistance of Clement, *Central Bank Cooperation*, 101, 515 n. 90.

26 Telegram no. 185/31, June 19, 1931, from Norman to Harrison. CUL, HP, Box 9, binder 20, Bank of England, January–December 1931.

27 Note, June 20, 1931, of telephone conversation between Harrison and Norman, June 19, 1931, at 3.30 p.m. FRBNY, no. 3115.2, Harrison Papers, Harrison's conversations with M. Norman, 1931.

28 Note, June 20, 1931, of telephone conversation between Harrison and Norman, June 19, 1931, at 3.30 p.m. FRBNY, no. 3115.2, Harrison Papers, Harrison's conversations with M. Norman, 1931.

29 Telegram no. 152, June 19, 1931, from Luther to Harrison. CUL, HP, Box 3, binder 7, Reichsbank (Germany), January 7–December 1931.

30 Note, June 20, 1931, of telephone conversation between Harrison and Norman, June 20, 1931, at 11 a.m. FRBNY, no. 3115.2, Harrison Papers, Harrison's conversations with M. Norman, 1931.

31 Note, June 19, 1931, on telephone conversation on 'Chile' between Harrison and C.E. Mitchell. CUL, HP, Box 27, binder 59, Office Memoranda: Volume II, 1928–31.

32 Telegram no. 358, June 20, 1931, from McGarrah to Harrison. CUL, HP, Box 1, binder 2, Bank for International Settlements, April 2, 1930–December 1931.
33 Telegram no. 204/31, June 20, 1931, from Harrison to Norman. CUL, HP, Box 9, binder 20, Bank of England, January–December 1931. See also telegram no. 12, June 20, 1931, from Harrison to McGarrah. CUL, HP, Box 16, binder 36, Personal Cables, 1930–35.
34 Telegram no. 156, June 20, 1931, from Luther to Harrison. CUL, HP, Box 3, binder 7, Reichsbank (Germany), January 7–December 1931.
35 Cable #41, June 13, 1931, from Fraser to McGarrah. BISA, 17.8.2. MCG.5. Correspondence regarding Leon Fraser's trip to New York in June 1931.
36 Cable #47, June 14, 1931, from McGarrah to Fraser and cable #43, June 15, 1931, from Fraser to McGarrah. BISA, 17.8.2. MCG.5. Correspondence regarding Leon Fraser's trip to New York in June 1931.
37 Letter, June 17, 1931, from Fraser to McGarrah. BISA, 17.8.2. MCG.5. Correspondence regarding Leon Fraser's trip to New York in June 1931. See also 'The Financial Situation', *Commercial and Financial Chronicle*, June 20, 1931, and Bennett, *Germany and the Diplomacy*, 132–65.
38 For the Hoover moratorium, see Gerhard Peters and John T. Woolley, 'The President's News Conference. Herbert Hoover, June 20, 1931', The American Presidency Project, www.presidency.ucsb.edu/documents/the-presidents-news-conference-671 (accessed March 24, 2022); Straumann, *1931*, 152–68.
39 See *The New York Times*'s account of how the Hoover moratorium was contemplated: Richard V. Oulahan, 'Hoover's Debt Move', *The New York Times*, July 12, 1931.
40 Horn, *J. P. Morgan & Co.*, 34–35.
41 Chernow, *The House of Morgan*, 328; Horn, *J. P. Morgan & Co.*, 80–82. For the process and the reception of Hoover's plan, see Straumann, *1931*, 160–78.
42 'Text of the President's Statement Proposing Suspension of Debts', *The New York Times*, June 21, 1931.
43 'Text of the President's', *The New York Times*, June 21, 1931.
44 Boyce, in contrast, argues that Hoover had an isolationist purpose of containing European pressure for American concessions on war debts, see Boyce, *The Great Interwar Crisis*, 305–6.
45 Note, July 3, 1931, of telephone conversation between Harrison and Norman, June 21, 1931. FRBNY, no. 3115.2, Harrison Papers, Harrison's conversations with M. Norman, 1931. For a less optimistic version, see Kunz, *The Battle for Britain's Gold Standard*, 59–60.
46 'France', *The Economist*, June 27, 1931, 1376; 'France', *The Economist*, July 4, 1931, 19.
47 Bennett, *Germany and the Diplomacy*, 169–71.
48 'World Bank Lauds Offer by Hoover', *The New York Times*, June 22, 1931. For a recent discussion of the French position on the Hoover Moratorium, see Banholzer and Straumann, 'Why the French Said "Non"'. For an overview of the financial effects of the Hoover Moratorium, see Eichengreen, *Golden Fetters*, 278.
49 P. J. Philip, 'France Not Ready to Make Sacrifice', *The New York Times*, June 22, 1931.
50 Quoted from Boyce, *The Great Interwar Crisis*, 308.

51 Telegram #87.514, June 22, 1931, from Morgan et Cie. to Parker Gilbert, J.P. Morgan & Co. ARC 1221, Box 14, Morgan Bank European Papers. Folder, Cables received, May 16–June 30, 1931, 4-B, (114–254).
52 Telegram #66.690, June 23, 1931, from Morgan & Co. to Morgan et Cie. ARC 1221, Box 14, Morgan Bank European Papers. Folder, Cables received, May 16–June 30, 1931, 4-B, (114–254).
53 'The Financial Situation', *Commercial and Financial Chronicle*, July 4, 1931.
54 Note, July 3, 1931, of telephone conversation between Harrison and Norman, June 21, 1931. FRBNY, no. 3115.2, Harrison Papers, Harrison's conversations with M. Norman, 1931.
55 Telegram no. 187/31, June 22, 1931, from Norman to Harrison. CUL, HP, Box 9, binder 20, Bank of England, January–December 1931.
56 'Memorandum: Meeting of Executive Committee, June 22, 1931'. CUL, HP, Box 23, binder 50, Discussion Notes: Volumes I, II & III, April 17, 1930–September 21, 1933.
57 'Memorandum: Meeting of Executive Committee, June 22, 1931'. CUL, HP, Box 23, binder 50, Discussion Notes: Volumes I, II & III, April 17, 1930–September 21, 1933.
58 'Memorandum: Meeting of Executive Committee, June 22, 1931'. CUL, HP, Box 23, binder 50, Discussion Notes: Volumes I, II & III, April 17, 1930–September 21, 1933.
59 Personal and confidential letter, June 22, 1931, from McGarrah to Harrison. FRBNY, Box 128149, folder 797.3, Bank of International Settlements, April–June 1931.
60 'World Bank Lauds Offer by Hoover', *The New York Times*, June 22, 1931.
61 Cable #55, June 22, 1931, from Quesnay to Fraser. BISA, 17.8.2. MCG.5. Correspondence regarding Leon Fraser's trip to New York in June 1931.
62 Cable #52, June 23, 1931, from Fraser to Quesnay. BISA, 17.8.2. MCG.5. Correspondence regarding Leon Fraser's trip to New York in June 1931.
63 'Note of a telephone conversation with Dr. Luther at 10.35 a.m. on the 22nd June, 1931'. #75 by Siepmann. BEA, OV34/80, Germany Reichsbank, January 2–July 14, 1931.
64 'Note of a telephone conversation of Dr. Luther with the Governor at 3 p.m. on 22nd June, 1931'. #76 by Siepmann. BEA, OV34/80, Germany Reichsbank, January 2–July 14, 1931.
65 Telegram, June 22, 1931, from Luther to Harrison. CUL, HP, Box 3, binder 7, Reichsbank (Germany), January 7–December 1931.
66 'Germany', *The Economist*, June 27, 1931, 1378.
67 Telegram, June 23, 1931, from Luther to Harrison. CUL, HP, Box 3, binder 7, Reichsbank (Germany), January 7–December 1931. See also telegram no. 162, June 24, 1931, from Reichsbank to Harrison. FRBNY, C261, Germany, Reichsbank, Policy and Procedures 1931–32.
68 Letter #77B, June 22, 1931, from Crump in Berlin to Harvey. BEA, OV34/80, Germany Reichsbank, January 2–July 14, 1931.
69 Letter #83, June 22, 1931, from Crump in Berlin to G. Vallace and forwarded to Siepmann. BEA, OV34/80, Germany Reichsbank, January 2–July 14, 1931.

70 Note #81, June 23, 1931, by Siepmann. BEA, OV34/80, Germany Reichsbank, January 2–July 14, 1931. See also letter, June 22, 1931, from Layton to P. Noel Baker and forwarded to Norman. BEA, OV34/2, Country Files, Germany, February 14, 1930–July 31, 1931.
71 Quote from 'Telephone conversation with Mr. Harrison' at 3.45 p.m., June 23, 1931. BEA, OV32/7, Federal Reserve Bank of New York, Confidential Cables, 1931. See also 'Germany' #84, June 23, 1931, by Siepmann; 'Note of a telephone conversation between Dr. Vocke and Vice-President Dreyse at 6.10 p.m. on 23rd June, 1931'. BEA, OV34/80, Germany Reichsbank, January 2–July 14, 1931.
72 'Telephone conversation with Mr. Harrison' at 3.45 p.m., June 23, 1931. BEA, OV32/7, Federal Reserve Bank of New York, Confidential Cables, 1931.
73 Note, June 24, 1931, on telephone conversation, June 23, 1931, at 10:45 a.m., between Harrison and Norman. FRBNY, no. 3115.2, Harrison Papers. Harrison's conversations with M. Norman, 1931.
74 Telegram no. 188/31, June 23, 1931, from Norman to Harrison, and telegram no 207/31, June 23, 1931, from Harrison to Norman. BEA, OV32/7, Federal Reserve Bank of New York, Confidential Cables, 1931.
75 Note, June 24, 1931, on telephone conversation, June 23, 1931, 12.45 p.m., on 'Germany' between Harrison and Governor Meyer. CUL, HP, Box 21, binder 45, Harrison, Conversations, vol. 1, 1926–31.
76 Note of June 23, 1931, on telephone conversation, June 23, 1931, at 1 p.m., on 'Germany' between Harrison and Lacour-Gayet. CUL, HP, Box 21, binder 45, Harrison, Conversations, vol. 1, 1926–31.
77 Note, June 23, 1931, on telephone conversation, June 23, 1931, 2.45 p.m., on 'Germany' between Harrison and Lacour-Gayet. CUL, HP, Box 21, binder 45, Harrison, Conversations, vol. 1, 1926–31.
78 Note, June 23, 1931, on telephone conversation, June 23, 1931, 2.45 p.m., on 'Germany' between Harrison and Lacour-Gayet. CUL, HP, Box 21, binder 45, Harrison, Conversations, vol. 1, 1926–31.
79 Note, June 24, 1931, on telephone conversation, June 23, 1931, 4 p.m., between Harrison and Norman. FRBNY, no. 3115.2, Harrison Papers. Harrison's conversations with M. Norman, 1931.
80 Note, June 24, 1931, on telephone conversation, June 23, 1931, 4 p.m., between Harrison and Norman. FRBNY, no. 3115.2, Harrison Papers. Harrison's conversations with M. Norman, 1931.
81 Note, June 24, 1931, on telephone conversation, June 23, 1931, 5 p.m., on 'Germany' between Harrison and Governor Meyer. CUL, HP, Box 21, binder 45, Harrison, Conversations, vol. 1, 1926–31.
82 Telegram no. 207/31, June 23, 1931, from Harrison to Norman. CUL, HP, Box 9, binder 20, Bank of England, January–December 1931.
83 Cables #53 and #54, June 23, 1931, from Fraser to McGarrah. BISA, 17.8.2. MCG.5. Correspondence regarding Leon Fraser's trip to New York in June 1931.
84 Note #88, June 24, 1931, 12.40 p.m., by Siepmann. BEA, OV34/80, Germany Reichsbank, 2 Jan 1931–14 Jul 1931. See also Clement, 'Between Banks and Governments', 143–44.

85 Telegram, June 24, 1931, from Luther to McGarrah. BISA, 7.18.2. MCG.1. Reichsbank, 1930–31.
86 Letter #89, June 24, 1931, from Norman to McGarrah and Luther (#89b). BEA, OV34/80, Germany Reichsbank, January 2–July 14, 1931.
87 'Reichsbank rediscount credit' #85, June 24, 1931, 1.40 p.m., by Siepmann. BEA, OV34/80, Germany Reichsbank, January 2–July 14, 1931.
88 Telegram #57, June 25, 1931, from McGarrah to Fraser. BISA, 7.18.2, Correspondence regarding Leon Fraser's trip to New York in June 1931. MCG.5. 1931.
89 Note, June 24, 1931, on telephone conversation, June 24, 1931, 12 noon, on 'Germany' between Harrison and Lacour-Gayet. See also note, June 24, 1931, 10 a.m. CUL, HP, Box 21, binder 45, Harrison, Conversations, vol. 1, 1926–31.
90 Note, June 24, 1931, on telephone conversation, June 24, 1931, 12.30 noon, on 'Germany' between Harrison and Norman. FRBNY, no. 3115.2, Harrison Papers. Harrison's conversations with M. Norman, 1931. See also Bank of England's note on the same conversation: 'Telephone conversation with Mr. Harrison' at 5.30 p.m., June 24, 1931. BEA, OV32/7, Federal Reserve Bank of New York, Confidential Cables, 1931; telegram no. 191/31, June 24, 1931, from Norman to Harrison. CUL, HP, Box 9, binder 20, Bank of England, January–December 1931. For the 'extremely critical' quote, see meeting, June 24, 1931, of Bank of England's Committee of Treasury. BEA, G8/60, Minutes of the Committee of Treasury – March 1931 to June 1932.
91 Note, June 24, 1931, on telephone conversation, June 24, 1931, 12.30 noon, on 'Germany' between Harrison and Norman. FRBNY, no. 3115.2, Harrison Papers. Harrison's conversations with M. Norman, 1931. See also Bank of England's note on the same conversation: 'Telephone conversation with Mr. Harrison' at 5.30 p.m., June 24, 1931. BEA, OV32/7, Federal Reserve Bank of New York, Confidential Cables, 1931.
92 Telegram #203, June 25, 1931, 8.53 p.m., from BIS to Bank of England. BEA, OV34/80, Germany Reichsbank, January 2–July 14, 1931.
93 Note on telephone conversation, June 24, 1931, 5 p.m., between Harrison and Norman. FRBNY, no. 3115.2, Harrison Papers. Harrison's conversations with M. Norman, 1931.
94 Telegram no. 94, June 24, 1931, from Harrison to Luther. CUL, HP, Box 3, binder 7, Reichsbank (Germany), January 7–December 1931.
95 Telegram no. 162, June 24, 1931, from Luther to Harrison. CUL, HP, Box 3, binder 7, Reichsbank (Germany), January 7–December 1931.
96 Telegram no. 368, June 25, 1931, from BIS to FRBNY, and telegram no. 241, June 26, 1931, from FRBNY to BIS. CUL, HP, Box 1, binder 2, Bank for International Settlements, April 2, 1930–December 1931.
97 Notes on telephone conversations, June 25, 1931, 11:45 a.m. and 1:15 p.m., between Harrison and McGarrah. CUL, HP, Box 21, binder 45, Harrison, Conversations, vol. 1, 1926–31. See also 'draft of announcement to be made by B.I.S.' FRBNY, No. 3013.1, Harrison Papers. Harrison's conversations with G.W. McGarrah, 1930–33.
98 Telegram no. 97, June 25, 1931, from Harrison to Luther. CUL, HP, Box 3, binder 7, Reichsbank (Germany), January 7–December 1931. See also telegram no. 239,

June 25, 1931, from FRBNY to BIS. CUL, HP, Box 1, binder 2, Bank for International Settlements, April 2, 1930–December 1931.

99 Telegram no. 164, June 26, 1931, from Luther to Harrison. CUL, HP, Box 3, binder 7, Reichsbank (Germany), January 7–December 1931.

100 Telegram #98a, June 26, 1931, from Luther to Norman; and response letter '98b from Norman to Luther, June 26, 1931'. BEA, OV34/80, Germany Reichsbank, January 2–July 14, 1931.

101 Note on telephone conversation, June 25, 1931, 10:45 a.m., between Harrison and Norman. FRBNY, no. 3115.2, Harrison Papers. Harrison's conversations with M. Norman, 1931.

102 'International Bank Notes (Letter no. 17)', June 26, 1931. NARA, RG39, Box 104, Entry 145, Folder: 'G783.5 Special Report Confidential Letters (1-24)'.

103 Letter of December 16, 1930 from Fraser to McGarrah, BISA. MCG.3. Correspondence between Fraser and McGarrah, 1930–31.

104 'France', *The Economist*, June 27, 1931.

105 'The Break in the Clouds', *The Economist*, June 27, 1931.

## Chapter 13

1 Letter, June 11, 1931, from van Hengel to McGarrah. BISA, 7.18.2. MCG.1. Papers Gates W McGarrah and Leon Fraser. Credit Anstalt Crisis, 1931.

2 'Note of a telephone conversation with Monsieur Quesnay at 11.30 a.m. on the 2nd July, 1931', July 2, 1931, 1.45 p.m., by Siepmann. BEA, OV34/2, Country Files, Germany, February 14, 1930–July 31, 1931; 'Note of a telephone conversation with Monsieur Quesnay at 11.35 a.m. on 3rd July, 1931', July 3, 1931, by Siepmann. BEA, OV34/80, Germany Reichsbank, January 2–July 14, 1931.

3 'The German Banking Situation', *The Economist*, June 20, 1931.

4 'Germany', *The Economist*, June 20, 1931.

5 Telegram (31), June 19, 1931, from Bruins to Norman. See also 'Note of a telephone conversation with Dr. Bruins at 12.15. p.m. on 20th June, 1931' (36), by Siepmann. BEA, OV28/4, Austria Country File, June 16–July 30, 1931.

6 'Austria' (23), note, June 19, 1931, 6.45 p.m., by Siepmann. BEA, OV28/4, Austria Country File, June 16–July 30, 1931.

7 Note on telegram, June 27, 1931, from Harrison in Washington to Norman. CUL, HP, Box 51, Norman, Montagu Collet, Governor of the Bank of England, I (May 1926–December 1931).

8 Telegram no. 195/31, June 27, 1931, from Norman to Harrison. CUL, HP, Box 9, binder 20, Bank of England, January–December 1931.

9 Note, July 3, 1931, of telephone conversation, June 27, 1931, between Harrison and Norman. FRBNY, no. 3115.2, Harrison Papers. Harrison's conversations with M. Norman, 1931.

10 Note on 'Telephone conversation with Governor Harrison' at 3.15 p.m. Saturday, June 27, 1931. BEA, OV32/7, Federal Reserve Bank of New York, Confidential Cables, 1931.

11 'Note of a telephone conversation with Dr. Vocke at 2 p.m. on the 27th June, 1931' (#242). BEA, OV34/2, Country Files, Germany, February 14, 1930–July 31, 1931.

12 'Telephone conversation with Vice-President Dreyse at 4 p.m. on the 27th June, 1931' (#243). BEA, OV34/2, Country Files, Germany, February 14, 1930–July 31, 1931.
13 Telegram no. 196/31, June 27, 1931, from Norman to Harrison. CUL, HP, Box 9, binder 20, Bank of England, January–December 1931.
14 Note of June 30, 1931, on telephone conversation of June 29 at 1:50 p.m. between Harrison and Lacour-Gayet. CUL, HP, Box 21, binder 45, Harrison, Conversations, vol. 1, 1926–31.
15 Note of June 30, 1931, on telephone conversation of June 30 at 11:20 a.m. between Harrison and Lacour-Gayet. CUL, HP, Box 21, binder 45, Harrison, Conversations, vol. 1, 1926–31.
16 Note, June 30, 1931, on telephone conversation, June 30, 1931, 11:20 a.m., between Harrison and Lacour-Gayet. CUL, HP, Box 21, binder 45, Harrison, Conversations, vol. 1, 1926–31.
17 Note, June 30, 1931, on telephone conversation, June 30, 1931, 11:20 a.m., between Harrison and Lacour-Gayet. CUL, HP, Box 21, binder 45, Harrison, Conversations, vol. 1, 1926–31.
18 Note, June 30, 1931, on telephone conversation, June 30, 1931, 11:20 a.m., between Harrison and Lacour-Gayet. CUL, HP, Box 21, binder 45, Harrison, Conversations, vol. 1, 1926–31.
19 See also Toniolo, *Central Bank Cooperation*, 103.
20 Telegram no. 177, June 30, 1931, from Luther to Harrison. CUL, HP, Box 3, binder 7, Reichsbank (Germany), January 7–December 1931.
21 Telegram #87.540, June 29, 1931, from Morgan et Cie. to J.P. Morgan & Co., and #66.983, June 29, 1931, from J.P. Morgan & Co to Morgan et Cie. ARC 1221, Box 14, Morgan Bank European Papers. Folder, Cables received, May 16–June 30, 1931, 4-B, (111-248).
22 Meeting, July 1, 1931. BEA, G8/60, Minutes of the Committee of Treasury – March 1931 to June 1932.
23 Telegram no. 201/31, July 1, 1931, from Norman to Harrison. BEA, OV32/7, Federal Reserve Bank of New York, Confidential Cables, 1931.
24 Note, July 1, 1931, of telephone conversation of July 1 at 12.35 noon between Harrison and Norman. FRBNY, no. 3115.2, Harrison Papers. Harrison's conversations with M. Norman, 1931.
25 See Norman's diary, July 2, 1931, www.bankofengland.co.uk/-/media/boe/files/archive/montagu-norman-diary/1931/july-1931.pdf (accessed December 26, 2023).
26 Note, July 2, 1931, of telephone conversation, July 2, 1931, 5 p.m., between Harrison and Norman. FRBNY, no. 3115.2, Harrison Papers. Harrison's conversations with M. Norman, 1931.
27 Telegram no. 206/31, July 3, 1931, from Norman to Harrison. BEA, OV32/7, Federal Reserve Bank of New York, Confidential Cables, 1931.
28 Telegram no. 220/31, July 3, 1931, from Harrison to Norman. BEA, OV32/7, Federal Reserve Bank of New York, Confidential Cables, 1931.
29 Telegram no. 208/31, July 4, 1931, from Norman to Harrison. BEA, OV32/7, Federal Reserve Bank of New York, Confidential Cables, 1931.
30 Telegram no. 207/31, July 4, 1931, from Norman to Harrison. BEA, OV32/7, Federal Reserve Bank of New York, Confidential Cables, 1931.

31 Note of July 3, 1931. FRBNY, no. 2690.2, Harrison Papers. Meetings with committees or groups of bankers, 1931–36.
32 'Note of a telephone conversation with Dr. Vocke at 10.30 a.m. on the 4th July 1931', #128, by Siepmann; and 'The Governor', #129, by Siepmann. BEA, OV34/80, Germany Reichsbank, January 2–July 14, 1931. See also cable no. 194, July 4, 1931, from Luther to Harrison. CUL, HP, Box 3, binder 7, Reichsbank (Germany), January 7–December 1931.
33 'The Money Market', *The Economist*, July 4, 1931; 'The Monetary Half Year', *The Economist*, July 4, 1931.
34 Cable, July 5, 1931, from Luther to McGarrah. BISA, 7.18.2. MCG.1. Reichsbank, 1930–31.
35 Bennett, *Germany and the Diplomacy*, 177.
36 'France', *The Economist*, July 11, 1931, 69.
37 'Germany', *The Economist*, July 11, 1931, 69.
38 'Note of a telephone conversation with Dr. Vocke at 2 p.m. on 7th July 1931', #138, by Siepmann. BEA, OV34/80, Germany Reichsbank, January 2–July 14, 1931.
39 Telegram #107, July 7, 1931, from Harrison to Luther. CUL, HP, Box 3, binder 7, Reichsbank (Germany), January 7–December 1931.
40 'Note of a telephone conversation with Dr. Vocke at 2 p.m. on 7th July 1931', #138, by Siepmann. BEA, OV34/80, Germany Reichsbank, January 2–July 14, 1931.
41 Telegram in two parts, July 8, 1931, from Luther to Harrison. CUL, HP, Box 3, binder 7, Reichsbank (Germany), January 7–December 1931. Two telegrams translated into English, July 8, 1931, from Luther to Norman. BEA, OV34/80, Germany Reichsbank, January 2–July 14, 1931.
42 'Note of a telephone conversation with Dr. Vocke at 2 p.m. on 7th July 1931', #138, by Siepmann. BEA, OV34/80, Germany Reichsbank, January 2–July 14, 1931.
43 'Telephone conversation with Vice-President Dreyse on the 8th July 1931', #145, by Siepmann. BEA, OV34/80, Germany Reichsbank, January 2–July 14, 1931.
44 'Germany. Note of telephone conversation with Dr. Luther, Mr. McGarrah, and Monsieur Moret between 4.30 and 7 p.m. on the 8th July, 1931', by Siepmann, July 9, 1931, 11.40 a.m. BEA, OV34/80, Germany Reichsbank, January 2–July 14, 1931.
45 'Germany. Note of telephone conversation with Dr. Luther, Mr. McGarrah, and Monsieur Moret between 4.30 and 7 p.m. on the 8th July, 1931', by Siepmann, July 9, 1931, 11.40 a.m. BEA, OV34/80, Germany Reichsbank, January 2–July 14, 1931.
46 Note, July 9, 1931, of telephone conversation between Harrison and Norman, July 8, 1931, 2 p.m. FRBNY, no. 3115.2, Harrison Papers, Harrison's conversations with M. Norman, 1931. See also Note of 'Telephone conversation with Mr. Harrison', 6.15 p.m., July 8, 1931. BEA, OV32/7, Federal Reserve Bank of New York, Confidential Cables, 1931.
47 Note of 'Telephone conversation with Mr. Harrison', 6.15 p.m., July 8, 1931. BEA, OV32/7, Federal Reserve Bank of New York, Confidential Cables, 1931.
48 Note, July 10, 1931, of telephone conversation, July 8, 1931, 3.20 p.m., between McGarrah and Harrison. FRBNY, no. 3013.1, Harrison Papers. Harrison's conversations with G.W. McGarrah, 1930–33.

49 Telegram no. 225/31, July 8, 1931, from Harrison to Norman. BEA, OV32/7, Federal Reserve Bank of New York, Confidential Cables, 1931.
50 'Memorandum: Meeting of Executive Committee, June 1, 1931'. CUL, HP. Box 23, binder 50, Discussion Notes: Volumes I, II & III, April 17, 1930–September 21, 1933.
51 Telegram no. 225/31, July 8, 1931, from Harrison to Norman. BEA, OV32/7, Federal Reserve Bank of New York, Confidential Cables, 1931.
52 Telegram no. 225/31, July 8, 1931, from Harrison to Norman. BEA, OV32/7, Federal Reserve Bank of New York, Confidential Cables, 1931.
53 Telegram #94, July 9, 1931, from Harrison to Moret. CUL, HP, Box 14, binder 29, Bank of France, 1931. Note, July 9, 1931, 10.45 a.m., of telephone call from Lacour-Gayet to Harrison. CUL, HP, Box 21, binder 45, Harrison, Conversations, vol. 1, 1926–31.
54 Note, July 8, 1931, 4.45 p.m., on telephone call from Dreyse to Harrison, and note, July 9, 1931, 10.45 a.m. of telephone call from Lacour-Gayet to Harrison. CUL, HP, Box 21, binder 45, Harrison, Conversations, vol. 1, 1926–31.
55 Telegram # 209, July 9, 1931, from Luther to Harrison. CUL, HP, Box 3, binder 7, Reichsbank (Germany), January 7–December 1931.
56 Telegram # 114, July 10, 1931, from Harrison to Luther. CUL, HP, Box 3, binder 7, Reichsbank (Germany), January 7–December 1931.
57 See Eichengreen, *Golden Fetters*, 276; Toniolo, with the assistance of Clement, *Central Bank Cooperation*, 111–12. For an excellent discussion of the history of austerity (deflation, economy) as ideology, see Mark Blyth, *Austerity: The History of a Dangerous Idea* (Oxford: Oxford University Press, 2013).
58 Kunz, *The Battle for Britain's Gold Standard*, 63–64.
59 'Memorandum: Meeting of Executive Committee, July 13, 1931'. CUL, HP, Box 23, binder 50, Discussion Notes: Volumes I, II & III, April 17, 1930–September 21, 1933.
60 Note, July 9, 1931, of telephone conversation, July 9, 1931, between Harrison and Norman. FRBNY, no. 3115.2, Harrison Papers. Harrison's conversations with M. Norman, 1931. See also Clarke, *Central Bank Cooperation*, 194–97.
61 Meeting, July 9, 1931. BEA, G8/60, Minutes of the Committee of Treasury – March 1931 to June 1932.
62 Memorandum, July 7, 1931, by Rodd. BISA, 7.18.2. MCG.2. Banking Department, 1930–31.
63 Note, July 9, 1931, of telephone conversation, July 9, 1931, between Harrison and Norman. FRBNY, no. 3115.2, Harrison Papers. Harrison's conversations with M. Norman, 1931.
64 Note, July 9, 1931, of telephone conversation, July 9, 1931, between Harrison and Norman. FRBNY, no. 3115.2, Harrison Papers. Harrison's conversations with M. Norman, 1931. See also Clarke, *Central Bank Cooperation*, 194–97.
65 Hans Luther, *Vor Dem Abgrund. 1930–1933. Reichsbankpräsident in Krisenzeiten* (Berlin: Propyläen Verlag, 1964), 185–87.
66 'A Week of Crisis Continued', *The Economist*, July 11, 1931, 62; Charles A. Selden, 'Loan of $400,000,000 Is Sought by Luther in London and Paris', *The New York Times*, July 10, 1931.

67 Letter, July 9, 1931, from Harrison to Governors of the Federal Reserve. FRBNY, FR credits'31, . . . 1931–32, 1936, 1939.
68 Letter, July 10, 1931, from Seay to Harrison. FRBNY, FR credits'31, . . . 1931–32, 1936, 1939.
69 See also James, *The German Slump*, 295 n. 19, 303–4.
70 Letter, July 10, 1931, from Seay to Harrison. FRBNY, FR credits'31, . . . 1931–32, 1936, 1939.
71 Quoted from Burk, *Morgan Grenfell*, 146.
72 Horn, *J. P. Morgan & Co.*, 66–67.
73 Kunz, 'American Bankers', 40. For Jack Morgan's dislike of Germany, see Chernow, *The House of Morgan*, 310; Burk, *Morgan Grenfell*, 143. Martin Horn notes how J.P. Morgan's telegram to Morgan Grenfell demonstrated the partners' 'obtuseness regarding political conditions in Germany' and that the attitude was an expression of fear on behalf of the partners about contagion to New York among other things; see Horn, *J. P. Morgan & Co.*, 131–32.
74 Telegram #87.572, July 15, 1931, from Morgan & Cie to J.P. Morgan & Co. JPM, ARC 1221, Box 14, Morgan Bank. European Papers, folder, Cables sent July 1–August 31, 1931, 5A (1-133).
75 Telegram #87.572, July 15, 1931, from Morgan & Cie to J.P. Morgan & Co. JPM, ARC 1221, Box 14, Morgan Bank. European Papers, folder, Cables sent July 1–August 31, 1931, 5A (1-133).
76 Letter, July 10, 1931, from E. Rowe-Dutton to Leith-Ross. BEA, OV34/2, Country Files, Germany, February 14, 1930–July 31, 1931.
77 Quoted from Bennett, *Germany and the Diplomacy*, 225–28.
78 Note, July 11, 1931, 6.30 p.m., on phone call from Lacour-Gayet to Harrison. CUL, HP, Box 21, binder 45, Harrison, Conversations, vol. 1, 1926–31.
79 Note, July 10, 1931, on telephone conversation between Harrison and McGarrah. FRBNY, no. 3013.1, Harrison Papers, Harrison's conversations with G.W. McGarrah, 1930–33.
80 Note, July 14, 1931, on telephone conversation, July 11, 1931, 1.30 p.m., between Harrison and McGarrah. FRBNY, no. 3013.1, Harrison Papers, Harrison's conversations with G.W. McGarrah, 1930–33.

## Chapter 14

1 'Hope Revived?', *The Economist*, July 11, 1931.
2 Note, July 11, 1931, on phone call from Dreyse to Harrison, July 11, 1931, 10.30 a.m. CUL, HP, Box 21, binder 45, Harrison, Conversations, vol. 1, 1926–31. In his memoirs, Luther clearly states that the French posed political conditions for assisting Germany. Clarke and Bennett seem to support this argument. See Luther, *Vor Dem Abgrund*, 186–88; Bennett, *Germany and the Diplomacy*, 229–31; Clarke, *Central Bank Cooperation*, 195–96.
3 Note, July 11, 1931, on phone call from Dreyse to Harrison, July 11, 1931, 10.30 a.m. CUL, HP, Box 21, binder 45, Harrison, Conversations, vol. 1, 1926–31.
4 'Telegraphic report from Berlin', July 11, 1931. CUL, HP, Box 21, binder 45, Harrison, Conversations, vol. 1, 1926–31.

5 'Telegraphic report from Berlin', July 11, 1931. CUL, HP, Box 21, binder 45, Harrison, Conversations, vol. 1, 1926–31. It is not entirely clear whether the report comes from the Reichsbank or the German government. See also Robert L. Hetzel, 'German Monetary History in the First Half of the Twentieth Century', *Economic Quarterly-Federal Reserve Bank of Richmond* 88, no. 2 (2002): 28–32.
6 Confidential telegram, July 11, 1931, from Dreyse to Harrison. CUL, HP, Box 3, binder 7, Reichsbank (Germany), January 7–December 1931.
7 Telegram, July 12, 1931, from Dreyse to Harrison. CUL, HP, Box 3, binder 7, Reichsbank (Germany), January 7–December 1931.
8 Telegram, July 12, 1931, from Luther to Harrison, and telegram, July 12, 1931, from Dreyse to Harrison. CUL, HP, Box 3, binder 7, Reichsbank (Germany), January 7–December 1931.
9 Telegram #116, July 12, 1931, from Harrison to Luther. CUL, HP, Box 3, binder 7, Reichsbank (Germany), January 7–December 1931. See also two notes on Harrison's conversations with Otto Kiep, July 11 and 12, 1931. CUL, HP, Box 21, binder 45, Harrison, Conversations, vol. 1, 1926–31. They basically repeat the information contained in Harrison's telegram to Luther.
10 Telegram, July 11, 1931, from Moret to Harrison. CUL, HP, Box 14, binder 29, Bank of France, 1931.
11 Note, July 14, 1931, of telephone conversation, July 12, 1931, noon, between Otto Kiep and Harrison. CUL, HP, Box 21, binder 45, Harrison, Conversations, vol. 1, 1926–31.
12 Telegram #209, July 9, 1931, from Luther to Harrison. CUL, HP, Box 3, binder 7, Reichsbank (Germany), January 7–December 1931.
13 Note, July 14, 1931, of telephone conversation, July 12, 1931, noon, between Otto Kiep and Harrison. CUL, HP, Box 21, binder 45, Harrison, Conversations, vol. 1, 1926–31.
14 Letter, July 12, 1931, from Moore to E.C. Douglas. FRBNY, Box 189130, folder Correspondence with Wiggin Committee in Basle + Bank for International Settlements, May–July 1931.
15 Harold James, 'The 1931 Central European Banking Crisis Revisited', in *Business in the Age of Extremes: Essays in Modern German and Austrian Economic History*, ed. Hartmut Berghoff, Jürgen Kocka and Dieter Ziegler (Cambridge: Cambridge University Press, 2013), 123, 125. For further discussions about the origins of the German twin crisis, see Born, *Die Deutsche Bankkrise 1931*; Harold James, 'The Causes of the German Banking Crisis of 1931', *The Economic History Review* 37, no. 1 (1984): 68–87; Theo Balderston, 'The Banks and the Gold Standard in the German Financial Crisis of 1931', *Financial History Review* 1, no. 1 (1994): 43–68; Thomas Ferguson and Peter Temin, 'Made in Germany: The German Currency Crisis of July 1931', *Research in Economic History* 21 (2003); Temin, 'Currency Crises'; Toniolo, with the assistance of Clement, *Central Bank Cooperation*; Isabel Schnabel, 'The German Twin Crisis of 1931', *The Journal of Economic History* 64, no. 03 (2004): 822–71; Thomas Ferguson and Peter Temin, 'Comment on "The German Twin Crisis of 1931"', *The Journal of Economic History* 64, no. 03 (2004): 872–76.
16 'Reported Decision at Basle', *Financial Times*, July 14, 1931.

17 'Note of a conversation this afternoon with Mr. Gurney of the B.O.B.' July 13, 1931. BEA, OV34/2, Country Files, Germany, February 14, 1930–July 31, 1931.
18 'Translation. Frankfurter Zeitung, 15.7.1931. The New Emergency Decree', #270, July 16,1931, by J.B.R. BEA, OV34/2, Country Files, Germany, February 14, 1930–July 31, 1931; 'Germany', *The Economist*, July 18, 1931; 'Coming to Grips', *The Economist*, July 18, 1931; 'A Diary of the Crisis', *The Economist*, July 18, 1931; Guido Enderis, 'Reich Situation Calmer', *The New York Times*, July 14, 1931. See also Eichengreen, *Golden Fetters*, 275–76; Tooze, *The Deluge*; Boyce, *The Great Interwar Crisis*, 309–10; Accominotti and Eichengreen, 'The Mother of All Sudden Stops'; Tobias Straumann, Peter Kugler and Florian Weber, 'How the German Crisis of 1931 Swept across Europe: A Comparative View from Stockholm', *Economic History Review* 70, no. 1 (2017): 243–44; Kirsten Wandschneider, 'The Stability of the Interwar Gold Exchange Standard: Did Politics Matter?', *Journal of Economic History* 68, no. 1 (2008): 157.
19 'Germany', *The Economist*, July 25, 1931, 171.
20 Harold Callender, 'Reich Bankers See Ruin Unless Aided', *The New York Times*, July 14, 1931.
21 'The Financial Situation', *Commercial and Financial Chronicle*, July 18, 1931. See also the Chronicle's narrative of the crisis, pp. 339–43. On the basis of legal and domestic financial reasons, the *Chronicle* was a persistent opponent to the Federal Reserve's involvement in credits to Austria, Hungary and Germany.
22 Telegram, July 13, 1931, from Dreyse to Harrison. CUL, HP, Box 3, binder 7, Reichsbank (Germany), January 7–December 1931; Clement, 'Between Banks and Governments', 147.
23 'Minutes of the thirteenth meeting of the board of directors of the Bank for International Settlements held in Basle on July 13, 1931'. BEA, OV 5/3, Bank for International Settlements. Minutes of Meetings of Board of Directors. 8.6.31 to 12.10.31.
24 Richard V. Oulahan, 'Hoover Will Leave Action to Bankers', *The New York Times*, July 13, 1931.
25 Note of July 14, 1931, on telephone conversation July 13 at 10.35 a.m. between Harrison and McGarrah. FRBNY, no. 3013.1, Harrison Papers, Harrison's conversations with G.W. McGarrah, 1930–33. See also Clarke, *Central Bank Cooperation: 1924–31*, 195.
26 Bennett, *Germany and the Diplomacy*, 240; Clarence K. Streit, 'World Bank Pledges Aid', *The New York Times*, July 14, 1931.
27 Clement, 'Between Banks and Governments', 148.
28 'Memorandum: Meeting of Executive Committee, July 13, 1931'. CUL, HP, Box 23, binder 50, Discussion Notes: Volumes I, II & III, April 17, 1930–September 21, 1933. See also Meltzer, *A History of the Federal Reserve*, 357 and n. 68.
29 Note of July 14, 1931, on telephone conversation July 13 at 3 p.m. between Harrison and McGarrah. FRBNY, no. 3013.1, Harrison Papers, Harrison's conversations with G.W. McGarrah, 1930–33.
30 Note of July 14, 1931, on telephone conversation July 13 at 5.20 p.m. between Harrison and Norman. FRBNY, no. 3115.2, Harrison Papers, Harrison's conversations with M. Norman, 1931.

31 Meeting, July 15, 1931. BEA, G8/60, Minutes of the Committee of Treasury – March 1931 to June 1932.
32 Quoted from Boyce, *The Great Interwar Crisis*, 309.
33 Note on 'Telephone conversation with Mr. Rodd at 12.5 p.m. Tuesday, 14th July, 1931'. (#166). BEA, OV34/80, Germany Reichsbank, January 2–July 14, 1931.
34 Kynaston, *The City of London*, 227–30. The Bank of England also performed open market operations in order to increase market liquidity after July 15, see Accominotti, 'London Merchant Banks', 24, 30 et passim; Sayers, *The Bank of England*, 503–12. Lazard's crisis was mostly due to a 'rogue trader' in the Belgian branch, see Cohan, *The Last Tycoons*, 29–34.
35 Telegram no. 427, July 14, 1931, from BIS to FRBNY. FRBNY, C261.1, National Bank (Austrian Nat'l Bank) Credit, May 1931–December 1932, 1 of 2. See also Marcus, *Austrian Reconstruction.*
36 'Note of a telephone conversation with Mr. Rodd at 11.40 a.m. on 16th July, 1931'. #97, July 16, 1931, 12.5 p.m. by Siepmann. BEA, OV28/4, Austria Country File June 16–July 30, 1931.
37 Letter, July 18, 1931, from Bruins to McGarrah. BISA, 6.30. II/1 Granting of Credit of 100,000,000 Schilling to Austrian National Bank, 1931.
38 'Facing Realities', *The New York Times*, July 14, 1931.
39 Streit, 'World Bank Pledges Aid', *The New York Times*, July 14, 1931.
40 Note of July 21, 1931, on telephone conversation between Harrison and McGarrah on July 14 at 11 a.m. FRBNY, no. 3013.1, Harrison Papers, Harrison's conversations with G.W. McGarrah, 1930–33.
41 Note of July 21, 1931, on telephone conversation between Harrison and McGarrah on July 14 at 11 a.m. FRBNY, no. 3013.1, Harrison Papers, Harrison's conversations with G.W. McGarrah, 1930–33.
42 'Dr. Vocke telephoned at 5.20 p.m.', July 14, 1931, by Siepmann. BEA, OV34/80, Central Bank, Reichsbank Direktorium, January 2–July 14, 1931.
43 Memorandum of July 21, 1931, of telephone conversation, July 15, 1931, 11.45 a.m., between McGarrah and Harrison. FRBNY, no. 3013.1, Harrison Papers, Harrison's conversations with G.W. McGarrah, 1930–33.
44 'Note of a telephone conversation with Dr. Vocke 6.20 p.m., Wednesday, 15th July, 1931', by Siepmann. BEA, OV34/81, Central Bank, Reichsbank Direktorium, July 15–December 1931.
45 Note of July 21, 1931, on telephone conversation, July 15, 1931, 9.30 a.m., between Harrison and Norman. FRBNY, no. 3115.2, Harrison Papers, Harrison's conversations with M. Norman, 1931; note, July 21, 1931, of meeting between Harrison and New York City Bankers, July 15, 1931, 12.15 p.m.; note, July 16, 1931, of meeting at 10.30 a.m. between Harrison and New York City Bankers, and Exhibit C attached to note, July 16, 1931, of meeting at 10.30 a.m. between Harrison and New York City Bankers. FRBNY, FR credits'31, . . . 1931–32, 1936, 1939; telegram no. 231/31, July 15, 1931, from Harrison to Norman. BEA, OV32/7, Federal Reserve Bank of New York, Confidential Cables, 1931.
46 Telegram no. 224/31, July 16, 1931, 6.15 p.m., from Norman to Harrison. BEA, OV32/7, Federal Reserve Bank of New York, Confidential Cables, 1931.
47 Telegram no. 234/31, July 16, 1931, from Harrison to Norman. BEA, OV32/7, Federal Reserve Bank of New York, Confidential Cables, 1931.

48 Telegram #124, July 15, 1931, from Harrison to Luther. See also telegram #241, July 14, 1931, from Luther to Harrison. CUL, HP, Box 3, binder 7, Reichsbank (Germany), January 7–December 1931. See also telegram #23, July 14, 1931, from McGarrah to Harrison. CUL, HP, Box 16, binder 36, Personal Cables, 1930–35.

49 Note and 'Memorandum', exhibit B, of meeting with bankers at the New York Fed, July 16, 1931, 10.30 a.m. FRBNY, FR credits'31, . . . 1931–32, 1936, 1939.

50 Copy of strictly private and confidential letter, July 16, 1931, from The Bankers' Clearing House to member banks. BEA, OV34/2, Country Files, Germany, February 14, 1930–July 31, 1931, #278.

51 Telegram #24, July 16, 1931, from McGarrah to Harrison. BIS, HA, Box 16, binder 36, Personal Cables, 1930–35.

52 In Great Britain, merchant banks were most exposed to Central Europe, while in the United States, it was the large commercial banks that had lent to Europe. The latter, however, were never threatened by the European crisis. See Accominotti, 'London Merchant Banks'; Accominotti, 'International Banking'; Richardson and Van Horn, 'In the Eye of a Storm'; Billings and Capie, 'Financial Crisis'. Barry Eichengreen writes that the German crisis meant that at least £70 million of English claims were frozen; see Eichengreen, *Golden Fetters*, 280. See also Moggridge, *Maynard Keynes*, 520; Skidelsky, *John Maynard Keynes*, 393; Boyce, *The Great Interwar Crisis*, 313–14.

53 Leith-Ross, *Money Talks*, 137; Dulles, *The Bank for International Settlements*, 398–401. The standstill agreement was renewed annually until 1939, see Sayers, *The Bank of England*, 503–12; Neil Forbes, 'London Banks, the German Standstill Agreements, and "Economic Appeasement" in the 1930s', *The Economic History Review* 40, no. 4 (1987): 571–87.

54 'The Financial Situation', *Commercial and Financial Chronicle*, July 18, 1931.

55 'Note of a telephone conversation between Dr. Brüning and Dr. Schober late last night about the situation in their respective countries'. #100, July 16, 1931, 4.20 p.m., by Siepmann. BEA, OV28/4, Austria Country File, June 16–July 30, 1931.

56 'Memorandum: Meeting of Board of Directors, July 16, 1931'. CUL, HP, Box 23, binder 50, Discussion Notes: Volumes I, II & III, April 17, 1930–September 21, 1933.

57 Department of State, *Papers Relating to the Foreign Relations of the United States, 1931, Volume I* (Washinghton DC, 1931), 256–57. See also Bennett, *Germany and the Diplomacy*, 246–49.

58 Memorandum, July 21, 1931, of telephone conversation between Harrison and Norman, July 16, 1931, 3.50 p.m. FRBNY, no. 3115.2, Harrison Papers, Harrison's conversations with M. Norman, 1931. For the French plan for a government loan, see Office of the Historian, 'Memorandum by the Secretary of State of Conversations With M. Flandin and With Mr. Jay, of Morgan & Company, at the Residence of the American Ambassador in France, July 17, 1931', *Papers Relating to the Foreign Relations of the United States, 1931*, https://history.state.gov/historicaldocuments/frus1931v01/d229; Office of the Historian, 'Memorandum by the Secretary of State', *Papers Relating to the Foreign Relations of the United States, 1931*, https://history.state.gov/historicaldocuments/frus1931v01/d217.

59 Memorandum, July 21, 1931, of telephone conversation between Harrison and Norman, July 16, 1931, 3.50 p.m. FRBNY, no. 3115.2, Harrison Papers, Harrison's conversations with M. Norman, 1931. See also James, *The German Slump*, 304.
60 Note from telephone call, July 16, 1931, 4.10 p.m., from Harrison to Mills. CUL, HP, Box 27, binder 59, Office Memoranda: Volume II, 1928–31.
61 Office of the Historian, 'Memorandum of Telephone Conversation', *Papers Relating to the Foreign Relations of the United States, 1931*.
62 Note from telephone call, July 17, 1931, 11.10 a.m., from Mills to Harrison. CUL, HP, Box 27, binder 59, Office Memoranda: Volume II, 1928–31. See also Office of the Historian, 'Memorandum by the Secretary of State'.
63 'Coming to Grips', *The Economist*, July 18, 1931.
64 'Germany', *The Economist*, July 18, 1931.
65 'The financial crash in Germany', July 17, 1931, by E. Rowe-Dutton. BEA, OV34/2, Country Files, Germany, February 14, 1930–July 31, 1931, #320.
66 Telegram #435, July 17, 1931, from McGarrah to Harrison. BIS, HA, Box 1, binder 2, Bank for International Settlements, April 2, 1930–December 1931.
67 Telegram #258, July 18, 1931, from Luther to Harrison. CUL, HP, Box 3, binder 7, Reichsbank (Germany), January 7–December 1931.
68 Memorandum, July 21, 1931, of telephone conversation, July 20, 1931, 2.45 p.m., between Harrison and McGarrah. FRBNY, no. 3013.1, Harrison Papers, Harrison's conversations with G.W. McGarrah, 1930–33.
69 Office of the Historian, 'The Acting Secretary of State to the Chargé in Great Britain (Atherton)', *Papers Relating to the Foreign Relations of the United States, 1931*.
70 Office of the Historian, 'The Acting Secretary of State to the Chargé in Great Britain (Atherton)', *Papers Relating to the Foreign Relations of the United States, 1931*.
71 Telegram #67.024, July 17, 1931, from J.P. Morgan & Co. to Morgan & Cie. JPM, ARC 1221, Box 14, Morgan Bank. European Papers, Folder 5-A, Cables Received, July 1–August 31, 1931 (1-120). See also Bennett, *Germany and the Diplomacy*, 260–61.
72 Telegram #67.024, July 17, 1931, from J.P. Morgan & Co. to Morgan & Cie. JPM, ARC 1221, Box 14, Morgan Bank. European Papers, Folder 5-A, Cables Received, July 1–August 31, 1931 (1-120). See also Bennett, *Germany and the Diplomacy*, 260–61.
73 Office of the Historian, 'Memorandum by the Secretary of State of Conversations With M. Flandin and With Mr. Jay, of Morgan & Company, at the Residence of the American Ambassador in France, July 17, 1931'. See also 'U.S. Cites Its Steps to Halt'31 Crisis', *The New York Times*, December 7, 1946.
74 Telegram #67.028, July 18, 1931, from J.P. Morgan & Co. to Morgan & Cie. JPM, ARC 1221, Box 14, Morgan Bank. European Papers, Folder 5-A, Cables Received, July 1–August 31, 1931 (1-120).
75 Telegram #87.584, July 18, 1931, from Morgan & Cie. to J.P. Morgan & Co. JPM, ARC 1221, Box 14, Morgan Bank. European Papers, folder, Cables sent July 1–August 31, 1931, 5A (1-133).
76 Cable #200, July 20, 1931, 6.35 p.m., from Morgan Grenfell to the Corsair. JPM, ARC 1216, Box 38A, Folder 34.
77 Note on telephone conversation between Harrison and Stewart, July 21, 1931, 4.05 p.m., by Harrison. CUL, HP, Box 21, binder 45, Harrison, Conversations, vol. 1, 1926–31.

78 Telegram #25, July 21, 1931, from McGarrah to Harrison. BIS, HA, Box 16, binder 36, Personal Cables, 1930–35.
79 Cable #134, July 21, 1931, from Harrison to Luther. CUL, HP, Box 3, binder 7, Reichsbank (Germany), January 7–December 1931.
80 'Note of a conversation between the Governor and Dr. Vocke held at the Bank of England on 21st July, 1931', by Siepmann. BEA, OV34/80, Central Bank, Reichsbank Direktorium, January 2–July 14, 1931.
81 Note on telephone conversation between Harrison and Stewart, July 21, 1931, 4.05 p.m., by Harrison. CUL, HP, Box 21, binder 45, Harrison, Conversations, vol. 1, 1926–31.
82 Cable #5, July 22, 1931, 8.20 a.m., from J.P. Morgan to the Corsair. JPM, ARC 1216, Box 38A, Folder 34.
83 Cable #4, July 22, 1931, from Jack Morgan to J.P. Morgan & Co. JPM, ARC 1216, Box 38A, Folder 34.
84 Cable #203, July 22, 1931, 7.10 p.m. from Morgan Grenfell to the Corsair. JPM, ARC 1216, Box 38A, Folder 34.
85 Cable #204, July 23, 1931, received 9 p.m., from Morgan Grenfell to the Corsair. JPM, ARC 1216, Box 38A, Folder 33.
86 Cable #103, July 24, 1931, from Jack Morgan to Morgan Grenfell. JPM, ARC 1216, Box 38A, Folder 33.
87 'The Conference and the Crisis', *The Economist*, July 25, 1931. For a historian's perspective on the London Conference, see Bennett, *Germany and the Diplomacy*, 249.
88 'The Conference and the Crisis', *The Economist*, July 25, 1931.
89 Cable #204, July 23, 1931, received 9 p.m., from Morgan Grenfell to the Corsair. JPM, ARC 1216, Box 38A, Folder 33.
90 Cable #103, July 24, 1931, from Jack Morgan to Morgan Grenfell. JPM, ARC 1216, Box 38A, Folder 33.
91 Letter, July 23, 1931, from Waley to Rodd. DB, Morgan Grenfell papers: Box 50595324/folder Correspondence with the British Treasury. I am grateful to Martin Horn for drawing my attention to this letter.

## Chapter 15

1 'The Financial Situation', *Commercial and Financial Chronicle*, August 8, 1931, 847–48.
2 'The Financial Situation', *Commercial and Financial Chronicle*, August 15, 1931, 1008.
3 Telegram no. 469, August 3, 1931, from McGarrah to Harrison. FRBNY, C261.1, National Bank (Austrian Nat'l Bank) Credit, May 1931–December 1932.
4 Confidential letter, August 6, 1931, from W. Randolph Burgess to J.E. Crane. FRBNY, Box 189130, folder, US Problems + Credits to Austria, Germany, Hungary August–December 1931.
5 'London Takes the Strain', *Financial Times*, July 14, 1931.
6 Clement, 'Between Banks and Governments', 148.
7 Sayers, *The Bank of England*, 389–92; Kunz, 'American Bankers', 39.
8 'The Financial Situation', *Commercial and Financial Chronicle*, July 18, 1931.

9 Telegram no. 231/31, July 15, 1931, from Harrison to Norman. BEA, OV32/7, Federal Reserve Bank of New York, Confidential Cables, 1931.

10 Telegram no. 223/31, July 16, 1931, 3.20 p.m., from Norman to Harrison. BEA, OV32/7, Federal Reserve Bank of New York, Confidential Cables, 1931. See also Williams, who argues that the loss of confidence in London as a banking centre took the Bank of England by surprise, David Willams, 'London and the 1931 Financial Crisis', *The Economic History Review* 15, no. 3 (1963): 524.

11 Memorandum, July 21, 1931, of telephone conversation between Harrison and Norman, July 16, 1931, 3.50 p.m. FRBNY, no. 3115.2, Harrison Papers, Harrison's conversations with M. Norman, 1931.

12 'The Money Market', *The Economist*, July 18, 1931, 102. According to Bennett, Norman 'in a passion . . . called Harrison and poured out his feelings' in an attempt to weaken France's position vis-à-vis Germany. Bennett, *Germany and the Diplomacy*, 257–58. See also Boyce, who shows how British media blamed France for the pressure on sterling while evidence suggests that the Banque de France and Moret supported sterling, Boyce, *The Great Interwar Crisis*, 315–17.

13 'London Is Cheered despite Gold Loss', *The New York Times*, July 17, 1931.

14 Telegram no. 231/31, July 21, 1931, 7 p.m., from Norman to Harrison. BEA, OV32/7, Federal Reserve Bank of New York, Confidential Cables, 1931.

15 Norman's handwritten note is on the telegram. Unfortunately, I have not been able to locate other records of the phone call. Telegram no. 231/31, July 21, 1931, 7 p.m., from Norman to Harrison. BEA, OV32/7, Federal Reserve Bank of New York, Confidential Cables, 1931.

16 'Bank Rate Raised to 3 1/2 per Cent', *Financial Times*, July 24, 1931.

17 Copy of text of telegram sent to all Federal Reserve Bank governors on July 24, 1931. FRBNY, Office correspondence: Subject: United States Correspondance, FRB Subcommittee, etc., May 1931–December 1932, 1936, 1939.

18 Memorandum, July 24, 1931, of telephone conversation, July 22, 1931, between Harrison and Meyer. FRBNY, FR credits '31, . . . 1931–32, 1936, 1939.

19 Telegram no. 243/31, July 23, 1931, received July 24, 1931, 1.20 a.m., from Harrison to Norman. BEA, OV32/7, Federal Reserve Bank of New York, Confidential Cables, 1931.

20 Telegram #103, July 24, 1931, from Crane to Moret. FRBNY, C261, France, Bank of France, 1931.

21 Note on telephone conversation between Lacour-Gayet and Crane, July 25, 1931. FRBNY, C261, England, Bank of England, 1931–32, General.

22 Telegram no. 243/31, July 27, 1931 (but written on July 25), from Norman to Harrison. BEA, OV32/7, Federal Reserve Bank of New York, Confidential Cables, 1931.

23 www.bankofengland.co.uk/-/media/boe/files/archive/montagu-norman-diary/1931/july-1931.pdf (accessed December 26, 2023). See also Boyle, *Montagu Norman*, 266.

24 Telegram no. 247/31, July 28, 1931, 4.10 p.m., from Norman to Harrison. BEA, OV32/7, Federal Reserve Bank of New York, Confidential Cables, 1931. See also Kunz, *The Battle for Britain's Gold Standard*, 84.

25 Meeting, July 27, 1931. BEA, G8/60, Minutes of the Committee of Treasury – March 1931 to June 1932.

26 Note of call from Fraser to Crane, July 27, 1931. FRBNY, Box 128149, folder 797.3, Bank of International Settlements, July–December 1931.

27 Telegram #27, July 28, 1931, from McGarrah to Harrison. CUL, HP, Box 16, binder 36, Personal Cables, 1930–35. On July 29, 1931, Harvey wrote to Moret that certain difficulties had arisen but that he worked to overcome them. See Morrison, 'Shocking Intellectual Austerity . . . Extended Citations', note 106.

28 Note, July 29, 1931, 12.40 p.m., of telephone conversation between Harrison and Norman. FRBNY, no. 3115.2, Harrison Papers. Harrison's conversations with M. Norman, 1931. See also Sayers, *The Bank of England*, 392–93; Janeway, 'The 1931 Sterling Crisis', 263.

29 Carlisle MacDonald, 'Britain Is Assured of French Credits', *The New York Times*, July 29, 1931.

30 Kunz, *The Battle for Britain's Gold Standard*, 85–86.

31 Note, July 29, 1931, 12.40 p.m., of telephone conversation between Harrison and Norman. FRBNY, no. 3115.2, Harrison Papers. Harrison's conversations with M. Norman, 1931. See also Sayers, *The Bank of England*, 392–93; Janeway, 'The 1931 Sterling Crisis', 263.

32 Note, July 29, 1931, 12.40 p.m., of telephone conversation between Harrison and Norman. FRBNY, no. 3115.2, Harrison Papers. Harrison's conversations with M. Norman, 1931.

33 Note, July 29, 1931, 12.40 p.m., of telephone conversation between Harrison and Norman. FRBNY, no. 3115.2, Harrison Papers. Harrison's conversations with M. Norman, 1931.

34 Meeting, July 29, 1931, of Bank of England's Committee of Treasury. BEA, G8/60, Minutes of the Committee of Treasury – March 1931 to June 1932. James Ashley Morrison argues that a conflict erupted between Norman and Harvey at the Bank's Committee of Treasury meeting on Wednesday, July 29, the same day Norman told Harrison about the two schools. However, Norman had also cabled about the two schools to Harrison the day before, so this discussion between a credit and a discount rate increase did not begin at the Committee meeting. In fact, the Committee meeting agreed to raise the rate to 4½ per cent and to let Moret know that preliminary discussions about a credit had also been taken up with New York. Morrison, 'Shocking Intellectual Austerity', 185–86; Morrison, 'Shocking Intellectual Austerity . . . Extended Citations', notes 97 and 98. For the Committee of Treasury meeting, see Meeting, July 29, 1931, of Bank of England's Committee of Treasury. BEA, G8/60, Minutes of the Committee of Treasury – March 1931 to June 1932.

35 www.bankofengland.co.uk/-/media/boe/files/archive/montagu-norman-diary/1931/july-1931.pdf (accessed December 26, 2023). See also Boyle, *Montagu Norman*, 266; Sayers, *The Bank of England*, 392. For Thorpe Lodge, see Jonathan Foyle, 'The Renovation of a Former Bank of England Governor's Historic Home', *Financial Times*, August 28, 2020.

36 Note, July 31, 1931, of call to Lacour-Gayet from Harrison, July 29, 1931, 6.30 p.m. CUL, HP, Box 21, binder 45, Harrison, Conversations, vol. 1, 1926–31.

37 Telegram #31/2350, July 29, 1931, from J.P. Morgan & Co to Morgan Grenfell & Co., received July 29, 1931, 10 a.m. JPM, ARC 1216, Box 38A, Folder 34.

38 Telegram #31/4894, July 29, 1931, 6.15 p.m., from Morgan Grenfell & Co. to J.P. Morgan & Co. JPM, ARC 1216, Box 38A, Folder 34.
39 'The Bank Rate Increase', *The Economist*, August 1, 1931.
40 'Steadying up the Exchanges', *Financial Times*, July 30, 1931.
41 'Memorandum: Meeting of Board of Directors July 30, 1931. Subject: Bank of England Credit'. CUL, HP, Box 23, binder 50, Discussion Notes: Volumes I, II & III, April 17, 1930–September 21, 1933.
42 Note, July 30, 1931, of call from Harrison to Harvey, July 30, 1931, 4.48 p.m. CUL, HP, Box 21, binder 45, Harrison, Conversations, vol. 1, 1926–31.
43 Sayers, *The Bank of England*, 398.
44 Telegram #256/31, July 30, 1931, from Harvey to Harrison. BEA, OV32/7, Federal Reserve Bank of New York, Confidential Cables, 1931. Morrison argues that 'following the collapse of the Bank's governor, the deputy governor shifted Bank strategy from making defensive rate hikes to pursuing fiscal austerity'. According to this argument, Harvey, who did not share Norman's network and connections with the City's merchant bankers, pursued a 'relentless campaign to badger the politicians into balancing the budget'. See Morrison, 'Shocking Intellectual Austerity', 182, 185–87. See also Simmons, *Who Adjusts?*, 230. Diane Kunz, in contrast, argues that the Bank of England's hesitation to use the discount rate during the crisis had already been present in the 1920s; Kunz, *The Battle for Britain's Gold Standard*, 18. It is also worth noting that Norman would not necessarily have been against Harvey's campaign and pressure on the British government to deal with the budget deficit. See James, Harold, 'The Ideology of Central Banking', 48.
45 Note, July 31, 1931, by Harrison on call to Lacour-Gayet, July 30, 1931, 6.30 p.m. CUL, HP, Box 21, binder 45, Harrison, Conversations, vol. 1, 1926–31. See also Clarke, *Central Bank Cooperation*, 206.
46 Note, July 31, 1931, by Harrison on call to Lacour-Gayet, July 30, 1931, 6.30 p.m. CUL, HP, Box 21, binder 45, Harrison, Conversations, vol. 1, 1926–31. See also Clarke, 206.
47 Note, August 3, 1931, telephone conversation on July 31, 1931, 7.00 p.m. between Harrison and Harvey. CUL, HP, Box 27, binder 59, Office Memoranda: Volume II, 1928–31.
48 'France', *The Economist*, August 1, 1931.
49 Telegram #108, August 1, 1931, from Harrison to Lacour-Gayet. CUL, HP, Box 14, binder 29, Bank of France, 1931.
50 Telegram #262/31, August 1, 1931, from Harrison to Harvey. CUL, HP, Box 9, binder 20, Bank of England, January–December 1931.
51 Telegram #111, August 4, 1931, from Moret to Harrison. CUL, HP, Box 14, binder 29, Bank of France, 1931.
52 See also Sayers, *The Bank of England*, 388.
53 Telegram, August 5, 1931, from Lacour-Gayet to Harrison. CUL, HP, Box 14, binder 29, Bank of France, 1931.
54 'The Exchange Crisis', *The Economist*, August 8, 1931.
55 'The Financial Situation', *Commercial and Financial Chronicle*, August 8, 1931.
56 'France', *The Economist*, August 8, 1931, 267–68.
57 Mouré, *The Gold Standard Illusion*, 194–97; Kunz, 'American Bankers', 41.

58 Clavin, *The Great Depression in Europe*, 131–32; Ahamed, *Lords of Finance*, 425–26.

59 Quoted from Moggridge, *Maynard Keynes*, 523–24. See also Skidelsky, *John Maynard Keynes*, 393–94.

60 Note, August 5, 1931, of telephone conversation between Siepmann and Moret, August 5, 1931, 7.10 p.m. BEA; OV45/82, Banque de France, January 1, 1931–February 25, 1932. See also Meeting, August 6, 1931, of Bank of England's Committee of Treasury. BEA, G8/60, Minutes of the Committee of Treasury – March 1931 to June 1932. See also Mouré, *Managing the Franc Poincare*, 66–68.

61 Telegram #2, August 5, 1931, from Sproul to Crane. CUL, HP, Box 16, binder 34, European Trips, 1927–32. See also notes, August 5 and 6, 1931, on telephone conversations between Sproul and Catterns. BEA, C261, England, Bank of England, 1931–32, General.

62 Telegram #2, August 6, 1931, from Crane to Sproul. CUL, HP, Box 16, binder 34, European Trips, 1927–32. See also notes of August 5 and 6, 1931, on telephone conversations between Sproul and Catterns. FRBNY, C261, England, Bank of England, 1931–32, General.

63 Note, August 8, 1931, on telephone conversation, August 6, 1931, 6.00 p.m., between Lacour-Gayet and Harrison. CUL, HP, Box 21, binder 45, Harrison, Conversations, vol. 1, 1926–31.

64 Meeting of August 6, 1931, of Bank of England's Committee of Treasury. BEA, G8/60, Minutes of the Committee of Treasury – March 1931 to June 1932.

65 Sayers, *The Bank of England*; Janeway, 'The 1931 Sterling Crisis', 260; Willams, 'London and the 1931 Financial Crisis', 519.

66 Meeting of August 6, 1931, of Bank of England's Committee of Treasury. BEA, G8/60, Minutes of the Committee of Treasury – March 1931 to June 1932. Eichengreen and Jeanne argue that the Bank did not raise the bank rate beyond 4.5 per cent because it would increase unemployment, see Eichengreen and Jeanne, 'Currency Crisis', 15–20. See also Willams, 'London and the 1931 Financial Crisis', 519–20; Harris, *Monetary War and Peace*, 43. For a different and not heavily substantiated interpretation arguing that central bank cooperation made compliance with credits more important than bank rate, see Nicholas Dimsdale and Nicholas Horsewood, 'The Financial Crisis of 1931 and the Impact of the Great Depression on the British Economy', in *British Financial Crises since 1825*, ed. Nicholas Dimsdale and Anthony Hotson (Oxford: Oxford University Press, 2014), 122–23, 135. For an international political economy perspective, see Jack A. Seddon, 'Between Collapse and Decline: The Dissolution of International Monetary Systems in Comparative Historical Perspective' (St. John's College, University of Oxford, 2015), 99–135. For a discussion and social network perspective that emphasizes the role of intersubjective trust, see Aykens, '(Mis)Trusting Authorities'.

67 Confidential letter, August 6, 1931, from Harvey to Snowden. BEA, G1/468, Governor's Papers – Miscellaneous, January 1931–December 1931.

68 Note, August 8, 1931, on telephone conversation, August 6, 1931, 6.00 p.m., between Lacour-Gayet and Harrison. CUL, HP, Box 21, binder 45, Harrison, Conversations, vol. 1, 1926–31.

69 Note, August 8, 1931, of telephone conversation between Lacour-Gayet and Harrison, August 7, 1931, 7.00 p.m. CUL, HP, Box 21, binder 45, Harrison, Conversations, vol. 1, 1926–31.

70 For discussions and different views of the event, see Boyce, *The Great Interwar Crisis*, 318–19; Sayers, *The Bank of England*, 394–96. See also Mouré, *The Gold Standard Illusion*, 196–97; Kunz, *The Battle for Britain's Gold Standard*, 91–92; Morrison, 'Shocking Intellectual Austerity'.

71 Note of telephone conversation with Harrison, August 7, 1931, 4.30 p.m. BEA, OV32/7, Federal Reserve Bank of New York, Confidential Cables, 1931.

72 'The Course of the Exchanges', *Financial Times*, August 6, 1931.

73 Note, August 8, 1931, of telephone conversation between Lacour-Gayet and Harrison, August 7, 1931, 7.00 p.m. CUL, HP, Box 21, binder 45, Harrison, Conversations, vol. 1, 1926–31.

74 Telegram #2371, August 8, 1931, from J.P. Morgan & Co. to Jack Morgan via Morgan Grenfell. JPM, ARC 1216, Box 38A, Folder 34.

75 Telegram #2371, August 8, 1931, from J.P. Morgan & Co. to Jack Morgan via Morgan Grenfell. JPM, ARC 1216, Box 38A, Folder 34.

76 Telegram #2372, August 8, 1931, from J.P. Morgan & Co. to Jack Morgan via Morgan Grenfell. JPM, ARC 1216, Box 38A, Folder 34.

77 Telegram #2372, August 8, 1931, from J.P. Morgan & Co. to Jack Morgan via Morgan Grenfell. JPM, ARC 1216, Box 38A, Folder 34.

78 Telegram #31/4913, August 8, 1931, from J.P. Morgan & Co. to Morgan Grenfell. JPM, ARC 1216, Box 38A, Folder 34.

79 Telegram #4, August 10, 1931, from Crane to Harrison. FRBNY, Box 189130, folder, US Problems + Credits to Austria, Germany, Hungary, August–December 1931.

80 Telegram #67.057, August 11, 1931, from J.P. Morgan & Co. to Morgan & Cie. JPM, ARC 1221, Box 14, Morgan Bank. European Papers, Folder 5-A, Cables Received, July 1–August 31, 1931 (1-120).

81 Telegram #87.612, August 12, 1931, from Morgan & Cie to J.P. Morgan & Co. JPM, ARC 1221, Box 14, Morgan Bank. European Papers, folder, Cables sent July 1–August 31, 1931, 5A (1-133).

82 Meeting of August 11, 1931, of Bank of England's Committee of Treasury. BEA, G8/60, Minutes of the Committee of Treasury - March 1931 to June 1932.

83 Meeting of August 11, 1931, of Bank of England's Committee of Treasury. BEA, G8/60, Minutes of the Committee of Treasury - March 1931 to June 1932.

84 Meetings of August 12, 13 and 14, 1931, of Bank of England's Committee of Treasury. BEA, G8/60, Minutes of the Committee of Treasury - March 1931 to June 1932; Kunz, *The Battle for Britain's Gold Standard*, 97; Janeway, 'The 1931 Sterling Crisis', 264.

85 Telegram #7, July 12, 1931, from Crane to Harrison. CUL, HP, Box 16, binder 34, European Trips, 1927–32.

86 Letter, August 14, 1931, from Siepmann to Henry Clay. BEA, ADM25–6 Papers of Harry Arthur Siepmann correspondence July 2–December 24, 1931, #97.

87 'Note of a Discussion with French Treasury Experts 11th August, 1931', by Leith-Ross, 13th August, 1931. BEA, OV45–4 France Country File, January 6–October 31, 1931.

88 'Note of conversation with Governor Moret on August 28, 1931', by Jay Crane. FRBNY, Box 189130, Folder: US Problems + Credits to Austria, Germany, Hungary August–December 1931.

89 'Note of conversation with Governor Moret on August 28, 1931', by Jay Crane. FRBNY, Box 189130, Folder: US Problems + Credits to Austria, Germany, Hungary August–December 1931.

90 According to Sayers, Harrison 'repeatedly advised against a rise' in the bank rate, while Sprague recommended 'successive advances of Bank Rate "to, say, 7 or 8%"'. Sayers cites no evidence, see Sayers, *The Bank of England*, 405.

91 Telegram #31/4894, July 29, 1931, 6.15 p.m., from Morgan Grenfell & Co., to J.P. Morgan & Co. JPM, ARC 1216, Box 38A, Folder 34.

92 Note, August 8, 1931, 1.55 p.m., of telephone conversation between Vocke and Siepmann, August 7, 1931, 6 p.m. BEA, OV34/3, Country Files, Germany, August 4, 1931–March 22, 1932. For Norman's diary, see www.bankofengland.co.uk/-/media/boe/files/archive/montagu-norman-diary/1931/august-1931.pdf (accessed December 26, 2023).

93 Note, August 8, 1931, of telephone conversation between Harrison and Harvey, August 8, 1931, 10.30 a.m. CUL, HP, Box 21, binder 45, Harrison, Conversations, vol. 1, 1926–31.

94 Letter of August 14, 1931, from E.R. Peacock to Harrison. CUL, HP, Box 51, Norman, Montagu Collet, Governor of the Bank of England, I (May 1926–December 1931). According to Chernow, *The House of Morgan*, 329–30, it was Edward Grenfell and Jack Morgan who 'decided to smuggle Norman out of England'. I haven't seen any evidence in support of this.

95 Cited from 'Mr Montagu Norman', *The Economist*, August 22, 1931. Whether Norman's departure from London was only due to medical advice is disputed. It has been argued that he was told to go away in order not to stand in the way of Ernest Harvey, or that he was smuggled out on the initiative of Jack Morgan and Edward Grenfell. See, for instance, Philip Williamson, 'A "Bankers' Ramp"? Financiers and the British Political Crisis of August 1931', *English Historical Review* 99, no. 393 (1984): 772 n. 4; Chernow, *The House of Morgan*, 329–30.

96 'Mr. Montagu Norman', *The Financial Times*, August 17, 1931; 'Mr Montagu Norman', *The Economist*, August 22, 1931.

97 Copy of telegram, August 18, 1931, 3.40 p.m., from Teddy Grenfell to Norman, JPM, ARC 1216 J.P. Morgan Jr. Papers, ca. 1875–1943. BOX 38A.

98 Copy of telegram, August 18, 1931, 3.40 p.m., from Teddy Grenfell to Norman, JPM, ARC 1216 J.P. Morgan Jr. Papers, ca. 1875–1943. BOX 38A.

99 Telegram #31/4919, August 18, 1931, from E.C. Grenfell to R.C. Leffingwell. JPM, ARC 1216 J.P. Morgan Jr. Papers, ca. 1875–1943. BOX 38A.

100 Meetings, August 14 and 17, 1931, of Bank of England's Committee of Treasury. BEA, G8/60, Minutes of the Committee of Treasury – March 1931 to June 1932.

101 Meeting, August 18, 1931, of Bank of England's Committee of Treasury. BEA, G8/60, Minutes of the Committee of Treasury – March 1931 to June 1932.

102 'British issue abroad to consolidate position of Sterling', note, August 20, 1931, probably by B.G. Catterns. See also notes on the same issue, August 13 and August 18, 1931. BEA, OV45/4 France Country File, January 6–October 31, 1931.

103 Moggridge, *Maynard Keynes*, 525–26; Kunz, *The Battle for Britain's Gold Standard*, 100–1.
104 Confidential memorandum, August 19, 1931, by Harry Siepman. LRRA, Folder 59, 'A few Bank of England Papers'.
105 Personal and confidential letter, August 21, from Rodd to Siepmann. LRRA, Folder 59, 'A few Bank of England Papers'.

## Chapter 16

1 Telegram #31/2380, August 21, 1931, from J.P. Morgan & Co. to Morgan Grenfell. JPM, ARC 1216, Box 38A, Folder 34.
2 Telegram #31/4923, August 21, 1931, from Morgan Grenfell to J.P. Morgan & Co. JPM, ARC 1216, Box 38A, Folder 34.
3 Mouré, *The Gold Standard Illusion*, 183–84; Mouré, *Managing the Franc Poincare*, 53–54.
4 'The British "Crisis"', *The Economist*, August 22, 1931.
5 Letter, August 21, from Edward Grenfell to Jack Morgan. JPM, ARC 1216, Box 38A, Folder 34.
6 Telegram, #301/31, August 21, 1931, from Harrison to Harvey. BEA, OV32/7, Federal Reserve Bank of New York, Confidential Cables, 1931.
7 Telegram #31/2382, received August 22, 1931, 7.50 a.m., from J.P. Morgan & Co. to Morgan Grenfell. JPM, ARC 1216, Box 38A, Folder 34.
8 'International Bank Notes (Letter No. 28)', October 6, 1931, from Merle Cochran to William R. Castle. NARA, RG39, Box 104, Entry 145, Folder: G783.5 Special Report Confidential Letters (25-50); Clement, 'Between Banks and Governments', 150–52; Albert H. Wiggin, 'Text of the Wiggin Report on the German Financial Crisis', *The New York Times*, August 20, 1931.
9 Telegram #31/2382, received August 22, 1931, 7.50 a.m., from J.P. Morgan & Co. to Morgan Grenfell. JPM, ARC 1216, Box 38A, Folder 34.
10 Meeting, August 22, 1931, of Bank of England's Committee of Treasury. BEA, G8/60, Minutes of the Committee of Treasury – March 1931 to June 1932.
11 Telegram #343/31, August 22, 1931, 10 p.m., from Harvey to Harrison. BEA, OV32/7, Federal Reserve Bank of New York, Confidential Cables, 1931. See also Kunz, who argues that both the Bank of England and the Morgans wanted the government to survive: Kunz, *The Battle for Britain's Gold Standard*, 99–100.
12 Note, August 24, 1931, of telephone conversation, August 23, 1931, between Harrison and Norman. FRBNY, no. 3115.2, Harrison Papers, Harrison's conversations with M. Norman, 1931.
13 Meeting, August 23, 1931, of Bank of England's Committee of Treasury. BEA, G8/60, Minutes of the Committee of Treasury – March 1931 to June 1932.
14 Quoted from Kunz, 'American Bankers', 42–43.
15 Meeting, August 24, 1931, of Bank of England's Committee of Treasury. BEA, G8/60, Minutes of the Committee of Treasury – March 1931 to June 1932.
16 Telegram #347/31, August 24, 1931, 5.10 p.m., from the Bank of England to Sproul. BEA, OV32/7, Federal Reserve Bank of New York, Confidential Cables, 1931.
17 Telegram #304/31, August 24, 1931, 10.15 p.m., from Harrison to Harvey. BEA, OV32/7, Federal Reserve Bank of New York, Confidential Cables, 1931.

18 Telegram #13, August 24, 1931, from Crane to Harrison. CUL, HP, Box 16, binder 34, European Trips, 1927–32.
19 Telegram #13, August 24, 1931, from Crane to Harrison. CUL, HP, Box 16, binder 34, European Trips, 1927–32.
20 Telegram, #307/31, August 24, 1931, from Harrison to Harvey. BEA, OV32/7, Federal Reserve Bank of New York, Confidential Cables, 1931.
21 Meeting, August 25, 1931, of Bank of England's Committee of Treasury. BEA, G8/60, Minutes of the Committee of Treasury – March 1931 to June 1932.
22 'U.S. Banks' Demands on Britain', *Daily Herald*, August 25, 1931; 'The Outlook for Sterling', *The Economist*, August 29, 1931. For a discussion of the bankers' ramp claim, see Burk, *Morgan Grenfell*, 147–56; Williamson, 'A "Bankers' Ramp"?'; Kynaston, *The City of London*, 240–41; Chernow, *The House of Morgan*, 332–34; Boyce, *The Great Interwar Crisis*, 319–24; Morrison, 'Shocking Intellectual Austerity'.
23 Telegram #359/31, August 26, 1931, from Harvey to Harrison. BEA, OV32/7, Federal Reserve Bank of New York, Confidential Cables, 1931.
24 'The Financial Situation', *Commercial and Financial Chronicle*, August 29, 1931, 1335.
25 Meeting, August 27, 1931, of Bank of England's Committee of Treasury. BEA, G8/60, Minutes of the Committee of Treasury – March 1931 to June 1932.
26 Note, August 25, 1931, telephone conversation between Harrison and Lacour-Gayet, August 25, 1931, 11.45 a.m. CUL, HP, Box 21, binder 45, Harrison, Conversations, vol. 1, 1926–31.
27 Note, August 25, 1931, telephone conversation between Harrison and Lacour-Gayet, August 25, 1931, 11.45 a.m. CUL, HP, Box 21, binder 45, Harrison, Conversations, vol. 1, 1926–31.
28 Telegram, August 25, 1931, from Moret to Harrison. CUL, HP, Box 14, binder 29, Bank of France, 1931.
29 'Note of conversation with Monsieur Moret at the Bank of France at 5 p.m. on Wednesday, the 26th August 1931'. BEA, OV45/4 France Country File, January 6–October 31, 1931.
30 'Note of conversation at the French Ministry of Finance at 6.30 p.m. on Wednesday, the 26th August, 1931'. BEA, OV45/4 France Country File, January 6–October 31, 1931.
31 Notes #82 and #83 of conversations in Paris on August 27 and 28, 1931'. BEA, OV45/4 France Country File, January 6–October 31, 1931.
32 Telegram #67.072, August 28, 1931, 7.55 p.m., from J.P. Morgan & Co. to Morgan & Cie. JPM, ARC 1221, Box 14, Morgan Bank. European Papers, Folder 5-A, Cables Received, July 1–August 31, 1931 (1-120).
33 Quoted from Kunz, 'American Bankers', 43.
34 Telegram #575/31, August 31, 1931, from Harvey to Harrison. CUL, HP, Box 9, binder 20, Bank of England, January–December 1931. See also Telegram #31/2410, August 29, 1931, from J.P. Morgan & Co to Morgan Grenfell. JPM, ARC1195, Box 5: Folder 5/18, 1931. See also Kunz, *The Battle for Britain's Gold Standard*, 113–19.
35 Letter, August 29, 1931, from Edward Grenfell to Jack Morgan. JPM, ARC1195, Box 5: Folder 5/18, 1931.

36 Letter, August 31, 1931, from Harvey to Morgan Grenfell. JPM, ARC1195, Box 5: Folder 5/18, 1931.
37 Meeting, August 31, 1931, of Bank of England's Committee of Treasury. BEA, G8/60, Minutes of the Committee of Treasury – March 1931 to June 1932.
38 Letter, September 1, 1931, from Snowden to Whigham. JPM, ARC1195, Box 5: Folder 5/18, 1931.
39 'Maintenance of the Pound's Value', *Financial Times*, September 2, 1931.
40 'International Bank Notes (Letter No. 25)', September 3, 1931, from Merle Cochran to William R. Castle. NARA, RG39, Box 104, Entry 145, Folder: G783.5 Special Report Confidential Letters (25-50).
41 Telegram #20, September 3, 1931, from Crane to Harrison. CU; Harrison Papers, Box 16, binder 34, European Trips, 1927–32 (F.R.Bk. Officers and others). See also Meeting, August 31, 1931, of Bank of England's Committee of Treasury. BEA, G8/60, Minutes of the Committee of Treasury – March 1931 to June 1932.
42 'International Bank Notes (Letter No. 25)', September 3, 1931, from Merle Cochran to William R. Castle. NARA, RG39, Box 104, Entry 145, Folder: G783.5 Special Report Confidential Letters (25-50).
43 Note, September 3, 1931, from Burgess to Harrison. FRBNY, Box 189130, Folder: US Problems + Credits to Austria, Germany, Hungary [see also Great Britain, Germany (?) ???] August–December 1931.
44 Note, September 3, 1931, from Burgess to Harrison. FRBNY, Box 189130, Folder: US Problems + Credits to Austria, Germany, Hungary August–December 1931.
45 Quoted from Kunz, *The Battle for Britain's Gold Standard*, 122–23.
46 Telegram #402/31, September 4, 1931, from Harvey to Harrison; #411/31, September 8, 1931, from Harvey to Harrison. BEA, OV32/7, Federal Reserve Bank of New York, Confidential Cables, 1931. See also Telegrams #334/31, September 3, 1931, from Harrison to Harvey and #338/31, September 4, 1931, from Harrison to Harvey; #414/31, from Catterns, Chief Cashier, to Harrison. CUL, HP, Box 9, binder 20, Bank of England, January–December 1931.
47 Aykens, '(Mis)Trusting Authorities', 328.
48 'The Treasury Credits', *The Economist*, September 5, 1931.
49 Telegram #23, September 9, 1931, from Crane to Harrison. CUL, HP, Box 16, binder 34, European Trips, 1927–32.
50 Letter, September 9, 1931, from Siepmann to Popovics. BEA, ADM25–6 Papers of Harry Arthur Siepmann Correspondence July 2–December 24, 1931.
51 Telegram #29, September 10, 1931, from Sproul to Crane. CUL, HP, Box 16, binder 34, European Trips, 1927–32.
52 Note, September 12, 1931, from Burgess to Harrison. FRBNY, Box 189130, Folder: US Problems + Credits to Austria, Germany, Hungary August–December 1931.
53 Note, September 12, 1931, from Burgess to Harrison. FRBNY, Box 189130, Folder: US Problems + Credits to Austria, Germany, Hungary August–December 1931.
54 Letter, September 19, 1931, from Burgess to King. See also Letter, September 13, 1931, from Burgess to King and letters, September 17 and 22, 1931, from King to Burgess. FRBNY, Box 189130, Folder: US Problems + Credits to Austria, Germany, Hungary August–December 1931.

55 Note on conversation, September 16, 1931, between Harrison and Harvey, September 17, 1931. CUL, HP, Box 21, binder 45, Harrison, Conversations, vol. 1, 1926–31.
56 Quoted from Kunz, *The Battle for Britain's Gold Standard*, 126.
57 Quoted from Kunz, *The Battle for Britain's Gold Standard*, 127. For a discussion of the Bank of England's policy, see Moggridge, *British Monetary Policy*, 193–96; Janeway, 'The 1931 Sterling Crisis', 267–68.
58 Telegram #456/31, September 17, 1931, from C.P. Mahon to Harrison. CUL, HP, Box 9, binder 20, Bank of England, January–December 1931.
59 Letter, September 17, 1931, from Edward Grenfell to Jack Morgan. JPM, ARC1195, Box 5: Folder 5/18, 1931.
60 Letter, September 17, 1931, from Edward Grenfell to Jack Morgan. JPM, ARC1195, Box 5: Folder 5/18, 1931.
61 'The First Lap', *The Economist*, September 12, 1931.
62 'The Bank Loses More Gold', *Financial Times*, September 17, 1931.
63 'International Bank Notes (Letter No. 26)', September 18, 1931, from Merle Cochran to William R. Castle. NARA, RG39, Box 104, Entry 145, Folder: G783.5 Special Report Confidential Letters (25-50).

## Chapter 17

1 'Note on visit in England', September 16, 1931, by Jay E. Crane. The note is part of 'Confidential memorandum of European visit. August and September, 1931', September 16, 1931, by Jay E. Crane. FRBNY, Box 189130, folder, US Problems + Credits to Austria, Germany, Hungary August–December 1931.
2 Ibid.
3 Telegram, September 18, 1931, from Harrison to Norman. FRBNY, C261, England – Bank of England, 1931–32.
4 Meeting, September 16, 1931, of Bank of England's Committee of Treasury. BEA, G8/60, Minutes of the Committee of Treasury – March 1931 to June 1932.
5 Meeting, September 17, 1931, of Bank of England's Committee of Treasury. BEA, G8/60, Minutes of the Committee of Treasury – March 1931 to June 1932.
6 Meeting of September 18, 1931, of Bank of England's Committee of Treasury. BEA, G8/60, Minutes of the Committee of Treasury – March 1931 to June 1932.
7 'Devaluation Delusions', *The Economist*, September 19, 1931.
8 'The Honest Alternative', *The Economist*, September 19, 1931.
9 'Liquidity of the Banks', *Financial Times*, September 21, 1931.
10 Meeting, September 19, 1931, of Bank of England's Committee of Treasury. BEA, G8/60, Minutes of the Committee of Treasury – March 1931 to June 1932.
11 Meeting, September 19, 1931, of Bank of England's Committee of Treasury. BEA, G8/60, Minutes of the Committee of Treasury – March 1931 to June 1932.
12 Note, September 19, 1931, 6.30 a.m., of conversation, between Harvey and Harrison. CUL, HP, Box 27, binder 59, Office Memoranda: Volume II, 1928–31.

13 Note, September 19, 1931, 8.30 a.m., of conversation between Harvey and Harrison. CUL, HP, Box 27, binder 59, Office Memoranda: Volume II, 1928–31.
14 Telegram, September 20, 1931, 9 p.m., from Harvey to Harrison. BEA, OV32/7, Federal Reserve Bank of New York, Confidential Cables, 1931.
15 Handwritten note, probably by Rodd, no date. LRRA, Folder 59, 'A few Bank of England Papers'.
16 'The British Government's Statement', *The New York Times*, September 21, 1931.
17 'The Financial Situation', *Commercial and Financial Chronicle*, September 26, 1931, 1961.
18 'Morgan Holds Gold Decision a "Hopeful Event"', *The New York Times*, September 22, 1931; 'Calls Step a Stage Toward Revival of Trade', *The New York Times*, September 22, 1931.
19 Telegram, September 21, 1931, from Owen D. Young to J.P. Morgan Jr. JPM, ARC 1216, Box 38A, Folder 34.
20 Quoted from Chernow, *The House of Morgan*, 335–36.
21 Quoted from Burk, *Morgan Grenfell*, 139. Martin Horn downplays the significance of Lamont's letter and argues that Jack Morgan may not have read it; see Horn, *J. P. Morgan & Co.*, 142–44.
22 'Gold Exports Stopped', *Financial Times*, September 21, 1931.
23 Morrison, 'Shocking Intellectual Austerity', 192, 193–97. See also Kunz, *The Battle for Britain's Gold Standard*, 184, 188 et passim; Seddon, 'Between Collapse and Decline', 131–32. Interestingly, on the basis of modelling, Wandschneider argues that Britain 'abandoned the gold standard at a time when the economic conditions did not necessarily warrant such a move'. For the financial centres in general, politics were more important than 'the rules of the game', for the decision to abandon gold. Wandschneider, 'The Stability', 170, 175–76.
24 Meetings, September 21, 22 and 23, 1931, of Bank of England's Committee of Treasury. BEA, G8/60, Minutes of the Committee of Treasury - March 1931 to June 1932.
25 'Memorandum: Meeting of the Board of Directors September 24, 1931. Subject: Consequences of British suspension of gold payments; policy to be followed by this bank'. CUL, HP, Box 23, binder 50, Discussion Notes: Volumes I, II & III, April 17, 1930–September 21, 1933.
26 'The Money Market', *The Economist*, September 26, 1931.
27 Letter, September 20, 1931, from Harvey to Moret. BEA, OV45/82, Banque de France, January 1, 1931–February 25, 1932.
28 'International Bank Notes (Letter No. 27)', September 24, 1931, and letter no. 28, October 6, 1931, from Merle Cochran to William R. Castle. NARA, RG39, Box 104, Entry 145, Folder: G783.5 Special Report Confidential Letters (25-50). See also the note 'Bank of France's loss on its sterling holding', September 28, 1931, by Catterns, and with Siepmann's comment in handwriting; letters, October 6, 1931, from Moret to Harvey and to the French Minister of Finance. BEA, OV45/82, Banque de France, January 1, 1931–February 25, 1932.
29 'International Bank Notes (Letter No. 27)', September 24, 1931, from Merle Cochran to William R. Castle. NARA, RG39, Box 104, Entry 145, Folder: G783.5 Special Report Confidential Letters (25-50).

30 'Note of telephone conversation with Mr. Rodd at 4.40 p.m. and 6.50 p.m. on Wednesday, 23rd September, 1931', by Siepmann, September 23, 1931, 8 p.m. BEA, OV34/3, Country Files, Germany, August 4, 1931–March 22, 1932.
31 Personal letter #84, September 28, 1931, from Harvey to Moret. BEA, OV45/82, Banque de France, January 1, 1931–February 25, 1932.
32 Meetings, September 28, 1931, of Bank of England's Committee of Treasury. BEA, G8/60, Minutes of the Committee of Treasury – March 1931 to June 1932.
33 'The Money Market', *The Economist*, September 26, 1931.
34 Cable #67.208, October 17, 1931, from J.P. Morgan to Morgan et Cie. BISA, 7.18.2. MCG.1. Correspondence with and regarding JP Morgan & Co, Morgan Grenfell & Co, 1930–31.
35 Accominotti notes that the forward sterling quotations indicated strong devaluation expectations, despite the support of the pound, see Accominotti, 'London Merchant Banks', 33.
36 Quoted from Moggridge, *Maynard Keynes*, 523–24. See also Skidelsky, *John Maynard Keynes*, 393–94.
37 See Morrison, 'Shocking Intellectual Austerity', 182, 185–87.
38 Telegram #31/2491, received September 29, 1931, 10 a.m., from J.P Morgan & Co. to Jack Morgan and Morgan Grenfell. JPM, ARC 1216, Box 38A, Folder 34.
39 Telegram #31/5036, September 30, 1931, 3.30 p.m., from Jack Morgan at Morgan Grenfell to J.P Morgan & Co. JPM, ARC 1216, Box 38A, Folder 34. See also Sayers, *The Bank of England*, 406–7. Sayers commented on the discussion that 'when it came to the crunch, personal judgments had to be exercised. Central banking is an art, not a book of rules'.
40 'The End of an Epoch', *The Economist*, September 26, 1931.
41 Einzig, *Montagu Norman*, 185.
42 'New Problems for the Investor', *The Economist*, September 26, 1931, 571.
43 'Norman in London; Public Held Back', *The New York Times*, September 24, 1931. There is some discussion as to whether Norman had been in touch with Harvey during his sick leave and to what extent Norman was aware of what was going on in London. See Kunz, *The Battle for Britain's Gold Standard*, 132–34; Morrison, 'Shocking Intellectual Austerity'.
44 Boyle, *Montagu Norman*, 268; Morrison, 'Shocking Intellectual Austerity', 196; Morrison, 'Shocking Intellectual Austerity ... Extended Citations', notes 200 and 201.
45 Morrison, 'Shocking Intellectual Austerity', 196; Morrison, 'Shocking Intellectual Austerity ... Extended Citations', notes 199, 200 and 201; Boyle, *Montagu Norman*, 268.
46 Note, October 2, 1931, of telephone conversation between Harrison and Norman and Harvey. FRBNY, no. 3115.2, Harrison Papers, Harrison's conversations with M. Norman, 1931.
47 Meetings, October 14, 1931, of Bank of England's Committee of Treasury. BEA, G8/60, Minutes of the Committee of Treasury – March 1931 to June 1932.
48 Letter, October 27, 1931, from Norman to Rodd. LRRA, Folder 59, 'A few Bank of England Papers'.
49 Letters, November 16, 1931, from Siepmann to George Ottlik and to Baron Franckenstein. BEA, ADM25-6 Papers of Harry Arthur Siepmann

Correspondence July 2–December 24, 1931. Norman wrote in his diary that Siepmann would be going to South Africa.

50 Copy of telegram, February 20, 1932, from Rodd to Stewart. Handwritten note, probably by Rood, no date. LRRA, Folder 146/4.

51 Note, September 30, 1931, from Miss Carrick to the Administration Department. CUL, HP, Box 27, binder 59, Office Memoranda: Volume II, 1928–31.

52 Friedman and Schwartz, *A Monetary History*, 315–17.

53 Meetings, November 11, 1931, of Bank of England's Committee of Treasury. BEA, G8/60, Minutes of the Committee of Treasury – March 1931 to June 1932.

54 Telegram, November 13, 1931, from Harrison to Norman. FRBNY, 3115.2 Harrison Papers – Conversations with M. Norman, 1930–31.

55 Morrison explicitly applies a counterfactual argument claiming that 'Had Norman remained healthy – or had he returned sooner – he would have ruthlessly raised interest rates. Such increases probably would have bolstered confidence'. Morrison also claims that the choice to leave gold 'was the final maneuver in a campaign Harvey waged to save conservatives in Parliament from electoral defeat. Harvey, simply put, suspended the gold standard to save it'. See Morrison, 'Shocking Intellectual Austerity', 192, 199.

56 Telegram #31/2686, November 30, 1931, from J.P. Morgan & Co. to Morgan Grenfell. BEA, OV28/5, Austria Country File, August 5–December 29, 1931.

57 Telegram #31/5252, December 4, 1931, from Morgan Grenfell to J.P. Morgan & Co. BEA, OV28–5, Austria Country File, August 5–December 29, 1931. In fact, Otto Niemeyer was strongly against the decision to leave gold. He wrote a memorandum, where he argued that the traditional measures – that is, a high bank rate – could have saved the gold standard, see Sayers, *The Bank of England*, 406–7.

58 Boyle, *Montagu Norman*, 327–28.

59 'Summary of an Address by Mr. Pierre Quesnay at the Ecole de la Paix, Paris', February 18, 1931. FRBNY, 797.3 Bank for International Settlements, January–March 1931. See also Feiertag, 'Les Banques d'émission', 719–20.

60 Letter, October 20, 1931, from Siepmann to Rodd. BEA, ADM25–6 Papers of Harry Arthur Siepmann Correspondence July 2–December 24, 1931. See also Seddon, 'Between Collapse and Decline', 132.

61 Letter, October 23, 1931, from Rodd to Siepmann. DB Morgan Grenfell papers: Box 50595324/folder Correspondence with H.A. Siepmann. I am grateful to Martin Horn for drawing my attention to this letter.

62 Wesley and Siepmann, *Darling Pol*, 53, 155.

## The End

1 Neil deGrasse Tyson, *Astrophysics for People in a Hurry* (New York: W. W. Norton, 2017), 13.

2 John H. Williams, 'The Crisis of the Gold Standard', *Foreign Affairs* 10, no. 2 (1932): 173.

3 Geertz, 'Thick Description', 7.

4 Examples from newspapers and magazines are many after the financial crisis of 2007–9, where the Credit Anstalt failure was used as an analogy to make sense of the present. The events of 1931 are also – and rightly so – considered important for

understanding the Great Depression and are therefore often referred to and used in historical analyses. Three examples of important books that nevertheless get some detail wrong are Martin, *The Meddlers*, 127; Eichengreen, *Hall of Mirrors*, 141–42; Eichengreen and Kakridis, 'Interwar Central Banks', 18–19; James, *The End of Globalization*, 54–55. In contrast, Piet Clement presents a brief but concise introduction to the role of BIS in the Credit Anstalt crisis. See Clement, 'Institutionalizing Central Bank Cooperation', 94–99.

5 Levi, 'On Microhistory', 98.

6 See Flyvbjerg and his references for a discussion, Bent Flyvbjerg, 'Five Misunderstandings about Case-Study Research', *Qualitative Inquiry* 12, no. 2 (2006): 237–38, 240.

7 To be sure, 'the end' is something I impose upon history. History never ends, and if you want to read what happened after, Max Harris has written about just that. See Harris, *Monetary War and Peace*. As for my approach, see Abolafia, 'Narrative Construction'; Abolafia, *Stewards of the Market*; Weick, *Sensemaking in Organizations*; Weick, 'Sensemaking in Organizations'; Weick, 'The Collapse of Sensemaking'; Jens Beckert, *Imagined Futures: Fictional Expectations and Capitalist Dynamics* (Cambridge, MA: Harvard University Press, 2016); Beckert and Bronk, *Uncertain Futures*; Beckert and Bronk, 'Uncertain Futures'; Haas, 'Introduction'; Haas, 'Epistemic Communities'; Shiller, 'Narrative Economics'; Shiller, *Narrative Economics*; Hansen, 'Making Sense of Financial Crisis and Scandal'; Hansen, 'Organizational Culture'; Hansen, 'From Finance Capitalism'; Per H. Hansen and Anne Magnussen, 'Making Sense of Business and Community in Hollywood Films, 1928–2016', *Business History Review* 92, no. 2 (2018): 307–37.

8 On writing history forwards, see also Schuker, 'The Gold-Exchange Standard', 82.

9 See, however, Marcus's defense of writing history backwards. Marcus, *Austrian Reconstruction*, 339–41.

10 New York Times, 'Leon Fraser Back. Seeks Upturn Signs', *The New York Times*, June 3, 1931.

11 Eichengreen, *Golden Fetters*; Temin, *Lessons from the Great Depression*; Eichengreen and Temin, 'The Gold Standard'; Eichengreen and Temin, 'Fetters of Gold and Paper'. For the 1931 crisis as catalyst for making the Great Depression longer and deeper, see Grossman, *Unsettled Account*, 246; Straumann, *1931*, xxii. Part of this narrative blames the French and to some extent the United States for not following the rules of the game. Instead of cooperating, they sterilized gold inflows and contributed to the devastating deflationary policies that devastated societies. See Douglas A. Irwin, 'Did France Cause the Great Depression', NBER Working Paper Series, 2010; Johnson, *Gold*. Other scholars such as Schuker and Boyce have focused more on the role of politics in their respective work, but it still comes down to a lack of cooperation. Schuker blames Germany and Chancellor Brüning in particular and argues that they used the reparations issue to obstruct any attempts to solve the crisis in 1931 and beyond. Boyce on the other hand is critical of the British and Norman and their lack of cooperation with and dislike of the French.

12 For a definition and discussion of central bank cooperation, see Cooper, 'Almost a Century of Central Bank Cooperation', 79–80. In contrast to the gold exchange standard, the classical gold standard was assumed to be an automatic system tending towards equilibrium, see Barry Eichengreen and Marc Flandreau, *The*

*Gold Standard in Theory and History* (London: Routledge, 1997), 11; David Hume, 'On the Balance of Trade', in *The Gold Standard in Theory and History*, ed. Barry Eichengreen and Marc Flandreau (London: Routledge, 1997), 33–43; Mouré, 'The Limits to Central Bank Co-operation', 260. For contrasting views, see Eichengreen, *Golden Fetters*; Flandreau, 'Central Bank Cooperation'.

13 Clarke, *Central Bank Cooperation*, 220. See also Grossman and Rockoff, 'Fighting the Last War', 253–54; Schubert, *The Credit-Anstalt Crisis*, 181. For other contributions along the same lines, see Eichengreen, 'Central Bank Co-operation', 114; Eichengreen, *Golden Fetters*, 160, 259. See also Mouré, 'The Limits to Central Bank Co-operation', 262–67, 273; James, 'The Creation of a World Central Bank', 165, 170; Michael D. Bordo, 'Monetary Policy Cooperation/Coordination and Global Financial Crises in Historical Perspective', NBER Working Paper, Cambridge, MA, 2020, 8; James, *The End of Globalization*, 55. See also Kenneth A. Oye, '"The Sterling-Dollar-Franc Triangle": Monetary Diplomacy, 1929–1937', in *Cooperation under Anarchy*, ed. Kenneth A. Oye (Princeton: Princeton University Press, 1986), 191; Simmons, *Who Adjusts*, 31; Simmons, 'Why Innovate'; Simmons, 'Rulers of the Game'; James, 'The Creation of a World Central Bank', 165; James, *The End of Globalization*, 55; Kindleberger, *The World in Depression*, 144–47, 290–91; Donald Moggridge is sceptical of Kindleberger and argues that the structural problems were so serious that intervention by France or the United States would not have prevented the breakdown of the gold standard, see Donald E. Moggridge, 'Policy in the Crises of 1920 and 1929', in *Financial Crises: Theory, History, and Policy*, ed. Charles P. Kindleberger and Jean Pierre Laffargue (Cambridge: Cambridge University Press, 1982), 171–87. For a more positive interpretation of central banks' actions, see Toniolo, with the assistance of Clement, *Central Bank Cooperation*, 110–11. For a view on Austria only, see Marcus, *Austrian Reconstruction*, 331 et passim. Meltzer is also sceptical of Eichengreen's and others' argument that international cooperation failed, and stresses that Harrison did cooperate, see Meltzer, *A History of the Federal Reserve*, 336. See also Catherine Schenk and Tobias Straumann, 'Central Banks and the Stability of the International Monetary Regime', in *Central Banks at a Crossroads: What Can We Learn From History?*, ed. Michael D. Bordo et al. (Cambridge: Cambridge University Press, 2016), 331–36.

14 Friedman and Schwartz, *A Monetary History*, 407, 412–13. With variations, this narrative is still the dominant monetarist explanation for the perceived failure of the Federal Reserve Bank to stop the Great Depression. Meltzer is sceptical that Strong would have made such a difference and blames the orthodoxy at the time, which meant that the New York Fed subscribed to a faulty real bills doctrine and the so-called Riefler-Burgess framework, Meltzer, *A History of the Federal Reserve*, 273–74, 400–13. See also Singleton, *Central Banking*, 80–82. Interestingly, a NBER director took exception to Friedman and Schwartz' basic assumptions and judgement of the Fed; see Albert J. Hettinger Jr, 'Director's Comment', in *A Monetary History of the United States*, ed. Milton Friedman and Anna J. Schwartz (Princeton: Princeton University Press, 1963), 809–14. For a recent convincing and comprehensive critique of Friedman & Schwartz, see O'Sullivan, 'History as Heresy'.

15 O'Sullivan, 'History as Heresy', 323–24, 330. See also Peter Temin, *Did Monetary Forces Cause the Great Depression?* (New York: W. W. Norton, 1976). Both

Friedman and Schwartz's money supply explanation and Barry Eichengreen's and Peter Temin's gold standard-based contribution are, what Harold James has called 'in its account of causation, above all a monetary history'. James, 'Financial Flows', 594, 607, 611–12. According to James, capital movements did not play a significant role in the 1931 crisis. He argues instead that the crisis was due to 'uncertainty about public budgets'. This argument is part of much larger partly ideological discussion, which was also present in the interwar period. See also Claudio Borio, Harold James and Hyun Song Shin, 'The International Monetary and Financial System: A Capital Account Historical Perspective', in *Central Bank at a Crossroads: What Can We Learn from History?*, ed. Michael Bordo et al. (New York: Cambridge University Press, 2016), 356–86; Harold James, 'The Ideology of Central Banking in the Interwar Years and Beyond', in *The Spread of the Modern Central Bank and Global Cooperation, 1919–1939*, ed. Barry Eichengreen and Andreas Kakridis (Cambridge: Cambridge University Press, 2023), 40–56.

16 O'Sullivan, 'History as Heresy', 323–24, 330.

17 Liaquat Ahamed's widely read *Lords of Finance* pushes the hindsight and the judgement beyond the sustainable as he argues that more 'than anything else . . . the Great Depression was caused by a failure of intellectual will, a lack of understanding about how the economy operated'. Ahamed, *Lords of Finance*, 405–6, 501–4. See also Singleton, *Central Banking*, 69, 80. For a devastating review of *Lords of Finance*, see Schuker, 'Central Bankers in the Dock'.

18 Forrest Capie, Terence Mills and Geoffrey Wood, 'What Happened in 1931?', in *Financial Crises and the World Banking System*, ed. Forrest Capie and Geoffrey Wood (London: Macmillan, 1986), 145. To be sure, they were certainly not alone with this judgement. In fact, blaming the central bankers, their worldview and their understanding of the gold standard is probably the dominant narrative when it comes to explaining the 1931 financial crisis. It also plays a powerful role in the conflicting narratives of the Great Financial Crisis.

19 Forrest Capie, 'Disintegration of the National Economy between the Wars', in *The Great Depression of the 1930s: Lessons for Today*, ed. Nicholas Crafts and Peter Fearon (Oxford: Oxford University Press, 2013), 152. The full question is whether the breakdown 'should be seen either as a response to the difficulties in international finance at the time, or as part of the disintegration of the system, about which little or nothing could be done'.

20 Still, the legacy of central bank action during the interwar period blamed them for the 'severity of the Depression', which effectively ended the idea of central bank independence for half a century. See James, 'The Ideology of Central Banking', 51–52.

21 Bagehot, *Lombard Street*, 27–28, 97. Richard Grossman and Hugh Rockoff argue that 'Bagehot's Lombard Street . . . still reigns supreme' and that experience 'has not led to rapid progress. . . . Economists, it turns out, are like generals, always fighting the last war'. Grossman and Rockoff, 'Fighting the Last War', 273.

22 For perplexing conditions, see letter, April 20, 1931, from Norman to Harrison. CUL, HP, Box 51, Norman, Montagu Collet, Governor of the Bank of England, I (May 1926–December 1931). For cause and effect, see telegram no. 152/31, May 28, 1931, from Norman to Harrison. FRBNY, C261.1, National Bank (Austrian Nat'l Bank) Credit, May 1931–December 1932, 1 of 2.

23 Indeed, the word 'crisis' in itself is performative in that it enables specific logics, practices and actions. See Graf, 'Either-or'; Reinhart Koselleck and Michaela Richter, 'Crisis', *Journal of the History of Ideas* 67, no. 2 (2006): 357–400.
24 For an analysis of financial networks and trust, see Pak, *Gentlemen Bankers*.
25 For exceptions, see for instance, Aguado, 'The Credit Anstalt Crisis'; Schubert, *The Credit-Anstalt Crisis*; Stiefel, *Finanzdiplomatie und Weltwirtschaftskrise*; Kernbauer, *Währungspolitik*, 306–8.
26 Among the exceptions that have to some extent examined private bankers are Horn, *J. P. Morgan & Co.*; Burk, *Morgan Grenfell*; Kunz, 'American Bankers'; Kunz, *The Battle for Britain's Gold Standard*.
27 George L.S. Schackle, *The Nature of Economic Thought: Selected Papers, 1955–1964* (Cambridge: Cambridge University Press, 1966), 126 (italics in original). See also Charles Carter, 'George Shackle and Uncertainty: A Revolution Still Awaited', *Review of Political Economy* 5, no. 2 (1993): 127–37; Popp, 'Making Choices in Time'.
28 Brine and Poovey, *Finance in America*.
29 Beckert and Bronk, *Uncertain Futures*; Kay and King, *Radical Uncertainty*; Levy, 'Radical Uncertainty'; King, 'Monetary Policy'.
30 Flyvbjerg, 'Five Misunderstandings', 221–23, 240. Flyvbjerg is paraphrasing Cheryl Mattingly, 'Narrative Reflections on Practical Actions: Two Learning Experiments in Reflective Storytelling', in *The Reflective Turn: Case Studies in and on Educational Practice*, ed. Donald A. Schön (New York: Teachers College Press, 1991), 237.
31 Weick, 'The Collapse of Sensemaking', 633.
32 I refer here to what Reinhart Koselleck calls 'space of experience' and 'horizon of expectation'; see Koselleck, *Futures Past*, chapter 14.
33 Abolafia, *Stewards of the Market*, 51.
34 Abolafia, *Stewards of the Market*, 77.
35 Abolafia, *Stewards of the Market*, 134.
36 Michael Kirk, 'Inside the Meltdown', PBS Frontline, 2009.
37 Ben S. Bernanke, Timoty Geithner and Henry M. Paulson Jr (eds.), *First Responders: Inside the U.S. Strategy for Fighting the 2007–2009 Global Financial Crisis* (New Haven: Yale University Press, 2020), 4; Ben S. Bernanke, Timothy Geithner and Henry M. Paulson Jr, *Firefighting: The Financial Crisis and Its Lessons* (London: Profile Books, 2019), 60.
38 Gillian Tett, 'Wall Street's Crash Course', *Financial Times*, August 26, 2007.
39 Eichengreen, 'Economic History and Economic Policy'.
40 See the memoirs from three of the main actors in the United States: Hank Paulson, *On the Brink: Inside the Race to Stop the Collapse of the Global Financial System* (New York: Headline Business Plus, 2010); Timothy Geithner, *Stress Test: Reflections on Financial Crises* (London: Random House Business Books, 2014); Ben S Bernanke, *The Courage to Act: A Memoir of a Crisis and Its Aftermath* (New York: W.W. Norton, 2015). See also Andrew Ross Sorkin, *Too Big to Fail: Inside the Battle to Save Wall Street* (New York: Allen Lane, 2009). For films, see for instance, John Wells et al., *The Company Men*, 2010; J.C. Chandor et al., *Margin Call*, 2011; Oliver Stone, *Wall Street. Money Never Sleeps*, 2010. On Hollywood films and the Great Financial Crisis, see Hansen and Magnussen, 'Making Sense of Business and

Community'; Andrea Werner, '"Margin Call": Using Film to Explore Behavioural Aspects of the Financial Crisis', *Journal of Business Ethics* 122, no. 4 (2014): 643–54.

41 Bernanke, *The Courage to Act*, 264. See also Sorkin, *Too Big to Fail*. For films, see for instance, Wells et al., *The Company Men*; Chandor et al., *Margin Call*; Stone, *Wall Street. Money Never Sleeps.*

42 See, for instance, Barry Eichengreen and Kevin O'Rourke, 'What Do the New Data Tell Us?', https://voxeu.org/article/tale-two-depressions-what-do-new-data-tell-us-february-2010-update (accessed December 29, 2023); Crafts and Fearon, *The Great Depression of the 1930s*; Michael D. Bordo et al., *Central Banks at a Crossroads: What Can We Learn from History?*, ed. Michael D. Bordo et al. (Cambridge: Cambridge University Press, 2016); Eichengreen, *Hall of Mirrors*; Per H. Hansen, 'Review Essay: Barry Eichengreen, Hall of Mirrors. The Great Depression, The Great Recession and the Uses – and Misuses – of History', *Business History Review* 89, no. 3 (2015): 557–69; Eichengreen and Temin, 'Fetters of Gold and Paper'; Michael Bordo and Harold James, 'The Great Depression Analogy', *Financial History Review* 17, no. 2 (2010): 127–40; Harold James, *The Creation and Destruction of Value. The Globalization Cycle* (Cambridge, MA: Harvard University Press, 2009); Harold James, 'How Not to Solve a Financial Crisis', *International Affairs* 98, no. 5 (September 6, 2022): 1575–93; William A. Allen and Richhild Moessner, 'The International Propagation of the Financial Crisis of 2008 and a Comparison with 1931', *Financial History Review* 19, no. 2 (2012): 123–47. For a somewhat different perspective, Amin Samman, 'Making Financial History: The Crisis of 2008 and the Return of the Past', *Millennium: Journal of International Studies* 42, no. 2 (2014): 309–30 and Amin Samman, 'The 1930s as Black Mirror: Visions of Historical Repetition in the Global Financial Press, 2007–2009', *Journal of Cultural Economy* 5, no. 2 (2012): 213–29. See also European Commission, 'Economic Crisis in Europe: Causes, Consequences and Responses', *European Economy*, 2009. See also two EU funded research projects led by Catherine Schenk and Youssef Cassis respectively: UPIER, https://upier.web.ox.ac.uk/ (accessed September 15, 2023), and MERCATOR, https://mercator.eui.eu/ (accessed September 15, 2023).

43 'There Could Be Trouble Ahead', *The Economist*, December 10, 2011.

44 For a discussion of historical analogies, see Eichengreen, 'Economic History and Economic Policy'; Eichengreen, *Hall of Mirrors*. For uses of history, see R. Daniel Wadhwani et al., 'History as Organizing: Uses of the Past in Organization Studies', *Organization Studies* 39, no. 12 (2018): 1663–83.

# Bibliography


'A Diary of the Crisis'. *The Economist*, July 18, 1931.

'A Week of Crisis Continued'. *The Economist*, July 11, 1931.

Abolafia, Mitchel Y. 'Narrative Construction as Sensemaking: How a Central Bank Thinks'. *Organization Studies* 31, no. 3 (2010): 349–67.

*Stewards of the Market: How the Federal Reserve Made Sense of the Financial Crisis*. Cambridge, MA: Harvard University Press, 2020.

Accominotti, Olivier. 'The Sterling Trap: Foreign Reserves Management at the Bank of France, 1928–1936'. *European Review of Economic History* 13, no. 3 (2009): 349–76.

'London Merchant Banks, the Central European Panic, and the Sterling Crisis of 1931'. *Journal of Economic History* 72, no. 1 (2012): 1–43.

'International Banking and Transmission of the 1931 Financial Crisis'. *Economic History Review* 72, no. 1 (2019): 260–85.

Accominotti, Olivier, and Barry Eichengreen. 'The Mother of All Sudden Stops: Capital Flows and Reversals in Europe, 1919–32'. *Economic History Review* 69, no. 2 (2016): 469–92.

Aguado, Iago Gil. 'The Credit Anstalt Crisis of 1931 and the Failure of the Austro-German Customs Union Project'. *The Historical Journal* 44, no. 1 (2001): 199–221.

Ahamed, Liaquat. *Lords of Finance: The Bankers Who Broke the World*. New York: The Penguin Press, 2009.

'Aktion Der Regierung Für Die Creditanstalt'. *Neues Wiener Tagblatt*, May 12, 1931.

Allen, William A., and Richhild Moessner. 'The International Propagation of the Financial Crisis of 2008 and a Comparison with 1931'. *Financial History Review* 19, no. 2 (2012): 123–47.

'And After Chequers . . .?' *The Economist*, June 13, 1931.

Anderson, Benedict. *Imagined Communities: Reflections of the Origin and Spread of Nationalism*, rev. ed. New York: Verso, 1991.

'Austria'. *The Economist*, June 6, 1931.

'Austria Fights off Financial Crash'. *The New York Times*, May 28, 1931.

'Austrian Bank Bills'. *Financial Times*, May 21, 1931.

Aykens, Peter. '(Mis)Trusting Authorities: A Social Theory of Currency Crises'. *Review of International Political Economy* 12, no. 2 (2005): 310–33.

Baffi, Paolo. *The Origins of Central Bank Cooperation: The Establishment of the Bank for International Settlements*. Rome: Editori Laterza, 2002.

Bagehot, Walter. *Lombard Street: A Description of the Money Market*. Westport, CT: Hyperion Press, 1962 [1873].

Balderston, Theo. 'The Banks and the Gold Standard in the German Financial Crisis of 1931'. *Financial History Review* 1, no. 1 (1994): 43–68.

Banholzer, Simon, and Tobias Straumann. 'Why the French Said "Non": A New Perspective on the Hoover Moratorium of June 1931'. *Journal of Contemporary History* 56, no. 4 (October 1, 2021): 1040–60.

Bank for International Settlements. 'Second Annual Report. April 1, 1931–March 31, 1932'. Basle, Switzerland, 1932.

'Bank of England and Austria: Resolving a Crisis'. *Financial Times*, June 19, 1931.

'Bank Rate Raised to 3 1/2 per cent'. *Financial Times*, July 24, 1931.

Beckert, Jens. 'How Do Fields Change? The Interrelations of Institutions, Networks, and Cognition in the Dynamics of Markets'. *Organization Studies* 31, no. 5 (2010): 605–27.

*Imagined Futures: Fictional Expectations and Capitalist Dynamics*. Cambridge, MA: Harvard University Press, 2016.

Beckert, Jens, and Richard Bronk. 'An Introduction to Uncertain Futures'. In *Uncertain Futures: Imaginaries, Narratives, and Calculation in the Economy*, edited by Jens Beckert and Richard Bronk, 1–333. Oxford: Oxford University Press, 2018.

*Uncertain Futures: Imaginaries, Narratives, and Calculation in the Economy*. Edited by Jens Beckert and Richard Bronk. Oxford: Oxford University Press, 2018.

'Uncertain Futures: Imaginaries, Narratives, and Calculative Technologies'. MPIfG Discussion Paper, Cologne, 2019.

Bennett, Edward W. *Germany and the Diplomacy of the Financial Crisis, 1931*. Cambridge, MA: Harvard University Press, 1962.

Bernanke, Ben S. *The Courage to Act: A Memoir of a Crisis and Its Aftermath*. New York: W.W. Norton, 2015.

Bernanke, Ben S., and Harold James. 'The Gold Standard, Deflation, and Financial Crisis in the Great Depression: An International Comparison'. In *Essays on the Great Depression*, edited by Ben Bernanke, 70–107. Princeton: Princeton University Press, 2000.

Bernanke, Ben S., Timoty Geithner, and Henry M. Paulson Jr. *Firefighting: The Financial Crisis and Its Lessons*. London: Profile Books, 2019.

Bernanke, Ben S., Timoty Geithner, and Henry M. Paulson Jr (eds.). *First Responders: Inside the U.S. Strategy for Fighting the 2007–2009 Global Financial Crisis*. New Haven, CT: Yale University Press, 2020.

Billings, Mark, and Forrest Capie. 'Financial Crisis, Contagion, and the British Banking System between the World Wars'. *Business History* 53, no. 2 (2011): 193–215.

Blyth, Mark. *Austerity: The History of a Dangerous Idea*. Oxford: Oxford University Press, 2013.

Bonavia, Michael. *London before I Forget*. Upton-upon-Severn: The Self Publishing Association, 1990.

Boobbyer, Philip. 'Francis Rodd, Lord Rennell (1895–1978)'. In *Geographers: Bibliographic Studies*, edited by Hayden Lorimer and Charles W.J. Withers, 35: 10–31. London: Bloomsbury, 2016.

*The Life and World of Francis Rodd, Lord Rennell (1895–1978): Geography, Money and War*. London: Anthem Press, 2021.

Bordo, Michael D. 'An Historical Perspective on the Quest for Financial Stability and the Monetary Policy Regime'. *Journal of Economic History* 78, no. 2 (2018): 319–57.

'Monetary Policy Cooperation/Coordination and Global Financial Crises in Historical Perspective'. NBER Working Paper, Cambridge, MA, 2020.

Bordo, Michael D., and Harold James. 'The Great Depression Analogy'. *Financial History Review* 17, no. 2 (2010): 127–40.

Bordo, Michael D., Øyvind Eitrheim, Marc Flandreau, and Jan F. Qvigstad. *Central Banks at a Crossroads: What Can We Learn from History?* Edited by Michael D. Bordo, Øyvind Eitrheim, Marc Flandreau, and Jan F. Qvigstad. Cambridge: Cambridge University Press, 2016.

Borio, Claudio, Gianni Toniolo, and Piet Clement. *Past and Future of Central Bank Cooperation*. Cambridge: Cambridge University Press, 2008.

Borio, Claudio, Harold James, and Hyun Song Shin. 'The International Monetary and Financial System: A Capital Account Historical Perspective'. In *Central Bank at a Crossroads: What Can We Learn from History?*, edited by Michael Bordo, Øyvind Eitrheim, Marc Flandreau, and Jan F. Qvigstad, 356–86. New York: Cambridge University Press, 2016.

Born, Karl Erich. *Die Deutsche Bankkrise 1931: Finanzen Und Politik*. Münich: R. Piper & Co. Verlag, 1967.

Boyce, Robert. *The Great Interwar Crisis and the Collapse of Globalization*. Basingstoke: Palgrave Macmillan, 2009.

Boyle, Andrew. *Montagu Norman: A Biography*. London: Cassell, 1967.

Brine, Kevin R., and Mary Poovey. *Finance in America: An Unfinished Story*. Chicago: The University of Chicago Press, 2017.

Brown, Andrew D., Ian Colville, and Annie Pye. 'Making Sense of Sensemaking in Organization Studies'. *Organization Studies* 36, no. 2 (2015): 265–77.

Bruner, Jerome S. *Acts of Meaning: Four Lectures on Mind and Culture*. The Jerusalem-Harvard Lectures. Cambridge, MA: Harvard University Press, 1990.

Burchill, S. *The National Interest in International Relations Theory*. London: Palgrave Macmillan, 2005.

Burk, Kathleen. *Morgan Grenfell, 1838–1988: The Biography of a Merchant Bank*. Oxford: Oxford University Press, 1989.

Callender, Harold. 'Reich Bankers See Ruin Unless Aided'. *The New York Times*, July 14, 1931.

'The Diplomat of Threadneedle Street'. *The New York Times*, November 6, 1932.

Capie, Forrest. 'Disintegration of the National Economy between the Wars'. In *The Great Depression of the 1930s: Lessons for Today*, edited by Nicholas Crafts and Peter Fearon, 141–87. Oxford: Oxford University Press, 2013.

Capie, Forrest, Terence Mills, and Geoffrey Wood. 'What Happened in 1931?' In *Financial Crises and the World Banking System*, edited by Forrest Capie and Geoffrey Wood, 1st ed., 120–48. London: Macmillan, 1986.

Carré, Emmanuel, and Laurent Le Maux. 'Financial Instability and International-Lender-of-Last-Resort Theory from the Gold Standard to the Dollar System'. *Jahrbuch Für Wirtschaftsgeschichte* 63, no. 2 (2022): 311–44.

Carter, Charles. 'George Shackle and Uncertainty: A Revolution Still Awaited'. *Review of Political Economy* 5, no. 2 (1993): 127–37.

Cassis, Youssef. *Crises & Opportunities: The Shaping of Modern Finance.* Oxford: Oxford University Press, 2011.

Chandler, Lester V. *Benjamin Strong: Central Banker.* Washington DC: Brookings Institution, 1958.

Chandor, J. C. *Margin Call*, 2011.

Chernow, Ron. *The House of Morgan: An American Banking Dynasty and the Rise of Modern Finance.* New York: Grove Press, 1990.

Clarke, Stephen V.O. *Central Bank Cooperation: 1924–31.* New York: Federal Reserve Bank of New York, 1967.

Clavin, Patricia. *The Great Depression in Europe, 1929–1939.* London: Macmillan, 2000.

Clay, Henry. *Lord Norman.* London: Macmillan, 1957.

Clement, Piet. 'Between Banks and Governments: The Records of BIS'. In *European Banking Overseas, 19th–20th Century*, edited by Ton de Graaf, Joost Jonker, and Jaap-Jan Mobron, 139–62. Amsterdam: ABN AMRO Bank N.V., 2002.

'Introduction: Past and Future of Central Bank Cooperation'. In *Past and Future of Central Bank Cooperation*, edited by Claudio Borio, Gianni Toniolo, and Piet Clement, 1–15. Cambridge: Cambridge University Press, 2008.

'Institutionalizing Central Bank Cooperation: The Norman-Schacht Vision and Early Experience of the Bank for International Settlements, 1929–1933'. In *The Spread of the Modern Central Bank and Global Cooperation, 1919–1939*, edited by Barry Eichengreen and Andreas Kakridis, 80–102. Cambridge: Cambridge University Press, 2023.

Cohan, William D. *The Last Tycoons: The Secret History of Lazard Freres & Co.* New York: Doubleday, 2007.

Colville, Ian, Annie Pye, and Mike Carter. 'Organizing to Counter Terrorism: Sensemaking amidst Dynamic Complexity'. *Human Relations* 66, no. 9 (2013): 1201–23.

'Coming to Grips'. *The Economist*, July 18, 1931.

'Conversations at Chequers'. *The Economist*, June 6, 1931.

Cooper, Richard N. 'Almost a Century of Central Bank Cooperation'. In *Past and Future of Central Bank Cooperation*, edited by Claudio Borio, Gianni Toniolo, and Piet Clement, 76–112. Cambridge: Cambridge University Press, 2008.

Costigliola, Frank C. 'Anglo-American Financial Rivalry in the 1920s'. *The Journal of Economic History* 37, no. 4 (1977): 911–34.

Cottrell, Philip L. 'Austria between Diplomats and Bankers 1919–1931'. In *Konstellationen Internationaler Politik 1924–1931*, edited by Gustav Schmidt, 292–311.Bochum: Studienverlag Dr. N. Brockmeyer, 1983.

'The Bank of England in Its International Setting, 1918–1972'. In *The Bank of England: Money, Power & Influence, 1694–1994*, edited by Richard Roberts and David Kynaston, 83–139. Oxford: Clarendon Press, 1995.

'Norman, Strakosch and the Development of Central Banking: From Conception to Practice, 1919–1924'. In *Rebuilding the Financial System in Central and Eastern Europe, 1918–1994*, edited by Philip L. Cottrell, 29–73. Aldershot: Scolar Press, 1997.

'The Bank of England and Credit-Anstalt's Collapse, Spring 1931'. In *Auf Heller Und Cent: Beiträge Zur Finanz- Und Währungsgeschichte*, edited by Karl Bachinger and Dieter Stiefel, 407–33. Vienna: Uberreuter Wirtschaft, 2001.

Crafts, Nicholas, and Peter Fearon, eds. *The Great Depression of the 1930s: Lessons for Today*. Oxford: Oxford University Press, 2013.

'Credit Anstalt Affairs. International Bankers' Committee'. *Financial Times*, June 2, 1931.

'Credit Anstalt Affairs. London Committee Appointed'. *Financial Times*, May 27, 1931.

Cross, Mai'A K. Davis. 'Rethinking Epistemic Communities Twenty Years Later'. *Review of International Studies* 39, no. 1 (2013): 137–60.

Darwin, John. *The Empire Project: The Rise and Fall of the British World-System, 1830–1970*. Cambridge: Cambridge University Press, 2009.

Davis, Natalie Zemon. *Fiction in the Archives: Pardon Tales and Their Tellers in Sixteenth-Century France*. Stanford: Stanford University Press, 1987.

Department of State. *Papers Relating to the Foreign Relations of the United States, 1931, Volume I*. Washington DC, 1931.

'Devaluation Delusions'. *The Economist*, September 19, 1931.

Dimsdale, Nicholas, and Nicholas Horsewood. 'The Financial Crisis of 1931 and the Impact of the Great Depression on the British Economy'. In *British Financial Crises since 1825*, edited by Nicholas Dimsdale and Anthony Hotson, 116–38. Oxford: Oxford University Press, 2014.

Doerr, Sebastian, Stefan Gissler, José-Luis Peydró, and Hans-Joachim Voth. 'Financial Crises and Political Radicalization: How Failing Banks Paved Hitler's Path to Power'. *The Journal of Finance*, June 22, 2022.

Dulles, Eleanor Lansing. *The Bank for International Settlements at Work*. New York: Macmillan, 1932.

'The Bank for International Settlements'. *American Economic Review* (June 1938): 292–304.

Eichengreen, Barry. *Golden Fetters: The Gold Standard and the Great Depression, 1919–1939*. Oxford: Oxford University Press, 1992.

'Central Bank Co-operation and Exchange Rate Commitments: The Classical and Interwar Gold Standards Compared'. *Financial History Review* 2, no. 2 (1995): 99–118.

*Exorbitant Privilege: The Rise and Fall of the Dollar*. Oxford: Oxford University Press, 2011.

'Economic History and Economic Policy'. *The Journal of Economic History* 72, no. 2 (2012): 289–307.

*Hall of Mirrors: The Great Depression, the Great Recession and the Uses – and Misuses – of History*. New York: Oxford University Press, 2015.

Eichengreen, Barry, and Marc Flandreau. *The Gold Standard in Theory and History*. London: Routledge, 1997.

Eichengreen, Barry, and O. Jeanne. 'Currency Crisis and Unemployment: Sterling in 1931'. In *Currency Crises*, edited by Paul Krugman, 7–43. Chicago: University of Chicago Press, 2000.

Eichengreen, Barry, and Andreas Kakridis. 'Interwar Central Banks'. In *The Spread of the Modern Central Bank and Global Cooperation, 1919–1939*, edited by Barry

Eichengreen and Andreas Kakridis, 3–39. Cambridge: Cambridge University Press, 2023.

Eichengreen, Barry, and Kevin O'Rourke. 'What Do the New Data Tell Us?' https://voxeu.org/article/tale-two-depressions-what-do-new-data-tell-us-february-2010-update, 2010 (accessed December 23, 2023).

Eichengreen, Barry, and Peter Temin. 'The Gold Standard and the Great Depression'. *Contemporary European History* 9, no. 2 (2000): 183–207.

'Fetters of Gold and Paper'. *Oxford Review of Economic Policy* 26, no. 3 (2010): 370–84.

Einzig, Paul. *Montagu Norman: A Study in Financial Statesmanship*. London: Kegan Paul, 1932.

Enderis, Guido. 'Germans Skeptical of Norman's Plan'. *The New York Times*, April 21, 1931.

'Reich Situation Calmer'. *The New York Times*, July 14, 1931.

European Commission. 'Economic Crisis in Europe: Causes, Consequences and Responses'. *European Economy*, 2009.

'Facing Realities'. *The New York Times*, July 14, 1931.

Feiertag, Olivier. 'Les Banques d'émission et La BRI Face à La Dislocation de l'étalon-or (1931–1933): L'entrée Dans l'âge de La Coopération Monétaire Internationale'. *Histoire, Économie et Société* 18, no. 4 (1999): 715–36.

Feiertag, Olivier, and Pablo Martin Acena. 'The Delayed Modernization of the Central Banks of France and Spain in the Twentieth Century'. In *The Emergence of Modern Central Banking from 1918 to the Present*, edited by Carl-L. Holtfrerich, Jaime Reis, and Gianni Toniolo, 38–68. Aldershot: Ashgate, 1999.

Feinstein, Charles H., Peter Temin, and Gianni Toniolo. *The European Economy between the Wars*, 1st ed. Oxford: Oxford University Press, 1997.

Ferguson, Thomas, and Peter Temin. *Made in Germany: The German Currency Crisis of July 1931. Research in Economic History*, vol. 21, 2003.

'Comment on "The German Twin Crisis of 1931"'. *The Journal of Economic History* 64, no. 03 (2004): 872–76.

Fisher, Irving. 'The Debt-Deflation Theory of Great Depressions'. *Econometrica* no. 1 (1933): 337–57.

Flandreau, Marc. 'Central Bank Cooperation in Historical Perspective: A Sceptical View'. *The Economic History Review* 50, no. 4 (1997): 735–63.

'Money and Doctors'. In *Money Doctors: The Experience of International Financial Advising 1850–2000*, edited by Marc Flandreau, 1–9. Taylor & Francis, 2003.

Fligstein, Neil, Jonah Stuart Brundage, and Michael Schultz. 'Seeing Like the Fed: Culture, Cognition, and Framing in the Failure to Anticipate the Financial Crisis of 2008'. *American Sociological Review* 82, no. 5 (2017): 879–909.

Flores Zendejas, Juan, and Gianandrea Nodari. 'Central Bank Cooperation 1930–1932, A Reappraisal'. *Economic History Working Papers*. Genève: Paul Bairoch Institute of Economic History, 2023.

Flyvbjerg, Bent. 'Five Misunderstandings about Case-Study Research'. *Qualitative Inquiry* 12, no. 2 (2006): 219–45.

Forbes, Neil. 'London Banks, the German Standstill Agreements, and "Economic Appeasement" in the 1930s'. *The Economic History Review* 40, no. 4 (1987): 571–87.

Foyle, Jonathan. 'The Renovation of a Former Bank of England Governor's Historic Home'. *Financial Times*, August 28, 2020.
'France'. *The Economist*, June 27, 1931.
'France'. *The Economist*, July 4, 1931.
'France'. *The Economist*, July 11, 1931.
'France'. *The Economist*, August 1, 1931.
'France'. *The Economist*, August 8, 1931.
Friedman, Milton, and Anna J. Schwartz. *A Monetary History of the United States, 1867–1960*. Princeton: Princeton University Press, 1963.
Friedman, Walter A. *Fortune Tellers: The Story of America's First Economic Forecasters*. Princeton: Princeton University Press, 2014.
Funke, Manuel, Moritz Schularick, and Christoph Trebesch. 'Going to Extremes: Politics after Financial Crises, 1870–2014'. *European Economic Review* 88 (September 1, 2016): 227–60.
'G.L. Harrison Heads Reserve Bank Here'. *The New York Times*, November 24, 1928.
Geertz, Clifford. *The Interpretation of Cultures: Selected Essays*. New York: Fontana Press, 1973.
'Thick Description: Toward an Interpretive Theory of Culture'. In *The Interpretation of Cultures*, edited by Clifford Geertz, 3–30. London: Fontana Press, 1973.
Geithner, Timothy. *Stress Test: Reflections on Financial Crises*. London: Random House Business Books, 2014.
'George L. Harrison Dead at 71; Headed Federal Reserve Here'. *The New York Times*, March 6, 1958.
'Germany: Ein Feste Burg'. *Time*, July 27, 1931.
'Germany'. *The Economist*, June 20, 1931.
'Germany'. *The Economist*, June 27, 1931.
'Germany'. *The Economist*, July 11, 1931.
'Germany'. *The Economist*, July 18, 1931.
'Germany'. *The Economist*, July 25, 1931.
Geyde, G.E.R. 'Vienna Bank Crisis Laid to Paris Plot'. *The New York Times*, June 7, 1931.
'Gold Exports Stopped'. *Financial Times*, September 21, 1931.
Graf, Rüdiger. 'Either-or: The Narrative of "Crisis" in Weimar Germany and in Historiography'. *Central European History* 43, no. 4 (2010): 592–615.
Grossman, Richard S. *Unsettled Account: The Evolution of Banking in the Industrialized World since 1800*. Princeton: Princeton University Press, 2010.
Grossman, Richard S., and Hugh Rockoff. 'Fighting the Last War: Economists on the Lender of Last Resort'. In *Central Banks at a Crossroads: What Can We Learn from History?*, edited by Michael Bordo, Øyvind Eitrheim, Marc Flandreau, and Jan F. Qvigstad, 231–79. New York: Cambridge University Press, 2016.
Gyöngyösi, Győző, and Emil Verner. 'Financial Crisis, Creditor-Debtor Conflict, and Populism'. *The Journal of Finance* 77, no. 4 (2022): 2471–523.
Haas, Peter M. 'Introduction: Epistemic Communities and International Policy Coordination'. *International Organization* 46, no. 1 (1992): 1–35.
'Epistemic Communities'. In *The Oxford Handbook of International Environmental Law*, edited by Daniel Bodansky, Jutta Brunnée, and Ellen Hey, 792–805. Oxford: Oxford University Press, 2008.

Hansen, Per H. 'From Growth to Crisis: The Danish Banking System from 1850 to the Interwar Years'. *Scandinavian Economic History Review* 39, no. 3 (1991): 20–40.

'Organizational Culture and Organizational Change: The Transformation of Savings Banks in Denmark, 1965–1990'. *Enterprise & Society* 8, no. 4 (2007): 920–53.

'Business History: A Cultural and Narrative Approach'. *Business History Review* 86, no. 4 (2012): 693–717.

'Cooperate or Free Ride? The Scandinavian Central Banks, Bank for International Settlements and the Austrian Financial Crisis of 1931'. *Scandinavian Journal of History* 37, no. 1 (2012): 87–107.

'Making Sense of Financial Crisis and Scandal: A Danish Bank Failure in the First Era of Finance Capitalism'. *Enterprise & Society* 13, no. 3 (2012): 672–706.

'From Finance Capitalism to Financialization: A Cultural and Narrative Perspective on 150 Years of Financial History'. *Enterprise & Society* 15, no. 4 (2014): 605–42.

'Review Essay: Barry Eichengreen, Hall of Mirrors: The Great Depression, the Great Recession and the Uses – and Misuses – of History'. *Business History Review* 89, no. 3 (2015): 557–69.

Hansen, Per H., and Anne Magnussen. 'Making Sense of Business and Community in Hollywood Films, 1928–2016'. *Business History Review* 92, no. 2 (2018): 307–37.

Harris, Max. *Monetary War and Peace: London, Washington, Paris, and the Tripartite Agreement of 1936*. Cambridge: Cambridge University Press, 2021.

Hawtrey, R.G. *The Gold Standard in Theory and Practice*. London: Longmans, Green and Co., 1927.

*The Art of Central Banking*. London: Longmans, Green and Co., 1932.

Hay, Colin. 'Narrating Crisis: The Discursive Construction of the "Winter of Discontent"'. *Sociology* 30, no. 2 (1996): 253–77.

'Constructivist Institutionalism'. In *The Oxford Handbook of Political Institutions*, edited by R.A.W. Rhodes and Sarah A. Binder. Oxford: Oxford University Press, 2006.

Helleiner, Eric. *States and the Reemergence of Global Finance: From Bretton Woods to the 1990s*. Ithaca: Cornell University Press, 1994.

Hernes, Tor, and Sally Maitlis. 'Process, Sensemaking, and Organizing: An Introduction'. In *Process, Sensemaking, and Organizing*, edited by Tor Hernes and Sally Maitlis, 27–37. Oxford: Oxford University Press, 2010.

Hettinger Jr, Albert J. 'Director's Comment'. In *A Monetary History of the United States*, edited by Milton Friedman and Anna J. Schwartz, 809–14. Princeton: Princeton University Press, 1963.

Hetzel, Robert L. 'German Monetary History in the First Half of the Twentieth Century'. *Economic Quarterly-Federal Reserve Bank of Richmond* 88, no. 2 (2002): 1–35.

Ho, Karen. 'Disciplining Investment Bankers, Disciplining the Economy: Wall Street's Institutional Culture of Crisis and the Downsizing of Corporate America'. *American Anthropologist* 111, no. 2 (2009): 177–89.

*Liquidated: An Ethnography of Wall Street*. Durham: Duke University Press, 2009.

'Hope Revived?' *The Economist*, July 11, 1931.

Horn, Martin. *J. P. Morgan & Co. and the Crisis of Capitalism*. Cambridge: Cambridge University Press, 2022.

Hume, David. 'On the Balance of Trade'. In *The Gold Standard in Theory and History*, edited by Barry Eichengreen and Marc Flandreau, 33–43. London: Routledge, 1997.

Imlay, Talbot C., Jonathan Kirshner, Sally Marks, Kenneth Mouré, Stephen A. Schuker, and Robert Boyce. 'H-Diplo Roundtable Review of Robert Boyce. The Great Interwar Crisis and the Collapse of Globalization'. H-Diplo, 2011.

'In The Thick of The Storm'. *The Economist*, June 20, 1931.

'International: Again Gold, Gold'. *Time*, December 15, 1930.

'International: Gold, Gold, Gold'. *Time*, December 1, 1930.

'International: Nothing Resounding'. *Time*, August 24, 1931.

Irwin, Douglas A. 'Did France Cause the Great Depression'. NBER Working Paper Series, no. 16350. NBER, 2010.

Jackson, Gardner. 'The American Signer of the Basle Report'. *The New York Times*, January 3, 1932.

James, Harold. 'The Causes of the German Banking Crisis of 1931'. *The Economic History Review* 37, no. 1 (1984): 68–87.

*The German Slump: Politics and Economics, 1924–1936*. Oxford: Oxford University Press, 1986.

'Financial Flows across Frontiers during the Interwar Depression'. *The Economic History Review* 45, no. 3 (1992): 594–613.

*The End of Globalization: Lessons from the Great Depression*. Cambridge, MA: Harvard University Press, 2001.

'The Creation of a World Central Bank? The Early Years of the Bank for International Settlements'. In *The Interwar Depression in an International Context*, edited by Harold James, 159–70. München: R. Oldenbourg Verlag, 2002.

*The Creation and Destruction of Value: The Globalization Cycle*. Cambridge, MA: Harvard University Press, 2009.

'The 1931 Central European Banking Crisis Revisited'. In *Business in the Age of Extremes: Essays in Modern German and Austrian Economic History*, edited by Hartmut Berghoff, Jürgen Kocka, and Dieter Ziegler, 119–30. Cambridge: Cambridge University Press, 2013.

'How Not to Solve a Financial Crisis'. *International Affairs* 98, no. 5 (September 6, 2022): 1575–93.

'The Ideology of Central Banking in the Interwar Years and Beyond'. In *The Spread of the Modern Central Bank and Global Cooperation, 1919–1939*, edited by Barry Eichengreen and Andreas Kakridis, 40–56. Cambridge: Cambridge University Press, 2023.

Janeway, William H. 'The 1931 Sterling Crisis and the Independence of the Bank of England'. *Journal of Post Keynesian Economics* 18, no. 2 (1996): 251–68.

Jobst, Clemens, and Hans Kernbauer. *The Quest for Stable Money: Central Banking in Austria, 1816–2016*. Frankfurt: Campus Verlag, 2016.

Johnson, H. Clark. *Gold, France, and the Great Depression, 1919–1932*. New Haven, CT: Yale University Press, 1997.

Jones, Geoffrey. 'Public Policy and British Multinational Banks, 1914–1982'. *Business and Economic History* 21 (1992): 209–18.

Josephson, Matthew. 'Money Men Are Different Now'. *The Saturday Evening Post*, February 26, 1949.

Kapstein, Ethan Barnaby. 'Between Power and Purpose: Central Bankers and the Politics of Regulatory Convergence'. *International Organization* 46, no. 1 (1992): 265–87.

Kay, John, and Mervyn King. *Radical Uncertainty: Decision-Making beyond the Numbers*. New York: W.W. Norton, 2020.

Kernbauer, Hans. 'The Policy of the Austrian National Bank before and during the 1931 Crisis'. *The 1931 Crisis and Its Aftermath*, 1982.

*Währungspolitik in Der Zwischenkriegszeit: Geschichte Der Oesterreichischen Nationalbank von 1923 Bis 1938*. Wien: Der Oesterreichischen Nationalbank, 1991.

'Central Bank Policy under Foreign Control: The Austrian National Bank in the 1920s'. In *The Spread of the Modern Central Bank and Global Cooperation, 1919–1939*, edited by Barry Eichengreen and Andreas Kakridis, 105–38. Cambridge: Cambridge University Press, 2023.

Keynes, John Maynard. *The Economic Consequences of the Peace*. London: Macmillan, 1919.

'The Economic Consequences of Mr. Churchill'. In *Essays in Persuasion*, edited by John Maynard Keynes, Norton Lib., 244–70. London: W.W. Norton, 1925.

Kindleberger, Charles P. *The World in Depression, 1929–1939*, 2nd ed. London: Penguin, 1986.

Kindleberger, Charles P., and Robert Z Aliber. *Manias, Panics and Crashes: A History of Financial Crises*, 6th ed. New York: Palgrave Macmillan, 2011.

King, Mervyn. 'Monetary Policy in a World of Radical Uncertainty'. *Economic Affairs* 42, no. 1 (February 28, 2022): 2–12.

Kirk, Michael. 'Inside the Meltdown'. PBS Frontline, 2009. www.pbs.org/wgbh/pages/frontline/meltdown/etc/script.html (accessed December 29, 2023).

Knight, Frank H. *Risk, Uncertainty and Profit*. New York: Sentry Press, 1921.

Koselleck, Reinhart. *Futures Past: On the Semantics of Historical Time*. New York: Columbia University Press, 2004.

Koselleck, Reinhart, and Michaela Richter. 'Crisis'. *Journal of the History of Ideas* 67, no. 2 (2006): 357–400.

Kunz, Diane B. *The Battle for Britain's Gold Standard in 1931*. London: Croom Helm, 1987.

'American Bankers and Americas Fall from Gold'. In *International Financial History in the 20th Century*, edited by Marc Flandreau and Carl-Ludwig Holtfrerich, 35–48. Cambridge: Cambridge University Press, 2003.

Kynaston, David. *The City of London: Volume III Illusions of Gold, 1914–1945*. London: Pimlico, 1999.

Leith-Ross, Frederick. *Money Talks: Fifty Years of International Finance*. London: Hutchinson of London, 1968.

Levi, Giovanni. 'On Microhistory'. In *New Perspectives on Historical Writing*, edited by Peter Burke, 93–113. Cambridge, MA: Polity Press, 1991.

Levy, Jonathan. 'Radical Uncertainty'. *Critical Quarterly* 62, no. 1 (2020): 15–28.

'Liquidity of the Banks'. *Financial Times*, September 21, 1931.

'London Is Cheered despite Gold Loss'. *The New York Times*, July 17, 1931.

'London Takes the Strain'. *Financial Times*, July 14, 1931.

Luther, Hans. *Vor Dem Abgrund. 1930–1933: Reichsbankpräsident in Krisenzeiten.* Berlin: Propyläen Verlag, 1964.

MacCormac, John. 'Austrian Cabinet Quits on Bank Deal', June 17, 1931.

MacDonald, Carlisle. 'French Seek to Win Vienna with a Loan'. *The New York Times*, May 18, 1931.

'World Bank Offers Austria $14,000,000'. *The New York Times*, May 19, 1931.

'90-Day Debt Notice by Reich Forecast'. *The New York Times*, June 2, 1931.

'Paris Fears Abate on German Crisis'. *The New York Times*, June 16, 1931.

'Britain Is Assured of French Credits'. *The New York Times*, July 29, 1931.

Macher, Flora. 'The Austrian Banking Crisis of 1931: A Reassessment'. *Financial History Review* 25, no. 3 (January 10, 2018): 297–321.

Mackenzie, Donald. *An Engine, Not a Camera: How Financial Models Shape Markets.* Cambridge, MA: MIT Press, 2008.

'Maintenance of the Pound's Value'. *Financial Times*, September 2, 1931.

Maitlis, Sally. 'The Social Processes of Organizational Sensemaking'. *Academy of Management Journal* 48, no. 1 (2005): 21–49.

Maitlis, Sally, and Marlys Christianson. 'Sensemaking in Organizations: Taking Stock and Moving Forward'. *The Academy of Management Annals* 8, no. 1 (2014): 57–125.

Malmendier, Ulrike, and Stefan Nagel. 'Depression Babies: Do Macroeconomic Experiences Affect Risk Taking?' *Quarterly Journal of Economics* 126, no. 1 (2011): 373–416.

Marcus, Nathan. *Austrian Reconstruction and the Collapse of Global Finance: 1921–1931.* Cambridge, MA: Harvard University Press, 2018.

Martin, Jamie. *The Meddlers: Sovereignty, Empire, and the Birth of Global Economic Governance.* Cambridge, MA: Harvard University Press, 2022.

Mattingly, Cheryl. 'Narrative Reflections on Practical Actions: Two Learning Experiments in Reflective Storytelling'. In *The Reflective Turn: Case Studies in and on Educational Practice*, edited by Donald A. Schön, 235–57. New York: Teachers College Press, 1991.

McCracken, Grant. 'Culture and Consumption: A Theoretical Account of the Structure and Movement of the Cultural Meaning of Consumer Goods'. *Journal of Consumer Research* 13 (1986): 71–84.

Meltzer, Allan H. *A History of the Federal Reserve. Volume 1: 1912–1951.* Chicago: The University of Chicago Press, 2003.

Moggridge, Donald E. *British Monetary Policy, 1924–1931: The Norman Conquest of $4.86.* Cambridge: Cambridge University Press, 1972.

'Policy in the Crises of 1920 and 1929'. In *Financial Crises: Theory, History, and Policy*, edited by Charles P. Kindleberger and Jean Pierre Laffargue, 171–87. Cambridge: Cambridge University Press, 1982.

*Maynard Keynes: An Economist's Biography.* London: Routledge, 1992.

Moggridge, Donald, and Robert Skidelsky. 'Critique of Schuker "J.M. Keynes and the Personal Politics of Reparations"'. *Diplomacy & Statecraft* 26, no. 4 (January 1, 2015): 736–44.

Mordhorst, Mads, and Stefan Schwarzkopf. 'Theorising Narrative in Business History'. *Business History* 59, no. 8 (2017): 1155–75.

Moreau, Emile. *The Golden Franc. Memoirs of a Governor of the Bank of France: The Stabilization of the Franc (1926–1928)*. Boulder, CO: Westview Press, 1991.

Morgan, Mary S. and Thomas A. Stapleford, 'Narrative in Economics: A New Turn on the Past'. *History of Political Economy* 55, no. 3 (2023): 395–421.

'Morgan Holds Gold Decision a "Hopeful Event"; Calls Step a Stage Toward Revival of Trade'. *The New York Times*, September 22, 1931.

Morrison, James Ashley. 'Shocking Intellectual Austerity: The Role of Ideas in the Demise of the Gold Standard in Britain'. *International Organization* 70, no. 01 (December 14, 2016): 175–207.

'Shocking Intellectual Austerity: The Role of Ideas in the Demise of the Gold Standard in Britain. Extended Citations'. *International Organization*, 2016. https://static.cambridge.org/content/id/urn:cambridge.org:id:article:S0020818315000314/resource/name/S0020818315000314sup001.docx (accessed December 23, 2023).

Mouré, Kenneth. *Managing the Franc Poincare: Economic Understanding and Political Constraint in French Monetary Policy, 1928–1936*. New York: Cambridge University Press, 1991.

'The Limits to Central Bank Co-operation, 1916–1936'. *Contemporary European History* 1, no. 3 (1992): 259–79.

*The Gold Standard Illusion: France, the Bank of France, and the International Gold Standard, 1914–1939*. Oxford: Oxford University Press, 2002.

'Mr Montagu Norman'. *The Economist*, August 22, 1931.

'Mr. Montagu Norman'. *The Financial Times*, August 17, 1931.

'New Problems for the Investor'. *The Economist*, September 26, 1931.

New York Times. 'World Bank Names M'Garrah as Head'. *The New York Times*, April 23, 1930.

New York Times. 'Leon Fraser Back. Seeks Upturn Signs'. *The New York Times*, June 3, 1931.

'Norman in London; Public Held Back'. *The New York Times*, September 24, 1931.

North, Douglas C. 'Institutions and the Performance of Economies over Time'. In *Handbook of New Institutional Economics*, edited by Claude Menard and Mary M. Shirley, 21–30. Dordrecht: Springer, 2005.

O'Sullivan, Mary A. 'History as Heresy: Unlearning the Lessons of Economic Orthodoxy'. *The Economic History Review* 75, no. 2 (2022): 297–335.

'Obituary: Lord Rennell of Rodd, KBE, CB, JP'. *The Geographic Journal* 144, no. 2 (1978): 392–93.

Office of the Historian. 'Memorandum by the Secretary of State'. Papers Relating to the Foreign Relations of the United States, 1931. https://history.state.gov/historicaldocuments/frus1931v01/d217 (accessed December 29, 2023).

Office of the Historian. 'Memorandum by the Secretary of State of Conversations with M. Flandin and with Mr. Jay, of Morgan & Company, at the Residence of the American Ambassador in France, July 17, 1931'. Papers Relating to the Foreign Relations of the United States, 1931. https://history.state.gov/historicaldocuments/frus1931v01/d229 (accessed December 29, 2023).

'Memorandum of Telephone Conversation'. Papers Relating to the Foreign Relations of the United States, 1931. https://history.state.gov/historicaldocuments/frus1931v01/d226 (accessed December 29, 2023).

'The Acting Secretary of State to the Chargé in Great Britain (Atherton)'. Papers Relating to the Foreign Relations of the United States, 1931. https://history.state.gov/historicaldocuments/frus1931v01/d231 (accessed December 29, 2023).

'The Acting Secretary of State to the Chargé in Great Britain (Atherton)'. Papers Relating to the Foreign Relations of the United States, 1931. https://history.state.gov/historicaldocuments/frus1931v01/d233 (accessed December 29, 2023).

Oliver, Michael J. 'Financial Crises'. In *Economic Disasters of the Twentieth Century*, edited by Michael J. Oliver and Derek H. Aldcroft, 182–235. Cheltenham: Edward Elgar, 2007.

Oulahan, Richard V. 'Hoover's Debt Move'. *The New York Times*, July 12, 1931.

'Hoover Will Leave Action to Bankers'. *The New York Times*, July 13, 1931.

Oye, Kenneth A. 'The Sterling-Dollar-Franc Triangle: Monetary Diplomacy, 1929–1937'. In *Cooperation under Anarchy*, edited by Kenneth A. Oye, 173–99. Princeton: Princeton University Press, 1986.

Pak, Susie J. *Gentlemen Bankers: The World of J. P. Morgan*. Cambridge, MA: Harvard University Press, 2013.

Pares, Bernard. 'Sir Peter Bark'. *The Slavonic and East European Review* 16, no. 46 (1937): 189–93.

Paulson, Hank. *On the Brink: Inside the Race to Stop the Collapse of the Global Financial System*. New York: Headline. Business Plus, 2010.

Peters, Gerhard, and John T. Woolley. 'The President's News Conference. Herbert Hoover, June 20, 1931'. The American Presidency Project. www.presidency.ucsb.edu/documents/the-presidents-news-conference-671 (accessed December 29, 2023).

Philip, P.J. 'France Not Ready to Make Sacrifice'. *The New York Times*, June 22, 1931.

'Political Stress in England and Germany – The Reparations Issue'. *Commercial and Financial Chronicle*, June 20, 1931.

Popp, Andrew. 'Making Choices in Time'. *Enterprise and Society* 14, no. 3 (2013): 467–74.

'Prof. O. M. W. Sprague, Financial Adviser to Bank of England, Said to Be at Odds with Sir Josiah Stamp'. *Commercial and Financial Chronicle*, June 20, 1931.

'Reported Decision at Basle'. *Financial Times*, July 14, 1931.

Richardson, Gary, and Patrick van Horn. 'In the Eye of a Storm: Manhattan's Money Center Banks during the International Financial Crisis of 1931'. *Explorations in Economic History* 68 (2018): 71–94.

Riefler, Winfield W. 'The Dilemma of Central Banking as Illustrated in Recent Literature'. *Quarterly Journal of Economics* 50, no. 4 (1936): 706–18.

Ritschl, Albrecht. 'Reparations, Deficits and Debt Default: The Great Depression in Germany'. In *The Great Depression of the 1930s: Lessons for Today*, edited by Nicholas Crafts and Peter Fearon, 111–39. Oxford: Oxford University Press, 2013.

Roches, Jérôme de Boyer des, and Ricardo Solis Rosales. 'R.G. Hawtrey on the National and International Lender of Last Resort'. *European Journal of the History of Economic Thought* 18, no. 2 (2011): 175–202.

Rockoff, Hugh. 'Walter Bagehot and the Theory of Central Banking'. In *Financial Crises and the World Banking System*, edited by Forrest Capie and Geoffrey E. Wood, 160–80. London: Macmillan, 1986.

'O.M.W. Sprague (the Man Who 'Wrote the Book' on Financial Crises) and the Founding of the Federal Reserve'. *Journal of Financial Stability* 17 (April 1, 2015): 35–45.

'O.M.W. Sprague (the Man Who 'Wrote the Book' on Financial Crises) Meets the Great Depression'. *Jahrbuch Für Wirtschaftsgeschichte* 63, no. 2 (2022): 527–557.

Rodd, Francis Rennel. *People of the Veil*. London: Macmillan, 1926.

Rosenhek, Zeev. 'Diagnosing and Explaining the Global Financial Crisis: Central Banks, Epistemic Authority, and Sense Making'. *International Journal of Politics, Culture, and Society* 26, no. 3 (2013): 255–72.

Rothbard, Murray N. *Economic Depressions: Their Cause & Cure*. 2009th ed. Mises Institute, 1969.

Samman, Amin. 'The 1930s as Black Mirror: Visions of Historical Repetition in the Global Financial Press, 2007–2009'. *Journal of Cultural Economy* 5, no. 2 (2012): 213–29.

'Making Financial History: The Crisis of 2008 and the Return of the Past'. *Millennium: Journal of International Studies* 42, no. 2 (2014): 309–30.

'Sanierung Der Creditanstalt'. *Neues Wiener Tagblatt*, May 12, 1931.

Sayers, R.S. *The Bank of England, 1891–1944*. Cambridge: Cambridge University Press, 1976.

Schackle, George L.S. *The Nature of Economic Thought: Selected Papers, 1955–1964*. Cambridge: Cambridge University Press, 1966.

Schenk, Catherine, and Tobias Straumann. 'Central Banks and the Stability of the International Monetary Regime'. In *Central Banks at a Crossroads: What Can We Learn From History?*, edited by Michael D. Bordo, Øyvind Eitrheim, Marc Flandreau, and Jan F. Qvigstad, 319–55. Cambridge: Cambridge University Press, 2016.

Schnabel, Isabel. 'The German Twin Crisis of 1931'. *The Journal of Economic History* 64, no. 3 (2004): 822–71.

Schubert, Aurel. *The Credit-Anstalt Crisis of 1931*, 1st ed. New York: Cambridge University Press, 1991.

Schuker, Stephen A. 'Money Doctors between the Wars: The Competition between Central Banks, Private Financial Advisers, and Multilateral Agencies, 1919–39'. In *Money Doctors: The Experience of International Financial Advising 1850–2000*, edited by Marc Flandreau, 49–77. London: Routledge, 2003.

'The Gold-Exchange Standard: A Reinterpretation'. In *International Financial History in the 20th Century: System and Anarchy*, edited by Marc Flandreau, Carl-Ludwig Holtfrerich, and Harold James, 77–93. Cambridge: Cambridge University Press, 2003.

'Central Bankers in the Dock. H-Diplo Review Essay on Liaquat Ahamed. Lords of Finance: The Bankers Who Broke the World'. *H-Diplo*, 2011.

Seddon, Jack A. 'Between Collapse and Decline: The Dissolution of International Monetary Systems in Comparative Historical Perspective'. St. John's College, University of Oxford, 2015.

Selden, Charles A. 'Loan of $400,000,000 Is Sought by Luther in London and Paris'. *The New York Times*, July 10, 1931.

'Settlements Bank. Board and Credit Anstalt Affairs'. *Financial Times*, June 9, 1931.

'Settlements Bank. Support for the Credit Anstalt'. *Financial Times*, May 21, 1931.

Shiller, Robert J. 'Narrative Economics'. *American Economic Review* 107, no. 4 (2017): 967–1004.

*Narrative Economics: How Stories Go Viral & Drive Major Economic Events*. Princeton: Princeton University Press, 2019.
Siepmann, Harry. *Echo of the Guns: Recollections of an Artillery Officer, 1914–18*. London: Robert Hale, 1987.
Simmons, Beth A. 'Why Innovate? Founding the Bank for International Settlements'. *World Politics* 45 (April 1993): 361–405.
*Who Adjusts? Domestic Sources of Foreign Economic Policy during the Interwar Years*. Princeton: Princeton University Press, 1994.
'Rulers of the Game: Central Bank Independence during the Interwar Years'. *International Organization* 50, no. 3 (1996): 407–43.
'The Future of Central Bank Cooperation'. In *Past and Future of Central Bank Cooperation*, edited by Claudio Borio, Gianni Toniolo, and Piet Clement, 174–210. Cambridge: Cambridge University Press, 2008.
Singleton, John. *Central Banking in the Twentieth Century*. Cambridge: Cambridge University Press, 2011.
'Sir Harry Goschen, British Banker, 79'. *The New York Times*, July 10, 1945.
Skidelsky, Robert. *John Maynard Keynes: The Economist as Saviour, 1920–1937*. London: Macmillan, 1992.
Sorkin, Andrew Ross. *Too Big to Fail: Inside the Battle to Save Wall Street*. New York: Allen Lane, 2009.
'Steadying up the Exchanges'. *Financial Times*, July 30, 1931.
Stiefel, Dieter. *Finanzdiplomatie und Weltwirtschaftskrise: Die Krise der Credit-Anstalt für Handel und Gewerbe 1931*. Frankfurt am Main: Verlag Fritz Knapp, 1989.
Stone, Deborah A. 'Causal Stories and the Formation of Policy Agendas'. *Political Science Quarterly* 104, no. 2 (1989): 281.
Stone, Oliver. *Wall Street. Money Never Sleeps*, 2010.
Straumann, Tobias. *Fixed Ideas on Money: Small States and Exchange Rate Regimes in Twentieth-Century Europe*. New York: Cambridge University Press, 2010.
*1931. Debt, Crisis, and the Rise of Hitler*. Oxford: Oxford University Press, 2019.
Straumann, Tobias, Peter Kugler, and Florian Weber. 'How the German Crisis of 1931 Swept across Europe: A Comparative View from Stockholm'. *Economic History Review* 70, no. 1 (2017): 224–47.
Streit, Clarence K. 'World Bank Pledges Aid'. *The New York Times*, July 14, 1931.
'The World Bank Feels Europe's Pulse'. *The New York Times Magazine*, 1931.
t' Hart, Paul. 'Symbols, Ritual and Power: The Lost Dimensions of Crisis Management'. *Journal of Contingencies and Crisis Management* 1, no. 1 (1993): 36–50.
Temin, Peter. *Did Monetary Forces Cause the Great Depression?* New York: W. W. Norton, 1976.
*Lessons from the Great Depression*. Cambridge, MA: MIT Press, 1989.
'Currency Crises: From Andrew Jackson to Angela Merkel'. In *The Oxford Handbook of Banking and Financial History*, edited by Youssef Cassis, Richard S. Grossman, and Catherine R. Schenk, 461–80. Oxford: Oxford University Press, 2016.
Tett, Gillian. 'Wall Street's Crash Course'. *Financial Times*, August 26, 2007.
'Text of the President's Statement Proposing Suspension of Debts'. *The New York Times*, June 21, 1931.
'The Austrian Credit Anstalt'. *The Economist*, June 27, 1931.

'The B.I.S. at Work'. *The Economist*, February 28, 1931.
'The Bank for International Settlements'. *The Economist*, May 9, 1931.
'The Bank Loses More Gold'. *Financial Times*, September 17, 1931.
'The Bank Rate Increase'. *The Economist*, August 1, 1931.
'The Break in the Clouds'. *The Economist*, June 27, 1931.
'The British "Crisis"'. *The Economist*, August 22, 1931.
'The British Government's Statement'. *The New York Times*, September 21, 1931.
'The Conference and the Crisis'. *The Economist*, July 25, 1931.
'The Course of the Exchanges'. *Financial Times*, August 6, 1931.
'The Credit-Anstalt'. *The Economist*, May 16, 1931.
'The Credit-Anstalt'. *The Economist*, May 30, 1931.
'The Credit-Anstalt'. *The Economist*, June 6, 1931.
'The End of an Epoch'. *The Economist*, September 26, 1931.
'The Exchange Crisis'. *The Economist*, August 8, 1931.
'The Financial Situation'. *Commercial and Financial Chronicle*, May 23, 1931.
'The Financial Situation'. *Commercial and Financial Chronicle*, May 30, 1931.
'The Financial Situation'. *Commercial and Financial Chronicle*, June 13, 1931.
'The Financial Situation'. *Commercial and Financial Chronicle*, June 20, 1931.
'The Financial Situation'. *Commercial and Financial Chronicle*, July 4, 1931.
'The Financial Situation'. *Commercial and Financial Chronicle*, July 18, 1931.
'The Financial Situation'. *Commercial and Financial Chronicle*, August 8, 1931.
'The Financial Situation'. *Commercial and Financial Chronicle*, August 15, 1931.
'The Financial Situation'. *Commercial and Financial Chronicle*, August 29, 1931.
'The Financial Situation'. *Commercial and Financial Chronicle*, September 26, 1931.
'The First Lap'. *The Economist*, September 12, 1931.
'The German Banking Situation'. *The Economist*, June 20, 1931.
'The Honest Alternative'. *The Economist*, September 19, 1931.
'The Monetary Half Year'. *The Economist*, July 4, 1931.
'The Money Market'. *The Economist*, July 4, 1931.
'The Money Market'. *The Economist*, July 18, 1931.
'The Money Market'. *The Economist*, September 26, 1931.
'The Outlook for Sterling'. *The Economist*, August 29, 1931.
The Reich Government. 'Text of the German Manifesto'. *The New York Times*, June 7, 1931.
'The Treasury Credits'. *The Economist*, September 5, 1931.
'There Could Be Trouble Ahead'. *The Economist*, December 10, 2011.
Thompson, Charles T. *The Peace Conference Day by Day*. New York: Brentano's Publishers, 1920.
Toniolo, Gianni, with the assistance of Piet Clement. *Central Bank Cooperation at the Bank for International Settlements, 1930–1973*. Cambridge: Cambridge University Press, 2005.
Tooze, Adam. *The Deluge: The Great War and the Remaking of Global Order*. London: Allen Lane, 2014.
Toynbee, Arnold J. *Survey of International Affairs 1931*. London: Oxford University Press, 1932.
Trautwein, Hans Michael. 'International Lending of Last Resort in Historical and Theoretical Perspectives: Introduction'. *Jahrbuch Für Wirtschaftsgeschichte* 63, no. 2 (2022): 303–10.

Tuckett, David. 'Conviction Narrative Theory and Understanding Decision-Making in Economics and Finance'. In *Uncertain Futures: Imaginaries, Narratives, and Calculation in the Economy*, edited by Jens Beckert and Richard Bronk, 62–82. Oxford: Oxford University Press, 2018.

Tuckett, David, Douglas Holmes, Alice Pearson, and Graeme Chaplin. 'Monetary Policy and the Management of Uncertainty: A Narrative Approach'. *SSRN Electronic Journal*. Bank of England, Staff Working Paper, 2020.

Tyson, Neil deGrasse. *Astrophysics for People in a Hurry*. New York: W. W. Norton, 2017.

'U.S. Banks' Demands on Britain'. *Daily Herald*, August 25, 1931.

'U.S. Cites Its Steps to Halt '31 Crisis'. *The New York Times*, December 7, 1946.

'Vienna Credit Bank Still in Need of Aid'. *The New York Times*, May 27, 1931.

Wadhwani, R. Daniel, Roy Suddaby, Mads Mordhorst, and Andrew Popp. 'History as Organizing: Uses of the Past in Organization Studies'. *Organization Studies* 39, no. 12 (2018): 1663–83.

Wandschneider, Kirsten. 'The Stability of the Interwar Gold Exchange Standard: Did Politics Matter?' *Journal of Economic History* 68, no. 1 (2008): 151–81.

Weick, Karl. 'The Collapse of Sensemaking in Organizations: The Mann Gulch Disaster'. *Administrative Science Quarterly* 38, no. 4 (1993): 628–52.

*Sensemaking in Organizations*. Thousand Oaks, CA: Sage, 1995.

'Sensemaking in Organizations: Small Structures with Large Consequences'. In *Making Sense of the Organization*, edited by Karl Weick, 3–31. Malden, MA: Blackwell, 2001.

Weitz, John. *Hitler's Banker: Hjalmar Horace Greeley Schacht*, 1st ed. Boston: Little, Brown and Company, 1997.

Wells, John. *The Company Men*, 2010.

Werner, Andrea. '"Margin Call": Using Film to Explore Behavioural Aspects of the Financial Crisis'. *Journal of Business Ethics* 122, no. 4 (2014): 643–54.

Wesley, Mary, and Eric Siepmann. *Darling Pol: The Letters of Mary Wesley and Eric Siepmann 1944–1967*. Edited by Patrick Marnham. London: Harvill Secker, 2017.

White, Hayden. 'The Burden of History'. *History and Theory* 5, no. 2 (1966): 111–34.

Widmaier, Wesley W. 'Constructing Monetary Crises: New Keynesian Understandings and Monetary Cooperation in the 1990s'. *Review of International Studies* 29, no. 1 (2003): 61–77.

Wiggin, Albert H. 'Text of the Wiggin Report on the German Financial Crisis'. *The New York Times*, August 20, 1931.

Willams, David. 'London and the 1931 Financial Crisis'. *The Economic History Review* 15, no. 3 (1963): 513–28.

Williams, John H. 'The Crisis of the Gold Standard'. *Foreign Affairs* 10, no. 2 (1932): 173–87.

Williamson, Philip. 'A "Bankers' Ramp"? Financiers and the British Political Crisis of August 1931'. *English Historical Review* 99, no. 393 (1984): 770–806.

Wolf, Nikolaus. 'Europe's Great Depression: Coordination Failure after the Great Depression'. In *The Great Depression of the 1930s: Lessons for Today*, edited by Nicholas Crafts and Peter Fearon, 74–109. Oxford: Oxford University Press, 2013.

Woodlock, Thomas F. '"Post-War War"'. *Wall Street Journal*, May 7, 1931.
'World Bank Lauds Offer by Hoover'. *The New York Times*, June 22, 1931.
'World Bank Plans Meeting April 22'. *The New York Times*, April 11, 1930.
'World Bank's Aid Sought by Austria'. *The New York Times*, May 13, 1931.
Yago, Kazuhiko. *The Financial History of the Bank for International Settlements*. London: Routledge, 2013.
Yohe, William P. 'The Mysterious Career of Walter W. Stewart, Especially 1922–1930'. *History of Political Economy* 14, no. 4 (1982): 583–607.

# Index


Abolafia, Mitchell, 15
action
  British crisis and, 319
  need for, 106, 181
action, enabling, 16. *See also* knowledge, actionable
adviser to Austrian government, 115, 117. *See also* Rist, Charles A.
adviser to Austrian National Bank, 102, 108, 113, 115. *See also* Bruins, Gijsbert W.J.
  acceptance of, 110
  Schacht proposed as, 115
air travel, 152, 349
alarm, feeling of, 153. *See also* urgency
ambiguity, 11, 13, 168, 217, 347. *See also* uncertainty
analysis
  framing of, 344
  narrative as, 343
analytical strategy, 17
Anglo-International Bank, 73
archives, 18
*Art of Central Banking, The* (Hawtrey), 15, 24
"at all costs" statement, 93–94, 99, 103, 110
Austria, 2, 167, 251. *See also* customs union, Austro-Germany; deficit countries; Europe; government, Austrian
  BIS support for, 141
  critical conditions in, 108, 236
  failure of to halt Credit Anstalt crisis, 103
  flight from, 121–22
  German crisis and, 268
  hyperinflation in, 82, 128, 132
  inflation in, 8, 141
  morale in, 129, 152
  possible bank holiday in, 269
  reconstruction of, 86
Austrian authorities. *See also* Austrian National Bank; government, Austrian,attitude of, 206
  concerns of, 76
Austrian crisis. *See also* bridge loan to Austria
  assessment of, 271
  Austrian National Bank and, 52, 87
  avoiding bank failure and, 91
  as banking crisis, 231
  BIS and, 324
  BIS's ability to deal with, 154
  efforts to contain, 5
  Germany and, 163
  improvement in, 206, 232
  lack of authority and, 172
  main issues related to, 51
  need to keep Austria going and, 147
  perceptions of, 349
  plan to avoid breakdown, 128
  rationales for action and, 103
  reconstruction plan, 54–55
  rediscounting and, 143, 150, 177, 191
  uncertainty and, 97
Austrian Finance Ministry, 2. *See also* Juch, Otto
Austrian National Bank, 2–3, 56, 81, 160. *See also* Brauneis, Viktor; Reisch, Richard,BIS credit to, 64, 75–76, 103, 105, 109, 111–12, 127, 131
  BIS credit to, second, 127, 129–30, 135, 138–41, 143, 168, 180, 187, 200–1, 281
  central bank cooperation and, 47
  confidence in managing crisis, 56
  cooperation and, 47
  Credit Anstalt crisis and, 53, 55, 87

Austrian National Bank (cont.)
credit risk of Credit Anstalt and, 94
deposits with BIS, 140
deposits with Credit Anstalt, 77
desire to avoid BIS credit, 56
discount rate and, 128
discounting and, 93
gold deposits with Bank of England, 139
lack of confidence in, 140
lack of information from, 92
loan portfolio of, 60
losses of, 127, 154, 176, 191, 193
reassurances from, 3
rediscounts of, 56
request for help from BIS, 99
risk of losses, 93
solvency of, 177
statements of, 56, 60, 101, 168, 193
symbolic value of, 128
Austrian public. *See also* confidence
BIS credit and, 61
blamed for crisis, 186
crisis and, 134
psychology/confidence of, 140
Quesnay on, 140
response of, 54, 56
Austrian Tobacco Monopoly, 123
authority
lack of, 172
Azzolini, Vincenzo, 62, 142

Bagehot operating model, 7, 10, 13, 16, 326, 352. *See also* bank rate (discount rate); cultural blueprint
assessment of response to crisis and, 347
Austrian crisis and, 11, 92, 133
belief in, 346
British crisis and, 289, 326
central bankers' use of, 15, 43, 49
criticism of central banks and, 346
dealing with combined internal and external drain in, 156, 245, 249, 263
as default blueprint, 6–7, 10–11, 217
discount rate and, 128
discounting and, 53
German crisis and, 244, 274
halting financial crises and, 165
Harrison's position and, 261
limitations of, 79
size of loans and, 291
Bagehot, Walter, 6, 15, 33, 79, 129, 220
on external drain, 91
Lombard Street, 43
state of discredit, 321
unprecedented crisis and, 92
Bank for International Settlements (BIS), 3, 259. *See also* central bankers; central banks; Fraser; Leon; McGarrah, Gates; Quesnay, Pierre; Rodd, Francis; Simon, Hans von
"at all costs" statement;, 94, 99, 103, 110
archives of, 18
Austrian confidence and, 140
Austrian crisis and, 63, 94, 113, 123, 141, 154
Austrian currency and, 105
Austrian National Bank credit, 109, 111–12, 127, 131
Austrian National Bank credit, second, 127, 129–30, 133, 135, 138–41, 143, 165, 168, 180, 187, 200–1, 281
Austrian National Bank deposits with, 140
Austrian National Bank's expectations of, 101
Bank of England's balance at, 318
on Banque de France, 331
board meetings, 61–62, 64, 139
Brauneis's request for increased credit, 129
Britain's departure from gold and, 336
British crisis and, 285, 324
central bank cooperation and, 26
communication and, 32
community and, 32
concerns of, 349
conditions imposed on Credit Anstalt by, 101
creation of, 6
Credit Anstalt crisis and, 103
Credit Anstalt's foreign creditors and, 75, 87
Credit Anstalt's requested credit and, 76
delay of Austrian National Bank credit, 348
deposits for emergencies, 240
focus on, 3
general meetings, 64
German attempt to bypass, 209
German crisis and, 211, 254, 262–64, 266, 269
German railway loan, 271
governor's meeting, 62–63
Hungary and, 179, 216
independence of central banks and, 143
international position of, 285
limitations of, 6, 74–75, 215
loans to Britain and, 318
marginalization of, 208

McGarrah's vision for, 7
meetings of central bankers and, 7
need for support of member banks, 151
Norman and, 32, 45, 221, 225, 227, 234, 318
opening of, 47
Reichsbank credit and, 221–22, 224–27
risk of losses and, 93
Rodd at, 23–24
on seriousness of British crisis, 318
sterling supported by, 292
United States and, 58
van Hengel and, 157
visions for, 47, 64
bank holidays
Austria and, 269
in Germany, 263, 268, 270
in Hungary, 268–69
Bank of America, 114
Bank of England, 9, 134, 180, 200, 284, 287. *See also* bridge loan to Austria; Britain; British crisis; Harvey, Ernest M.; Kindersley, Robert; loan, Bank of England; Norman, Montagu; Siepmann, Harry
Anglo-International Bank and, 73
archives of, 18
Austrian crisis and, 75
Austrian loan and, 134, 152
balance at BIS, 318
bank rate and, 280, 285
bankers' ramp story, 314
Banque de France and, 31, 298, 300
BIS credit to Austrian National Bank and, 65, 124
bridge loan to, 313
Bruins and, 151
compared to other central banks, 25
conditions imposed on Austria, 113
Court of Directors, 25
Credit Anstalt and, 3, 74, 76, 79
discounting and, 93
Dutch banks and, 318
focus on, 19
Germany and, 210, 257, 263, 282
gold standard and, 34
government and, 299, 317
importance of, 75, 151
independence of, 74, 144, 204–5
information about foreign creditors and, 90
losses of, 280, 283, 286, 293–94
national interests and, 30
Norman made governor of, 25
Norman's absence from, 287, 299
Norman's return to, 336
note on Austrian government borrowing powers, 2
optimism of, 320
pessimism of, 44
politics and, 296, 298, 326
position of, 26, 31, 337
priorities of, 25
professionalization of, 25
Reichsbank and, 215
resources of, 312
risk of losses and, 93
sale of securities, 312–13
Bank of Italy, 65
bank rate (discount rate), 6, 13, 38, 45
Austrian, 180
Austrian crisis and, 131, 133, 142, 190
Austrian National Bank and, 128
Bank of England and, 283, 285, 300, 323, 326, 338, 340
Banque de France and, 301
Britain and, 280
British crisis and, 283, 289, 294, 323
financial crises and, 261
German, 248, 270, 274
German crisis and, 278
Reichsbank and, 159, 165, 167, 207, 209, 278
unemployment and, 13
bank, international, 38
bankers, private
Austria and, 78
central bankers and, 28
bankers, US
perception of European crisis and, 176
Bankers' Clearing House, 270
bankers' ramp story, 313, 319
banking restrictions, German crisis and, 274
banks
politics and, 213
banks, Austrian, 111
possible closures, 128
run on, 52, 161
banks, Belgian, 318
banks, British
Austrian loan and, 67, 143, 149, 151
German crisis and, 270, 279, 282
withdrawal of credit from Germany, 285

banks, central, 3. *See* Bank for International Settlements (BIS); central banks
banks, Dutch, 318
British crisis and, 322
banks, French. *See also* Banque de Paris et des Pays-Bas
placing Austrian loan and, 68
withdrawals by, 72
banks, German, 160, 263, 270. *See also* Danatbank; Gold Diskont Bank; Reichsbank
banks, international
German crisis and, 270
loans to Austria and, 63
banks, private, 19, 39. *See also individual banks*
additional Reichsbank credit and, 246
Austria and, 67, 80, 206
Austrian loan and, 143
Austrian National Bank's expectations of, 101
Bank of England loan and, 289
central banks and, 70, 79, 350
concern about European situation, 170
Credit Anstalt's request for ten million pounds and, 82
in crisis of 1931, 349
failures of, 48
Germany and, 246, 266–67
interference with markets and, 39
Kindersley Plan and, 39
state ownership of, 57
worldview of, 40
banks, Swiss, 322
British crisis and, 318
banks, universal, 62. *See also* Credit Anstalt
banks, US, 91. *See also* Federal Reserve Bank of New York; Federal Reserve System; *individual banks*
Austrian loan and, 68, 149, 151, 165, 173, 205
Bank of England loan and, 288
bankers' ramp story and, 314
BIS and, 58
BIS credit to Austrian National Bank and, 165
British crisis and, 288–89
British government loan and, 303
Credit Anstalt and, 54, 90–91, 97, 104–6
crisis in, 337
criticism of, 157
fragility of, 158
German crisis and, 247, 253, 265, 270, 276, 278–79
Germany and, 159, 242–43, 245
International Committee and, 107
responsibility for European crisis and, 275
rumours about, 336
van Hengel on, 157
view of Austrians, 207
Banque de France, 26, 30–31. *See also* France; Lacour-Gayet, Robert; Moret, Clément
Bank of England and, 31, 298, 300
Bank of England loan and, 287–88, 290, 293, 295
bank rate and, 301
BIS credit to Austrian National Bank and, 65
bridge loan to Austria and, 204
Britain's departure from gold and, 331
British crisis and, 284
British government loan and, 308–9
credit to Hungary and, 234
distrust of theory at, 30
epistemic community and, 204
financial leadership and, 31
French government and, 121, 204, 216, 220, 242, 348
German crisis and, 215, 257, 261, 263
gold standard and, 34
information and, 32
Norman and, 31, 223, 225–26
participation in loans, 348
Reichsbank and, 32
Reichsbank credit and, 220–22, 224–27
reparations and, 39
Rodd's narrative and, 197
sterling supported by, 292, 318
Banque de Paris et des Pays-Bas, 67, 88, 174. *See also* Moreau, Emile
Austrian loan and, 68, 89, 149–50, 152
Bark, Peter, 73, 76, 78–79
Basle. *See* Bank for International Settlements (BIS)
Bear Sterns, 354
Beckert, Jens, 16
Belgium, 62, 142, 339
Austrian loan and, 58, 66
BIS credit to Austrian National Bank and, 65
British crisis and, 318
gold standard and, 331
beliefs, causal. *See* epistemic community
Beneduce, Alberto, 142
Bernanke, Ben, 353–54
blackmail, 78
Blessing, Karl, 123, 149

blind spots, 17, 159, 199, 344
McGarrah's, 99
Norman's, 227, 240
blueprint, cultural. *See* cultural blueprint
bond loan. *See* loan, Austrian
Brand, R.H., 42
Brauneis, Viktor, 50, 70, 81, 160. *See also* Austrian National Bank
acceptance of BIS conditions, 102
adviser and, 109
on conversation with Stephany, 83
on Credit Anstalt's request for credit, 81
request for increased credit, 129
requests for help, 81
Siepmann and, 93
statement and, 60
threat to resign, 159, 161
breakdown, financial. *See* collapse, economic/financial
Briand, Aristide, 243
bridge loan to Austria, 143, 149, 180, 182, 185, 196, 200–1, 216, 232
French view of, 203
motivation for, 205
need to repay, 281
politics and, 204
purpose of, 184
responses to, 205–6
source of, 202
bridge loan to Bank of England, 313
Britain, 9. *See also* Bank of England; British crisis; budget, British; deficit countries; finances, British; gold standard, Britain and; government, British; sterling
Austrian crisis and, 120, 181
Austrian interests and, 199
Austrian loan and, 58, 116, 119, 123, 142, 166, 178, 188, 191–92
Austrian reconstruction and, 86
balance of trade, 331
contagion and, 124, 243, 272, 283
debt of, 37
deflation and, 167
deposits with Credit Anstalt, 55
France and, 120, 196
German crisis and, 268
German visit to, 126, 135–36
Gilbert's view of, 71
gold and, 9, 34, 37, 272
Hoover moratorium and, 213, 227
imperial worldview of, 242
Lacour-Gayet and, 307
London Conference and, 278
money doctors from, 10
power of, 9
rescuing, 181
Royal Navy, 324
Versailles Treaty and, 12
British crisis. *See also* gold standard, Britain and; loan, Bank of England; loan, British government; sterling
bank rate and, 285, 289, 294, 300, 323, 326
BIS and, 285
British government and, 288, 295, 298–99
budget and, 287, 294–95, 303, 320
central bankers and, 289
Committee of Treasury and, 303
confidence and, 319–20
Crane on, 325
deflation and, 301, 304
drain of sterling, 319
Dutch demands for gold and, 327
extent of, 292
framing of, 287
France and, 284, 300, 327
Harvey's handling of, 322
interconnectedness of financial system and, 292
J.P. Morgan & Co., 287, 297
Keynes and, 292
Lacour-Gayet and, 307
New York Fed and, 293
optimism about, 320
relations between Bank of England and Banque de France and, 298
rumours and, 296, 299
sale of securities and, 312–13
seriousness of, 318, 324–25
US and, 322, 327
British Foreign Office. *See* government, British
British Treasury. *See* government, British; Leith-Ross, Frederick
Bronk, Richard, 16
Bruins, Gijsbert W.J., 117–18, 128, 150
analysis of Austrian crisis, 134
Brauneis and, 159
demands of, 123
France and, 117
guarantee and, 124, 161
plan to avoid breakdown, 128–29
proposal of, 143

Bruins, Gijsbert W.J. (cont.)
response to Austrian bridge loan, 205
in Rodd's memo, 190
sensemaking by, 132
view of Austrian situation, 131
Brüning, Heinrich, 99, 108, 126, 136, 160, 209, 243, 256. *See also* government, German
German crisis and, 274
Norman and, 233
opposition to, 209
reparations statement, 137, 159, 207, 229
on seriousness of situation, 271
visit to Britain, 136
budget, Austrian, 127
budget, balanced, 252
budget, British, 287, 292, 294, 301, 304, 309, 334. *See also* British crisis; finances; British; government, British
confidence and, 320
Crane on, 325
cuts in social benefits, 310–11
National Government and, 312, 324
Norman and, 310
Royal Navy protest and, 324
sterling crisis and, 287, 295, 303, 320
taxes and, 310
budget, German, 99, 160, 183, 207
Burgess, W. Randolph, 36, 42, 281, 319, 321
Butcher. *See* controller for Credit Anstalt

Capie, Forrest, 346
capitalism, 5
fear of fall of, 15
future of, 33
Great Depression as crisis of, 345–46
Norman's fear for, 26
state-owned enterprises and, 84
threats to, 12, 35, 176, 197, 321
Castle, William R. Jr., 212, 214, 264–65, 269, 275
catastrophe narrative. *See* collapse narrative
Catterns, Basil G., 75, 304
causal relationships, 15
causality, 344
cause and effect, 44, 98, 175, 297, 335, 347, 351
Austrian crisis and, 99
German crisis and, 273
central bankers, 7, 10. *See* budget; epistemic community of central bankers; gold standard
Britain's departure from gold and, 332–33
British crisis and, 289
conflict among, 32
constraints on, 58
first international meeting of, 62
identity of, 30
judgment of, 353
learning through experience and, 30, 43
national interests and, 30, 202, 229, 241
neglect of in historical literature, 348
politics and, 254
priorities of, 7, 242
private bankers and, 79
professional, 77
sensemaking by, 17
Siepmann's view of, 8
struggle to maintain gold standard, 345
central banks, 3–4, 12, 26, 47, 259. *See also* Bank for International Settlements (BIS); cooperation/coordination; gold standard; lender of last resort; *individual banks*
ability to manage economy, 353
Austrian currency and, 105
Austrian National Bank's expectations of, 101
Bagehot operating model and, 7
concerns of, 3, 26, 76, 134
constraints on, 164, 204
consultation with boards of, 251
Credit Anstalt's proposal and, 73
of creditor nations, 70
currency crises and, 119
German crisis and, 259, 267, 269
governments and, 149, 349
independence of, 26, 28, 32, 140, 143, 205, 314
individual action by, 3
lack of comprehensive program of financial relief, 216
as lender of last resort, 6
limitations of, 208
loans by, 10
national interests and, 349
Norman's vision of, 8
politics and, 30, 164, 239, 241
private banks and, 28, 70, 350
purpose of, 296
Chancellor of the Exchequer. *See* Snowden, Philip
Chanler, L.S., Jr., 107
Chase National Bank, 173. *See also* Gannon, James H.; Wiggin, Albert H.
Credit Anstalt and, 97, 104
Germany and, 242
importance of, 173
International Committee and, 107

Chatham Phoenix National Bank & Trust Co., 90, 114
Chemical Bank and Trust Co., 97
Chile, 211
Churchill, Winston, 9
City of London. *See* Britain; *individual banks*
Clarke, Stephen, 345
Claudel, Paul, 242
Clay, Henry, 325
Cochran, Merle, 36, 110, 112, 202
  on Hoover moratorium, 229
  on Kindersley Plan, 38
  on Quesnay's narrative of Austrian crisis, 199
collapse narrative, 82, 168, 172, 176
collapse, economic/financial
  avoiding, 240, 246, 266
  effects of, 241
  German crisis and, 257
  gold standard and, 346
  impending, 241
  possibility of, 237
Cologne Gazette, 44
*Commercial and Financial Chronicle, The*, 108
  on Bank of England loan, 292
  on bridge loan to Austria, 203
  on Britain's departure from gold, 329
  on France, 215
  on German crisis, 263
  on Germany, 139
  on pressure on sterling, 282
commitment, willingness to make, 321. *See also* confidence
Committee of Treasury, 124, 285. *See also* Bank of England; British crisis; government, British
  Bank of England loan and, 285
  sterling crisis and, 294, 303
communication, 18, 32, 85, 153, 349. *See also* cooperation/coordination; information
  between Harrison and Luther, 259
  between Norman and Harrison, 250
  central bankers and, 37, 166
  complexity of, 150
  contradictory reports and, 83
  Harrison and, 235
  lack of coordination of, 73
  sensemaking and, 80
  telephone and, 152
community, epistemic. *See* epistemic community of central bankers
conceptual framework, 350–51, 355. *See also* emplotment; future, imagined; narrative(s); sensemaking; uncertainty
confidence, 64, 219. *See also* optimism; runs
  Austrian crisis and, 70, 91, 100–1, 103, 127, 129–30, 132, 134–35, 139–40, 142, 151
  Bank of England loan and, 288
  Britain's departure from gold and, 334
  British crisis and, 288, 291, 296, 312, 319–20, 334
  Burgess on, 319
  depression and, 321
  Gannon's plan and, 170
  German crisis and, 244, 260, 264, 275, 279, 291
  Hoover moratorium and, 219–20
  rumours and, 66
  uncertainty and, 134
confidence. restoring
  Gannon's plan and, 170
contagion, 5, 134, 164. *See also* house of cards scenario
  air travel and, 152
  Austrian crisis and, 97, 103, 120, 122, 130
  Austrian moratorium and, 182
  avoiding, 70, 168
  BIS and, 63
  bridge loan and, 180
  Britain and, 124, 272, 283
  compression of time and, 349
  concerns about, 76
  emplotment and, 166
  fear of, 4–5, 53, 59, 61, 91, 126
  Germany and, 54, 59, 124, 232, 243, 268
  Hungary and, 159
  increased risk of, 80
  International Committee and, 85
  Norman's fear of, 84, 86
  Norman's prediction of, 340
  preventing, 207
  telephone and, 152
context
  assessment of financial crisis and, 346
  of crisis of 1931, 11
  erased by hindsight, 355
  importance of in central banking, 258, 292
  provided by history, 356
Control Committee. *See* League of Nations
controller for Credit Anstalt, 102, 108, 110, 113–14, 120. *See also* van Hengel, Adrianus
cooperation/coordination, 11, 31, 47, 348. *See also* Bank for International Settlements

(BIS); communication; information; International Committee
Austrian crisis and, 122
Austrian guarantee and, 124
Bank of England loan and, 291–92
communication and, 73
cracks in, 170
Credit Anstalt and, 105
French action and, 205
German crisis and, 262
importance of, 96
need for, 104
Norman's belief in, 26
perceived failure of, 12
Reichsbank credit and, 242
second BIS credit and, 169
coordination. *See* cooperation/coordination
cover ratio
Austrian, 128
Reichsbank's, 207, 209–10, 215, 219, 226, 228, 244, 253, 263, 274
Crane, Jay, 37, 294, 325
Credit Anstalt, 54. *See also* creditors, Credit Anstalt
administration of, 84
Austrian National Bank and, 55
balance sheet, 59
business model, 1
conditions imposed on, 101
controller for, 108
effects of failure of, 144, 178
foreign deposits of, 54, 76
foreign liabilities of, 55, 73, 78, 87
frustration with, 92
government and, 145
lack of information from, 92
liquidity of, 52, 62
losses of, 1, 52, 142
merger with Bodencreditanstalt, 77
new credits and, 101
real position of, 75
reconstruction of, 2, 52, 55, 132, 156
request for ten million pounds, 76, 80–82
secrecy of management, 62
short-term credits and, 2
size and importance of, 2
solvency of, 62, 156
survival of, 80
US withdrawals from, 90
van Hengel on, 157
Credit Anstalt crisis, 11, 97
Bernanke on, 355
novelty of, 5
credit bank, international, 39. *See also* Kindersley Plan
credit restrictions, Austrian, 133, 189–90, 192
credit restrictions, German, 208, 219, 238, 246–49, 251–52, 255, 257–58, 273–74
credit stability, Federal Reserve System and, 42
credit system, 36
credit, Credit Anstalt's request for, 81
creditor nations, 39, 48–49. *See also* France; United States
central banks of, 70
responsibility of, 216
creditors, Credit Anstalt, 60, 69–70, 74, 76, 78, 87, 91, 97, 107, 112, 122, 126, 134–35. *See also* guarantee, Austrian; International Committee; London Committee; moratorium, Austrian; *individual banks*
amounts owed to, 90
Austrian government and, 87
committee of, 86
concerns of, 76, 134
Credit Anstalt's future and, 207
identity of, 90–91
Juch and, 162
lack of agreement with, 122
organization of, 78, 82, 84, 87, 89
refusal to follow International Committee policy, 114
risk of run and, 84
Rodd's concerns about, 59
rumours about, 126
standstill agreement, 127, 133, 144, 157, 160
taking of losses by, 158
uncertainty about, 125
US, 97, 104–6
van Hengel on, 119
withdrawals by, 52, 61
creditors, Germany's, 231
organizing, 231
standstill agreement, 271, 281, 285, 290
Creditors' Committee. *See* International Committee; London Committee
credits, last-resort, 119

credits, long-term, 37
credits, short-term, 37
crises, economic/financial, 11. *See also* uncertainty
central bankers' idea of, 15
lack of plan for dealing with, 45
responding to, 11
crisis of 1931, 11. *See also* Austrian crisis; British crisis; German crisis
actors in, 14
approach to understanding, 344
causes of, 348
context of, 11
dates of, 14
as first international crisis, 6
Great Financial Crisis and, 354
new understanding of, 344
as political/structural problem, 282, 303
"Crisis of the Gold Standard, The" (Williams), 342
crisis, twin, 352
cross deposits, 122
Crump, Norman, 220
cultural approach, 350
cultural blueprint, 7, 10, 44. *See also* Bagehot operating model; knowledge, actionable; worldview
Austrian crisis and, 130
Bagehot's operating model as, 10
failure of, 13
German crisis and, 272
lack of, 6, 217
lack of knowledge for, 83
plans and, 73
cultural lens, 99
currency. *See* Reichsmark; schilling, Austrian; sterling
currency contraction
Austrian, 150, 180, 184
German, 160, 257
internal drain and, 156
currency crises
averting, 168
central banks and, 119
Curtius, Julius, 136, 243
customs union, Austro-German, 2, 45, 120, 136, 254, 257, 259. *See also* politics
France and, 41, 53, 64, 169, 194, 196
Czechoslovakia, 65–66
*Daily Herald*, bankers' ramp story in, 313
Danatbank (Darmstädter und Nationalbank), 245. *See also* German crisis
concern about, 248
failure of, 257, 259, 263, 268, 276
guarantee to creditors of, 265
merger with Dresdner Bank, 281
Nordwolle trouble and, 247, 253
uncertainty about, 249
Danske Landmandsbanken, 90, 105
Darmstädter und Nationalbank (Danatbank). *See* Danatbank; German crisis
data, 14, 16. *See also* information; knowledge, actionable
Davies, H.E., 109
Dawes Plan, 9, 29, 32, 209
debt, 12, 37, 48, 165, 212, 229. *See also* Hoover moratorium; politics; reparations
effects of, 44
French, 175
German, 207, 263, 278
Germany, 60
lack of plan for dealing with, 45
London Conference and, 273, 278
need for money and, 211
need for political action and, 168
Norman and, 165, 280
US position on, 229
debt, short-term
Kindersley Plan, 37
van Hengel and, 157
debt suspensions, 167
debtor nations. *See* Austria; Britain; Germany; deficit countries
decision-makers, 168. *See also* central bankers; individual governments
collapse narrative and, 168
decision-making, 73. *See also* cultural blueprint
British crisis and, 319
German crisis and, 272
imagined consequences and, 351
uncertainty and, 344, 351
deficit countries, 35, 39, 48–49, 167. *See also* Austria; Britain; Germany, blamed for financial crises, 251
deflation and, 167
gold standard imbalances and, 167
deflation (economy), 9, 12, 34, 36, 41, 251, 303
bankers' view of, 252
Britain and, 301, 304, 309, 311, 314, 325

deflation (economy) (cont.)
effects of, 263
in Germany, 247
Germany and, 99, 137, 207, 238, 247, 258, 263, 280
gold standard and, 9, 167, 249
Siepmann on, 305
Denmark, 90, 105
depression, 137
confidence and, 321
psychology and, 321
description, thick, 14, 17, 343, 350
description, thin, 342
Dictator. *See* adviser to Austrian National Bank
disarmament, German, 136
discounting, 53, 82
Austrian National Bank and, 93
discredit, state of, 321
Dresdner Bank, 270
merger with Danatbank, 281
Dreyfus, Armand, 69–71, 79
Dreyse, Friedrich (Fritz), 96, 209, 258. *See also* Reichsbank
on German crisis, 256
Hoover moratorium and, 233
request for help from Harrison, 264

economics
central banks' limitations and, 208
politics and, 10, 211
*Economist, The*
on Austrian crisis, 61, 108, 121
Bagehot and, 6
on Bank of England loan, 290–91
Britain and, 283, 335
British government loan and, 320
on budget, 324
on Credit Anstalt, 1
on crisis of 1931, 355
on French view of Hoover moratorium, 243
Germany and, 136, 220, 230, 232, 256, 263, 274, 288
Great Financial Crisis and, 355
on Hoover moratorium, 214, 230
on leaving gold standard, 327, 331
on London Conference, 279
on need for political action, 164, 168, 262
on Reichsbank credit, 242
economists, 30
economy (deflation). *See* deflation (economy)
economy (system). *See also* worldview
anxiety about, 34
rescuing, 181
Eichengreen, Barry, 345, 354
Einzig, Paul, 25
emplotment, 14–15, 98, 355. *See also* narrative(s); sensemaking
Austrian crisis and, 98, 141, 186
Britain's departure from gold and, 331, 335
British crisis and, 297
contagion and, 166
decision-making and, 351
difficulty of, 44, 175
German crisis and, 272
Harrison and, 119, 148
need for, 217, 347
Norman and, 164
recognition of political problems and, 164
Stephany's memo and, 80
uncertainty and, 20
epistemic community of central bankers, 7, 15, 30, 349
Austrian crisis and, 148
Bagehot operating model and, 347
Bank of England and, 151
Bank of England loan and, 291
Banque de France and, 204
BIS and, 32
central bank independence and, 140
central banks' purpose and, 296
gold standard and, 330
Harrison in, 223, 227
Hoover moratorium and, 237
narratives and, 16
national interests and, 31
Norman in, 223, 227
van Hengel and, 158
worldview of, 161
Europe. *See also individual countries*
avoiding breakdown in, 237, 240
blamed for own problems, 251
Harrison's narrative about problems of, 251
money needed for, 211
seriousness of situation in, 163
stability of, 179
US self-interest and, 211
European debt crisis, 355
exchange controls, 270, 281

exchange crisis, 294. *See also* Austrian crisis; British crisis; German crisis
exchange rate
British crisis and, 320
leaving gold standard and, 305–6
protecting, 25
expectations
experience and, 353
managing, 56
expectations, fictional, 47, 49, 237. *See also* future, imagined
Austrian crisis and, 180
changing, 353
Hoover moratorium and, 237
narrative as, 73
rules and, 352
experience, 15, 30, 49, 353. *See also* historical analogies
expectations and, 353
limitations of, 346
need for, 352
export markets, Germany and, 33

fear, 104
Federal Open Market Committee (FOMC), 353
Federal Reserve Bank of New York, 28, 36, 58. *See also* Burgess, W. Randolph; Harrison, George L.; Strong, Benjamin
archives of, 18
assistance to Europe and, 216, 240
autonomy of, 28
Bank of England loan and, 284, 287, 289–90
BIS credit to Austrian National Bank and, 58, 65, 168
bridge loan to Bank of England, 313
Britain's departure from gold and, 330
British crisis and, 286, 292–93
Credit Anstalt rescue plan and, 3
Credit Anstalt's foreign creditors and, 72
economic theory and, 320
focus on, 18
Geithner, 354
German crisis and, 166, 210, 265, 271
Germany and, 261
gold and, 42
Harrison's leadership at, 28
Hungary and, 211, 216
independence of, 28
monetary policy, 207
pessimism of, 44
Reichsbank credit and, 224, 228
responsibility of, 218
role of, 164
sterling supported by, 284, 293
Federal Reserve Bank of Richmond, 252
Federal Reserve banks
blamed for Great Depression, 345
German crisis and, 263
Federal Reserve Board, 353. *See also* Bernanke, Ben
BIS loan and, 58
Harrison on, 27
New York Fed and, 28
Reichsbank credit and, 224
Federal Reserve System
Austrian loan and, 58
Bank of England loan and, 292
BIS and, 58
credit policy, 41
credit stability and, 42
opening of, 27
sterling supported by, 284
finance
politics and, 34, 37, 314
finances, British, 292, 300. *See also* budget, British
financial system, 10. *See also* worldview
interconnectedness of, 216–17, 292
possible revolt against, 282
*Financial Times, The*, 56
on BIS board meeting, 141
on bridge loan to Austria, 204
on Britain's departure from gold and, 330
on British situation, 327
on financial and economic system, 297
on French credit to Bank of England, 288
on German crisis, 263
on gold standard, 331
on historical knowledge, 354
on International Committee, 107
on leaving gold standard, 317
on London, 282
on London Committee, 88
on Royal Navy, 324
First National Bank of Boston, 97
Flandin, Pierre-Étienne, 316
Fleuriau, Aimé-Joseph de, 268
Flyvbjerg, Bent, 343, 352
Fodor, M.W., 53
*Foreign Affairs*, 342
Fournier, Pierre-Eugène, 309

franc, pegging of, 334
France, 3, 27, 67, 174. *See also* Banque de France; Banque de Paris et des Pays-Bas; Lacour-Gayet, Robert; Moret, Clément; Morgan & Cie; Quesnay, Pierre; reparations
  assistance to Credit Anstalt, 83
  Austrian loan and, 58, 64, 66–68, 86, 89, 116–17, 120, 123–24, 147, 149, 151–53, 169, 173–74, 178, 182, 186, 191–93, 199, 201–2, 241
  Austrian reconstruction and, 86
  BIS and, 65
  blamed for Austrian crisis, 53, 186
  bridge loan to Austria and, 201, 203–4
  Britain and, 120, 179, 196, 242, 307
  British crisis and, 283–84, 300, 327
  British government loan and, 303, 314
  Castle on, 214
  conditions for assisting Germany, 275
  conditions in, 12
  credit proposal, 239–40
  customs union and, 41, 53, 169
  debt and, 175
  economic/financial importance of, 26, 31
  economy of after Great War, 9
  franc Poincaré, 334
  German crisis and, 220, 252, 254, 257, 259, 261–62, 273, 275
  Germany and, 32, 37, 166, 169, 272
  Gilbert's view of, 71
  gold and, 9, 35, 166–67, 251, 293, 306–7, 332
  gold standard and, 34, 36, 136, 331
  Great War and, 215
  Hoover moratorium and, 214, 221–23, 226, 229, 232–35, 237–38, 241–42, 258
  International Committee and, 108
  Kindersley Plan and, 38
  London Conference and, 275, 277
  Luther in, 250
  money doctors from, 10
  Norman and, 30–31, 86, 181, 215, 221, 227, 229, 241, 254, 286
  potential US action and, 208
  public opinion in, 226, 235
  Reichsbank loan and, 222
  reparations and, 136, 175
  Schacht and, 116–17
  security of, 319
  Versailles Treaty and, 12
Franck, Louis, 62, 142–44
franc Poincaré, 334
Francqui, Emile, 45
Fraser, Leon, 4, 29, 87. *See also* Bank for International Settlements (BIS)
  communication and, 32
  on creditors, 97
  involvement of, 87
free riding, 171
French Note, 193
Friedman, Milton, 345
future, 13
  anxiety about, 34, 41
  consolidating, 134
future, imagined, 10, 15–16, 54, 59, 355. *See also* contagion; expectations, fictional; gold standard; narrative(s) uncertainty
  action and, 180
  Austrian crisis and, 98, 127, 129, 180
  collapse narrative and, 168
  contagion and, 54, 124
  creditors' losses and, 158
  crises and, 11
  crisis of 1931 and, 340
  emplotment and, 15
  establishing, 97
  German crisis and, 261, 265–66, 280
  Germany and, 121
  gold standard and, 158, 304, 331–32
  Hoover moratorium and, 220, 237
  house of cards scenario and, 5
  importance of visualizing, 217
  leaders and, 321
  Morgan's, compared to Grenfell's, 27
  pessimism about, 44
  plans and, 73, 272
  politics and, 165
  Rodd's evaluation and, 59
  silencing of, 346
  Simon's note and, 59
future-planning, actionable knowledge and, 129

Gannon, James H., 169, 189–91
  on International Committee, 107
  International Committee agreement and, 171, 193
  on seriousness of situation, 176
  plan for Austrian loan, 192
  Rodd's memo and, 198
Geertz, Clifford, 14, 342
Geithner, Tim, 354

German crisis, 29, 164, 212, 249, 316. *See also* customs union, Austro-German; deficit countries; Dreyse, Friedrich (Fritz); Europe; government, German; Luther, Hans; moratorium, German; Reichsbank; Reichsmark; reparations; Versailles, Treaty of
Austrian crisis and, 136, 163, 175
awareness of, 262
Bank of England and, 210, 282
Bank of England loan and, 282
bank rate and, 248, 278
as banking matter, 264
BIS and, 254, 262, 264, 266, 269
BIS on seriousness of, 324
British banks and, 270, 282
central banks and, 259
confidence and, 245, 260, 275
credit restrictions and, 208, 238, 246, 248, 252, 273
critical conditions in, 238
currency contraction and, 257
decision against requesting more money, 278
deflation and, 258
described, 209
exchange controls and, 270, 281
external drain, 211
focus on, 182
France and, 243, 254, 259, 262, 275
German responsibility for, 243, 247–48, 251–52, 275
gold standard and, 245
Harrison and, 259, 262
imagined future and, 266
impending collapse and, 257
improvement in, 298
interest rate and, 245
internal and external drain in, 279
international banks and, 270
J.P. Morgan & Co;, 278
lack of actionable knowledge and, 271–72
lack of plan to address, 271
loan needed, 274
London Conference and, 272
losses in, 233
McGarrah and, 275
need for plan to address, 272
New York Fed and, 166, 210, 271
Nordwolle trouble and, 253
Norman and, 208, 253, 267, 273
politics and, 163, 256–57, 261–62, 264–65, 267, 269, 271–72, 274–75
possibility of improvement in, 324
pressure on sterling and, 282
preventing banking crisis in, 231
private banks and, 246
relations between Bank of England and Banque de France and, 298
rumours and, 288
Schacht and, 269
seriousness of, 183, 271
speed needed for, 238
uncertainty and, 249, 272, 275–76
US and, 266
US banks and, 242, 247, 253, 270
German public, 235
Germany, 2, 4–5, 26, 30, 41, 96, 98, 126, 139, 158, 167, 251. *See also* customs union, Austro-German; deficit countries; Dreyse, Friedrich (Fritz); Europe; government, German; Luther, Hans; moratorium, German; Reichsbank; Reichsmark; reparations; Versailles, Treaty of
ability to withstand financial trouble, 138–39
Austrian crisis and, 5, 96
Austrian loan and, 58, 165, 169, 192
bank holiday in, 263, 268, 270
battleships, 254, 257, 259
BIS and, 65
bridge loan to Austria and, 200
concerns about, 99, 108, 121
conditions in, 12, 119, 137, 153, 207, 236
contagion and, 54, 59, 124, 159, 268
credit of, 233
Dawes Plan and, 9
debt of, 37, 60
deflation and, 238, 247
deflation in, 263
disarmament, 136
economic situation and, 136
fragile situation in, 125
France and, 32, 37, 166, 169, 272
Gilbert's view of, 71
gold standard and, 263
hyperinflation in, 8
impending collapse in, 246, 257
importance of, 218
inflation and, 12
Kindersley Plan and, 40
London Conference and, 278
McGarrah on, 98

Germany (cont.)
Norman and, 30
political issues and, 234, 319
Rodd's concerns about, 59
Schacht, 117
Siepmann on, 45
syndicate of companies in, 244, 253
van Hengel on, 156
Versailles Treaty and, 12
withdrawals from, 237
Gilbert, Seymour Parker Jr., 9, 29, 33, 71
Kindersley Plan and, 39
gold, 6, 34, 42–43
accumulation of, 35, 251
Bank of England and, 283, 293, 301
Bank of England loan and, 293
Britain and, 34, 272
British crisis and, 291, 293
distribution of, 306
drain of, 6, 35
France and, 35, 167, 251, 293, 307
inability to create, 6
Reichsbank and, 166
US and, 35, 167, 207, 251, 337, 342
Gold Diskont Bank, 209, 244, 253
credit to, 267
guarantee of foreign credits, 265
gold exchange standard, 33
gold standard, 13, 33, 106, 134. *See also* cultural blueprint; house of cards scenario
abandonment of, 14, 306
BIS and, 63
central banks and, 3
collapse of financial system and, 346
commitment to, 8, 26, 31–32, 36, 42–43, 118, 161, 181, 237, 251–52
as cultural construct, 9
currency flight and, 3
defense of, 94
fear of fall of, 15
France and, 36
Germany and, 245, 263
after Great War, 9
Great War and, 8
Harrison on, 43
Hungary and, 298
imaginaries for saving, 249
imbalances of, 44, 166–67
lack of faith in, 36
maintaining, 7, 179, 218, 345
national interests and, 31, 34
as natural, 9
Norman's belief in, 25, 27
possible breakdown of, 54, 158
possible revolt against, 282
rules of, 346
scepticism of, 42
standard operating procedure and, 249
Strong on, 31
threat to, 176, 197
US and, 36
gold standard mentality, 345
gold standard narrative, 16
as performative, 16
gold standard, Britain and, 5, 9, 26, 124, 299–300, 325
ability to maintain, 292, 326
departure from gold, 9, 43, 299, 304, 307, 325, 327, 342
*Financial Times* on departure from gold, 317
Norman on departure from gold, 335
reaction to departure from gold, 329
returning to gold, 305, 331, 335
Siepmann on departure from gold, 338
*The Economist*, 327
victim narrative and, 330
gold sterilization, 34–35, 37, 207
*Golden Fetters* (Eichengreen), 345
Goschen, Harry, 101, 106
gossip. *See* rumors
government. *See also* politics; social issues
central banks and, 349
government, Austrian, 3, 51, 103, 123, 144, 268. *See also* guarantee, Austrian; Juch, Otto; loan, Austrian
adviser to, 115
attitude of, 152, 154, 161, 177, 199, 206
Bruins's criticism of, 132
Credit Anstalt and, 145
Credit Anstalt promoted by, 1
Credit Anstalt's liabilities and, 89
fall/resignation of, 173, 178, 183, 192–93, 195, 200
guarantee and, 87, 183
International Committee's agreement with, 177, 185, 190, 193, 200
lack of trust in, 140
money needed by, 138
need for loan, 2
new, 206
private banks and, 57

socialist, possibility of, 145
Winkler's resignation, 191
government, British, 126, 179, 292, 324, 342. *See also* budget, British; finances, British MacDonald, Ramsay; Snowden, Philip
Austrian bridge loan and, 205
Bank of England and, 299, 317
Bank of England loan and, 285–86
confidence and, 320
general election, 322–23, 326–27, 332
Harvey and, 294
Labour Party, 313
May Report, 292
National Government, 312, 323–24
Norman's views and, 273
proposed economies, 309
resignation of, 311
Socialist Party, 317
statement on departure from gold, 328
sterling crisis and, 287–89, 294–95, 298
government, French
Banque de France and, 121, 204, 216, 348
Hoover moratorium and, 235–38
mixing of politics and finance by, 204
government, German, 126, 136, 160, 256. *See also* Brüning, Heinrich; Germany; German crisis
British visit, 126, 135–36
confidence in Reichsmark and, 261
Danatbank failure and, 263
German crisis and, 265
possible fall of, 256–57
stability of, 183
government, US, 163. *See also* Hoover moratorium; Hoover, Herbert; Mellon, Andrew; Mills, Ogden; Stimson, Henry L.
action expected from, 211–12
British crisis and, 322
concern about European situation, 163
German crisis and, 211, 276
role of, 164
Grant, D.B., 107, 120
Great Britain. *See* Britain
Great Depression, 1, 11, 354
counterfactual argument about, 346
as crisis of capitalism, 345–46
Federal Reserve blamed for, 345
as historical analogy, 355
narratives about causes of, 345
Great Financial Crisis of 2007–2009, 353
crisis of 1931 and, 354
Great War, 5, 11. *See also* politics; reparations; Versailles, Treaty of
effects of, 44
France and, 215
gold standard and, 8
repercussions of, 174
Siepmann in, 23
Greece, 65
Grenfell, Edward, 26
guarantee, Austrian, 74, 76, 89–90, 94, 106, 112–13, 126–27, 152, 206. *See also* government, Austrian; moratorium, Austrian
assistance and, 103, 124
BIS and, 94, 102
Bruins and, 133
conditions for, 93
conflicting narratives of, 349
Credit Anstalt's future and, 207
creditors' demand for, 91
credits covered by, 100, 106, 110
expectations for, 120
extent of, 126
France and, 89
in Gannon's plan, 169
government and, 161, 173, 183, 349
internal deposits and, 150, 160–61, 177, 191, 206
International Committee and, 171
loan and, 126
need for, 90, 122, 125
optimism and, 98
period for maintaining deposits and, 144
possibility of, 95–96, 98
pressure for, 103, 109
preventing moratorium and, 74
Rothschild on, 145
socialist party and, 173
time needed for, 81
uncertainty about, 91, 105, 111, 119, 122, 126, 135
urgency of, 126
Whigham on, 145
guarantee, Danish, 105
guarantee, German, 265, 273
guarantee, international, 93
Guaranty Trust Co., 90, 92, 107

Hambros Bank, 106
Harrison, George L., 4, 25. *See also* Federal Reserve Bank of New York
after 1931 crisis, 337

Harrison, George L. (cont.)
additional Reichsbank credit and, 247
background of, 27
Bank of England loan and, 289–92
bankers' ramp story and, 314
British crisis and, 294, 297
British loan and, 303
in community of central bankers, 223, 227, 291
conflict between Reichsbank and Banque de France and, 32
constraints on, 58
Credit Anstalt creditors and, 97, 101
in Europe, 34
French and, 242
German crisis and, 259–60, 262, 264–65, 267, 272
Harvey and, 323
information and, 4, 29, 32, 88, 148, 235
international cooperation and, 107
international outlook of, 216
Lacour-Gayet and, 314
London Conference and, 278
narrative about Central Europe's problems, 251
national interests and, 32
Norman and, 28, 39, 233, 239, 270, 276, 280, 311, 337
Norman's request for help from, 283
Reichsbank credit and, 221, 224, 259
after Wall Street crash, 28
worldview of, 10, 249
Harvey, Ernest M., 66, 76, 81, 303. *See also* Bank of England; British crisis
Bank of England loan and, 287, 296
bank rate and, 326
Britain's departure from gold and, 328
budget plan and, 310
Credit Anstalt crisis and, 3
government and, 294, 333
handling of sterling crisis, 322
Harrison and, 323
ineffectiveness of, 319
Norman and, 323
re-appointment of, 337
use of government loan and, 320
Hawtrey, Ralph, 10, 15, 24, 35, 43, 308
Hay, Colin, 17
hearsay. *See* rumors
hindsight, 13, 343, 346, 355
historical analogies
Bank of England loan and, 291–92
Britain's departure from gold and, 334
French credit to Bank of England and, 288
Great Depression and, 355
Great Financial Crisis and, 355
lack of, 6, 36, 42, 60
limitations of, 346
history, 355
context provided by, 356
forward-looking, 343
Great Financial Crisis and, 355
learning from, 355
making sense of, 355
writing forwards, 21, 346–47, 350
Hoesch, Leopold von, 254
Hoover moratorium, 202, 212, 214, 275, 342. *See also* reparations
announcement of, 232
British response to, 227
community of central bankers and, 237
conditional/unconditional payments and, 214, 233, 239, 271
delay in, 251
Dreyse and, 233
*The Economist*, 230
effects of, 228, 238
France and, 215, 221–23, 229, 232–38, 241–42, 258
French public opinion and, 235, 243
German crisis and, 262
German public and, 233
German request for assistance and, 264
Germany's credit and, 233
Harrison and, 223
implementation of, 271
J.P. Morgan & Co;, 238, 277
legitimizing narrative, 235
Luther and, 218
need for, 236
Norman and, 233–34, 238
opposition to, 241
political conditions and, 269
Hoover, Herbert, 34, 163
London Conference and, 272
J.P. Morgan & Co. and, 213
London Conference and, 276
horizon of expectation, 353
house of cards scenario, 4–5, 15, 54, 56, 70, 85, 181. *See also* contagion; gold standard; narrative(s)
Britain's departure from gold and, 330
contagion and, 124

foreign credits and, 88
Germany and, 99, 258, 263
threat of Austrian moratorium and, 70
human beings, focus on, 20
humanistic approach, 350
Hungary, 121, 151, 153, 164, 179, 211, 215, 238. *See also* Europe
bank holidays in, 268–69
BIS on seriousness of situation, 324
conditions in, 208, 236
contagion and, 159
credit to, 209, 234
gold standard and, 298
lack of assistance for, 241
need to repay loan, 281
New York Fed and, 211, 216
hyperinflation, 8, 82, 128, 132

ideas, need for, 166
identity, 8
India, 153
inflation
Austria and, 8, 85, 127–28, 132, 140–41, 152
fear of, 41
Germany and, 8, 12, 274
Harrison on, 104
risk of, 81–82
information, 32, 85. *See also* communication
about Austrian crisis, 148
about German crisis, 276
BIS's marginalization and, 208
contradictory, 83
difficulties getting and processing, 73
evaluating, 80
exchange of, 32
Harrison and, 29, 98, 148, 229, 235, 239
importance of, 96
lack of, 11
need for, 166
Norman and, 239, 241
problems in, 349
sources of, 73, 85
US bankers and, 272
interest rate. *See also* bank rate; discount rate
Bagehot on, 6
Germany crisis and, 245
International Acceptance Bank, 90, 97, 107, 242
International Committee, 107, 113, 144, 148, 150–51, 188–89. *See also individual bankers*
agreement with Austrian government, 171, 177, 185, 190, 193, 200
controller for Credit Anstalt and, 114, 120
France and, 108
guarantee and, 124
standstill agreement and, 160, 232
US representatives on, 107
van Hengel and, 146
international relations, 12. *See also* politics
interventions, 9. *See also* politics
investments, long-term, 37
investors, foreign, 48. *See also* creditors, Credit Anstalt; creditors, Germany's
Italy, 65, 121, 142, 151
S. Japhet & Co.
deposits with Credit Anstalt, 74, 76
tainted money and, 122

Jay, Nelson Dean, 86, 150, 276. *See also* Morgan & Cie
on Hoover moratorium, 214
Juch, Otto, 3, 53, 70, 111, 123, 134, 152. *See also* government, Austrian
attitude of, 154
guarantee and, 133
internal guarantee and, 161, 177
International Committee agreement and, 193
Morgan firms and, 68
placing of Austrian loan and, 152
view of Austrian situation, 162

Kassenscheine, 128, 142, 188
Keynes, John Maynard, 9, 137, 325, 333
Crane on, 325
leaving gold standard and, 305
on May Report, 292
Siepmann and, 24
sterling crisis and, 292
Kienböck, Viktor, 123
Kindersley Plan, 37, 43, 65
Kindersley, Robert, 115, 150, 153, 170, 189, 191
Bank of England loan and, 284–85
British crisis and, 285
on improvements in Austria, 232
on International Committee, 107
International Committee agreement and, 171, 178, 193
on London Committee, 105
response to Rodd's memo, 198
on socialist government, 145
view of Austrian approach to crisis, 198
King, Willford I., 321
Knight, Frank, 351

knowledge, actionable, 92. *See also* International Committee; London Committee
access to, 148
action and, 180
Austrian crisis and, 158, 180
collapse narrative and, 168
establishing, 17
future-planning and, 129
lack of, 44, 83, 92, 125
lack of, German crisis and, 271–72
need for, 97
Norman's need for, 135
Norman's plan for providing, 92
produced by Rodd, 44, 57
knowledge, context-dependent, 352
knowledge, historical, 354. *See also* historical analogies
knowledge, rule-based, 352
Koselleck, Reinhart, 353
Kredit Anstalt. *See* Credit Anstalt
Kreditanstalt. *See* Credit Anstalt

Lacour-Gayet, Robert, 222, 226, 291. *See also* Banque de France
Bank of England loan and, 290–91, 295
British crisis and, 294
on British problems, 307
in community of central bankers, 291
Harrison and, 242, 314
Hoover moratorium and, 235
national interests and, 229
Lamont, Thomas, 213, 276, 329. *See also* J.P. Morgan & Co; Morgan and Co.
Kindersley Plan and, 39
last-resort credits, 119
Laval, Pierre, 243
Layton, Walter, 220
Lazard Brothers & Co., 145, 170. *See also* creditors, Credit Anstalt; International Committee; Kindersley, Robert; London Committee
Credit Anstalt and, 97
organization of creditors and, 79
leadership, 31, 321. *See* Bank of England; Banque de France; United States
lack of, 172
League of Nations, 86, 188. *See also* politics
Austrian loan and, 2, 51, 53, 55, 57, 63, 66
French conditions and, 194
in French Note, 195
reluctance to involve, 86
stabilization loan to Austria, 9
Leffingwell, Russell C., 9, 28
Lehman Brothers, 354
Leith-Ross, Frederick, 58, 66, 300, 308
British government loan and, 315
lender of last resort, 352
central banks as, 6
lender of last resort, international, 6
need for, 24
lending, international
Siepmann's pessimism about, 44
stability and, 37
lending, short-term
German crisis and, 275
*Lessons from the Great Depression* (Temin), 345
Levi, Giovanni, 343
Lindenberg, Paul, 77
loan, Austrian, 63, 103, 122, 129, 179–80. *See also* Austrian National Bank; bridge loan to Austria; government, Austrian
avoiding moratorium and, 168
Bank of England and, 134
Britain and, 58, 123, 142, 166, 178, 188, 191
British banks and, 143
Federal Reserve System and, 58
France and, 58, 66, 86, 89, 116, 123–24, 147, 149, 151–53, 169, 173–74, 178, 182, 186, 191–92, 199, 201
French conditions for, 173, 193, 202, 205, 241
Gannon's plan for, 169, 172–73, 192
Germany and, 165, 169
guarantee and, 126
insufficiency of, 126
international participation, 123
Juch and, 162
League of Nations and, 2, 53, 55, 57, 66, 188
moratorium and, 172
need for, 51, 63, 167
negotiator for, 183
opposition to, 66
placing, 52–53, 58, 64–65, 67–68, 116–17, 119, 122–24, 127, 138–39, 141, 143, 148, 151, 159, 169, 173, 180–81, 201
placing, delay in, 162–63
placing, failure of, 177, 181, 185, 204, 207, 281
politics and, 123
Rodd and, 56, 68, 186

second BIS credit and, 169, 180, 187, 200–1
socialist party and, 173
uncertainty and, 68, 105, 135
urgency of, 55
US and, 165–66, 183
US banks and, 173, 205
loan, Austrian stabilization, 9, 63, 188, 199
loan, Bank of England, 284, 286–87, 303, 318. *See also* British crisis
Banque de France and, 290
Harrison and, 289–90
historical analogies for, 288, 291
Lacour-Gayet and, 290
New York Fed and, 289–90
private banks and, 289
size of, 289, 291,
US banks and, 288
use of, 293, 295, 297, 299, 303, 312
loan, British government
Banque de France and, 309
BIS and, 318
budget plan and, 310
France and, 314
government delay and, 308
J.P. Morgan & Co. and, 307, 309
need for, 294, 296–97, 301, 303–4, 313
need for Parliamentary action, 309
size of, 308, 310, 315, 320
urgency of, 315
US and, 310
US banks and, 316
use of, 320, 322–23, 326, 333
loan, Bank of England
*The Economist* on, 290
loans
by central banks, 10
size of, 291
*Lombard Street* (Bagehot), 6, 49. *See also* Bagehot operating model
London. *See* banks, British; Britain
London Committee, 90–91, 97–98, 104, 106. *See also* creditors, Credit Anstalt; International Committee
London Conference of Ministers, 40, 272, 276–77, 279, 283, 309
France and, 277
long-term capital, lack of, 291
Luther, Hans, 31, 33, 38, 62, 160, 166
Austrian crisis and, 96
BIS and, 264
credit restrictions and, 246
discouragement of, 320
in France, 250
Harrison and, 262
Hoover moratorium and, 218, 234
lack of plan, 265, 267, 269
leadership of, 250
Norman and, 212, 244, 253
pressure on, 261
Reichsbank credit and, 228, 244–45
Schacht and, 269
Länder Bank, 188–89

MacDonald, Ramsay, 126, 167. *See also* Britain; government, British
budget and, 310–11
German visit and, 126
London Conference and, 273
on options for Britain, 326
resignation of, 311
Macmillan Committee, 31, 282, 335
Macmillan report, 282–83, 286
Magyan Nemzeti Bank, 211. *See also* Hungary
market, 31
Austrian crisis and, 135
belief in, 36
intervention in, 26, 39
material, empirical, 18
May Committee, 310
May Report, 292
McCracken, Grant, 8
McGarrah, Gates W., 7, 29, 37, 47
Austrian bridge loan and, 205
communication and, 32
Federal Reserve and, 58
German crisis and, 274
on Germany, 98
Hoover moratorium and, 218
Norman and, 225
optimism about Austrian crisis, 98
second Reichsbank credit and, 247
van Hengel and, 155
vision for BIS, 7
meaning construction, 20
meaning loss, 15, 36, 42, 352
crisis of 1931 and, 340
failure to place Austrian loan and, 177
spread of, 281
Melchior, Carl, 40
Mellon, Andrew, 208, 234, 277
Mellon–Berenger agreement, 175

Mendelsohn, Franz, 253
Meyer, Eugene, 42, 58, 271
  Reichsbank credit and, 222, 224
micro-level perspective, 17, 21, 343
Mills, Ogden, 163, 238, 273, 275
Minister of Finance, Austrian. *See* Juch, Otto
Mitchell, Charles, 104, 118, 211, 275
  Britain's departure from gold and, 331
  criticism of US banking, 157
  second BIS credit and, 169
  view of Austria, 207
models. *See also* Bagehot operating model
  inadequacy of, 352
monetary policy, 32
monetary system, 10. *See also* worldview
money doctors, 10, 109, 115. *See also* central bankers; individual bankers
money, creating, 6
money, new, 96
money, tainted, 76, 80, 122
Moore, Ernest, 262
morale, 129. *See also* confidence
moratorium, Austrian, 70, 74, 89, 134, 143, 152, 170, 177. *See also* creditors, Credit Anstalt; guarantee, Austrian
  assistance and, 103
  Austrian National Bank's duty and, 94
  Austrian preference for, 91
  avoiding, 74, 79, 94, 112–13, 168, 180, 206
  BIS and, 102
  concerns about, 79, 179
  conflicting narratives of, 349
  contagion and, 70, 182
  effects of, 70, 78, 190
  fear of, 86, 91, 97, 103
  government's concerns and, 349
  International Committee's agreement and, 190
  likelihood of, 76, 95, 189
  loan and, 173
  Louis Rothschild, 80
  Norman's efforts to avoid, 182
  opposition to, 81
  placing of loan and, 172
  plans for, 193
  possibility of, 70, 74, 76, 79, 84, 87, 89, 91, 96, 103, 154, 173
  possibility of, effects of, 80
  postponement of decision about, 191, 193
  purpose of, 78
  repercussions of, 176
  in Rodd's memo, 189
moratorium, German, 41, 238, 266
  French view of, 243
Moreau, Emile, 252
  Norman and, 30
Moret, Clément, 26, 31, 38, 62, 142, 144. *See also* Banque de France
  on Austrian loan, 143
  Bank of England loan and, 291, 293, 295
  bridge loan to Austria and, 204
  British crisis and, 301
  British government loan and, 315–16
  in community of central bankers, 291
  German crisis and, 260
  on gold sold by Reichsbank, 166
  Harrison and, 35
  London Conference and, 277
  national interests and, 229
  Reichsbank loan and, 223
  Schacht and, 117
Morgan & Cie, 27, 85, 149. *See also* Jay, Nelson Dean; Morgan firms
  on Austrian loan, 149
  Austrian loan and, 67
  communication and, 32
  Hoover moratorium and, 214, 238
  information and, 85
J.P. Morgan & Co., 27, 58, 144. *See also* creditors, Credit Anstalt; International Committee
  Austrian loan and, 67, 105, 206
  on Austrians, 207
  Britain's departure from gold and, 333
  British crisis and, 287, 297
  British government loan and, 307, 309, 316
  central banks and, 350
  Credit Anstalt and, 71, 89, 97
  French connections, 173
  German crisis and, 278
  Germany and, 242
  Hoover and, 213
  on Hoover moratorium, 215
  Hoover moratorium and, 238, 277
  London Conference and, 278
  Norman and, 86
  views of Europe, 349
Morgan firms, 27
  Austrian loan and, 67–68
  Britain's departure from gold and, 333
  German crisis and, 276
  Germany and, 252
  information and, 85

London Conference and, 279
pessimism about Europe, 319
role of in crisis of 1931, 349
Morgan Grenfell, 27–28, 144–45. *See also* creditors, Credit Anstalt; Grenfell, Edward; International Committee; Whigham, Charles
on Austrians, 206
central banks and, 350
Credit Anstalt's proposal and, 72–73
information and, 85
organization of creditors and, 79
Morgan, Jack, 26, 298
Britain's departure from gold and, 329, 333, 335
British crisis and, 287
Kindersley Plan and, 39
Norman and, 280
Mouré, Kenneth, 9

narrative(s), 14–15, 20. *See also* emplotment; future, imagined; house of cards scenario
action and, 180
as analysis, 20, 343
Burgess's call for, 321
central bankers' use of, 352
coherent, lack of, 83
diverging, 92
epistemic community and, 16
as fictional expectation, 73
Hoover moratorium and, 235
house of cards scenario and, 85
imagined futures and, 16
moratorium threat and, 70
need for, 92, 97, 351–52
perceiving world and, 347
as performative, 16, 348
narratives, about Britain's departure from gold, 330
narratives, about crisis of 1931
Norman's, 348
narratives, dominant, 42, 345
narratives, forward-looking, 343
narratives, legitimizing
Hoover moratorium and, 235
narratives, of Austrian crisis, 183
British point of view in, 197
contagion and, 124
difficulty constructing, 98
heroes in, 197
Norman's, 103, 181
Quesnay's, 199
Rodd's, 185, 201–2
Siepmann's attempt to create, 122
van Hengel's, 158
villains in, 196, 199
narratives, of Britain's departure from gold, 333
narratives, of British crisis, 297
Harvey's, 295
narratives, of Central Europe, 251
narratives, of collapse, 82, 168, 172, 176
narratives, of crisis of 1931
differences in, 348
Norman's, 338, 340–41
politics and, 165
Rodd's, 340
Siepmann's, 338, 340–41
Williams's, 342
narratives, of German crisis, 258
conflicting, 249
difficulty establishing, 272
German responsibility in, 252, 262
lack of, 265
Norman's, 275
Rowe-Dutton's, 253
shift in, 244
US, 275
narratives, of Great Depression, 345
narratives, of Hoover moratorium, 237
narratives, stereotyping, 243
National Bank of Hungary, 209, 211. *See also* Hungary
National Bank, Austrian. *See* Austrian National Bank
National City Bank, 90, 92, 97, 104, 169, 242. *See also* Mitchell, Charles
national interest/feeling, 8, 319. *See also* politics
central bankers and, 30, 241
central banks and, 31
gold standard and, 34
nationalism, 12
Nazis, 118. *See also* politics, German
Netherlands
BIS credit to Austrian National Bank and, 65
British crisis and, 318, 322
demand for gold from, 327
Netherlands Bank, 318
networks, 349. *See also* epistemic community of central bankers
Neues Wiener Tagblatt, 2
Neurath, Konstantin von, 239
Neurath, Ludwig, 62

neutrality, 10
New York. *See* banks, US; Federal Reserve Bank of New York; Harrison, George L.; United States
New York Fed. *See* Federal Reserve Bank of New York; Harrison, George L.
New York Stock Exchange, 4
*New York Times*
on Austrian crisis, 88, 120
on Austrian loan, 2, 64, 181
on Bank of England loan, 286
on BIS, 7
on BIS credit to Austrian National Bank, 65
on British loss of gold, 283
on Castle William R. Jr., 264
on Credit Anstalt creditors, 183
on German crisis, 136, 263, 268
on Hoover moratorium, 214, 218
on Kindersley Plan, 43
New York Trust Company, 97, 101, 104
Nordwolle company, 244–45, 247, 249, 253
Norman Plan. *See* Kindersley Plan
Norman, Montagu, 3, 10, 97, 283. *See also* bridge loan to Austria; British crisis; Bank of England; London Committee
absence from Bank of England, 338, 341
additional Reichsbank credit and, 245, 249
adviser/controller and, 108
after 1931 crisis, 338
assistance requested from, 74
background of, 24
Banque de France and, 31, 223
on BIS, 32
BIS and, 221, 225, 227, 234
Britain's departure from gold and, 335
budget plan and, 310
call for currency contraction, 160
central bank cooperation and, 291
communication and, 32
in community of central bankers, 151, 223, 227
on conditions in Austria, 84
creditor committee and, 78, 84, 97
criticism of, 318
distrust of theory, 30
France/French and, 30–31, 86, 181, 215, 221, 225–27, 229, 241, 254, 286
future and, 35
on general problems in Europe, 234
German crisis and, 212, 267
Germany and, 30, 253, 261–62, 273
gold standard and, 9, 31, 335
Harrison and, 29, 32, 39, 233, 239, 270, 276, 280, 311, 337
Harvey and, 323
health of, 287, 291, 299, 301, 310, 324
Hoover moratorium and, 233–34, 238
intervention by, 79, 179, 185
Jack Morgan and, 280
Kindersley Plan and, 38
length of tenure, 319
London Conference and, 273, 279
Morgan firms' reliance on, 86
motivation of, 205
narratives of, 275, 348
national interests and, 32
network of, 27
pessimism of, 135, 338
politics and, 240–41
re-appointment of, 337
Reichsbank credit and, 220, 224, 227
request for Harrison's help, 283
return to Bank of England, 336
return to London, 326
role of, 27, 151
Schacht and, 116, 118
on seriousness of European situation, 163
Siepmann and, 24
sterling crisis and, 288
Strong and, 31
temperament of, 25
tenure at Bank of England, 338
Versailles Treaty/reparations and, 272, 275
vision of, 8, 26
worldview of, 10, 25, 161, 249
'you and I' statement;, 118–19, 164
Norris, George W., 53
nostalgia, Britain's departure from gold and, 332
note circulation, Austrian, 128, 142, 161
note issue, gold exchange standard and, 34

O'Sullivan, Mary, 345–46
observation, point of, 14
Oesterreichische Nationalbank. *See* Austrian National Bank
Old Lady of Threadneedle Street. *See* Bank of England
operating models, 7, 15–16, 33, 94. *See also* Bagehot operating model; gold standard historical analogies
opportunities, in crises, 13

optimism
  about preventing spread of crisis, 348
  Austrian crisis and, 98, 121, 190–91, 193, 232
  of Bank of England, 320
  British crisis and, 288
  German crisis and, 209, 228, 232
  Hoover moratorium and, 219, 243
  Kindersley's, 172
  McGarrah's, 155
  Reichsbank credit and, 242
  Rodd's, 57, 154
  Simon's, 126
Ottoman Bank, 171
outlook, 11

panic, 5, 10, 130, 193, 195. *See also* Bagehot operating model
  Austrian crisis and, 128, 130, 193
  avoiding, 10, 128, 130, 158, 176
  Bagehot on, 6, 10, 347
  central banks and, 9
  fear of, 100
  in Germany, 219, 230, 253, 262, 266, 279, 305
  possibility of, 59
  Williams on, 342
Paris. *See* Banque de France; Banque de Paris et des Pays-Bas; France
Parliament, Austrian, 103. *See also* government, Austrian; guarantee, Austrian
Paulson, Hank, 354
payments, conditional. *See* Hoover moratorium; reparations
pegging
  of franc, 334
  of sterling, 320, 322–23, 333–34
perception. *See also* operating models
  divergence of, 243
  framework for, 16
perspective, micro-level, 17, 21, 343
pessimism, 36, 44
  about future, 44, 319
  about German crisis, 274
  of Austrian public, 132
  Bank of England loan and, 282
  Norman's, 135
  spread of, 281
plans, 73, 353
Poland, 65
politics, 86, 319. *See also* customs union, Austro-German; debt; League of Nations; reparations; Versailles, Treaty of; individual governments,Austrian crisis and, 89, 134
  Austrian loan and, 53, 116, 123, 173, 201
  Bank of England and, 296, 326
  bank rate and, 13
  banks and, 213
  bridge loan to Austria and, 204
  British crisis and, 289, 298
  central bankers and, 229, 254
  central banks and, 30, 165, 208, 239, 241
  crisis and, 120–21, 165, 213, 233, 303, 309
  economics/finance and, 10, 32, 34, 37, 54, 108, 136, 156, 174, 204, 314
  European financial stability and, 227
  French withdrawals and, 72
  Gannon's plan and, 170
  German crisis and, 163, 254, 256–57, 262, 264–65, 267, 269, 271–72, 274–75
  German public and, 233
  German visit to Britain, 135
  London Conference and, 272–73
  need to address issues of, 168, 319
  Norman and, 240–41
  in Norman's narrative, 341
  Norman's narrative and, 338, 340, 348
  polarization in, 12
  preventing collapse and, 237
  recovery and, 256
  second Reichsbank credit and, 249
  solution to problems and, 321
politics, Austrian, 112
politics, German, 118, 160, 207. *See also* customs union, Austro-German; reparations; Versailles, Treaty of
  extremism in, 258
  Nazis, 118
  polarization in, 99, 234
Portugal, 135
pound. *See* British crisis; sterling
practices, bankers', 7. *See also* epistemic community
  challenges to, 15
present, 353
presentism, 346
protectionism, 12
psychology, 261. *See also* confidence
  Austrian crisis and, 132, 134, 140
  Austrian guarantee and, 161

psychology (cont.)
  Bank of England loan and, 290, 293
  depression and, 321
  German crisis and, 277
  of lender of last resort actions, 289
  support of sterling and, 284
public, 321. *See also* confidence
public opinion, French, 226
  Hoover moratorium and, 235
public, Austrian, 132

Quesnay, Pierre, 3, 26, 125. *See also* Bank for International Settlements (BIS),"at all costs" statement, 99
  on Austrian guarantee, 110
  on Austrians, 140
  communication and, 32
  on German creditors, 232
  Hoover moratorium and, 229
  narrative of Austrian crisis, 199
  national interests and, 203, 229
  pessimism of, 35

reconstruction plan. *See* loan, Austrian
rediscounting, 52
  Austrian crisis and, 57, 60, 64, 111, 126–27, 142–43, 150, 177, 180, 189, 191, 268
  Reichsbank and, 219
reforms, money in exchange for, 10
Reichsbank, 96, 158, 209. *See also* Blessing, Karl; Dreyse, Friedrich (Fritz); German crisis; Germany; Luther, Hans; Schacht; Hjalmar; Vocke, Wilhelm
  additional credit to, 244, 247, 249, 267
  Bank of England and, 215
  bank rate (discount rate) and, 159, 165, 167, 207, 209, 270, 274, 278
  Banque de France and, 32
  BIS credit to Austrian National Bank and, 65
  cover ratio, 207, 209–10, 215, 219, 226, 228, 244, 253, 263, 274
  Credit Anstalt and, 4, 82
  credit restrictions, 219, 246–47, 249, 255, 257–58, 274
  credit through Gold Diskont Bank, 209
  credit to, 220, 231–32, 234, 237, 242, 269
  currency contraction and, 160
  gold sold by, 166
  impending collapse of, 241
  leadership of, 30, 96, 250
  likelihood of needing help, 138
  losses of, 160, 165, 210, 228, 274
  Norman and, 30, 220
  rediscounting and, 219
  responsibility of, 248
  run on, 248
  withdrawals from, 158, 234, 238
Reichsmark. *See also* Germany
  flight from, 246, 248–49, 253, 259
  weakness of, 98
Reichstag. *See* government, German
Reisch, Richard, 3, 63, 116. *See also* Austrian National Bank
relationships, 349
reparations, 9, 26, 32–33, 136, 164. *See also* France; Germany; Hoover moratorium; politics, German; Versailles, Treaty of; Young Plan
  Brüning's statement on, 137, 159, 207, 229
  credit and, 210
  criticism of, 30
  disagreement about, 300
  economic conditions and, 136
  effects of, 44
  France and, 39, 136, 175,
  Gannon and, 169–70
  German crisis and, 268
  London Conference and, 273, 278
  need for money and, 211
  need for political action and, 168
  need to address, 139, 165
  Norman and, 165, 280
  possible postponement of, 98, 126, 136, 175
  possible reconsideration of, 272
  Reichsbank credit and, 234, 237, 250
  Schacht on, 118
  uncertainty about, 160
  unconditional payments, 271
  US initiative and, 212, 229
Reusch, Paul, 340
Riksbanken (Sweden), 47
*Risk, Uncertainty and Profit* (Knight), 351
Rist, Charles A., 115–18, 120–21
  as adviser to Austrian government, 117
  Austrian loan and, 149
  national interests and, 230
  pessimism of, 35
  pressure from, 124
  renewal of credits and, 125

Rodd, Francis, 3, 56. *See also* Austrian crisis; central banks; Bank for International Settlements (BIS)
after 1931 crisis, 337
background of, 22
at BIS, 24, 141
Britain's departure from gold and, 331
clarity provided by, 97
communication and, 32
demands of, 123
departure from Vienna, 205
departure for Vienna, 3
evaluation of Credit Anstalt crisis, 51
on guarantee, 109
on leaving gold standard, 306
narrative of 1931 crisis, 340
narrative of Austrian crisis, 185, 201–2
optimism of, 57
plan to avoid breakdown, 128
politics and, 121
role of, 18, 22–23
Siepmann and, 24
in Vienna, 110
worldview of, 10, 23
Rooth, Ivar, 47
Rosenhek, Zeev, 15
Rothschild committee. *See* London Committee
Rothschild house
Austrian, 2
promotion of Credit Anstalt, 1
Rothschild, Anthony de, 105
Rothschild, Lionel de, 105. *See also* London Committee
creditor committee and, 79, 84, 86–87
guarantee and, 145
on International Committee, 107
on need to keep Austria going, 147
on need to restore confidence, 139
on van Hengel, 146
Rothschild, Louis, 80
N.M. Rothschild & Sons, 55. *See also* creditors, Credit Anstalt
central banks and, 350
deposits with Credit Anstalt, 74, 76
information about foreign creditors, 90
interest in Credit Anstalt, 80
role of in crisis of 1931, 349
tainted money and, 122
Rowe-Dutton, Ernest, 253, 274
Royal Geographical Society, 23
rules, 352
rumours, 2, 66
about Germany, 98
about Norman, 336
about postponement of reparations, 126
about US banks, 336
Austrian crisis and, 122
British crisis and, 296, 299, 308
Credit Anstalt creditors and, 126
German crisis and, 288
uncertainty and, 53
runs, 72. *See also* confidence; withdrawals
on Reichsbank, 248
runs, Austrian crisis and, 64, 84, 161
on Credit Anstalt, 76
expected, 81
external, 64
internal, 52, 64
on schilling, 97, 100, 203

Sargent, Orme, 55, 205
scale of observation, 14, 343, 347
micro-level perspective, 21
Schacht, Hjalmar, 30, 33, 115, 269. *See also* Reichsbank
Schackle, George, 351
schilling, Austrian
Austrian public and, 132
BIS and, 94, 123
confidence in, 52
fear of collapse of, 100
flight from, 82, 111, 134, 141, 160
lack of confidence in, 139, 142
need to protect, 162
possible breakdown of, 127
problems with, 92
risk of run on, 84
run on, 100, 203
stability of, 126
support/defense of, 93–94, 99, 105
Schober, Johan, 82, 271
Schwartz, Anna, 345
Schweizerischer Bankverein, 69
Seay, George J., 252
sensemaking, 13, 15–16, 352, 355. *See also* emplotment; future, imagined; narrative(s)
Austrian crisis and, 98–99, 103, 141, 197
Britain's departure from gold and, 331–32, 335
British crisis and, 297, 319
Bruins's note and, 132
Burgess's, 321

sensemaking (cont.)
  by central bankers, 17
  collapse narrative and, 168
  communication and, 37, 80
  difficulty of, 86
  efforts at, 5
  Great Financial Crisis and, 355
  lack of, 44
  London Conference and, 279
  need for, 217, 347
  Norman and, 164, 340
  passing judgment and, 343
  planning and, 353
  political issues and, 164–65
  retrospective, 342, 355
  Rodd and, 18, 23, 127, 154, 185, 197
  Siepmann and, 47, 122, 340
  Stephany's memo and, 80
  uncertainty and, 20, 351
  worldview and, 10
Shawmut Corporation, 90
short-term funds, 2
  Credit Anstalt and, 2
Siepmann, Harry L., 10. *See also* Bank of England; central banks
  after crisis of 1931, 341
  Austrian National Bank and, 93
  background of, 23
  Bank of England loan and, 293
  Britain's departure from gold and, 304, 331
  British government loan and, 315
  central bankers and, 8, 349
  communication and, 32
  Credit Anstalt crisis and, 3
  on Harvey's policy, 338
  holiday of, 337
  house of cards scenario, 4–5
  narrative of crisis of 1931, 340–41
  Norman and, 24
  optimism of, 320
  Rodd and, 24
  role of, 22
  worldview of, 10
signification, 18
Simon, Hans von, 50, 61, 240
  January note, 47, 49, 52, 144, 346, 352
  "Lessons of the Austrian Crisis" note, 121–22, 241, 346
  optimism of, 126, 130
  in Vienna, 61
Smoot-Hawley Tariff, 12, 34
Snowden, Philip, 179, 181, 273, 285, 299, 317. *See also* government, British
social issues. *See also individual governments*
  need to address, 319
Socialist Party, 317
space of experience, 353
speed, need for, 236, 238. *See also* urgency
Sprague, Oliver M. W., 36, 39, 304
Sproul, Allan, 34, 293
stability
  central bankers and, 26
  Federal Reserve System and, 42
  gold standard and, 7
  need for, 37
standstill agreement
  Austrian, 157, 160, 232
  for Europe, 170
  German, 231, 271, 281, 285, 290, 342
  International Committee and, 171
state, 32
  central bank and, 28
state-owned enterprises, capitalism and, 84
statesmen. *See* politics; *individual governments*
Stephany, Samuel, 77–78, 80, 119
  on London Committee, 105
  memo on seriousness of situation, 80
stereotypes, 243
sterilization. *See* gold sterilization
sterling
  after Britain's departure from gold, 331
  drain of, 319
  as fiat money, 330
  pegging of, 322–23, 333–34
  pressure on, 181, 312
  privilege of, 25
  support of, 284, 286, 293
sterling crisis. *See* British crisis; loan, Bank of England; loan, British government
Stewart, Walter W., 10, 51, 109, 116, 202, 281, 286, 337
  Austrian loan and, 134
  London Conference and, 278
Stimson, Henry L., 41, 58, 167, 175
  London Conference and, 275–76
  on Norman, 273
Stolper, Gustav, 220
stress, 11
Strong, Benjamin, 28, 31–32, 223
structural issues. *See also* debt; reparations; Versailles, Treaty of;
  crisis in Europe and, 213

European financial stability and, 227
Norman's narrative and, 348
supply and demand, 305
surplus countries. *See* creditor nations; France; United States
Sweden, 47
Swiss National Bank, 65
Switzerland
Austrian crisis and, 65, 106
British crisis and, 318, 322
gold standard and, 331
syndicate, of German companies, 244, 253

Tardieu, André, 35
tariff union. *See* customs union, Austro-German
telegraph, 349
telephone, 152, 349
Temin, Peter, 345
*Le Temps*, 292
Tett, Gillian, 354
Thaa, Gustav, 70, 99, 116. *See also* Austrian National Bank
theory, 11, 320, 353. *See also* Bagehot operating model
distrust of, 30
limitations of, 346
thin ice metaphor, Germany and, 99
time, 24, 74, 167–68, 173, 176, 349. *See also* speed; urgency
Trades Unions, 317
treasury bills. *See* loan, Austrian
treasury bond loan. *See* loan, Austrian
Troubled Asset Relief Program (TARP) bill, 354
trust, 349
Tyrrell, William, 273

UK. *See* Britain
uncertainty, 7, 10–11, 13, 15, 41, 83, 355. *See also* Bagehot operating model; future, imagined
Austrian crisis and, 92, 97, 118, 121, 125, 130, 136, 197
Austrian guarantee and, 91, 105, 111, 122, 126
Austrian loan and, 68, 105
awareness of, 350
blueprint for action under, 10–11, 13
British crisis and, 297
capitalism and, 33, 321
collapse narrative and, 168
Credit Anstalt's future and, 4
dealing with, 13
decision-making and, 344, 351
erased by hindsight, 355
European situation and, 309
expression of, 352
financial crises and, 331
Francqui on, 45
German crisis and, 207, 249, 259, 272, 274–76, 280
in Germany, 263
Great Financial Crisis and, 354
of global financial situation, 319
Harrison on, 35
Hoover moratorium and, 232
increase in, 80, 86
indicators of, 305
interconnectedness of financial system and, 217
lack of plan and, 45, 217
leaving gold standard and, 304, 331
marginalized in mainstream economics, 351
need for sensemaking and emplotment and, 347
outcome of decisions and, 15, 175
passing judgment and, 343
pervasiveness of, 44
planning and, 73, 353
reduced by bridge loan to Austria, 206
reducing, 134, 272
reparations and, 160
responding to, 11
risk of runs and, 64
Rodd's memo and, 185
rumours and, 53, 66
sensemaking and, 16, 351
Siepmann's note and, 47, 50
silencing of, 346
understanding actions and, 15
vs calculable risk, 351
widespread sense of, 36
withdrawals from Credit Anstalt and, 74
unemployment, 12–13, 207
United States. *See also* banks, US; Federal Reserve Bank of New York; Fraser, Leon; Great Depression; Harrison, George L.; Hoover moratorium; McGarrah, Gates W.
action needed from, 208
Austria and, 199

United States. (cont.)
Austrian loan and, 165–66, 183, 192
banking difficulties in, 2, 337
BIS and, 58
British crisis and, 327
British government loan and, 316
Credit Anstalt and, 4
debt of, 37
economic/financial importance of, 10, 26, 31
economy of after Great War, 9
Europe and, 12, 213, 309, 319
fear of contagion in, 243
German crisis and, 266
gold and, 35, 43, 167, 207, 251, 306, 332, 342
gold standard and, 36, 136, 331
Hoover moratorium's effects on, 238
interventions by, 9
Kindersley Plan and, 38
London Conference and, 278
money doctors from, 10
short-term credit in Britain, 38
war debt and, 229, .
unpredictability, 175
urgency, 168, 174. *See also* speed; time
Austrian crisis and, 106, 134, 136, 153, 162
Britain's departure from gold and, 332
British crisis and, 313, 326
British government loan and, 315
Brüning's reparations statement and, 207
Credit Anstalt crisis and, 44
erased by hindsight, 355
lack of, 44
reduced by bridge loan to Austria, 206
withdrawals from Credit Anstalt and, 74

van Hengel, Adrianus, 114, 117–20, 217, 270
authority of, 120
on Credit Anstalt, 157
creditors and, 125, 144
demands of, 123
dismissal of, 159
on Germany, 156, 231
International Committee and, 146
letter to Norman, 155
McGarrah and, 155
on US banks, 157
Versailles Peace Conference, Siepmann at, 24
Versailles, Treaty of, 5, 11, 165, 227. *See also* politics; reparations
Austria and, 165, 207
dealing with legacy of, 165
Germany and, 30, 262
Norman and, 26
opposition to revisiting, 276
possible reconsideration of, 269, 272, 275
problems caused by, 12, 44, 165
revision of, 268
Vienna. *See* Austria
Vissering, G., 318
Vocke, Wilhelm, 122, 159, 209

Waley, S.D., 280, 315
Wall Street. *See also* banks, American; United States
Credit Anstalt and, 4
Wall Street crash (October 01929), 28
*Wall Street Journal*, 43
Warburg, Max, 55, 67, 91
Warburg, Paul, 90
Western Civilization, rescuing, 181
Whigham, Charles F., 28. *See also* Morgan Grenfell
Austrian loan and, 68, 174, 179
on creditors' committee, 88
on guarantee, 105, 145
on International Committee, 107
on London Committee, 105
Whitmarsh, Theodore, 216–17, 231
Wiener Bankverein, 189
Wiggin, Albert H., 169, 173, 176, 192–93, 309
Austrian loan and, 206
Wiggin Report, 309, 316
Williams, John H., 342
withdrawals, 69, 72. *See also* runs
effects of, 69–70, 74
fear of, 71, 76, 80
Woodlock, Thomas F., 43
Woolley, Clarence M., 119, 271, 330
World War I. *See* Great War
world, changes in, 7
worldview, 10
British, 216, 242
central banks and, 10, 161
differences in, 249
Harrison's, 10
imperial, 30, 242
narratives and, 199
Norman's, 10, 25, 84, 161, 241
of private bankers, 40
Rodd's, 10, 23
Siepmann's, 10
writing history and, 344

Young, Owen, 266, 289, 291, 329
Young Plan, 98, 136, 214. *See also* reparations
  acceptance of, 214
  conditional/unconditional payments and, 214, 223, 226, 233, 239, 271
  Hoover moratorium and, 214
  need for reconsideration of, 269
Young, Roy A., 28

Zinovstenska Banka, 189
Österreichische Credit Anstalt für Handel und Gewerbe (Credit Anstalt). *See* Credit Anstalt

For EU product safety concerns, contact us at Calle de José Abascal, 56–1°,
28003 Madrid, Spain or eugpsr@cambridge.org.

www.ingramcontent.com/pod-product-compliance
Lightning Source LLC
Chambersburg PA
CBHW070148211025
34312CB00004B/113
* 9 7 8 1 0 0 9 5 0 5 3 1 4 *